CSWE's Core Competencies and Practice Behavior Examples in this Text

Competency	Chapter
Professional Identity	
Practice Behavior Examples...	
Serve as representatives of the profession, its mission, and its core values	10,16
Know the profession's history	1
Commit themselves to the profession's enhancement and to their own professional conduct and growth	16
Advocate for client access to the services of social work	10
Practice personal reflection and self-correction to assure continual professional development	
Attend to professional roles and boundaries	16
Demonstrate professional demeanor in behavior, appearance, and communication	16
Engage in career-long learning	
Use supervision and consultation	16
Ethical Practice	
Practice Behavior Examples...	
Obligation to conduct themselves ethically and engage in ethical decision-making	10,12, 13
Know about the value base of the profession, its ethical standards, and relevant law	11
Recognize and manage personal values in a way that allows professional values to guide practice	10, 12. 13
Make ethical decisions by applying standards of the National Association of Social Workers Code of Ethics and, as applicable, of the International Federation of Social Workers/International Association of Schools of Social Work Ethics in Social Work, Statement of Principles	
Tolerate ambiguity in resolving ethical conflicts	10, 11
Apply strategies of ethical reasoning to arrive at principled decisions	12, 13
Critical Thinking	
Practice Behavior Examples...	
Know about the principles of logic, scientific inquiry, and reasoned discernment	
Use critical thinking augmented by creativity and curiosity	12, 13
Requires the synthesis and communication of relevant information	10, 11
Distinguish, appraise, and integrate multiple sources of knowledge, including research-based knowledge, and practice wisdom	12, 13
Analyze models of assessment, prevention, intervention, and evaluation	10, 16
Demonstrate effective oral and written communication in working with individuals, families, groups, organizations, communities, and colleagues	10, 11

Competency	Chapter
Diversity in Practice	
Practice Behavior Examples...	
Understand how diversity characterizes and shapes the human experience and is critical to the formation of identity	1, 2, 10
Understand the dimensions of diversity as the intersectionality of multiple factors including age, class, color, culture, disability, ethnicity, gender, gender identity and expression, immigration status, political ideology, race, religion, sex, and sexual orientation	2,10–13
Appreciate that, as a consequence of difference, a person's life experiences may include oppression, poverty, marginalization, and alienation as well as privilege, power, and acclaim	2, 4,5
Recognize the extent to which a culture's structures and values may oppress, marginalize, alienate, or create or enhance privilege and power	10,11
Gain sufficient self-awareness to eliminate the influence of personal biases and values in working with diverse groups	16
Recognize and communicate their understanding of the importance of difference in shaping life experiences	
View themselves as learners and engage those with whom they work as informants	2
Human Rights & Justice	
Practice Behavior Examples...	
Understand that each person, regardless of position in society, has basic human rights, such as freedom, safety, privacy, an adequate standard of living, health care, and education	10,11
Recognize the global interconnections of oppression and knowledge about theories of justice and strategies to promote human and civil rights	8
Incorporates social justice practices in organizations, institutions, and society to ensure that these basic human rights are distributed equitably and without prejudice	
Understand the forms and mechanisms of oppression and discrimination	
Advocate for human rights and social and economic justice	
Engage in practices that advance social and economic justice	16
Research-Based Practice	
Practice Behavior Examples...	
Use practice experience to inform research, employ evidence-based interventions, evaluate their own practice, and use research findings to improve practice, policy, and social service delivery	10, 12, 13
Comprehend quantitative and qualitative research and understand scientific and ethical approaches to building knowledge	
Use practice experience to inform scientific inquiry	1
Use research evidence to inform practice	1

CSWE's Core Competencies and Practice Behavior Examples in this Text

Competency	Chapter
Human Behavior	
Practice Behavior Examples...	
Know about human behavior across the life course; the range of social systems in which people live; and the ways social systems promote or deter people in maintaining or achieving health and well-being	3, 2,
Apply theories and knowledge from the liberal arts to understand biological, social, cultural, psychological, and spiritual development	3–8
Utilize conceptual frameworks to guide the processes of assessment, intervention, and evaluation	3
Critique and apply knowledge to understand person and environment	3, 10–15
Policy Practice	
Practice Behavior Examples...	
Understand that policy affects service delivery and they actively engage in policy practice	10, 11, 14
Know the history and current structures of social policies and services; the role of policy in service delivery; and the role of practice in policy development	1,10,16
Analyze, formulate, and advocate for policies that advance social well-being	16
Collaborate with colleagues and clients for effective policy action	16
Practice Contexts	
Practice Behavior Examples...	
Keep informed, resourceful, and proactive in responding to evolving organizational, community, and societal contexts at all levels of practice	4–8,10,11
Recognize that the context of practice is dynamic, and use knowledge and skill to respond proactively	
Continuously discover, appraise, and attend to changing locales, populations, scientific and technological developments, and emerging societal trends to provide relevant services	14
Provide leadership in promoting sustainable changes in service delivery and practice to improve the quality of social services	16

Competency	Chapter
Engage, Assess Intervene, Evaluate	
Practice Behavior Examples...	
Identify, analyze, and implement evidence-based interventions designed to achieve client goals	12,13
Use research and technological advances	
Evaluate program outcomes and practice effectiveness	
Develop, analyze, advocate, and provide leadership for policies and services	
Promote social and economic justice	
(A) ENGAGEMENT	
Substantively and effectively prepare for action with individuals, families, groups, organizations, and communities	4–8
Use empathy and other interpersonal skills	10,11,14,15
Develop a mutually agreed-on focus of work and desired outcomes	
(B) ASSESSMENT	
Collect, organize, and interpret client data	4–8,10
Assess client strengths and limitations	4–8,10
Develop mutually agreed-on intervention goals and objectives	10,12–14
Select appropriate intervention strategies	10,12,13
(C) INTERVENTION	
Initiate actions to achieve organizational goals	
Implement prevention interventions that enhance client capacities	16
Help clients resolve problems	10,12–15
Negotiate, mediate, and advocate for clients	10,12–14
Facilitate transitions and endings	12–14
(D) EVALUATION	
Critically analyze, monitor, and evaluate interventions	

Ninth Edition

Understanding Child Abuse and Neglect

Cynthia Crosson-Tower

PEARSON

Boston Columbus Indianapolis New York San Francisco Upper Saddle River
Amsterdam Cape Town Dubai London Madrid Milan Munich Paris Montréal Toronto
Delhi Mexico City São Paulo Sydney Hong Kong Seoul Singapore Taipei Tokyo

Editor in Chief: Ashley Dodge
Editorial Assistant: Nicole Suddeth
Managing Editor: Denise Forlow
Program Manager: Carly Czech
Program Project Manager: Doug Bell,
   PreMediaGlobal, Inc.
Executive Marketing Manager: Kelly May
Marketing Coordinator: Courtney Stewart
Director, Digital Media: Brian Hyland
Digital Media Project Manager: Tina Gagliostro

Creative Art Director: Jayne Conte
Cover Designer: Suzanne Behnke
Interior Design: Joyce Weston Design
Manager, Rights and Permissions: Paul Sarkis
Cover Art: © Nastya Pirieva
Full Service Project Management:
   PreMediaGlobal, Inc./Murugesh Namasivayam
Procurement Manager: Mary Fisher
Procurement Specialist: Eileen Corallo
Printer/Binder: Courier Westford

Credits and acknowledgments borrowed from other sources and reproduced, with permission, in this textbook appear on appropriate page within text.

Library of Congress Cataloging-in-Publication Data

Crosson-Tower, Cynthia.
   Understanding child abuse and neglect / Cynthia Crosson-Tower. — Ninth edition.
      pages cm
   Includes bibliographical references and index.
   ISBN-13: 978-0-205-39969-7 (alk. paper)
   ISBN-10: 0-205-39969-X (alk. paper)
 1. Child abuse—United States.   2. Abused children—Services for—United States.
   3. Social work with children—United States.   I. Title.
   HV6626.52.T69 2014
   362.760973—dc23

                                                                        2013013464

10 9 8 7 6 5 4 3

ISBN-10: 0-205-39969-X
ISBN-13: 978-0-205-39969-7

Contents

3. Maltreatment and the Developing Child   42

4. The Neglect of Children   60

8. Extrafamilial Sexual Abuse, Misuse, and Exploitation   166

14. Foster Care as a Therapeutic Tool   316

15. Adults Abused as Children   324

Preface

For Chay, Andrew, Becky, and Ruby

We live in a culture that values comfort and a sense of well-being. Even in today's difficult economy, the expectation is that, despite having to make some sacrifices, each citizen has the opportunity to achieve this sense of well-being. Yet many members of our culture—our children—are being beaten, neglected, and sexually exploited in alarming numbers. Every 10 seconds, a child is being abused or neglected.

Granted, child abuse and neglect have existed for centuries. And although some sources suggest that the incidence of child maltreatment has actually decreased slightly in the last few years, the fact remains that children are still being abused—in some cases more seriously than ever. Why has child maltreatment become such a serious issue? The answer may lie in several areas. We live in a more violent society than ever before. We are barraged with violent images, both in the news and in our entertainment. Crime statistics attest to the impact of this desensitization. The intensity and seriousness of the abuse perpetrated against children does, as well.

Does the answer also lie in the fact that the child protection system, set up to safeguard the lives of the children at risk for maltreatment, is not achieving its goal? As a former protective services worker, I recognize that individual professionals within protective services are often dedicated and well meaning, but the system as a whole is still not adequately protecting children, nor are these services often our fiscal priority.

What can be done to reverse the disturbing fact of child maltreatment? And how can society, and more specifically the child welfare system, better protect the children at risk?

These questions can be addressed from several vantage points. We look not only to raise societal awareness and increase research into causes of abuse and neglect, but we must also change social policy, triage the child welfare system, and provide better training for protective workers, not only in the skills important to do their job but in culturally sensitive ways to approach a variety of people from many different backgrounds.

After over 30 years of teaching courses on child abuse and neglect, many years in the child protection system, and over 40 years in the field of social services, I have written this book, now in the nineth edition, to prepare future and even current professionals to better intervene and treat the children and families at risk. This book draws on my years of practice to present an all-encompassing view of maltreatment, in its various guises, from symptoms of abuse and neglect to motivations of those who abuse and neglect children, as well as how the social services system intervenes. The questions asked of me by students, social service workers, and trainees have helped to shape the direction of the book. My experiences not only as a protective social worker but also as a therapist treating victims, families, and perpetrators and now a clergywoman have helped to provide ideas for the illustrations and examples.

New to This Edition

There are many new and updated materials throughout the text. Below are a few of the most exciting changes:

1. The text has been reorganized into 16 chapters to correspond with the typical academic semester.
2. CSWE's Core Competencies and Practice Behavior Examples grid added to front matter
3. Chapter 8 features the new topics of sexting and sexual trafficking.
4. Chapter 10 now covers the full range of intervention from reporting through case management.
5. Chapter 16 outlines what it is like to work in the child protection system from the everyday experiences of a social worker through the need for workers to use their knowledge to address effective prevention as well as planning for the future.
6. Additional pedagogical materials and specially correlated multimedia available in the eText included with the purchase of MySearchLab.

    - New learning objectives, self-study assessment including key topic quizzes and chapter reviews
    - Multimedia including videos, readings, weblinks, and more

Plan for the Text

Chapter 1 lays a framework for the discussion of abuse and neglect by tracing the history of child maltreatment from biblical times to the present. Chapter 2 considers the responsibilities of families and what rights society accords families and children. Maltreatment and the developing child are the focus of Chapter 3, which examines the effects of abusive and neglectful behavior on children's progress, or lack of progress, through developmental stages.

Chapters 4 through 9 outline the symptoms of neglect, physical abuse, sexual abuse, and emotional/psychological abuse, and they examine the needs and motivations of abusive and neglectful parents. Chapter 7 looks more closely at the incidence of incest, or sexual abuse within the family setting. Since sexual abuse can also be perpetrated by strangers, Chapter 8 considers abuse outside the family, including a discussion of child pornography, abuse on the Internet, prostitution, and sex rings. Chapter 9 considers the psychological abuse of children.

Chapters 10 and 11 focus on how to combat the problem of abuse. Chapter 10 discusses the intervention process—from the report through the investigation and case management—and highlights such important elements of protective work as home visiting, investigative interviewing, case management issues, and the roles of other professionals. The court system and how it might be called on to address abuse, neglect, and sexual abuse are considered in Chapter 11, distinguishing between intervention through the juvenile court process and prosecution through the criminal court system.

Chapters 12 and 13 outline the models of treatment available for abused and neglected children and their families. Therapy approaches for each type of maltreatment are considered separately. Chapter 14 discusses foster care as a therapeutic tool.

Following this examination of intervention, Chapter 15 provides a view of the experiences of adults who, as children, never reported abuse. The treatment available for these survivors is discussed.

The experience of working in child protection is the subject of Chapter 16—from a typical day in the life of a protective social worker and the challenges the work to the part that workers must play in prevention and in planning for the future.

In this ninth edition, I have continued to search more current research. Majority of the most recent research is now coming from Britain, Australia, and Europe as these countries meet the challenges of responding to child abuse and neglect. I have used these sources when the information appeared to be applicable to the United States. I have also continued to use classic writings in the field as well as a few more recent, albeit smaller, studies.

In response to reviewer requests, this edition has been reorganized into 16 chapters to correspond with the typical academic semester. The information on intervention as well as case management is now contained in Chapter 10. A new Chapter 16 focuses on the important aspects of child protection work including the need for social workers to not only pay attention to prevention but also to use their expertise to anticipate the best solutions for the future.

There continues to be the attention to military families reflected in the eighth edition. Additional topics such as sexting, and sexual trafficking have also been added.

Understanding Child Abuse and Neglect can be used as a text for undergraduate as well as graduate courses in social work, human services, psychology, and sociology or in counseling, family studies, and education programs.

Acknowledgments

Many people have contributed directly or indirectly to the writing of this book. My thanks go first to my family—especially to my husband, Jim; my sons, Chay and Andrew; and my daughter in-law, Becky. They continue to encourage me. In addition, my granddaughter, Ruby Louise has reminded me of the promise of childhood and how it must be protected.

I have learned a great deal from my students, both those in the behavioral sciences and those in theology, whose interest, enthusiasm, and inquiries have done much to stimulate this endeavor. As graduates, they have continued their support, often as close friends. My special thanks also go to Stephanie Flynn for her encouragement and willingness to chat about the frustrations of writing. I thank my able research assistant, Peggy Prasinos, who knows more about computers and how to find information than I ever hope to. Her support, as well as her computer-generated cartoons, was essential in keeping me on task. And she is always ready to tackle a new task with an enthusiasm that is contagious.

I thank the following reviewers for their helpful comments: Pam Reid, University of Akron; Rachel Happel, Missouri State University; Beth Walker, Western New Mexico University; Melody Loya, West Texas A&M University; and Brian Flynn, Binghamton University.

I also thank Carly Czech, my Pearson editor, and Mary Stone and Doug Bell of PreMediaGlobal, Inc., and all the dedicated and hard-working folks who worked to make this edition possible.

Cynthia Crosson-Tower
Harvest Counseling and Consultation

This text is available in a variety of formats—digital and print.
To learn more about our programs, pricing options, and customization,
visit **www.pearsonhighered.com.**

Chapter 1

The Maltreatment of Children from a Historical Perspective

Maltreatment of children is deeply entwined with historical values and perspectives. The concept of child maltreatment has been defined and redefined throughout history. Society is slowly evolving from viewing children as property, subject to the whims of the family and society, to at least recognizing that children may have rights of their own. Each period in history—as well as each culture—has a concept of how children should be treated.

CHILDREN AS PROPERTY

Early in history, children were seen as the property of their families—usually headed and ruled by fathers. Children looked to their fathers for their very existence. Fathers had the right to determine not only the manner in which their child was cared for but also if the child were to live or die.

Issues of Life and Death

Infanticide, or the killing of infants and young children, has occurred since early times. The Bible cites Abraham's intention to sacrifice his son, Isaac, to God. In early Rome, the father was given complete power to kill, abandon, or even sell his child. In Greek legend, Oedipus was doomed to death until he was rescued by a family retainer. In Hawaii, China, and Japan, many female and disabled children were killed to maintain a strong race without overpopulation.

Infanticide was practiced for many reasons. Like the Hawaiians, Chinese, and Japanese, some cultures saw the practice of infanticide as a means of controlling and regulating the population so that society's resources could be expended on the strongest and most valued. As in the case of Abraham, babies were offered to appease gods, and infanticide was in some ways associated with religious beliefs. Attempts to limit family size or ensure financial security were also used as rationales for killing children (deMause, 1998).

In early England, as in many other cultures, infanticide was an unwed mother's solution to her act of shame. A well-known ballad tells of Mary Hamilton, lady-in-waiting to the queen, who had the misfortune to become pregnant by the "highest Stewart of all," ostensibly the queen's consort. As she bemoans her disgrace, the balladeer sings:

> She tyed it in her apron
> And she's thrown it in the sea;
> Says, "Sink ye, swim ye, bonny wee babe
> You'll ne'er get m'air o' me." (Friedman, 1956)

In Germany, newborns were sometimes plunged into frigid water to test their ability to survive. A similar ritual was practiced by some tribes of Native Americans. The child was fit to live only if he or she surfaced and cried. Records in England in the 1620s attest to the burial of infants murdered by drowning, burning, and scalding.

Issues of Dependence

Children were dependent on their families not only for their early existence but also for their later survival. The feudal system in Europe established a concept of ownership and articulated a hierarchy of rights and privileges. Children were at the bottom, and the children of poor families fared the worst. If parents were unable to support themselves and their children, the fate of the family was often the poorhouse. Poorhouses offered a meager subsistence, which often ended in death for the weaker members of the family.

In 1601, the Elizabethan Poor Law sought to give some help to families and children by dictating that relief must be offered to the destitute. The poor were separated into three categories:

1. The able-bodied poor—those who were considered capable and were, therefore, forced to work

2. The impotent poor—those who were old, disabled, or mothers, who were excused from work and for whom aid was provided by the state

3. Dependent children—those who were orphaned or abandoned and for whom aid was provided

The fate of children still depended largely on their family constellation. Able-bodied people were sent to work. In some cases, mothers and their children were provided for at home by contributions of food and clothing but never money. Education was not viewed as a right or privilege of such families (Popple and Leighninger, 2010).

For those who were not poor, children fared as their families saw fit. Still seen as property, some children were slaves to their guardians, performing whatever tasks were expected of them. Certainly, the family life of a farming culture required that each member take part. For most children, this arrangement was satisfactory, but some children were assigned jobs far beyond their abilities or were beaten or neglected.

The early United States saw the arrival of immigrants other than Europeans. African slaves contributed greatly to the economic development of the new country, not only in the South but also in New England. The children of southern plantation slaves owed their allegiance to their parents as well as the masters who owned them. They were thought of as property and had little control over whether they worked, were sold (often without parents or siblings), or were used sexually by those more powerful. In the North, black children were not exempt from almshouses until 1822, when the Quakers in Philadelphia established the first orphanage for such children (Ambrosino et al., 2011; Popple and Leighninger, 2010; ten Bensel, Rheinberg, and Radbill, 1997).

Asian and Pacific Island immigrants came to the United States with their own values about dependent children. One significant value was that the family was involved with the care of the individual from the time of birth until death (Mass and Yap, 2000), which meant that dependent children were often absorbed into the ethnic community. Native American children were also generally regarded as the responsibility of the community. In addition, Hispanic children relied on extended family members or friends to supplement or substitute for parental nurturance.

Issues of Discipline

The subject of discipline has always been controversial. Many methods used in early Western culture would certainly be open to censure today. The philosophies of our fore-bears, however, differ from those of most modern-day societies. Not only in the home but in the classroom, corporal punishment was a means to mold children into moral, God-fearing, respectful human beings. Parents were expected to raise religious, dedicated, morally sound, and industrious contributors to the community. Obedience was the primary virtue to develop in children. Disobedience often carried significant fines; even older children were subject to such rules. An 1854 Massachusetts law stated,

> If any children above sixteen years old and of sufficient understanding shall curse or smite their natural father or mother, they shall be put to death, unless it can be sufficiently testified that the parents have been unchristianly negligent in the education of such children or so provoked them by extreme and cruel correction that they have been forced thereunto to preserve themselves from death or maiming. (Bremner, 1970, p. 68)

The schoolmaster or mistress was accorded the same right to use corporal punishment:

> School masters in colonial Boston were conscious of the need to maintain the great English tradition of "education through pain" and, if anything added refinements to the flagellant tools they had inherited from the old country. One Bostonian invented an instrument called a "flapper"—a heavy piece of leather six inches in diameter with a hole in the middle which was fixed to a wooden handle. Every stroke on a bare bit of flesh raised an instant blister. (Inglis, 1978, p. 29)

Theologian John Calvin was of no help to children in the treatment accorded them by their elders. Calvin spoke of breaking a child's will in the hope of saving the spirit from evil. Discipline was severe in the hope that children could be transformed into God-fearing individuals.

For a short period during the eighteenth century, the treatment of children improved. Philosopher Jean-Jacques Rousseau spoke of children as inherently good and encouraged educational methods that would enhance their positive development, not break their spirit (Lenoir-Degoumois, 1983).

Other cultures had their own interpretations about discipline. Many (e.g., Asian/Pacific, Hispanic) stressed the dominance of elders or males who had the right to determine how to deal with children. The strong kinship relationships of African Americans and the community responsibility inherent in Native American cultures indicated that the care and discipline of children were shared by parent figures.

CHILD LABOR

One of the earliest forms of child labor was *indenture*—a system in which parents apprenticed their children to masters who taught them a trade but who were free to use them as virtual slaves in exchange for room and board. Indenture began at a very young age and continued until 14 or 16 years of age for boys and 21 years for girls. Writings by historians, novelists, and social reformers show that apprentice masters could be cruel—concerned more for the work they could extract than for the development or abilities of their juvenile charges. Charles Dickens wrote of Oliver Twist's days as an apprentice to an undertaker. Exposed to death in its basic forms, fed very little, and chided and belittled by his master's older apprentice, Oliver thought he had little recourse. In fact, English society assumed he had inherited a good lot and one for which he should be most thankful.

Indenture and child labor were also issues in early United States. As the Industrial Revolution progressed, the practice of prematurely bringing children into the labor market began to be a concern. Children were brought to the colonies to work until they were 24 years old. Child labor was seen as an inexpensive boon to the labor market, since a child could be hired for less wages than an adult. Some jobs, such as chimney sweeping and mining, were suited to children's small bodies (Hindman, 2002; Mintz, 2006; Rose and Fatout, 2003; ten Bensel et al., 1997).

As the 1800s dawned in the United States, the role of children remained little changed. They continued to be the property of their parents, who could choose to beat them, neglect them, or send them out to work. As the population increased and society became more impersonal, assaults on children were more easily hidden.

In the late 1880s, the settlement house movement evolved. It contributed much to the future of children and their families and had a substantial impact on the reduction of child labor. The settlement houses became known through the establishment of Toynbee Hall, as a result of the influence of Arnold Toynbee in London. Inspired by the dedication of such an act, Jane Addams established Hull House in the Chicago slums. Hull House not only bridged the gap between new and more established immigrants, but it was the impetus for later reforms of benefit to children. One of Addams's special concerns was child labor:

> Our very first Christmas at Hull House, when we as yet knew nothing of child labor, a number of little girls refused the candy which was offered them as part of the Christmas good cheer, saying simply that they "worked in a candy factory and could not bear the sight of it." We discovered that for six weeks they had worked from seven in the morning until nine at night and they were exhausted as well as satiated. The sharp consciousness of stern economic conditions was thrust upon us in the midst of the season of good will. (Addams, 1910, p. 148)

Addams also described the dangerous conditions:

> During the same winter three boys from the Hull House club were injured at one machine in a neighborhood factory for lack of a guard which would have cost but

a few dollars. When the injury of one of these boys resulted in death, we felt quite sure that the owners would share our horror and remorse, and that they would do everything possible to prevent the reoccurrence of such a tragedy. To our surprise they did nothing whatever, and I made my first acquaintance then with those pathetic documents signed by the parents of working children, that they will make no claim for damages resulting from "carelessness." (Addams, 1910, p. 148)

Although Addams and her staff at Hull House fought hard for changes in these conditions, it wasn't until much later that laws protecting children from unreasonable labor were enacted.

In addition, African American children were largely excluded from settlement house programs and from the predominantly white Charity Organization Societies (Jackson, 1978). As a result, until legislation was later passed, there was little to protect them from being used as laborers.

SEXUAL VALUES, ATTITUDES, AND EXPLOITATION

Early History

The definition of *sexual exploitation* has evolved throughout history. Although we might today consider the values and attitudes of the past as exploitive, the fact remains that our current customs exploit children in other ways.

In ancient times, the child, especially the female, was considered the property of her father, to do with as he saw fit. His permission was required for all her dealings. She was something with which he could barter for lands and money. With the father's permission, a betrothal could be sealed by intercourse with the underage (under 12 years) daughter. Marriage of extremely young girls was not uncommon. Since early times, fathers paid dowries for the marriage of their daughters. When dowries could not be provided for all female children, some girls entered the convent, sometimes by the age of 9, to take their vows by age 13. Rush (1992) relates a prioress's confession that young nuns were treated like wives by the monks associated with the convent. The girls were threatened with excommunication if they told of this sexual exploitation.

Boys were not immune to sexual misuse in early history either. In Greece, pederasty (men using boys for sexual relationships) was practiced widely. Boys were taken for their attractive appearance, their softness, and their youth but were expected to show strength in battle. In fact, pederasty was the training ground for future soldiers. Most sons of noble families were actually compelled to take adult lovers, and in turn, the boys were protected and plied with gifts. The protector was teacher and counselor, accepted and approved by the boy's family (Rush, 1992). In early Rome, however, sex or sexual relationships were not seen as a means of elevating children, as in Greece. In Rome, the rape of a child was a humiliation rather than a means of owning a treasured plaything (Rush, 1992).

It was not until 1548 that any legal protection from sexual abuse was offered to children. In that year, England passed a law protecting boys from forced sodomy. In 1576, another law was enacted that prohibited the forcible rape of girls under the age of 10 (Conte and Shore, 1982, p. 22). In the 1700s, some educators warned parents to protect their children from abuse by supervising them at all times and by ensuring that they were never nude in front of adults and in general suggested enforced modesty (Conte and Shore, 1982). This warning was one of the earliest indications that the larger society recognized children could be sexually exploited.

The Nineteenth Century

The rigid standards of the Victorian era also colored society's attitudes toward sexuality and children. Masturbation was vehemently condemned as being a precursor of insanity, growth retardation, and early death for boys; for girls, it was said to promote precocious sexual development, promiscuity, and nymphomania. Attempts to curb this practice of self-gratification were extreme—surgery to remove the clitoris, slitting the penis, or cutting the nerves of the genitalia in both sexes. With these measures came the message that children should not be seen as sexual beings.

The Victorian era, however, was replete with contradictions. On one hand, society was undergoing unbelievable advances in industrial enterprise and scientific discoveries; it was a time of deep thought and analysis. Yet behind the closed doors of so-called God-fearing homes, sexual abuse apparently flourished. Child molesters, even those who took their interests outside the family, seem to have been well protected. Numerous revered men in the public eye were taken with the charms of little girls, some to the point of acting on their desires. William Wordsworth expounded on his admiration of nubile young girls, and at age 26, Edgar Allan Poe wed his 13-year-old cousin (Rush, 1992). Victorian morals viewed this union as scandalous, even though girls marrying at a young age had been a common practice. Lewis Carroll was well known for his interest in children. He is said to have had an entourage of whom he took nude photos. Biographers and critics have questioned whether his activities extended beyond taking pictures, telling stories, and playing games with the children (Lennon, 1972; ten Bensel et al., 1997).

Pornography and child prostitution also increased during the Victorian period. Men who dared not "prevail upon their wives to do their duty too often" and who shielded their children from explanations of sexuality thought nothing of frequenting child prostitutes in city slums. In the early nineteenth century, U.S. slave owners delighted in "breaking in" their young slaves or using them for breeding. Often, 11-, 12-, and 13-year-old girls were impregnated (Olafson et al., 1993; Rush, 1992).

Into this scene came a man who was to be the father of modern psychoanalysis. Sigmund Freud, a therapist in nineteenth-century Vienna, treated women who were diagnosed as having hysterical neuroses and exhibiting a variety of symptoms from compulsive vomiting, sneezing, and coughing to blindness, deafness, and paralysis. In the course of therapy, a large number of patients reported having been sexually abused at a young age. In response to this phenomenon, Freud (1966, p. 584) wrote, "Almost all my women patients told me that they had been seduced by their fathers. I was driven to recognize in the end that these reports were untrue and so came to understand that the hysterical symptoms are derived from phantasies and not from real occurrences."

Note, however, that in 1905, in the case of "Dora," Freud included a vivid description of the 14-year-old girl's seduction by her father and her subsequent use as a "pawn in [his] elaborate sex intrigues" (Herman, 1997, p. 14). From his account, the abuse obviously seems to have occurred so that it is difficult to believe Freud later discounted the credibility of the situation (Rush, 1992). We will never know what caused Freud's reversal of his theories,[1] since he destroyed his notes and diaries. Certainly, his attitudes have had an influence on our current denial or reluctance to recognize the symptoms of sexual abuse in children.

The Twentieth Century

Over the years, literature has reflected a preoccupation with sexual activity and children. In 1955, Vladimir Nabokov's novel *Lolita* shocked the public and was banned from numerous bookstores and libraries. People's fascination with this type of story was obvious, and the book became a popular seller and later a movie. At age 12, Lolita is seduced by 50-year-old Humbert Humbert, who had become captivated with her. Unfortunately, the story perpetrated the belief that children—especially young girls—knowingly seduce older men, who are helpless to resist. As such, this novel—and later ones like it—likely provided rationalization for incestuous fathers and added to the misconceptions of the general public. *Greek Love*, by J. Z. Eglinton (1965), recounted love and sexual tutelage of boys by adult men and how such a relationship prepares boys for adult sexual experiences. Lawrence Sanders's *The Case of Lucy Bending* (1982) gave the impression of an adult abused by a disturbed child who had instigated the relationship.

It is clear that our current society harbors a contradiction in its view of children and sexuality. On one hand, we state that children should not be exploited sexually; on the other hand, child pornography thrives, both in print and on the Internet, and the courts are often more likely to believe molesting adults than molested children. Television commercials use nubile girls posed seductively. The Internet provides an excellent vehicle for perpetrators to contact children for sex. Such practices can only give molesters and children a mixed message about what society believes about sexual abuse and the sexual exploitation of children.

Newly immigrated cultures bring with them their own contradictory practices. For example, father–daughter incest is rare in India. Rather, an Indian father finds his power in his ability to offer a virginal daughter in marriage—hopefully, one that will improve her economic status. However, sexual abuse of young boys is not uncommon though rarely discussed. Indians often bring these taboos and attitudes with them as they immigrate to other cultures.

THE INCEST TABOO

History

In some form, the taboo against incest appears to be universal. Historically, prohibitions of marriage and sexual relations with one's immediate blood relatives are found even in early writings. In the Bible, Leviticus outlines those individuals whom one could

---

[1]Some theorists (e.g., Rush, 1992) attribute Freud's shift to personal experiences, whereas others (e.g., Meiselman, 1992; Olafson et al., 1993) suggest that collegial pressure was the primary reason.

not uncover: "You shall not uncover the nakedness of your father, which is the naked-ness of your mother; she is your mother, you shall not uncover her nakedness" (Lev. 18:7). Throughout the scripture, sisters, granddaughters, stepsisters, aunts, and daughters-in-law are specifically cited as protected from sexual contact with relatives (Lev. 18:9–18). Marriage with particular individuals was also discouraged. This taboo may actually be the basis of current mores in the United States. The Greeks and Romans prohibited sexual relationships between cousins. Emperor Claudius of Rome married his niece, Agrippina, making uncle–niece marriages acceptable for a time (Weinberg, 1955). In Egypt, during the Pharaonic and Ptolemaic periods, brother–sister unions among royalty were not un-usual, with Cleopatra's marriage to two of her brothers perhaps the best known. There is some indication that during their conquest of Egypt, Romans also saw sibling marriages as acceptable (Middleton, 1962).

Christianity and the early Catholic Church in Europe reestablished and strengthened taboos on incest and intermarriage. Historically, the penalties for incest ranged from se-vere censure to decapitation (in eighteenth-century Scotland). By the early 1900s, punish-ment through "penal servitude" or other types of incarceration were favored, and thus the offense became civil rather than religious (Weinberg, 1955).

Reasons for Taboo

Religious laws and legal writings have devoted much attention to the commission of in-cest. How did this taboo originate? Several possible explanations have been offered for the taboo of incest.

Biological

In *Ancient Society* (1877), L. H. Morgan suggested that incestuous marriages created de-fective offspring. His information appeared to be based on the experiences of animal breeders who discovered that constant inbreeding created a variety of physical and mental disabilities.

The biological theories of Morgan and his contemporaries were later discounted, however, on the basis of several factors and beliefs. First, geneticists argued that although one can create dysfunctional characteristics by inbreeding and thus giving more oppor-tunity for recessive genes to combine, it is also possible to create superior individuals through the same process. Some breeders of animals practice inbreeding to produce a stronger and better species. Second, it is difficult to detect whether the inferior offspring are a result of weaknesses on the part of the founders of the strain or if the process of inbreeding is at fault. Third, since animals use little selection in mating, they would be extinct if Morgan's theories were true.

Sexual Aversion

Meiselman (1992) discussed the theories of E. Westermarck and J. K. Fox. Despite a funda-mental belief in the biological interpretation, Westermarck in 1922 suggested that another explanation could be that people who live together constantly develop a sexual aversion. This theory was later supported by Fox, who in 1962 used the example of children raised in the Israeli kibbutzim. Thrown together from birth, these children seek sexual partners elsewhere.

Family Disruption

Family disruption was the basis for Malinowski's theory (1927) of the origin of the incest taboo. This anthropologist suggested that the family could not tolerate the ambiguity, blurred role definitions, and confusion of feelings brought on by the sexual involvement of its members. Interestingly enough, family disruption is considered today to be one of the major causes as well as one of the effects of incestuous behavior.

Multidimensional Theories

In *Incest*, Meiselman (1992) reported that in the 1940s, L. A. White contributed to the incest controversy, and G. P. Murdock created his own multidimensional theory. White contended that survival in early societies was difficult and often depended on ingenuity and cooperation with others. As language developed, people became better able to exchange goods and ideas with other cultures. Marriage with other cultures increased networks and enhanced the possibilities for survival. Intermarriage created isolation and reduced the number of individuals available for marriage outside the tribe, thus limiting the chances of networking.

Murdock later used White's theory but suggested that it be combined with the premise that family members had a repressed desire for each other and that the family itself had to preserve its stability by keeping confusion and sexual jealousy to a minimum. This stability was most likely achieved by prohibiting incestuous behavior.

Subsequently, a variety of theorists reemphasized the importance of the incest taboo to the family structure and suggested the influence of such a taboo on the child's development. As noted by Justice and Justice (1980), Talcott Parsons wrote in 1954 that the incest taboo helped the child develop autonomy and social roles necessary to eventually leave the family. Prohibited from having sexual relations with family members, the child must then seek others outside the family structure. Carl Jung also mentioned the incest taboo as part of the child's vital struggle for individualization. Freud also spoke of the necessity of the child giving up incestuous wishes in order to succeed and procreate outside the family system (see also Turner, 2005).

Legal and Social Prohibition

Today, marriages with blood relatives are prohibited by law in the United States. Individual states differ in prohibitions against marriages between cousins, stepparents, and stepsiblings. The penalty for breaking this cultural and legal taboo is a jail or prison sentence. Perhaps more powerful, however, is the social stigma attached. Culturally, Weinberg (1955, p. 31) describes the stereotype as having four components:

1. An inner revulsion to incest
2. Disgust with the participants
3. Perception that participants are mentally or emotionally abnormal
4. Perception of a disorganized or even absent family life

In fact, the taboo is violated in our modern society. Current studies support the idea that incestuous relationships are barriers to children's autonomous development. Incestuous families demonstrate disorganization and dysfunction suggested by early theorists.

RECENT HISTORY OF HELPING THE ABUSED AND NEGLECTED CHILD

So far, the historical perspective has not included the individuals and movements that preceded our current child welfare systems. One of the first organized attempts to protect children was the Elizabethan Poor Law. This law was enacted not so much for the children but for society to deal with the impoverished parents. Churches and communities were often expected to provide for children who did not come under the jurisdiction of the law.

Voluntary child welfare services sprang up in isolation during the seventeenth and eighteenth centuries. Convents, churches, and philanthropists led the efforts in early child protection, but the advocates for children did not always arise from the expected quarters of religious and humanitarian groups. From firsthand knowledge, Charles Dickens spoke up for child protection. At age 12, Dickens was sent from his family to a workhouse in London. His father was frequently in debtors' prisons, and his mother's rejection of him was a fact that would greatly influence his life and later writings. In 1838, he wrote *Oliver Twist*, a largely autobiographical novel about a young boy who goes from the poorhouse to apprenticeship and finally to live among a band of juvenile thieves. As Gardner (1980) reports, this book represented Dickens's first social protest and was to be followed by other novels concerned with abused, abandoned, and crippled children. By midcentury, Dickens's work had spread and was influential throughout the United States. In 1858, Dickens began his campaign for child protection with a speech supporting the Great Ormond Street Hospital for Children in London. He graphically detailed a neglected, dying child he had seen in the slums of Edinburgh. His oration had such impact that it was published as a pamphlet for distribution.

Several years after Dickens's speech, events were taking shape to transform the course of child protection. New York City was the backdrop for a scene featuring Henry Bergh, who was gaining much attention as the first president of the Society for the Prevention of Cruelty to Animals (SPCA). A writer, lecturer, and administrator, Bergh had so aroused the sentiments of community leaders in intervening in the maltreatment of animals that his efforts were known as Bergh's War. In the midst of this "war" came the case of Mary Ellen Wilson (Shelman and Lazoritz, 2003). In 1874, Mary Ellen lived with Francis and Mary Connelly and was the illegitimate daughter of Mrs. Connelly's first husband. On several occasions, a neighbor had observed the ill-clad 8-year-old shivering outside a locked door. But Mary Ellen's screams as she was beaten with a leather strap were more than the neighbor could bear. She reported her observations to Etta Wheeler, a church worker from St. Luke's Methodist Mission, who, not knowing where else to turn, took the matter to Henry Bergh at the SPCA.

Although most reports are that Bergh intervened on behalf of the SPCA, more recent sources quote Bergh as saying that he acted as a private citizen. Whatever his motivation, Mary Ellen was removed from the home, and Bergh's close friend, attorney Elbridge Gerry, was asked to prosecute. For Mrs. Connelly, the outcome was a year of labor in prison, and for Mary Ellen, the result was the end of the abuse she had been suffering and eventual placement in the Sheltering Arms children's home.[2] For the nation, however, Mary Ellen Wilson's abuse set into motion an organized effort to combat child maltreatment. Thus, in 1875, the Society for the Prevention of Cruelty to Children (SPCC), under the leadership of Elbridge Gerry, began an impressive movement toward protecting children.

The New York branch of the SPCC was eventually duplicated in Philadelphia and Chicago. The SPCC not only intervened in cases of child abuse and neglect but also advocated for child protection in a variety of arenas. Many chapters sponsored shelters for women and children who were in economic distress or victims of family violence. Later, the Boston chapter emphasized *family rehabilitation*, a new concept in protective services. This total family approach would eventually be the predominant philosophy of child protection agencies.

Dedication to this family-centered treatment was obvious from the White House Conference on Dependent Children in 1909. The conference supported the plan for a Children's Bureau, enacted in 1912, to oversee the welfare of children. The bureau did not, however, deal with individual cases of maltreatment but entrusted investigation and treatment of individual children to public agencies, thus diminishing the original strength of the SPCC movement (Smuts, 2005). Another organization dedicated to seeing that children's needs were met was an indirect result of this first White House conference. The Child Welfare League of America (CWLA), a product of Carl Christian's 1915 paper, proposing standards for services and aid provided to children, continues to exist today as one of the foremost advocates for children.

Although World War I temporarily diverted attention from child protection, as the nation braced itself for a different conflict, the American Humane Association added children to its list of concerns and continued to gather support from anticruelty societies from every part of the United States.

By 1930, the cause of children's rights and the treatment of abused children was revived in the Social Security Act that mandated "child welfare services for neglected dependent children and children in danger of becoming delinquent." Although intervention was mandated, the detection of child abuse and neglect was left largely to social workers. Physicians had not entered the war against child maltreatment, possibly because of an unfortunate diagnosis made in 1868 by Dr. Athol Johnson. This London physician observed repeated fractures in hospitalized children and misdiagnosed them as rickets, thus opening the door for almost a century of future misinterpretations.

In the mid-1940s, at Columbia University, a radiology professor, John Caffey (1946), noted that the x-rays of some infants demonstrated unexplained multiple fractures. He also noted an increased number of victims with subdural hematoma (a collection of blood under the skull). The case histories did not indicate any falls or events serious enough to

---

[2]Many wondered what happened to Mary Ellen after her much-publicized case. The Sheltering Arms was, in fact, a home for disturbed girls—not orphans like Mary Ellen. Thus, Mary Ellen became a victim of the system's mistreatment as well. Still concerned with her, Etta Wheeler, recognizing the inappropriate placement, petitioned Judge Lawrence to be Mary Ellen's appointed guardian. Lawrence allowed Wheeler to place the child with Wheeler's mother, Sally Angell, on a farm outside Rochester, New York. When Angell died, Mary Ellen continued to be raised by Angell's daughter. Years later, Mary Ellen's own daughter would write to the then director of SPCC, asking to know more of her mother's history (Lazoritz, 1990).

explain these medical findings. Caffey wondered if these traumas had been somehow inflicted by the parents. He stated his suspicions:

> In each case unexplained fresh fractures appeared shortly after the patient had arrived home after discharge from the hospital. In one of these cases the infant was clearly unwanted by both parents and this raised the question of intentional ill treatment of the infant; the evidence was inadequate to prove or disprove this point. (p. 166)

Caffey's theory was supported by several other physicians in the early 1950s. Both Parton (1985) and ten Bensel et al. (1997) note that F. N. Silverman, along with P. V. Wooley and W. A. Evans, reported they had explored Caffey's work and felt there was strong evidence that parents were responsible for many of these injuries.

Physicians continued to study the phenomenon. In 1962, Dr. C. Henry Kempe, chairman of the Department of Pediatrics at the University of Colorado School of Medicine, and his colleagues published in the *Journal of the American Medical Association* the now-famous article entitled "The Battered-Child Syndrome." Kempe and colleagues used this syndrome to refer to a condition in young children who had apparently been victims of severe physical abuse, generally at the hands of a parent or foster parent. The condition has also been described as "unrecognized trauma" by radiologists, orthopedists, pediatricians, and social service workers. Kempe cited the age of the children involved as under 3 years and suggested that diagnosticians look for a discrepancy between clinical findings and historical data supplied by the parents as a primary indicator (ten Bensel et al., 1997). Although experts now include within this syndrome children older than 3 years, the difference between clinical findings and data supplied by parents is still thought to be significant in the identification of maltreatment. Kempe went on to establish one of the first child protection teams in 1958 at the Colorado General Hospital in Denver (Myers, 2011; ten Bensel et al., 1997).

The identification of the phenomenon by name and definition provided a means to publicize the problem. *Battered-child syndrome* was talked about by almost every professional concerned with children, and an increasing number of studies were undertaken to determine the magnitude of the problem. The studies conducted by Kempe and associates uncovered that in 71 hospitals, at least 302 cases of child abuse had occurred; 33 of these children subsequently died and 85 suffered permanent brain injury. Following Kempe's work, Vincent DeFrancis, the new director of the American Humane Association, discovered that in the year 1962 alone, 662 cases of child abuse were reported to the press (ten Bensel et al., 1997).

Further Efforts on Behalf of Children

The fervor of the 1960s caused professionals, who had not thought of child abuse as a problem within their particular domain, to recognize their need to be involved. Ray Helfer, a collaborator with Henry Kempe and a fellow physician, outlined the reasons that physicians in the past had been reticent to report abuse. Helfer felt that physicians were both unaware of their legal obligations and unable to recognize parental abuse because of close ties to the family (Richardson, 2003; ten Bensel et al., 1997). By the early 1970s, through the efforts of Helfer and others, physicians had been made well aware of their responsibilities to children and their families.

In 1972, the National Center for the Prevention of Child Abuse and Neglect was established with financial aid from the University of Colorado Medical Center. The purpose of this office was to provide a newsletter, engage in research, and offer training for recognizing and preventing child abuse to interested professionals.

By 1973, the need for a federal stand on the issue became obvious. The Child Abuse Prevention bill (S. 1191) was proposed on March 13, 1973, largely under the sponsorship of Senator Walter Mondale, chairman of the Subcommittee on Children and Youth. Ellen Hoffman (1978), primary author of the Child Abuse Prevention and Treatment Act proposal, was greatly influenced by C. Henry Kempe. Hoffman's proposal to establish a National Center on Child Abuse and Neglect under the auspices of the Department of Health, Education and Welfare (HEW) was in four parts:

1. The center would be responsible for research, establishment of a clearinghouse, and distribution of training materials.

2. Demonstration projects to "prevent, identify and treat child abuse and neglect" would be encouraged by the provision of $10 million in 1973 and $20 million for the next four years to be used for grants and contracts.

3. To study the effectiveness of child abuse and neglect-reporting laws and "the proper role of the federal government" in assisting state and local efforts, a board, known as the National Commission on Child Abuse and Neglect, would be established.

4. States would be required to adopt specific procedures to identify, treat, and prevent child abuse and to maintain information and report to HEW on the efficiency of these procedures. States would also be required to cooperate with state health education and other agencies in the interest of coordinating the treatment of child abuse and neglect cases. Complying with these standards would protect the states' eligibility for certain funds under the Social Security Act.

Hearings for the adoption of this bill went on for four days in Washington, Denver, and New York. Slides of abused and neglected children were shown, and experts attested to the need for such a law. A witness who made a substantial impact was Jolly K., the founder of Parents Anonymous. She candidly described how she had at one time beaten her own children. What she did not tell the assembled group, however, was that she had been a victim herself of beatings, abandonment, and rape. Her testimony had a phenomenal impact, and in January 1974, the Child Abuse Prevention and Treatment Act was passed. This act mandated the reporting of child maltreatment, provided funds for research, mandated training, and made provisions for the treatment of child abuse and neglect. It was 100 years after Mary Ellen Wilson shivered on the steps of her foster home that the nation officially recognized the need to provide for all children like her.

The Child Abuse Prevention and Treatment Act, although perhaps the most far reaching, would not be the last legislation to influence services to abused and neglected children. The Adoption Assistance and Child Welfare Act of 1980 (P.L. 96-272) sought to prevent removal of children from their families by making "reasonable efforts" to keep families together or to unify families in a timely manner if placement could not be avoided. When reunification was not possible, this act mandated that the best permanent plan (often adoption) be sought.

Three years later, the Family Preservation and Support Services Act was passed as part of the Omnibus Budget Reconciliation Act of 1993 (P.L. 103-66), building on the previous legislation by expanding the services available to strengthen families as well as providing additional supports for children who must be placed outside the home (Jackson and Brissett-Chapman, 1999).

Professional Awareness and Response to the Movement to Protect Children and Families

As the movement to provide safe environments for children attracted more and more national attention, various professionals began to emphasize the importance of their discipline's involvement in intervention. Kempe and his colleagues led the way in helping fellow physicians and other medical personnel recognize the vital role they could play in detecting and reporting child abuse. The 1962 article "Battered-Child Syndrome" stimulated increased interest in the phenomenon, research, and programs within medical communities. In 1977, Kempe and several of his colleagues created the International Society for the Prevention and Treatment of Child Abuse and Neglect in an effort to

> to promote opportunities, facilities and organizations which will enable the children of all nations to develop physically, mentally and socially and in a normal manner . . . and in particular, to promote the protection of every child, in every country against all forms of cruelty and exploitation. (ISPCN, 2012)

This organization continues to support efforts in the area of treatment and research largely through the publication of the *International Journal of Child Abuse and Neglect.*

Sexual abuse was not widely studied until the late 1970s, when David Finklehor surveyed New England College students to determine if they had been sexually abused as children. About the same time, Diana Russell's study of 940 San Francisco women uncovered that 38 percent reported sexual abuse as children. As researchers looked for indications that children were being sexually abused, survivors began speaking out. Butler's *Conspiracy of Silence* and Brady's *Father's Days* recounted abuse perpetuated against children by their fathers.

Physician Suzanne Sgroi urged those in the medical community to pay closer attention to venereal disease in children as an indicator of child sexual abuse (1988). In 1983, Roland Summit, thought by many to be the initiator of our current understanding of the dynamics of sexual abuse, published his now well-known article "The Child Sexual Abuse Accommodation Syndrome," in which he outlined his theory of how children are affected by such abuse. Thus, sexual abuse, once a concept foreign to most of us, had become a household phrase by the 1980s and 1990s.

As society became more aware of the need to protect children from a variety of types of maltreatment, the importance of having schools involved became more obvious. In the early 1980s, the National Education Association commissioned Crosson-Tower, a former protective services worker and then an educator, to write a book to help to bridge the gap between schools and protective service agencies. *Child Abuse and Neglect: An Educator's Guide to Recognition, Reporting, and Classroom Management* (Tower, 1984) soon gave rise to a multimedia training package for educators. Since this time, schools have become significantly involved in responding to child maltreatment issues.

Other professions were also urged to enhance the training and knowledge of professionals. Publications began to address not only the medical, psychiatric, and educational professions but the criminal justice and legal arenas as well.

Professionals within community organizations, such as churches and civic groups, have also recognized the need for involvement. Increasingly, a variety of religious denominations are recommending or requiring that churches develop Safe Church policies to protect children who worship there (see Crosson-Tower, 2006).

Today, a glance at the book sellers' booths at any major child abuse conference confirms that much has been written for a variety of readers. In addition to texts, a variety of clearinghouses available through websites offers resources for professional and layperson alike.

The Child Welfare Information Gateway (http://childwelfare.gov) offers a wealth of information along with sites sponsored by the Kempe Center (www.kempe.org) and the American Humane Association (www.americanehumane.org). Prevent Child Abuse America (www.preventchildabuse.org) also helps to coordinate and circulate information on child abuse prevention. Currently numerous journals, including the *International Journal of Child Abuse and Neglect, Child Maltreatment*, and the *Journal of Child Sexual Abuse* serve to keep professionals better informed.

Professionals now realize that their strength in combating the problem of child abuse and neglect is through communication.

CHILD PROTECTION TODAY

Current Framework

A significant problem in child abuse intervention is the fact that there is no universally agreed-on way to define maltreatment nor is there just one framework used to understand the focal point at which intervention should be initiated or how this intervention should proceed. Brissett-Chapman (Jackson and Brissett-Chapman, 1999) expressed her concern over this issue by commenting that

> [the] no universal operational definition of child abuse and neglect, and the multiple and overlapping definitions challenge the very ability of professional helping systems to adequately and universally address the assessment of risks, the allocation of resources, the accurate assessment of the need for the child's removal from the family, or the opportunity to engage the involvement of other actors (i.e., neighbors, family, community institutions, allied disciplines) in ensuring that children are safe and adequately cared for. (p. 53)

Intervention ideologies can be broken down into three basic orientations: penal, medical, and social welfare (see Table 1.1). Each of these has a characteristic way of viewing the abuser, the act, and the type of intervention necessary. As you continue reading this text, it will be important to bear these differences in mind. As the field builds a more multidimensional set of intervention strategies, it is hoped that these views can borrow from and influence one another. Certainly, the ideal would be a universally accepted framework, but that is not something that appears to be immediately on the horizon.

Table 1.1 Alternative Child Abuse Ideologies

Framework	Penal/Legal	Medical/Scientific	Social Welfare/Humanistic	
			(a) traditional	(b) radical
Presupposition	individual has free will	behavior is determined	(a) traditional	(b) radical
Definition	cruelty	battered-child syndrome	child abuse	child abuse
Attitude to problem	punitive; deviance is conscious defiance of rules; moralistic	results from forces beyond control of individual	compassionate; individual/family cannot cope with situation	relative but results from social processes
Social rationale	justice; due process; individual rights	cure; treatment of needs of the child	prevention; rehabilitation by adjustment	social liberation by reorganization
Focus of attention	act of abuse; deprivation	disease process, pathology syndromes	the person; family, social situation; "cycle of deprivation"	social processes, structural inequality
Tools	legal code, courts	medical expertise and technology	counselling, therapeutic relationships, social experts	social change
Conception of parents	responsible	irresponsible or not responsible	psychologically, emotionally, and socially inadequate	socially victimized
Stated purpose of intervention	punishment of guilt	treatment of dysfunction	personal, family rehabilitation, physical and emotional safety of child	equality and redistribution
Some practicing groups	police, judiciary	doctors, some psychiatrists	social workers; some doctors, e.g., pediatricians	some social workers and some sociologists

Source: From Nigel Parton, *The Politics of Child Abuse*, Table 1.2, p. 17. Copyright © 1985. Reprinted by permission of Macmillan London and Basingstoke (world rights) and St. Martin's Press (U.S. rights).

The Role of Child Protective Services

Contrary to the provision of services for maltreated children in the past, it is the child protective services (CPS) agency that currently serves the pivotal role in responding to reports of abuse and neglect. Depending on the state that it serves, CPS is known by a variety of titles, including the Department of Social Services, the Department of Health and Human Services, the Department of Family and Children's Services, and others. The fact that this agency acts as a division of the state or county has both positive and negative points.

From the 1960s to the mid-1980s, CPS enjoyed relative autonomy, while also becoming an entity feared by parents for its ability to "take kids away." Despite this belief, CPS was largely dependent on the legal arm of the juvenile court to remove children. Only in a case of severe emergency or abandonment did CPS have the authority to place children for a specified period (usually 72 hours) while their parents were sought or plans were made for their welfare. (For those early years, see Crosson-Tower's *From the Eye of the Storm: The Experiences of a Child Welfare Worker*, 2002.)

Throughout the 1980s and 1990s, the role of CPS shifted in scope and emphasis. Part of the responsibility for the shift can be attributed to the Adoption Assistance and Child Welfare Act of 1980 and later the Family Preservation and Support Services Act (both mentioned previously). Weber (1997) suggests that there were several other underlying causes for the transformation in the role of CPS. First, there was a lack of consensus about the role of CPS, as parents whose children were removed began to protest through legal channels. Lawsuits argued that CPS had not had enough evidence to prove the need for removal, and this led to the formation of Victims of Child Abuse Legislation (VOCAL), a group that advocated for themselves and others. The court actions complaining of insufficient evidence forced CPS to hone its investigative procedures and ensure that the lawyers responsible for representing their contention that children needed to be better protected were better trained (Weber, 1997).

These events came to the attention of the media. Because the parents protesting their innocence saw media attention as a way to publicly plead their cases, whereas CPS was bound to silence by the agency regulation requiring confidentiality, the agency did not fare well in public opinion. When a child was finally identified as the victim of severe abuse or died, Weber (1997) suggests that the scenario was amazingly predictable. CPS was portrayed as a

> government agency with no public accountability which had not done its job of protecting children. The scenario was usually followed by a mayor's or governor's task force or blue-ribbon commission. One or more CPS staff members were then found not to have taken every reasonable action to protect the child; a reorganization of the CPS agency was instituted; the task force recommended smaller caseloads, more training and clearer policies; and elected officials provided the funds for CPS programs which might have been requested and denied earlier. (p. 124).

At the same time, as children's rights became more widely debated, advocates for children argued that injuring a neighbor could subject the perpetrator to criminal charges, while beating or abusing your wife or children would result in merely being referred to a protective agency. As a result, numerous states began to pass legislation making child maltreatment a criminal offense. The attention of the general public also focused on the phenomenon of the sexual abuse of children. Until the late 1970s, this type of maltreatment had rarely been discussed. Now, the call to investigate sexual abuse allegations began to far outweigh the reports of physical abuse and neglect (Weber, 1997).

The debates surrounding child maltreatment did bring three positive challenges: the search for risk assessment tools; the development of child abuse registers; and the formation of child protection teams. Risk-assessment protocols came about as an effort to standardize the collection of information in maltreatment cases, with the hope of allowing CPS workers to make more effective decisions that would be more reliable if legally challenged (Righthand, Kerr, and Drach, 2003; Sameroff and Gutman, 2004; Weber, 1997). Child abuse registers sought to track abusive parents who might move from city to city or state to state. Those who were found to have abused children were registered in a central database that could be accessed by other concerned CPS staff. Knowing that abusers had been identified by CPS in other jurisdictions gave investigators support in their efforts to intervene with the abusive family or protect children who might come in contact with an abuser (Weber, 1997). Some of these registries met with controversy, but a number still facilitated CPS intervention in maltreatment cases.

Perhaps one of the most successful innovations for CPS agencies has been the use of child protection multidisciplinary teams. At a macro level, a multidisciplinary team is composed of a variety of community professionals, including medical, law enforcement, legal, and psychiatric/mental health representatives as well as other professionals who, using their own individual perspectives, aid CPS in their intervention with child protective cases. At a micro level, schools and other organizations have created school- and agency-based child protection teams to facilitate effective reporting of maltreatment situations.

Today, CPS agencies have the following functions:

- to receive reports of child maltreatment made by mandated reporters
- to screen the accepted reports
- to intervene directly in emergency situations
- to investigate alleged maltreatment cases
- to determine the risk to the child of maltreatment
- to make a disposition as to the likelihood of maltreatment and need for service
- to formulate case plans for cases
- to facilitate court intervention when necessary
- to provide case management
- to provide or contract for social services for families and children
- to facilitate out-of-home placement and supervision when necessary
- to make "reasonable efforts" to keep families together or reunite them
- to provide the least restrictive permanent plan for children who are unable to remain at home
- to close cases and provide aftercare when needed (Myers, 2011; Weber, 1997).

Those envisioning the future of CPS agencies express concern that they will be forced, due to the severity and number of child maltreatment cases, to take on more of an investigative role, forcing workers to slight their social work backgrounds, which emphasize family treatment. In addition, with the increased emphasis on client rights, some fear that protective workers will be increasingly hampered in the roles of protecting children. Weber (1997) expresses the hope that CPS agencies will develop a way to offer more than one response as they enlist the support from and collaboration of other community agencies. Only through community efforts can children be truly protected from maltreatment.

Child Rearing, Maltreatment, and Public Opinion

How the general public sees child abuse and efforts to intervene has a significant influence on the support and funding of programs to address the needs of children. It is clear that the general public is concerned about children and child maltreatment, even if this concern does not always manifest itself through providing funds for prevention programs.

A 2003 study (see Public Knowledge LLC, 2003) on the perception of the public on parenting, child development, and child maltreatment sheds some interesting light on contemporary attitudes. The majority of those surveyed feel that life has gotten worse for children in recent years. In addition, when asked their opinion of teens and children, 71 percent of the respondents describe teens negatively, using such terms as *rude*, *irresponsible*, and *wild*, and 53 percent of adults and 58 percent of parents have negative views of younger children (p. 6). When asked to pinpoint the causes of such problems, the public asserts that the parents are responsible and complains that they are not "paying attention to what is going on in their children's lives" (83 percent call this very serious; p. 6). Although parents protest that they are teaching their children important values (97 percent say they are), the general public (61 percent) holds parents in a very negative light (p. 7).

Despite changing values, the majority of those surveyed feel that a significant contribution to poor parenting is the fact that mothers need to work outside the home. Eighty percent feel strongly that one parent should be at home with children. The public does not feel that a child is worse off only because both parents work, however. If parents take the time, it is possible to provide a healthy environment for their children (63 percent agree), and many feel a woman can be both a mother and have a career (71 percent; p. 11).

The researchers in the Public Knowledge study also look at people's perceptions of child development and conclude that the general public harbors numerous misconceptions in this area. Many feel that children will be "spoiled" if attended to too quickly. For example, a significant number of respondents (42 percent) feel that a 3-month-old baby will develop good coping skills if his or her cries are not immediately responded to (p. 15). Could this, these authors wonder, be a factor contributing to neglect?

When looking specifically at child abuse issues, most people equate maltreatment with physical abuse (55 percent), which is somewhat surprising, given the recent media coverage of child sexual abuse (only 9 percent mention sexual abuse, and 8 percent neglect). At the same time, a significant number (81 percent) of the general public believe that abusing drugs during pregnancy is a form of child abuse. In addition, 75 percent of people also feel that drinking alcohol, smoking marijuana (75 percent), and smoking cigarettes (57 percent) during pregnancy are also abusive to the unborn child (p. 19). When sexual abuse *is* mentioned, most respondents, not surprisingly, brought up the recent scandal in the Catholic Church (p. 23).

Americans continue to be conflicted about what constitutes abuse and what constitutes discipline. Many do not feel that spanking is abusive. Most parents feel they rely more on nonphysical discipline (e.g., grounding, time-outs), but many describe themselves as too lenient with their children, with 60 percent saying that how they respond depends on the circumstances, rather than consistency (p. 20). Might not concerns about leniency lead to increased physical punishment?

If people are asked what they feel are the causes of child abuse, 69 percent point to increased alcohol and drug use among parents, 67 percent to lack of parenting experience and skills, 64 percent to abuse of parents when they were children, and 48 percent to the presence of nonfamily members in the home (p. 25). Because most people see child abuse as a crime, the emphasis is on accusation, and criminal sanction, rather than education and support.

The attitudes held by the public today have a significant impact on the treatment of and prevention efforts for child abuse and neglect. It is clear that there is need for increased education and community awareness if CPS and communities are to join together in the protection of children and the provision of help for abusing families.

SUMMARY

The maltreatment of children is a long-standing problem. Since ancient times, children have been viewed as property to be sold, given, or exploited by adults. Throughout history, children have been overworked, prostituted, and physically maltreated for a variety of reasons. Severe beatings administered with religious fervor were inflicted to gain the child's salvation and to exorcise evil. Employers used children to further their own economic interests.

Despite the widespread sexual exploitation of children, the one taboo has been incest. The origins of this taboo seem to have been economic. An untouched female child was insurance for later barter with other tribes and cultures. Today, we also recognize the family disorganization that the breaking of the incest taboo creates.

There have been crusaders for children throughout history, however. Charles Dickens used his own painful background to speak out against child maltreatment. Then the case of Mary Ellen Wilson and crusader Henry Bergh set in motion a mechanism for the future protection of children. Bergh's efforts on behalf of Mary Ellen gave birth to the SPCC, which provides help for children even now.

The discovery by radiologists of multiple, unexplained fractures and the coining of the phrase *battered-child syndrome* in the 1960s added impetus to the child protection movement. In 1974, the Child Abuse Prevention and Treatment Act required that states intervene in abuse situations and provided financial and material resources to aid the states.

Today, we know that child abuse is seen from the view of three ideologies—penal, medical, and social welfare. From the social service perspective, child protective agencies are responsible for direct intervention from investigation and case management to case closure. These agencies can be hampered if there is not community and public support for their work. Toward this end, there needs to be more extensive community awareness and education.

Chapter 2

The Family
Roles, Responsibilities, and Rights

THE DEFINITION AND FUNCTION
OF THE FAMILY

The family as an institution has changed significantly over the years. Each culture has a different interpretation of what it expects a family to be. No matter what the culture, society has particular expectations of a family and, in some cases when those expectations are not met, is entitled to intervene. The changes in society itself have put additional pressures on families and can make functioning and meeting societal expectations of a stable unit even more difficult.

What factors in today's culture have altered families' functioning? An industrialized, impersonal climate has increased mobility, as wage earners follow the expansion or relocation of businesses in search of satisfying, better-paying, or continuing positions. Moves frequently promote further isolation of families. Emphasis on faster, more competitive, more affluent lifestyles produces stress.

Amidst the stresses of living in a high-pressured world, the family has had to make adjustments. The *nuclear family* (mother, father, and children), which for a time had all but replaced the *extended family* (parents and children often living with grandparents or adult siblings), is now decreasing (Berk, 2012). The current divorce rate, once the highest level ever, has now leveled out, but recently the single-parent family represents a large percentage of the parenting population. One in four families is headed by a single mother (Fabes and Martin, 2003; Skolnick and Skolnick, 2010). Today there are numerous constellations that can be considered a family—each with its own strengths and weaknesses and issues. In the blended family, husband and wife care for children from their previous marriages and perhaps their children from their present marriage. Within this context, cohabitation, or two people living together without legal sanction and caring for children, is practiced widely today, and gay and lesbian families (two same-sex partners) are increasingly more common. Communal living, more popular during the 1960s than today, joins several adults and their various offspring in one living arrangement (Berk, 2012; Fabes and Martin, 2003; Zinn, Eitzen, and Wells, 2010).

African American families rely extensively on kinship networks—that is, blood relatives or friends who become kinsmen and often take on the duties of family members. African American children are also more frequently taken into the homes of grandparents to be raised (Goode, Jones, and Jackson, 2011). Hispanic families have the institution of *compadres*, or companion parents. Compadres, godparents named at baptism, have an integral part in children's upbringing (Lum, 2003; McAdoo, 2006; Zuniga, 2011). Members of Hopi Indian tribes may practice *bifurcate merging*; in other words, the father's or mother's relatives are divided into separate lineages. Relatives of the same sex and generation are then grouped together in helping clusters. For example, the mother's sister would be seen as a close relation and would behave toward the child as the biological mother would (Glover, 2001; Lum, 2003).

Whatever the type, here the term *family* refers to a group of people who live together (or at least have regular contact) and who are expected to perform specific functions, especially in reference to the children involved. In the context of this book, the primary function of the family is the task of raising children. The parents, or parenting adults, are assigned certain responsibilities. Parental responsibilities are not, for the most part, recorded in a book of how-to's. However, mores and customs are passed from generation to generation and now are considered by popular opinion to be tasks and roles for parents to undertake. The way in which these responsibilities are characterized may vary widely. Some family texts outline the parental functions as follows:

1. Reproduction
2. Socialization
3. Assignment of social roles (social order)
4. Economic production and consumption
5. Emotional support (Berk, 2012; Berns, 2012).

Basically, the family prepares the child to take his or her place as a functional adult within society. If this relationship continues to foster the child in the way that society demands, the family unit is promised relative autonomy and freedom from government intervention. Therefore, the parent–child relationship is expected to provide stability and integrity; financial security; health and education; and morality and respect.

Stability and integrity mean parents need to provide a secure, stable, constant relationship on which their children can base their expectations and model their future relationships. Within this realm of security, parents have an opportunity to teach their children what society and their own culture will expect from them as adults. To enable the child to learn these lessons, parents are expected to provide comfort—the comfort of being properly housed, clothed, and fed. The assurance of these comforts requires financial security, which should be provided by the parents. Emotional well-being also necessitates being healthy and educated. A healthy future adult will benefit society as a whole.

THE FAMILY AS A SYSTEM

The family, especially in its role of raising children, is a complex and ever-changing system. Like any system, families must maintain some type of balance, continue a flow of information, and monitor the communication among their members. Families do this through a series of subsystems, boundaries, roles, and communication patterns. Another important piece of family life is the fact that family interactions set the stage for the child's future relationships, through the ability of members to attach or bond with one another (Berk, 2012).

Subsystems and Boundaries

A subsystem consists of smaller units that carry out specific functions and together make up the whole. In a healthy, functioning family, the parents unite in a major subsystem responsible for making decisions and regulating family activities.

Parents are expected to understand and adapt to developmental needs and to explain the rules they impose. They must guide and control, keeping in mind the child's need to mature and gain autonomy. The parents provide models, not only of behavior but of the use of authority. They must also introduce children to their own culture and serve as interpreters to explain differences between that culture and that of the larger society.

The sibling subsystem helps children experiment with the complexities of peer relationships. Here, they have an opportunity to fight, accommodate, isolate, negotiate, compete, and basically learn from each other. In later life, children transfer their interactions with siblings into their dealings with extrafamilial peers.

In addition to these two major subsystems, the family is composed of numerous others. For example, all the females in the family comprise one subsystem, all the males another, and there may be expectations of each of these. Subsystems exist by virtue of sex, age, interest, and function, and each family member is simultaneously part of several subsystems. *Boundaries*, which are divisions between *subsystems*, allow these minisystems freedom to operate. Boundaries also define who can interact with whom and how. These are also influenced by cultural values. For example, in many cultures, the boundary around the spouse or parent subsystem allows children access to each parent but not to interfere in the relationship between these parents. The parents' closed bedroom door is one symbol of this boundary and says to the children that the parents are then maintaining their right to privacy.

In some families where the boundaries are extremely rigid, there is little interaction between subsystems, and family members appear unresponsive to each other. For example, parents whose lives have little involvement with their children and who fail to perform such normal family rituals as eating meals with their children are probably not overly responsive to their children's needs. At the other end, the family with unclear or too flexible boundaries may also present problems. Often, the incestuous family has unclear generational boundaries. Relationships, especially those that are sexual and normally kept to the older generation, begin to involve the rest of the family.

Boundaries can also be maintained between the family and the external world. Those that are too rigid create isolation for the family, but if the boundaries with the outside are poorly defined, nonfamily members may float in and out of the family constellation to the confusion of all. Some families join together in cultural groups, moving freely within that ethnic heritage but remaining relatively isolated from the external world.

Roles

Each family member is given or assumes a series of *roles*. These roles may enhance family functioning or may cause dysfunction. Roles in a family shape how people think of themselves, how others see them, and how they function or behave within a family. One parent may be the breadwinner, while the other is the stay-at-home nurturer. In other families, parents share both roles. Sometimes, the roles others expect us to take shape how we behave. For example, the mother may respond to her child's misbehavior by saying, "Wait until your father gets home." This sets up her spouse as the disciplinarian, so there is pressure for him to assume this role, which he may do willingly or reluctantly. If, however, he chooses not to take this role and does not confront his wife, the issue is clouded and confusion results.

Some families find that their cultural values impose roles on them that they have difficulty maintaining. For example, Asian/Pacific immigrant parents may find it difficult to maintain the unquestioned position of respect, authority, and leadership given to them in their native countries. While their children are learning the value of independence in their U.S. schools, the parents cling to their regard for family and for their "old-world ways." Fathers who worked as engineers and doctors perhaps may find that, due to their inability to speak English well enough to pass licensing exams, they must take jobs that they deem inferior. The respect they were once given is further impacted when their wives find it easier to find work. For these fathers, the experience is one of losing face (Chan and Chen, 2011; Lum, 2003; Webb and Lum, 2001).

Children are often cast in dysfunctional roles. For example, a child can become the scapegoat for the family's stresses and thus sometimes the victim of abuse. Another child may be expected to assume parental roles and is seen as the parent for the rest of the family, including the adults.

The delegation or assumption of roles can be extremely complex. Numerous motivations cause family members to assume or accept roles. Through analyzing the roles in a family, it becomes more clear why one child is abused or why another family is neglectful.

Communication

The regulation of subsystems and boundaries and even the assignment of roles are accomplished through communication patterns. *Communication* is not always one family member talking to another. Silences, body movements, facial expressions, voice tone, and posture all convey messages. For example, a mother may say, "Stop that," with little conviction in her voice or facial expression. The child gets several messages. Verbally, he or she is being told to cease the behavior, but the mother's lack of affect is saying not much will happen if it does not stop. Communication patterns within the total family can become complex and unclear. Using another example, a father's attempt to control his son may be met with his being ignored while the mother looks on smugly, conveying the message "I told you that kid couldn't be controlled!" In such a situation, the child's deviant behavior may well escalate.

Communication patterns in families of different cultures may also differ. Some cultures (e.g., Asian, Hispanic) stress communication patterns that are hierarchical. Young people may be expected to listen to their elders, not contradict them. The feelings and opinions of children are not shared with elders. For example, in the Asian tradition, people who show their emotions are considered to lack strength or self-control. The difference in these communication patterns is especially difficult for minority children growing up in the United States. They see their friends or characters on television who openly share feelings with their parents and they may actually feel unloved or neglected by parents who communicate according to a different set of rules (Lum, 2003; Mass and Geaga-Rosenthal, 2000).

Part of family communication has to do with family rules. *Family rules* are repetitive patterns of interaction that family members develop with each other. These patterns begin to be accepted by the family as a code of behavior or assumptions about how to act. For example, a family rule that the son is uncontrollable may have evolved because the mother has been ineffective, and she may even have undermined the father's attempts at discipline.

A family rule in another family might be "Go to Dad if you're upset; he's more understanding." Incestuous families often develop the rule that no one outside the family can be trusted, so that the family secret of incest can be protected. Rules may be functional or dysfunctional, but they regulate the way the family communicates.

To be truly effective, communication and rules must be clear cut, open, and consistent, as accepted by that particular culture. Often, families with problems practice incomplete communication—that is, sending a partial message that assumes the receiver perceives the remainder of the message. For example, in a voice loud enough to be heard by her husband and children watching TV, a tired mother may say, "Dishes, dishes! As soon as I do them, there are more to do!" On the surface, she is making a statement about the abundance of dirty dishes generated by the family. However, her angry look at the assembled family and the resentment in her voice betray her real feelings of being overworked and needing some help. She assumes that her verbal statement has made the message clear and may be furious that no one offers help. In fact, a more complete message might be, "I'm really tired after doing dishes all day, and I'd like you to help me." Or better still, "Do these dishes so I can relax too." (The mother may also be disrupting the family rule of "Mom's the dishwasher—she'll do the dishes. Just ignore her complaints.") Making a request for help might have to be followed by a command for someone specific to do the job, but the mother will have made her desires known.

When family members communicate unclearly or inadequately yet expect others to understand their meaning and perceive their needs, the result is often frustration, resentment, and anger. Communication is therefore an important element of family functioning or dysfunctioning.

Bonding and Attachment

One vital aspect provided by the family and influencing the child's entire life is that family members usually provide the infant with an opportunity to bond. When parents provide adequate care and nurturing, most babies form this attachment easily. This then enables them to replicate this attachment with others in their lives as they go on to forge new relationships. But when babies are inconsistently parented within their family of origin or are abused or neglected, they may not develop a healthy attachment to others (Bee and Boyd, 2011; Berk, 2012; Fabes and Martin, 2003; Hughes, 2006).

This is often called *attachment disorder* and creates not only an inability to bond with others but also self-destructive behaviors, cruelty to others, poor impulse control, habitual lying, and an inability to discern cause from effect (Levy and Orlans, 1998). Some have called those suffering this disorder "children without a conscience," for they do not demonstrate the behavior expected of them by society. Without help, such children may become teens or adults who offend against others (Rich, 2006).

Increasingly, attachment-disordered children are seen in the child protection system. When professionals seek to help these children, they learn that without initial attachment within the family, forming healthy relationships will be extremely difficult. These become the children who bounce from one part of the social service system to another, from foster home to residential treatment. Only when ways are found to provide healthy attachment experiences for young children will a solution be provided to this problem.

Rituals

When one strives to understand families, especially in the context of their individuality often influenced by their culture, it is important to recognize the presence, absence, or importance of family rituals. *Rituals* are repetitive behaviors that families may practice as a vital part of their communication. Imber-Black, Roberts, and Whiting (2003) identify four types of rituals: *day-to-day essentials* that govern how members eat, sleep, greet each other, and perform other daily tasks; *family traditions* that involve the manner in which families celebrate or choose not to celebrate birthdays, anniversaries, and other milestones as well as vacation times; *holiday rituals* that revolve around calendar holidays such as Christmas, Hanukkah, Ramadan, Three King's Day, New Year's, Fourth of July, and others; and *life cycle rituals* that recognize important birth to death events like naming ceremonies, baptisms, adoption days, Bar and Bat Mitzvahs, weddings, retirement, and funerals (also see Bevin, 2001; Garcia, 2001; Glover, 2001).

Understanding what part these rituals play in the life of a given family and/or their cultural heritage may enlighten a worker as to how well the family is integrated and functions. Disengaged families may have few obvious rituals, although some rituals may not be as obvious and are even dysfunctional. For example, total inattention to special days that the rest of their culture honors may in itself be a ritual and may signify the family's lack of nurture toward its members. Therefore, the question may arise, Can this family begin to value itself, or does this lack of value make it unable to protect and care for its children? Although there are no stock answers to such questions, the recognition of the place of family rituals, especially in understanding cultural differences, may play an important piece in the intervention with this family.

MINORITY FAMILY SYSTEMS

Families develop communication patterns and roles according to their own cultural values; however, even families of a specific culture may differ. For example, within the Hispanic cultures, Cuban, Puerto Rican, and Mexican families may all have different values (see Bevin, 2001; Garcia, 2001; Morales and Salcido, 2007; Zayas, Canino, and Suarez, 2001; Zuniga, 2011). Even among one group (e.g., Puerto Ricans), there will be variations.

How a particular family functions will depend on several variables:

1. The culture in which the family has originated
2. The subgroup of that culture (India, Puerto Rico, and many other countries from which immigrants come have caste systems. Individuals from these cultures often feel strongly about not being grouped with those from a lower caste.)
3. The individual characteristics of family members

4. The family's method of adapting to the stresses placed on it by living within the family unit

5. How the family functions within that culture (e.g., compliance or deviance) (see Webb and Lum, 2001)

Leiberman (1990) points out that, in contrast to the individualistic culture emphasized in the United States (i.e., the idea "that a person's highest calling is to be true to him or herself" [p. 107]), many minority cultures value collectivism. Lieberman compares the two value systems by saying,

> An individualistic culture is one where a person's social behavior is shaped primarily by personal goals and needs which do not necessarily overlap with the goals and needs of their in-group. Competition is stressed and cooperation is not. In contrast, in a collectivist culture the person's behavior is shaped primarily by the goals, needs, and values of the in-group, even when this involves giving up personal pursuits. These cultures tend to stress cooperation and avoid competition. There is also a high personal identification with the family and a sense of mutual obligation and responsibilities among extended family members. Personal sacrifices are expected on behalf of family welfare.... In individualistic cultures, people who sacrifice important personal goals for the sake of others may be considered masochistic, immature or overly dependent.... In a collective culture a person who fails to sacrifice personal goals for the welfare of others is often rebuked as selfish, disloyal, and untrustworthy.

It is this fundamental difference that creates conflict for many minority families. Due to the extent of these differences, as well as the previously mentioned variables, it is impossible to assume that any one minority family is like another. However, to begin to understand how certain minorities function within the culture, we may generalize the values espoused by each group—recognizing that it is then necessary to be particularly sensitive to the variations of individual families.

African American Families

Kinship Bonds

African American families rely heavily on the mutual aid of those beyond the nuclear family structure. Extended family members and friends are accepted as kinsmen who provide support for the family, including such things as child care, advice, financial aid, and emotional support (Goode et al., 2011; Hildebrand, Gray, and Phenice, 2007; Lum, 2003; McAdoo, 2006; Prater, 2000; Scott and Shears, 2007; Waites, 2008). According to research, African American families take children from extended families or friends into their households more frequently than whites, and older black women take in the highest proportion of children. It is this reliance on kinsmen and close community spirit—perhaps originating in African tribal cultures and carried into plantation life—that has protected the children to some degree against racism by keeping them within the confines of their own community.

Self-Help and Self-Esteem

The strong reliance on community for support and mutual aid has benefited the development of African American children's self-esteem. In the African American culture, children are seen as representing the continuity of life and are prized and nurtured by the whole community (Goode et al., 2011; Hildebrand et al., 2007; Hill, 2003; McAdoo, 2006; Prater, 2000; Scott and Shears, 2007; Waites, 2008).

Adaptable Family Roles

A primary value among African American families is that everyone is expected to work. There is equality among family members, although over the years, it has become the mother who keeps the family together (Lum, 2003; McAdoo, 2006). Largely due to the ability of these women to find work more easily than their men, women are often the primary breadwinners.

The lower socioeconomic status of African American families with working mothers has necessitated that children perform a substantial amount of household duties. While their parents work, children may be expected to care for younger siblings, much like their own mother did in her youth. The concept of *parentified child*, with its pejorative connotation, does not take into consideration the need for these families to adjust in any way they can to ensure survival (McAdoo, 2006). Indeed, most poor African American families would fail to understand why expecting so much of their children might be considered neglectful by white social workers.

Achievement and Work Orientation

Like many minority groups, African American families realize that the only means for a better life for their children is through achievement and hard work. There are, however, constraints on their ability to achieve. Educational systems are not always receptive to what African American children have been taught to value. For example, such families often teach children to be assertive and independent at an early age. Such attitudes frequently conflict with the values of modern classrooms. Racism and the failure to be sensitive to cultural differences compound the picture (Goode et al., 2011; McAdoo, 2006; Prater, 2000; Scott and Shears, 2007; Waites, 2008).

Religious Orientation

The role of the church in African American families goes beyond the spiritual. Religion provides not only a social context but also a mechanism for survival. Throughout history, religion has fortified blacks against racism from a hostile white world (Goode et al., 2011; Hill, 2003; Lum, 2003). Ministers often have close ties with African American families, serving as spiritual teachers, advisors, counselors, political advocates and spokespersons, and often kinsmen. Church services frequently provide an arena where pent-up emotions can be released and supported by others in the congregation. The African American family's assumption that "the Lord will provide" in the face of crisis is often misinterpreted as a lack of motivation.

Communication

African American families often communicate in analogies, rather than identifying or expressing their feelings. For example, instead of identifying feelings of loneliness or depression, a mother might say, "I feel like I have no one in the world." The abstract nature of such communication is often interpreted as an inability to recognize feelings or as a lack of insight (McAdoo, 2006; Scott and Shears, 2007). On the contrary, African American families are often very much in tune with their feelings and those of others, though this may be expressed in their own characteristic manner.

Hispanic American Families

Thought to be the fastest growing ethnic group in the United Stated today, Hispanic Americans are from one of several different cultures, including Mexican American (63 percent), Puerto Rican (9.2 percent), Cuban (3.5 percent), Salvadoran (3.3 percent), Dominican (2.8 percent), and others from Central and South America (U.S. Census Bureau, 2011). Despite the differences in the origins of these groups, it is possible to make some generalizations about the values and functioning of Hispanic families.

Family Ties, Values, and Rituals

Many Hispanic American families are more likely to be living as single-parent families than the general population (Delgado, 2000; Zayas et al., 2001). Some, explains Garcia (2001), have been able to live in the United States while their male partners have not, due to work or immigration requirements. Increasingly the numbers of households with a couple as opposed to a single parent is increasing. There is also strong reliance on the extended family. *Extended families* not only consist of blood relatives but may also include friends (often the children's godparents) and those who share living space. For example, it is not uncommon for families to buy an apartment complex together and maintain strong survival-oriented or cultural bonds.

The *compadrazgo*, or the system of using *compadres*, is an integral institution among Hispanic American families, especially Mexican American and Puerto Rican. *Compadres* are godparents or sponsors (*padrinos*) to children who are named at baptism and maintain an extremely close relationship to both the parents and children. Children are treated as if they are the *compadre's* own and even given a home, if the need arises (Delgado, 2000; Garcia, 2001; Hildebrand et al., 2007; Lum, 2003; Morales and Salcido, 2007; Smith and Montilla, 2006; Zuniga, 2011). Too often, these important individuals are overlooked by child welfare workers, who instead place children in unrelated foster homes.

Within the family itself, the father is the undisputed authority. He receives respect and allegiance. One value that is much misunderstood is that of *machismo*. This value, often given a negative interpretation by the larger society, is more positively and accurately associated with a male's sense of honor, courage, and responsibility to his family, both nuclear and extended. It is the father's (or older male's) role to keep the family together—to protect and provide for them. Family is all important to the Hispanic father's role. His inability to have children, especially sons, leads to questions about his maleness (Zayas et al., 2001; Zuniga, 2011). Unfortunately, this sense of pride and family position is greatly threatened in the Hispanics' adopted culture of the United States. Because it is easier for the women to find employment, Hispanic men often feel depressed and thus unable to command respect from their families (Bonilla-Santiago, 2007; Delgado, 2000; Smith and Montilla, 2006). Family tension and sometimes violence may result as aggression is condoned when a man's machismo is challenged (Bevin, 2001; Bonilla-Santiago, 2007; Zuniga, 2011).

Zayas et al. (2001) suggest that the position of the Puerto Rican women is often overlooked. This Latina has more power in her home than her white counterparts and is often vital to family decision making.

Other important values of the Hispanic family are *dignidad, respecto*, and *personalismo*. *Dignidad* refers to dignity or the inherent unique importance of each individual. *Respecto* involves adherence to hierarchical relationships; elders must be respected. *Personalismo* describes the Hispanic value of person-to-person contact and close relationships. Hispanic families shun large impersonal bureaucracies, instead preferring close personal involvements with individuals (Bonilla-Santiago, 2007; Smith and Montillo, 2006).

Sometimes, the values of ethnic groups are directly opposite from the majority culture and may be questioned. For example, after years of hardship in their native Cuba, older generations of Cubans see robust, healthy children as symbols of their new prosperity. Now in a country that values thinness and seems to worship the practice of dieting, Cuban parents strive to *cebar a un crio*, or literally "fatten the child" (Bevin, 2001), resulting in children who tend to be chubby. For those not familiar with this value, encouraging a child to be chubby might be seen as not being in the child's best interests.

Hispanic parents tend to expect their children to behave and are not above a spanking to get the point across. The Cuban saying *"una nalgadaa tiempo hace milagros"* ("A timely spanking can work miracles"; Bevin, 2001, p. 193) mirrors the sentiments of other Hispanic cultures as well. In some cases, such a value may bring these families to the attention of CPS.

Ritual plays a major role in both maintaining family ties and child rearing in Hispanic families. Family centered rituals strengthen *familismo*, or the closeness of the extended family. If not already living together, family members may come together regularly for fellowship and connection (Bevin, 2001; Fong, 2003; Garcia, 2001; Hildebrand et al., 2007; Smith and Montillo, 2006; Zuniga, 2011).

Not only do most Hispanic families celebrate a child's baptism with great joy, but they may also celebrate when a child reaches a certain age. For example, Cuban and Mexican families have a party (called a *quince* in Cuban culture and *la quincianera* in Mexican culture) when a daughter turns 15. This celebration, which can be as extravagant and expensive as a wedding ceremony, marks the young woman's receptivity for suitors (Bevin, 2001; Garcia, 2001).

Religion

Catholicism, the predominant religion of Hispanics, plays an extremely important role in family life. Within the Puerto Rican culture, especially, other fundamental Protestant religions have also made inroads (Zayas et al., 2001; Zuniga, 2011). The church provides support and comfort as well as often the focus of social activities. Much of *barrio* (Hispanic community) life revolves around the church. Besides teaching about moral and ethical behavior, churches within the community also provide services such as financial aid, housing, rehabilitation programs, and a host of other social services (Delgado, 2000; Garcia, 2001; Lum, 2003; Morales and Salcido, 2007).

In addition, spiritual practices pervade all aspects of family life. Zayas, Canino, and Suarez (2001) describe the practice of *la bendicion*. When a child enters a room in many Hispanic households, he or she is expected to say *"Bendicion!"* to the parents or adults present. The request is that they give the child their blessing and indicates that they are held in respect. The implications of cultural values for practice with Hispanic families include the following:

- to recognize the importance of family and respect the need for clients to include family in conversations
- to recognize the importance of religion and the church for most Hispanic families
- to seek resources first within the family or cultural community
- to demonstrate respect for the family and its hierarchy (e.g., father as head, mother as nurturer)
- to use titles (Mr., Mrs.) rather than first names
- to respect families' need to trust the outsider and discuss neutral subjects before getting to the problem
- to understand that families have respect for those in authority, which gives the worker power that should not be abused (Hildebrand et al., 2007; Lum, 2003; Morales and Salcido, 2007; Smith and Montilla, 2006; Zuniga, 2011)

Folk Healers

In addition to dependence on organized religion, Hispanic families also espouse the concept of folk healers. Mexican Americans, particularly in the Southwest, are known for their use of *curanderismo*. Perhaps due to the firm belief in folk medicine or the folk healers' understanding of their clients, these practices appear to be especially effective (Delgado, 2000; Garcia, 2001; Morales and Salcido, 2007; Zuniga, 2011).

Communication

The concept of *respecto*, as it governs attitudes toward authority figures, may distort the Hispanic family's relationship with the larger culture. For example, Hispanic mothers' belief in graciousness and sociability and the social worker's lack of understanding of this interfere with the communication between client and worker. Mothers asked to schedule appointments with workers (whom they see in an authority position) may feel compelled to comply but not see the need to keep the appointments. It is important that the worker be in tune with cultural variations.

Hispanics placed under extreme stress and unhappiness appear to translate their distress into somatic complaints. Rather than openly admit their psychological suffering, they are more likely to complain of headaches, stomach distress, or other physiological ailments (Bevin, 2001; Garcia, 2001).

Asian and Pacific Islander Families

Asian and Pacific Islander families are perhaps the most difficult to generalize because of the variety of cultures included in this category. When one speaks of *Asian*, the reference may be to Chinese, Japanese, Filipino, Vietnamese, Cambodian, Thai, Laotian, Indian, Indonesian, Korean, or Pakistani. *Pacific Islanders* encompass Hawaiian, Tamoan, Malasian, Tongon, Guamanian, and Micronesian cultures (Chan and Chen, 2011; Jacob, 2011; Lum, 2003; Mass and Geaga-Rosenthal, 2000).

Mass and Geaga-Rosenthal (2000) identify two major cultural orientations: "(1) Confucianism, which predominates in northern Asian countries such as China, Japan, Korea, and Vietnam, and (2) a combination of Hindu/Malayan/Polynesian cultures that predominate in the southern countries such as India, the Philippines, Indonesia, Malaysia, as well as the Pacific Islands" (p. 149). Although there are some similarities (discussed later), each cultural orientation must also be understood as being unique. This short explanation cannot hope to fully capture all the nuances and values of this cultural group.

Family Ties and Values

The Asian/Pacific Island culture is another that demonstrates a hierarchical structure with male dominance and well-defined roles. One particular people espousing these values is the Hmong—one of the newest groups of refugees. Unlike many of those immigrating to the United States, the Hmongs' exodus is involuntary. Most of these immigrants state that they would have preferred to stay in their native Laos or Thailand, where many fled initially, but these countries were unable or unwilling to let them stay. Now, large groups of extended families or clans have settled, primarily in the areas of California, Texas, Minnesota, Wisconsin, and Rhode Island, in numbers that exceed 100,000 (Culhane-Pera, Xiong, and Vawter, 2003). Since the Hmong come from agrarian, isolated areas, their enculturation into the United States has been difficult. They are often seen as part of public assistance caseloads, as they are at a loss for understanding how to survive on their own in this industrialized society.

Clan leaders still maintain a strong hold over family members and act as arbitrators between the clan and the outside world. Family members often will not cooperate with social service systems unless the clan leader is intimately involved in the process. From a subculture that condones severe physical punishment of children, Hmong parents do not understand why protective service agencies intervene. Only by enlisting the support and trust of clan leaders can social workers hope to be effective with these families (Culhane-Pera et al., 2003).

In Asian cultures, the older generation is revered. Whether these individuals are clan leaders, as among the Hmong, or merely the family's grandparents, family ties bind each member in an intricate hierarchy of respect. Filial piety (parents are respected and obeyed) is of primary importance, but the male of the oldest generation has the highest rank (Fong, 2003; Hildebrand et al., 2007; Lum, 2007; Shibusawa, 2001; Wu, 2001). Individuals, although important, see themselves in relationship to the family and its well-being. Autonomous behavior on the part of an individual is considered a rejection of family values. Accomplishments are not individual endeavors but efforts to bring honor to the family. Family honor is greatly valued, and shame (over the possible compromise of this honor) is a powerful method used to ensure that children and adults do nothing to disgrace the family. The sometimes intense use of shaming children is often interpreted by non-Asian professionals as emotionally abusive (Lum, 2003; Mass and Geaga-Rosenthal, 2000; Okamura et al., 1995; Shibusawa, 2001).

One type of loss of family honor avoided at all cost by Asian families is the sexual misuse of female children. For example, the highest priorities for a Vietnamese female child growing to adulthood are her virginity and good behavior. Many Southeast Asian cultures believe that a female who has been sexually violated is not honorable enough to be allowed to marry and she becomes an outcast (Cheung and Nguyen, 2001; Jacob, 2011).

Families may also feel that there is dishonor brought upon them when they come to the attention of an agency such as CPS, and workers must keep this in mind when initially approaching them.

In seeming paradox to these values is the pervasive but rarely discussed problem of domestic violence among Asian families. (see Nguyen, 2007). It is crucial that workers be sufficiently aware of normal family values so that the incidences of domestic violence and the impact on children can be discerned.

Harmony and Self-Esteem

Harmony is a dominant aspect especially of the Confucian value system. Individuals are expected to subordinate their needs to the group and to use self-control and self-restraint in the expression of their own needs. Self-esteem is tied into how well one is able to avoid conflict and to submit to the needs of others (Mass and Geaga-Rosenthal, 2000). Asian/ Pacific Islander children are taught that to take a middle position gives them a sense of belonging and togetherness with others (Chan and Chen, 2011; Lum, 2003, 2007).

Religion and Fatalism

The religions of Asians vary. Confucianism and Buddhism are the foundation for the moral principles of respect for one's ancestors, filial piety, and the avoidance of shame (Lum, 2003). Hindus and Moslems are also often involved with their religions as more of a code of living than any actual worship. More recently, some Asians have been integrated into the Roman Catholic and Protestant faiths (Lum, 2003).

Most Asian cultures practice some type of *fatalism*—or an adapted philosophical detachment. Whether this is the Indian belief in karma (the belief that behavior in one life affects one's fate in the next) or the resignation of people who have been buffeted by political events over which they have had little control, the Asian may treat events as inevitable. This fatalistic acceptance not only makes the Asian family less likely to seek help but is also often interpreted by nonculturally aware professionals as resistance or a lack of caring (Lum, 2007; Shibusawa, 2001).

Communication

The hierarchical nature of the family necessitates that communication begins at the top (oldest male) and filters down. Western professionals, schooled by culture to be direct and open, may find the nature of communication with Asian/Pacific Islanders difficult.

In Japanese culture, for example, people are expected to use *ki* (energy) to understand and relate to others without open discussion. The Japanese may put more emphasis on what is *not* said than what is said (Shibusawa, 2001), which can be especially confusing to the Western worker. In addition to the need to address the highest in authority, direct questions or eye contact are often seen as disrespectful.

The Asians' attempt at self-control will keep their affect calm. Some clients' response of "yes" to an idea or suggestion means only "Yes, I heard you," rather than compliance with the suggestion.

It is particularly important to understand the cultural values of the particular client in order to facilitate communication. The Coalition for Asian American Children and Families (2001) suggests that language barriers may be a significant impediment for families involved with CPS. Having a child translate can lead to distortions, as a child will feel obligated not to shame or upset family members. Competent translators should be used.

Native American Families

Native American tribes vary almost as much as the Asians previously discussed. Customs are based on centuries of culture that has been adopted according to geographic location and individual tribal rituals. Once again, an understanding of the particular tribe is important.

Family Ties and Values

Native American families are structured not so much with the inclusion of extended family members as with total reliance on grandparents as the official and symbolic leaders of the family and their community. Grandparents have the ultimate say in child-rearing practices and are rarely contradicted by parents (Glover, 2001; Hildebrand et al., 2007; Joe and Malach, 2011; Lum, 2003).

Sharing is perhaps the primary value of Native Americans. Accumulation of goods is a foreign concept; what one has is given freely to others. By the same token, child rearing is a shared activity. Children are allowed to roam freely throughout the community, with the assumption that they are the responsibility of the entire group. It is also felt that children learn from experience.

Native American families also believe that one must endure the natural happenings that affect one's life, and thus suffering is an integral part of growing up. They contend that in spite of this suffering, or perhaps because of it, people will triumph because they are ultimately good. This philosophy, perhaps based on the attempts to survive amidst extreme poverty and land disputes, has been called by some a kind of "optimistic toughness."

Native American families teach their children to control their emotions. As adults, they are expected to relate to others with poise, self-containment, and even aloofness. Indeed, the family keeps its problems to itself. Noninterference is important. To protest a perceived injustice, the Native American will use silence or withdrawal.

Religion/Spirituality

The beliefs of the Native American are based in a complex manner on the healing power of nature. Nature is associated with life itself, and the two must remain in harmony. Community religious rites are a fundamental part of living. The type of ceremonies enacted depend largely on the customs of each particular tribe (Edwards and Edwards, 2007; Glover, 2001; Lum, 2003).

Communication

Native Americans believe in the dignity of the individual, but that the individual is an integral part of the universe. Each person should respect and revere another.

Another fundamental view is the virtue of patience. With the knowledge and recognition that the universe is unfolding as it should, parents teach their children that one may have to wait for what is desired. In today's fast-paced society, with its instant gratification, this quality is sometimes interpreted erroneously by outsiders as laziness.

Along with patience, Native American children learn a different perception of time. Time is not measured by the clock but rather by natural events (moons, seasons, etc.). Congeniality is more valuable than time; thus, if one meets a friend on the way to an appointment, conversation will take precedence (Edwards and Edwards, 2007; Joe and Malach, 2011).

THE CHALLENGES OF DEVELOPING CULTURAL AWARENESS

The importance of knowing the demographic makeup of the area in which one works has become increasingly complex. Even census reports fail to accurately identify the cultural variations present in geographic areas. For example, families whose roots are based in the Middle East are categorized with other Caucasians on Census reports but customs may differ significantly.

The Middle East is generally understood to include countries such as Syria, Lebanon, Israel, Palestine, Bahrain, Iraq, Iran, Egypt, Jordan, Kuwait, Oman, Qatar, Sudan, Saudi Arabia, Turkey, Yemen, and the United Arab Emirates, although the languages, values, and religions are also shared with some of the surrounding nations. There is increasingly an Arab-American identity claimed by have come to the United States from the Middle East to settle here (Sharifzadeh, 2011).

Family plays a significant role among families with Middle Eastern roots. Extended families often live together with as many as three generations in one dwelling. Loyalty is first to one's family and kin. Families tend to be patriarchal with the dynamics of family functioning influenced predominantly by their religious affiliation. Achievement is valued in Middle Eastern families and as a group they tend to be some of the best educated of any minority group. But it is often the collective achievement of a family group that is held up with pride rather than that of any one member (Sharifzadeh, 2011).

Family systems also provide the social supports that some ethnic groups seek from formal organizations. It is expected that one will have children and not to do so is a source of unhappiness. Male children are prized and in some household elevate the status of the family. The birth of a male child is an event to celebrate. Most families hope to have numerous children, perhaps because it is expected of adult children to care for their parents in old age.

Religion among those from Middle Eastern countries can be varied. Religious practices may reflect Judaism, Zoroastrianism, or Islam. The increased number of Muslims living in the United States requires that workers learn more about Islamic values and customs.

Changing Families

Although the preceding discussion considered the general characteristics of a variety of diverse families, it cannot be stressed enough that each family is unique. In addition, anthropologist Stephanie Bird (2009) contends that the new American culture is bicultural and tricultural. The election of a biracial president highlights the changes in the demographics of American culture and the challenges faced by this generation that some are now referring to as Generation MIX. Bird also suggests that the increased rate of biracial and triracial births affect the composition of the family of tomorrow.

FAMILY PROBLEMS AND DYSFUNCTION

Every family faces problems in its day-to-day life. Many are able to overcome them, but those families that cannot conquer their problems cease to function in a manner that encourages the positive growth of their members. Failing to meet common problems compounds the problems. These failures can be organized into four categories:

1. Failure to complete basic family tasks
2. Failure in dealing with changes associated with developmental tasks
3. Failure to deal with crises
4. Failure to deal with societal pressures (which may include pressures from a different culture)

Failure to complete basic tasks includes the family's inability to provide food, shelter, protection, and education for its members. When they are unable to handle the most basic of needs, such families may come to the attention of agencies. Some families lack the basic ability to nurture their offspring and bond with each other, robbing their children of the skill of attachment to others—the underpinning of later relationships.

Other families are able to complete the tasks expected of them until some member or members reach developmental milestones, presenting behavior that upsets the family balance. The most obvious, perhaps, is the family whose children are becoming teenagers. Suddenly, the autonomy the children expect and the manner in which they behave to get it are too distressing for the parents, and the family may well have difficulties. The budding sexuality of the teenager can also create problems for other members of the family.

For example, one incestuous father described his problems as beginning when his daughter approached adolescence. His wife, unable to cope with the girl's rebelliousness, retreated into her own career. The father began to have quiet talks with his daughter in an attempt to understand her. He described being stimulated by these talks and suddenly realized she had become quite sexually attractive. The pathology of this abuser and the emotional neediness of the daughter created a family atmosphere that necessitated intervention.

Even before a child reaches adolescence, some parents have difficulty with developmental milestones. The birth of a child, the autonomy sought by a 2-year-old, and a child's entrance into school—all have the potential for changing the family balance and creating problems.

Crises can also tax a family's ability to cope. Illness, death, unemployment, and natural disasters (e.g., fire or flood) force a family to mobilize its resources in order to deal with the event and its consequences. Some families do this well, whereas others are unable to make the necessary adjustments and need outside help.

Another problem confronting some families is prejudice. The minority family faced with the constant need to overcome the societally imposed stigma of color, race, or nationality may have difficulty functioning. For example, some families in a predominantly

Puerto Rican neighborhood had adapted themselves to their new society, but Carmen Valasquez had difficulty. Her family had come from Puerto Rico, where they enjoyed a certain status in their society. Now, finding herself a member of a minority, she resented what she perceived as her family's demotion in social status and was frustrated with the housing and employment she seemed forced to accept. Her depression permeated the family.

The Greybank family experienced similar resentments. Life on the reservation had its own pressures, not totally conducive to a family's well-being. Migrant workers, newly immigrated Asians, and other minorities find that it is not easy to raise children in a culture that does not reflect their views. In an immigrant family, the teen's desire to belong in his or her new culture often meets with conflict especially when the parents cling to traditional cultural values.

Another stigma not related to race or culture is society's attitude about who can and cannot raise children effectively. The mentally retarded and the mentally ill are two populations that have fought hard to prove their ability to be parents.

Sometimes, family problems and the failure to cope with them overlap, and the family moves in and out of constant crisis. Often referred to as the *multiproblem family*, these families invariably need help and are frequently the clients of protective services workers.

THE FAMILY AND CHILD MALTREATMENT

Along with the functions, roles, and responsibilities of the family, two factors are associated with the family's position that actually contribute to the continuation of child maltreatment. These are society's belief in the sanctity of the family, and the disproportionate emphasis afforded the rights of parents compared to the rights of children.

Parents' Rights

Goldstein, Freud, and Solnit, in their controversial book *Beyond the Best Interests of the Child* (1998), argue vehemently for the sanctity of the family. The parent–child relationship, they contend, is the basis on which a child's emotional growth depends. Only when parents fail to nurture that child's growth in the most minimal way should intervention be considered.

In 1981, a bill was considered in the Senate that would have made even more private the interactions between children and their parents, even including the parents' right to physically punish at will. Had the bill passed, children might have been even less protected from abuse than they are now (Nelson, 1990). The actual consideration of such a bill, however, is indicative of our nation's continued support for the parents' right to do with their children what they will. Our comfort with allowing parents complete jurisdiction over children is based on our expectations of adequate parenting, rather than our recognition of the painful statistics of the incidences of child maltreatment and parental failure. Certainly, most parents would feel extremely hampered if the government intervened randomly. The assumption is made by parents that "We are doing our job; leave us alone," and in a large percentage of homes, this is true.

But what of the parents who vehemently contend they are doing their jobs but are, in fact, subjecting their children to behavior that is considered by the greater society as abusive? What of the child whose premature introduction to adult sexuality is rationalized by a parent as educating or being affectionate toward the child? This is where children's rights enter the picture.

Children's Rights

In an era when society is obsessed with the discussion of individual rights, the rights of children are often overlooked. Despite a few attempts to clearly delineate these entitlements, children's rights are more likely to be defined by virtue of what their parents do or do not do for them. The family, as mentioned, is expected to provide for the basic needs of the child. From the birth of their children, parents have the right to and are entrusted with the care, custody, and control of their children. For young children, parents are also the link with the outside world. These children, therefore, may have no opportunity to have any needs met except those their parents decide are important.

Given this reality, what are the rights of children and how do we define them? Goldstein, Freud, and Solnit list some of the child's needs:

> The child's body needs to be tended, nourished and protected. His intellect needs to be stimulated and alerted to the happenings in his environment. He needs help in understanding and organizing his sensations and perceptions. He needs people to love, receive an affection from and to serve as safe targets for his infantile anger and aggression. He needs assistance from adults in curbing and modifying his primitive drives (sex and aggression). He needs patterns for identification by the parents, to build up a functioning moral conscience. As much as anything else, he needs to be accepted, valued, and wanted as a member of the family unit consisting of adults as well as other children. (1998, pp. 12–13)

Outlining the child's needs makes the assumption that these will be met by virtue of parental responsibilities. But to what is the child actually *entitled*? What of society's obligation to provide for children? A parent may have every intention of meeting his or her children's needs. The problem arises if that parent is poor or of a racial/ethnic minority (which some refer to as *structured racism*) and cannot provide an adequate income or housing. How, then, are children's rights defined?

Some would say that children's only rights are the provision of financial aid and education. But even when it comes to the right to financial support and education, some children fall through the cracks. Children, in fact, have no clearly established rights. The only rights are negative—rights expressed when the parents fail to meet their responsibilities. Only after parents do not properly care, control, or maintain custody is the child seen to have rights. When the parents have failed to supply this care and if the system works as it should, then the child will be provided with medical care (through Medicaid), financial security (through Transitional Assistance to Needy Families), and shelter (with foster home placement).

Thus, children are seen as potential adults, but they do not benefit from the rights given to adults. Instead, it is assumed that they have no real rights but only needs, unless the adults to whom they are entrusted are found to have failed. If these adults fail because of the inequities of the society they live in, the children are the ultimate sufferers.

There have been attempts to further delineate the rights of children. In 1959, the General Assembly of the United Nations formulated the Declaration of the Rights of the

---

Figure 2.1   Summary of the Universal Declaration of Human Rights[1]

The Preamble states that the child, because of his [or her] physical and mental immaturity, needs special safeguards and care, both before and after birth, and that individuals and groups should strive to achieve children's rights by legislative and other means. [Humanity], it says, owes the child the best it has to give.

In ten carefully worded principles, the declaration affirms that all children are entitled to

1. the enjoyment of the rights mentioned, without any exception whatsoever, regardless of race, color, sex, religion, or nationality;

2. special protection, opportunities, and facilities to enable them to develop in a healthy and normal manner, in freedom and dignity;

3. a name and nationality;

4. social security; including adequate nutrition, housing, recreation, and medical services;

5. special treatment, education, and care if handicapped;

6. love and understanding and an atmosphere of affection and security, in the care and under the responsibility of their parents whenever possible;

7. free education and recreation and equal opportunity to develop their individual abilities;

8. prompt protection and relief in times of disaster;

9. protection against all forms of neglect, cruelty, and exploitation;

10. protection from any form of racial, religious, or other discrimination, and an upbringing in a spirit of peace and universal brotherhood.

Finally, the General Assembly resolved that governments, nongovernmental organizations, and individuals should give this declaration the widest possible publicity as a means of encouraging its observance everywhere.

Source: Based on the United Nations, General Assembly Resolution 1386 (XIV), November 20, 1959, published in the *Official Records of the General Assembly, Fourteenth Session, Supplement No. 16,* 1960.

Child (see Figure 2.1). Unfortunately, few have heard of these suggestions of children's rights, nor have they been made into law or operational. In fact, many advocates for children suggest that children's rights are still often disregarded.

Various groups have sought to delineate children's rights. Most of these mention that children have the right to have their basic needs met (i.e., physical care, nurture, food, clothing, safety). Further, children have the right to education and medical care as well as an opportunity for recreation. Children have the right to be respected, to be guided, and

---

[1]A five-point Declaration of the Rights of the Child was stated in 1923 by the International Union for Child Welfare, with 1948 revisions in a seven-point document. The League of Nations adopted the IUCW declaration in 1924. The Declaration of the Rights of the Child was adopted by the United Nations General Assembly in 1959.

to be provided with adult models who promote healthy moral development. These rights should be available to all children regardless of race, color, sex, religion, or social status.

One of the difficulties in the adoption of a declaration of rights for children is in the interpretation. For example, some Bills of Rights state that a child has the right to receive good adult examples. What constitutes a good example? This is hardly as tangible as an adult's right to vote or to own a driver's license. It would be difficult, therefore, to protect children when their stated entitlements are subject to interpretation.

Impact on the Child Protection Movement

What impact does our failure to delineate children's rights have on the efforts to protect them from abuse? Perhaps one is to find other methods of primary prevention. Until recently, society assumed that if no one noticed otherwise, the child's growth and development were progressing as expected. Only when contrary evidence was obvious was there intervention. Thus, children are not protected until the damage is done. Intervention—before the problem exists—through giving the family more support through primary prevention is clearly needed.

A solution to one type of maltreatment—physical abuse—might be to pass a law, as Sweden has done, prohibiting corporal punishment of children. In the United States, lawmakers are hesitant to limit adult rights or intervene in family life in this manner. Some critics outlining the problems this law has created for Sweden argue against implementing such a statute in the United States. Apparently, most people are not ready or able to create a Bill of Rights for children that can be adopted. Thus, people are left with the framework of the family unit as vital to the growth of children but with the need to further protect children where families fail.

The debate continues: How can we best protect our children and still continue to give the family room to function? Until this question is answered, professionals can only improve their intervention and treatment practices and look for new methods of prevention.

SUMMARY

The family, despite numerous changes, remains the fundamental societal unit responsible for the care and nurturing of children. Today, the family may be nuclear, extended, blended, single parent, communal, or cohabitant. Families can also be defined by virtue of their function, their legal ties, their biological ties, the members' perceptions of who is family, and the members' long-term commitment to each other.

Parents are expected to have specific responsibilities in the areas of reproduction, socialization, assignment of social roles, economic production and consumption, and emotional support. The family is a complex system made up of smaller subsystems. The boundaries between these subsystems give members freedom to operate and promote better functioning of the total family unit. Each family member is assigned or assumes a series of roles that also promote family functioning. Some of these roles are helpful, but others are dysfunctional and add to or create family problems. Within these roles, a family communicates. Communication can be overt or indirect and unclear. Patterns of communication repeated over time become family rules—or the standards that dictate the behavior of family members.

Every family has problems in everyday living, but some fail to solve these problems effectively. The four types of issues that prevent adequate family functioning are (1) failure to complete basic tasks, (2) failure to adapt to changes brought on by developmental tasks, (3) failure to deal with crises, and (4) failure to deal with societal pressures.

Once people understand how the family operates, they see its place in society today. But two factors in the agreement between society and the family actually contribute to child maltreatment. The first is society's belief in the sanctity of the family: As long as the family appears to be completing the tasks expected of it (especially in relation to the children), society will not intervene. The problem is that many abusive or neglectful families hide their behavior. The second is that society places little value on children, affording them few rights compared to those for parents. Perhaps the solution lies partly in better prevention efforts.

Chapter 3

Maltreatment and the Developing Child

The development of a child from conception and birth to adulthood is a complex journey fraught with obstacles. Not only must the child master myriad physical challenges such as crawling, walking, running, speaking, controlling bowels and bladder, writing, and so on, but he or she must also contend with numerous social tasks. As development progresses, the child is faced with issues of trust, getting needs met, making friends, developing a positive self-image, setting priorities, and numerous other tasks that prepare him or her for the adult world. But healthy development requires consistent guidance on the part of the adults in the child's world, an experience not always available to abused and neglected children.

In studies with abused and neglected children, researchers and practitioners have found two types of parenting that affect the development of the abused child. The first type of parent–child relationship is fraught with conflict. Unstable, immature parents, whose own childhood needs are still unmet, are faced with children who demand their time and limited psychological energies. The result is impaired bonding, emotional deprivation, and eventually role reversal as these parents place their children in the position of meeting the parents' needs. From these homes come children who have difficulty with attachment and thus an impaired ability to form future relationships. Neglectful—as well as some sexually and physically abusive—parents often exhibit this type of parent–child relationship. For the physically abused child, this deprivation in parenting has a more profound effect than the physical abuse itself.

The second type of parent–child relationship pattern is more likely to be exhibited by physically and sometimes sexually abusive parents. In the physically abusive family, the child is wanted and expected, but the desire carries with it a complex set of extremely high expectations. For the physically abusive parent, it can be the child's failure to meet these expectations that creates anger and frustration and results in abuse. Or the abuse is seen by the parent as normal discipline designed to create obedience or mold the child to meet the parent's expectations (Berk, 2012; Davies, 2010; Myers, 2011).

For sexually abusive parents, the abuse often results from the parents' disillusionment with themselves and others in their lives, whom they perceive as having failed to meet their expectations. Life is not what they had envisioned. The unmet needs that these parents harbor, but hide so well, surface and return to the child for satisfaction of these needs. Thus, the idealized child becomes the target for the sexual exploitation.

Children learn in several ways: by association, through outcome, and by observation. When a child learns by association that a parent's angry voice means that he or she will also be hit, that child may then generalize and demonstrate a fear of all adults. A toddler who attempts to demonstrate his or her autonomy by running when the parent says "come" may discover that the outcome is a beating. The child then learns that autonomy is not encouraged, and an important part of his or her growth suffers. And finally, children who observe their parents using violence to express frustration or anger learn that violent behavior is acceptable. Children whose parents explicitly demonstrate the answers to sexual questions by rationalizing that they are "lovingly teaching their children" are robbed of the ability to differentiate between sexuality and affection.

To add to the complexity of development for children in the United States, they are influenced not only by the expectations of the greater society but also by the culture of their parents. An issue as seemingly simple as where an infant sleeps differs from culture to culture (Webb and Lum, 2001). While furniture stores feature a wide variety of cribs for babies, some cultures believe that expecting infants to sleep in a bed by themselves, and often in a separate room, is tantamount to abuse. One young woman who had come from India to study in an American university stayed in the home of one of her professors:

> *"I could not believe it!" she confessed. "The wife had just had a baby and they expected him to sleep in this huge crib in a room by himself! No wonder he cried and cried and would not sleep. This couple seemed like such concerned parents with their six-year-old, and this is what they were doing to their baby. I wanted to take him in bed with me!"*

When she could tolerate what she saw as abusive no longer, the young woman asked her hostess why the baby was expected to sleep alone. In her country, children slept with their parents until they were about 5 years old, at which time it was felt that they were ready to sleep on their own. Webb and Lum (2001) explain that there are other cultures, such as Japanese and Mexican, where it is expected that infants will sleep with their parents until they are 6 or even longer. Such congregate sleeping may actually set the stage for the interdependence among family members that is an integral part of the fabric of these cultures.

Taking into consideration that normal child development differs significantly among cultures, it is still possible to identify some of the ways maltreatment influences the growth of children.

DEVELOPMENTAL STAGES

Pregnancy and Birth

Even before the birth of a child, the future relationship between parents and child is determined. The atmosphere, attitudes, and expectations surrounding the conception of the baby are the first factors that influence the potential bonding experience. The mother's and father's motivations for conception must be considered: Was conception a planned or hoped-for event? Were the reasons for this anticipation healthy? Is the child a replacement for another or a last effort to solve a failing marriage? Was the pregnancy a mistake, a dreaded inconvenience? How does the parents' culture view such a pregnancy? Or do the parents disagree on any of these questions? The relationship of the mother and father has an impact on their ability to accept and want the baby, as does the maturity, stability, and mental health of each of the parents. In fact, their own past experiences may have a significant impact on their ability to parent.

Pregnancy can be a time of trauma for many mothers. Not only does a woman's body change, but there is also a realignment of her perceptions, her needs, and her relationships with others. The mother who finds these changes extremely difficult may attribute her discomfort to her baby. Another mother, feeling a need for nurturing, may welcome pregnancy as a time when she is pampered and coddled but forget the true significance of her situation—that she is incubating a new life. In some cultures, the mother is well supported emotionally, while in others, she is expected to underplay her condition until it comes to fruition. Culture plays a major role in how the pregnancy is received (Fabres and Martin, 2002).

Pregnancy requires a mother to adapt in two ways. First, she must recognize the fetus as a part of herself; second, she must accept that the fetus is also a separate individual. The second phase becomes more obvious when the fetal movements begin. The mother's style of handling these adaptations can be significant. Fetal movements impress on the parents that the imminent arrival of the child is a reality. Any conflict the mother has in her attitude toward this new individual can be embodied in her reaction to fetal movements.

Culture plays a significant part in how both mother and father are viewed, greatly influencing how they react to the impending birth. The father's contribution during pregnancy should not be underestimated. His presence, his ability to support, and his acceptance of both mother and baby can greatly influence the later parent–child relationships for both him and the mother. This necessity of supporting the mother creates upheaval for the father as well. Rarely does he feel that he has others who support him (Lamb, 2010).

The expectations built up during pregnancy by both mother and father are significant to the later relationship. The potentially neglectful or abusive parent—especially the mother—may not be considering the joys of caring for a helpless dependent baby so much as the satisfaction to be gained from the baby. These mothers have described anticipating how much the babies will love *them*. They have spoken of reveling in the thought of how good and how idyllic their babies will be. For most of these mothers, reality means disillusionment. The birth itself is not what they had anticipated.

Control is an important issue for the abusing parent. Fear of being out of control permeates his or her life. Yet modern technology often takes control from this mother at a time when she most needs it. Anesthesia, an emergency or unplanned caesarean, and the often unexplained procedures of modern medicine render the mother feeling helpless and out of control. The mother who actively participates in her delivery—through natural childbirth or controlled breathing—is more likely to transfer the comfort in her own control over the birth to a positive relationship with her infant. Again, culture plays such an important role in how the birth process is viewed. Families who are denied their cultural traditions in order to satisfy the policies of a particular medical community may feel the strain in their future relationship with their children.

Studies have underlined the significance of the timing and circumstances of the first contact between mother and child and the effect of this early interchange on bonding. Studies have found that a significant number of abused mothers and infants were separated early in the child's life.

Other authors stress the importance of how well the child meets the mother's expectations: Does the baby look as the mother had expected? Is he or she attractive? Is he or she as light or dark as the mother has hoped? Is the mother aware that the baby cannot as yet make eye contact, smile, or behave in what could be perceived as a loving way? The father may be influenced by these same factors. His ability to handle the differences between his expectations and his baby can have an influence on the mother's perception as well. The congenitally malformed infant creates conflicts for any parent, but for the already conflicted mother or father, the effect can be devastating.

Eva is an excellent example of a parent who had difficulty in the early stages of bonding.

Eva Davis, a young African American woman, was raised by two alcoholic parents and had one older sibling. She had had no experience with babies but always felt she would "like a baby to love."

At age 17, Eva left high school and got a job as a waitress. She met Joe not long afterward. Joe was a regular customer, a big brusque Swedish longshoreman who ate lunch and dinner at the restaurant in which Eva worked. Before long, Eva began going home with him after work and staying the night. Accustomed to abusive treatment at home, Eva did not mind when he "slapped her around," and in fact, she saw it as indicative of his love for her.

Eva heralded her pregnancy with enthusiasm. Although not sure if Joe would "kick her out," she saw a baby as someone who would be totally hers and thoroughly loving. Joe was not as enthusiastic, however, and for the first time questioned their interracial union. Later, Eva observed that despite his anger over the coming baby, "He did stop knockin' me around."

Joe began leaving Eva alone for extended periods. She would return to his apartment but would end up spending the night alone. She described feeling warm and comforted, though, as if "she had company" in the baby. Uneducated about nutrition or the necessity for prenatal care, Eva ate poorly and sought no medical advice. Fetal movement was a surprise to Eva. She had not been prepared for the sensation and found the movement distressing. When assured by a co-worker that this was normal, Eva hesitantly suggested that Joe "feel her belly." The reality of the situation was impressed on the father, and in a fit of temper, he threw Eva out, insisting that she "get rid of it or don't come back!"

Overwhelmed, Eva returned to her parents' home and attempted to abort. Her older sister found Eva hemorrhaging and called an ambulance. Assured by hospital staff that she had not lost the baby, Eva cried hysterically. She was referred to the hospital social service, which arranged for a visiting nurse to follow her for the remainder of her pregnancy.

Eva spent the rest of her pregnancy in her parents' home, avoiding their abuse by staying in her room and going to work. She remained depressed and withdrawn. Joe no longer came to the restaurant, perhaps himself dreading a confrontation.

Three weeks prior to her due date, Eva began labor just after arriving at work. Panic stricken, she had to be calmed down by a co-worker, who took her to the hospital when her labor pains increased in intensity. Once at the hospital, however, her labor stopped. After another 24 hours, the fetal monitors indicated fetal distress and the baby was delivered by caesarean section. For the first few hours after birth, the baby boy remained in "guarded condition." Finally rallying, the infant was brought to his mother the next morning. She greeted him with suspicion, insisting that he was not hers. "He's supposed to be light, like his father!" she protested. The small, dark baby had little energy after his long ordeal and lay listlessly in the nurse's arms. He showed little interest in eating, and his mother had no inclination to nurse him.

For Eva, what had been initially anticipated as a marvelous event in her life had climaxed in disappointment. She had produced a baby who in no way met her expectations and was forced to return with him to an environment that gave no support to either mother or child. The result was that 3-month-old Toby Davis was admitted to the hospital after his mother had shaken him severely to "make him stop his damn cryin'!"

Birth to One Year

The average child exhibits certain behaviors throughout the phases of his or her development. These normal developmental milestones (see Table 3.1 on page[s] 47–48) depend on the consistency of the child's experience as well as his or her relationship with the primary caregiver—usually, the mother.

When mother and child do not make a good adjustment to each other, the infant often develops an irritable high-pitched cry, which can be particularly upsetting to a caregiver, especially an already uncomfortable mother. Not only is the pitch and intensity of the cry unnerving, but it does not vary according to the child's needs. Although most mothers can quickly differentiate their child's cry from hunger from that of being tired or wet, mothers of babies with the high-pitched cry are not given such clues. Thus, the mother perceives herself a failure, feels even more out of control of her situation, and may target the child as the cause.

Consider, too, that most new mothers have support systems, people to whom they can go with their problems or fears. It is not uncommon for the neophyte parent to consult her own mother, mother-in-law, friend, other relative, or physician for advice. These individuals provide emotional support or models for the behavior and attitudes necessary to parent. In some cultures, the parenting behavior of others close to the mother allows for the baby's needs to be met.

Mothers who are abusive are women who have not developed this important support system. As a result, they feel very much alone and isolated, with no models to emulate. The only models available to them may have been those in their own abusive pasts. To make matters worse, they are grieving the loss of the attention they received when they were pregnant. Now it is the baby over whom everyone fusses.

Mothers within large extended families may feel pushed aside in favor of their babies. Conchita Juarez never felt accepted by the large family she married into. Throughout her pregnancy, she got conflicting messages about how to care for herself and her baby. When the baby was born, it seemed that she no longer mattered. She began to resent her small offspring for the attention he received.

The mother's conflicts and sometimes depression may mean the baby's needs are not met adequately by her. The mother may be ignorant of the baby's needs, or she may be caught up in her own unmet needs. Sometimes, the cries are met with satisfaction, but other times, they provoke only anger in the parent, who shuts out the cries by leaving, ignoring them, or striking out in anger (Bee and Boyd, 2011; Berk, 2012; Fabres and Martin, 2002).

Table 3.1   **Normal Developmental Accomplishments of the First Two Years**

Age	Physical	Mental	Language	Social
0–3 months	Demonstrates sucking and other reflexes While awake, turns head to one side Turns head toward food source	Learns to focus in seeming concentration Discriminates some individual voices	Coos Develops differentiated cry	Grasps fingers Focuses on faces
3–6 months	Rolls over from stomach to back Keeps head steady and does not fall back when pulled to sitting position Beginning to reach for and grasp objects Can lift shoulders or lift head and look around when on stomach Can sit with support	Looks at objects in hand Can follow visually when toy dropped Uses both hands to grasp toys or objects Looks at small objects Turns head to human voice and can follow with eyes	Coos Squeals Laughs out loud Chuckles Makes expressive noises	Exhibits social smile Can pat bottle with both hands Anticipates being fed
6–9 months	While on back, can lift head up Rolls over from back to stomach Can put feet in mouth Able to sit alone without support for more than a minute Can stand if grasping hands of another Attempts to creep or crawl When sitting can reach forward to grasp without falling over	Can transfer toys from one hand to other Can reach for toy with one hand Able to bang toys in play Able to pick up dropped toy consistently Can pull a toy toward self if attached to a string	Responds to own name Responds to social stimuli by vocalizing Can say single consonants like *ma, da, ba* Is able to combine syllables—*Ma-ma, Da-da* Enjoys toys that make sounds Imitates sounds	Discriminates between known adults and strangers Anticipates stimuli being repeated Eats solid food Smiles at self in mirror Chews and bites toys Begins to enjoy playing peekaboo

(conitnued)

Table 3.1

Normal Developmental Accomplishments of the First Two Years *(Continued)*

Age	Physical	Mental	Language	Social
9–12 months	Can sit steadily for over 10 minutes Crawls proficiently Can stand if holding onto furniture Can pull self up to sitting position Walks, holding onto a hand or to furniture	Able to uncover a toy when seen covered Grasps small objects between thumb and forefinger Can put things into and take them out of containers Goes for an object with out-stretched index finger Likes to drop toys deliberately Demonstrates an interest in pictures	Comprehends the word *no* Can say *Mama* and *Dada* and begins to attach meaning to the words By 12 months, knows at least one word Can put meaning to one to three words	Can cooperate in games Tries to roll a ball to another person Plays patty-cake and peekaboo Can wave goodbye May offer toy without releasing it Enjoys interacting with adults in play
12–18 months	Begins to walk well unaided Can crawl up stairs Can get to sitting position unaided Can stoop to pick up an object While walking, can pull a pull-toy Can seat self on chair	Can scribble with a crayon or pencil Can look at pictures in a book Can use a spoon Can drink from a cup Can follow one or more direc-tions (e.g., "give me the ball")	Can say three to five words with understanding Can point to one part of body Will point to at least one picture Has own language with inflections Imitates some words	Can cooperate in dressing Can hold own bottle or cup Able to feed self with fingers Points or vocalizes to make wishes known Shows off or offers a toy
18–24 months	Runs stiffly Can walk up and down stairs with one hand held Can jump with both feet Awkwardly throws ball Is able to kick a ball or other object Can stand on one foot if one hand held	Can turn pages of a book Can build a tower of two or more small blocks Tries to imitate what an adult draws Able to point to two to three body parts	By 2 years, has at least 20 words By 2 years, can combine two words in a phrase Can make wishes known through words	Able to use a spoon adequately Can drink well from a cup Able to remove one piece of clothing Imitates adults more and more

Sources: Adapted from Berk, 2012; Bee and Boyd, 2011; and Davies, 2010.

It is not entirely clear how much of the baby's own inherent personality and how much of the unsupportive environment contribute to this early lack of communication between mother and child. Brazelton's (1969) classic work demonstrated that there are distinct differences in the personalities of infants from birth. People still can only speculate about the effects of a particular infant's personality on the mother's inability to parent effectively.

Babies' personalities can be influenced by their in utero environment. Increased research on the effects of perinatal substance abuse indicate that babies whose mothers were using alcohol or drugs during pregnancy have a greater chance of exhibiting such complications as fetal alcohol syndrome, neurological damage, prematurity, and other problems. These babies have been observed to be more irritable; to exhibit high-pitched crying; to have excessive vomiting, diarrhea, seizures, and uncoordinated sucking; and to demonstrate either increased or decreased muscle tone (Bee and Boyd, 2011; Connor, Sampson, Bookstein, Barr, and Streissguth, 2001; Fabres and Martin, 2002). Thus, the parent who may either be continuing to abuse substances herself or be dealing with her own attempts to now remain substance free is faced with a baby who is not easy to care for. For this mother, hampered by her own past or current problems, caring for an infant may seem like an overwhelming task. She may withdraw from this challenge at the baby's expense.

At one time, it was felt that the child who was not sufficiently stimulated may develop *failure to thrive syndrome* and withdraw from the world that he or she sees as hostile. Batchelor (2008) notes the importance of recognizing that failure to thrive—or *faltering growth*, as she prefers to call it—results exclusively from the child's not receiving the requisite number of calories to sustain growth. In these cases, it must then be determined the reason for this low calorie intake. Faltering growth can be caused by an organic problem requiring medical attention. If an organic cause is ruled out, the immediate assumption by professionals is that nonorganic failure to thrive is a result of maternal neglect.

Caretakers who are uncomfortable nursing or feeding infants, who have fears about obesity themselves, or who are ambivalent or rejecting of the infant can communicate this while feeding, which may cause the infant to withdraw. Negative interactions at feeding times in general can result in the infant refusing to consume ample calories. Malnourished babies may then develop poorly.

Stereotypes that equate neglect with lower socioeconomic levels also mean that this condition is not often diagnosed in the middle and upper class. Yet faltering growth spans all socioeconomic levels.

For the abused or neglected child, the lack of social responsiveness between 6 and 12 months becomes more striking. A disturbance in object relations becomes marked. When the child is given a toy, for example, he or she plays with it passively. When the toy is removed, however, the child accepts the loss with the same passivity. Children from inadequately parenting families may also fail to develop separation anxiety and later stranger anxiety. *Separation anxiety* is demonstrated by children crying or acting fearful when their caregiver leaves. Their anxiety is based on their assumption that if out of sight, the caretaker no longer exists. The child must distinguish a loved person or parent from others, which is done by recognizing those who are there to consistently satisfy the needs. Once a child has distinguished the caregiver, he or she fears being abandoned when that person leaves. At the same time, the child fears strangers (*stranger anxiety*) who have not proved themselves as caregivers and may therefore not be trusted.

A child whose needs are not met consistently does not look to the caregiver as the provider of comforts. And without this directed trust, the child does not see strangers as suspect. Therefore, the child seeks the attention of anyone who is a potential need satisfier. Children who have been inconsistently parented often seek attention indiscriminately. By the same token, they may indicate subtly that they are already convinced that these needs will not be met.

If one uses Erikson's theory of development, this is the stage at which the consistency of caretaking is developing in him or her a sense of trust (Bee and Boyd, 2011; Webb and Lum, 2001). But not having had this consistency, a sense of mistrust becomes obvious in abused children. Again, the development of trust necessitates consistency. Lack of consistency may convince the child that the environment and those in it are not to be trusted.

Language should be beginning to develop as the child draws closer to the year-old mark. At age 6 or 7 weeks, the first intentional vocalizations (other than cries) lay the ground for language development. When the caregiver talks to the infant, the child watches intently, preparing to mimic these sounds in later months. The child who is not talked to frequently or whose babblings are not encouraged learns to take little pleasure in verbalizing. Therefore, language development is slow.

It was mentioned earlier that while one type of parent emotionally neglects, another type stimulates. The latter parent may heavily invest in the child's first year, but with that investment comes great expectations. Before the year is out, the child will be expected to talk, walk, and even be toilet trained. Caretakers may also have controlled and distinct ideas of what the baby's schedule should be, regardless of the baby's inner timing. Unmet expectations sometimes result in abuse.

One to Four Years

By age 1 year, the poorly parented baby shows little interest in toys or exploration in general. The ways in which children use toys mirror what they see in others. Children who have nothing to observe—who are not stimulated through mutual play—lack the ability to use toys or to show interest in playing. Many abused adults demonstrate the inability to play and enjoy life. This inability may stem from as early as this first year.

Children also demonstrate *frozen* (or *passive*) *watchfulness*, whereby the child lies immobile, watching the actions of others (Cicchetti and Toth, 2000). These children have learned that the world is not predictable and sometimes not even friendly. In the course of a day, these children learn that sometimes they are struck for their behavior and that other times that same behavior is ignored. Therefore, children from abusive and neglectful homes develop an uncanny knack of reading their environment. They become acutely aware of stimuli and what they mean. This ability to assess and often predict their environment requires a skill not always developed by the average child. Unfortunately, this skill is not measurable, so that in later years, when the intelligence of abused children is in question—or felt to be lower than other children—no points are given for this demanding ability. Thus, the young child's ability to read the environment—so basic for survival at home—is a detriment in learning situations.

The child between ages 1 and 3 continues to demonstrate delays in motor activity and social development. He or she appears to have little investment in relationships and fails to make eye contact. He or she has learned that adults are all powerful and that autonomy is discouraged. To displease an adult by exerting one's own will may mean abuse.

Around the age of 2, a toddler especially needs a consistent, loving mother (parent) figure. It is a time when the task is to separate from the caregiver and to begin to develop a sense of autonomy. For this, the child needs a mother who is secure enough to encourage individual growth. The mother must be able to send the child off but be available when the child needs to return to her arms—to check if she is still there. The mother, in return, must be confident that her child will return periodically and be pleased by his or her growth, for, indeed, this represents the beginning of the child's final separation and individuation from her (Bee and Boyd, 2011; Berk, 2012).

For still other infants, babyhood was a time when the parent was able to give. The tasks of feeding and nurturing were not much of a burden to the mother. After infancy, however, some of these mothers have difficulty. Once the child becomes more of an individual, the mother, who is not confident in her own abilities, may be threatened by her child's need to differentiate. She may see attempts at separation, no matter how brief, as a rejection, and she may either withdraw from her child or strike out in anger. The child for whom the parent–child relationship has been inadequate may not be comfortable enough to attempt this separation. So the child will remain half involved and half uninvolved with the withholding parent.

This inability to wholly test independence also hampers the child's ability to test reality—and to learn to trust himself or herself. When the child is learning the "rules" of his or her environment and is attempting to internalize these rules to eventually become his or her own standards, then the child who is not given full opportunity to test the limits in relative safety will not internalize adequately.

Autonomy in children must also be considered within a cultural context. In cultures that encourage interdependence, rather than autonomy, this stage may look somewhat different. Still, it will be necessary for the child to be confident that caretakers are there when needed (Webb and Lum, 2001).

Some cultures believe more strongly than others that the parents should be in charge. The method of child rearing in relation to discipline and the encouragement of independence depends on the cultural values to which the family ascribes. Thus, when one sees a child of another culture who does not appear to be developing independence, it is important to look deeper into the values of that culture. Erickson (see Bee and Boyd, 2011) described the age between 2 and 3 as a time when a child either develops autonomy or experiences shame and doubt. Yet there are some cultures that use shame as a method of teaching children and promoting family loyalty (Shibusawa, 2001).

Although much research has focused on the mother's influence on the developing child, paternal influence is also important. Different stages of development are affected differently by paternal absence or by a dysfunctional father–child relationship. These effects are also culture dependent. Recent studies on the importance of attachment suggest that fathers as well as mothers are significant in building secure attachment (Bee and Boyd, 2011; Fabes and Martin, 2002).

The importance of the father as well as the mother in sexual development of both male and female children is also worth noting. Between 1 and 3 years of age, the child's sexual development is progressing. By age 3, the average child will have learned of sexuality through seeing, touching, and doing. He or she may have bathed with children of both sexes and have an early understanding that there are differences. The parents' reaction to toilet training, exposure and touching of the genitals, and masturbation gives the developing child a clear indication of what is normal and expected. Most children wonder about their parents' breasts and penises and ask that the names and functions be identified. The way in which the child's own culture views the discussion of sexuality is also crucial to his or her development in this area.

Sexually abusive parents rationalize that this curiosity necessitates touch or demonstration. The child who experiences this early distortion in teaching is frequently indiscriminate in touching others' genitals or acts out the demonstration on peers.

Finding pleasure in their own bodies is a normal part of development in most children. A parent who severely punishes a child for masturbation gives the child a message that that part of the body is "dirty," "sinful," or not to be touched. It must also be noted that this, too, is culture dependent. For example, Shibusawa (2001) comments that the lack of openness toward sexuality in Japanese families, combined with mixed messages about sex in the United States today, can be problematic for children later in adolescence. The sexually abusive parent, on the other hand, may encourage masturbation and develop the practice into mutual manipulation as a progression toward other sexual interplay. The way in which children are treated by the parent of the opposite sex is important in the development of a healthy sexual attitude. Overstimulation impedes the child's ability to incorporate knowledge pertinent to his or her level of understanding. The result is confusion, guilt, and often a later inability to distinguish between sexuality and affection.

By 4 years of age, average children are well within the period when they are attempting to sort out their own concepts of sexuality. Although the boy is attracted to his mother as a love object (Oedipal conflict) and the girl to her father (Electra complex), both are beginning to recognize that these parents are already attached. The solution then is found in modeling the parent of the same sex in the hope of some day finding someone like the beloved opposite-sex parent (Bee and Boyd, 2011).

Abuse and neglect impede these vital learnings in several ways. To progress to wanting to identify with the same-sex parent, the child must perceive that the parents condone this growth and that the same-sex parent is emotionally attractive enough to identify with. For example, in order for a girl to model herself after her mother, she must perceive that both her mother and father applaud this behavior. Parents who are threatened in some manner by the child's development may communicate discomfort, thus impeding the child's desire to grow. The mother's attractiveness as a model for the little girl may be diminished if she is emotionally unapproachable, too harsh in her discipline, or is constantly being criticized—or even battered—by the father. In addition, to allow the girl to pull herself away from her immature sexual attachment to her father, he must behave toward her in a nonseductive manner. The female child whose father is not only seductive but sexually abusive does not have an opportunity to develop an appropriate attitude toward sexuality.

The male child sexually abused by the mother faces similar issues. Sexual abuse of a boy by the father often creates fears of homosexuality and gender confusion. Similar conflicts—and apparently more intense—are evident in the female abused by her mother.

By age 4, abused and neglected children demonstrate difficulty in relating to others—especially in the area of trust, a diminished capacity for play, low self-esteem, and often fears and phobias. Language development is not comparable to other children their age. One of the most marked observations of children who have experienced inadequate parenting, however, is their extreme passivity. Their disinclination to reach out or explore makes the scope of their activities extremely limited. Survival has taken so much energy that they have little left for other pursuits.

Four to Eight Years

The developmental delays continue to be obvious in the child between ages 4 and 8. The hallmark of this period should be learning, but the child whose early development has been punctuated with abuse or neglect may not have sufficient energy or interest for this activity. These children come to school unable to trust the teacher, and the success of their education often depends on the quality of this relationship. Their relationships with peers are frequently poor.

By age 8, children who have experienced consistency in their lives are beginning to develop the concept of cause and effect. For the abused child, however, causal relationships may not be clear. A particular action or event one day elicited a specific response from the mother or father, but the next day, the same action caused a totally different result. Thus, the child's sense of predictability has been distorted, and an inability to understand some of the most basic learning principles has been created.

Verbal explanations may be difficult for the understimulated child to comprehend. Used to one-word commands at home, the teacher's complicated set of instructions creates only confusion in the child's underdeveloped mind. The hypervigilance developed for survival again proves more of a liability than an asset at school. The child becomes so preoccupied with the teacher's perceived intention that he or she has difficulty grasping cognitive material.

The rules of life and games, including the cultural context on which these are based, are firmly embedded in most children's minds by the development of the superego (i.e., the incorporation of past parental restrictions that eventually form a conscience and a concept of the ideal self). These rules may be hazy for the abused and neglected child. Whether you get caught is often of more concern than any inner morality. Getting caught is symbolic of failure, and there is little remorse about the actual deed. This is the experience of the child deprived of consistency and adequate nurturing.

Another type of child—a member of the rigid, physically abusing family—has developed a superego, but it, too, is faulty. Rigid and uncompromising, this child's superego outlines strict rules, but again the control is external. The child may comply because he or she has learned that not to comply brings on abuse. The child may have begun to internalize some of these unrealistically high expectations—not through any sense of independence but because the parents' admonishments echo in his or her mind. These children often demonstrate an intense need to succeed in their schoolwork. Failure is totally unacceptable.

"Craig reminded me of a little robot," remarked the teacher of a compulsive 8-year-old. He was immaculately dressed, right down to the unfailingly white section of the saddle shoes he wore. His movements were definite. Each task would be undertaken with intense concentration. I often felt he was "programmed" at home to do superior schoolwork. When hard work and concentration were the only prerequisites to a job well done, Craig was fine. But when the task required deductive reasoning, Craig faltered. Failure to answer a question correctly or a low grade on a paper resulted in a rigid body posture so intense that I was concerned. Several failures in one day usually brought on an asthma attack.

Craig's parents had high expectations of their son. Their own fear of failure (his father was in sales with a company that pitted its employees in fierce competition with each other for quotas) had translated into physical abuse when Craig displeased them. (It was later learned that his numerous bruises were not the result of accidents but caused by this abuse.)

Craig was indeed a child whose internalized expectations, as well as the abuse he suffered, left him all but unable to learn.

Eight to Twelve Years

The abused or neglected child whose parents have difficulty in nurturing is probably well established as the nurturer by now. The parents have long since indicated their expectations that the child assume their roles and meet their needs. The unsure child thus cares for younger siblings, assumes household tasks, and caters to parental whims. While this role reversal usually commences as soon as the child is able (often as early as age 4 or 5), the preadolescent becomes skilled in these tasks. To complete these tasks often requires returning home right after school or taking days off. Already feeling alienated from peers, the child's isolation is intensified by his or her lack of opportunity to participate in peer activities.

The child who has been having school problems may be beginning to be disillusioned with the educational system. Behavior problems within school and truancy are indications of the inability to cope. The way in which the school deals with these issues can be of utmost importance in the child's future attitude toward learning and toward authority figures. Suspension or expulsion provides the isolated maltreated child with one more proof of rejection and failure.

It is important to note that some cultures expect that children will care for younger siblings at an early age. The need to work several jobs, for example, might mean that a mother leaves her 9-year-old as the sole caregiver of 6-, 4-, and 2-year-olds from 7:00 P.M. to 3:00 A.M. when the mother returns home. Although protective agencies state that under the law this practice is neglectful, parents like this mother argue that it is a necessity. In addition, some cultures have different ideas regarding the age at which it is appropriate to leave children on their own or to care for younger children (Webb and Lum, 2001), but this should not be confused with the child who has been put in the role of parent.

A *parentified child* (one who takes a parent's place as caregiver), especially the preadolescent girl, is particularly vulnerable to the onset of sexual abuse. She has often been placed in a position at home where she has assumed more and more household responsibilities, culminating in a role reversal with her mother. This role reversal, as well as her budding sexuality, is perceived by the abusive father as signals of her availability. Since incest is a family issue, it is important to examine the dynamics of family life for the preadolescent and adolescent girl. There are several factors that influence the onset of an incestuous affair.

The parents of a sexually abused child are caught up in their own marital disputes, which often originate or culminate in their sexual adjustment. At the same time, the female child is developing sexually and is realizing her own sexuality. Threatened by this aspect of her child's development, the mother may further alienate herself from the parent–child relationship. (Some degree of alienation usually exists prior to this time.) The father, at the same time, is attracted by his daughter's sexuality and sees her as a nonconflictual sexual substitute. So complex are the patterns of this dysfunctional family that it is difficult to outline in other than a simplistic manner. The problems inherent in a father's seduction of his daughter and a mother's further isolation are present prior to the child's overt sexual development. While in most families, there exists the inclination toward such feelings, the censoring mechanism of the healthy ego quickly represses them. The potentially incestuous father and his mate, however, are plagued by remnants of childhood scars that inhibit this censoring (Child and Adolescent Development [CAD] and Diamond, 2006; Ryan, 1998).

Adolescence

The same factors just mentioned operate during adolescence. But during adolescence, the sexually abused girl is likely to try to extricate herself from an incestuous relationship—especially if the onset of the abuse occurred after she had established some peer connections. Her desire for age-appropriate peer relationships and her guilt over her perceived complicity, along with the normal adolescent quest for identity, often cause her to attempt to stop the behavior herself or to tell someone else. The boy who has witnessed his sister's abuse may either identify with the aggressor—acting out abusively on either his sister or other siblings or, less frequently, attempting to be protective of his sister. The boy who is being sexually abused may feel the same need to free himself for reasons of peer connections. Abuse by a male often elicits myriad homosexual fears, desires, and conflicts.

Todd was abused by his father from the age of 9. The middle of three brothers, he also remembers his older brother approaching him sexually. This angered Todd, and after initially complying, he rebuffed his older brother's attention. Todd does remember, however, that on several occasions, he instigated sexual contact between his younger brother and himself.

The main recipient of his father's attention, Todd remembers feeling "special" and "loved." At age 13, however, he was attracted to an older girl but worried that he was homosexual. His father ridiculed his concerns, causing Todd to feel "belittled and humiliated." In a fit of anger, he told his mother of his relationship with his father. She became angry and apparently confronted the father, but the subject was never discussed again.

Angered by Todd's "betrayal," the father ceased all attention to his son. He ignored the boy in every way. Todd was devastated. In desperation, he became involved with drugs, but his mother was delegated to handle any trouble he got into. Finally, two years later, Todd reapproached his father sexually in a desperate attempt to terminate the silence. The relationship became sexual once again and lasted well into the boy's twenties.

Todd resolved his conflicts by bartering sexuality for the attention he received from his father. This was the first of a series of homosexual relationships in which he chose the attention of men, rather than chance trusting a woman again.

Body image is another important dynamic for adolescents and plays a particular role in the behavior of the sexually abused child. In a conscious or unconscious compulsion to feel less sexual in response to their developing bodies, some sexually abused girls develop anorexia nervosa. When this condition persists, it can inhibit menstruation and the further development of secondary sex characteristics (Berk, 2012; Dolgin, 2010). Other types of self-abuse are also common among this age group (Winkler, 2003).

For the adolescent, sexual abuse has a decided impact on development in other ways. In their classic work, Finkelhor and Browne (1985) postulate that sexual abuse has four types of traumatic effects:

1. Traumatic sexualization
2. Betrayal
3. Powerlessness
4. Stigmatization

Traumatic sexualization is a result of a child's exposure to sexual behavior inappropriate to the level of development. She or he has been rewarded for participation in this activity and therefore sees sexuality as a method of manipulating others to meet his or her needs. The adolescent may also view his or her own value as synonymous with being sexual. Promiscuity is often a part of the abused adolescent's pattern.

The adolescent has also developed cognitively, recognizing the possibility of alternatives and choices. The abused adolescent begins to recognize that the perpetrator also made choices and, in choosing to exploit, has betrayed the victim's trust. The sense of betrayal felt by the developing adolescent can be profound and can contribute to self-abusive or rebellious behavior.

Having been unwillingly violated again and again and, compounding the assault, not having been believed when trying to tell someone, the sexually abused adolescent feels a sense of powerlessness. The stigmatization comes when the adolescent recognizes that being abused makes him or her different. The resulting shame and guilt further intensify the isolation and low self-esteem, which are already a burden for the developing child.

Control and self-mastery are issues not only for the sexually abused but for all maltreated children. The child who has received inadequate parenting may not have learned to internalize control. Neglecting families do not provide sufficient role models for standards and moral development. Overly rigid, abusive families maintain the locus of control that makes it difficult for the adolescent to do anything but mimic their rigidity. For physically abused adolescents, control has been ensured through violence. It is not surprising, therefore, that studies have found that exposure to violence predisposes children to delinquent behavior.

Separation is difficult for the adolescent whose needs have not been met. For these children, the break with parents is often abrupt—through running away, early pregnancy, premature marriage, or total alienation. Although unequipped with the proper models, these adolescents often promise they will be better parents than their own.

The search for identity, pursued with full force during adolescence, is built on testing internalized values and the final resolution of an individualized code of ethics. Such a hazardous, emotional pilgrimage necessitates some degree of self-esteem, room for growth, and positive models to emulate. For the child whose family life has been disorganized and dysfunctional, the search for identity can be exceedingly painful. Too often, this adolescent, hampered by insecurity and robbed of good self-esteem, gives up the pursuit and immerses himself or herself in the parents' values. Thus, the cycle of abuse and neglect may repeat itself.

Fortunately, in adolescence, children have access to other role models. Contact with a concerned teacher, relative, friend, or counselor may enable the child to develop alternative values.

DEVELOPMENT, MALTREATMENT, AND RESILIENCY

Manny and Gerry were brothers. Only 11 months apart, the two boys were inseparable. They looked so much alike that people often thought that they were twins. But Manny, the older of the two, was the more daring. He felt his position as the oldest of his five siblings was an important role. Both Manny and Gerry tried to protect their younger sisters from their parents' constant fights. When their mother began to pick at their father about his drinking and frequent absences from home, both boys knew what would come next. They would corral their sisters into a closet to keep them out of harm's way. Fights began with their parents screaming at each other, but it would not be long before their father's angry words would erupt into punches, which their mother would return with equal vehemence. Sometimes, it seemed that their parents were not happy unless someone was bloodied and the police had to drag one parent away screaming abuse and promises to "get even." Both Manny and Gerry were to have nightmares about those fights for years to come.

Years later, the fact that they had been almost identical in their youth would have been difficult to imagine. Manny's gravitation toward a gang won him a deeply scarred face from the myriad of fights he had fought. He dropped out of school and developed a drug habit that robbed his body of nourishment, and he became thin, emaciated, and sickly. Despite this, he was quick to pick a fight with anyone who displeased him. He drifted from place to place, often in trouble with the law.

Gerry, on the other hand, finished high school, met a girl at 16, and moved in with her family. They were poor, but there was none of the violence that he had experienced in his own home. Gerry found a job, married his girl, and did his best to care for her and their children.

What caused two brothers so similar in age and from the same background to seek such different paths in adulthood? Some researchers would attribute Gerry's more positive outcome to what is termed *resilience*. Resilience refers to a child's ability to adapt to adversity and function adequately despite its existence (Erickson and Egeland, 2011). No one is sure exactly how some children develop resilience and why some do not fare as well, but recent research has sought to isolate several factors.

Gilgun (2003) suggests that when children are hurt and their healthy development is threatened, they seek to regain control and mastery over themselves and their environments. Children may do this in one of three ways: through prosocial efforts (finding comfort, seeking out trusted adults, adopting positive behavior such as participation in sports, or searching for positive ways to interpret negative events); through antisocial efforts (through violence, destruction, stealing, and other crimes); or through self-injurious efforts (cutting, eating disorders, substance abuse, suicide attempts, etc.). The resilient child is more likely to seek prosocial ways to cope with stress.

What makes a child resilient? Theorists postulate that the child's own temperament or personal characteristics, combined with a close relationship with at least one parent or other nurturing adult and social support outside the family, make the difference (Goldstein and Brooks, 2006; Masten, 2001; Quyen, Bird, Davies, Haven, Jensen, and Goodman, 1998). Gilgun (2003) adds the influence of an affirming ethnic and cultural identification, the ability to engage in self-soothing behaviors (like music, affirming self-talk, or daydreams about a positive future), and the ability to choose people who model prosocial behaviors. Bancroft and Silverman (2002), considering children who have witnessed domestic violence, would concur. They also point to the development of talents and interests, scholastic aptitudes, and positive peer relationships (see also Allen-Meares and Fraser, 2004). Iwaniec (2006) suggests that other qualities to be factored in are a child's problem-solving ability and social competence.

For Gerry, his physical abilities gave him an opportunity to participate in sports, which in turn provided him with positive peer relationships. Ironically, his ability to depend on Manny through most of their early years gave him the support of a confidant that he needed to develop positive self-esteem. And his more even temperament helped him to cope more effectively with his violent home. Manny, on the other hand, who was more intense and aggressive, shunned school and antagonized his classmates. Disenchanted, he dropped out early. His anger at his home life spilled over, making him seek escape, rather than prosocial means of coping.

Bancroft and Silverman (2002) caution professionals to be attentive to batterers who undermine resilience by isolating the child to prevent peer relationships, verbally abusing the child about his or her abilities, or attempting to sabotage personal strengths.

Little research has considered the effects of culture on resiliency among maltreated children. Addressing what they described as "the fastest growing minority in the United States," Flores, Cicchetti, and Rogosch (2005) studied 133 low-income Latino children from an urban area of upstate New York to assess the characteristics associated with resilience among both maltreated and nonmaltreated children. These authors concluded that maltreated Latino children, like their African American and European American counterparts, have increased difficulty with interpersonal relationships and are more prone to behavioral problems. The female children demonstrated more resiliency than the males, but this may not have been an accurate finding due to the low number of females in the study. The authors further postulated that strong gender roles and cultural values such as *machismo* may promote feelings of shame and frustration among maltreated boys. Latinas, on the other hand, who are socialized to be more obedient and self-sacrificing, may be better able to cope with environmental adversity. Much more research is needed, these authors conclude, about the fine points of the influence of culture on resiliency.

A child's resilience is not always entirely predictable, but identification of the above factors enables helping professionals to more effectively foster these traits and hopefully help a child in doing more to overcome the residual effects of abuse and threatened development.

SUMMARY

Developing normally is a difficult task for the abused and neglected child. Two parenting patterns occur in maltreating families, both of which hamper the development of the child. One type of family is composed of adults who continually strive to get their own needs met, neglecting the needs of the child and eventually forcing the offspring into the role of nurturing them. A second type of family is rigid in its standards with unrealistically high expectations for the child. Although they are able to give the child more nurturing, the result of their unmet demands is abuse and confusion for the developing child.

Each developmental period provides new conflicts for the maltreating family. Pregnancy is marked with hopes for an infant who will be miraculously loving and giving in every way. The relationship between mother and father frequently determines the couple's ability to accept the infant. Birth and early bonding are complicated by the emotional immaturity of the mother, the relationship or lack of relationship between the mother and significant others, and other environmental factors. Inadequate bonding leaves the child at risk for abuse.

The abused or neglected child between birth and 1 year demonstrates poor motor control, a lack of social responsiveness, slow language development, and a general mistrust of the environment. From 1 to 4 years of age, the child develops a passivity combined with hypervigilance about his or her surroundings. This child is slow to reach out or explore and has little interest in developing autonomy.

Fathers, too, have an effect on the child's development. Studies indicate that young children demonstrate affiliative behavior with their fathers, and fathers who are absent or unavailable can negatively influence their children's cognitive development and self-esteem.

Early sexual development is impeded by inappropriate exposure to sexuality during these years. Children who are sexually abused develop confusion about their own sexuality and the way in which they are expected to relate to others.

By 4 to 8 years, the child's development delays appear more significant. He or she has difficulty relating to peers and is unable to make the transition to structured learning in the classroom. Abused children have difficulty internalizing standards—some because they have observed no consistent standards at home and others because the rigidity in their home life does not allow them the autonomy to be self-directed.

The maltreated child between ages 8 and 12 may well have developed into the nurturer of the parents. School problems and behavior problems may be part of the child's life. Preadolescence is a classic age for sexual abuse to commence. The child's budding sexuality augments the parents' own conflicts, and abuse may be the result. Maltreated children of this age group often feel isolated and alienated from their peers.

Adolescence marks the quest for control, separation, and identity—a quest hampered by maltreatment. The abused child demonstrates poor self-esteem and a poor body image, which often leads to self-injurious behavior. Adolescents frequently separate abruptly from the family of origin through running away, becoming pregnant, or some other method of separation.

Why does abuse and neglect affect some children profoundly and others to a lesser degree? Recent studies have pointed to the resilience of some children, which is based on a variety of factors.

Chapter 4

The Neglect of Children

A 5-year-old child sits on a city doorstep in early January, clad only in a thin, dirty sweater; ragged slacks; and holey sneakers. With grimy fingers, she listlessly picks a potato chip from a half-empty bag. Her hair is matted, and her eyes stare into the distance; she is indifferent to her surroundings. Beside her sits a 2-year-old, pulling idly at the threads on his already frayed socks. He, too, is ill clad, despite the temperature. In the apartment above, no one is home. In fact, no one has been home since morning. Small, emaciated, dirty representatives of a world that pays little heed to their welfare, the children appear oblivious.

THE NEGLECT OF THE CONCEPT OF NEGLECT

If one compares the literature on various types of child maltreatment, it becomes obvious that there is a dearth of information on the concept of child neglect, despite the fact that a large number of children are neglected each year. In fact, the term *neglect* is usually subsumed under the generic description of maltreatment as in "child abuse and neglect." Although neglect can underlie not only physical and sexual abuse but domestic violence, it has its own unique characteristics. Why has this phenomenon been so infrequently studied?

Garbarino and Collins (1999) suggest that there are several reasons why neglect has not demanded, as a research topic, the attention given to every other type of maltreatment. First, *neglect is less dramatic* than the bruises of physical abuse or the thought of a father having sexual relations with his own child. Instead, the *problems of neglect are less obvious* and therefore more difficult to see. In addition, *the intervention needed in neglectful situations is not the cessation of assault but rather a gradual process* that teaches a neglectful parent how to meet his or her own and the child's needs. Thus, intervention is not clear cut in many cases and certainly not short term. And finally, the *misconception is that neglect is born of poverty*, and poverty is a condition that the general public tries hard to ignore. In fact, although neglect can stand alone without poverty, it is often the unavailable energy of neglectful parents that drives them into a life of being poor (Cantwell, 1997; Dubowitz, 2007; Erikson and Egeland, 2011; Smith and Fong, 2004; Stevenson, 2007; Taylor and Daniel, 2005). The lack of connection with the greater society, characterized by the lack of social supports and social isolation, causes them to be discounted and ignored until their children come to the attention of social agencies because of parental neglect.

DEFINITION AND MEASUREMENT OF NEGLECT

Defining *child neglect* in legal or social terms can in no way give an accurate picture of the neglected child. Such children must be seen to appreciate the true hopelessness of their existence. For years social workers and legal authorities have debated the definition of *neglect* and the magnitude of the problem (Erickson and Egeland, 2011).

The difficulty in defining neglect is threefold. First, it differs from other forms of maltreatment in that it is an act of omission rather than an assault or act of commission (Cantwell, 1997; Haworth, 2007; Joffe, 2002; McSherry, 2011). Second, there are many types of behavior or omissions in childcare and supervision that can be included under the term *neglect*. These may differ significantly. And finally, neglect must be considered as it relates to the developmental level of the child in question (De Panfilis, 2006; Zuravin, 1999; Erikson and Egeland, 2011; McSherry, 2011). For example, leaving a 10- or 12-year-old without adult supervision might not be construed as neglect, whereas leaving an infant alone for any period of time certainly would be defined as such.

Neglect is seen by most experts as an act of omission often related to parental deficits, which some divide into three categories: *physical neglect*, *educational neglect*, and *emotional neglect* (Black and Dubowitz, 1999; DePanfilis, 2006; DePanfilis and Salus, 2003; Smith and Fong, 2004).

Joffe (2002) divides neglect into three categories: *physical neglect*, which encompasses nonorganic failure to thrive, inadequate supervision, abandonment, and failure to meet a child's basic physical needs; *medical neglect*, which involves refusal to provide health care or a delay in getting health care; and *educational neglect*, which involves permitting truancy, failure to send a child to school or enroll him or her in school, and inattention to special educational needs (see also DePanfilis, 2006; Pearl, 2002). Erickson and Egeland (2011) add *emotional neglect*, which involves inattention to a child's emotional needs, and *mental health neglect*, whereby the caretaker refuses to tend to a child's serious emotional or behavioral disorder. Some authors suggest that community deficits may also inhibit the parents from meeting the child's needs (Smith and Fong, 2004; Kaplan, Schene, DePanfilis, and Gilmore, 2009).

Cantwell (1997) takes a more functional view in her definition, outlining in more detail what neglectful parents fail to provide for their children. The emotional neglect mentioned earlier involves, in this author's view, the failure of the parent to help the child develop competence by failing to adequately bond with that child and neglecting his or her development of self-esteem. Cantwell discusses the various aspects of emotional neglect that are detrimental to the child. The child experiences *stimulation neglect*. Neglectful parents often demonstrate an inability to provide stimulation for their offspring, thus endangering their emotional and neurological development. For example, when a baby's bottle is propped, as often happens in a neglectful home, the child is robbed of the touching and interaction with the caretaker that is so basic to attachment. In addition, being held during feeding provides a foundation for hand–eye coordination and other perceptual skills; the baby whose bottle is propped loses out here as well.

Neglected children also experience *language neglect*, in that their parents may communicate only in commands and do not read to them or talk to them at any length. When adults converse with children, they are helping them to internalize language, preparing them for future social relationships, and arming them with the ability to solve problems. Children who do not have this vital beginning in terms of their language are ill equipped to function adequately in school or in later social relationships (Cantwell, 1997; McSherry, 2011).

Neglected children are also robbed of the opportunity to develop both gross motor skills and fine motor skills (*gross motor* and *fine motor neglect*). Children develop gross motor skills by playing, jumping, cavorting, and enjoying the world in the boisterous manner that is typical of healthy children. If a child's noisy play bothers a parent, this type of activity may well be prohibited. Fine motor control is perfected as early as infancy when a feeding baby reaches for its mother's face and touches it with delicate, searching fingers. Later, normal children will be encouraged to do puzzles or turn pages or scribble with crayons. Children whose lives are more concerned with keeping out of the way of a neglectful or intoxicated parent who has little time for such childish needs will not develop their fine motor skills (Cantwell, 1997). Both of these skills are necessary for a variety of tasks in learning, schoolwork, and later life.

Admittedly, the definition of neglect at any given time in history is influenced greatly by the mores and values of that particular period. Not only the contemporary standards but the cultural values significantly frame the definition. Current society holds parents responsible for giving their children adequate food, shelter, and clothing; medical care; education; supervision and protection; and moral and social guidance (DePanfilis, 2006; Garbarino and Collins, 1999; Gaudin, 1999; Joffe, 2002; McSherry, 2011).

During the 1960s and 1970s, Norman Polansky and his colleagues documented their extensive research with both urban and rural neglectful mothers. Despite the age of this research and the fact the families have changed to some extent, Polansky's work is classic in the field and provides a foundation for our current understanding of neglect. Polansky, Hally, and Polansky provided a more concise working definition of this phenomenon:

> Child neglect may be defined as a condition in which a caretaker responsible for the child either deliberately or by extraordinary inattentiveness permits the child to experience available present suffering and/or fails to provide one or more of the ingredients generally deemed essential for developing a person's physical, intellectual, and emotional capacities. (1975, p. 5)

In 1967, to further define the concept of *neglect*, Polansky and his colleagues developed the Childhood Level of Living Scale (CLL), originally as a result of research done among families in rural Appalachia and later applied to low-income families in Philadelphia. The CLL was designed to assess families with children between the ages of 4 and 7 but has also been used for a wider range of ages. Geared predominantly toward maternal care—because in a majority of households only the female parent was available for study—the CLL presented nine descriptive categories, five of which assessed physical care and four the emotional, cognitive, and psychological factors. Under physical care, consideration was given to such factors as meal planning, medical care, safety issues, leaving the child alone, house or shelter adequacy and safety, appropriateness of sleeping and living conditions, and cleanliness. The psychological assessment considered the type of stimulation the child was given, the parents' emotional availability to the child, quality of discipline, the mother's concern for the child, and her own stability (Hally, Polansky, and Polansky, 1980, pp. A-2–A-8).

Despite the fact that Polansky and his fellow researchers purportedly used different types of families to draw the composite that became the CLL, experts in multicultural studies protested that the scale would make some functional minority families appear neglectful. For example, Amy Iwasaki Mass, an expert in Asian/Pacific studies, comments that the CLL would be totally inappropriate in assessing an immigrant Hmong family. The Hmongs are hill people from Laos who worked with American service personnel after the fall of Saigon. Some have more recently immigrated to the United States but often have difficulty acclimating to this culture. The CLL scale would be problematic in assessing their childcare for several reasons: First, this culture passes information orally from one generation to the next instead of having written language. For this reason, they would not have magazines or books available. Nor would they be likely to take their children to historical sites to enhance their education. Such daily tasks as shopping at a large super market or using public transportation would be challenging (Mass, 1991).

Native American, Hispanic American, and African American families also often place emphasis on child-rearing practices that do not conform to the CLL scale. Certainly, these cultural differences should not be enough to label them neglectful.

Recognizing the limitations of the CLL scale, a panel of experts on child maltreatment in Ontario developed the Child Neglect Index (CNI) to aid protective workers in Ontario as they make determinations of neglect. Although geared specifically to Ontario statutes, the scale can be applicable to other geographic locations (Trocmé, 1996).

The CNI (see Figure 4.1) assesses neglect in the following areas: (1) supervision, (2) food and nutrition, (3) clothing and hygiene, (4) physical health care, (5) mental health care, and (6) developmental/educational care (Trocmé, 1996). The index was originally tested by intake workers dealing with neglect cases and was found to be as reliable, if not in some instances more reliable, than the field trials used with the Child Well-Being Scales. Perusal of the short instrument attests to the latitude available to see cases in cultural contexts, rather than impose on clients a particular cultural bias. However, Trocmé (1997) comments that the brevity of the index is both a strength and a weakness. Use of the CNI presupposes some degree of training on the part of the protective worker in order to make judgments. It is especially important that the worker be familiar with the cultural background of the family in question (Korbin and Spilsbury, 1999).

During the last 10 years, a bit more attention has been given to the need to measure neglect. Journals dedicated to intervention in child maltreatment (such as *Child Maltreatment* and *Child Abuse and Neglect*) have published more articles specifically related to neglect in the last decade.

Dubowitz and his colleagues (2011) renewed the efforts to develop categories of neglect through the use of information collected from the self-reports of youth about their parents' neglectful behaviors. Responses to the 25 questions were then categorized into a 3-factor model, referring to the meeting of the youth's physical needs, emotional support, and parental supervision or monitoring. Although not a thorough classification, the study did provide some interesting data from the perspective of the victims of neglect.

Polansky and his colleagues' studies were largely based in lower socioeconomic areas. But what of the family of the busy professionals whose 6-, 8-, and 10-year-old children let themselves in from school and prepare their own meals before the parents return home? The neighborhood is affluent and supposed to be idyllic. Yet these parents and children have little contact, and while well provided for materially, the children lack the attention

Figure 4.1   Child Neglect Index

20	15	5	0

CHILD'S NAME: _____   AGE: 0–2   3–5   6–12   13–16

FILE #:

WORKER'S NAME: _____   DATE: _____

SUPERVISION

The two factors to be considered in assessing level of supervision are avoidability (i.e. extent to which a caretaker can be expected to anticipate and prevent) and severity of harm, or potential harm. CFSA identifies three specific types of harm that may result from failure to supervise:

Physical Harm	Sexual Molestation	Criminal Activity/Child Under 13
S.37(2)(a&b)	S.37(2)(c&d)	S.37(2)(k)

na	Unknown/Does not Apply
0	1. Adequate; provisions made to ensure child's safety, caretaker knows child's whereabouts and activities, clear limits set on activities.
25	2. Inconsistent; child is occasionally exposed to situation that could cause moderate harm (e.g. young school-aged child occasionally left alone, parents do not monitor whereabouts of adolescent who occasionally comes home late in evening).
50	3. Inadequate; child is often exposed to situations that could cause moderate harm, or there is a slight possibility that child could suffer serious harm (e.g. young school-aged child often left unsupervised, or infant occasionally left alone while sleeping).
60	4. Seriously Inadequate; child is often exposed to situations that could cause serious harm; (e.g. abandonment, home used as "crack house" & drugs left within reach of child, child often left to wander in dangerous neighbourhood, toddler often exposed to hazardous situations).

PHYSICAL CARE

Physical harm or substantial risk of physical harm due to the caretaker's "failure to care and provide for... the child adequately" CFSA 37(2)(a&b).

FOOD/NUTRITION

na	Unknown/Does Not Apply
0	1. Regular and nutritional meals provided.
20	2. Meals irregular and often not prepared, but child's functioning is not impaired.
40	3. Meals irregular and often not prepared, child's functioning is impaired (e.g. child is hungry and has difficulty concentrating in class).
50	4. Inadequate food provided, there is a substantial risk that the child will suffer from malnutrition (e.g. infant given diluted formula).
60	5. Child displays clinical symptoms of malnutrition; medical attention and/or rehabilitative diet required (e.g., weight loss, anaemia, dehydration, etc.).

CLOTHING & HYGIENE

na	Unknown/Does Not Apply
0	1. Child is clean and adequately clothed.
20	2. Inadequate clothing or hygiene, but this does not appear to affect child's functioning.
40	3. Inadequate clothing or hygiene limits child's functioning (e.g. unable to go outdoors because of lack of clothing, isolated by peers because of hygiene or appearance).

Figure 4.1 Child Neglect Index *(Continued)*

50	4. Inadequate clothing or hygiene likely to cause illness requiring medical treatment (e.g. infestation of head lice).
60	5. Illness requiring medical treatment due to inadequate clothing or hygiene (e.g. serious infection due to poor diaper care, intestinal disorder).

PROVISION OF HEALTH CARE

For the following three scales "not provided" means "does not provide, or refuses or is unavailable or unable to consent to..." (CFSA S.37(2)(e, f, g, h, & j). The extent to which harm could be avoided should be carefully considered in rating these three scales. Three factors should be examined: (a) whether a reasonable layman would recognize that a problem needs professional attention; or (b) whether a professional has recommended services or treatment; or (c) a vailability and/or effectiveness of treatment or services (e.g. the questionable effectiveness of services for chronic teen runners).

PHYSICAL HEALTH CARE   *CFSA S.37(2)(e)*

na	Unknown/Does Not Apply
0	1. Basic medical care provided.
20	2. Preventive medical care not provided (e.g. no regular checkups).
40	3. Medical care not provided for injury or illness causing avoidable distress.
50	4. Medical care not provided for injury or illness causing avoidable distress and interfering with child's functioning (e.g. chronic absence from school due to untreated illness).
60	5. Medical care not provided for injury or illness which could lead to permanent impairment or death (e.g. infant vomiting or diarrhea leading to dehydration).

MENTAL HEALTH CARE   *CFSA S.37(2)(f, g, & j)*

na	Unknown/Does Not Apply
0	1. Parents anticipate and respond to child's emotional needs.
25	2. Inconsistent response to emotional distress (e.g., responds only to crisis situations).
50	3. Services or treatment not provided in response to emotional distress, child at substantial risk of severe emotional or behavioural problems (anxiety, depression, withdrawal, self-destructive or aggressive behaviour, child under 13 engaging in criminal activity).
60	4. Services or treatment not provided in response to emotional distress, child experiencing severe emotional or behavioural problems.

DEVELOPMENTAL AND EDUCATIONAL CARE   *CFSA S.(2)(h)*

na	Unknown/Does Not Apply
0	1. Child's developmental and educational needs are met.
25	2. Child's developmental and educational needs are inconsistently met (e.g. limited infant stimulation, child could benefit from remedial help in one or two subjects, child having academic difficulties due to poor school attendance).
50	3. Services or treatment are not provided in response to identified learning or developmental problems (e.g. learning disability diagnosed but caretakers refuse remedial help).
60	4. Child has suffered or will suffer serious/permanent delay due to inattention to developmental/educational needs (e.g. Non-Organic Failure To Thrive identified but caretakers refuse remedial help).

For further information contact Nico Trocmé (416–978–5718; nico@fsw.utoronto.ca), Faculty of Social Work, University of Toronto (Version 5: Toronto,1995).
Funding provided by the Child, Youth & Family Policy Research Centre & the Social Sciences & Humanities Research Council.

Reprinted with permission from Nico Trocmé, "Development and Preliminary Evaluation of the Ontario Child Neglect Index," *Child Maltreatment,* 1(2) (1996) pp. 145–155, pp. 153–154.

necessary for healthy growth. In the more affluent family, even if the parents are not able to meet the children's needs adequately, they probably have many more resources available to them than a poor family. There may be more support within neighborhoods and among families and friends. Families with money may be more able to pay for the care of their children (Trocmé, 1997). Thus, status and income level may not only protect children from not having their needs met but also protect a family from being defined and therefore reported as neglectful. The chances of an affluent white family being reported to a protective agency are probably quite slim. Poor or minority families, on the other hand, are more likely to come to the attention of the social service system. Therefore, this chapter deals with the families more likely to be reported—those with lower incomes and with fewer resources.

Clearly, it becomes increasingly perplexing as to how to develop a scale to measure neglect that will encompass all socioeconomic and ethnic groups. Neglect is a type of maltreatment that is highly dependent on cultural child rearing values as well as variations in the neighborhood, the community, and indeed the cultural, economic, and political values of society itself.

CAUSES OF NEGLECT

Where does neglect begin? Does it commence when a family resigns itself to experiencing poverty or struggling to live with inadequate welfare benefits? Does neglect emanate from a decaying neighborhood that attracts those who care as little for themselves as they do for their surroundings? Or is neglect an individual phenomenon practiced by a parent or parents for whatever complex psychological reasons, resulting perhaps from their own unmet needs, stresses, or mental health problems?

Polansky and colleagues suggest that the causes can all be grouped within three theories:

> The economic, emphasizing the role of material deprivation and poverty; the ecological, in which a family's behavior is seen as responsive to the larger social context in which it is imbedded; and the personalistic, which attributes poor child care to individual differences among parental personalities, particularly their character structures. (1983, p. 21)

Economic Causes

Proponents of the economic view suggest that neglect is a response to stress, and poverty is an all-pervasive stress. The most overwhelming feature noted by numerous theorists and researchers is the extreme level of poverty of these families (Cantwell, 1997; Dubowitz, 1999; Joffe, 2002; Smith and Fong, 2004; Stevenson, 2007).

Poverty obviously has a deleterious effect on the parents' ability to care for their children. It cannot be denied that these families are among the poorest. Does neglect then stem from poverty? Or is poverty inevitable, given deficits in personality structure and the ability to cope with everyday tasks? Most authors are clear that not all families living in poverty are neglectful (Cantwell, 1997; Erickson and Egeland, 2011; Joffe, 2002; Smith and Fong, 2004; Taylor and Daniel, 2005).

It should be noted in a discussion of the correlation between neglect and poverty that being poor may cause the onlooker to *suspect* neglect. Based on the U.S. Census Bureau reports, the rate of African American children below the poverty line is 35.3 percent compared to 17 percent for white children (U.S. Census Bureau, 2012). And yet, according to the Children's Bureau (2011), 44.8 percent of the abused and neglected children were white, while 21.7 9 percent were African American and 21.4 percent Hispanic; 1.1 percent were Native American, and 1.1 percent were Asian/Asian Pacific (U.S. Department of Health and Human Services, Administration for Children and Families, Administration on Children, Youth and Families, Children's Bureau, 2011). Thus, to be poor does not mean that a child is neglected. Why then do some poor families neglect while the majority does not? The answer must be found in other variables.

Crittenden (1999) grappled with this somewhat deceptive correlation between poverty and neglect and pointed out some interesting observations. She comments that

> because of its association with neglect, low socioeconomic status has been identified as a major cause of child neglect. . . . Low socioeconomic status, however, includes a wide range of factors associated with poverty, such as unemployment, limited education, social isolation, large numbers of children, and childbirth to unmarried adolescents. (p. 48)

Crittenden goes on to say, however, that efforts to improve the economic status of neglectful families by providing them with material goods have neither ended their poverty nor prevented them from neglecting their children. Therefore, she concludes that "it is unlikely that the income or the lack of material goods is the primary impediment to successful parenting" (p. 49).

Ecological Causes

The ecological view originated with similar questions. According to an early study by Wolock and Horowitz (1979), neighborhoods of maltreating parents appeared to be more run down and more unfriendly, creating low morale among respondents. More recent studies have found similar environments (DePanfilis, 2006; Drake and Pandy, 1996; Korbin, Coulton, Lindstom-Ufiti, and Spilsburt, 2000).

Again, does the low morale of unfriendly, poorly kept neighborhoods severely stress parents and sap their strength for adequate child care? Or does the obvious lethargy in those unable to parent lead to other undone tasks, such as proper housekeeping and adequate home repair, and to their inability to support and communicate with neighbors? Do neighborhoods fail to understand the practices of newly immigrated parents and therefore isolate them? When vulnerable families fall prey to slum landlords, are they too overwhelmed to band together and protest? Or has their own development hampered their ability to relate to others, even in this basic way? If parents' ability to care for their children is influenced by the total social context in which they live, then feeling unsupported by their surroundings could well create parents who neglect.

Today, the ecological perspective is widely favored as a sufficiently encompassing theory to deal with a form of maltreatment that has as many variables as neglect. The ecological view in social work practice sees the individual as part of and interacting with the environment. From the perspective of neglect, this view would lead to several assumptions. First, the neglectful family must be seen within the context of the neighborhood, their culture, and the society. An understanding of cultural and racial values is vital in assessing the family's ability to function. The family is seen as a complex system, and the strengths they exhibit are as important as the problems they have. And finally, the family's issues are seen in relation to the community's ability to provide resources and social supports for them. The ecological approach to neglectful families puts more emphasis on interventions, which stress social supports.

The ecological perspective invites us to look at how society contributes to neglect. From a societal perspective, we have difficulty accepting that our values and institutions actually stimulate neglectful situations. Recent welfare reform legislation has created challenges for some populations of parents. For example, the requirement that parenting teens must return to their homes may throw them back into the same dysfunctional, possibly neglectful, environment they sought to escape.

The welfare system (now called Temporary Assistance for Needy Families, or TANF) is not the only contributor to neglect. The conversion of low- and moderate-income apartments into high-priced condominiums and the construction of condominiums, shopping malls, and professional buildings on formerly affordable housing sites leave families homeless or force them into decaying neighborhoods. These injustices burden the family with additional stresses. As immigrant and minority populations are forced into confined areas, their bitterness and frustration increase, and the energy they have available for child rearing decreases. Lives punctuated by long-term oppression often prevent parents from performing their roles adequately.

The contributors to neglect are many. Not only are neglectful families difficult for society to accept, but they also present problems for the system in its attempts to intervene.

Personalistic Individual Causes

Instead of looking at the economic status of neglectful parents or at how the neighborhood or societal institutions contribute to neglect, Crittenden (1999) and Cantwell (1997) suggest that the roots of neglect lie deep in the development of the individual parent and the way in which he or she has learned to process information. The way we process the information we receive from the world largely influences how we relate to that world and how we behave. The two types of information we receive relate to cognition and affect.

Cognition is information that tells us what actions will cause what effects, and this will influence the behavior that we adopt in most situations. *Affect* has to do with information about safety or danger in specific situations. Affect "is experiences in feeling states that motivate protective or affectionate behavior, and when feelings of distress are low, that promote exploration and learning" (Crittenden, 1999, p. 51).

With these two forms of information in mind, Crittenden (1999) theorizes that there are three types of neglect, based on how the parents and later their children process information: *disorganized neglect, emotional neglect*, and *depressed neglect*. These specific types of neglect are discussed later under the heading "Neglectful Parents." Suffice it to say at this point that Crittenden believes that her theory goes a long way toward explaining why child protection agencies find neglectful parents such a challenge. The processing of information is so basic that we sometimes find it difficult to relate to those who do not see the world as we do.

PROBLEMS IN INTERVENTION

Intervention with neglectful families presents myriad problems. First, neglectful families are numerous. An average social worker's caseload has a considerable number of neglect cases. Second, many neophyte workers find these cases elusive; they don't know what to expect from the parents, and the neglect is difficult to document. Too often, neglect is equated with material deprivation. If a family appears affluent, it is easier to ignore the emotional and physical neglect of the children. Third, coordination of these cases is extremely difficult. The organization that social workers feel is so desperately needed is alien to these clients. Social workers describe acute frustration with clients who have few skills or little ability to carry out the plans recommended for them. And frustration mounts because neglect often permeates generation after generation in these families. Fourth, if we are to consider Crittenden's (1999) theory, neglectful parents process information in a faulty manner that makes communicating with them extremely difficult. And finally, when professionals do recognize neglect and mobilize the families, they have few tangible resources to offer them. With cutbacks in funds, programs, and personnel, how can they hope to meet the ever-growing needs?

Yet despite frustration with parents and insufficient resources, professionals are constantly motivated to try to intervene so that at least the children will have a chance.

NEGLECTED CHILDREN

Neglect is a phenomenon that usually involves the entire family. If one child is neglected, usually all will be. Certainly, as children grow older and are more able to care for themselves, they are less likely to be dependent on parental care, but the neglect of earlier years has usually taken its toll emotionally. The Children's Bureau's report on child maltreatment in 2010 indicates that 78.3 percent of the victims of maltreatment suffered neglect. The highest percentage of these were under the age of 7 years, with the highest rate of 36.9 percent found between ages 0 and 4 years. It should also be noted that this report indicates that 58.2 percent of the reports of maltreatment made to child protective services go unsubstantiated (U.S. Department of Health and Human Services, Administration for Children and Families, Administration on Children, Youth and Families, Children's Bureau, 2011).

The picture of a neglected child is not soon forgotten. This impression was aptly characterized by physician Vincent Fontana, who became concerned about neglected children when he came to the New York Foundling Hospital in the late 1960s. Although some of the 320 children then sheltered at the hospital had been battered, a substantial number showed signs of neglect. Fontana describes making the rounds:

> What my associates and I saw were dull-eyed children who turned their faces to the wall, who could not respond to a friendly touch. Children with infections that had gone untreated. Children who had had lice removed from their hair. Children who were slightly bruised, perhaps had a minor dislocation or two, whose eyes were big in hollow faces. Children who had been dehydrated almost to the point of death. Small children barely capable of speech who used the most incredible gutter language. Children who had been fed totally unsuitable foods. Children who showed

traces of medication never intended for children. Children who gave every appearance of being physically healthy, yet looked terribly lost and who never laughed and seldom cried. (1976, p. 20)

Symptoms and Effects of Neglect

Children who have been neglected demonstrate numerous symptoms and effects, including those described by Fontana. Some physical symptoms are not obvious, but others are—to a painful degree.

Infancy and Early Childhood

The *nonorganic failure to thrive* (*NFTT*) *syndrome* is a condition found in infants and diagnosed by the presence of several factors: (1) The infant has fallen below the fifth percentile in weight and often in height. (The percentile scale is used by physicians to determine normal height and weight of infants and children. Below the fifth percentile means that 95 percent of babies weigh more than this.) (2) The baby was once of a weight and height within the expected norm. (3) The infant demonstrates a delay in psychomotor development (Dubowitz and Black, 2002; Joffe, 2002; Oates and Kempe, 1997; Wright, 2005).

Joffe (2002) is quick to point out that failure to thrive can also be organic, resulting from a variety of medical conditions. Although organic and nonorganic failure to thrive may coexist in the same infant, it is NFTT that is more likely indicative of neglect.

Wright (2005) differentiates between the child who is demonstrating a low weight and the child who is failing to thrive and thus necessitates protective services intervention. A child who continues to lack interest in eating, whose development continues to lag behind what is expected for his or her age, and who demonstrates little response to the environment is of particular concern for having failure to thrive.

NFTT syndrome may be caused by parental inexperience in not knowing how to feed properly or how much babies eat or by diluting the formula for lack of money. NFTT can also be a more deeply rooted problem. Infants quickly sense the feelings and attitudes of caregivers. If the parent feels ambivalence or hostility toward the infant, lacks attachment, or sees the child as too demanding, the infant may react negatively. NFTT infants often exhibit little affect. They are difficult to feed because of poor ability to suck and little interest in food. Some infants vomit after feedings. These babies appear to turn inward, and parents describe them as unlovable or unwilling to be held. If untreated, the syndrome can result in death as the infant depends less and less on the environment and simply wastes away. Maternal deprivation has largely been held accountable for the NFTT syndrome. Family systems proponents suggest this condition is symptomatic of total family maladaptation and of family disengagement characterized by distancing and lack of communication within the total family unit (DePanfilis, 2006; Dubowitz and Black, 2002; Joffe, 2002; Kaplan, Schene, DePanfilis, Gilmore, and 2009; Wright, 2005). In neglectful households, poor communication and the inability to get one's needs met are typical.

Infants with NFTT who are removed from home are likely to gain up to a pound a week when fed and stimulated properly. There is some controversy, however, about the maximum level of normalcy that can be attained.

Children from 18 months to 16 years may suffer from a related syndrome known as *psychosocial dwarfism* (*PSD*) or by a variety of other terms, including *hyposomatotropism*, *deprivational dwarfism*, and *abuse dwarfism*. The symptoms are similar to those of NFTT in that emotional deprivation promotes abnormally low growth. PSD children are also below the fifth percentile in weight and height, exhibit retarded skeletal maturation, and have a variety of behavioral problems. Bizarre eating patterns, which may include voracious overeating, indiscriminate eating, or stealing food, are compounded by failure to sleep, night wanderings, hyperactivity, or extreme fatigue. Enuresis (uncontrolled urination) or encopresis (fecal soiling) may further complicate the condition. Underlying the physical symptoms, children afflicted by PSD have reacted to the disturbed environment in which they live by their own disturbance of growth, development, speech, and social relationships. Removed from the distressing environment, most PSD victims recover.

Not all symptoms of neglect are as pronounced. Lack of emotional stimulation and poor nutrition affect weight gain but are not always immediately discernible. Moreover, not all children are neglected from infancy, but to understand this is to comprehend the parental needs and patterns of neglect discussed later in the chapter.

Infants who are neglected may also demonstrate poor muscle tone and an inability to support their own weight in later months. If the infant lies unattended for long periods, hair rubs off the back of the head, and the back of the head may become flattened. The infant fails to gain weight properly. Infants who have little confidence in their environment are unwilling to make eye contact and do not smile, babble, or squeal as normal babies do. Babies who are not changed or who are left in their own excrement or vomit develop rashes and infections that may go untreated.

Young Children

Poor motor skills and language development delays appear in neglected children at all ages. Continued lack of attention to diet, as well as to emotional needs, creates a child with poor skin clarity and dull hair. Severe malnutrition creates the distended stomach and emaciated limbs that are associated with children from countries experiencing famine. Lack of emotional stimulation promotes flat affect or extreme passivity.

Under normal circumstances, these impairments in development would be detected by the child's physician. Neglectful parents, however, often leave medical problems unattended let alone attend to regular checkups. Immunizations, as well as screenings for anemia and lead poisoning, may never be completed, and avoidable childhood diseases often become a painful part of the neglected child's life.

Another persistent medical problem in the neglectful home is *pediculosis*, or lice. Children's lice-infested hair may infect the body as well. Getting rid of these pests is a time-consuming process of shampoos and combings, which can be beyond the abilities of the already overwhelmed parent.

Behaviorally, neglected children present a sad picture.

> Lori Sue Samson sits in front of an old TV, rocking her frail body while sucking on two fingers and clutching a dirty, tattered blanket. The blanket, much loved and fiercely guarded, is her only memory of a time when her mother rewarded her spasmodically with fervent attention. But by the time Lori Sue was 18 months, Mama had another baby, and then another two years later, and the last six months ago. Now 5-year-old Lori Sue is the designated caregiver while Mama shops, visits, and meets friends at their hang-out, the bowling alley. Small for her age, the child twists dull, tangled hair around one

finger. After occasional admonishments about not combing her hair, both mother and child have become tired of the struggle. Lori Sue has not yet lost a tooth, and her baby teeth are fragile and decayed. Idly, she drags the blanket with her as she retreats to the kitchen, searching for something to eat.

In a crib at the far side of the kitchen is 6-month-old Franny, naked but for an undershirt. The baby is awake, but pays little attention to her older sister. She is listless and small. A full bottle of now-curdled milk lies beside her, but the infant makes no move to reach it. The mattress on which she lies is soiled and lacks a sheet. Lori Sue gazes at her baby sister and goes quickly into the next room to assure herself that her 3-year-old brother is still asleep on his mattress.

The Samson children are alone and have been for several hours. It is not that 21-year-old Ella Samson does not care about her children. She does, in her own inconsistent way. She did not think that parenting would be too much for her. When she became pregnant with Lori Sue at age 16, Ella had been jubilant. She hadn't expected that her boyfriend would leave her after impregnating her once again, nor that a new boyfriend would later do the same. Ella Samson is sure she is a victim—just as others feel her children are.

Within the year, Lori Sue Samson will go to school. Her hair, too tangled to comb, will have to be cut. Her teacher will report that she is dirty, smells, has lice, and has an impossibly short attention span. And Lori Sue will have difficulty understanding the most basic commands given to her at school. The cognitive development of neglected children has been impaired in numerous ways (DePanfilis, 2006; Smith and Fong, 2004; Stevenson, 2007; Strathearn, Gary, O'Callaghan, and Wood, 2001; Taylor and Daniel, 2005).

Cantwell (1999) suggests that neglected children do not do well in school partly because their home environment has robbed them of the ability to understand the messages being given in the classroom. The teacher may say, "Now sit in your seats, put your feet on the floor, take out your notebook, and copy this word off the board." Children like Lori Sue, who are accustomed to hearing one-command statements (e.g., Sit down! Shut up! Shut the door!), do not have the experience to conceptualize the number of commands given in the teacher's instructions. But they have also learned that not to respond to a command may result in being hit or at least a stern admonishment. So the child complies with as much of the message as he or she has heard—"Sit in your seat." How this seeming lack of compliance is handled by the teacher differs. If the teacher reacts with annoyance, the child, in time, will conclude that nothing he or she does is correct. In time, this child may experience school as a series of frustrations. If the teacher recognizes the child's lack of comprehension, there may be a happier ending (see also Pearl, 2002).

Impaired socialization is not uncommon in neglected children. Impairment in language development (mentioned earlier) manifests itself in the child's inability to conceptualize beyond the most basic level. This lack leads to poor communication with others who have the ability. Thus, as the neglected child grows older, he or she feels isolated from all but those who are similarly lacking in this ability.

Another aspect of socialization is the internalization of standards. Due to the inconsistency in the home setting, the neglected child is never sure what to expect. Without defined and consistent rules, neglected children face punishment when their actions annoy the caregiver. Little attention is given to what is best for the child. Therefore, neglected children do not develop an internalized set of standards to guide them. Instead, they respond to external stimuli. For these children, whether stealing is wrong is less important than the prospect of getting caught.

Along with this impaired thinking goes a need to "have it now." Neglected children are never sure if their pleasures or prizes will be available tomorrow. If Mom fixes dinner one day, it does not mean she will the next—or the next. Therefore, the children learn to take it when it comes. These children develop an inability to delay gratification, which in turn results in impulsive behavior, stealing, promiscuity, and a variety of other frustrations both for the individual and for society.

Adolescents

It is not uncommon in neglectful homes for older children to strike out on their own at an early age. Early emancipation through moving out, running away, or becoming pregnant often sets the cycle of neglect in motion once again. Neglected children with unmet needs are isolated from those who have learned to compete in society. They seek out others with similar backgrounds and begin the pattern again with their children.

NEGLECTFUL PARENTS

The neglectful parent has long been an enigma to the greater society. It is difficult for most of us to understand how a family can slip to the level of disorder, confusion, indifference, and filth exhibited by some neglectful households. Yet there is a segment of our population that knows little else, and being sufficiently isolated from others, save those with similar values, they have little chance to learn another style of living.

The typical neglectful parent is an isolated individual who has difficulty forming relationships or carrying on the routine tasks of everyday life. Burdened with the anger and sadness over unmet childhood needs, this parent finds it impossible to consistently recognize and meet the needs of her or his children. Most neglecting households are headed by women, due largely to the inability of these individuals to maintain lasting heterosexual relationships. Always at the commencement of a relationship is the hope that this new lover or helpmate will meet the unmet needs from childhood. When neither the man nor woman is able to ease the burden of sorrow carried by the other, the man moves on, leaving the woman to try to mother the children they have created.

Studies undertaken with neglectful parents describe them as seemingly indifferent to their children, disciplining them (if at all) more out of their own need for quiet or convenience than out of a concern for what the child is learning and having a poor capacity to problem solve or set goals for the future. Their own backgrounds have not equipped them to perform these tasks. Their relationships with their own mothers have usually been poor. Such parents have been described as drifting aimlessly and passively through a world that feels hostile to them. Because of their own inadequate childhoods, negative experiences with school, and unsatisfying adult relationships, they are ill equipped to instill hope in their children, encourage them in school, or model for them the roles that society expects of functioning adults. This picture of a neglectful home has challenged professionals for years and has given rise to some attempts to understand the symptomology and etiology of this problem.

Recent studies suggest that neglectful parents are less involved with others, less able to control impulses, less verbally accessible, less able to organize or plan, and less equipped with pride in their accomplishments or workmanship. In these studies, neglectful parents have been found to test lower on intelligence scales and higher on scales for *anomie*, or an absence of social norms or values (Hally, Polansky, and Polansky, 1980; Smith and Fong, 2004; Stevenson, 2007; Taylor and Daniel, 2005).

Cantwell (1999) suggests that neglectful parenting can be attributed to a lack of knowledge, lack of judgment, and lack of motivation, and she outlines some examples. Parents lack knowledge in the areas of attending to their children's needs (e.g., a baby must be fed every three to four hours), housekeeping and cooking skills, nutrition, child development, including the need for stimulation and nurturing, medical care, and the need to set limits for children. Parents may also lack judgment in perceiving when a child is really ill, knowing when to leave a child alone, recognizing when children are unable to act like adults, and knowing what roles are appropriate for parents and children. Parents may also lack motivation in the form of energy to attend to their children or because they feel that they are the best judge of what is best for their children. These parents may have little desire or energy to learn. Their behavior may well be based on the fact that they have no standard for comparison. If they were raised in neglectful families, they may not see that anything is wrong. Once again, it is vital that the assessment of parental limitations be seen within their context of their culture.

Whether or not we understand the apparent indifference of these parents toward their children, many theorists feel that parents who neglect have disturbances in their personality structure. Neglectful parents have often been described as having infantile personalities. The word *infantile*, despite its negative connotation, refers simply to a regression or fixation to childhood concerns or being burdened with remnants of unfinished business of one's childhood. The parents' need to attain or mourn the love and concern expected but not given them in their family of origin explains, to some extent, their inability to give to their own children (Polansky, Borgman, and DeSaix, 1972; Stephenson, 2007; Taylor and Daniel, 2005).

Perhaps another reason these parents present themselves as infantile is not only that they have not had their needs met in childhood but also that their parenting career has begun prematurely. Hampton (2003), in his study of African American families, found that neglectful parents were more likely to have their children at a younger age, more likely to have more live births spaced closely together, and more likely to have these births unplanned (p. 55). The comparison group of white neglectful parents was similar except that white mothers had their children at a slightly older age. Thus, we find an overburdened parent, usually a mother, who finds herself unprepared and unsupported in the important task of parenting. It is not surprising, therefore, that given the likelihood of coming from a dysfunctional family herself, the pattern of neglect repeats itself.

Efforts to Explain the Behavior of Neglectful Parents

Personalities of Neglectful Mothers: Polansky and Colleagues

One of the earliest and most comprehensive efforts to study and explain the parents of children who are neglected was made by Polansky and various of his colleagues (DeSaix, Sharlin, Borgman, Chalmers, Buttenwieser, Hally, Williams, and N. Polansky). These researchers studied women, feeling that it was the mother who was more available for study and whose presence was more stable in the children's lives. They concluded that one contributor to neglect was found in the personality deficits of neglectful mothers.

In 1972, Polansky, DeSaix, and Sharlin developed a set of types of neglectful mothers: (1) apathetic–futile; (2) impulse ridden; (3) mentally retarded; (4) women in reactive depression; and (5) women who are borderline or psychotic. Of these types, the authors felt that most women fell into the apathetic–futile and impulse-ridden categories. While Polansky's studies focused on the households of single-parent women, he later researched the influence of the father (Polansky, Chalmers, Buttenwieser, and Williams, 1983). The results Polansky and his colleagues concluded showed that the quality of child care and whether a family is considered neglectful or not still rests largely on the personality structure of the mother.

Apathetic–Futile   The women who are characterized as apathetic–futile (Polansky, Chalmers, Buttenwieser, and Williams, 1983) seem to have given up on living. They are withdrawn, flat in affect, with a feeling that nothing is worth doing. "What is the point of changing the diaper?" the mother asks. "She'll just get it dirty again." She is lonely, emotionally numb, and isolated. The relationships she does attempt are superficial and chaotic, giving her little real pleasure. She is typically stubbornly negative. This mother fears commitment but may comply with requests in a hostile passive–aggressive manner. Her thinking is doggedly concrete. She thinks in terms of black or white because she lacks the ability to conceptualize except on the most basic level. Her limited conceptualization ability and underdeveloped language skills make her verbally inaccessible. She may be annoyed when people don't understand her when she uses inappropriate words. One mother described how the lifeguard gave her son "artificial perspiration" and was openly angered when a social worker didn't immediately comprehend. Yet inherent in her problem is an inability to gain insight. She is almost incapable of self-observation.

The Brent family exemplifies the apathetic–futile syndrome:

The Brents came to the attention of social services when City Hospital reported that 2-month-old Gordon had just died. The cause of death was determined to be severe neglect.

The Brent family lives on the second floor of a run-down, three-story house in an urban area. There is trash on the porch, and the backyard is cluttered with car parts, an old refrigerator, and assorted items. The social worker encountered a very dirty little boy, probably about age 4 or 5, standing outside. He was dressed in a tattered, soiled undershirt, and shorts. He did not greet the worker but watched furtively.

There was no response to the knock at the door. The worker knocked again and still received no response. Wordlessly, the little boy came forward, opened the door, and went in, leaving the door open. It appeared to be an invitation, so the worker followed him into the kitchen, which was strewn with various bits of food. A strong smell appeared to be a combination of garbage and urine. Another child about 3 years old was crawling on the floor after a cat but showed no reaction to the social worker. The older child went over, picked up the younger, and sat him on a chair.

They both stared at the worker. On the table were several beer cans and an empty potato chip bag. A sound from a bedroom made it obvious there was someone else in the house. At the same moment, a child cried in another room off the kitchen. The worker observed a baby about 1 year old sleeping on a bare mattress badly soiled with urine and feces. The baby was naked from the waist down and wore only a dirty shirt. Mrs. Brent emerged from the bedroom and wondered at the worker's presence. Mrs. Brent did express sorrow when told of Gordon's death and explained that he had always been sickly. When questioned about the 1-year-old's lack of a diaper, the mother stated there was no point in keeping a diaper on as the child would only get it dirty.

At 5 years old, Ricky Brent is small for his age. He appears to be the primary caregiver for Peter, 3, and Alfred, 11 months, who rests on his mattress for hours without making a sound. Mrs. Brent rejected any suggestion that she might be having trouble coping with her children or the home situation, but she accepted the agency's intervention in a hostile but passive manner.

Mrs. Brent is a small, stocky woman who appears to be in her 30s but in fact is barely 20. She was dressed in a torn bathrobe and apparently nothing else. She was disheveled and somewhat incoherent and had apparently been sleeping, as she reported doing much of the time. She immediately lit a cigarette and continued to chain smoke, flicking her ashes on the floor.

Lorraine Blake Brent is the youngest of 13 children. Her family of origin had a history of involvement with the welfare system, and as a child, Mrs. Brent was placed in a foster home for a short time as a result of "deplorable conditions" in her mother's home. Mrs. Brent calls herself her "mother's mistake," the result of her mother's attending a party for a group of sailors. At an early age, Mrs. Brent was left alone while her mother and older siblings pursued their own interests.

Currently, Mrs. Brent is a single parent. Her husband, Richard, age 29, works sporadically, sometimes collecting unemployment or welfare. He reportedly is able to accept little or no responsibility and is currently serving a jail term for auto theft. He is the middle of seven children, and his family also has had frequent contacts with social service agencies. The Brents grew up in the same neighborhood and have known each other since childhood. When Lorraine became pregnant at age 14, the couple was married, and since that time, Richard has come and gone as he pleased.

The difficulty for social workers is that such a mother's feelings of futility are quite contagious. Her lack of insight creates doubts in the inexperienced worker's mind as to the diagnosis. Even the most experienced workers relate the contagion of "nothing is worth doing." Without using the simplest language, the worker will not be understood (and even then may be blocked out), and intervention is extremely difficult.

Impulse Ridden   The impulse-ridden mother is one who has a low frustration tolerance, has little ability to delay gratification, and uses extremely poor judgment in her actions (Polansky, Chalmers, Buttenwieser, and Williams, 1983). She may demonstrate more energy in her undertakings, but this energy is usually directed toward getting her own needs met rather than meeting the needs of her children. Her home may not be as dirty and disorganized as that of the apathetic mother, but her consistency is in question. Characteristically, she has used faulty judgment and is erratic in her treatment of her children. She has failed to protect or nurture her children adequately. Over the years, the children have learned that the only thing they can count on is that tomorrow will be different.

Today, their mother may be loving, but tomorrow, she may be irritable and rejecting. Maria exemplifies such a parent:

> The school voiced its concern over the Harper family, alleging that 7-year-old Alice and 6-year-old Karen had not been in school for most of the past two months. Both girls had severe coughs, which appeared to be untreated.
>
> The social worker was greeted by Beverly Harper, an attractive African American woman, who said she was the children's grandmother. She recounted with some annoyance that her 28-year-old daughter Maria, the children's mother, had just gotten home after being away for several days. Maria apparently had no address of her own and dropped the girls off unannounced and left them for extended periods.
>
> Maria Harper was an attractive young woman who behaved more like a teenager than the mother of two. She was neatly dressed, relatively clean, and babbled enthusiastically about her latest boyfriend, with whom she and the girls "were going to live." In fact, they had stayed there several times "just to try it out." Ms. Harper appeared extremely nervous and bit her nails. She reported having had several addresses over the last year, usually taking the girls with her to stay with her boyfriend of the moment. She did not perceive this as a problem for the girls. She spoke of the girls' fathers. Alice's was a migrant worker from Puerto Rico, whom she had dated for a short time, and Karen's was a white college student, with whom she had been particularly impressed.
>
> When it was pointed out that the girls had persistent coughs, Maria seemed genuinely concerned and said she might take them to the clinic. Assuming that the school had made the report, Ms. Harper embarked on a tirade of perceived injustices by the school personnel. These perceived injustices caused her to rationalize not sending the children to school more often. She felt that her children were being discriminated against in the predominantly white school.
>
> Discussion was difficult with this nervous, flighty young woman. The girls' welfare reminded her of a myriad other stories, which she recounted excitedly. Throughout the meeting, Ms. Harper's mother grumbled to herself, picking up accumulated clutter in the small apartment, all the while smoking incessantly. At one point, Maria Harper suggested that if social services preferred, she would leave the children with her mother until she became "settled." "Like hell you will!" came almost inaudibly from her mother.

Although she obviously cares for her children, Maria Harper has difficulty perceiving and meeting their needs. Her inability to recognize inappropriate situations and living conditions exposes her children to an erratic, potentially harmful lifestyle. Despite her caring for the girls on numerous occasions, Maria's mother appears to give little real support.

Mentally Retarded Mental retardation or developmental delay certainly does not negate the possibility of adequate parenting. In fact, only a small percentage of neglectful mothers are mentally retarded. However, without proper supervision and education, it is possible for neglect to become an issue. Consider the case of Terry:

> Terry Taylor and her infant daughter Michelle came to the attention of social services when Michelle was hospitalized after being fed whole milk rather than a formula. The baby was also extremely thin and had a severe diaper rash that had become infected. Ms. Taylor, at age 23, had the mental age of 12. She reported living on her own in an

apartment across town. Extremely distraught and agitated over the illness of her baby, whom she obviously adored, Ms. Taylor was difficult to talk with, but her background was eventually uncovered.

Brain damaged at birth, Terry Taylor had attended a series of schools and programs for people who are mentally retarded. Her older parents were obviously so pleased with her progress that they repeatedly told her older married siblings how self-sufficient Terry was. The parents died in quick succession 18 months ago, and Terry's care was relegated to her older sister, who lived in a small town some distance away. "I didn't want her to have to leave her sheltered workshop," the sister later reported, but she also admitted that she "didn't trust my bum of a husband" around attractive Terry.

For whatever reasons, the sister set Terry up in her own apartment in the city and returned home. Confused, lonely, and disoriented, Terry did not return to the workshop and was befriended by a male neighbor who subsequently impregnated her and left. Disgusted by Terry's plight, the sister arranged to have a family care for her during her pregnancy. She delivered a healthy baby girl and returned to her own apartment. Why neither the foster family nor the hospital intervened for support is unclear. A visiting nurse did stop by on several occasions, but she felt the young mother was doing fine.

Lonely and depressed, Terry had difficulty caring for her infant. When money was not forthcoming from her sister, she tried to feed the baby whole milk. The baby became ill, and Terry, in frustration and panic, began screaming hysterically. A neighbor urged her to open the door and, alarmed by the baby's overall poor condition, took the mother and child to the hospital.

With supervision, Terry Taylor might have been able to care for infant Michelle. Without it, however, this young mother was overwhelmed and unable to adequately parent.

Reactive–Depressive   Characterized by the mother's inability to adjust to some aspects of her life and the resultant depression over that inability, the reactive–depressive mother is left incapable of parenting adequately. Other factors such as the birth of another child, desertion by a spouse, or death of a loved one can trigger such a depression. For Jane Wales, the depression was a result of a change in lifestyle:

The building is extremely run down and situated over a liquor store. There is no glass on the outside door, and the stairs up to the third floor are extremely dirty. When the worker arrived at the apartment, Mrs. Wales had apparently just returned and was wearing a soiled, torn housedress. She stated that she had been downstairs at a neighbor's "getting her husband cigarettes." Mrs. Wales is an obese young woman who looks much older than 23 years. Her hair is uncombed and appears dirty. She is softspoken with little or no affect and, in fact, expresses little emotion about anything.

Mrs. Wales made no objection when the worker suggested they go into the apartment. Inside were two children, a baby about 8 months old and a girl about 2. Both were in cribs in one section of a small, unlighted apartment, which appeared to have only one large room, an alcove containing a double bed and the two cribs, and a kitchen. There were tattered curtains at the windows and several broken panes of glass that had newspaper over them. There were only a couch and one table in the main room and a dinette set in the kitchen. The smell in the apartment was overwhelming. The kitchen table was cluttered with dishes, and there were piles of dirty dishes on the sink and on the stove. The entire kitchen was littered with scraps of food; the chairs and table were crusted.

The couch had a ripped and dirty cover. On the table were several packs of cigarettes and matches. The floor appeared not to have been cleaned for some time.

Both children were scantily clad, the baby in a diaper and light shirt and the little girl in a light sleeveless nightgown and diaper. Sitting in her crib, the little girl played with her toes. The baby was crying and banging his head against the bars of his crib. The mother made no attempt to comfort either child but finally got a bottle from the table and gave it to the baby. He retired to the far side of the crib to drink it. The little girl fussed and was given a cupcake. Both mattresses were sheeted but quite dirty.

Mrs. Wales answered the worker's questions but volunteered little. She spoke in an even, quiet tone with little or no inflection. She stated that her husband worked at a nearby mill, and although he had changed jobs frequently in the past, he was a fairly steady worker and provided a meager income for the family. She also stated she did occasionally go to the neighbors and leave the children alone, but she thought they were fine if left in their cribs. At no time did she look at her children until the baby, bottle finished, began to cry again. Mrs. Wales picked him up and put him on the floor. She then did the same for the little girl, who began searching for crumbs to eat.

At one point, the mother looked furtively at the clock and suggested that the worker leave before her husband got home. When asked why, she could only respond that he would not like finding the worker there. Mrs. Wales agreed that the worker might return on another occasion. During the next few visits, the worker learned the following about the Wales family.

Jane Foster Wales, mother of Marlene, 23 months, and Ronald Jr., 8 months, is a daughter of Mary and Harold Foster, successful real estate brokers in town. Mrs. Wales has not seen her mother nor father since her marriage four years ago. Mrs. Wales is a high school graduate who completed one year of college before her marriage. She was an excellent student and reportedly of above-average intelligence.

Mrs. Wales is the younger of two children. Her brother, she assumes, is still in business with their father, but she has not seen him since her marriage either. She reports that she met her husband while he was working in a gas station. Her car broke down on her way home from college one weekend, and Mr. Wales was the attendant at the garage. They dated for several months, and Mrs. Wales discovered she was pregnant. The couple's decision to marry met with the complete disapproval of Mrs. Wales's parents, who said they would never see her again. They kept their word, and Mrs. Wales's several attempts to contact them have been to no avail. "My father wanted me to be a doctor," Mrs. Wales once said, "and he was really angry when I quit school."

The Waleses had a baby boy who was born with a heart problem. His death at 3 months brought about severe depression for Mrs. Wales. She gained more than 100 pounds, stayed at home, and remembers feeling alone and isolated at first. After a while, "it didn't matter." Now Mrs. Wales rarely goes out of the apartment building and only occasionally goes to the neighbors, who buy cigarettes for her husband. She is obviously a very depressed young woman.

Ronald Wales, 23, is the oldest of 10 children. He left home at age 16 when he felt put upon because his alcoholic father had disappeared, leaving him again to help support his mother. He states he was "sick of it" and longed to be on his own. The local welfare department records numerous contacts with the family, including several for severe neglect. There has been no contact between Wales and his family.

After leaving home, Mr. Wales had numerous odd jobs, the longest of which was attendant in the gas station. He appears to be an extremely immature young man who requires that his wife wait on him hand and foot. Although there is no evidence that he has ever abused his wife, Mrs. Wales seems afraid to displease him. She makes sure that he is always well stocked with cigarettes. Mr. Wales seems oblivious to his wife's depression, weight problem, and insufficient care of the children. He pays little attention to the children except to make sure they are out of his way.

Psychotic   Psychosis is present in only a small percentage of neglectful families. Frequently, the neglect stems from the parents' inability to see beyond their delusional world. Detection is not always easy. When the parent is not hallucinating, she or he may be conscious of the needs of the child. This inconsistency is damaging in and of itself. Some parents have a borderline reality orientation. Such individuals drift in and out of psychosis or practice delusional thinking, once again causing confusion for the child. Norma Spitz is such an individual:

Social services received a call that Norma Spitz needed immediate hospitalization and a placement for her 3-year-old son, Georgie. When the worker arrived at the Spitz home, the police were already there, having been summoned by neighbors. The house was dark, and shrieks were heard from behind the locked doors. A small, naked boy dashed excitedly from window to window calling inaudible phrases to the assembled group. He was finally prevailed upon to open the door and turn on the lights.

The small house was extremely dirty and scattered with a mixture of food, dog food, and animal feces. Mrs. Spitz, dressed in shorts and a torn blouse in spite of the midwinter chill, sat on a stool in the kitchen, rocking and mumbling to herself, "God is dead. God is dead." Georgie dashed about in a frenzy, repeating his mother's exclamation, and asked the worker, "Did you know God is dead?"

This was not the first time social services had been involved with the Spitz family. At 35, Norma Spitz was the mother of five children, all of whom had spent their lives in and out of foster homes. Mrs. Spitz had been in and out of hospitals since she was 15 years old. During her first stay, she had met Herman Spitz, whom she later married. Spitz was diagnosed schizophrenic and was himself hospitalized on several occasions. He also frequented detoxification centers for treatment of his alcoholism. Twenty years older than his wife, Herman Spitz had drifted away and was now assumed by Mrs. Spitz to be dead.

Mrs. Spitz had been treated as an outpatient during several periods of her motherhood. During visits with her children, she appeared to be a concerned, loving mother. Returning the children to her, however, usually resulted in her rehospitalization.

At his birth, Georgie had been cared for by an itinerant sister of Mr. Spitz's. At 18 months, Georgie was returned to Mrs. Spitz when the sister moved to another city. Seen regularly at a community mental health center, Mrs. Spitz had appeared to do well with her son. It was unclear exactly what had sparked her breakdown, but a reorganization at the health center had caused a change in her treatment.

It is often extremely difficult to work with or predict the future behavior of psychotic parents. Hospitalization causes interruptions in child care and can be extremely confusing for children. If the parent is capable of stabilizing, it is usually only through close supervision and support from community agencies.

The Processing of Information and Neglect: Crittenden

Neglect and the characteristics of neglectful parents have not had a central place in either research or literature since Polansky and his colleagues studied neglectful mothers in the 1970s. Instead, neglect was most often included in texts as just one type of child maltreatment. But in 1999, Dubowitz edited an important new book dedicated exclusively to neglect. As part of this volume, Crittenden (1999), a familiar author in the field, postulated that neglectful parents, especially mothers, can be characterized as having difficulty with the way they process information (see "Personalistic Individual Causes" on page 68) and that this fact alone makes working with them a challenge.

Crittenden suggests that neglectful parents fall into three categories: as perpetrators of disorganized neglect, of emotional neglect, and of depressed neglect. Parents who exhibit *disorganized neglect* are inconsistent with their children, live from crisis to crisis, and are often seen by the child welfare system as being multiproblem families. For these families, affect (feelings) is dominant. Cognition (processing facts about cause and effect) is minimized. As a result, family members emote but do not reason. The most dramatic emotions warrant the mother's attention, as shown by this case:

> The social workers who visited the Menendez house usually left in frustration. Their visits were punctuated by a blaring television that was never turned off or down, a perpetually ringing phone, a dog who barked nonstop despite efforts to calm him or suggestions that he be put outside, six constantly fighting children, and a mother who spent her time screaming at the loudest of her brood. The family lived from crisis to crisis.
>
> The most immediate crisis received Mom's attention. While 3-year-old Maria was walking precariously on the back of the couch, Mrs. Menendez chose to deal with 5-year-old Homer, who was screaming that he didn't want to put on his shoes. It was not until Maria fell, splitting open her head and then bleeding profusely, that Mrs. Menendez noticed that her child might be in any danger. The same negative behavior on the children's part would in one instance be met with a sharp retort from their overwhelmed mother and at another time be totally ignored.
>
> Mrs. Menendez presented her own requests to the workers in loud dramatic tones, often in Spanish, frightening the neophyte Anglo social worker. The case was reported again and again to social services, always requiring one more visit to assess the home for neglect. Mrs. Menendez argued in angry tones that she couldn't possibly keep up with all these kids. She was constantly being threatened with having her utilities cut off because a simple piece of paper constituting the bill was not a dramatic enough reminder to get her attention. Only when the electric or telephone company cut off her service did she fight to have it reinstated.
>
> Mrs. Menendez had a history of suicidal gestures and an abundance of men in her life who would move in and soon leave, often precipitating the mother's threats to kill herself. The Menendez family presented a significant challenge for the local child protection agency.

For the Menendez family, crisis was a way of life. Because Mrs. Menendez's response to her children was so unpredictable and usually governed by the urgency of their requests, they learned to be explosive and dramatic. They also learned how to manipulate and cajole her into acquiescing to whatever they requested. As a result, she had no control over her six offspring. Her attempts to bribe or threaten them were unsuccessful mainly because they had learned that she never followed through. For the Menendez family, affect was dominant. They were incapable of planning or even of recognizing the effect of their behaviors or actions. Mrs. Menendez's neglect of her children was based largely on her inability to do anything but react to feelings.

The family who demonstrates *emotional neglect* falls at the opposite end of a continuum from the Menendez family. This family uses cognition to the exclusion of affect. Because they are unable to make emotional connections with others, they "must depend on cognitive information as their organizing structure, as a way to make sense of the world" (Crittenden, 1999, p. 57). Emotionally neglectful homes exist in all socioeconomic statuses, and children may not be deprived of possessions. Yet as very small infants, children from these homes have learned that their parents are emotionally unavailable. If they protest, they are punished for their affect, so they learn not to express any feelings. These qualities describe the daughter of Mrs. Warren:

> *Mrs. Warren presented herself as an extremely well organized woman whose household was run by myriad strict rules. She showed little affect when her child's school called her in for a meeting to discuss Jerusha's inability to learn. Eight-year-old Jerusha seemed to have little energy for learning. Her teacher described her presence in class as "existing there" and was frustrated that she could raise little or no response from the child. None of this was surprising when she met Mrs. Warren. The mother was cold to her child but ready to discuss her progress in an intellectual manner. It was clear to all attending the meeting that there were little nurturing and no warmth in the Warren home.*

The family characterized as exhibiting *depressed neglect* demonstrates some of the "nothing is worth doing" attitude described by Polansky et al. (1978), as prevalent in his apathetic–futile mothers. These families guard against both cognition and affect, appearing withdrawn and dull. Because their parents have not responded to them since birth, children learn that their behavior has no meaning, so they, too, become withdrawn and devoid of any emotion. Because they have shut off both their feelings and their perceptions, intervening with them will be difficult (Crittenden, 1999).

Only when we begin to understand how the families just described perceive the world can we begin to recognize how to help them care for their children in ways that are not neglectful. Crittenden would argue that although the influence of poverty cannot be overlooked, processing difficulties may be central not just to parents' neglect of their children but also to creating or maintaining their poverty status.

Substance-Abusing Families

Substance abuse on the part of parents, like domestic abuse, can lead to any type of child maltreatment. Parents under the influence of drugs or alcohol can physically, sexually, or emotionally abuse their children and often do. It is certainly true that even if they do not abuse their children in one of these ways, they are not fully available to be adequate parents. Because the influence of substances hampers parents in parenting and therefore implies neglect, the subject of substance-abusing parents is included in this chapter.

Consider the case of Dolores:

Dolores, 18 years old and 5 months pregnant, appeared at the free prenatal clinic at the insistence of her TANF social worker. This was the girl's second pregnancy. During her first pregnancy, she had been kicked out of her closely knit Puerto Rican family. She began to use alcohol and drugs. When the baby was born, she gave it up for adoption after it was diagnosed with fetal alcohol syndrome. The social worker advised the clinic that not only was Dolores continuing to drink, but the father used cocaine and had "turned on" Dolores to the drug. Despite staff counseling, Dolores continued to drink and use drugs until she gave birth to a premature baby who was diagnosed with fetal alcohol syndrome and went through drug withdrawal at birth.

Prenatal Abuse

Although over the years, some women have ingested substances known to be harmful to unborn fetuses; it is only recently that this has been identified as child abuse. Experts identify numerous medical complications that can be caused by prenatal substance abuse. Children born of substance-abusing mothers may be premature, have infectious diseases, be infected with human immunodeficiency virus (HIV) or AIDS, demonstrate such syndromes as fetal alcohol syndrome (FAS), FTT, sudden infant death syndrome (SIDS), intrauterine growth retardation (IUGR), or central nervous system disorders. Neurological disturbances may cause babies to demonstrate such symptoms as irritability, tremors, high-pitched crying, increased or decreased muscle tone, problems with sucking or frantic sucking, seizures, diarrhea, excessive vomiting, rapid and unusual eye movements, and disturbed sleep patterns (Chasnoff and Lowder, 1999; Kelly, 2002; Spohr and Steinhausen, 2011; Straussner and Fewell, 2006).

FAS and *fetal alcohol effects* (*FAE*—not the full syndrome but several effects associated with it) are conditions which have frequently been seen by protective services workers over the years. The diagnosis of FAS is based on three criteria: low birth weight, an abnormally small head, and prenatal and postnatal growth retardation. Later, the child will be identifiable by abnormalities of the face, intellectual impairment, developmental delays, and neurological problems. These children have difficulty learning, remembering, problem solving, and being aware of cause and effect. They are often uncoordinated, hyperactive, and impulsive (Kelly, 2002; Spohr and Steinhausen, 2011; Straussner and Fewell, 2006).

It is also important to mention in this context the incidence of the HIV virus and AIDS among young children. The virus can be transmitted not only in utero but also at delivery or through breast milk. Mothers who are injection drug users, who are prostitutes, or who have had multiple sexual partners have the ability to transmit this disease to their babies before or at birth. The prognosis for these infants is poor. Newborns may test negative and later show evidence of infection. Currently, the outcome for these children is uncertain (Kelly, 2002; Sharpe, 2005).

Substance Abuse and Children

Not all mothers abuse substances during pregnancy. For some, their abuse does not become problematic until the child is older. That was the case with Penny:

> *Penny was 14 when she had her first baby, Joanne. At 16, when she became pregnant with her second child, Eddie, the father of this child, suggested that they get married. After the birth of Amy, Penny and Eddie found that parenting was not what they had imagined. When a friend suggested they try crack, it seemed like an exciting new experience. Smoking crack using devices that Eddie made from old beer cans provided a unique form of entertainment. Penny found that she could get extra money for crack through having sex with dealers. Eddie didn't seem to mind, as long as she brought home the crack to him.*
>
> *Neither noticed when their lives changed. They became absorbed in their habit to the point where they cared little about themselves, each other, and their two children. When 4-year-old Joanne was found wandering the neighborhood by a local police officer, protective services was called in. Social workers found two ill parents who in no way could cease their bingeing on drugs to care for their children.*

Like Penny and Eddie, those addicted to crack tend to neglect the basics of eating and sleeping until their physical health is in jeopardy. They have little interest in either their appearance or their well-being, often trading sex for drugs or money and harming themselves through burns and falls (Sharpe, 2005).

Although other drugs are equally as damaging to one's ability to parent, crack is perhaps one of the most popular street drugs due to its availability and affordability. Heroin, hallucinogens, cocaine, and morphine are also available. The effects of any of these substances are that the parents under their influence become ineffective caretakers. Their dulled reactions, euphoria, sleepiness, and general neglect of their children's needs can also expose these children to possible sexual or physical abuse. Often, drug- and alcohol-abusing parents are so addicted to the substance and their way of life that social service intervention can do little to effect change. It is only when the parent sees a reason to be helped that change can occur. For some, their children may not be reason enough.

Domestic Violence and Neglect

Although domestic violence is addressed, it is important to recognize that a family that is caught up in its own violent struggles may well have little time to attend to the needs of the children. Describing the male batterer, Ritchie, Silverman, and Bancroft (2011) explain that this man usually sees his children as a hindrance or annoyance. Unable to compromise his own needs, the batterer will rarely be able to meet those of his children. He often knows little about them, from their schedules to their progress in school to their interests, strengths, or ambitions. He is certainly unaware of the effect of his violent behavior on his children (p. 32). At other times, the batterer entreats his children to side with him against their mother. The abused party in domestic violence, usually the mother, may be so caught up in protecting herself that she, too, is unable to meet her children's needs.

Plight of the Parent and the Social Worker

When professionals see the effects that parents' problems and deficits have on their children, it is easy to condemn the neglectful parent as the adversary or enemy. This attitude must be counteracted because the parent is all the child knows, and children see the condemnation of their parents as a rejection of themselves. It is important to remember that the parent is like a child. Given a neglectful family of four, there are not two adults and two children but rather four children. Children grow emotionally when their needs are met. Unmet needs result in retarded emotional growth. Only by seeing the omissions of the neglectful parent as a cry for help can we truly understand them.

New social workers, especially, want to remove children from their neglectful families. In some situations, this is the only solution. Yet in a great number of neglectful homes, the solution is not that simple. The cycle must be broken to ensure that the next generation has a chance to grow into healthy adults. To achieve this, it is not so much placement that is needed as "parenting" of the parents so they can take care of their children. Unfortunately, this takes time and a great deal of energy.

Neglectful families elicit the same feelings of futility and hopelessness in those who try to help them. The degree of stress experienced by neglecting parents often strikes the worker as overwhelming. Progress with this type of client is extremely slow. Since the average social worker has more neglect than abuse cases, it is vital to understand the neglectful parent.

SUMMARY

Neglect of children is a result of parental failure to meet basic human needs—adequate food, shelter, safety, and affection. Several authors have attempted to define *neglect*—first by the creation of the CLL, developed by Polansky and colleagues, and later by the creation of Trocmé's CNI.

It is difficult to determine the cause or causes of neglect. Some theorists feel the economic factors should be considered, along with deficits in the personality structure of the parent. Today, many theorists favor an ecological view—that is, the parent within the context of the environment.

Children who have been neglected demonstrate retarded growth, poor motor and language development, flat affect, indications of malnutrition, unattended medical problems, and an inability to conceptualize. Older children often seek early emancipation and may begin the cycle all over again.

Neglectful parents are largely children themselves. Their infantile personalities seem to be largely the result of their own unmet childhood needs. They are isolated, have difficulty maintaining relationships, are verbally inaccessible, and lack the knowledge, judgment, and maturation to adequately parent their children. From their studies of neglectful mothers, Polansky and colleagues identified five types of personalities: the apathetic–futile, the impulse ridden, the woman in reactive depression, the mentally retarded, and the psychotic. Parents may also neglect (or abuse) under the influence of drugs or alcohol. Neglect may also go hand in hand with domestic violence.

Knowledge about maltreatment is increasing. We need to strive to understand the large numbers of neglectful families and, by understanding, hope to break the cycle.

Chapter 5

The Physical Abuse of Children

The physical abuse of children is a phenomenon that can only be defined by considering the total social and cultural context with special emphasis on some specific factors. The historical prevalence of physical abuse and the influence different historical periods had on the definition of abuse were discussed earlier. The structure of society must also be considered. For example, as part of their heritage, other cultures have practices that by Western standards would be considered abusive. Finding a definition, therefore, depends largely on the source culture or the prevailing sentiment. It is agreed, however, that the physical abuse of children refers to nonaccidental injury inflicted by a caregiver. Although protective services try to understand different cultural practices, the fact remains that those living in the United States must live within state and federal statutes.

The medical community sees abused children by virtue of the bruises, welts, broken bones, and burns they present in a hospital or other medical setting. Spurred on by the adoption of the term *battered-child syndrome*, medical professionals define abuse in light of the child's *ailments*, which must be healed, and the parents' *illness*, which must be treated (Reece, 2009, 2011).

The legal community, including the police, defines child abuse more in terms of intent. Parents have particular legal (and moral) responsibilities. Failure to comply with the acceptance of these duties is to defy the statutes set up by society and is therefore punishable. The child is the victim; the parent is either the perpetrator or accomplice. This is not to imply that compassion does not enter into the disposition of abuse cases. Nevertheless, the legal definition is deeply entangled with the debate over individual rights.

Amid the healing of the injured and the punishment of the guilty appears the social worker, who is taught over time to see the family as a total system—a system influenced in turn by larger and more complex systems (i.e., the neighborhood, the social strata, the state, and the culture). Thus, child abuse is again defined with respect to anticipated outcome—that is, to restore in some manner the delicate balance of family continuity so that the nurturing of children can continue. If this is not possible—if the family system is too grossly distorted by stresses or individual pathologies—placement of the child may be the only solution.

These three very different approaches to the nonaccidental injury of children combine to create the helping climate of today.

Several agencies have been involved in the compilation of statistics on child abuse and neglect. From 1976 until 1987, the children's division of the American Humane Association was largely responsible for collecting statistical data. More recently, however, the Children's Bureau of the U.S. Department of Health and Human Services has published periodic reports on the incidence of child maltreatment.

The Children's Bureau (2011) reported that a survey of state protection agencies there were 2,607,798 reports of maltreatment received in 2010. Of these, 1,581,882 (or about 61 percent) were screened in (to be investigated by Protective services.) and 1,025,916 were not. Of these, physical abuse (17.6 percent) was the second most common type of maltreatment with neglect as the first (78 percent) (U.S. Department of Health and Human Services, Administration for Children and Families, Administration on Children, Youth and Families, Children's Bureau, 2011).

What do these statistics mean? It is important to remember that these figures are based on the reports made to state protective agencies and do not reflect the abused children whose abuse is never reported. Some states define physical abuse as an injury that leaves a mark, while children can still be victims of abusive treatment that is not observable. In addition, since most courts do not find sufficient evidence to take action in emotional abuse cases, many protective agencies do not encourage the reporting of these. In some states, the disposition of prenatal substance abuse (when the mother is abusing substances during pregnancy) is still in controversy.

Whatever we choose to assume from statistics, millions of children are subjected to some form of abuse and neglect in the United States today. The question remains, why?

CAUSES OF PHYSICAL ABUSE

The search for the underlying causes of physical abuse has been an arduous one. In the 1970s, 1980s, and 1990s, a variety of models evolved that might be loosely categorized into the following categories: the *psychodynamic* or *character-trait models*, both of which attribute the abuse to characteristics of the abusive parent; the *interactional models*, which consider how the interactions between the victim and the abuser or the dynamics within the family give rise to an abusive situation; and the *environmental/sociological/culturally based models*, which focus on the part that the environment and stressors within it play in the abuse.

Today, there is consensus among experts that child abuse is not caused by one or two factors but by an interconnected group of characteristics and events (Black, Heyman, and Smith-Slep, 2001; Casselles and Milner, 2000; Cohen, Berliner, and Mannarino, 2000; Dopke and Milner, 2000; Ford et al., 1999; Graham-Berman and Howell, 2011; Giardino, Lyn, and Giardino, 2010; Howe, 2005; Howes, Cicchetti, Toth, and Rogosh, 2000; Minns and Brown, 2006; Runyon and Urquiza, 2011; Saunders and Goddard, 2010; Swenson and Kolko, 2002; Wigg, Windom, and Tuell, 2003). Allen-Meares and Fraser (2004) suggest that a framework for looking at these factors has three categories: the microsystem, which describes the parent–child interactions; the meso or exosystems or those networks in which that parent and child are involved (e.g., relationships and institutions), and the macrosystem, which is the umbrella of social structure under which the previous two systems are situated. Most experts now agree that a contemporary view of child physical abuse emphasizes the interplay among the psychology of the individual, of the dynamics of the family and variables involving the cultural and society.

Another way to outline the underlying causes of abuse is to look at them from the perspective of interactional variables, environmental/life stress variables, and social/cultural/economic variables.

Interactional Variables

When we speak of *interactional variables*, we are referring to the interplay between the victim and the abuser that set up the abuse situation. Some authors see abuse as resulting from a cyclical pattern of parent and child relations. For example, the parent sees the child as difficult and is stressed by the child's behavior. The parent punishes the child, who in turn becomes more difficult (Bugental, Blunt, Judith, Lin, McGrath, and Bimbela, 1999; Howe, 2005; Runyon and Urquiza, 2011; Swenson and Kolko, 2002). The following is an example of such a cycle:

> *Eloise had just turned 20 when she discovered that she was pregnant. The baby's father, Melvin, agreed reluctantly to marry her and Eloise excitedly awaited the baby's birth. The girls at work even gave her a shower, which surprised her because she wasn't really that friendly with them. But she had decided to leave her job at the copy center anyway so it was a nice going-away gesture. Melvin was rarely home, but Eloise didn't care. She worked and then came home and watched her TV shows. If he wasn't home, he couldn't hassle her about them. In her third trimester, she began feeling poorly and having a lot of cramps. She decided that it was time to see a doctor, so she made an appointment at the clinic. They assured her that there were no problems, but still she worried.*
>
> *Baby Leo was born in the middle of a snowstorm, three weeks before he was due. Melvin wasn't even home, and Eloise had to call a taxi to get her to the hospital. The delivery was difficult and complications took their toll on both baby and mother. Melvin hadn't even made it until well after Eloise had been sedated. Then, Eloise was unable to see her infant for two days. Finally, she could visit him in neonatal intensive care. She was shocked by what she saw. Leo was tiny and old looking, with tubes coming from every part of him. She was afraid even to touch him.*
>
> *Eloise was allowed to go home after several days, but Leo remained in the hospital. Eloise was cranky and sore, and this was not what she thought new motherhood would be like. She usually had to get a taxi to get to the hospital to see her son and became increasingly angry with Melvin. Finally, after a fight, he told her that he had met someone else and was leaving.*
>
> *When Leo finally came home, it was to a hurt disillusioned mother who had no idea how to care for him. Eloise had grown up in a series of foster homes herself and realized that she had been depending on Melvin, the oldest of seven children, to help her out. She felt inept. And Leo cried constantly. Nothing she did seemed to make him happy. Her initial attempts to nurse were unsuccessful. Putting him on formula gave him a reaction. Even the visiting nurse could not help.*

Eloise began to feel like a failure and saw Leo as too demanding a baby. With a different baby, she reasoned, she would have been okay. "I'll show him!" she thought. She began putting ear plugs in her ears and ignoring his cries. He became fussier, and Eloise began to spank him when he cried. One day, in total frustration, she shook him violently. When the visiting nurse arrived and could not awaken the baby, she insisted that he be rushed to the hospital. He was diagnosed with a subdural hematoma.

Already feeling inept, the baby's crying, typical of many premature infants, was too much for this inexperienced mother who had no support systems. Her inability to care for her child and her disillusionment at a less than ideal experience caused her to feel depressed. This further hampered her ability to parent. The baby's response to her neglect of his needs was to intensify his demands (see also Field, 1998). When such a pattern begins for potentially abusive parents, it often spirals downward.

Ford et al. (1999) also point to such conditions as attention-deficit hyperactivity disorder and oppositional defiant disorder as other factors that might create interactional difficulties between overstressed parents and children. Disabilities put children at significant risk for abuse (Beckett, 2007; Howe, 2005; Rodriguez and Murphy, 1997). Other authors look at other components of the parent–child relationship that could become problematic and a precursor for abuse (Cadzow, Armstrong, and Fraser, 1999; Casselles and Milner, 2000; Dopke and Milner, 2000; Howes et al., 2000; Runyon and Urquiza, 2011; Algood, Hong, Gourdine, and Williamsold fractures, 2011).

As part of the interactional pattern with their children, many abusive parents have had their own abusive or otherwise dysfunctional childhoods. These experiences leave them less able to cope with the demands of parenting (Howe, 2005; Loiselle, 2002; Mufson and Kranz, 1994; Zielinski and Bradshaw, 2005). In addition, abuse of children may occur within the context of inter-partner violence (Graham-Berman and Howell, 2011).

Environmental/Life Stress Variables

Abusive parents frequently experience a variety of stressors. Poverty is often correlated with abuse. Although not all poor parents are abusive, poverty does rob one of both self-esteem and often the drive to rise above their situation. This, in turn, may create anger, which can be directed toward others, including the children. Multiple moves, unsupportive neighborhoods, and an insufficient support system can put parents under pressure. Unemployment, stressful family relationships, and domestic violence also take their toll (Azar and Gehl, 1999; Bancroft, 2005; Black et al., 2001; Feldman, 1997; Howe, 2005; Runyon and Urquiza, 2011; Zielinski and Bradshaw, 2005).

Social/Cultural/Economic Variables

Child-rearing patterns across cultures can differ significantly. What one culture considers abusive, another may not. Differences in values around the boundaries between parents and children, the use of shame, corporal punishment, folk practices, medical care, and reactions to psychiatric issues may all be interpreted differently depending on the culture of the family of origin. In some instances, the practices of minorities might be seen as abusive in the United States (Fontes, 2008; Lustig and Koester, 2009; Lynch and Hanson,

2011; Webb and Lum, 2001). For example, the propensity of some cultures to use objects to hit children conflicts with some state regulations that define abuse as hitting with the use of an object. Or widely practiced folk remedies may create bruises that are mistaken for abuse (Fontes, 2008; Lynch and Hanson, 2011; Webb and Lum, 2001). For example, the cupping or coin rubbing practice by some Asian communities is often misdiagnosed as evidence of intentional abuse by parents, rather than a cultural remedy believed to help the child.

In addition to cultural influences, other societal factors put children at risk for abuse. The current economic climate, for example, puts families under a great deal of stress. This, combined with individual parental characteristics, such as low frustration tolerance or an already poor self-concept, may set the stage for abuse. And the climate of violence in which we currently live lowers the sensitivity to aggressive acts and may, in some individuals, be channeled into violence within the family.

There is no simple way to determine why abuse happens in a family. Instead, one must consider all the variables.

RISK ASSESSMENT AND PHYSICAL ABUSE

The practitioner looks at child abuse in terms of the risk to the child through what is often termed *risk assessment*. Risks are divided into categories, and it is understood that an abundance of high or moderate risks across several categories puts the child at high risk. The research over the last few decades has identified components of risk for children to be abused, for the parents to be abusive, and for the family system to foster such behavior.

More recently, in an effort to identify those strengths that might be enhanced in treatment, assessment has also included those factors that protect the child or can be used to protect him or her. These are known as *protective* factors. Weighing the balance between risk factors and protective factors enables child protection workers to determine what type of intervention will be necessary.

Child Risk and Protective Factors

Research has found that children are more vulnerable to abuse the younger they are. Premature infants present inexperienced parents with a dependent who needs extra care, thus putting additional stresses on the caregiver. The baby may be particularly sensitive to stimuli, cry more, be smaller, be perceived as more fragile, and be generally more difficult to care for than a full-term baby. In addition, the mother may perceive that child as being somehow abnormal because it is premature. Finally, parental expectations about behavior at specific ages may not take into consideration that a premature infant is not as developmentally advanced as a full-term child.

Although it might be difficult for most of us to imagine abusing a small baby, the fact is that, according to the Children's Bureau (2011), 34 percent of the children abused are between birth and 3 years. In addition, 23.4 percent are between 4 and 7 years, 18.7 percent are between 8 and 11 years, 17.3 percent are between 12 to 15 years, and 6.2 percent are between 16 and 17 years old. That means that children under the age of 7 years represent 57.4

percent of those abused. Thus, it can be said that increased age is a protective factor (U.S. Department of Health and Human Services, Administration for Children and Families, Administration on Children, Youth and Families, Children's Bureau, 2011).

In recent years, experts have begun to emphasize that it is not so much an individual child's characteristics that put him or her at risk for abuse but rather that child within the caretaking environment. The importance of attachment cannot be understated (Howe, 2005). Children who have not been able to bond adequately with their caretakers are at high risk (Barker and Hodes, 2004; Howe, 2005; Howes et al., 2000; Swenson and Kolko, 2002). Children whom the parents see as difficult (e.g., colicky, difficult to feed, resists being held) or who have specific disabilities that tax parental patience are more likely to be vulnerable to abuse (Black et al., 2001; Casselles and Milner, 2000; Dopke and Milner, 2000; Howe, 2005; Swenson and Kolko, 2002). Health problems, in both children and parents, as well as allergic reactions and nutrition deficits, may produce irrationality, nervousness, or hyperaggressive symptoms, the misunderstanding of which causes potentially abusive situations (Azar and Gehl, 1999; Hobbs, Hanks, and Wynne, 1999; Howe, 2005; Monteleone, 1998; Reece, 2011).

In later years, learning problems, whether based on sensory difficulties, neurological damage, or psychological connections, may place children at risk from parents who are unaware of or misunderstand their child's behavior. Finally, in the adolescent years— marked by the child's striving toward autonomy, which may take on rebellious overtones, and his or her reliance on peer cultures, not always a positive influence—children are once again vulnerable to seemingly invite their parent's abuse (Farrington and Welsh, 2008; Flowers, 2008; Hobbs et al., 1999; Kaplan, Pelcovitz, Salinger, Mandel, and Weiner, 1998; Monteleone, 1998; Wigg et al., 2003).

Protective factors (see Friends National Resource Center [FNRC], 2008) related to the child might be his or her personality (including resiliency), advanced developmental level, healthy attachment, and ability to reach out to other adults. In sum, the consensus among most authors is that children do not actually invite abuse, but some of the reasons listed earlier put them at higher risk for it.

Parental Risk and Protective Factors

Although the abusive parent is discussed in more depth later in the chapter, it is important to note here the factors that put parents at risk for being abusive. Recent studies have found some of the risk factors found in earlier studies but not others. For example, Miller, Fox, and Garcia-Beckwith (1999), in their study of severe abuse cases, found that the parents exhibited depression, personality disorders, and serious life problems, including domestic violence. However, parents in the research sample denied being abused as children. Cadzow et al. (1999), studying stressed and abusive parents of infants, pointed to financial stress, less education, housing concerns, and domestic violence as risk factors. They discounted the influence of single parenthood, poverty, the youth of parents, and childhood abuse. An earlier attempt by Coohey and Braun (1997) to create an integrated framework in order to understand physical abuse caused these authors to suggest that the major factors influencing physical abuse were a parent's exposure to aggression in childhood or at the hands of a partner, exposure to environmental stressors, and fewer interpersonal resources.

It is generally agreed that parents who abuse their children usually have a dearth of coping mechanisms. They may not have achieved the degree of social competence of non-abusive parents and lack their problem-solving abilities. Some authors see these parents as less flexible and more easily overwhelmed (Ford et al., 1999; Howe, 2005; Howes et al., 2000; Swenson and Kolko, 2002). Although some studies do not find a history of abuse or dysfunctional childhoods, others suggest that they might be in evidence (Bancroft, 2005; Black et al., 2001). This may lead them to less appropriate disciplinary standards (Casselles and Milner, 2000). A number of abusive parents are inconsistent and approach child rearing with negativity (Azar and Gehl, 1999; Runyon and Urquiza, 2011). Their attitude leads them to feel less effective and overwhelmed, and as a result, they tend toward more aggressive models of discipline (Casselles and Milner, 2000; Dopke and Milner, 2000; Runyon and Urquiza, 2011).

Although it is commonly believed that abusive parents are mentally ill, this is not the case in the majority of situations. There is often an element of depression, although it can be situational rather than chronic, and there is some correlation between physical abuse of children and substance abuse (Black et al., 2001; Swenson and Kolko, 2002).

Protective factors for physically abusive parents might include the presence of some type of support system or adequate models of parenting responsibilities by another adult, the ability to channel anger in appropriate ways, and having been raised in a functional family (FNRC, 2008).

Family System Risk and Protective Factors

Families in which physical abuse takes place are often isolated and have poor relationships with extended family and others in the community. If one measured their support system (confidants or the people they turn to in times of need or in times of joy), it would be sorely lacking. Relationships within the family are also strained, negative, in conflict, or operating on a coercive or aggressive model. It is not uncommon to find unemployment, illness, estrangement, or other stressors that affect the entire family (Bancroft, 2005; Black et al., 2001; Graham-Berman and Howell, 2011; Howes et al., 2000; Runyon and Urquiza, 2011; Swenson and Kolko, 2002). Communities that provide outreach to such families provide protective factors.

SYMPTOMS OF PHYSICAL ABUSE

Physical abuse is behavior that results from a complex web of attitudes, variables, and factors. It is difficult to predict accurately which families might be abusive and which might re-offend. For some families, it is that one last stress that tips the scale and results in violent behavior.

Physical Symptoms

Bruises

Although play can cause bruises, particular bruises are indicative of abuse. Bruises prior to a child's becoming ambulatory are suspect. Granted, it is possible to bruise an infant accidentally, but it is not as likely as with an older child. Bruises on various parts of the body may indicate that a child has been hit from several directions. Bruises on the backs of the legs, the upper arms and chest, neck, head, or genitals are often manifestations of abuse. Investigators are cautioned to look for bruises that are covered by clothing and that indicate a clear pattern—a hanger, a palm print, a buckle print, or an imprint going around the body that would suggest the child had been hit with a rope, belt, or cord (Loiselle, 2002; Reece, 2011).

Bruises that vary in color indicate they have been inflicted at different times. On white or light pigmentation, a new bruise is red and turns blue after 6 to 12 hours. About 12 to 24 hours later, the injury becomes blackish-purple, and in 4 to 6 days, a dark greenish tint appears. In 5 to 10 days, the bruise looks pale green or yellow (Brittain, 2005; Feldman, 1997; Hobbs et al., 1999; Loiselle, 2002; Monteleone, 1998; Runyon and Urquiza, 2011). Bruises are not always easy to detect, however. On darker skin pigmentation, for example, bruises may be less discernible or not follow the above-mentioned patterns. Human bite marks (especially adult size) are of concern. Other indications of abuse can be choke marks, pinch marks, grab marks (often indicating that the child has been grabbed to be shaken), and fingernail scratches (Brittain, 2005; Feldman, 1997; Hobbs et al., 1999; Loiselle, 2002; Reece, 2011).

Fractures

Fractures in infants under age 12 months are a strong indication of abuse. Spiral fractures (especially in children under age 3) should be studied carefully. Many abusive parents' explanations do not fit the injury and cause investigators to be suspicious. Numerous fractures, either healed or current, may indicate repeated battering. Radiologists can detect previously healed breaks by the calcium deposits formed around them. A number of old fractures, improperly healed, give support to findings of abuse (Reece, 2011).

Fractures or skeletal injuries may take many forms. Multiple fractures can be seen, indicating that there are two or more fractures on one bone. The fracture most widely seen with abuse is the epiphyseal/metaphyseal chip fracture. Feldman (1997) also points out that jerking or shaking the limbs of a child can result in a "bucket handle" fracture, in which the ligament connections at the end of the bone are torn away (p. 208). Greenstick fractures result when one side of the bone is broken while the other is bent. These can be caused by twisting. Dislocations may result when a child is forcibly picked up or thrown by an arm or a leg (Brittain, 2005; Feldman, 1997; Loiselle, 2002; Monteleone, 1998; Reece, 2011).

In general, small children do not demonstrate numerous fractures under nonabusive conditions. Toddlers are most likely to exhibit greenstick fractures when they fall in play. For most children, however, a broken bone is accompanied by swelling, discomfort, discoloration, and a need to be comforted. It is unlikely that such an injury could be overlooked. If a parent displays little knowledge of previously acquired breaks picked up by x-rays, there should be further investigation (Feldman, 1997; Hobbs et al., 1999; Swenson and Kolko, 2002).

Head and Internal Injuries

Head injuries can be extremely serious and are often associated with abuse, especially in infants. Skull fractures may result from hitting the head against an object or throwing the child. In a depressed fracture, the bone fragments are pressed into the skull cavity. This type of injury is produced by a severe blow. Hematomas are collections of blood that form around the surface of the brain. In a subdural hematoma, blood collects between the brain and the tissue (dura) surrounding the brain. This is usually caused by a jolt (such as a slap) or severe shaking, which breaks veins and releases blood. The child may vomit, feel listless, or have seizures before the injury is diagnosed. In an epidural hematoma, the blood collects beneath the skull; this is caused by the rupture of an artery covering the brain. The child may vomit or lose consciousness soon after the assault (Brittain, 2005; Cobley and Sanders, 2006; Feldman, 1997; Hobbs et al., 1999; Loiselle, 2002; Reece, 2011).

Abused children may also experience injuries to the abdomen, such as a ruptured liver or spleen, intestinal perforation, kidney or bladder injury, torn arteries, or injury to the pancreas. Physicians note that peritonitis (inflammation of the abdominal lining) has often set in by the time the child is seen in a medical facility (Brittain, 2005; Hobbs et al., 1999).

Shaken baby syndrome has been well reported in the media over the last few years and is responsible for 50 percent of the nonaccidental deaths of children (Minns and Brown, 2006; Monteleone, 1998). Even if shaking a baby or young child severely does not cause death, it often results in significant damage. Shaking is especially detrimental for several reasons. First, in infants under 2 years, the head is large in comparison to the rest of the body and the neck muscles supporting it are relatively weak, so the head moves violently. Second, the infant's brain has more water content than an adult's and is less well protected. Since the bones are not yet solidified and firmly attached to one another, the skull is unstable (Cobley and Sanders, 2006; Monteleone, 1998). Therefore, jarring the skull with any kind of force means that there will certainly be damage. The results may be retinal detachment, nerve damage, hemorrhages, and subdural hematoma (Feldman, 1997, Hobbs et al., 1999; Minns and Brown, 2006; Reece, 2011; Vincent and Kelly, 2010). Eye damage can also be caused by either being hit directly in the eye or a blow to another part of the head. Strangulation, acute chest compression, or pressure to the thorax can create a hemorrhage in the area of the eye (Feldman, 1997; Loiselle, 2002; Minns and Brown, 2006).

Burns

Burns are also common in child abuse but not always easy to evaluate. The infant or small child is most likely to be a victim of burning. Among the most common types of burns are those inflicted by cigarettes. Although it is possible for burns to be accidental, cigarette burns that appear on the abdomen, genitals, bottoms of feet, or other more inaccessible spots are more likely to be intentionally inflicted. The recent popularity of the wood-burning stove has created more frequent reports of burns made by pressing the child's hands, legs, or buttocks against a hot stove.

What does it actually take to cause a burn? Monteleone (1998) gives some indications of what it takes to burn with hot water. Using results based on the burning of adult skin, he notes the following:

- At 120°F (the lowest setting on most gas hot water heaters), it takes 5 to 10 minutes to cause a deep burn.
- At 124°F, burns occur in 4 minutes.
- At 125°F, burns occur in 2 minutes.

- At 130°F, burns occur in 30 seconds.
- At 140°F (the average temperature for most households), a scald burn will occur in 5 seconds.
- At 158°F, a burn will occur in 1 second. (pp. 24–25)

These facts are based on adult skin; children's skin can be much more sensitive, so it can burn more quickly and more severely.

Tap water burns often result from parents' frustrations over child behavior—especially problems with toilet training. The child may be forcibly immersed in hot water. If the child's buttocks touch the bottom of the receptacle, they may not be burned, thus creating an unusual looking donut-shaped burn (Loiselle, 2002). Burns more pronounced in the middle and radiating out represent hot liquid having been poured on the spot. Glovelike or sacklike burns indicate that the hand or foot has been immersed in hot liquid (Brittain, 2005; Feldman, 1997; Hobbs et al., 1999; Loiselle, 2002). If the burn occurred accidentally, there are likely to be splash marks from the child's attempt to avoid the spill or the parents' attempt to protect the child. Some children show signs of burns from steam or direct contact with flame.

Patterned burns indicate that a hot object has been used on the child. Hot pokers, irons, heating grates, and other utensils are sometimes used (Loiselle, 2002). Rope burns are also common. Again, attention should be given to the location of the burn. Is it feasible in light of the parents' explanation?

It may not always be easy to differentiate the accidental injury from the intentional one. The wise investigator, however, armed with a knowledge of indicators, considers other factors as well. It is vital to have a complete explanation of how the injury occurred. Is it possible for the injury to have occurred in the proposed manner? Is the parent willing to discuss the injury or does he or she seem secretive and defensive? (Certainly, the interviewer must guard against putting the family on the defensive.) It is also important to consider the family's cultural background, where some practices may be indications of abuse.

Behavioral Indicators of Abuse

Children's behavior often mirrors the atmosphere at home. Abused children exhibit particular behaviors that are indicative of their dysfunctional environment.

Some of the first behavioral indicators of abuse are observed by physicians in hospital settings. Young children brought in with broken limbs, bruises, welts, and other suspect injuries appear different from the normal pediatric patient. The abused children cry little, on the whole, but cry hysterically when being examined. They are often apprehensive when other children cry and demonstrate a passive watchfulness—lying quietly in their cribs and observing their surroundings intently. These children show no expectations of being comforted by parents but constantly search for tangible comforts like food. One nurse described the release of such a child:

I knew there was something wrong, but we couldn't quite put our finger on it. He just lay there in his crib, with one leg in a cast and those big eyes just staring at everyone. Two years old and he never smiled, never talked. At first, I thought he was just homesick, but the day his parents came to get him was a real mystery. They seemed excited to pick him up, but he hardly reacted. He almost seemed reluctant to go with them. It was only later, when we learned that the broken leg was a result of abuse that I understood.

Children who are abused early in their infancy may develop a shrill cry that is not differentiated according to their particular need. The high-pitched quality of this cry is described by abusive parents as extremely unnerving, often precipitating further abuse. The motor development and social development of these infants are slow. They do not begin to crawl, sit, or reach for toys when others of their age do. The passive watchfulness described earlier is especially obvious among abused infants. Passivity permeates their attitude toward their world. They show little interest in toys and accept losses with little reaction. As they grow, this same passivity demonstrates itself in their attitude toward schoolwork (Swenson and Kolko, 2002).

One of most striking characteristics noted by those working with abused children is their impaired capacity to enjoy life. These children often seem old for their age (pseudomature); they lack the ability to play. Life for them had been unrewarding, and they demonstrate this clearly in their attitudes. Symptoms such as enuresis (inability to control bladder functions), encapresis (fecal soiling), temper tantrums, and bizarre behavior can be classified under psychiatric symptoms. Low self-esteem becomes obvious not only at home but in the school setting as well. Abused children have little confidence in their own abilities, and school learning problems are the result (Fraser, 2004; Giardino et al., 2010; Howes et al., 2000; Algood, et al., 2011).

Withdrawal is another common characteristic of abused children. Often used as a defense to avoid further punishment, abused children carry this withdrawal into every aspect of their lives. What some authors refer to as *oppositional behavior* has been termed *aggression* or *overt hostility* by others. Abused children harbor a suppressed anger over their lack of control of their lives. In addition, they see their parents using violence as a way of handling problems and taking out aggression. Some children act out their anger against peers, animals, or even adults, whereas others harbor it and turn their anger inward.

Over the years, researchers have pointed to abused children's demonstrating *hypervigilance*, sometimes referred to as *passive watchfulness*. They also note that some children demonstrate *compulsivity*. If abuse is an issue of control and children cannot control the abuse, it follows that they may attempt to control other aspects of their lives. Children may reason (more unconsciously than consciously), "I cannot control Daddy's hitting me, but I do have control in my own room or in my play. I can fix my room just as I want it, or I can stack the blocks precisely one on another. In this way, *I* can maintain *some* control." Many abusive families have immaculate homes and lead well-ordered lives—both manifestations of their intense need to control. Feeling out of control is disturbing to all the family members.

One characteristic of abused children is their *unusual ability to adapt* to a variety of people and settings. For these children, this ability has meant survival. It has been important for them to perceive, with almost psychic ability, the needs of those around them and adapt accordingly: "If Dad doesn't want to see you after a hard day at work, get out of his way." "If Mom doesn't want to be disturbed, leave her alone." One particularly adaptive 5-year-old boy discovered that if his father had several beers when he got home, he would fall asleep and thus spare the family his tirades and possible abuse. The boy soon learned that greeting Dad with a beer, and following that by several more, was all that was needed to ensure the family a relatively peaceful evening.

Abused children are particularly *fearful of failure*. Again, this quality may relate to being adaptable and not wishing to displease others. It may also be that children perceive abuse as a deserved retribution for their failure. When psychological testing is done, abused children also demonstrate difficulty attending to instructions, a behavior that carries over into school and is a frustration to both teacher and pupil. This behavior may exist for several reasons. First, there are numerous stimuli in a test situation. Hypervigilance in the child means that he or she has taken in all of these stimuli and may be confused. Further, the child is faced with a collection of objects that are not his or hers. The admonishment at home has been not to touch without first asking. Therefore, the child's anxiety is raised. Similar situations in the school setting add to the child's learning problems.

The abused child may also *demonstrate verbal inhibition*. At home, talking too much can be dangerous. Verbalization is also a step in cognitive development. Organizing thoughts and conceptualizing increase in complexity as the child matures. If a child's development, self-esteem, opportunity to converse, and trust are hampered by abuse, poor language development may be the result.

Regression is often used by abused children as a defense. Children may find it more comfortable to return in some way to an earlier stage—a stage perhaps where they did feel nurtured and loved. Baby talk, wetting the bed, and sucking fingers or thumb are methods children sometimes unconsciously use to cope with their situations.

Poor peer relationships are often marked among maltreated children. These children with poor object relations have not learned the give-and-take of relationships, and they may be hesitant to share lest friends uncover the magnitude of their unhappiness. Abused children sometimes exhibit behavior that does not appeal to other children— pugnaciousness or extreme shyness. And finally, what if they attempt to make a friend and are rejected? The anticipation of this hurt is enough to prevent abused children from even trying.

Parents may prohibit their children from participating in activities, which keeps the children even *more isolated* from others of their age. With their own insecurity and lack of support system, the parents do not allow their children to have friends. Lacking confidence to make friends themselves, these parents feel threatened when their children do. Abusers are also fearful that confidences between children and their friends will uncover the abuse. Poor peer relationships carry into adolescence.

The abused adolescent was, until recently, all but overlooked. It may have been assumed that adolescents were not as vulnerable to abuse because of their strength, weight, size, and age. Adolescents are also seen as being able to run away, avoid the abuse, protect themselves, or get help. Yet every year, numerous adolescents are abused. The abuse may have been long term, persisting throughout childhood and continuing into adolescence, or the maltreatment may begin or intensify during adolescence because of the parents' own current conflicts, which are possibly brought on by the stresses of adolescence (Kaplan et al., 1998).

Separation and control are important factors in the life of the adolescent as well as the parents. Abuse often represents the battle being waged over these issues. A fervid attempt at control used by the abused adolescent is running away. Feeling deeply fused with his or her family yet unable to stop the abuse, the desperate teen forces the separation by escape. Some adolescents run to someone or some place, but most, aware of their own isolation, run aimlessly and are often picked up by pimps and drug dealers. Another form of escape for abused adolescents is through drugs and alcohol. These substances dull the mind or heighten the fantasy world and allow adolescents to ignore or deny the abuse.

Other adolescents, rather than escape, conversely provoke abuse from adults or peers. The underlying need is again to maintain control. To provoke abuse is to bring it on one-self or to control the situation. Such adolescents may be assaultive, aggressive, or pugna-cious. Their acting out causes schools and parents to label them incorrigible. The mood swings of adolescents are especially visible in the abused child. Acute hostility gives way to withdrawal, as the adolescent strives to cope with the abuse as well as the conflicts of development. The same type of attention-seeking devices seen in the younger child are ob-vious in the adolescent. Low self-esteem and depression are hallmarks of adolescent abuse.

Some authors suggest that child abuse can be a precursor of delinquent behavior (Far-rington and Welsh, 2008; Flower, 2008; Kaplan et al., 1998). "Trigger" Collins, so called because he had gained the reputation of being the faster to "trigger his switchblade," is an example of an abused adolescent who turned to delinquency:

Trigger Collins, a handsome, tall, African American 16-year-old, remembers little else of his home life except the abuse. The youngest of five children, Trigger knew from his early years that he was unplanned and unwanted. His father was an alcoholic who beat the boy regularly. His mother took a job as an elevator operator to provide an income for the family.

His siblings, the youngest of whom was 10 years his senior, paid little attention to him unless they required errands to be run. Oldest brother Jake thought it amusing, and later profitable, to teach his brother to shoplift. When he was 8, Trigger's mother interrupted the transaction of stolen goods between brothers, and when Jake denied knowledge of the theft, she beat Trigger severely with a strap. His refusal to continue stealing was met by his older brother's assaults.

Trigger, the only child still at home, was also expected to maintain the house in his mother's absence. This often meant finding his father's hidden bottles and putting his father to bed when he came home drunk. Mrs. Collins was a compulsively well-organized and immaculate housekeeper. She found Trigger's attempts at housekeeping totally unac-ceptable. Failure to maintain her standards meant "a walloping" and admonishments about being a "stupid, lazy, dirty kid."

The abuses Trigger suffered for his own apparent misdeeds were compounded by the marital discord of his parents. Parental fights meant thrown pots, broken bottles, and an array of verbal assaults. The victor, usually his mother, accused the bystanders of being "just like your father" and sent them "out of my sight" while she recuperated. If pressed, Trigger can remember some calm periods when his father stopped drinking and his mother was more amenable.

At age 13, after a particularly painful beating by his father, Trigger decided he had had enough. He stole money from his father's pants pocket and his brother's switchblade, which had been carefully hidden from his mother, and ran. A bus ride took him into the city, where his large size and agility with the switchblade quickly brought him to the attention of Arnold, a small-time thief who maintained an apartment for homeless boys and required them to steal for him to earn their keep. Trigger, already an adept thief, thanks to the tutelage of Jake, fit in well. Brief skirmishes with the police brought his whereabouts to the attention of his parents, but by mutual agreement, he did not return home. With Arnold's final arrest came Trigger's chance to assume his place at the head of the small gang of boys. Fierce street fighting and myriad different crimes punctuated his career for the next year until at age 16, Trigger was arrested for armed robbery.

Throughout his childhood, Trigger Collins had been written off as difficult, unwilling to learn, and developmentally slow. His later actions, therefore, mirrored the only behavior he knew—violence.

Like Trigger, isolated, withdrawn, or aggressive attention-seeking children mature into individuals much like their own parents.

In the detection of abuse, it is extremely important that one be aware of the child's culture heritage (Fontes, 2008; Lynch and Hanson, 2011). Helpers must first discover what are the practices and/or customs of a particular culture. For example, in a culture where children are expected to be obedient and respectful, the Wu family found that 4-year-old Byron's hyperactivity was impossible for them to understand and difficult for them to cope with. In the detection of abuse, one must assess the mother's (and father's) own history and background in a cultural context. Knowledge of cultural customs and individual histories may then aid in determining if the behavior in question is idiosyncratic and abusive, requiring intervention, or is part of cultural practice, requiring education on the parenting expectations of American culture.

And finally, cultural sensitivity also necessitates that one look at the current environment of the family. A mother whose husband had died soon after the family immigrated from India, now faced life as a widow. Since her own son was only 5 and not old enough to care for her, she was forced to live with relatives in crowded quarters. Their resentment of her was obvious, and the resulting stress may have been a significant factor in her abuse of her year-old daughter.

ABUSIVE PARENTS

Although the abusive family is a complex system influenced by sociological, cultural, psychological, and interactional variables, many authorities feel that parents who abuse demonstrate some particular personality characteristics. Low self-esteem is universal among abusive parents. These parents feel unloved and unworthy themselves. Their lives have usually been fraught with rejection and losses, with the loss of nurturing in childhood as the foundation (Cadzow et al., 1999; Howe, 2005; Howes et al., 2000; Iwaniec, 2006; Swenson and Kolko, 2002; Miller et al., 1999; Saunders and Goddard, 2010). Other parents may have had relatively accepting childhoods, but find they must now cope with circumstances for which they feel totally unprepared. For example, parents who are newly immigrated from a different culture may not know what is expected of them. Some experts also point to the difficulty for mothers raising children with developmental disabilities as a possible stressor that could correlate with abuse in some instances (Rodriquez and Murphy, 1997).

Both types of parents, those with dysfunctional childhoods and those thrust into a totally foreign environment, are excessively dependent on others and often have a symbiotic attachment to their spouse or family of origin. Feeling incapable of autonomous behavior, the parents cling to others. When their needs are not met, frustration ensues.

By the same token, isolation from the outside—the absence of an adequate support system—is of vital importance in understanding abuse. Overwhelmed by the tasks of parenting, these parents have few outlets through which to vent their tensions. To compound these stresses, many abusive parents have rigid superegos and feel they need to tightly control their behavior and the behavior of those around them. Their inability to control themselves and others causes them great distress.

Parents' Unlearned Tasks from Childhood

Ray Helfer, noted advocate for abused children, stated that there are five tasks abusive parents have not learned: (1) to get their needs met in appropriate ways; (2) to separate feelings from actions; (3) to determine they are responsible for their own actions and not for the actions of others;[1] (4) to make decisions; and (5) to delay gratification (Helfer, 1979; Helfer, 1989; Helfer and Krugman, 1997). Although his theory was postulated several decades ago, it still has a great deal of validity when attempting to understand parents who abuse. For this reason, each of these tasks will be considered here.

Getting Needs Met

In their own childhoods, abusive parents learned that to have their needs noticed, they had to express them in the extreme. For example, a quiet request for attention from their own parents was ignored, but a tantrum was acknowledged, if only by a slap. Becoming extremely ill or trying to commit suicide also elicited a response. Thus, the now-abusive adult learned that if you want to be heard, you must exhibit behavior that cannot be ignored. Because abusive parents learned early to overact or overreact, they do not know how to make their wishes and feelings known in appropriate, less dramatic ways. They feel so insignificant that they are sure no one will listen if they merely tell how they feel. These parents find themselves directing these attitudes in their children. More than one abusive parent has said, "But my child doesn't listen if I just *tell* her no!"

Separating Feelings from Actions

Hitting instead of telling a child about the misbehavior is also related to the parents' inability to separate the feelings from the action. In childhood, when the mother was angry, she hit. Anger for these parents translates into action. Verbally expressing the anger is a foreign concept to them.

Determining Limits of Responsibility

"I don't know how many times my mother told me," recounted one abusive mother, "'If it hadn't been for you, your father wouldn't have left.' For years I was convinced that I was the cause of every rotten thing that happened to our family."

Unable to accept the responsibility for their own actions, abusive parents blame everyone else, especially their children: "If you hadn't done that, I wouldn't have beaten you." There is a stage in development when children feel all powerful—able to cause or

---

[1]There may be some cultures in which it is accepted that individuals are responsible for each other's actions.

affect anything in their environment. Eventually, healthy children recognize they are not that powerful and, in fact, that people make choices about what they do. The child who is constantly blamed continues to believe that he or she is the cause, especially of unpleasant happenings. Because the events are always negative, the child would like to deny his or her contribution but feels powerless to do so. Thus begins one more conflict in the area of control. As an adult, the individual feels inherently responsible for the negative aspects of life, regardless of the role others play. For example, a wife is liable to believe she drove her husband away, not that her husband left because he was irresponsible and couldn't settle down. Overwhelmed by blame and in a last attempt at control, a parent projects the blame on his or her own children, and the cycle repeats itself.

In cultures where an individual's actions *are* expected to affect the family or community, abuse may result from the child's failure to meet these expectations. For example, 9-year-old Jon Chen's theft of candy from a local store was seen by his father as a deliberate attempt to make the family "lose face." The abuse that resulted was an effort to tell Jon that he, too, was responsible for the family's honor.

Making Decisions

Healthy families teach children how to make daily decisions. "What kind of cereal would you like for breakfast?" asks a mother of her sleepy charges. So fearful are some parents of losing control, however, that they do not allow their children to make decisions. When the children become adults, they may lack the ability to make decisions. Since every aspect of life requires making decisions (frequently, immediate ones), the indecisive individual again feels powerless and out of control.

Delaying Gratification

Children presented with consistency in their lives learn that life is predictable; a pleasure one would like now will be attainable if one has patience. Yet the childhoods of abusive parents have not been characterized by consistency. One minute their parent was loving, and the next he or she struck out in anger. Pleasurable things make one feel good, but abusive parents, unable to trust what will come in the future and needing so desperately to feel good now, have difficulty putting off until tomorrow what can be had today. They live in a world geared toward instant results—instant solutions to their problems and instant obedience from their children. When these instant results are not forthcoming, the parents once again feel powerless and react.

These five factors promote unrealistic expectations of the child. Abusive parents expect their children to nurture them, perform household tasks, excel in school, and generally be mini-adults. (The parent becomes involved in role reversal with the child.) These parents demonstrate impulsivity and tenuous control and are easily provoked to anger. Since abusive parents usually seek mates who are developmentally similar, both expect the other to meet their needs. When this is not possible, marital discord is the result. Yet the family is so deeply fused that neither parent can leave. In fact, as one parent abuses, the other stands by (a kind of co-abuser) unable to significantly intervene. Perhaps conflicts go unaddressed because neither of the spouses has learned to handle issues except with violence. Much of the therapy practiced with abusing dyads involves teaching these parents how to communicate their frustrations and resolve conflicts verbally and without excessive hostility.

Munchausen Syndrome by Proxy

Protective service agencies are often faced with a condition referred to as *Munchausen syndrome by proxy* (*MSBP*; sometimes also called *factitious disorder by proxy*, or *FDP*). Affecting predominantly mothers and their infants or young children, this distortion in parenting created a sufficient amount of public attention and was the subject of several studies. Related to adult Munchausen, this syndrome nonetheless has variations.

Adult Munchausen involves an adult who seeks attention at a hospital for symptoms that are often self-induced. This individual is extremely demanding of drugs and hospital attention but also seems resentful of those who attend him or her. The conclusion made by those studying this syndrome is that it is based on rage directed toward what the patient has perceived (symbolically) as abandoning parents (Lasher and Sheridan, 2004; Main and Coolbear, 2002; Parnell, 2002; Roesler and Jenny, 2008; Shapiro and Nguyen, 2011).

Munchausen syndrome by proxy is manifested by mothers, who have sometimes been Munchausen patients themselves. (Although fathers may demonstrate this pathology, the incidence is rare.) These mothers present a picture to the world of caring and concerned caretakers, while they are administering to their children large doses of such substances as ipecac (producing vomiting), phenolphthalein (causing diarrhea), insulin or glucose (affecting blood sugar), or even fecal matter. Some mothers try to smother their children. Children may also appear to fail to thrive. The intent on the mother's part is to induce a condition that necessitates hospitalization and the attention rendered by medical staff. Because this mother seems so attentive, albeit demanding, and so intensely interested in hospital procedures during the child's hospital stay, it often requires several hospitalizations and sometimes results in the death of the child before medical personnel recognize what is occurring (Hobbs et al., 1999; Lasher and Sheridan, 2004; Main and Coolbear, 2002; Shapiro and Nguyen, 2011). MSBP has also been misdiagnosed as sudden infant death syndrome (SIDS).

It may be difficult to understand the mother who would inflict harm on her child so that she could benefit from the attention the child receives. But this mother has developed, usually as a result of her own childhood, a pathological way of getting her needs met.

Although physical abuse is often not discernible in the childhoods of these mothers, emotional abuse and abandonment are. Feeling the rage over not having her needs met, this mother uses her child to gain attention and protection from the figure who is associated with life and death. At the same time, she resents this professional, feeling that nothing he does (usually a male physician) is enough (Main and Coolbear, 2002; Parnell, 2002). Other authors suggest that this mother's own perceived or real rejections by others may have created in her a rage that is turned against her child. Some researchers also suggest that she is unable to differentiate herself from her child and her own pathology spills over onto him or her (Lasher and Sheridan, 2004; Main and Coolbear, 2002; Parnell, 2002; Shapiro and Nguyen, 2011).

Munchausen syndrome by proxy is a difficult type of abuse to diagnose. The first suspicion occurs when the medical community is stymied by the child's failure to respond to treatment. Often, covert video monitoring is needed to detect the real cause of the problem. Subsequently, good communication among staff and efficient gathering of relevant information, not only about the child's medical history but also the mother's background, are necessary (Main and Coolbear, 2002). A multidisciplinary team approach is the only method that seems to achieve both diagnostic and treatment results.

The emotional impact of the child that survives Munchausen syndrome by proxy has not been sufficiently researched as yet. In addition to medical treatment to reverse any physical harm that has been done, the child will also need psychiatric assessment to determine if he or she has attachment disorders, difficulty with trust, or other residual effects. The treatment for the perpetrator is usually much more intense, given the depth of her pathology (Lasher and Sheridan, 2004; Main and Coolbear, 2002; Parnell, 2002).

Roseler and Jenny (2008) make a strong case that the diagnosis of Munchausen syndrome by proxy should be retired and subsumed under the classification of medical child abuse.

Abusive Parents and Adolescents

Although the abuse of adolescents was mentioned briefly in this chapter, it requires more attention. Adolescence is a difficult period for abusive parents. For all parents, adolescence marks the time when they watch their children blossom with sexuality and autonomy just at the time they are beginning to face or anticipate middle age. For example, immigrant parents may find that their adolescents have become well acclimated to the new culture, often accepting values that are foreign to their parents. Recognizing perhaps what they have not accomplished in their own lives, parents see their children as now having the opportunity to accomplish these or similar things. Healthy parents may see this as an extension of their own accomplishments, but abusive parents, in competition with their child, see the child's growth as a threat. For these parents the frustration and fear of losing control manifest in striking out at the perceived symbol of their failure—the adolescent.

Separation is also an important factor for parents and their teenagers. Anxious to be on their own, teens pull away from home in a manner that may be especially difficult for the insecure parent. Abusive parents, often hopelessly fused with their offspring and scarred by previous rejections, see separation as a major crisis often surrounded by much emotional conflict. Perhaps an element of guilt enters into the already complex picture. Determined to exert control over the child and confused by anger, guilt, and fear over the impending loss, the parent abuses.

Sheri and her mother were locked in a conflict stimulated by the girl's adolescence:

"I don't know what happened!" protested Sheri tearfully in the therapy session. Sheri had been abused from ages 14 to 16 by her 40-year-old mother. She had run away at age 16 and was, for a period of time, placed in a foster home. Now at 17, she was living at home and was, with her family, in therapy. Sheri's attempted suicide necessitated individual therapy as well.

"It was like she turned into a mad woman," recounted the pretty, full-figured teenager, referring to her mother. "We never got along too well, but one day she caught me drinking and she just spaced out. She took this belt and started hitting me and hitting me. She wouldn't stop! I was really afraid of her!"

Sheri's mother had been treated for severe depression a year before the abuse began. Mrs. Meade had supported herself and her daughter since her divorce five years before. Dependent and immature, Mrs. Meade clung to her daughter for support. Sheri had always been immature, but at age 13, she suddenly blossomed and began an intense interest in boys. She went out often and became sexually active. Mrs. Meade admitted being desperately lonely and felt unable to handle Sheri's flippant attitude and rebellious behavior.

She met and, within three months, married Frank Meade in the desperate hope that together they would solve her problems with Sheri. Meade, a retired army officer, set down firm rules in an attempt to control his new stepdaughter. Feeling rejected by her mother's marriage and overwhelmed by her new stepfather's intensity, Sheri ran away and went to live with a boyfriend. She returned of her own accord, however, and was met by a violently angry stepfather and a hysterical mother. The next few months Sheri describes as "pure hell." Her stepfather ignored her and attempted to regiment his now bewildered wife. Mrs. Meade's hospitalization for depression created even more tension between Sheri and her stepfather, and Sheri began once again staying out late.

When her mother returned, Sheri said she "felt bad." Although they had never been close, the adolescent now felt a need to make amends and became "really nice" to her mother. Annoyed by "this pretty picture that leaves me out," Frank Meade left the home. Mrs. Meade was devastated, feeling that she couldn't possibly survive without him. The feeling was apparently mutual, because Meade called her daily but refused to return until "that kid gets out." A month later, Mrs. Meade smelled liquor on her 14-year-old daughter's breath when Sheri returned from a party. A beating ensued, leaving Sheri bruised and crying and Mrs. Meade hysterical. Finally composing herself enough to call her husband, she begged him to return.

The next two years were marked by episodes of abuse, Mr. Meade's leaving and returning, and Sheri's more and more rebellious behavior. Eventually, Sheri sought help from a teacher who reported the situation to social services. So enraged were her parents that the resulting arguments led Sheri to attempt suicide.

Not unlike other abusive families, the Meades represent a complex system of confused, unhappy individuals. Mrs. Meade, the product of an extremely close family, transferred her need to be taken care of to her first husband. When he failed and even eventually left her for another (equally needy) woman, she turned to her daughter. Adolescent Sheri, however, was just beginning to come into her own and found her mother's dependence too intense. Sheri began pulling away in the only way she knew—her interest in boys and staying out late. It is not surprising that Mrs. Meade then discovered another individual on whom she felt she could depend.

For parents new to this culture, the separation expected of adolescents takes on more complexities:

Eduardo Hernandez had immigrated to the southwestern United States as a young man. He was easily accepted into the closely knit Mexican American community. He met and married Carmelita, who had newly immigrated from another part of Mexico. Together, they raised three sons.

Eduardo had no complaints about his new life. Originally a clerk in his uncle's small grocery store in the Mexican community, Eduardo eventually became the owner when his uncle died. The community was a strong one—perhaps protecting itself from the discrimination they saw outside. Eduardo's two older sons naturally began working at the store. But with Alphonso, the youngest, the family reached an impasse. Alphonso had long questioned the family's values. He had learned English early—unlike his parents, who still had difficulty conversing in anything other than Spanish. At age 13, he had become rebellious and argumentative, qualities not accepted by his patriarchal community.

Initially, Eduardo managed to punish his son in ways that would not be considered abusive. The father found himself greatly conflicted. On the one hand, he admired his son's ability to acclimate to the non-Hispanic culture and to make non-Hispanic friends; on the other hand, Eduardo feared that he was losing his son and resented the boy's failure to recognize his authority. The result was that Eduardo began severely beating his son. After one such beating, Alphonso fled to a friend's house. The friend's parents contacted protective services.

Only a small percentage of abusive parents are actually psychopathic. They, too, have experienced an interruption in nurturing in early life and have difficulty when faced with parenting. Psychotic parents see the child as part of their delusional system and present a high risk of abuse.

The Impact of War on Family Violence

As previously mentioned, stress is one significant factor in a parent's perpetrating physical abuse against his or her children, as is witnessing or being taught violence through childhood victimization. Exposure to violence desensitizes individuals and serves to normalize this behavior.

Today, numerous parents—both mothers and fathers—are serving in the military. It is not unusual for these parents to have to leave their children when they are deployed. No matter how long the deployment, the lives of these individuals and those of their families are often wrought with numerous problems. First, these individuals have been trained for combat, desensitizing them to violent behavior. In addition, returning veterans face a myriad of stresses from realigned family roles, difficulties with partners, mounting bills, and their own internal conflicts about having been in combat and returning to family life. A significant number of returning veterans are being diagnosed with *post traumatic stress disorder (PTSD)*, which puts further stress on both the individual and the family as the veteran tries to heal (Paulson and Krippner, 2007; Hall, 2008; Crosson-Tower, 2013).

A recent study that compared maltreatment among military families to nonmilitary families documented that the emotional impact of war on military personnel is profound and affects the incidence of child maltreatment. This study found that the rate of child maltreatment in military families increased by approximately 30 percent with each 1 percent increase in the proportion of soldiers with at least one child who departed to or returned from operational deployment. The rate in nonmilitary families was essentially static over the time period of the study (three years). Thus, it is not only the return but also the initial deployment that affects family stability and maltreatment (Rentz, Marshall, Loomis, Casteel, Martin, and Gibbs, 2007, p. 1204). Since few studies of this type currently exist, it will be important for practitioners and researchers to be conscious of this trend as long as deployment to combat is a part of our way of life in the United States (see Crosson-Tower, 2013, for a more complete look at the military family).

From the characteristics suggested here, it is obvious that abusive parents are themselves in need of help. With the exception of a few sadistic individuals, they do not intend to harm their children. However, their own conflicts, compounded by the stresses of day-to-day living, result in abuse.

DOMESTIC VIOLENCE AND OTHER ABUSE WITHIN THE FAMILY

Inter-partner Domestic Violence

It is difficult to determine where to include the issue of domestic or family violence in a book on child abuse and neglect. Certainly, violence in the family has a severe emotional impact on the children and can be seen as a form of *emotional maltreatment*. There is also the possibility that abused women will be so caught up in their own survival that they will *neglect* their children's needs. And finally, there is a high correlation between the incidence of the physical abuse of wives and the simultaneous *sexual abuse* of their female children. But since family violence is predominantly a physical act, it has been included in this section on physical abuse.

There is increasing evidence that children who witness physical violence within their homes between their mother and the adult male figure (father, stepfather, or boyfriend) demonstrate a number of reactions and lifelong effects (Bancroft, 2005; Ritchie, Silverman, and Bancroft, 2011; Cadzow et al., 1999; Graham-Berman and Howell, 2011; Miller et al., 1999; Mullender, Kelly, Haque, and Imam, 2003; Williams, 2002). Some children identify with the victim, becoming withdrawn, fearful, and depressed. Others demonstrate a phenomenon called *identification with the aggressor*, in which the child is so fearful of also being harmed that he or she chooses consciously or unconsciously to join with the abuser in the aggressive behavior. This may take the form of criticizing the mother (the usual victim) for not standing up to the abuse or the child actually abusing the victim himself or herself or assaulting a younger sibling (Bancroft, 2005; Ritchie et al., 2011; Graham-Berman and Howell, 2011; Hampton, 1998).

For all children brought up in violent homes, the seed of aggression has been planted, a seed that may well mature into violence in future generations (Bancroft, 2005; Ritchie et al., 2011). Consider this case:

> *Kanisha was in high school before she was able to remember the full extent of the violence that had gone on in her home when she was a small child. Now she confided to a trusted teacher that she was afraid to go home. "I can't stand what Jerome's doin' to Mama!" she wailed. Jerome, her 22-year-old brother, had recently returned home after a brief stay in jail for drug trafficking. Influenced by a very violent father who had left several years before, Jerome had now taken on the role of batterer. Although Kanisha was at first fearful for her mother's safety, she later admitted that she, too, was a victim of her brother's assaults.*

For children like Kanisha and Jerome, childhood is a nightmare. They worry about their own and their mother's safety. They view their father with hatred and fear but are confused by the moments when he seems kind and loving. They watch their mother with a mixture of compassion, pity, and resentment, realizing that she is too fearful for herself to give them much comfort.

Recent research on children who witness violence has found that between 3 and 10 million children are observers of domestic violence each year and suffer from a variety of residual effects (Williams, 2002). Children may be either observers of violence in the home or become intended or unintended victims of the abuse between the adults. A study done by Graham-Berman, Howell, and their colleagues (2011) noted that children in violent homes were exposed to different forms of psychological abuse as well as physical violence several times a week. Sometimes, children were used to manipulate or coerce the abused partner into complying with some demand on the part of the abuser. Not only are children harmed themselves if they try to intervene, but the rage of the batterer is also sometimes turned on the child (Graham-Berman and Howell, 2011). In addition, many children witness the brutal, sadistic abuse of pets and the murder of their mothers (Bancroft, 2005; Ritchie et al., 2011). Children who witness violence have been found to be more aggressive with peers and may go on to abuse their own children or partners. These children also have fewer friends, have significantly more behavioral problems, and exhibit hyperactivity, anxiety, withdrawal, and learning problems in school (Bancroft, 2005; Ritchie et al., 2011; Graham-Berman and Howell, 2011; Mullender et al., 2003).

It is not clear if there are cultural or racial differences in the incident of domestic violence. Although Hampton (1998) found that African American families had a higher incidence of domestic violence, the reality is that children of any racial or ethnic group may be victims. Ritchie et al. (2011) noted a study that pointed to a high incidence of domestic violence in Hispanic homes.

For any child who witnesses such severe family breakdown, the low self-esteem, developmental delays, depression, conduct disorders, acute anxiety, and violence against others are their legacy from these homes. The effects of violent homes can be equally as emotionally damaging to children as assaults perpetrated on them directly.

Abuse by Siblings

When Laura Allen found 2-year-old Stephen screaming and observed his cut and bleeding head, she could not imagine what had happened. Quickly grabbing the wounded child to her, she frantically surveyed the scene. It was not until she saw the metal truck with one bloody corner and 8-year-old Aaron sitting nearby that she realized what had happened.

"Did you hit your brother?" she asked angrily. Aaron looked up unperturbed. "He was bothering me!" the older child responded calmly. It was not the first time Aaron had injured Stephen, and Laura now realized that if she did not get him some help, it would not be the last.

Every year, the amount of violence between siblings increases. This is not to say that siblings over the years have not expressed their rivalry in physical terms, but today, in a society that is obsessed with violence, there is no doubt that children are learning that this is the way to deal with disagreements (Weihe, 2002; Kiselica and Morrill-Richards, 2007).

A survey of 2,143 families in the United States found that sibling physical abuse actually occurs more frequently than abuse by parents. It is estimated that 53 out of 100 children attack a sister or brother each year. Further, 138,000 children from ages

3 to 17 used a weapon on their sibling. Although this abuse may begin as hitting, biting, slapping, shoving, and punching, it may escalate to life-threatening action such as choking, smothering, or using guns and knives (Weihe and Herring, 1991). Often, this abuse is precipitated by witnessing domestic violence in the home (Johnstone and Marcinak, 1997).

More recently, Button and Gealt (2010) conducted a study of eighth and eleventh graders in a Delaware School system. The sample was composed of 26 percent African American children and teens, 64.7 percent Caucasian, and 9.1 percent Latino/a.

Of those living with siblings (4,548 eighth graders and 3,574 eleventh graders), 42 percent reported some form of sibling violence including pushing, shoving, slapping threats, and other forms of aggression. About 22 percent also experienced some type of abuse by their parents and 48 percent had witnessed violence between the adults in their homes (135). These authors suggested that these results were low compared to pervious studies.

What underlies such behavior? Weihe and Herring (1991) contend that sibling violence is about power. In our fast-paced, power-oriented world, violence is an easy way to take control. These authors also believe that power is a

> male-oriented issue in today's society. Many men still mistakenly believe that they must be in control. Feeling powerless creates problems for some of them. They think they are expected to be powerful, and they seek to satisfy that idea. . . . The sense of power they get from being abusive makes them want to repeat the experience. (p. 18)

Button and Gealt (2010) noted a correlation between sibling abuse and substance abuse, delinquency and other forms of aggression as well as general family violence.

While it is more likely for male children to physically abuse younger siblings, especially sisters, some females are also abusive. Children who abuse may also be mirroring the abuse in their family. For example, boys who see the father figure assaulting their mother may identify with the aggressor and abuse siblings.

There is not to date, an abundance of research on the characteristics of those who abuse their siblings physically. The perpetrators may enjoy the power that it gives them or be mirroring the aggression they have experienced or witnessed. Some are dealing with their own psychological issues, and a sibling becomes a target for their aggression and rage (Weihe, 2002; Kiselica and Morrill-Richards, 2007; Caffaro and Conn-Caffaro, 2005; Button and Gealt, 2010).

Parental reaction to abuse by siblings is extremely important. Parents like Laura Allen (mentioned earlier), who perceive the behavior as problematic and respond by trying to help the abuser, offer a chance for healing. But parents who are abused themselves, who perceive the extremes as *normal* sibling rivalry, or who are so caught up in their own issues that they can be of no help to their children, may be creating an abuser who will continue to fall back on this behavior as an adult.

Abuse by Peers

Although in years past, physical abuse has been, by definition, perpetrated within the family, increased recognition of abuse by peers has raised public concern and should therefore be discussed.

Bullying and Peer Violence

At first, I was afraid to Tell anyone why I was afraid to walk the six blocks between our house and my school. It started when Punky would come out of his house, a block from mine, and immediately insist that he go through my lunch pail. After he took out any treats that he liked, he would riffle through my back pack. I was afraid to say anything. Everyone knew he was a tough kid and you didn't cross him. He would hurl insults at me as well until I was in tears—comments about how I looked, what I wore, my choice of friends. I tried to get away from him, but he was always there. When we got to school, I would make up some excuse about going into the building early. Sometimes at recess, Punky would poke me or pinch me threatening me if I told anyone. It was when he failed an English test that—on our way home—he punch and hit me until I screamed for him to stop. A neighbor saw what he was doing, chased him off and took me inside to call my mother. Even then, I was afraid to tell them the full extent of it—afraid that Punky would come back and beat me up again.

Despite the obvious abuse depicted in the previous scenario, bullying is not always as easy to identify. Peers are often seemingly cruel to one another, but may not always intend to hurt. Bullying, on the other hand, is recognized by the intent to harm with the additional characteristics of being repetitive, intentional, chronic, with a difference of either physical or social power between the bully and the victim (Rivers, Duncan, and Besag, 2009; Potzner, 2010; Olweus, 2011). Olweus (2011) identifies way in which children might be bullied:

- Verbally through insulting comments or names
- By being isolated or excluded
- Being kicked, shoved or spit upon
- Through having vicious rumors or lies circulated about them
- Having possessions damaged or stolen
- Being threatened
- Being the brunt or racial slurs
- Subjected to sexual comments or pressure

Although not all of these involve physical abuse, bullying may escalate into becoming physical. The bully is believed to have a strong need for power, perhaps as a way of compensating or his or her own feelings of inadequacy. They often find pleasure in the suffering of their victims. And, the adults around them may knowingly or unknowingly collude by their inattention to what is happening (Rivers, Duncan, and Besag, 2009; Potzner, 2010; Olweus, 2011).

The effect on the victim may be profound. Victims suffer from diminished self-esteem, anxiety, fear, a sense of helplessness, and depression. Such symptoms may further escalate into psychosomatic problems, poor school performance, as well as suicidal thoughts or actions (Rivers et al., 2009; Potzner, 2010; Olweus, 2011). There is some indication that those involved in school shootings had previously been victims of bullying (Daniels and Bradley, 2011).

SUMMARY

Physical abuse is a concept that is difficult to define. Its definition depends largely on the mores and values of the times. Today, most specialists agree that abuse involves the nonaccidental injury of a child at the hands of the caregiver. Four professional fields are intimately involved in the investigation and treatment of child abuse: medical and psychiatric, legal, social services, and law enforcement. Causal theories are numerous but can be grouped into three categories: interactional variables, environmental/life stress variables, and social/cultural/economic variables.

Practitioners look at potential abuse situations in terms of both risk factors and protective factors. Particular children may be at higher risk for abuse than others.

In addition, bruises, fractures, head injuries, and burns provide primary physical indicators of abuse. Behaviorally, children demonstrate a variety of symptoms, such as passive watchfulness or hypervigilance, developmental delay, passivity, enuresis, encopresis, aggression, compulsiveness, regression, and fear of failure. Adolescent runaways are often overly aggressive, turn to drugs or alcohol, or become delinquent in behavior.

Abusive parents have carried into their adulthood the unmet needs of their own childhoods. They exhibit low self-esteem, excessive dependency, a failure to meet the challenges of parenting, unrealistic expectations of their children, role reversal with their children, and impulsivity. Parents abusing adolescents are frequently working out their own developmental conflicts. It is not only parents who are abusive. Siblings, too, can become abusers. Some children also observe violence within their homes, and this, too, can take its toll. More recently the issue of bullying has been recognized as a form of peer abuse.

Physical abuse, whether perpetrated by parents or siblings, peers or observed within the home, is difficult to understand. Once society fully understands the abuser and the family that harbors that abuse, however, people will be better able to help the abused child.

Chapter 6

The Sexual Abuse of Children

I s there anything wrong with sex between children and adults? Some writers have argued that not only are children unharmed by having sex but also sexual relationships with adults can be educational. Perpetrators contend their sexual tutelage is actually beneficial to the victims' development. Although a few may agree, most researchers argue against sexual activities between children and adults. First, some say a small girl's vagina is too small to accommodate an adult male's penis. Since sexual abuse often does not progress to the point of vaginal intercourse, this argument is not always valid. Second, many people are disgusted by the idea of child–adult sexual involvement and prefer to see children as innocent and untouched by adult sexuality. And third, most societies have some type of taboo against such a sexual liaison. Researchers and therapists alike feel that early sexual involvement with adults exposes the child to premature sexualization and may have long-term negative effects. Indeed, studies of survivors attest to the scars left by sexual abuse.

Researcher David Finkelhor presents the most convincing argument against adult–child sexual involvement. He contends (1984a) that U.S. society is based on consent and free will, and in order to consent, one must have knowledge and authority. Children do not have knowledge of the meanings of sexuality, information to enable them to anticipate the direction of the sexual relationship, or any idea of how others will react to their sexual involvement. Further, children have no authority in either a legal or psychological sense. Their natural awe of adults, perpetuated by their elders, renders them subject to the whims of these adults. Legally, children are unable to marry, drive a car, or enter into contracts prior to their maturity. Therefore, children are in no position to consent to relationships that carry so many implications as sexual liaisons with adults (see also Faller, 2003).

TWO GROUPS' APPROACHES TO CHILD SEXUAL ABUSE

Sexual abuse of children is not new to our culture. Even so, child sexual abuse is a major problem today. The concern is heightened when adult survivors report its impact on their lives.

Two groups have been instrumental in bringing this issue to the attention of the public and in championing the efforts toward effective treatment and prevention: the child protection movement and the feminist movement. Although currently, the two groups show evidence of combining their efforts in the interest of children and adult survivors, their fundamental difference must be understood (Finkelhor, 1984a).

Child Protection Movement

The child protection movement sees sexual abuse as the third form of child maltreatment, in addition to physical abuse and neglect (Berliner, 2011). Protective agencies deal primarily with *in-family abuse*, or *incest*, which is perpetrated by family members, surrogate parents, or caregivers. The etiology of this problem is believed to be in the family pathology, in which the whole family system is affected in some manner. Theorists describe family patterns that may repeat themselves if no intervention takes place. Protective agencies may also become involved in the treatment of parents of children abused outside the home. Alleviating parental guilt and strengthening the family unit provide protection for the child in the future. Thus, child protection advocates place emphasis on the family as the seat of pathology as well as the medium responsible for the child's protection. (For more historical information on this approach see Corwin, 2002.)

In terms of treatment, the child protective philosophy sees protection of the child as paramount and the family as the unit responsible for this protection. Toward this end, the whole family is seen in treatment, with emphasis on redefining generational boundaries and role definitions and enhancing communication. The ultimate goal is reuniting the family, if the perpetrator is able to take responsibility for his actions and the mother is able to protect her child in the future. Some agencies use the threat of prosecution of the perpetrator to engage him in treatment. Only when his cooperation is not forthcoming or when required by state law do most agencies favor incarceration.

Feminist Movement

Feminists, on the other hand, espouse the sociological view that considers the assault of children as representative of societal values. Because of the patriarchical social structure, women and children have inferior status and are subjected to male dominance (Bolen, 2007; Herman, 1997; Herman and Hirschman, 2000). It may be that patriarchy has not only set up boys to be sexually abused but has also caused abused boys to keep silent, because they fear that disclosure or their victimization will prevent them from being seen as "man enough" to eventually assume the role of patriarch. Further, advertisements in the media and the prevalence of child pornography suggest that children are exploitable. Although Finkelhor's studies argued that healthy, strong mothers can apparently prevent incest, Russell (1984) states, "Mothers should not have to protect their children from their fathers!" (p. 264). Thus, feminists see child sexual abuse as more of a societal than a familial issue (Russell and Bolen, 2000).

For treatment, feminists favor a rape crisis model with an emphasis on victim advocacy. Use of the criminal justice system to punish the perpetrator is seen as a deterrent to future abuse. The victim is helped through this process by a concerned advocate, who also strives for the establishment of protection for the child in the future. Family reconciliation is viewed with some reservation and favored only if protection of the child can be ensured (Finkelhor, 1984a).

It is not always easy to discern the orientation of a helper in the area of child sexual abuse. Although some workers concentrate on family dynamics, they may feel that separation and even incarceration of the perpetrator are better for all involved. Many also see the victim in need of a strong advocate. Whatever the position, both perspectives agree that protection of the child in the future is vital.

DEFINITION OF CHILD SEXUAL ABUSE

Child abuse, for reporting purposes, was defined in the 1974 Child Abuse Prevention and Treatment Act. In 1984, however, the U.S. Congress amended the previous definition to read as follows:

> The term sexual abuse includes: (i) the employment, use, persuasion, inducement, enticement, or coercion of any child to engage in any sexually explicit conduct (or any simulation of such conduct) for the purpose of producing any visual depiction of such conduct, or (ii) the rape, molestation, prostitution, or other form of sexual exploitation of children, or incest with children, under circumstances which indicate the child's health or welfare is harmed or threatened thereby. (Child Abuse Prevention and Treatment Act 42 as Amended by Public Law 98–457, 98th Congress, 9 October 1984)

Sexual abuse refers to the use of a child for the sexual gratification of an adult. Other authors say that sexual abuse is any sexual activity with a child under the legal age of consent (Berliner, 2011). Numerous other words are used synonymously with sexual abuse. *Sexual exploitation*, for example, can be not only the actual genital manipulation of a child and the request to touch an adult but also compelling the child to observe sexual acts or have pictures taken for pornographic purposes. Some authors use a variety of terms, including *assault, molestation, victimization*, and *child rape* (Finkelhor, 1981, 2008; Jones, 1997). *Rape*, in the commonly understood sense, denotes sexual intercourse usually undertaken with violence to the victim. The laws of many states, however, define *child rape* as the intrusion of any part of the perpetrator's body (e.g., penis, fingers, tongue) into an orifice of the child's body.

Haugaard (2000) argues that there is still no clear definition of child sexual abuse or terminology that fully captures the essence of the issue. This inhibits the treatment, research, and advocacy efforts necessary to combat the problem. He cites three obstacles in defining child sexual abuse. First, the term *child sexual abuse* is used by many different professionals within a variety of different contexts. The role of each professional dictates that he or she approach the subject with a particular mandate. Therefore, what to do in the face of child sexual abuse becomes problematic. Second, child sexual abuse falls on a continuum of behaviors involving sexuality, and there is disagreement about where exactly to place this type of abuse. What causes one type of sexual behavior to be abusive and another not to be? For example, when is it permissible for a father to bathe his daughter? At one age, it might be considered acceptable, yet several years later, some might consider it to be abusive. And third, there is much discussion about the contexts in which sexual behavior occurs and which of these make it abusive. For example, there has been much controversy of late about the slaps that coaches give their players on their bottoms in the course of a sports event. Previously assumed to be innocent in this context, some people have now complained that this represents suggestive behavior.

TYPES OF SEXUAL ABUSE

Whether termed *child sexual abuse* or *misuse*, this type of maltreatment is usually categorized based on the identity of the perpetrator.

Intrafamilial Abuse

Intrafamilial abuse, or *incest*, is sexual abuse by a blood relative who is assumed to be part of the child's nuclear family. An individual assuming the role of a surrogate parent, such as a stepfather or live-in boyfriend, may be included in a functional definition of incest. Older siblings, who differ significantly in age or by virtue of their power and resources, may also be considered abusive. Intrafamilial abuse may also encompass members of a child's extended family, such as uncles, aunts, grandfathers, cousins, and so on.

Bolen (2007) compares various studies on incest to determine the characteristics of this type of abuse. From her comparisons, this author concludes that feminist theory, family systems theory, and attachment theory all shed some light. Feminist theory points to fathers as more likely in the roles of perpetrators, using their power to be dominant over their daughters. Indeed, it is power and control that are at the center of incest, rather than sexuality. Bolen suggests that the fact that fathers exploit their power does not explain the levels of dysfunction in the rest of the family systems. She turns to family systems theory for this explanation.

According to family systems theory, incestuous families tend to be less organized, more isolated from the community, and more generally dysfunctional than those in which incest is not a factor (Berliner, 2011; Mannarino and Cohen, 1997; Ogilvie, 2004; Sgroi, 1982; Stone, 2005). There is some question as to whether this dysfunction is present before the incest or occurs as a result of it (Bolen, 2007).

Attachment theory sheds further light on the nature of the abusive family by explaining that insecure attachment puts families at greater risk for incest. Fathers who are not involved in child rearing have been found to be more likely to later abuse their daughters (Bolen, 2007; Rich, 2006).

Russell and Bolen (2000), comparing several studies, found that father–daughter incest represented only some of the abuse by family members. Other authors who have studied males as well as females feel that male children may also be vulnerable to abuse within the family, although perhaps not as much so as female children (Gartner, 2005; Lew, 2004).

Extrafamilial Abuse

Extrafamilial abuse, perpetrated by someone outside of the child's family, represents, according to many authors, a small proportion of sexual abuse. Bolen (2007) disagrees, arguing that there is much more sexual abuse perpetrated outside the family than previously believed. For example, if one compares statistics of the number of boys molested by perpetrators who target boys outside the home (Coxe and Holmes, 2001; Durham, 2006; Finkelhor, 1984a; Flora, 2001; Gartner, 2005), it becomes obvious that this is a highly underreported form of abuse. And this type of abuse is much less studied than incest for several important reasons. First, the first real theories postulated about child sexual abuse came from Freud, who saw women who had been abused within the family. Therefore, sexual abuse became synonymous with incest. When, in the later 1970s, survivors began to tell their stories, most were also victims of incestuous abuse. In an attempt to help the public recognize that abuse could be perpetrated by someone known and loved by the child, reports of abuse by strangers and acquaintances were minimized (Bolen, 2007).

Several other dynamics influenced the view that child sexual abuse was more frequently committed within the family. Family systems theory began to influence the field of child protection and in so doing put sexual abuse in the family in the spotlight. Child protection agencies, due to the sheer numbers of abuse reports, were forced to specialize. With the influence of family systems theory, child protection began to see only intrafamilial abuse situations; all others were referred to law enforcement. Due to the diversity of offenders and offender characteristics, it was easier to pinpoint the family and the body of knowledge that had already been developed than to look at individual patterns of offending. In short, says Bolen, it was more cost effective to study the breakdown of family dynamics than to recognize that society as a whole was not protecting children. Thus, as resources were developed, they tended to center around family intervention (Bolen, 2007).

Offenders who abuse outside of families (as well as a few within) are often referred to as *pedophiles*. *Pedophilia* literally means "love of children," although many authors question whether pedophiles can actually be said to love children (Bolen, 2007; Faller, 2003). *Pederasty* is sexual relations between an adult male and a male child (Jenkins, 2001; Rush, 1992).

Child pornography, an increasingly prevalent form of abuse, uses children to produce sexually explicit material, such as graphics, photographs, films, videos, slides, and books. Using the child for pornography may be part of the engagement process—a form of initiation of the child by the perpetrator—or the pornography may be an end in itself. Evidence gives credence to the possibility that child pornography actually stimulates perpetrators to commit sexually abusive acts, and most perpetrators have collections of such materials (Cooper, Giardino, Vieth, and Kellogg, 2006; Flowers, 2001; Jenkins, 2001; Taylor and Quayle, 2003; Gillespie, 2011).

PROGRESSION OF SEXUAL ABUSE

There is usually a progression in the sexual abuse of a child. The perpetrator may try out behaviors to measure the child's comfort. If the child allows the abuser to continue, the abuse will be intensified. This procedure is called *grooming*. Such a progression, or *grooming*, may begin with the adult disrobing or appearing nude in the presence of the child. The perpetrator may also expose him or herself or observe the child in more intimate past times such as bathing or undressing. Kissing the child in a sexual manor or fondling the child may follow. At some point in the progression, the perpetrator may masturbate or encourage the child masturbate him/her. Oral genital contact may also be a part of the abuse, referred to fellatio when the penis is orally stimulated and cunnilingus when done on a female.

Once the perpetrator has progressed to the point where the child is either desensitized to the abuse or too afraid to resist, the adult may either digitally or penilely penetrate the child (vagina or rectum). Instead of penetration, some offenders will rub their penises against the child (especially in the inner thighs, buttocks or genital area often to the point of ejaculation. This type of stimulation has been referred to as *frottage* or *dry intercourse* (Berliner, 2011; Gilgun, 2009; Sgroi, 1982).

Not every case of sexual abuse progresses in the same manner. In general Lyon and Ahern (2011) suggest that an offender had several steps in his modus operandi: He must befriend the child in order to gain opportunity to have physical contact. This may require patience and time on his part. Certainly, a longer-term relationship between the child and the perpetrator allows for a more leisurely progression over a period of time. Next, he must desensitize the child to more invasive sexual talk and contact. He then initiates the sexual acts and must accompany those with the effort to keep the child from disclosing the abuse. Some authors suggest that these steps can be categorized in five separate phases.

Engagement Phase

During the engagement phase, the perpetrator gains access to the child, engages him or her, and conveys to the child that the behavior is acceptable. (The pronouns *he* and *his* are used here for perpetrator since more than 95 percent of those reported are men.) Often, this is accomplished by his misrepresentation of moral standards. For example, he may say to a child, "This is what every father does with his daughter," or "This is the way adults teach kids about sex."

Perpetrators use a variety of methods to elicit cooperation. Basically, perpetrators play on children's need for human contact and affection, their need for adult approval, their enjoyment of games, and their interest in material rewards. Children's awe of adults and recognition of their own powerlessness provide the perfect opportunity for the perpetrator. Again, this process is referred to as *grooming*. Preble and Groth (2002) classify the method in which the perpetrator grooms the child according to that individual's motivational intent or the psychological aims underlying his behavior. Groth places these aims in two categories: pressured sex contacts and forced sex contacts (Groth, Birnbaum, and Brecher, 2002).

Pressured Sex

In a pressured sex contact, a perpetrator uses *enticement*, trying to persuade or cajole the child. "Come see the game I have for us to play" might be a lead line. *Entrapment* suggests that the perpetrator attempts to make the child feel indebted or obligated. He might say, "After I gave you that nice toy, the least you can do is make me feel good." This type of offender encourages the child to cooperate with the sexual activity by means of bribing or rewarding the child with attention, affection, or material goods. If the child refuses, he will not use force; he is attracted by the child as a loving, innocent, undemanding love object, and frequently knows the child prior to the assault (Burgess, Groth, Holstrom, and Sgroi, 1978; Preble and Groth, 2002; van Dam, 2006).

Forced Sex

Forced sex contacts, on the other hand, involve the threat of harm or the use of force to complete the abuse. A perpetrator may attempt to intimidate the child, using his position as an adult for this purpose. Although he does not intend to injure the child, his use of force to complete the sexual act sometimes harms the child. To him, the child is an object—a tool to carry out his sexual gratification or his need for control. As a result, he makes no attempt to engage his victim. A very small number of child molesters gain pleasure from hurting their victims. This sadistic child abuser sees the child as a target for his anger and cruelty. His crime is premeditated, and his intent is to degrade, hurt, or even destroy the child (Bolen, 2007; Burgess et al., 1978; Ward, Polaschek, and Beech, 2006).

Sexual Interaction and Secrecy Phases

The second phase is sexual interaction, or the actual sexual contact. The abuse may range anywhere from watching or fondling a child to sexual intercourse. Often, the longer the abuse has gone on, the more advanced and complex it becomes. The third, or secrecy phase, ensures that the abuse can continue as the perpetrator uses his power to dominate, bribe, emotionally blackmail, or threaten the child into keeping the secret.

Disclosure Phase

Disclosure may or may not occur during childhood. Many adult victims of child sexual abuse attest that this phase may not be realized until adulthood. During disclosure, the abuse is uncovered either purposefully (the child tells an adult or the perpetrator seeks help) or accidentally (the participants are observed or the child demonstrates physical or emotional trauma resulting from the abuse). Children with genital or vaginal tears, venereal disease, or age-inappropriate sexual behavior or knowledge often give clues that are interpreted as indicators of abuse.

Suppression Phase

The final phase, suppression, occurs when those close to the child—as a result of their own abhorrence of the issue or fear of scandal, stigma, or consequences—encourage and often compel the child to recant or forget the abuse. The pressure the child feels often elicits a recantation, and treatment or prosecution becomes difficult or impossible. The case of Georgia provides an example:

> *Georgia's abuse followed the classic progression. Soon after her divorce, Georgia's mother's boyfriend, Chip, moved in with the family. Alone with Georgia and her infant brother while the mother worked evenings, Chip appeared to be the ideal babysitter. He engaged 7-year-old Georgia in games and encouraged her trust. After several months of tickling, fondling, and bathing—interspersed with a variety of innocent games—Chip suggested they play a new game. He demonstrated to Georgia the "inflatable quality" of his penis and encouraged her to "play with it." Such play was followed by Chip's statement that this was "their little game" and she must not tell anyone. If she did, he told her, he would have to leave, and her mother would never forgive her.*

When her mother observed Georgia rubbing her baby brother's penis sometime later, she questioned her. Georgia's response was that she "wanted to see if it got big like Chip's." Not wanting to admit to herself that her boyfriend could be guilty of any wrong-doing, the mother passed off the remark by telling her daughter that she "shouldn't talk like that." Several years later, when Georgia developed extreme tenderness in her vaginal area, the mother took her to a doctor, who, in conference alone with Georgia, managed to uncover the story. The mother reacted in disbelief and sobbingly ordered Georgia to "take back your awful lies." Fortunately, the mother was eventually able to support her daughter, but once social services closed the case, she told Georgia "to put it all out of your mind."

For such abused children, there are interviewing techniques that include preparing children for the possibility they will be asked to recant. With this preparation and support from the helping system, fewer children are placed in the position of feeling they must deny what has happened to them.

Whatever the semantics or the categories citing its damage and progress, *sexual abuse* is the use of sex by an adult to gain power, dominance, and control over a child. The child is manipulated through force, coercion, cajoling, enticement, or threat to comply with the adult's desires. It is natural for children to participate because of their awe, trust, respect, or love for the adult.

INCIDENCE OF SEXUAL ABUSE

Studies of Abuse

One of the major problems with studies of child sexual abuse is that most with samples of any magnitude were done from the late 1970s to the mid-1990s. Therefore, most of the data are already a decade old. Some authors still use these statistics, contending that they have not changed appreciably (Bolen, 2007).

There are also several methods of gathering data. Some studies are based on current information collected from child protection agency statistics or information gleaned from convicted perpetrators. These may be skewed in that the individuals have come to the attention of CPS or the criminal justice system and do not reflect how many have not. Random surveys depend on the readiness of the respondents to talk about an area as delicate as sexual abuse, and retrospective studies (usually talking to survivors about their past experiences) are based on information that is already a decade or two old. Thus, it is difficult to determine the real facts about child sexual abuse.

One of the earliest studies was done in 1919 by deFrancis (Finkelhor, 1981) in association with the American Humane Association (Children's Division). From 263 cases studied in the New York City area, deFrancis discovered a much higher incidence of sexual abuse than had been previously assumed. Kinsey and his associates, in their random survey of 14,000 women in the 1950s, discovered that at least 25 percent had had some sexual encounter prior to the age of 13 (Pomeroy, Kinsey, Gebhard, and Martin, 1998, p. 25).

Pursuing adults' experience of abuse in their childhoods, Finkelhor (1984a) studied 796 college students in the 1970s and disclosed that of the 530 females, 19.2 percent reported having been victimized in childhood, as did 8.6 percent of the 266 males. In a survey of 930 San Francisco women, Russell (1984) found 647 cases of child sexual abuse, but only 30 had ever been reported to the police.

In Finkelhor's 1981 study of 700 households in Boston, researchers conducted interviews with 521 parents to discover whether they or their children had ever been victimized. Of the 63 people, 21 percent (15 percent female and 6 percent male) reported that they themselves had been sexually abused. Parents reported that 4.5 percent of their children had been abused and another 4.5 percent of their children had been victims of attempted abuse. Overall, 47 percent of the subjects studied had some knowledge or experience of sexual abuse (Finkelhor, 1984a). From the various studies of adults reporting their own past experiences, it was found that between 9 and 52 percent of the females and between 3 and 9 percent of the males had some sexual abuse exposure as children (Finkelhor, 1984a).

With the recognition that males are abused almost as frequently as females have come recent studies on male victimization. In 1988, Urquiza found that of the 2,016 male students studied at the University of Washington, 17.3 percent reported some type of sexual abuse prior to the age of 18. Murphy, in 1989, conducted 777 telephone interviews in Minnesota and came up with an 11 percent abuse rate among males. Many theorists and clinicians would argue that these statistics are extremely low compared to the actual suspected incidence of abuse (Urquiza and Keating, 1990).

The National Child Abuse and Neglect Data System (Children's Bureau, 2011) reports that, in 2010, approximately 9.2 percent of the 1,927,599 children who were reported to be victims of maltreatment were sexually abused. This does not account for the number falling into the category of multiple types of abuse (U.S. Dept of Health and HUS, Children's Bureau, 2011). And how many more children are sexually abused than are estimated or reported? Of the numbers, the majority of *reported* sexual abuse victims are female. Males are still sexually exploited at younger ages with the highest incidence of boys abused at age 4 to 6 years and the highest number of girls between ages 11 to 14.

Today, it is not always easy to compile statistics to indicate the prevalence of children involved in pornography and prostitution. Computer technology has significantly affected the incidence of child pornography. There are many reasons the computer and being online present children with more potential to be sexually exploited. Healy (1996) suggests several reasons. First, there is anonymity on the Internet, which may lower the resistance of perpetrators. There is also a certain thrill for children using this technology, as they feel that they can take a risk while feeling protected at home. The cost and risk of producing pornography are reduced. Pictures and video clips can be scanned into the computer without any loss of quality. New technology makes this process faster and more efficient. Built-in microphones and speakers will soon enable enhanced capacity for production and distribution of home videos. And finally, the Internet provides an excellent opportunity for perpetrators to groom their victims over a period of time, thus lowering the children's resistance gradually.

How does the Internet involve children in pornography and abuse? Finkelhor, Mitchell, and Wolak (2000), in their extensive report *Online Victimization: A Report on the Nation's Youth*, report that of the 1,501 youths from ages 10 to 17 included in their survey, one in five had received a sexual solicitation over the Internet in the last year (p. 1). The survey was repeated in 2005, and in 2010 when it was discovered that there was a decrease in the number of youths receiving unwanted sexual solicitations (from 19 percent in 2000 to 9 percent in 2010), while youth exposure to unwanted pornography went from 25 percent in 2000, to 34 percent in 2005 and back down to 23 percent in 2010 (Jones, Mitchell, and Finkelhor, 2012).

The Keene, New Hampshire, Police Department, as part of the Regional Task Force on Internet Crimes Against Children for New England, conducted a three-year Internet law enforcement project to attempt to intervene in this increasingly serious form of child victimization. During the course of the project, over 200 offenders from 12 different countries were arrested and over 2 million pieces of child pornography were intercepted (McLaughlin, 1999), attesting to the magnitude of the problem.

Due to the secrecy and transient nature of child prostitutes, it is not always easy to collect statistics about child prostitution. In 1999, Klain estimated, that there were about 300,000 runaway and throwaway children living on the streets and prostituting for food, drugs, money, shelter, and survival (see also Flowers, 2001). In 1998, Flowers (2001) reported that 3,869 teens were arrested for prostitution. Of these, 2,372 were female and 1,497 were male. Although many of these were 18 or 19, 257 were 16, 134 were 15, and 106 were 13 or 14 years of age (pp. 98–99).

A more recent study published by the U.S. Department of Justice reported that between 1997 and 2000, only 29 of the 13,814 incidents of prostitution known to the police were committed by juveniles (Finkelhor and Ormrod, 2004). The researchers did note that there may have been some discrepancy in the manner of characterizing the statistics, thus distorting the final outcome. For example, when adults act as pimps for juveniles, the teen prostitutes are then categorized as victims rather than offenders. The significant finding of those who were classified as prostitutes was that 61 percent were male and 39 percent were female, differing markedly from adult statistics (p. 5). However, one might argue that it is girls who are more likely to be managed by adult pimps than boys (see also Wortley and Smallbone, 2012).

As a result of the passing of the Victims of Trafficking and Violence Protection Act of 2000 (TVPA, P.L. 106-386), there has been increased attention given to child prostitution and pornography within the United States. *Human trafficking*, the subject of this law, refers to the exploitation for individuals for commercial sexual use or forced labor. The TVPA makes the sexual trafficking of children, even within their own communities, a federal crime. Between January 1 of 2008 and January 1 of 2010 there were 2,515 investigated cases of human trafficking, 82 percent of which were sexual. Of these, 40 percent were children believed to be involved in prostitution or sexual exploitation (Finklea, Fernandes-Alcantara, and Siskin, 2012).

Influence of Reporting on Statistics

Although the incideonce of sexual abuse of children seems significant, the reported cases represent a very small portion of the children actually abused. There are several reasons for this:

1. Sexual abuse is difficult to identify and prove and easy to deny.

2. Children are given few legal rights and are often not believed.

3. Efforts to treat focus on punishing the offender. In family situations, the other family members are less likely to report because prosecution upsets the family balance, both economically and physically.

4. Those investigating cases feel discomfort in talking about sexual issues and do not screen cases properly or recognize signals that sexual abuse is occurring.

5. Treatment methods are not coordinated or sufficiently effective to elicit a desire for treatment on the part of families or victims. Investigators, too, feel treatment is not effective enough to warrant the trauma children are exposed to when the case is reported.

6. Society's taboo on sexual deviations places a stigma on both victim and perpetrator; therefore, not to report is not to suffer disgrace (Berliner, 2011; Bolen and Scannapieco, 1999; Pecora, Whittaker, Maluccio, Barth, and Plotnick, 2000; van Dam, 2006).

Family members and other private citizens describe personal reasons for not wanting to report sexual abuse. Some people do not want to inform on or interfere in the affairs of others, especially when the perpetrator may be a respected member of the community or even a family member. Parents may feel they can handle the situation of their child's abuse on their own. Even if the fact of the abuse is accepted and help seems warranted, many adults do not know where to report. Perhaps the most universal reason more reports are not substantiated is adults' reluctance to believe children and their hesitancy to attribute such behavior to other adults (Bolen, 2007; Finkelhor, 1994; Jones, 1997).

False Allegations Movement

Currently, there is a movement underway that may also hamper the reporting of abuse now and in the future. This movement charges that the incidence of sexual abuse has been greatly exaggerated or even fabricated. While this sentiment has existed among some of the public and a few professionals for some time, it became formalized into what is known as the False Memory Syndrome Foundation when one particularly controversial case sparked supporters of an accused couple to protest their innocence.

Gardner (1991), a forensic psychiatrist, is one believer in the idea that our society has become preoccupied with sexual abuse to the point of obsession or hysteria. He contends that "the ubiquity of environmental sexual stimuli is playing a role in the epidemic of false sex abuse allegations that we have witnessed in the last decade" (Gardner, 1991, p. 19). Further, he suggests that several common mechanisms lead parents (often within the context of custody disputes) to influence their children to make false accusations. These, Gardner explains, are *vicarious gratification* (where the parent forms a visual image of a sexual encounter and attributes that encounter to the child); *projection* (where unacceptable thoughts or feelings are attributed to others); *reaction formation* (when an individual consciously takes on feelings which are the opposite of what he or she really feels); *voyeurism* (which is a compulsive need to observe sexual happenings or people); *a release of anger or displacement of blame* (which enables the parent to get back at the perpetrator by the accusation); and *substitution* (which allows the child to be substituted for the sexual object) (Gardner, 1991, pp. 25–37). Through these mental processes, the parent either suggests to the child that he or she has been abused or assumes that he or she has been.

Gardner also questions the use of anatomically correct dolls, the assumption that children never lie, and whether indicators of sexual abuse are in fact reliable (1991, pp. 46–68). It is his contention that not only do children lie but also they may seek notoriety and want to ingratiate themselves to adult authority figures. Some may also make reports because others of their peers have reported or embellish these reports for the same reasons (pp. 92–97).

Many traumatic stress proponents take issue with false memory assertions. They argue that those who espouse the false memory theory have not studied trauma or traumatic memory sufficiently and have overgeneralized the memory studies of normal events (Courtois, 2010; Mollon, 2003).

Although some authors believe that these ideas require additional debate, many clinicians express concern that voicing such arguments only serves to prevent those who might otherwise have sought help for their abuse from doing so (see also Courtois, 2010; Faller, 2003; Ney, 1995; Ofshe and Watters, 1998).

PROFILE OF THE ABUSED CHILD

Is there, in fact, a typical kind of child who is sexually abused? Research shows that girls are more likely to report as the victim of abuse than boys (Berliner, 2011). This fact appears to be not so much indicative of who is abused but of our culture, which tells males to be strong and run from danger (see Table 6.1). In the role of victim, boys may feel like sissies. Boys are less likely to have to account for their whereabouts and, therefore, not as likely to be confronted by parents about unusual behavior (Dorias, 2009; Durham, 2006; Gartner, 2005; Lew, 2004; Preble and Groth, 2002). Based on reports and stereotypes, the assumption has been that girls are the most frequent victims. It has now been shown that boys are almost equally as vulnerable. Studies show the incidence of abuse among male children is significantly higher than reported (Gartner, 2005). Until even more research has been done on male victimization, however, we cannot gather accurate statistics.

The average age of those abused is between 4 and 6 years for boys and 11 and 14 years for girls (Berliner, 2011). There may be more abused adolescents, but statistics are difficult to formulate for several reasons. First, adolescents are especially reluctant to report because they fear their parents will curb their freedom to punish or protect them in the

Table 6.1   How Society "Sets Up" Children as Victims

Girls	Boys
Taught by society to be vulnerable	Taught to believe they are powerful
Taught to feel guilt and shame	Taught not to be seen as victims
Taught to be clean and attractive	Taught that molestation may lead to homosexuality or to question manhood
Taught to be manipulative	Taught to think it is "cool" to be initiated by a female
Taught to please others	Taught to fear no one will believe them
	Taught to be "free" and that "freedom" will be repressed if molestation is reported to parents

future. Further, because of age, the offense, if reported, may very likely be categorized as adult rape. Our dating culture (i.e., early, unchaperoned dating as well as the popularity of singles bars) makes teens especially vulnerable to strangers, acquaintances, and so-called date rape.

Children at Risk

It is difficult to determine why some children are abused while others are not. What puts children at risk for sexual victimization?

Bolen (2007), coming from a feminist perspective and discussing risk mostly to female children, argues that we should not focus wholly on the factors that put children at risk as this is only "one part of the story." She writes,

> Victims are abused not because they possess factors that put them at greater risk, but because these factors place them at greater risk to be targeted by offenders. Some children with numerous risk factors escape abuse, whereas children with no risk factors are abused. They are abused because offenders target them for abuse.
> (p. 143)

Thus, we must look not only at the child risk factors but also at the offender. Risk can also be assessed in layers. There is what Bolen (2007), using an ecological perspective, outlined as the *macrosystem*, or the values and beliefs of the culture; the *exosystem*, or the community in which the victim resides; the *microsystem*, or the family of the victim; and the *ontogenic system*, or the individual victim.

In this culture, we give children very few rights. In addition, we assume that sexuality is an adult province and often overlook influences that would be harmful to children. For example, many parents think nothing of allowing children to view an inordinate amount of television, while critics suggest that the messages that children receive are highly suggestive or sexualized as well as extremely violent. Critics point to advertisements that encourage young girls to grow up too quickly and that emphasize sexuality in even the very young. Children's beauty pageants serve to objectify young girls, emphasizing aspects that some feel are harmful to girls' development (Olafman, 2008). This constant exposure desensitizes children to sexual and violent acts, making them often less likely to recognize sexually dangerous situations (Bancroft, 2004; Russell and Bolen, 2000).

Finkelhor (2008) suggests that when family patterns deviate from functional two-parent households, children are more at risk for sexual abuse. The reasons for this, he postulated, are several; that children may be exposed to more unrelated potentially predatory people; that there may be less supervision of the children; there may be more of a likelihood that the family has experienced conflict, loss or some other turmoil often resulting in dysfunctional interpersonal relationships; and such families may feel less in control of their immediate environment.

Bolen (2007) supports some of these conclusions by explaining that the presence of a stepfather in the home has been found to be a factor that makes a child more vulnerable, not only for abuse by the stepfather himself but for abuse by others (Bolen, 2007). Statistically, a girl, especially one whose mother had remarried, has probably been exposed to a variety of men (i.e., the mother's previous boyfriends) who may have had an opportunity to abuse her. Further, friends of a stepfather may not perceive as strong a taboo against molesting the adopted daughter of a friend as against a blood relative. This perception may result from the belief that the stepfather does not have as great an emotional investment in the child (Finkelhor, 1984a, 2008; Karson, 2001).

Other studies report that it is the isolation among families with dysfunction that puts their children risk for abuse. Child care and support services for children are also not always available in a given community. Children who are left alone, who are unsupervised, or who do not have the physical presence of numerous friends and neighbors are more likely to be abused (Berliner, 2011; Bolen, 2007; Iwaniec, 2006).

Families play a significant part in their children's vulnerability. Child sexual abuse may also be present in families in which there is also domestic violence (Bancroft and Miller, 2002; Ritchie, Silverman, and Bancroft, 2011). Substance abuse in families also has a negative influence on child safety (Bancroft and Miller, 2002; Bolen, 2007; Gartner, 2005; Karson, 2001). Some studies show that mothers may also influence risk. The mother who is absent, who is not close to her child emotionally, who is sexually punitive or religiously fanatic, who never finished high school, or who keeps herself isolated is more likely to have a child who may be abused (Finkelhor, 1984a; Sgroi, 1982).

Some authors (Berliner, 2011; Dorias, 2009; Gartner, 2005; Jones, 1997; Preble and Groth, 2002) have described risk factors associated primarily with the families of male children. Boys were found to be at higher risk for sexual abuse in either father–son or mother–son incest if the parents abused alcohol. Mothers were more likely to abuse their sons if they were single parents or the dominant parent, if the household was low income, and if these mothers exhibited other emotional or mental problems. Fathers were more likely to abuse their boys sexually if they were the dominant parent, if there was marital discord, if they had physically abused the wife or other children, if the household was low income, if the mother was emotionally distant and hostile toward males, and if the father feared homosexuality.

Female Victims

Why an individual child is chosen to be abused has long been a subject of debate. Some theorize that a father may approach his eldest daughter and if she refuses, he may go on to abuse other daughters (Meiselman, 1992; Sgroi, 1982). Children with disabilities (physical limitations or emotional disturbances) are particularly vulnerable to victimization (Higgins and Swain, 2009).

Most authors say that actual physical attractiveness of the daughter in incest situations seems to have little influence on whether or not she is abused, whereas Bolen (2007) argues that perpetrators do look at the attractiveness of their victims. There is some debate as to the seductiveness or promiscuity of the female incest victim prior to victimization. Although offenders often describe their victims as seductive, this allegation is usually viewed as part of the perpetrator's rationalization. Studies that question the promiscuity of the daughter as a contributor to incest (Bolen, 2007; Meiselman, 1992) show that the daughter's behavior was predisposed by her already character-disordered family. The patriarchal nature of the incestuous family may also have created a child limited in her ability to say no and thus vulnerable to all types of sexual exploitation (Herman, 1997; Herman and Hirschman, 2000; Meiselman, 1992).

Male Victims

A composite of male victims is more difficult to formulate. From five studies of adult men conducted to assess the incidence of abuse among boys, Finkelhor estimated that the prevalence of abuse reported among boys under 13 years was between 2.5 percent and 5 percent. "This should mean a total of 550,000 to 1,100,000 of the currently twenty-two million boys under thirteen (census estimate, 1980) would eventually be victimized" (Finkelhor, 1984a, p. 155). Yet, despite these figures, it is difficult to get a picture of the boy involved or the abuse he experiences.

Dube et al. (2005) estimated that 16 percent of all boys are sexually abused before eighteen. However, given the fact that perpetrators against boys reports more victims in their careers than those who abuse girls, this statistics seems inadequate.

The research thus far indicates that boys are abused at a younger age. Earlier research cited the median age for boys to be sexually abused was 8.46 years (as opposed to girls at 12.4 years) (Berliner, 2011; Finkelhor, 1984b). The abuse of boys takes place for shorter periods of time and is more likely to take place outside the family. Statistically, abused boys are from poorer socioeconomic backgrounds than girls. There is more likely to be physical abuse in their families, but why a particular boy is chosen (youngest, eldest) has not been fully researched. Some theorists believe that the less assertive boy is more likely to be victimized (Chandy, Blum, and Resnick, 1997; Dorias, 2009; Durham, 2006; Finkelhor, 1984a; Urquiza and Keating, 1990).

DEGREE OF TRAUMA

Not every child is affected by sexual abuse in the same way. The degree of trauma the child experiences depends on several variables:

1. *The type of abuse.* Some victims of family incest appear to be more deeply affected than those who were abused by someone outside the family. Yet abuse by nonfamily members who have either meant a great deal to the victim or who have been sadistic or violent can also have profound effects.

2. *The identity of the perpetrator.* When the relationship with the perpetrator is close, the victims describe being more significantly traumatized. This trauma is based on the betrayal of trust that abuse by a family member or trusted individual represents. Daughters abused by fathers demonstrate less trauma in adulthood than those abused by mothers. Sons molested by mothers report fewer effects of the abuse, but researchers are now finding abuse by mothers in the backgrounds of many rapists and homosexuals. The experiences of boys abused by fathers appears to be more negative (Dorias, 2009; Durham, 2006; Preble and Groth, 2002). Sibling incest is drawing increased attention as producing more trauma than previously recognized.

3. *The duration of the abuse.* Most abuse in incestuous families takes place from one to three years before disclosure. Abuse that continues for a period of time, rather than a one-time incident or series of incidents, seems to create more trauma. The exception is when the one-time incident involved violence or sadism.

4. *The extent of the abuse.* Although any type of misuse can cause traumas for children, a perpetrator who takes a child further along the progression or does more physical damage to the child creates more residual effects.

5. *The age at which the child was abused.* Developmentally, children pass many milestones. Each interrupted developmental stage will cause its own particular effects.

6. *The first reactions of significant others at disclosure.* Most children attempt to tell at least one adult of the victimization. Individuals who decide to tell a trusted adult may receive help that can lessen the impact. Securing therapeutic aid is often based, however, on the reactions of those who first hear of the abuse. If the adults in the child's life are not willing to believe the child, he or she may be blamed or forced to keep the guilty secret into adulthood (Berliner, 2011; Faller, 2003).

7. *The point at which the abuse was disclosed.* Children who try to tell and are not believed or who do not have the confidence in their protection to disclose may keep their secret to adulthood. Treatment of adult survivors indicates that keeping the secret does, in fact, compound the trauma.

8. *The personality structure of the victim.* Children differ in as many ways as perpetrators. One child abused in a similar manner as another might react totally differently (Tower, 1988).

PROFILE OF THE PERPETRATOR

Much debate surrounds the personality and, therefore, the treatment of the perpetrators of child sexual abuse. Between 95 and 98 percent are reported to be males (Bolen, 2007; Preble and Groth, 2002), but some authors question whether there are more female perpetrators who are unrecognized. Between 50 and 70 percent of offenders were themselves victimized as children, either sexually, physically, or by other significant psychological stressors (Baker, 2002; Bolen, 2007; Coxe and Holmes, 2001; Flora, 2001; Karson, 2001; Leberg, 1997; Ryan, 1997; Stevens, 2001; Weeks and Windom, 1998). Rich (2006) postulates that poor attachment is a root contributor to sexual offending in adults. These individuals may be married or unmarried, employed or unemployed, or at any educational level (Baker, 2002; Beech, Browne, and Craig, 2009; Flora, 2001; McLaughlin, 1999).

Clinically, sexual offenders have some similarities. Most theorists agree that a sexual interest in children is just one of several or even many paraphilias (sexual deviations). Most have an interest in and many collect pornography and use it to construct a rich sexual fantasy life (Baker, 2002; Beech, Browne et al., 2009; Flora, 2001; Stevens, 2001). Those who work with offenders describe them as manipulative individuals with low self-esteem and poor social skills who feel that they lack power and strive to achieve it. Unable to achieve intimacy with others, partially due to their inability to feel empathy, sexual abusers use denial, rationalizing in an attempt to deny responsibility for their behavior. In addition, they often project the blame onto their victims (Baker, 2002; Beech, Browne et al., 2009; Bolen, 2007; Flora, 2001; Karson, 2001; Leberg, 1997; Rich, 2006; Ryan, 1997; Stevens, 2001). This inability to recognize their own dysfunctional behavior also prevents them from seeking help voluntarily (Flora, 2001).

Over the last two decades, there has been an increasing amount of research that attempts to explain the characteristics of those who offend against children, resulting in the emergence of a variety of theories too diverse to summarize here. Suffice it to say that the general consensus is that sexually offending, especially against children, is a complex interplay of a variety of biological, social, behavioral, cognitive, and emotional factors. In addition, the behavior exhibited by offenders further involves interplay between the individual and his or her environment (Ward et al., 2006). But since it is important that we begin to understand the dynamics of sexual offending, several theories will be outlined.

Perhaps one of the earliest and most widely accepted typologies was based on the work of A. Nicholas Groth, a psychologist who studies offenders within the prison system. Groth's early work divided the male offenders with whom he worked into two distinct categories: fixated and regressed. The *fixated offender* was one whose primary orientation was to children, predominantly male children. His compulsive, premeditated abuse was based on his need to repeat or undo his own past victimization. Emotionally, he was considered to be fixated in adolescence, and his maladaptive resolution of life issues created an individual who was not stressed or guilty about his behavior. He expressed little heterosexual interest in agemates, unless the women had children of an age that interested him (Preble and Groth, 2002).

The *regressed offender* was one who had achieved a tenuous level of adult adjustment but who was motivated by conflicts and crises to regress to an interest in children, prominently female, whom he then saw as "little women." The abuse was impulsive and episodic, precipitated by stress. This offender was often looking for the "all-loving mother." He might co-exist with an adult female while still abusing children. Alcohol often played a part in the equation (Preble and Groth, 2002).

Despite the extensive reliance on this theory for some years, clinicians found that all offenders did not fit neatly into these categories. In addition, Groth's work had been done only with males who were incarcerated. Along with this theory were those theories that suggested that sexual abuse could be seen as an addiction (see Carnes, 2001). Although there are some addictive qualities, most theorists believe that child sexual abuse cannot be adequately described by addiction theory.

As a result, other theories emerged based on a variety of research. Ward et al. (2006) suggest that the existing theories can be divided into three categories: those that are based on multiple factors, those that highlight single factors, and those that describe the offense as a process (pp. 12–13). These authors also contend that in order for an offense to occur, one must take into account the vulnerability factors based on the offender's developmental experiences as well as his or her genetic inheritance (e.g., anxious temperament), which go to make up his or her traits as well as how these vulnerability factors interact with triggering events or processes to result in sexual offending.

Multifactor Theories

Perhaps one of the most widely used multifactor theories is still Finkelhor's *Precondition Model*. Finkelhor (1984a) (see Table 6.2) states there are four preconditions for sexual abuse to take place.

The first is that the perpetrator must be motivated to abuse. *Motivation* is based on three factors: emotional congruence, sexual arousal, and blockage of normal outlets. *Emotional congruence* is the need of the perpetrator for the child to satisfy some emotional

Table 6.2   Preconditions for Sexual Abuse

Level of Explanation

	Individual	Social/Cultural
Precondition I: Factors Related to Motivation to Sexually Abuse	*Emotional congruence* Arrested emotional development Need to feel powerful and controlling Re-enactment of childhood trauma to undo the hurt Narcissistic identification with self as a young child	Masculine requirement to be dominant and powerful in sexual relationships
	Sexual arousal Childhood sexual experience that was traumatic or strongly conditioning Modeling of sexual interest in children by someone else Misattribution of arousal cues Biological abnormality	Child pornography Erotic portrayal of children in advertising Male tendency to sexualize all emotional needs
	Blockage Oedipal conflict Castration anxiety Fear of adult females Traumatic sexual experience with adult Inadequate social skills Marital problems	Repressive norms about masturbation and extramarital sex
Precondition II: Factors Predisposing to Overcoming Internal Inhibitors	Alcohol Psychosis Impulse disorder Senility Failure of incest inhibition mechanism in family dynamics	Social toleration of sexual interest in children Weak criminal sanctions against offenders Ideology of patriarchal prerogatives for fathers Social toleration for deviance committed while intoxicated Child pornography Male inability to identify with needs of children
Precondition III: Factors Predisposing to Overcoming External Inhibitors	Mother who is absent or ill Mother who is not close to or protective of child	Lack of social supports for mother Barriers to women's equality

(continued)

Table 6.2	**Preconditions for Sexual Abuse** *(continued)*	

Level of Explanation		
	Individual	**Social/Cultural**
	Mother who is dominated or abused by father Social isolation of family Unusual opportunities to be alone with child Lack of supervision of child Unusual sleeping or rooming conditions	Erosion of social networks Ideology of family sanctity
Precondition IV: *Factors Predisposing to Overcoming Child's Resistance*	Child who is emotionally insecure or deprived Child who lacks knowledge about sexual abuse Situation of unusual trust between child and offender Coercion	Unavailability of sex education for children Social powerlessness of children

Source: Reprinted with the permission of The Free Press, a Division of Simon & Schuster, Inc., from *Child Sexual Abuse: Theory and Research* by David Finkelhor. Copyright © 1984 by David Finkelhor. All rights reserved.

need. His choice of a child is a result of his need to feel powerful and in control because of his arrested emotional development or his reenactment of his own childhood trauma. Society contributes to this need by its emphasis on male dominance in sexual relationships. A child is a person over whom dominance is assured.

The perpetrator must then be *sexually aroused by the child.* Again, a sexual trauma in his own childhood or his modeling of another's interest in the child can create such arousal. Some perpetrators misinterpret children's need for affection and attention and assume they are being sexually seductive. Child pornography, as well as the male tendency to sexualize emotions, may contribute to the perpetrator's sexual interests.

Further, the perpetrator's motivation to abuse is a result of a *blockage of normal outlets* for his sexual and affectional needs. A fear of adult females—based perhaps on an unresolved Oedipal conflict, castration anxiety, or early trauma, complicated by inadequate social skills—can create such a blockage. Marital problems and society's norms, which censure masturbation and extramarital sex, can also create an atmosphere of frustration for the potential perpetrator.

The second precondition to child sexual abuse is based on *the perpetrator's lack of internal inhibitors.* Alcohol, psychosis, senility, and an impulse disorder can all prevent his "inner voice" from prohibiting him from acting on the desire to abuse. He may not have received a clear message in his family of origin that sexual activities with children are prohibited. Society's weak sanction against offenders, support of patriarchal prerogatives, and toleration for acts committed under intoxication give a confused and easily rationalized message to the perpetrator.

The third precondition describes the *external inhibitors* that the perpetrator must overcome for the abuse to take place. The role of the mother of the potential victim is an important factor. Mothers who are emotionally distant, ill, or absent or who fail to supervise present less of a deterrent to the perpetrator. The lack of privacy and unusual opportunities for the abuser to be alone with the child can also contribute to the abuse. Families who are socially isolated are also more vulnerable to sexual abuse.

In the fourth precondition, *the perpetrator must overcome the child's resistance* to the abuse. Children who have a poor self-concept and lack knowledge of abuse are more vulnerable. The closeness between child and perpetrator may also place a child in a position where the abuse can take place. Children learn early that they have no rights or power.

Powerlessness makes children extremely vulnerable; a group of sex offenders describe this vulnerability:

> *Six inmates in a maximum security prison agreed to speak with the small group of students, assembled as part of a community awareness program. All convicted child molesters, these men spoke openly of their backgrounds and motivations.*
>
> *"What kind of child do you look for?" asked one young coed.*
>
> *The handsome, slightly built young man scratched his beard thoughtfully and smiled.*
>
> *"I look for the kid who looks like he needs attention. The one who hangs back; he reminds me of me a few years ago, thinking I was garbage and figuring I wasn't good enough to ask for anything."*
>
> *Another inmate spoke up. "I used to be awed at the power I could have over my victims, like they had no idea what I was doing. I couldn't believe someone hadn't told them something about sex! But at that time, I'm sure I was glad no one had."*
>
> *"What do you think could have protected kids from you?" baited an involved student.*
>
> *"Someone should have told them about guys like me. A couple of kids I approached said, 'No,' and I just backed off. I didn't want no hassle, you know. If someone had told them about sex and sex abuse or even watched them better, I'd have been sunk."*

Many of the earlier theories concentrated on males as offenders. This may be partially due to the sparse research available on female offenders as well as the fact that more identified offenders appear to be males.

Another theory of note—again, focusing on males—is Marshall and Barbaree's *integrated theory*, which was developed to explain a variety of types of sexual offending and not just child sexual abuse. They begin with the premise that a critical task during adolescence for males is to learn to discriminate between their aggressive and sexual impulses. Unable to do this due to offense-related vulnerabilities based on early development combined with the right trigger, these males may sexually offend. According to these theorists, the factors that cause sexual offending are *developmental experiences*, *biological processes*, *cultural norms* and *attitudes about sexuality*, and the *psychological vulnerabilities* as a result of these causes (Marshall and Barbaree, 1990; Ward et al., 2006, p. 34).

The process of the development of an offender, although in reality quite complex, can be somewhat simplified as follows. An individual is the victim of inadequate child rearing and faulty bonding or attachment with primary caretakers. As a result, he does not learn to trust and feels worthless and unloved. In addition, the individual does not learn effective problem solving, good judgment, self-regulation, and how to appropriately and effectively live his or her everyday life. This becomes an individual with low self-esteem, impulsivity, and poor judgment who tries to compensate for those deficiencies at the expense of others. The personality is further stressed in adolescence when he learns to meet previously unmet psychological needs through sexuality. Sexuality provides not only tension release but also enhances self-esteem and makes the individual feel more personally effective. Pornography m ay feed into this to normalize a distorted view of sexual relations. Sexuality and aggression also become fused in his mind. Cognitive distortions begin to develop that excuse any deviance that the individual might otherwise notice from peers (Beech, Browne et al., 2009; Flora, 2001; Karson, 2001; Marshall and Barbaree, 1990; Stevens, 2001; van Dam, 2006; Ward et al., 2006). Marshall and Barbaree conclude that the "more vulnerable a person is to committing sexual offenses the less intense stressors need to be for an offense to occur" (Ward et al., 2006, p. 38).

Ward and Siegert's *pathways model* adds additional insight to sexual offending by attempting to weave together several theories, including Finkelhor's and Marshall and Barbaree's. The theory is organized into four sets of problems or psychological mechanisms exemplified by sexual abusers: (1) *difficultly with identifying and controlling emotional states*, (2) problems with *social isolation, loneliness, and dissatisfaction*, (3) *deviant sexual fantasies and arousal patterns*, and (4) *cognitive distortions* (Ward et al., 2006, p. 62). These individuals often suffer from attachment difficulties that make it hard for them to develop adequate social skills or achieve true intimacy. Even those who do develop some level of social skills mask their inability to attain healthy relationships, often through achieving positions of power (van Dam, 2006). For example, the mayor of one small city allowed a group to create a child safety policy while he continued, unknown to his constituents, to sexually abuse children. The inability to relate effectively with other adults can lead to loneliness and isolation.

The sexual scripts—or expectations about and behavior in sexual situations—have often become distorted in childhood (interpersonal distortions), or they may be adversely affected by the myriad cultural messages that become, in the offender's mind, woven into a sexual script. For example, the advertisements featured at one time that portrayed small girls in a seductive manner were interpreted by some sexual offenders as justification for behaving sexually toward young children. Cognitive distortions are part of the mechanism of sexual offending. In addition to seeing children as sexual beings, offenders may feel that they are not harming children by abusing them, that they have a right to have their needs met above the needs of others, that the world is a dangerous place and others will reject them because of their own self-interests, or that they have no control over their impulses to abuse children (Flora, 2001; Karson, 2001; Stevens, 2001; van Dam, 2006; Ward et al., 2006).

According to the pathways model, each of these four psychological mechanisms plays a part in an offender's life, but each offender will have a primary pathway through which he will offend. Consider this example:

> Harry was abused by his uncle when he was 7. After fondling him and gaining his confidence, the uncle began to sodomize the boy. At first, Harry was frightened and disgusted. But he felt that he had no choice to resist. The uncle began to take more care not to hurt him and showered him with gifts and attention. Harry's home was a chaotic and unhappy one, and his uncle's attention was important to him. The abuse stopped abruptly when the uncle was badly crippled in a car accident and, relegated to a wheelchair, was kept at home by a controlling wife.

As an adult, Harry found that the only stimulation that he enjoyed was anal. When he attempted to get a young female partner to stimulate him anally, she was repulsed and he concluded that women did not like that. Since he believed strongly that he was not homosexual, Harry eventually turned to a boy in the neighborhood whom he had befriended. Much like his uncle had with him, Harry initiated the child into sex.

Single-Factor Theories

Some theorists base their theories primarily on one characteristic exhibited by sexual offenders. Perhaps the most popular of these is *cognitive distortions*, a key building block of the multifactor theories. Cognitive refers to the manner in which information is processed. For offenders, as indicated earlier, information that might be totally nonsexual to the average person becomes sexualized due to the manner in which the offender interprets it. The offender develops a belief system that both motivates him to offend and excuses or rationalizes his behavior after the fact (Flora, 2001; Rich, 2006; Ward et al., 2006; Yates, 2003). Some typical cognitive distortions were previously mentioned.

Another set of theories about sexual offending are based on the knowledge that offenders *lack empathy for their victims*. In order to empathize, one must first recognize the feeling involved. Many offenders, due to their dysfunctional and unsatisfying childhoods, are so sealed off emotionally that they are unable to recognize feelings for others. They may be so needy that to imagine that someone else is also in need of affection or attention is impossible for them. Any attention that they might give to a child is almost totally self-motivated.

In addition to recognizing a feeling and accepting that others might have it, to be empathetic, one must both put himself or herself in the other's place and decide to respond to the other's need. (For more detail see Ward et al., 2006.) Offenders, so totally caught up in their own needs, can often do neither. This fact leads some researchers to point to intimacy deficiencies as causal.

Some theorists believe that child sexual abuse is based on the offenders' *deviant sexual interest* in children. As mentioned earlier, it is well documented that sexual offenders who abuse children usually possess other paraphilias. The etiology of such deviance is usually traced to childhood, causing critics of sexual deviancy theories to argue that one must look at how this deviance developed.

Clearly, one cannot attribute the motivation to sexually abuse children to one explanatory hook. Most researchers today favor either the multifactor explanation or the process models.

Process Models

Process models use various ways to explain not only why the offender targets his victims but also how he does so. Ward, Polaschek, and Beech (2006) suggest that "cognitive elements—such as decision making—but also behavioural [*sic*] volitional and affective factors" (p. 213).

One particularly popular tool among clinicians has been the use of the relapse prevention model (RPM). The *RPM*, initially developed as a treatment strategy for the management of other addictive behaviors such as alcoholism, characterizes sexual abuse as a cycle or process and allows the clinician and offender to strategize toward halting the process at a given point. Zak demonstrates an abusive cycle:

> Zak was raised in a home that was well known by the local police for reports of domestic violence. As a child, Zak spent a good deal of time at his grandfather's, who lived several houses from his. He got used to the sexual favors that slowly became part of their relationship. Anything was better than the hell at home. When Zak was 14, his grandfather was diagnosed with a brain tumor that took him quickly. By this time, his father had also left his mother, so things were a bit less chaotic at home. At 18, Zak married Lurlene, and between their jobs at a local factory, they were able to find an apartment of their own.
>
> Zak looked forward to starting his own family and was disappointed when the first year and then the second of their marriage passed with no indication that they would have one. He and Lurlene began to fight regularly, each blaming the other for their lack of success. When they had a fight, Zak would storm out, get in his car, and drive.
>
> He does not remember when he picked up the first young boy, but the pattern was soon set. He would find a boy, bribe him with money to masturbate or perform oral sex, and then let him off with the promised reward when it was over. After these events, Zak felt soothed and ready to face his troubled marriage again. But the effect was the opposite. Before long, Zak found himself instigating fights so that he would have an excuse to go off and perpetrate his abuse as a self-soothing gesture.

But one boy did not keep the abuse a secret, and Zak was arrested and incarcerated. During treatment, he was able to recognize that his fights with his wife led to high stress and his driving around seeking out boys to abuse. He was able to recognize these precursors as part of a pattern and eventually to develop strategies that would avoid evoking a relapse.

Another popular process model is the *cycle of offending* developed by Wolf (1985). This model derives from the addiction cycle, which demonstrates the self-perpetuating nature of the abuse. The offender's poor self-concept feeds his expectation of rejection, which leads to his withdrawal and isolation from appropriate peers. In this isolation, he creates fantasies—usually sexual—to self-sooth. His masturbation to these fantasies soon is not enough, and he begins to groom a victim to play them out with him. Once he abuses a child, he often feels guilt, which then feeds back into his worthlessness and poor self-esteem. And the cycle repeats itself until there is intervention (Flora, 2001; Ward et al., 2006; Wolf, 1985).

There are numerous other process models (see Ward et al., 2006). As mentioned earlier, most of these models have been used to describe male offenders.

WHICH PEOPLE BECOME PERPETRATORS?

Numerous authors have outlined the reasons why an individual male might perpetrate, but what is it about certain men that they will abuse a child while others will not? Why do some, who were themselves molested as children, molest other children while other survivors find other ways to make sense of this trauma?

Gilgun (1990) has suggested a four-factor risk model that offers an explanation to this question. In her research, Gilgun, looking at men who were abusive and those who were not, found that differences in four areas seemed to account for why some went on to abuse and others did not. In *confidant relationships*, Gilgun discovered that abusers had had no one to confide in growing up and felt isolated or excluded by others. The nonabusive males (known as the controls) had these intimate relationships. Abusers, in the area of *sexuality*, used sex to maintain equilibrium, masturbated prior to the age of 12, and had repetitive, coercive, sexual fantasies. Controls began to masturbate later in adolescence and used the practice to release sexual tension along with appropriate peer-related and noncoercive sexual fantasies (Gilgun, 2009).

The *families of origin* of the sex offenders tended to be filled with maltreatment and domestic violence. If these offenders had not been abused themselves, they may have witnessed the abuse of a sibling or parent. Nonabusive controls had much more stable family environments. Anechiarico (1999) suggests that experiencing attachment in the family of origin has a significant effect on the offender's self-esteem. When this important bond with early caretakers is not healthy, the individual does not develop adequate self-esteem, thus remaining vulnerable to feelings of shame. Recent research has significantly correlated the concept of shame with sexual deviance and abuse.

And finally, *peer relationships* for abusers growing up tended to be centered around antisocial activities. Masculinity was also equated with sexual conquest. Controls, on the other hand, were involved in more social behavior and equated masculinity with a respect for women. As Gilgun and others continue their research, we will hopefully learn more about why some men abuse and some do not.

Female Abusers

The models just discussed are based predominantly on males as perpetrators. There is some question as to why women are not reported as perpetrators and whether they are, in fact, not as likely to abuse. The issue of female abuse (see Table 6.3) can be examined from several perspectives: (1) women may be able to mask their behavior through normal nurturing activities, such as bathing and dressing the victim; (2) victims are less likely to report because of their dependency on females, especially their mothers; and (3) the targets are often boys who are the most reticent to report (Baker, 2002; Beech, Parrett, Ward, and Fisher, 2009; Flora, 2001; Flora et al., 2008; Kasl, 1990; Salter, 2003; Seto, 2008).

Perhaps women are not as likely to abuse based on their socialization; women are socialized to prefer older, larger, more powerful sexual partners who initiate the relationship. Children do not fit this picture. Women are socialized to be more maternal, caring for needs of children and identifying with the pain they feel when harmed. Women are less likely to

Table 6.3   Why Women Are Less Likely to Abuse

1. Women are trained to be nurturers; they learn the "total child."
2. Traditionally, the child is always neat and clean and smells good when turned over to Dad.
3. Because of nurturing, a mother is more likely to have empathy for the child.
4. Men are trained for smaller, weaker partners.
5. Women are trained for bigger, stronger partners.
6. Men are trained to equate affection with sex.

perpetrate harm (Finkelhor, 1984a). Our culture teaches women that they are subject to domination and that they must sublimate their needs for sexual stimulation (Herman and Hirschman, 2000; Mathews, Mathews, and Speltz, 1990; Rush, 1992; Ford, 2006). And finally, Finkelhor (1984a) suggests that the basic differences between men and women account for the higher percentage of male perpetrators. (Men are more easily aroused by sexual stimuli such as pornography, and men appear to sexualize their emotions more than women.)

Characterizing Female Abusers

The fact remains that women do abuse children, though in comparison to their male counterparts, the research on female offenders is much less prevalent. Until recently, the information and classifications about such sexual abusers was gleaned primarily from three studies done by McCarthy, who studied the case records of 26 female offenders from an incest treatment center (published in 1986); Faller, who looked at 40 female offenders from an outpatient treatment facility (published in 1987); and Mathews, Mathews, and Speltz, who took their sample of 16 women from Genesis II, a female offender program (published in 1990) (see Davin, 1999; Faller, 2003).

These researchers all independently concluded that women who abused children fell into two general categories, with subgroupings within each. The first of these described a woman who is an *independent abuser*. Mathews et al. (1990) differentiated between the teacher/lover and the predisposed offender with a long intergenerational history of abuse. The second category suggested that many women abused children as *co-offenders or accomplices with a man* (Davin, 1999).

From this research, as well as more recent studies, a picture emerges of women who abuse children. Both independent abusers and coabusers have suffered significant psychological and physical abuse in their childhoods, a significant number at the hands of mothers. The majority have been sexually abused usually by uncles or brothers. Independent abusers tend to have emerged from this as more emotionally damaged, naive, and regressed (Mathews et al., 1990; Ogilvie, 2004; Rosencrans, 1997). Although agreeing that there was still some psychological impairment, Davin (1999) found that the coabusers appeared more normal (like nonabusers) in personality testing. Early research pointed to substance abuse as a factor in the abuse scenario, but later studies have not consistently concurred.

Multiple researchers have indicated that women are somewhat more likely to abuse girls than boys (Beech, Parrett et al., 2009; Davin, 1999; Flora et al., 2008; Ogilvie, 2004; Rosencrans, 1997; Seto, 2008) a fact that differs somewhat from earlier beliefs (see Finkelhor, 1984a). Coabusers are statistically more involved with their own children, whereas independent abusers offend with acquaintances. For those who abuse along with men (coabusers), fear is the engagement strategy used with the children; independent abusers, on the other hand, invite their victims to play games that become sexual (Davin, 1999).

Whether abuse is perpetrated by a male or female, it is nonetheless traumatic for the victim.

Juvenile Sexual Offenders

One population that, until recently, had been inadequately studied is the juvenile offender. Children and adolescents are not as likely to be reported as offenders, due to their ages and the perception of society that children are not sexual beings and teens are just working out their teen issues. As a result, most parents and many mental health professionals do not take sexual acting out by youth seriously enough, even though the impact on the victim may be significant. Yet early intervention for the young offender is essential. Studies of adult offenders point to the fact that many began their abuse in their teen years or as children (Barbaree and Marshall, 2008; Erooga and Masson, 2003; Flora, 2001).

What characterizes a juvenile who would sexually abuse younger children? Not all children and teens who act out sexually are to be considered juvenile offenders. Some are acting on curiosity that has been fanned by a sexualized society. Others exhibit reactive disorders, as they strive to understand their own histories of sexual abuse by acting it out on others. Children as young as 3 years have been reported to be sexually aggressive toward other children in their attempts to gain power over their own trauma and victimization (Araji, 1997; Erooga and Masson, 2003; Gil and Johnson, 1993; Rich, 2009).

Some children who have been sexually traumatized develop pervasive, deviant sexual patterns that may become compulsive. These children often engage other past victims in mutual sexual activities. The final category of acting out youth exhibit more anger and other deviant behavior. They target victims who are vulnerable and bribe, coerce, or force them into submission (Araji, 1997; Gil and Johnson, 1993). These are the juvenile offenders.

Rich (2003, 2009) describes an average juvenile offender as being around 14 years old, of low to average intelligence, and preferring girls as his victims. At the same time, this author cautions that one must also recognize that youthful offenders as a group range in age, interests, social skills, and behaviors. Rich and other researchers have identified several factors that appear to be common threads tying together those youths who offend sexually.

A *history of victimization*, both sexual and physical, often leads to juveniles who offend against others. Or these youths may *have witnessed family dysfunction*, such as domestic violence. Most exhibit *attachment difficulties*, a factor that current theorists feel should not be underestimated. *Mental health issues* are also apparent among juvenile offenders. About 80 percent of juvenile offenders have psychological disorders that are diagnosed in the *Diagnostic and Statistical Manual of Mental Disorders* (*DSM-IV-TR*; American Psychiatric Association [APA], 2000); conduct disorder and oppositional defiant disorder are the most frequent diagnoses (Rich, 2003, 2009; Ryan, 1997).

Socially, juvenile offenders demonstrate underdeveloped social skills, which often impede their ability to forge healthy peer relationships. The lack of these social skills, along with attachment difficulties, not only hampers relations with others but also impedes their ability to function effectively in many areas of living. In addition, they often demonstrate regressed moral development and, like their adult counterparts, a lack of empathy for their victims (Baker, 2002; Flora, 2001; Rich, 2003, 2009; Ryan, 1997).

Fanning the flames of problematic development among these young offenders are myriad sociocultural environmental factors. Children who have been introduced to sex inappropriately through poor boundaries or abuse are barraged with a quantity of sexualized material. The media play a significant role in exposing youth to a variety of sexual messages that not only stimulate them but also desensitize them to inappropriately use this information. Sexual roles and relationships are viewed through the media as distorted and often equated with violence. The Internet and video games add to this equation, creating an overwhelming consistency of sexualized messages that compound some youths' already distorted view of sexual appropriateness and add to the creation of significant cognitive distortion through which they abuse and/or justify their behavior (Rich, 2003, 2009; Ryan, 1997). For example, in a sample of sexually abusing girls, Kubick and Hecker (2005) found that these young female offenders were more likely to agree with statements reflecting the belief that the offender in a sexually aggressive vignette was not responsible for initiating the inappropriate sexual contact depicted (p. 62).

Sexual offending, even by juveniles, is multidimensional. Not all young offenders act out sexually with the same motivation. Rich (2003) divides motivators into four specific categories. Some offenders see *the sexual offending itself as the primary goal*. They coerce or force their victims to accomplish this goal. Another group sees the *aggression and violence as a primary motivator* and the sexual behavior as secondary. For others, the sexual contact falls more under *experimentation* or *exploration* that goes beyond the intended goal. And finally, some youthful offenders are *mentally ill or exhibit cognitive impairment* that renders them unable to make appropriate decisions about their sexual behavior (p. 87).

Whatever the motivation for a juvenile to offend, there is increasing recognition of the importance of early intervention with children and teens who act out sexually.

SUMMARY

The study and understanding of child sexual abuse have been promoted largely by two movements—the child protection movement and the feminist movement. The first sees abuse as part of total family dysfunction, or a failure of the family to protect, while the second holds that society victimizes its weaker members. Most authors agree that sexual abuse—whether through molestation within or outside the family, pornography, or prostitution—takes place for the gratification of the adult. Sexual abuse progresses over time, usually in five specific phases.

In the last few years, experts have seen an increasing number of sexual abuse cases, despite society's hesitancy to recognize its existence. Girls are more likely to report their victimization, although it is beginning to be known that more boys are abused than is reported. The degree of trauma a child experiences is based on a variety of factors, such as the identity of the perpetrator, the extent and duration of the abuse, and the point of and reactions to disclosure.

One of the earliest and most widely used typologies of offenders was Groth's fixated and regressed categories. The fixated abuser appears developmentally fixated in his interest in children, while the regressed abuser turns to children in response to the stresses and conflicts in his relationships with adults. In the last few decades, numerous other typologies have emerged. These can be divided into multifactor theories, single-factor theories, and process theories.

In one popular multifactor theory, Finkelhor describes four preconditions to sexual abuse: motivation on the part of the perpetrator, lack of internal inhibitors, weak external inhibitors, and overcoming the child's resistance. Two other popular multifactor theories are the integrated model and the pathways model. The single factors most commonly identified are cognitive distortions, inability to feel empathy for the victim, and deviant sexual interests. Two types of popular process models are relapse prevention and cyclical theories.

An increasing amount of information is available on female offenders, including some postulations about their characteristics. Although not as numerous as male perpetrators, they are nonetheless of concern. And finally, more is being learned about juvenile perpetrators. Although not all sexually acting out youths can be seen as chronic offenders, it is important that the cycle of abuse be interrupted early.

Chapter 7

Intrafamilial Abuse

I ntrafamilial abuse, commonly known as incest has long been an issue in our culture. It is not always possible, however, to define inappropriate sexual behavior between adults and children within families. Sexual intercourse and even overt handling of the genitalia are inappropriate in most cultures. Family nudity, however, is more controversial.

Perhaps the difficulty lies in the fact that child rearing involves aspects of sexuality. In many cultures, children are nurtured by their parents with hugs, kisses, and physical closeness. Nursing, some say, promotes sexual feelings. It is disturbing to realize that these well-intended and emotionally necessary components of child rearing can be seen as sexual by some, when, in fact, kept at the appropriate level, they are beneficial to the child and the parent. It is the abuse of these normal activities that differentiates the incestuous from the nonincestuous family.

Healthy families attend to raising children without seducing or overstimulating them, giving them affection while maintaining appropriate sexual boundaries. Privacy is a family right, and children are given explanations about sexual information in a nonstimulating and age-appropriate manner. Incestuous families involve children sexually for the gratification of the adults. Children are often introduced to adult sexuality disguised as parental affection and attention.

INTRAFAMILIAL ABUSE AS A PROBLEM TODAY

Prior to the late 1970s, intrafamilial abuse was referred to as *incest*—a word in our vocabulary, but one that was little used. As feminists brought the study of rape to the forefront, incestuous abuse seemed to be riding on its coat tails. Still, it rarely entered the public's consciousness as a national problem in and of itself (Jenkins, 1998).

Today, incest figures prominently in the media, although the term *incest* has given way to references to *abuse within the family* or *intrafamilial abuse*. Each year, a large number of familial abuse cases come to the attention of protective services. Researchers like Diana Russell (1999), who studied 930 California women, and David Finkelhor (1979), who surveyed 796 college students in New England, have proven that incest has gone unreported by victims for years. This realization brings so many questions to mind.

Contributing significantly to the early understanding of the dynamics of incest was the work of Roland Summit, a psychiatrist who had provided expert testimony in numerous sexual abuse cases. Summarizing his research as part of his testimonies, Summit suggested how children survive sexual abuse within the family system through the *Child Sexual Abuse Accommodation Syndrome*. According to this theory, (1) *secrecy* allows the abuse to continue and (2) causes a sense of *helplessness* for the child in his or her adult relationships. Thus, the child (3) begins to feel trapped (*entrapment*) and learns to live with the abuse (*accommodation*). Sometimes, (4) there are delayed, conflicted, and unconvincing disclosures that are often overlooked or misinterpreted by the nonabusing adults in the child's life. Finally, when the child does disclose, guilt, fear, or the reactions of those who are told may cause (5) him or her to retract (*retraction*) the report of sexual abuse (Conte, 2002; Olafson, 2002; Whetsell-Mitchell, 1995). This five-point theory became a helpful tool in the study and treatment of child sexual abuse.

What causes familial abuse? Why are some victims more traumatized than others? Why are some children chosen as victims while others are not? Not all of these questions can be definitively answered, but asking them has stimulated much important research over the years. Although much of the significant research was done in the 1980s and 1990s, it still appears applicable to today's understanding of incest.

SOCIETAL CONTRIBUTIONS TO INCEST

In most people's minds, the taboo against incest is still sacred. Why then, is it so often broken?

Part of the answer lies in society's preoccupation with sexuality. Attractive young bodies sell jeans, and sexy women drape themselves over cars and mattresses to provide more appealing advertisements. Many people feel we have sexualized our young female children for years suggesting that as young children, girls are taught to be cute, to be sexy, and to seek attention. This becomes a liability for incest victims who come to believe that they have somehow invited the abuse by their behaviors (Butler, 1996). Thus, society not only-teaches female children that sexuality is useful but plants the seeds for girls to feel they are to blame for whatever comes of acting sexual.

Society itself has fewer rules about sexual behavior. At one time, people could count on more clearly stated mores. Now with changing sexual values, confusion is rampant. Amidst this confusion about the rules, the perpetrators more easily justify their behavior or are themselves even unsure of appropriate limits.

Along with a shift in rules and an increased preoccupation with sexuality has come a greater emphasis on sexual performance. Magazine articles discuss improving sexual relationships, and numerous paperback books offer ways to enhance one's sexual prowess. For the average individual, this emphasis on sexual performance may create casual interest, but for a man already concerned about his own incompetence and powerlessness, the effect can be damaging. To compensate, he looks for a partner who is adoring and who will not measure his sexual competence. Often, that person is his daughter.

The stresses and constant changes in society provide another clue to why abuse within the family occurs. High technology also places emphasis on performance. Businesses grow quickly, and employees must frequently move. Immigrants still flock to our shores in search of better economic conditions. Families are often transferred from one location to another or immigrate from other cultures and are left with few roots and insufficient support systems. Some families adjust easily, making new friends and building new alliances. Other families are not so quick to respond, and their sense of isolation intensifies. The stresses of everyday life augment the feelings of failure these individuals already carry with them. The members find comfort within their own family structure—sometimes turning to children to meet their needs.

It should also be noted that culture plays a part in whether children are abused within the family. Some cultures believe that a female child must be protected, keeping her pure for her future marriage; this may well affect the status of the entire family. In such families, father–daughter incest is almost nonexistent. Boys may not be as lucky, however. Yet other cultures, in which masculinity is equated with strength and power, may see victimization of male children as unthinkable.

The characters in this drama are varied. The most widely discussed type of incest is perpetrated by fathers against their daughters. But mothers, siblings, uncles, grandfathers, and cousins are also abusers. The victims may be sons, daughters, or other siblings, and the degree of trauma each experiences depends on numerous variables. Since little has been written on the dynamics of incest in the last few years, we are dependent on previously postulated theories.

FATHER–DAUGHTER INCEST

Families in which a father abuses his daughter are characterized by family dysfunction and pathology. The family as a system gives up its dedication to the growth of each of its members and instead holds sacred the family secret—the abuse. So exhausting is the guarding of the secret that the family has little time or energy for other pursuits.

It is not surprising that children's needs go unmet. Instead, the perpetrator rationalizes that sexual attention is what the child desires. The family presents a picture of an isolated, enmeshed system, balancing precariously in what they perceive as a hostile environment. The role and characteristics of each family have been studied and restudied in an attempt to understand and intervene.

Family Patterns

Although there is generalization in the literature about family patterns in father–daughter incest, the dynamics of this type of abuse can be more easily studied through the classic typology of Stern and Meyer (1980). They suggest three interactional patterns among incestuous families: the possessive–passive, the dependent–domineering, and the dependent–dependent.

Possessive–Passive

The possessive–passive pattern is often referred to in feminist literature as the *patriarchal family*. Herman and Hirschman (2000) describe the fathers as "perfect patriarchs":

> Their authority with the family was absolute, often asserted by force. They were also the arbiters of the family's social life and frequently succeeded in virtually secluding the women in the family. But while they were often feared within their families, they impressed outsiders as sympathetic, even admirable men. (p. 71)

This father relies on intimidation and uses physical force to maintain submission of family members.

In the possessive–passive family, the father sees his wife and children as possessions. The mother tends to be passive, insecure, and often withdrawn. She acquiesces to her husband's domination and is often unable to protect her daughter, because she learned through her own childhood that this is the way men behave. Since the daughter has also learned to see her father as undisputed head of the family, she is vulnerable. The father turns to his daughter for sex for a variety of reasons but largely as an abuse of power (Deblinger, Hathaway, Lippman, and Steer, 1993; Faller, 1990).

Dependent–Domineering

This pattern is characterized by a strong, domineering woman and a weak, inadequate man. The father looks to his wife for support and nurturing, and she treats him as she does their children. The father often allies himself with his children much as he would with his siblings, so that many children of these liaisons describe their fathers as sharing and loving and their mothers as cold and rejecting. This father may be prone to outbursts of anger and spend much of his energies compelling others to meet his needs.

Eventually, the mother feels that her own needs are not being met and withdraws from the husband and the children. Since she is more outgoing than a dependent wife and has developed better social skills, she often seeks gratification outside her home through a job, activities, or education. The more the mother is absent, the more the daughter is required to perform housekeeping tasks, and the father then turns to her for his emotional and sexual needs (Stern and Meyer, 1980).

Dependent–Dependent

The third pattern is that of a dependent–dependent relationship between spouses. Two needy, dependent individuals come together, each with the anticipation that his or her needs will be magically met by the spouse. Both the mother and father experienced abuse or deprivation in their childhoods. The women have frequently been abused, while the men, if not themselves were abused, have observed maltreatment in their families of origin. As they escape from the deprivations of childhood, they unconsciously seek out individuals with similar backgrounds, not recognizing that other needy individuals cannot meet their needs (Hanson, Lipovsky, and Saunders, 1994). The couple clings to each other in desperation, but since they are of no emotional support to each other, they turn to their children for nurturance.

Often, the oldest daughter assumes the role of surrogate mother and sees her task as keeping the family together. As she continues in her role, the father sees her as a rival to his wife, and because his daughter appears to be more nurturing, he turns to her for comfort. The daughter in such a family is endowed with a great deal of power and status. Her siblings are liable to resent her for the position she holds. In turn, the victim represses anger toward her mother for not protecting her. The abusive behavior in each type of family serves some purpose for the equilibrium of the system.

Profiles of the Family

Families can also be characterized by how they handle conflict.

In *conflict-avoiding families*, the mother sets the emotional tone. Sexual and emotional problems are not discussed. In an effort to avoid problems, the mother tends to distance herself. Thus, the daughter emerges as nurturer and mother figure. The father and mother covertly agree with the arrangement, rather than bringing up the role-reversal problem for discussion or confrontation. The daughter, in turn, recognizes that she cannot go to her mother for help and has, in fact, been abandoned despite her mother's outward appearance of competence.

Conflict-regulating families sacrifice the daughter to regulate conflict and avoid family breakdown. In these families, the mother gives little or no support to her children. The daughter feels rejected by her mother and resentful of her lack of protection. There may be overt conflict in the family, and although there are more discussion and awareness of the problems, the family allows the daughter's abuse and does not seek help.

It is not surprising that children who are unnurtured and who are forced into pseudomaturity feel robbed of their childhoods. Emotionally deprived, they spend their adulthoods searching for someone who will meet their needs. When two people with these problems marry, the cycle of abuse may begin again.

Some theorists argue that relegating incestuous families to patterns is either passé (Jenkins, 1998) or does injustice to the family members (Strand, 2000). From the numerous studies on incest, profiles of the participants have been developed. Although they do not perfectly describe every family, they can be used to draw a mental picture.

The Father

Incestuous fathers share common characteristics—a deep-seated feeling of helplessness, a sense of vulnerability, and dependency. They are unprepared for adulthood, marriage, or fatherhood. Newly immigrated fathers are also unprepared for what *our* culture expects of them; failure in these roles only serves to intensify their feelings of inadequacy (Fontes, 2008; Fontes and Plummer, 2012; Hanson et al., 1994). The picture they present in their fervent attempts to control the demands of their life may differ, however.

The type of father most commonly described in the literature is one who overcompensates for his feelings of powerlessness by adopting an extremely rigid, controlling, authoritarian position as the undisputed head of his household (Baker, 2002; Bolen, 2007; Flora, 2001). He is described as the primary participant in the possessive–passive family pattern. He has frequently learned his behavior from his own father, since a large number of abusive fathers were parented by overbearing and often physically abusive fathers themselves.

Sometimes, tyrannical behavior is a father's exaggerated response to feeling that he has lost his importance within the family. Consider the Lee family:

The Lees were comfortably situated in their native Korea. Dr. Lee was on the staff at a large hospital. When the political situation necessitated that they leave the country, the Lees came to live with cousins in the United States. Dr. Lee soon discovered that his medical license was not readily recognized in this country. His wife, however, was offered secure employment as a companion housekeeper for an elderly woman. Dr. Lee was very much against his wife's working, especially in the role of domestic help. He argued that they had had servants in Korea, and his wife would not be one here. It went against family honor. But seeing no other way to support themselves, Mrs. Lee acted for the first time against her husband's wishes and took the job.

As Mrs. Lee became more involved outside the home, her husband grew more and more depressed at home. For the first time, he was forced into the role of caregiver of his two daughters, aged 5 and 9. The more out of control he felt, the more tyrannical he became. He was convinced that although his wife had "left him," his daughters were his to do with as he would. Eventually, he began to see his oldest daughter as a nurturing—and finally sexual—substitute for his wife.

Power and control are bywords in this type of abuser's orientation to the world. Some of these fathers have not had the success that Dr. Lee had once had. Many of them fit the profile of the man who, throughout his life, has felt out of control because of a father who dominated and used his power and a mother who was cold, unloving, and failed to protect. This abuser may also have witnessed the sexual abuse of his own siblings. In short, this individual never learned to share with a mate, to nurture, or to parent. His insecurity in his own masculinity convinced him that he must rule his family in every way. This father may also physically abuse his children (Bancroft and Sullivan, 2002).

Studies show that this father is alienated from his wife. In many cases, she is an individual as needy as he, who was scarred by her own childhood trauma and turned to him for nurturance and comfort. His unreasonable demands on her intensify her own sense of inadequacy, and she withdraws emotionally—unable to meet his needs and unable to nurture her children.

The second orientation is markedly different from "the tyrant." This type of man appears in the dependent–domineering and dependent–dependent family patterns. He does not project his insecurity through aggressive or violent behavior but instead withdraws from adult responsibilities and maintains a passive–dependent role, often seeming like a child himself (Bolen, 2007; Flora, 2001; Karson, 2001). Although some theorists suggest that this insecurity permeates his lifestyle, Herman and Hirschman (2000) argue that this father has the ability to assess situations and determine who has the power. In the face of other authority figures (such as police, prosecutor, therapist, or researcher), he presents himself as passive, helpless, and dependent.

Reports of daughters seem to substantiate that their mothers are in the dominant role and the perpetrators are more like siblings. Other survivors describe families in which both mother and father characteristically assume the role of nurtured children. Consider the following case of Art:

Art was raised by his mother and two aunts. He vaguely remembers his father but believes he left when Art was quite young. One of the aunts was divorced and the other had never married. Art's mother was extremely overprotective, not wanting him to go out with friends or participate in school activities. She did everything for him, allowing him to do little for himself. Art remembers that his mother chose his clothes and bought all his toiletries until he left home. She also bathed him until his teen years, seemingly with little resistance on Art's part.

When Art was 18, he joined the army with his mother's blessing, surprisingly. One of his aunts had recently died, and he thinks his mother was having difficulty coping. "I think she thought I'd be taken care of," he commented. Army life was extremely difficult for him; he had been surrounded by women, and being thrust into an all-male society created problems. He was teased about his indecisiveness, his lack of assertiveness, and his meticulous mannerisms.

After a year, Art was hospitalized after confessing suicidal feelings and demonstrating a severe inability to cope with everyday tasks. He received a medical discharge and went home to live. His mother suggested he enter the seminary, but remembering his past experiences living with males, he refused. Instead, Art got a job in a shoe store. Shortly thereafter, his mother developed cancer; her health rapidly deteriorated and she died. While his mother was ill, Art's aunt constantly berated him about "how thoughtless he was about his poor mother, who had done so much for him." He was confused and hurt by these admonishments, convinced that his presence was all his mother needed.

After his mother's death, Art was at a loss. He lived with his aunt for a short time but found this intolerable and moved to his own apartment. He continued at the shoe store, which was owned by a family who pampered and fussed over him. Art found living on his own difficult. He knew little about cooking or housekeeping, so when Sally, the young woman in the next apartment, started inviting him over for dinner, he was overjoyed. He praised her cooking and commented favorably on her every action. After a brief courtship, they were married. Art was sure he would be taken care of; Sally was convinced she had found someone to adore her as her parents never had.

The marriage was far from idyllic. Art demanded that their lives revolve around him. If Sally did not cater to him, he would develop an ailment to gain her pity and elicit her attention. The birth of twin girls further taxed Sally's coping abilities, and she invited her sister to live with them and help her. Once again, Art heard how lazy and ungrateful he was—this time from Sally's concerned sister. Her criticism drove him further into his own world emotionally. His relationship with Sally deteriorated, and they ceased sexual relations.

Art turned instead to the twins, especially Gabrielle—the younger of his daughters who had always been smaller and more timid. "She reminded me of myself," he commented. When the twins were 7, Sally's sister left to marry her long-time boyfriend. Sally found herself once more in the mothering role—mothering Art as well as their children. Art intensified his demands on her time and energies, but Sally had adopted her sister's habit of berating him.

Through the crisis of the family's attempt to rebalance, Sally became particularly involved in the church. She attended church meetings regularly and left Art to care for the girls. Gretchen, more assertive than her sister, would frequently antagonize her father, at which point he would send her to bed. This left Art and Gabrielle watching TV together and gave him the opportunity for sexual abuse.

Despite Art's more passive behavior, he, too, ruled his family by insisting that they meet his needs.

In describing incestuous fathers, experts note particular characteristics: These fathers tend to demonstrate poor impulse control, low frustration tolerance, and the need for immediate gratification. They often regress, exhibiting sexual or emotional immaturity and frustrated dependency needs. Such men have low ego-strength and self-esteem, often to the point of identity confusion. They may be passive–aggressive in their demonstration of anger, denying, rationalizing, and projecting blame for their actions. In their feelings of powerlessness and faulty superego operation, they seek to manipulate both the victim and other family members. In general, their interpersonal relations are poor (Baker, 2002; Brown, Cohen, Johnson, and Salzinger, 1998; Courtois, 2010; Flora, 2001; Karson, 2001; Kinnear, 2007).

We have considered characteristics of the perpetrators, but what motivates them to abuse children? Most authorities agree that this abuser is motivated by emotional rather than sexual needs. This man finds that adult relationships are too taxing on his already low self-esteem. He therefore misuses his power as an adult in an attempt to bolster his own ego. Groth (1982) suggests that incestuous behavior serves a number of motivations simultaneously for the father. It may serve to validate his sense of worth and bolster his self-esteem, as he tries fervently to compensate for the perceived rejection of him by his wife and other women. It often gives him an illusion of power and control and gratifies his need for attention, affiliation, and recognition. In short, it strengthens his sense of identity (p. 228).

Incestuous fathers present strangely different pictures. Some inspire empathy; others disgust. Regardless of an abuser's manner of presentation, and despite the family dynamics surrounding his abusive behavior, this individual is still responsible for his actions and cannot be exonerated. Much blame has also been placed on the mother in abusive situations.

The Mother

Many theorists contend that the mother is unjustly blamed for causing the incestuous relationship and for not intervening (Bolen, 2007; Herman and Hirschman, 2000; Strand, 2000). Some victims harbor as much, if not more, resentment toward their mothers for what they perceive as that parent's failure to protect them (Ricker, 2006). Jenkins (1998) suggests that the role of mothers has altered in the public and professional consciousness over the years.

Sgroi (1982), one of the earlier theorists to look at the role of the mother, contended that these women fell into one of two categories, dominant or dependent (see Table 7.1).

Table 7.1   Wives in Incestuous Families

Dominant Wives	Dependent Wives
More social skills	Few social skills
Self-assertive	Passive
Capable but unwilling to make it on their own	Highly dependent on husbands; fear outside world
Consciously turn away from spousal relationship	Remain dependent but may withdraw unconsciously
Feel in control and like mother to both father and children, often resentfully	Feel more like a child than a wife
Husbands describe them as "cold" and "unforgiving"	Husbands describe them as "dumb" or "silly"

Source: Adapted with the permission of The Free Press, Division of Simon & Schuster, Inc., from *Handbook of Clinical Intervention in Child Sexual Abuse* by Suzanne M. Sgroi, M.D. Copyright © 1982 by D.C. Heath & Co., All rights reserved.

Johnson (1992) categorizes mothers of incest victims somewhat differently. She identifies three categories of mothers: the collusive mother, the powerless mother, and the protective mother. The *collusive mother* is one who is withdrawn, cold, ill, or psychologically
impaired and who pushes her daughter into her own role in the family. In her withdrawal
from the family communication, this mother fails to enforce limits, so that not only are
generational boundaries blurred, but the perpetrator is afforded more opportunity to
abuse when another adult is not supervising. The daughter is then identified as the delegate to take over household tasks and decisions, eventually evolving into a pattern of role
reversal between mother and child. Anger permeates this relationship. As the actual sexual
abuse commences and then continues, the daughter then harbors anger at her mother for
failing to protect her. At the same time, the mother may see that she has become isolated,
unnecessary, and replaced, and as a result, she feels anger toward her daughter (Jacobs,
1994; Joyce, 1997; Ricker, 2006).

The *powerless mother* is one who feels helpless, defeated, victimized, and unable
to protect herself, let alone her daughter. The incestuous father in this home usually fits the pattern of the tyrant and may be physically abusive to his wife as well
as sexually abusive to his daughters. Although some theorists have called this a collusive stance, others point out that the fear that this mother feels totally paralyzes
her and renders her unable to act (Johnson, 1992; Ritchie, Silverman, and Bancroft,
2011; Schonberg, 1992). The feminist perspective would say that women are taught by
society to be victims so that this role becomes natural for them. Traditional female
sex roles dictate the subservience, say feminists, that secures the victim role from one
generation to the next.

The *protective mother* profile is one that is only recently emerging in the literature.
Our lack of a clear picture of this mother is based on an inability to define *protection*. Is
the protection a protection *from the incest* or protection from *future victimization* once
the incest has been disclosed? Obviously, when dealing with reported cases, the mothers
have not been able to protect their children from the abuse. Therefore, it is postdisclo-
sure behavior by the mother, which comes under scrutiny. Does the mother believe her
daughter, condemn the father's actions, report the incest, and protect her child in the
future?

Some authors argue that, before one judges the mother and her ability or inability
to recognize or intervene in the abuse of her child, one must consider a variety of factors that influence her life. The mother must be seen within her total context (Krane,
2003; Strand, 2000). *Cultural factors* influence how she sees her role, the role of the
male in her life, and her relationship with her children. In some cultures, to go against
the family or cultural group or to air one's problems openly is tantamount to emotional suicide (Alaggia, 2001; Fontes, 2008; Fontes and Plummer, 2012; Stone, 2005).
Where men are seen as dominant, the mother may hesitate to or be afraid to question
his behavior. In addition, a *mother's own background* may influence her. Mothers who
have grown up in abusive families themselves may be ill equipped to nurture effectively, so great are their own needs. Or their own incestuous childhoods may rob them
of the ability to face or intervene in the pattern that is being repeated (Joyce, 1997;
Strand, 2000).

Some mothers are *financially dependent* on their mates and cannot see themselves
as being cut off from this support. Mothers who *lack vocational skills* may not see

any way that they can maintain themselves and their children without their spouse (Alaggia, 2001; Fontes, 2008; Joyce, 1997; Strand, 2000). Dependence on *drugs or alcohol* may also blur her judgment and ability to protect her child. And a woman's *self-concept* also comes into play. Society expects that women will maintain the family balance and to admit that the family is dysfunctional can engender feelings of failure in the mother. In addition, until recently, it was expected that women would be in relationships and that they found their identity in that relationship. Therefore, their husbands' abuse may be too painful for them to acknowledge. What does the fact that a woman's husband is sexually involved with her daughter mean to her possibly already fragile ego?

There has long been a debate as to whether the mother in a family where there is incest knows of the abuse. When professionals observe such a family, they often assume that the mother did know and judge her accordingly. At the point of intervention, however, prior knowledge is not as much of an issue as whether this mother can protect her child once the abuse has been disclosed. Her ability to do this, even if it means separation from her husband, depends on how much ego strength she has and/or how much support she is given by the helping system (Krane, 2003; Strand, 2000).

The Daughter

The victim of a father–daughter incest, like her parents, usually has a *poor self-concept*. She is deeply in need of attention and nurturing and becomes a hostage in the conflict between her parents. If her mother withdraws, her father seeks her out as his undemanding partner. She may bask in the attention, for with the abuse may come gifts, money, or other special treats. She feels special, and it becomes easier to accept the sexual activity. In fact, the daughter begins to confuse sexuality with affection.

Experts in incest (Berliner, 2011; Bolen, 2007; Jacobs, 1994) provide several reasons as to why the daughter accedes to the abuse. She has the natural *awe of adults* instilled in most children in our society. Taught to submit to authority, she may *fear physical or emotional retaliation* if she does not submit. Her father may actually *physically force her*, and she is powerless to resist. Or this girl *may love and trust her father*. In her *need for attention*, she *becomes engaged in the games* he plays with her. She may also see herself as providing help to her troubled family by *keeping her parents' marriage* together or, by her submission, *protecting her younger siblings* from abuse.

Not all daughters are cajoled into incestuous activities. Beth describes how her father raped her when she was 5 years old:

> He just came in one night. I think I was half asleep. He frequently tucked me in, but this night he took me out of bed, not too gently, laid me on the floor, and raped me—or at least tried penetration. I only know I was stunned; we were close and I loved him.
>
> Later I found I was bleeding and asked what I should do. He just said, "You're disgusting; go wash!" I felt so hurt and so abandoned. I'd never felt close to my mother— even at that young age. I thought my father was wonderful. I couldn't fit that piece of behavior into my picture of him. So I blocked it out until it happened again—and again. When I was older, I convinced myself that he'd been drinking, and that explained it for me.

A few daughters also experience violence with the abuse. Doreen's father stood her on a chair in the attic with a hangman's noose around her neck:

First he'd fondle my genitals; I was afraid to move for fear the chair would tip. I was so scared. He'd masturbate, and then when he was finished, he'd run downstairs. He told me when he came back he'd pull the chair out and I'd hang. He would run up the stairs—just to the top—and then go back down. I never knew if he was coming in. I became more and more anxious and wet my pants. Then he'd beat me for wetting myself.

The daughter in incest often has a poor relationship with her mother. Her father may be a nurturer—or a tyrant—or somewhere in between. Whatever his approach, she is completely vulnerable when unprotected by her mother.

The victim of abuse may develop symptoms from stomach problems to enuresis (wetting). She exhibits behavior such as passivity, acting out, truancy, and promiscuity. She may become involved with substance abuse. Daughters present a picture of pseudomaturity, appearing older than their years, yet they are very vulnerable, nonassertive children who blame themselves for the family disruption. They also harbor repressed anger against both of the parents but especially toward the mother for failure to protect them (Berliner, 2011; Briere, 1992; Courtois, 2010; Faller, 2002; Ricker, 2006).

The burden of keeping the secret to herself is a heavy one for the abused child. For this reason, she isolates herself from her peers—a fact that intensifies her loneliness and forces her to turn once more to her abusing parent.

Daughters are abused at various ages. The average age at onset appears to be between 8 and 10, while the highest percentage of girls are abused between 11 and 14 (Bolen, 2007). Often these victims try to tell someone of the abuse, but they are frequently not believed. The ensuing feeling of powerlessness sets the girl up for victimization in later life (Brown et al., 1998; Fontes, 2008; Grauerholz, 2000; Herzberger, 1999; Messman-Moore and Long, 2000; Seto, 2008). The incest experience can be so disturbing to the daughter that she continues to exhibit symptoms in her adulthood.

The Siblings

In a family that cannot properly nurture its children, it is not surprising that more than one child is starved for attention. The siblings of the victim are often resentful of the attention given to the abused daughter. They are also conscious of the abusive behavior. They may not be aware that the victim feels her submission protects them from abuse. Therefore, the siblings may, in their resentment, set up the victim for further abuse. If violence is part of the family system, it may be safer for a sibling to aid the aggressor than to advocate for the victim (Browne and Herbert, 1997; Wiehe, 1997, 2002).

The importance of their own sense of security in the collusive behavior of siblings is undeniable. These brothers and sisters recognize that keeping the secret is necessary for the continuation of the family unit. If the abuse is disclosed, the family might be separated, and their fear of this is often enough to ensure their silence. This failure to protect the victim creates a feeling of guilt that siblings carry through adulthood. This guilt, combined with their witnessing the abusive behavior, may lead them to victimize or be victimized in their own adult years (Erooga and Masson, 2003; Flora, 2001; Grauerholz, 2000; Seto, 2008; van Dam, 2001; Wiehe, 2002).

Some siblings attempt to intervene on behalf of the victim, but because of their powerlessness as children, they are usually thwarted.

FATHER–SON INCEST

The victim of father–son incest suffers from the consequences of not only the broken incest taboo but the violation of the taboo against homosexuality. Since this type of abuse often includes sodomy (anal intercourse), the victim suffers physical pain as well as emotional conflicts. Unlike other forms of incest, this type emerges from the individual pathology of the perpetrator. His conflicts are usually scars from his childhood—disturbed reactions to feelings of inadequacy, an overbearing mother, or conflicts over homosexuality. Although Gartner (2001) states that most abusers of boys consider themselves to be heterosexual, many do experience confusion around their sexual identity. Instead of being motivated by a sexual orientation, the father in this type of incest is often trying to feel more powerful. He finds power in sexual exploitation.

Family Dynamics

While the father is seeking power through his relationship with his son, the mother in this family usually plays the role of silent partner. She may even have a vested interest in the abuse continuing. Her husband's sexual interest in her son relieves her of his sexual demands, or she may fear her husband and feel powerless to intervene. Whatever her motivation, this mother fails to protect her son, sometimes after she has been told of the abuse:

"I think I blame my mother almost as much as my father," recounted Todd bitterly. Todd's relationship with his father began when he was 12 years old.

"We were out camping. I had been thrilled when he'd wanted to take me and not my older brother. We began talking about sex and he said he'd show me some things that I didn't know. He showed me his penis along with a kind of lecture on how big I'd get and what I could do when I was older. Then we started fondling each other. I thought it was fun at first. The rest of the camping trip was great. My father was a really quiet guy; he'd been dominated by his own mother, and I guess that made him sort of meek. He really knew about the woods, though, and that knowledge plus the sexual stuff with me made him seem more alive—more forceful!

"I didn't think a lot about it when we got home, but then he started coming to my room when no one else was home. He got home around 4:00, and my brother was usually out and my sister at a friend's. My mother worked and didn't get home until 5:30.

"So, he started asking me to perform oral sex—actually, not asking—almost forcing. It was like he was on a power trip. But I just got sort of philosophical about it. I liked the attention, and if it made him feel good, it was okay. It went on occasionally for a few years.

"Then I heard some older guys at school talking about guys who fooled around with other guys being homosexual. That sort of shook me up. I asked my dad, and he said that I was being silly. Did he look like a 'fag'? He talked in a high voice, lisping and looking really effeminate, and strutted around the room. We laughed, and I said I guess we weren't like that. But it must have still bothered me because I asked my older brother one day. The first thing he said was, 'Has Dad been messing around with you?' I was shocked.

How did he know? But he said that Dad had tried it with him and he'd said no. I was really hurt. I thought I was so special, and I was angry, too.

"I wanted to hurt my father, so I told my mother. We never got along too well. I'd describe her, in retrospect, as kind of cold. She didn't seem too surprised when I told her, but she must have said something to my father, because suddenly he stopped coming to my room. As a matter of fact, he stopped everything—he no longer gave me any attention at all. He sort of ignored me. Then one day he said, 'You know, maybe you are a fag—only a fag would wreck a good thing like we had!' It didn't occur to me that the logic of that was screwy. I think he knew that a comment like that would really hurt and it did. I became really depressed. Some of my friends were on drugs, and I got into that scene for a while. I tried to make it up to my father, but he was really angry at me I think.

"When I was 16, my father had a stroke and was paralyzed for the next five years until he died. I tried to help him then, but he'd just glare at me and I'd know he didn't want me around.

"In my teens, I dated a few girls, but something was missing. Finally, after my father died, I started going to gay bars, but I hated that scene. Finally, I met a great guy at work. He's a lot older than me, but we get along good. We have a great apartment together. Sometimes the closeness we have reminds me of the good times between my father and me. But those memories are mixed with a lot of anger and bitterness, too."

Unlike Todd, many victims do not disclose the secret. Often, they are too afraid that they will be labeled homosexual. The father–son affair usually terminates without outside intervention. It is usually the son who refuses to participate.

Effects of Father–Son Incest

Like female victims, abused boys too tend to exhibit poor peer relations and self-destructive behavior (Briere, 1992; Brown, 1990; Dorias, 2009; Froning and Mayman, 1990; Gartner, 2001; Lew, 2004; Seto, 2008). Some note, however, that while female victims turn their anger inward, males express it outwardly. In fact, violence toward others may be an outlet for the repressed anger. Some authors also point to sexual dysfunction, depression, substance abuse, and perpetration of sexual assaults as residual effects of this type of abuse (Briere, 1992; Gartner, 2001; Lew, 2004).

Most experts agree that an early introduction to homosexual activity predisposes a boy to later fears of or to homosexual acting out. Father–son incest is not the only reason for homosexuality, but some victims, like Todd, later prefer a homosexual lifestyle. While not actively homosexual, others fear they will become so (Gartner, 2001).

MOTHER–DAUGHTER INCEST

Mother–daughter incest is an abusive relationship that researchers and clinicians find to be rare. Russell (1999), in her study of 930 women, uncovered only 10 cases of incestuous abuse by females, only one of which was by a mother. Although Finkelhor (1979) notes that victims of female perpetrators reported less trauma than those abused by males, later authors suggest that the victims they saw experienced disruption (e.g., self-abusive behavior, suicide attempts, and depression) in later life (Mitchell and Morse, 1997; Ogilvie, 2004;

Rosencrans, 1997). Perhaps the contradiction in the findings of various researchers depends on (1) the overall quality of the relationship between mother and daughter, (2) how much the daughter incorporated her mother's pathological attitudes and was therefore not traumatized by them, and (3) whether the activity was masked in otherwise maternally acceptable activities such as bathing or prolonged breast feeding (Bolen, 2007).

This type of incest is underreported in a general population survey, and because of its rarity, it has rarely been fully explored. It is known that in general women tend to be less likely to abuse children than men do. According to Russell (1999, p. 309), "Only five percent of all sexual abuse of girls and about twenty percent of all sexual abuse of boys is perpetrated by older females."

Rosencrans (1997) suggests that mother–daughter incest is well concealed in society today. In her study of 93 daughters victimized by mothers, most (77 percent) felt that this type of incest differed from other types in that it was even more isolating (p. 37). Most (53 percent) were unsure whether their nonabusing parent had any idea that they were being abused (p. 39). And the majority of the victims (70 percent) never tried to talk with their mothers about the abuse, nor was the abuse ever mentioned by the mother (91 percent of the cases). Thus, the girl remained not only in isolation but also in darkness as to whether anyone knew or cared about her plight.

What is known about the participants in mother–daughter incest?

Family Dynamics

Perhaps the most striking characteristic of the abusive mother is what many victims describe as her *differentness*. These mothers usually come from dysfunctional, depriving families themselves. Rosencrans (1997) reports that 51 percent of the victims believed that the mother had been sexually abused as a child and 39 percent were unsure (p. 61). Their own childhood trauma has rendered them incapable of adequately dealing with everyday living.

Ogilvie (2004) reports that victims experience their mothers as lonely, miserable, and isolated. Feeling inadequate, these women view their daughters as extensions of themselves—as their completion. Often unable to distinguish between their daughters and themselves, their abuse becomes almost masturbatory. The mother views her attention to her daughter as affection. Since this type of abuse often begins at a very young age, the daughter begins to equate sexuality with affection. She may bask in her mother's attention. She sees her mother's neediness and feels compelled to take care of her. Thus, the mother becomes the nurtured and the daughter the nurturer, which she may or may not resent (Mitchell and Morse, 1997; Ogilvie, 2004; Rosencrans, 1997; Schwartz and Cellini, 1995). The daughter feels she cannot hate this woman or even break away. She is so caught up in their symbiotic relationship that hating her mother seems like hating herself. Despite feeling trapped, the girl sees abandoning her mother as the ultimate rejection.

Ruby recounts her experience:

"I don't remember when it began—probably when I was really young. I just know that my earliest memories of my mother were of sleeping with her. I think it started out because my father was away a lot. He had a small orchestra and was on tours. It's all very muddled in my mind, but I know that my mother used to sing. He really encouraged her.

I think he pampered her and they worked together. She was his prize. Then she had some kind of throat operation and couldn't sing. I know she felt my father abandoned her. She was really unstable, I think. She always was, I guess, but my father kept her going so she would sing. I was just a baby when all this happened. I used to think I'd done something to her though, but she assured me I hadn't.

"*Anyway, we'd sleep together when my father was away—well, even when he was home, for that matter. My mother would masturbate me and get me to do it to her. And she wanted me to pamper her like my father had. We'd play little games—like she'd want her breakfast in bed with silver and a rose on the tray, sort of like a prima donna. She wanted me to sing. She really pushed me. It was as though she saw me as her chance.*

"*I really liked the attention—especially since when he was home, my father treated us the same. One minute he'd humor us, the next minute he'd be yelling. Finally, he just left—I think with the cellist from his orchestra. That was when I was 12. It was also about then that I began feeling trapped—suffocated. I think I pulled away. My mother started taking tranquilizers and she began drinking. It worried me. I felt I needed to take care of her, so I did. She was usually "out of it," so the sex stuff stopped. But sometimes I'd get in bed with her and just stroke her hair. She seemed so vulnerable.*"

Ruby finally attempted to leave home at age 17. Her mother overdosed on tranquilizers and was hospitalized. Ruby returned home and pursued a singing career until her mother died when Ruby was 28. Ruby married but was divorced five years later. She tried to return to her singing but had little success. She went through a period of extreme depression, but after treatment, she seemed to recover. At 38, Ruby is currently engaged in a lesbian affair with an older woman and describes herself as "relatively happy."

The fathers in the family supporting mother–daughter incest are, like Ruby's, either absent or emotionally unavailable. Their unavailability seems to support the need for the mother to cling to her daughter.

Effects of Mother–Daughter Incest

Mother–daughter incest appears to have a significant effect on the child victim. Ogilvie (2004) reports that survivors of mother–daughter incest speak of feeling shame, betrayal, grief, and, even into adulthood, a sense of being trapped and isolated as a result of their mother's attempts to control and manipulate. In addition, they struggle with, on one hand, identifying with mothers and, on the other, fighting to distance themselves from them. This constant conflict creates difficulties for these women not only in sexual relationships but also in coping with life in general. They feel powerless and out of control and often turn to substance abuse or self-injurious behaviors.

Rosencrans (1997) found that the daughters in her study all felt that the experience had been damaging. Forty-four percent felt that the abuse was so damaging that they questioned whether they would ever recover, 27 percent felt that the abuse was damaging but that they would recover, and 29 percent were in between these two positions (p. 124). Sexual identity (59 percent) and sexuality (48 percent) were problematic issues for these survivors (p. 130). Most (90 percent) suffered from adult trust issues (p. 161) and continued to feel isolated (85 percent) into adulthood (p. 163).

While Finkelhor (1979) and Russell (1999) have concluded that past victims of mother–daughter incest are not as severely traumatized, more recent studies have suggested more trauma and researchers suggest the need for another explanation. Some believe that when a child is deprived of adequate mothering as a result of mother–daughter incest, the problem is compounded by this maternal deprivation. The trauma or lack of trauma resulting would therefore depend on the overall quality of the mother–child relationship, aside from the incestuous behavior.

MOTHER–SON INCEST

Although romanticized and eroticized in literature and movies, mother–son incest appears to have as deleterious an effect on the victim as father–daughter incest. Only a small number of cases of this type of abuse have actually been reported. This may be the result of three factors: (1) mothers statistically do not abuse their sons as often as fathers do their daughters; (2) mothers are able to mask (through bathing and caressing for instance) some activities that might be considered sexual to a degree; and (3) sons are not as likely to report mother–son incest because of the severity of the taboo.

There are variations in mother–son incest from a seemingly benign arrangement where mother and son dress together, sleep in the same bed, and possibly bathe together to overt sexual contact from fondling and masturbation to possibly actual vaginal intercourse. The mother may couch her activities in normal caretaking tasks, such as washing her son long after this would be necessary and sometimes stimulating him sexually as she does so. Boys may actually believe that they are participating in such activities willingly and may perceive that they are taking the place of an adult male who is absent either physically or emotionally. Yet the heightened sexual stimulation by his mother is also confusing to the child (Dorias, 2009; Gartner, 2001; Lew, 2004).

Family Dynamics

Usually, no father is present in the family where a mother abuses her son. In the very few cases where a father is involved, he is inconsistent, unavailable, and, on learning of the incestuous relationship, is seemingly indifferent to it (Gartner, 2001). It is the absence of a father figure that often motivates the mother to abuse and encourage the boy to comply. Feeling his mother's sense of loss and needing to protect her, the boy responds to her overtures of "affection." His own Oedipal desires stimulate his need to be "the man of the house," so with his sexual involvement with his mother comes a pattern of role reversal.

Promiscuity may be a dynamic in the mother's personality. Many theorists feel that the mother's indiscriminate relations with other men are actually provocative for the son. Once their relationship begins, however, the mother becomes extraordinarily dependent on her son emotionally. For her the relationship may, in fact, be more emotional than physical.

Consider the next case:

Conrad Simons was 6 years old when his parents were divorced. It had been a stormy marriage, but his mother's reaction was one of acute grief. After several years of strife with the mother, Conrad's 15-year-old sister had chosen to live with her father.

Conrad believes this was a double blow for his mother. Financially comfortable, Mrs. Simons remained home and showered her son with attention. She started getting a neighborhood girl to come over after he was in bed and while she went out. Conrad remembers numerous men frequenting their apartment, and it was not uncommon for one of these men to be there in the morning when he got up. Despite the attention he got during the day, Conrad described feeling "very left out" by his mother's evening activities.

Whether actual or fabricated he cannot remember, but the boy began complaining of fears—of the dark and of being alone. His mother confessed that she too was afraid to sleep alone and invited her son to sleep with her. Conrad was delighted, especially since their arrangement seemed to preempt the invitations to other men. He felt safe and secure with his mother and eagerly participated in mutual body rubs. Conrad continued to sleep with his mother on a regular basis, but her ministrations to him evolved into fondling his penis and encouraging him to touch her genitals. She assured him of his importance to her, and, in retrospect, Conrad realizes how "crushingly dependent" she was on him. Their relationship evolved to include mutual masturbation, and Conrad was convinced of his role as her emotional as well as sexual partner.

During this time, Mrs. Simons was also a regular and avid church-goer. She took Conrad along and frequently pointed out pictures and statues of the Virgin Mary and Jesus, telling the boy how special the relationship between mother and son could be. She suggested that others might "taint" the purity of that relationship, and she urged him to tell no one of their "special moments" together.

When Conrad was 13, Mrs. Simons met a widower through church and began to date him. When they married a short time later, Conrad remembers feeling enraged but "afraid to show it for fear I'd lose her altogether." His difficulties with his stepfather resulted in a mutual decision that he be sent to boarding school. Although quiet and somewhat sullen, Conrad managed to repress his anger and remain an average student. He went directly to college and married shortly after graduation, maintaining very little contact with his mother and stepfather throughout.

At the birth of his first child, a boy, Conrad's mother suggested they see more of each other. Conrad felt that he had repressed much of their previous relationship, so he agreed. Seeing his mother with his infant son made him extremely anxious, however, and he always felt a "need for air" when she was in his home.

Conrad began taking walks on evenings when his mother came over. One evening, he saw through a window a young woman dressing. She emerged from the apartment with a young man, who had obviously just come to get her. Several nights later, he returned to the apartment, crawled through an open window, and raped the girl. "I just kept thinking about how mad that guy would be to see what I'd done," he later remarked.

This began a pattern of finding women who were involved with a man and raping them. Conrad's primary motivation seemed to be "taking something" that belonged to another man. The rapes were always followed by extreme remorse and severe depression. Soon after the first rape, he began to experience impotence with his wife. Only when he raped could he reach a climax. Conrad's rapes also began to take on bizarre religious overtones, and he would often fantasize raping the Virgin Mary.

Finally, when his wife threatened to leave if Conrad did not get over his depression, he sought the aid of a therapist.

Most incest of this type is initiated by the mother or occurs as a pathological extension of the mother's nurturing. The mother in this relationship is less disturbed than her son. Although many of these sons are found to be schizophrenic, the incest seems not to be a causal factor in this illness. The advances toward his mother may be part of an episode or, in some other manner, representative of his disturbance.

Effects of Mother–Son Incest

Finkelhor (1979) felt that men were not as deeply affected by this type of incest. The fact that the women used no force and inspired cooperation, combined with the fact that the boys were eager to explore sexuality, is what may account for this finding. In addition, society tends to view young males' involvement with older women as a form of initiation into sexuality, rather than a form of abuse. In reality, however, studies show that male victims of abuse by mothers do feel extreme guilt, which can create problems later. These sons report feelings of worthlessness, betrayal, rage, and fear. Some experience aggressive or sexual problems (Dorias, 2009; Flora, 2001; Flora et. al., 2008; Gartner, 2001; Lew, 2004).

For many cultures, sexual abuse by the mother causes additional conflict and trauma. For example, the Hispanic culture sees mother as "precious above all things" (Carrasco and Garza-Louis, 1995, pp. 13–18). She is supposed to be granted the child's absolute love and devotion. Imagine the confusion for the Hispanic boy who learns that the sexual contact between him and his mother is not acceptable. His confusion will be profound. In addition, shame is a powerful concept in this culture, being the opposite of much-prized honor (Fontes, 2007; Fontes and Plummer, 2012). Unfortunately, not enough data exist on the mother–son relationship or on the effects for the victim, so until more research is conducted, only speculation is possible.

BROTHER–SISTER INCEST

Brother–sister incest is surrounded by what Russell (1999) calls the "myth of mutuality." Despite this assumption that sexual contact between siblings is more than likely benign, 48 percent of the women in Russell's study reported that their experience with brothers was at least somewhat upsetting. Finkelhor (1980) found that 30 percent of his sample were left with negative feelings after an incestuous relationship with their brothers.

Distinguishing between peer sexual play and abusive incest is not always easy. Several authors have attempted to define what is incestuous and what is exploratory, as in this example from Forward and Buck (1988):

> Under certain very specific circumstances sibling incest may be a traumatic or even unpleasant experience. If the children are young and approximately the same age, if there is no betrayal of trust between them, if the sexual play is the result of their natural curiosity and exploration, and if the children are not traumatized by disapproving adults who stumble upon their sex play, sibling sexual contact can be just another part of growing up. In most such cases both partners are sexually naive. The game of show-me-yours-and-I'll-show-you-mine is older than civilization and between young siblings of approximately the same age it is usually harmless. (p. 85)

Herzberger (1999) contends that this type of incest is as serious and damaging as father–daughter incest.

Therefore, what factors create trauma for some children? Perhaps there are two styles of initiation in brother–sister incest. One type of brother is curious about sexuality and uses his sister as a kind of sexual guinea pig (Erooga and Masson, 2003; Rich, 2006; Seto, 2008; Wiehe, 1997). If she resists, he may cajole or even threaten in order to elicit her compliance. The sister, too, may be curious and perhaps even participate initially. At some time during the interaction, however, the sister may resist because she is confused or frightened by the intensity of the sexual experience, which is beyond her developmental years, or because she is overcome by the shame and guilt that the taboo of these activities arouses. Although one brother may be deterred from further exploration, another may intensify the pressure on his sister to continue.

Another personality type is fraught with unconscious conflict. This aggressor is a number of years older than his sister and knowingly exploits her for complex intrapsychic reasons. Brothers initiate incest with bribes or threats in addition to capitalizing on their sisters' regard for them. Although only 12 percent of the brothers in Russell's (1999) sample actually used physical force (though none with weapons), 44 percent used a less severe type of force such as pushing or pinning the sister down. This type of perpetrator seems motivated by his need to in some way dominate his sister. Often, he is in the role of surrogate father since this parent is absent, incapacitated, or emotionally unavailable. Sisters often describe their abusing brothers as "bullies" who teased them, used trickery, and liked to demonstrate their superior strength (Erooga and Masson, 2003; Rich, 2006; Wiehe, 1997, 2002).

The case of Nicki illustrates some of these traits:

Nicki was the youngest child and had three brothers. Her mother, divorced from Nicki's alcoholic father, worked long hours, entrusting Nicki's care to Will, her oldest brother. Although her two brothers were allowed by the domineering Will to go to a nearby play-ground after school, Nicki was not. Instead, Will invaded every aspect of her life, giving her little privacy. When she complained to him, he assured her that it was "only because he wanted to protect her." Complaints to her mother were met with defensive remarks such as "You kids don't know how hard it is for me to work all those hours and come home to this. Can't you get along?"

When Nicki was 9 and Will 17, he suggested they "play a game," which consisted of Will touching her genitals and she touching his. At first she resisted, but discovered that the sensation was not unpleasant. It wasn't long before she noticed that Will's attitude toward her changed during these sessions. He was almost loving, despite his commands for her to "try different things." She learned that she could "buy" freedom and privacy by complying with her brother's demands. "After a while," she commented, "the price got too high. He threatened all kinds of stuff, but I just wouldn't do it. Then he and my mother had a big fight and he left. My next oldest brother took care of me—but he never tried anything."

In retrospect, Nicki is extremely angry with Will. She feels she was exploited and that it colored her later attitude toward sex.

Perpetrators have several motivations in sibling incest. Exploration is the most common. This exploration is often framed in a game or in play (Wiehe, 1997, 2002). Although the activities may begin as games, Finkelhor (1980) makes the distinction that the brothers in his sample were too developmentally advanced to be involved in play. At least one of the partners in 35 percent of his sample was older than age 12, and in 73 percent of the cases, one partner was over 8 years old.

Retribution is not an uncommon motivator for abusers. The brother sought to humiliate his sister—to make up for perceived past injustices. His anger was expressed in his abuse of his sister. Power and control were also motivators. This brother sought to motivate and control more out of his need for dominance than for retribution. A few sisters described sadistic relationships with brothers. Such attacks were motivated by the brothers' own severe disturbances and often produced long-term effects for the victim (Wiehe, 1997).

Why does the sister become involved in sibling incest? Since most researchers (Finkelhor, 1980; Fontes, 2008; Herzberger, 1999; Russell, 1999; Wiehe, 1997) describe the sisters in their samples as younger than the brothers, the difference in power and resources might be the reason, and, undoubtedly, the ties of siblinghood, punctuated perhaps with affection, mutuality, and trust, give the perpetrator a significant edge. Older siblings are persuasive; they can convince younger, more naive children about sexuality or the possible physiological, pleasurable sensations of sexual exploration.

Fontes (2008) points out that in cultures where boys are more highly valued than girls, it is difficult to assign blame. Some victims describe their belief that the threats of their brothers—of harm or of telling the parents—frightened them sufficiently to ensure cooperation or at least compliance.

Family Dynamics

Most incest victims describe parents who are either absent or uninvolved in their children's lives. They certainly have not adequately protected their children or provided the familial restraints to prevent incestuous behavior. Some fathers were unavailable because of death, alcoholism, or psychosis. Theorists have found the fathers were physically in the home but described as emotionally absent. Families, in general, appeared dysfunctional and were either unaware or discounted the incest (Herzberger, 1999; Laviola, 1992; Wiehe, 1997).

The mothers in these situations were of two types. One type was not available to the victim. Some of these mothers were physically absent from the home, but those who were not were passive and ineffectual, apparently lacking the energy or inclination to supervise the children. Another type of mother was one whose extremely rigid, puritanical attitudes toward sex led her children to experiment on their own, rather than ask for information:

> Dora described her mother as a cold and unyielding fundamentalist who saw her religion as her life. (Dora's father died when she was a baby.) Dora's mother spent most evenings going to some function at the church, while Dora and her brother, three years her senior, were left at home. "She used to preach to us on the 'evils of sin,'" recounted Dora.
>
> "I believed her, but my brother apparently was talking to friends. He'd sneak out with his buddies when my mother was at church meetings, and I wasn't supposed to tell. When I was 11, he said he wanted to show me something. He showed me his penis and wanted me to undress. I was really naive. I was sure I'd burn in Hell. But finally, he convinced me. For a while it was fun—if you can call it that. Then I started feeling guilty again and wanted to stop. But he didn't; he threatened to tell my mother, and that really scared me.

If I'd had any smarts, I'd have realized that he would have been in as much trouble as me—but that never occurred to me.

Anyway, it kept on for a couple of years. He tried intercourse, but it hurt too much and I got really upset. I think he found some girl in the neighborhood after that, because he left me alone. It really changed our relationship. I still think of it when I see him today."

Unlike Dora's, families of the participants of sibling incest tend to be large, providing less privacy but less supervision, as well. The perpetrator often tends to be the oldest brother in this large family. Finkelhor (1980) found that his respondents were from large families, and Russell (1999) reiterated this finding by documenting that 77 percent of the victims of sibling incest in her sample of 930 San Francisco women came from families of six or more. This is especially understandable, considering that the greater the number of brothers in a girl's family, the higher the statistical chance of brother–sister incest (Bolen, 2007; Russell, 1999).

Effects of Brother–Sister Incest

Although some authors contend that brother–sister incest leaves little lasting effects, the latest research argues otherwise. An immediate effect of this type of sibling incest appears to be an increase in alienation from the parents. The siblings' recognition of their need to protect themselves from disclosure and the possible consequences of that disclosure accounts for some of this alienation (Erooga and Masson, 2003; Wiehe, 1997, 2002). The victim who feels exploited from the onset may also resent the lack of protection her parents have afforded her (Herzberger, 1999; Laviola, 1992).

Promiscuity was found to be a problem for some past victims. As it turned out with Dora, many lapsed into multiple relationships with married men following the cessation of their affairs with their brothers. Conversely, some adult past victims described an aversion to sex. Many have severe mistrust of men (Herzberger, 1999; Laviola, 1992; Wiehe, 1997).

Perhaps related is Russell's (1999) finding that 47 percent of her sample of victims never married. Of those who did marry, a high percentage (50 percent) were physically abused by husbands. Revictimization and the fear of revictimization are also obvious among past victims. Of Russell's respondents, 58 percent were sexually victimized by an authority figure, 90 percent were upset by a man's sexual comments or advances on the street, and 32 percent were asked to pose for pornographic pictures. Also, 79 percent of the victims of brother–sister incest in Russell's study expressed fears about being further sexually assaulted.

In contrast to the negative effects of brother–sister incest, Finkelhor (1980) discovered a higher level of self-esteem in the young women who had been involved in such a relationship. Finkelhor concluded that learning to combine sex and friendship is a crucial developmental task in adolescence and young adulthood. Women who had already learned to do this saw themselves better able to cope with new relationships. How this finding relates to Russell's suggestion that a high percentage of past victims do not marry is subject to speculation.

Not every girl involved sexually with her brother reports long-term traumatic effects, despite the increased number who have. If the intent is exploration not exploitation and the girl continues to maintain a trusting relationship with her brother, then traumatic effects are avoided.

HOMOSEXUAL SIBLING INCEST

Little has been written on either brother–brother or sister–sister incestuous relationships. Brother–brother incest may occur in the same family as father–son incest. The presence of this type of incest within the family may well indicate the permeation of sexuality between males as a result of the father's pathology. Incestuous behavior between brothers is often motivated by experimentation, a need for power on the part of the older brother, or homosexual leanings. If both participants are under age 7, the behavior is more likely to spring from sexual exploration and awakening. When the power differences between the participants become greater or when the brothers are over 7 years old, there is a possibility of homosexuality or bisexuality.

In Tower's (1988) sample of survivors of child sexual abuse, two were found to be victims of brother–brother incest. One was more traumatized by the simultaneous incestuous relationship with his father than by the seemingly incidental interaction with his brothers. This young man later pursued a homosexual lifestyle. The second victim was abused at an early age by a brother only. Despite feeling exploited, the individual continued the relationship with his brother intermittently and secretly well into midlife. His orientation, however, appeared to be heterosexual as he married, fathered children, and gave no indication of his relationship with his brother for many years.

With so few reported cases, the data about brother–brother incest are inconclusive. The victims who have disclosed reported suffering depression, self-loathing, and confusion over sexual identity in later life (Dorias, 2009; Lew, 2004; Wiehe, 1997; Seto, 2008).

Sister–sister incest seems to have less impact on the participants than other types of sibling incest. The sisters in Russell's (1999) sample did not see this type of sibling incest as creating problems for them in their lives. "Not only are girls much less likely to be sexually abused by a sister than a brother, but it appears that when sister–sister incestuous abuse occurs, it may be less upsetting and may have a less negative impact on the victim's lives" (p. 306). Some 50 percent of the women reporting sister–sister incest in Russell's sample saw it as a nonabusive relationship.

Since others have not researched sister–sister incest, it is not possible to draw any conclusions as to its frequency or the extent of trauma.

INCEST WITH UNCLES, GRANDFATHERS, AND COUSINS

The most common type of incestuous behavior, according to Russell's (1999) study (Bolen, 2007), occurs between uncles and nieces. Uncles, in fact, represented the primary perpetrator in slightly more cases than fathers. Kinsey and colleagues (1953), in their earlier study of female sexual behavior, also concluded that uncles abuse their nieces in more instances than fathers abuse their daughters. The degree of trauma experienced by these nieces has been the subject of controversy.

If an uncle is not an integral part of the family's everyday life, the impact on the child may not be as significant. On the other hand, when the uncle is closer to the family circle and perhaps more trusted, or if he employed violence, more trauma would be expected. Russell (1999), however, stated that in 96 percent of her cases, the abuse by uncles was unwanted and that 48 percent of the respondents reported being very or extremely upset by the incidents. The uncles involved appeared to have a variety of different relationships, ranging from surrogate parents to intense involvement with the family to infrequent interaction with the family. For those who saw their nieces infrequently, greetings and departures often provided opportunities for the uncles to overstep their bounds and fondle or inappropriately kiss their nieces (Russell, 1999).

An interesting statistic uncovered by Russell was that nieces who were abused by their uncles were more likely to be raised by surrogate parents, such as grandparents or the uncles' own families. Certainly, if an uncle was functioning as a surrogate father, the quality of the incest and its resultant trauma would more closely approximate father–daughter incest.

Uncles who abuse nieces for whom they were not surrogate parents are usually described as abusing other relatives as well. Family members frequently see them as troublemakers or problems apart from the abusive behavior. The victimized nieces tended to be dependent children often attached to their mothers (Bolen, 2007). Frequently the uncle is able to ensure compliance based on the niece's experience with domineering authority figures who insist on obedience. It is also highly likely that the girl's mother was herself an incest victim.

Gloria was abused by her Uncle Harry:

> Gloria's uncle was in the service during the years when the abuse first began. She describes her father as domineering and her mother as passive and docile but basically loving. Mother and daughter appeared to see their alliance as a protection against the father's wrath. Gloria's older sister was more like her father, "assertive and often overbearing." On occasion, this created real friction between the sister and her father.
>
> When Uncle Harry first started coming to their house on his leaves, Gloria was pleased. He was a carefree kind of person, quite different from her father. He would spend time with her, take her to a nearby playground, and push her on the swings. Sometimes, he would reach his hands in her shorts as he pushed her. Gloria doesn't remember being traumatized by this, thinking it was all part of the game.
>
> Uncle Harry was reassigned to a base near the family's home and frequently came over on weekends. He started engineering activities so that he and Gloria were alone. The abuse intensified, as he would openly touch her genitals and encourage her to touch him. "It began to frighten me," reports Gloria, "and finally I told my mother." The mother was angry but said that Gloria's father could not be told lest "he kill Uncle Harry." Gloria was so frightened that Uncle Harry, whom she did like, would be harmed that she felt terribly guilty about her disclosure. She withdrew from contact with her uncle, and soon after, he stopped coming to the house. Gloria became extremely depressed and is still convinced she "drove him away."
>
> In later years, Gloria's mother recounted that her brother had also abused her as a child. At the time, she felt powerless to stop it, but when her daughter was abused, she was able to intervene by suggesting he no longer come over.

Girls who are abused by uncles may develop a variety of after-effects. Some complain of psychosomatic ailments and their inability to openly handle the conflict. Still others report sexual difficulties or a general mistrust of men. Often, this trauma is not experienced until later in life (Bolen, 2007; Russell, 1999; Courtois, 2010).

Grandfather–granddaughter incest is another frequent type of abusive relationship. This abuse often takes place because society views the older person as nonsexual, beyond the age of interest in sexuality. In fact, age is often a contributor to the incest. Already unsure of his power and worth, the incestuous grandfather's self-doubts are intensified as society begins to view him as a less capable individual because of his age. He feels infanticized—especially if he lives with his adult children and needs to be looked up to. His granddaughter provides affection and attention, asks little of him, and usually looks up to him. The relationship provides him with an opportunity to assert his manhood, and his sexual performance will not be judged. It may be this need for his granddaughter's approval that explains another finding (Bolen, 2007; Courtois, 2010).

Not every grandfather is in the older-age range. A grandfather may be in his 40s or 50s and still at the height of his career and capabilities. For these men, the motivation is much like that for father–daughter incest. Often, their marriage has broken down and they are seeking a less-demanding, less-conflictual relationship. The man may also have incestuous wishes toward his own daughter—the child's mother—and find it easier not to break so clear-cut a taboo. A relationship with a female one generation removed appears to be less guilt provoking.

Grandfathers frequently abuse other relatives within their family circle. By the same token, the victims of grandfather incest tend to be involved in multiple victimizations, often abused by uncles and cousins. It is not unusual for the grandfather, however, to be the first in a string of abusers (Russell, 1999).

Many researchers feel that granddaughters are not as likely to experience trauma from abuse by a gentle grandfather as through other types of incest. Russell's (1999) respondents described fewer long-term effects, due perhaps to the grandfather's gentleness or only mild level of abuse. It would be a mistake, however, cautions Russell, to assume that all grandfather–granddaughter incest is benign.

Victims who report trauma from their grandfathers' abuse blame themselves, rather than the perpetrators:

Diona was 7 years old when her grandfather began his abuse of her and her sister. When the girls stayed at their grandparents' for the weekend, he would intentionally leave his robe open as they breakfasted. He would suggestively rub Diona's legs under the table while their grandmother fixed the food in the adjoining kitchen. The activity progressed to touching Diona's legs and breasts and finally her genitals when he was able to coax her into being alone with him. He had apparently not touched her sister, and although Diona felt pleased at the attention, she also felt enormous guilt that she had somehow provoked it. (She later learned that her sister was also abused.)

The abuse lasted over the course of a year, until Diona refused to comply. Her grandfather stopped, and they remained relatively close, but she describes "feeling weird about it" and wondering what was "wrong" with her. Everyone loved her grandfather, so Diona concluded she must be at fault.

In her teens, Diona began to binge and use laxatives excessively. She sought therapy for this behavior but never associated it with the abuse. When she became engaged in her early 20s, the bulimic behavior intensified. Again in therapy, she finally recognized that her new sexual relationship with her husband had intensified her self-guilt over the abuse.

Although the incest taboo is not quite as strong, sexual abuse by first cousins can also create conflict for the victim. The degree of conflict caused by male cousins' abuse appears similar to the conflict created by brothers' abuse. Cousins, however, are more likely to molest once (although some do abuse over extended periods), and significant long-term effects are less likely. Certainly, the degree of force used and the closeness of the perpetrator's relationship to the victim are important variables in considering the degree of trauma experienced (Russell, 1999).

WHY INCEST STOPS

Intervention is not always the reason incestuous relationships cease. Other factors can also account for its cessation. As the victims grow to adolescence, they may begin to feel trapped and constrained by the abuser's inability to let go. Victims describe a need to be involved in more peer activities, but the perpetrator, afraid to lose the relationship, may hold on even tighter. At some point, the adolescent refuses to continue. The price is too high.

In *Father's Days*, Katherine Brady (1979) describes that it was her engagement that finally enabled her to terminate the relationship:

> Finally my father was willing to relinquish me. Something had taken precedence over his need for sexual gratification: ownership, custody of me by another man. That was something he could understand, however, much as he resented it. (p. 120)

As adolescents grow in stature and strength, they also feel powerful enough to stop the abuse. "I told my father when I was 17, that if he touched me again, I'd kill him," reported Ed. "I think I would have, too. I was much bigger than he was by then and I'd had enough of being used and abused by him." The perpetrator may also lose interest in the child, who is becoming more like an adult. When this happens, abusers, especially fathers, turn to younger siblings.

For some older victims, leaving home is the only solution. Often harboring guilt that they leave their younger siblings vulnerable to the abuse, the victims flee in an attempt to resist further exploitation of themselves. The progression of abuse has been discussed. When the activity begins to include actual vaginal penetration, some children become frightened. If truly concerned about the child, the perpetrator may not continue. Or the abuser may perceive that a girl nearing puberty might become pregnant and not want to take that risk.

Recall that parents, especially, often abuse their children as a result of their own inability to cope with stressful situations, so when the stress subsides the abuse may, too:

> *Geri described the abuse she suffered from her father when he was unemployed. The family was in a great deal of conflict, especially when her mother, with great reluctance, was forced to work outside the home. A year later, the family pressures were somewhat relieved. Her father had been working for several months, had a renewed and more positive outlook on life, and her mother had given up her job. The abuse ceased.*

Not all situations are as clear cut as Geri's. Easing family conflict can, however, lessen or alleviate abusive behavior in some families.

Opportunity is another essential ingredient in abusive situations. If the perpetrator is robbed of the opportunity to sexually exploit, the abuse will stop. Geri's father's return to a job with long hours decreased her availability for the abuse. Better supervision of children minimizes the opportunities of the abusers.

And finally, some mothers recognize the problem and are able to intervene, either by better supervision and protection of the child or by actual confrontation with the perpetrator. Individuals for whom there was no overt intervention and treatment appear to suffer more profoundly from the effects of incest (Faller, 1990; Jacobs, 1994; Russell, 1999).

SUMMARY

Child rearing is accompanied by closeness and touching, which, in most families, serves only to provide the child with a sense of security and the feeling of being loved. Some families, however, are not able to confine their touching to appropriate limits and hence sexually abuse their children.

Familial abuse, or incest, has become recognized today as a national problem. Part of the explanation for the high incidence of incest lies in society's emphasis on sexuality and performance as well as its training little girls to see sexuality as a means to gain attention and favors. Increased mobility and confused values also lay the groundwork for sexually abusive behavior.

The most frequently discussed type of incest involves fathers and their daughters. This type of incestuous family exhibits three patterns: possessive–passive, dependent–domineering, and dependent–dependent. The incestuous father tends to be either controlling, rigid, and dominant or passive, dependent, and submissive. Underlying both these styles are a deep-seated vulnerability, helplessness, and low self-esteem. Mothers whose husbands abuse are either domineering or extremely dependent and passive. Some mothers appear to collude in the abuse, while others are powerless to stop it.

Both mother and father are usually from emotionally deprived families and both are seeking to be nurtured. Where the parents are unable to meet each other's needs, they both turn to their daughter—the mother through role reversal and the father through sexual abuse. As the mother withdraws from the family, her daughter feels abandoned and isolated. She looks to her father for support and is sexually exploited. Daughters then become hostages in the conflict between their parents. The siblings in this family also suffer. They are forced to choose between their father and their sister and suffer guilt as a consequence. Often, these siblings carry scars into their adult years and may later victimize or be victimized themselves.

Other types of incest include father–son (a pathological orientation of the father, based, perhaps, on his own latent homosexual drives or on his need for power); mother–daughter (the mother's overidentification with her daughter results in a masturbatory type of abuse); mother–son (the mother sees her son as the surrogate adult male in her life); and brother–sister (a brother uses his superior power over his sister as a means of meeting his exploration or exploitation needs). The incidence of homosexual sibling incest is relatively underreported and therefore difficult to document. Uncles, grandfathers, and cousins are also known to be abusers. The degree of trauma to the victim of each type of abuse depends largely on the relationship between abuser and victim, as well as on other variables.

Intervention is not the only reason abuse ceases. Victims may be able to protect themselves as they grow older. The perpetrator may be robbed of opportunity to abuse. Or the stressful situation that prompted the abuse may abate.

Incest, past victims tell us, often leaves scars. The residual effects will be discussed in a later chapter.

Chapter 8

Extrafamilial Sexual Abuse, Misuse, and Exploitation

The prevailing myth has been that children are sexually abused by strangers. It is now known that a significant percentage of sexual abuse is perpetrated by family members or by surrogate caregivers who are close to the child. Yet there is also danger that friends, acquaintances, and even strangers abuse and exploit children. This is especially likely as the Internet makes unrelated children more accessible to perpetrators.

Child sexual abuse in the broadest sense encompasses not only the inappropriate touching of children but also using children in sexual trafficking, pornography, and prostitution. Perpetrators may meet their victims in person or through the computer. Often, perpetrators abduct their victims. This chapter covers the wide range of extrafamilial sexual abuse—from molestation by acquaintances and strangers to the sexual exploitation of children through a variety of misuses of adult power. For the purpose of this chapter, *abuse* refers to the touching or molestation of a child by a perpetrator, whereas *misuse* and *exploitation* refer to the perpetrator's encouraging sexual contact with or photographing of the child for the perpetrator's own financial gain.

DYNAMICS AND CHARACTERISTICS OF SEXUAL ABUSE OUTSIDE THE FAMILY

It has been concluded that the greater the emotional bond between the perpetrator and the victim, the greater the potential for harm, but the trauma precipitated by an abuser outside the family cannot be minimized. Several factors are said to cause the greatest trauma in children who have been abused. Consider how each of these factors can be seen in relation to incest and to extrafamilial abuse.

From Table 8.1, it would seem obvious that children do experience trauma from extrafamilial abuse. The degree and types are explored later in this chapter. This table has also been updated to reflect the difference between the stranger who encounters the child initially in person and the offender who begins his or her engagement of the child online.

Table 8.1   Factors Influencing Degree of Trauma

Factor	Incestual	Extrafamilial		
		Acquaintance	Stranger	Online Victimization
Continues for a long period of time	Probable	Possible but often not as long as in familial	Usually not	Possible
Close emotional bond	Almost always	Possible but not always	Usually not	Often develops through online contacts
Involves penetration	More likely, due to progression and duration	Possible but may not	Possible but may not. If penetration, usually forcible rape	If offender and child meet, possible
Is accompanied by aggression	Majority of cases are not	Possible	Often	Usually not
Child's partici-pation to some degree	Usually	Possible	Unlikely but possible	Yes, the child is engaged and learns to trust through online contacts
Child is cognizant of taboo against or violation	Possible in older children	Possible	Probable (due to admonishments about strangers)	Often not due to being in security of home

It should be noted that there are cultural implications that also affect the degree of trauma felt by children who are sexually abused both within and outside the family. For example, children of a culture that has experienced a great deal of oppression or prejudice might be either hypervigilant to abuse from the outside or emotionally numb due to having dealt with nonfamilial emotional assaults throughout childhood (Ertz, 1995). This is important to consider when making an assessment of the degree of trauma experienced by an individual child.

Children are vulnerable to abuse from many different individuals. Although the majority of children are abused by family members, some abusers are from outside the home. The perpetrator's ability to molest in an extrafamilial situation often depends on lack of parental judgment or inadequate parental supervision. This statement seems to imply blame, but parents allow access to their children for different reasons, some unrelated to intent or irresponsibility. Why might a parent not perceive potential harm from a perpetrator?

First, the *perpetrator may have an emotional bond* with the parent. The individual may be a family friend who has gained the trust of the parent, or the abuser may be a babysitter who is assumed to be reliable.

Second, abuse is *not within the parents' frame of reference*. Parents who have had no experience with abuse or who have blocked the memory of their own experiences do not expect other adults to sexually abuse children. Native American families, for example, give children a great deal of freedom on the reservation, not expecting that they will come to any harm (Fontes and Plummer, 2012). Parents whose children use the Internet may not recognize how potentially dangerous unmonitored use can be for children. Because of current media attention, parents may be more cautious, but even cautious parents often tell themselves their fears are groundless.

Third, some parents *need the services of the potential abuser*. The increased reports of abuse in day care settings, in schools, and by babysitters point out that parents are not always discerning about the providers of those services. Even with thorough checking of references, it is not possible to know that these individuals are reliable. Financial constraints may necessitate using whatever facility or person is available.

And finally, the *parent may trust the potential abuser*. Parents who trust coaches, youth-group leaders, or even ministers and priests, for example, may not realize that these individuals could be harmful (Baker, 2002).

Parents may not provide adequate supervision for several reasons: They may *feel their children can care for themselves*. Parents who allow children freedom in walking home from school or playing in the neighborhood may not even consider the danger of potential abuse or may feel that the children can take care of themselves. Some parents have unrealistic expectations about their children's ability to care for themselves. In this era of the Internet, some parents may not realize that children need supervision when they are online. Today, the Internet provides an opportunity for children to be seduced into future abuse while they are on the computer in their own homes.

Parents *may feel unable to provide supervision*. Latchkey children, who come home to an empty house and remain alone until the parents return from work, are becoming the trademark of two-career families. Child care is expensive, and some parents feel financially unable to provide an alternative. In addition, the parents may not be able to find a program or a sitter to supervise.

Or parents *may be unaware of unsupervised periods*. The child who misses a ride or for some reason is left unsupervised is vulnerable despite the parents' good intentions. Some parents *may be otherwise occupied*. Caring for a child is a demanding and full-time job. For some parents, the responsibility is sometimes overwhelming. Others may be so involved in their own crises or conflicts that they are not able to concern themselves with their children's whereabouts.

And finally, the *child may initiate the separation*. Children who wander off, run away, or become distracted sometimes separate themselves from supervising caregivers.

The preceding discussion presupposes that a perpetrator meets a child and begins his or her seduction. But over the last decade, the complexion of seduction by nonfamilial perpetrators has changed. Today, the easiest way for an abuser to meet and engage a child for abuse, pornography, or prostitution is over the Internet. So parents may now have difficulty with supervision while the child is in their own home. While the parent innocently watches TV or goes about his or her household duties, a perpetrator could be luring a child into seduction in the very next room (Cooper, 2002; Hughes, 1998; Jenkins, 2001; Lin, 2002; Sher, 2008; Taylor and Quayle, 2003).

Finkelhor, Mitchell, and Wolak (2000) estimated that close to 24 million youths between the ages of 10 and 17 were online regularly in 1999. Between August 1999 and February 2000, these authors studied 1,501 of these youths and found that 1 in 5 had been approached for sexual solicitation during the past year. For 1 in 33 of these children, the solicitation was aggressive. One in 4 were exposed (unwantedly) to pictures of people who were nude or having sex (p. ix).

This study was repeated in 2005 and again in 2010. Fortunately, the number of youths receiving unwanted sexual solicitations decreased (13 percent in 2005 and 9 percent in 2010), and youths being exposed to unwanted pornography went from 25 percent in 2000 to 23 percent in 2010, but those being harassed online increased from 6 percent in 2000 to 11 percent in 2010 (Jones, Mitchell, and Finkelhor, 2012).

The fact that youths are still receiving *any* solicitations forces us to recognize that, whether a perpetrator has access to a child initially met in person or initially met on the Internet, children are vulnerable to abuse. Children may be exposed to one or more of the variety of types of abuse, misuse, or exploitation—from abuse at the hands of one perpetrator to involvement in sex rings and prostitution. Let us consider some of these forms of sexual deviation.

Pedophilia

Pedophiles are individuals who have a sexual interest in children. Although some incestuous fathers may be pedophiles in their orientation, the term is mostly reserved for the abuser whose victim is outside the family. Pedophilia is related to the individual pathology of the abuser.

A pedophile may be characterized in a variety of ways depending on the typology used and his choice of victim may reflect his particular type of pathology. Pedophiles seek a relationship with a child because they see children as nonconflictual partners who can satisfy their unmet emotional needs. Some perpetrators' interest in children begins early. He has become expert at engaging children. He becomes emotionally involved with these children and sees himself at their level. Outside his relationship with children, this pedophile views himself as helpless and ineffective (Flora, 2001; Holmes and Holmes, 2009; Laws and Donahue, 2008; Seto, 2008; van Dam, 2006; Ward, Polaschek, and Beech, 2006).

Fantasy is an important part of this individual's life. He may fantasize sexual and emotional involvement with children and often acts out his fantasies. Interestingly, the perpetrator projects his feelings of powerlessness and often perceives that it is the child who initiates the relationship (Flora, 2001; Holmes and Holmes, 2009; McLaughlin, 2000; van Dam, 2006). Children are often preoccupied by their own conflicts, family issues, self-esteem problems, and a variety of other issues that make them needy and vulnerable. They may crave affection and are therefore prime targets for adults who prey on such vulnerability.

Offenders often approach the children at their age level, often plying them with gifts or attention. Some pedophiles suffer from arrested psychosocial maturation, resulting from difficulties in development—including attachment issues (Groth, 1978; Laws and Donahue, 2008; Rich, 2006; Ward et al., 2006). This molester has failed to develop normally; he sees himself as a child and finds no gratification in the accomplishment of adult tasks. As children, these perpetrators' needs were unmet, and having lost faith in adults, they now look to children to meet their dependency and nurturing needs. They find themselves at ease with children and become "sexually addicted" to them (Flora, 2001; Groth and Birnbaum, 2001; van Dam, 2006; Ward et al., 2006).

Another pedophile may not demonstrate his interest in children until his relationship with adults breaks down; when relationships with peers are too conflictual, he chooses children. Frequently, the onset of his molestation behavior can be traced to a crisis in his life. His relationship with a child becomes an impulsive act that underlies his desperate need to cope:

> *Perry was 35 years old when his sexual abuse of children was discovered. He was married and had three sons, all of whom were good athletes and did well in school. Perry was proud of them but vaguely resentful, as he had never excelled at anything. His wife, Trudy, was employed by a large company, where she had worked herself up to a position of some importance. She frequently attended corporate meetings in the evenings and left Perry alone and feeling neglected. His sons were rarely home either, so he would often go out for a walk or a drive "to think." He was trained as a plumber and made good money. He was much in demand because his customers liked his efficiency and his quiet, friendly manner. Customers' children often watched him work, and he would explain what he was fixing.*
>
> *As Trudy became less and less of a companion, Perry's depression increased. He began to spend his evenings on the Internet talking to children. He found them interesting and somehow sexually stimulating. Often, he would think about these contacts as he took long nighttime drives. One night on one of his drives, he saw the daughter of a customer walking home. He pulled over and offered her a ride. The child had talked with him on numerous occasions and got in readily. The offer of an ice cream cone was also accepted, and Perry found himself stopping on a deserted road and molesting the child. When she became frightened, he took her home and urged her not to tell. When he arrived home several hours later, an irate Trudy and the police greeted him. The girl had told her parents.*
>
> *After his arrest, Perry admitted that he had "maybe done the same kind of thing before." He remembered molesting a girl while he was in the service, but she apparently never told anyone. He also remembered a brief relationship he had had with a child, when Trudy was pregnant with their last child. Neither he nor his wife had wanted another child, and there had been considerable friction between them. Perry described his relationship with these children as "comforting." He said they gave him something no adult could.*

As mentioned in Chapter 6, pedophiles approach children in a variety of ways. Some pressure their victims, and others threaten or physically force them.

The pedophile who pressures does so without using physical force. He may use *enticement* in which he cajoles the victim with gifts, treats, and affection. Or he may convince the child of how important he or she is to him. *Entrapment* is also used by abusers who try to make the child feel indebted or obligated to them in some manner. The pressuring pedophile hopes to gain the child's consent in the relationship and thus convince himself that the union is mutual rather than abusive or exploitive. If the child refuses, the perpetrator may intensify his efforts to cajole or entrap but will rarely force the child (van Dam, 2001, 2006; Seto, 2008).

The abusers who force their victims use either intimidation or physical aggression. Children are in awe of adults. The perpetrator who intimidates uses his power as an adult to commit the abusive act. Consider this case:

"He didn't say much," remembers Suzannah. "In fact, I'm not sure he spoke English well; but he was so overpowering." She spoke of the man who had worked at her father's ranch for a short while. Suzannah's family was strict. Her parents insisted that she respect adults. She describes not knowing what to do when the workman took her into the cabin and began undressing her. "His size scared me; he was so big. It was just understood that I'd comply."

Suzannah was molested on several occasions by the 6-foot, 7-inch ranchhand. Only after the man had drifted away at the end of the season was she finally able to tell her parents, who admonished her for "making up stories." Suzannah tried to forget. The memories, however, continued to haunt her.

The motivation of abusers who force themselves on their victims is to complete the sexual act. Force is used when the abuser perceives it necessary. Most likely, he intends no injury to the child, but sees her or him as an object to be exploited and manipulated to his own satisfaction. He is not concerned about the trauma for the victim, and he will usually not take no for an answer (Laws and Donahue, 2008; Pryor, 1999; van Dam, 2001, 2006).

Other abusers actually prefer physical aggression. They, too, are exploiting and plan to do so without the child's consent. This type of abuser is often called a *child rapist* because of the likelihood that his assault includes penetration. Any type of pedophile may reach the point of intercourse with his victim, but this individual's act more closely approximates the rape of an adult female. Two motivations seem to play a role in child rape—anger and the need for power (Bolen, 2007; Holmes and Holmes, 2009).

Anger toward a child or something that the child symbolizes may cause the perpetrator to use sex as a weapon. His purpose is to hurt the victim, and he often combines physical battering with the sexual assault. Often, he does not anticipate abuse but acts instead on impulse or emotion (Groth and Birnbaum, 2001; van Dam, 2006). One abuser was apprehended after raping the 6-year-old daughter of his girlfriend:

"I was so angry when she [the child's mother] broke up with me," he said, "that I just had to find a way to hurt her. The kid was there and it wasn't 'til after I raped her that I realized what I'd done."

The power rapist sees the child as weak, vulnerable, and unable to resist. The child, once again, is seen as an object that he uses and discards. Some rapists who have unsuccessfully tried to take their aggression out on adults may make children their targets (Groth and Birnbaum, 2001).

A small minority of child molesters are sadistic in their assaults. They are sexually stimulated by hurting the child. Their act is totally premeditated, often taking on an almost ritualistic pattern. The sadistic abuser uses more force than necessary to overcome the child and sometimes kills the child. The child sometimes symbolizes something the abuser hates in himself or perhaps evokes a memory of his disturbed childhood (Groth and Birnbaum, 2001; van Dam, 2001, 2006; Ward et al., 2006).

Statistics from a variety of agencies attest to the fact that numerous children are abducted and murdered each year. Many of these crimes have a sexual component.

Pederasty

Chapter 1 briefly discussed the practice of pederasty among early Greeks. But this practice is not confined to ancient times; pederasty thrives in our culture today.

Geiser (1979) speaks of pederasts as "eternal adolescents in their erotic life. They become fixated upon the youth and sexual vitality of the adolescent boy.... Pederasts love the boy in themselves and themselves in the boy" (p. 83). Rossman (1976) describes pederasts as males over age 18 who are sexually attracted to and involved with young boys who are between ages 12 and 16.

Are pederasts considered pedophiles? In England, the answer is affirmative. In the United States, however, the answer lacks clarity. Geiser (1979) differentiated by saying that pedophiles exploit children, whereas pederasts prey on "willing children." Many might disagree with this premise and the semantics, but most agree that pederasty is the abuse of boys, especially those between 12 and 16 years of age.

In the 1970s, Rossman (1976) used questionnaires and interviews with 300 adolescent boys who were sexually involved with adult men and reviewed the writings of more than 1,000 pederasts. Although there is a small fraction of promiscuous pederasts (called *chicken hawks*) who seek out boys between ages 12 and 16 for sexual exploitation, Rossman's study found a larger percentage drifted into sex play or sexual relationships with boys as a result of their fantasies or contacts with these youths. Rossman estimated that at least 1 million men in the United States have been sexually involved with teenage boys.

Rossman's study is dated, but there is a lack of similar recent studies. One reason for this is that the picture of child sexual abuse has been altered significantly by the Internet.

Although illegal in our society, pederasty may still be practiced through underground movements. Several organizations currently exist that are only half hidden from the public. The North American Man Boy Love Association, known as NAMBLA, was created in 1978 in response to the breakup of the "Revere Ring" outside Boston. The ring had operated for many years and included numerous professional men and more than 60 boys. After several of the men were charged with illegal sexual acts with boys, 32 men and 2 teenage boys organized to protect these kinds of sexual relationships and to defend the rights of these youths (Holmes and Holmes, 2009; Rush, 1992). NAMBLA, currently based in New York City and San Francisco, publishes newsletters and now has a website, both of which advocate for the "...for fundamental reform of the laws regarding relations between youths and adults." The website goes on to say, "Today, many thousands of men and boys are unjustly ground into the disfunctional [*sic*] criminal justice system. Blindly, this system condemns consensual, loving relationships between younger and older people." (NAMBLA, 2012). Through these, the organization provides a network for pederasts. The René Guyon Society believes that sexuality between men and boys is a natural type of education. Based in Beverly Hills, the group argues that the age of consent should be lowered, as reflected in their motto "Sex by eight is too late" (Freeman-Longo and Blanchard, 1998; Holmes and Holmes, 2009). The Child Sensuality Circle, formed in 1971, produces pamphlets attesting to their belief that children have the right to experience sensuality including sexual relationships "based on natural desires." The Pedophile Information Exchange (PIE) began in England in 1974 and insists that laws against sex with children are damaging to them. This group feels that the age of consent should be abolished, as children should be able to consent themselves (Holmes and Holmes, 2009).

Should pederasty be considered abusive? Since there is so little research available on male sexual victimization, it is only possible to speculate. Organizations of pederasts argue that their proponents neither abuse nor exploit boys. Some say that, unlike the fixated pedophile, the pederast is not reliving the trauma of a sexual assault in his own youth but rather is seeking a reciprocal relationship of sexual pleasure with a boy.

Because of this difference in motivation, the pederasts interviewed by researchers indicate that they see themselves as guided by a particular code of ethics. This ethical code suggests that the boys are not merely sexual objects but have feelings and interests of their own. Pederasts are admonished to keep photos taken of boys to themselves, a practice that appears to have changed. Further, the pederast is encouraged to protect the best interests of the boy by discouraging drugs and alcohol and encouraging him to stay in school (Freeman-Longo and Blanchard, 1998; Rossman, 1976). There is some question as to whether the ethical code first discovered by Rossman's study still operates.

On the other hand, many argue that a child under age 18, by virtue of his insufficient knowledge and lack of authority, cannot consent and that to ask consent is taking unfair advantage. Another issue for consideration is that of harm to the child. It is known that many boys involved with pederasts do not see themselves as exploited or harmed. The possibility of trauma increases when a boy has been forced. If he agrees to the alliance and is treated gently and with respect, is trauma precluded? While organizations as vocal as NAMBLA might argue for the sexual education of boys, survivor groups insist that, for some, trauma is still the result (Freeman-Longo and Blanchard, 1998; Gartner, 2001).

SEXUAL ABUSE BY CLERGY

An increased amount of attention has been given in the news media to the abuse of children by religious figures, such as priests and ministers. (Currently, no major news story has surfaced about a rabbi.) In August 1993, *Newsweek* featured major coverage of "Sex and the Church" with a discussion of priests who abuse. Jason Berry's book *Lead Us Not into Temptation* (2000) met with much controversy (when it was first published in 1992), as it chronicled the abuse by a number of priests during the 1980s:

> According to a recent study undertaken by John Jay College of Criminal Justice of the City University of New York, between 1950 and 2002 there were 10,210 reported incidents of sexual abuse of minors by priests. These statistics also showed that although a little over 1 in 10 incidents had been reported by victims quickly, 41 percent were reported after more than twenty-five years (Terry and Smith, 2006, p. 8).
>
> Although most of the priests reported targeted boys between the ages of 11 and 14, those representing only single-incident reports involved a slightly higher percentage of female children. (p. 27)

Over the last few decades, more and more reports of abuse by clergy have come to the surface. For example, former priest James Porter (discussed in more detail later), who left the priesthood and married, admitted to abusing between 50 and 100 children over a period of 30 years.

The Catholic Church should not be singled out as the only religious organization to be plagued by deviant activities among its clergy (despite the fact that in the relatively new body of literature, most has been aimed at abuse by priests). Across the nation, other religious orders and denominations are being disillusioned by reports of clergy abuse (Cozzens, 2002):

> *"When our minister was arrested,"* reported one mother, *"I couldn't believe it! He used to run the youth group. He was so great with the kids. He'd taken them on trips and was even involved with a Boy Scout troop. I refused to believe that this minister who we all loved could have molested kids. That is until my own son told me that he'd been abused too."*

Some critics contended that the reports of abuse by Roman Catholic clergy were "manufactured panic" (Jenkins, 2004). Jenkins (2004) pointed to the issue as providing a rationalization for the criticism of celibacy for Roman Catholic clergy. Jenkins believes that the magnitude of reports is really a movement, led to some extent by feminists, to question the authority of the church. Roman Catholic laypeople suggest that the need for more openness from the Church hierarchy, along with the call for more lay participation in decision making, was at the heart of the crisis.

Fogler, Shipherd, Rowe, Jensen, and Clarke (2008) believe that the crisis can be best termed *"an interactive dynamic process"* (p. 303). They go on to explain that clergy-perpetrated abuse

> includes a clergyperson's inappropriate sexual advances and behavior, but it also includes the cultivation of a relationship in which these behaviors occur, the theological and community context surrounding this usually secret and forbidden relationship, and the impact and psychological aftershock of abusive behavior on the survivor and the community. (p. 303)

Motivation of Perpetrators

What could possibly motivate a priest, minister, or other religious leader to sexually abuse children? This is a question that has been explored by a variety of authors of late. Perhaps the only way to deal with this conundrum is to consider what religious life offers and how this fits into the needs of a perpetrator.

First and foremost, church leadership brings with it respect and often unquestioned authority. Ministers and priests are usually held up as people who are trustworthy, loyal, and who want the best for those to whom they minister. For an insecure individual, which perpetrators appear to be (Flora, 2001; van Dam, 2006), this lauded position would hold great appeal. Further, the trust with which a clergyman or woman is surrounded offers opportunity to be alone with children, often in a close or nurturing role. Until recently, when abuse by clergy has come under scrutiny, being a religious leader also offered one some degree of protection. The church community has often gone to great lengths to deny that their leader is guilty of any deviance (Doyle, Sipe, and Wall, 2006; Fogler et al., 2008; Gerdes, 2003; Kearney, 2001). Like the mother quoted earlier, most parishioners find abuse by their priest or minister unbelievable. Some feel the media is just inventing a panic (Cozzens, 2002).

And finally, Freudian interpretation might suggest that the perpetrator, often abused, neglected, or abandoned by his own mother, is searching for the all-loving mother. What better candidate for this role than the "mother church"? Some might also argue that celibacy in the Catholic Church provides the perpetrator, who is not interested in adult women, with an acceptable alternative.

It should be made clear that despite the fact that the perpetrator may find a haven in the church for the above reasons, there are many healthy members of the clergy who have never and will never be abusive to children. Perpetrators seek out, whether consciously or unconsciously, situations and positions that give them opportunities to be with children. The position of church leader, like numerous other positions, provides that vehicle (see Table 8.2).

Crisis in the Catholic Church

Given the fact that there have been perpetrators found among the ranks of clergy of other denominations, why has the Catholic Church been blamed for so much of the current incidence of clergy abuse? Several researchers of the crisis contend that the responsibility

Table 8.2 Comparison of the Offerings of an Ecclesiastical Career and the Needs of Perpetrators

What Is Offered by the Priesthood/Ministry	What an Offender Searches for
Respected as priest or member of clergy due to faith of parishioners, usually unquestioned	Unquestioned acceptance/respect
Due to profession, is elevated in status	Respect in the community
Held apart from general community in minds of most	Some isolation from general community
Authority based on a higher power, an association that makes him powerful	Power
Head of the congregation	Control
Contact with youth in a variety of ways, often unsupervised, with the trust of both parents and youth	Opportunity with children
Under the protection of the "Mother Church," also nurtured by parishioners	An all-loving parent or nurturance
Provided with housing and structure in daily tasks	Limited self-care responsibility
Celibacy in some denominations. Ethical concern for not becoming romantically involved with congregation in others	Threatened by adult relationships and prefers not to have them on an intimate level

Source: Adapted from Berry, 2000; Cozzens, 2002; Flora, 2001; Flynn, 2003; Gartner, 1999; McGlone, 2003; Pryor, 1999; Sipe, 1999; van Dam, 2001.

lies not only within the structure of the denomination but also with the authorities within the Church who denied the crisis (Bruni and Burkett, 2002; Cozzens, 2002; Doyle et al., 2006; Flynn, 2003; Jost, 2003; Sipe, 1999). Bruni and Burkett (2002) suggest that

> in the end, the Roman Catholic Church wound up alone on the hot seat simply because it seemed to have done such a terrible job of coping with the problem. The United Methodist Church and Southern Baptists both conducted surveys to gage the extent of the problem in their ranks; the National Conference of Catholic Bishops insisted it did not even keep records of reported cases. The Presbyterians required background checks on pastors who relocate; the Catholics transferred known abusers. The Unitarians passed out pamphlets to their members on how to make complaints against abusive clergy and the Evangelical Lutheran Church spelled out a formal disciplinary process in its constitution; most Catholic dioceses keep their policies under lock and key. (p. 40)

In addition, several critics point to the structure of the Catholic Church, which may provide a harbor for perpetrators. The hierarchy so central to the administration of this denomination is encumbered with numerous layers of authority, amidst which reports of clergy misconduct can be lost. Instead of being answerable to their parishes, as is the case in many denominations, Catholic priests work for their bishops. If a bishop does not know what is transpiring at the parish level or if he chooses not to respond, an abusive priest may be allowed to continue his perpetration. And traditionally, priests were seen as representatives of God and therefore not subject to public scrutiny (Bruni and Burkett, 2002; Cozzens, 2002; Doyle et al., 2006; Flynn, 2003; Fogler et al., 2008).

Several analysts of the current crisis offer other explanations as to why it might have been inevitable for the Catholic Church. Bruni and Burkett (2002) point to a study undertaken by Eugene Kennedy in the 1970s and published under the title *The Catholic Priest in the United States: Psychological Investigations* (1972). This research found that 57 percent of the 218 priests in the sample had not passed through all of the developmental stages necessary for healthy adulthood and were, therefore, considered to have arrested psychological development (p. 54). Kennedy noted that "their lack of maturity involved not just sexual feelings but a poor sense of personal identity and command of interpersonal relationships" (Bruni and Brackett, 2002, p. 54). This may be the result of the fact that boys are often expected from childhood to become priests and, therefore, robbed of the typical developmental tasks available to their counterparts in the secular world. In addition, the seminary, with its absence of heterosexual relationships and emphasis on inner focus as well as celibacy, further stunts the young man's emotional growth (Bruni and Burkett, 2002; Kennedy, 2003).

Is celibacy a contributor to child sexual abuse? Amidst the scandal that has rocked the Catholic Church, there is an ongoing debate about the contribution of celibacy to child sexual abuse. Jenkins (2003) explains that celibacy, a product of the very early Church, was designed to ensure that priests focused on their spiritual life rather than on worldly concerns. "The idea of celibacy is based less on a fear of sexuality than on a deep respect for its power, and with proper training, a celibate could transform or channel this power into a source of strength (p. 33)." Jenkins does not feel that celibacy among Catholic priests contributes to child sexual abuse and argues that "there is no evidence that the rate [of perpetration] for these priests is higher than that for any other non-celibate group" (p. 34).

Kennedy (2002), author of *The Unhealed Wound: The Church and Human Sexuality* (2001), believes that although celibacy does not *cause* pedophilia, pedophiles, often intimidated by relations with adult women, may seek refuge in a profession where celibacy is required.

Whether celibate or not, clergy may often be placed in a position in which they feel they cannot be wholly themselves with those in their parishes. In fact, loneliness may contribute to the inevitability of perpetration by those with a tendency to abuse children. Because of their positions, members of the clergy may feel segregated from parishioners in a manner that promotes feelings of isolation and loneliness. Seeking to relieve this alienating emotion, a perpetrator may seek out affection in inappropriate ways from those who also seem vulnerable—children (Bruni and Burkett, 2002; Cozzens, 2002; Kennedy, 2003). Although mostly the Catholic Church has come under fire for scandals related to child abuse, this latter factor may be true of Protestant clergy as well.

Impact on Victims

Abuse by a minister or priest brings with it the same trauma as abuse by any other trusted adult. There may, however, be an additional factor compounding the trauma. As one survivor put it,

> I was so invested in the church as a kid. To me, being an altar boy was a big deal. It made me feel like somebody. At home, things weren't great. My dad left us when I was little. My mom had a whole string of boyfriends, most of whom had drug problems. And here was the church, where the minister made a big deal of me and I loved the attention. When he started touching my genitals, I didn't know what to think. Before it had gone too far, I found out that he was doing it to other kids. It made me feel like I didn't really count. It also rocked my faith. How could a man of God do that to me?

Survivors often report losing their faith and the desire for a spiritual life after they have been abused by a priest or minister. As many from troubled homes have sought the church as a form of comfort, these victims feel especially shaken by this betrayal. In addition, many wonder how their parents have not known. Why did these parents continue to allow them and even urge them to go to church? Some survivors describe feeling alienated from parents as a result of these feelings (Berry, 2000; Bruni and Burkett, 2002; Cozzens, 2002; Kearney, 2001; McGlone, 2003; Shea, 2008; Tracy, 2005).

Kearney (2001), writing about the treatment of sexually abused children and their families, proposes that abuse raises such questions as "Why does God let this happen?", "Has God abandoned me?", and "Am I being punished?" and creates theological concerns that are difficult for families to address. (See also Shea, 2008; Tracy, 2005.)

Today, organizations such as Survivors Network of those Abused by Priests (SNAP) offer support for and information to survivors on their websites (e.g., www.snapnetwork.org).

Addressing Clerical Perpetrators

What should be done when a member of the clergy has been found to be abusive? Until recently, such matters were handled within the church and did not always come to the attention of the civil authorities (Berry, 2000; Bruni and Burkett, 2002). As a result, clerical perpetrators were often moved from one parish to another in order to cover up their transgressions. The seeds of a scandal, sewn long before, began to sprout in the 1980s when reports of abuse by several priests began to appear in the media (Berry, 2000; Bruni and Burkett, 2002; Doyle et al., 2006; Jenkins, 1996). The states of Louisiana, California, Wisconsin, Illinois, Rhode Island, New Jersey, Washington, and Massachusetts all found themselves embroiled in particularly distressing scandals that pitted congregations against clergy and sent the authorities scrambling to expose what seemed to be an unending array of coverups.

One well-known case was that of James Porter, a Catholic priest who served in several parishes and left in his wake a multitude of victims and a number of other clergy who had either looked the other way or ensured that he was transferred. Serving in the communities of North Attleboro, Fall River, and New Bedford, Massachusetts, Porter molested both male and female children in numbers that some estimate amounted to 200 to 300 victims. After leaving Massachusetts and a brief stay in a treatment center, Porter was reassigned to a parish in Minnesota, where he continued to molest until he eventually left the priesthood in 1974. However, he continued to abuse children and was later reported to have molested a babysitter at his home in Minnesota (Berry, 2000; Bruni and Burkett, 2002; Doyle et al., 2006; Jenkins, 1996).

In 1989, Frank Fitzpatrick, an insurance investigator included among Porter's former victims, tracked down the former priest, called him, and tape recorded an interview in which Porter admitted to his myriad abuses. By 1992, the case, with its incriminating interview, had made the Boston television station and later the ABC news program *Primetime Live*. Finally tried for his Massachusetts and Minnesota crimes, Porter was sentenced to 18 to 20 years in prison after one of the most publicized cases in history (Berry, 2000; Bruni and Burkett, 2002; Doyle et al., 2006; Jenkins, 1996).

The Roman Catholic Church was not alone in uncovering the fact that clergy had abused children. Protestant churches of many denominations began to discover that some of their clergy were also guilty of sexual improprieties. Many of these church bodies scurried to survey the extent of the problem and began to explore ideas to address future instances of abuse (Bruni and Burkett, 2002; Jenkins, 1996).

Regardless, the Catholic Church's failure to take the same proactive stance did not bode well for the future. Fingers began to point at not only perpetrators but at those who had protected them under the veil of ecclesiastical secrecy as well. Hard hit by such criticism was the Archdiocese of Boston and its head, Cardinal Bernard Law. An investigative report from the Massachusetts Attorney General's Office documented that from 1940 to 2002, over 700 children were reported to have been abused by over 200 priests within the diocese (Office of Attorney General, 2003, p. 1).

In response to the crisis, in the spring of 2002, Cardinal Law sought out appropriate external expertise and impaneled the Cardinal's Commission for Child Protection to study what had transpired and to make recommendations as to how the archdiocese policies and procedures for the protection of children and the prevention and investigation of sexual misconduct could be strengthened. This commission brought together a wide variety of professionals in all aspects of child abuse as well as in judicial and canon law. Four subcommittees were formed to address policies and procedures, education and training in prevention (for both adults and children), screening for employment, volunteer ministry and entry into seminary programs, and outreach and service to abuse victims. Coincident with the completion of the commission's work and on its recommendations, the arch-diocese created the Office for Child Advocacy, Implementation, and Oversight, whose task it was to orchestrate the archdiocese's momentous prevention/educational initiative, review and revise policy, and respond to the ongoing needs of victims and survivors. An Implementation and Oversight Committee was also established to assist the office's ef-forts. The committee is comprised of professionals from both public and private sector organizations with expertise in the clinical, medical, educational, public policy, and social service fields. The parent of an abuse victim and several victim/survivors also sit on the committee (Rizzuto, 2003).

Cognizant of the increasing seriousness of the crisis of child abuse, as well as the criti-cism of both the media and national sentiments, the United States Catholic Conference of Bishops (USCCB) addressed the problem of perpetration by clergy in its 2002 meeting. From this came the Church's stance on the problem, which included the establishment of a National Review Board, the publication of the national Charter for the Protection of Children and Young People, and plans for national audit (see www.usccb.org/ocyp/char-ter.shtml).

As a result of concerns in both the sacred and secular communities, an increasing number of denominations have taken steps to create churchwide policies. Now, not only do many churches require that those who work with children undergo a criminal records check, but child abuse prevention is becoming increasingly a part of adult leader training. And Catholic dioceses have not only been challenged to recognize the problem and de-velop policies, but the traditional structure of the Church has become a subject of debate (Bruni and Burckett, 2002).

Addressing the overall issue, at least in the Roman Catholic Church, may require attitudinal and structural changes. Thomas Doyle, Richard Sipe, and Patrick Wall, all of whom are either formerly or currently priests or monks, suggest that the resolution must be through communication between clergy and laity. Victims want to be heard, and it will be necessary for bishops and other clergy to enter into dialogue that inspires trust and accountability (Doyle et al., 2006). All denominations are also considering the impact that future prevention of clergy abuse will have on seminary training and clerical formation.

SEXUAL ABUSE IN DAY CARE SETTINGS

A decade ago, much publicity was given to the sexual abuse of children in day care set-tings. The Manhattan Beach, California, case, one of the largest and most publicized, involved numerous children and their parents in lengthy investigation and court proceed-ings. Some of these day care settings involved ritualistic abuse (see Chapter 9). From this and other such situations evolved a near hysteria over day care.

"Is day care a safe alternative for child care?" asked many parents. Day care facil-ities, in general, became suspect. The reality is most adults have a sincere interest in taking care of children, but unfortunately, those who have the potential to be or are abusive gravitate to settings where children are available. Faller (2003) concludes that "although sexual abuse in day care is not rampant, it poses a significant problem for young children" (p. 217).

Types of Day Care Abuse

Of the cases of sexual abuse in day care settings to date, three patterns have been identified: single offender–single victim, in which one adult develops a relationship with a particular child that allows the abuse to occur; single offender–multiple victims, in which one adult, usually associated with the day care facility, abuses various children while supervising naps, or bathroom trips, before or after hours, and so on (these offenders are usually male pedophiles, and their victims have been of either gender [Faller, 2003; Schumacher and Carlson, 1999]); multiple offenders–multiple victims, in which a group of offenders has been found to be abusing a number of children, sometimes with sadistic or ritualistic overtones (Faller, 2003; Schumacher and Carlson, 1999). These cases have often received significant media attention—for example, the McMartin Preschool in California.

Reactions and Resulting Changes

High-profile cases resulting in parental concerns have stimulated changes—some positive and some negative—in the provision of day care service. On the negative side, day care centers have found their insurance rates have risen significantly. Centers may pass on this cost in their fees, so they become beyond the financial reach of some parents. Especially vulnerable to insurance hikes have been those facilities based in private homes. The increased rates have meant that some of these providers are no longer able to operate.

Relationships between children and staff members are also under closer scrutiny. Once available for comforting pats and hugs, some child care workers are now hesitant to touch their charges and thus deprive the children of a valuable means of communication and demonstration of caring.

Although both men and women have been found guilty in recent abuse trials, men seem to be more suspect. Children who have no male contact outside of day care centers may be denied this opportunity because of the center's hesitancy in hiring or retaining male employees. In addition, more stringent licensing regulations may be decreasing the number of centers available to parents.

On the other hand, some providers applaud the changes brought about by concerns of abuse. Many parents have become more positively involved in their children's substitute care arrangements. The media, as well as concerned organizations, have published guidelines for choosing a day care center. Parents are cautioned to interview staff attentively and be cognizant of policies about discipline, nap time, bathroom visits, and off-limits areas. Protective workers postulate that if just one child can be protected by such publicity, then it is warranted.

SEX RINGS

A *sex ring* is an arrangement in which at least one adult is involved sexually with several underage victims (Lanning, 1992). These rings may be dedicated to any or many of the following activities:

- Production of pornography
- Prostitution
- Molestation by adults of children in the ring (group)

- Sale or transportation of minors for sexual purposes
- Use of juveniles to recruit other youths into the ring
- Use of blackmail, deception, threats, peer pressure, or force to coerce or intimidate children into sexual activity.

Lanning (1992) has characterized sex rings as having four dynamics: (1) multiple young victims, (2) multiple offenders, (3) fear as a controlling tactic, and (4) bizarre and/or ritualistic activity (p. 126).

Before the dawn of the Internet, the organization of such rings ranged from small, informal neighborhood groups to intricate, national networks. One of the largest and best-publicized child sex rings was uncovered in December 1977 in Revere, Massachusetts. The media reported that 24 men, including a psychiatrist, a psychologist, and several educators, were indicted. The ring had allegedly exploited 63 boys between the ages of 8 and 13. The boys were reportedly plied with beer and marijuana to induce them into sexual activities. The adults paid between 30 and 50 dollars for their visits with the boys, and of this, the boys were allowed to keep 5 to 10 dollars. Along with the arrests, the police confiscated more than 100 pornographic photographs and films of young boys. The ring was obviously well organized and had been in operation for several years.

The case rocked Boston and brought to light a phenomenon that few had ever considered. The reactions prompted the Massachusetts House Subcommittee on Children in Need of Services to establish a statewide hotline to deal with other potential victims. A backlash of a different sort gave rise to Boston's NAMBLA, discussed earlier, which argued for the justification of sexual experience between men and boys (Geiser, 1979).

At one time, the adults who perpetrated through sex rings were already involved in the lives of the children. Some had met children in their capacities as teachers, coaches, youth-group leaders, or neighbors. Sex rings have also been discovered in day care centers.

How do children become involved in sex ring activities? Exposed to adults who play roles in their lives, children are often initiated into sex rings without recognizing the implications. They may observe sexual activity between adults and other members and be presented with the idea that such activities are part of group membership. Perpetrators may approach children by showing them pornographic pictures or allowing them to see the perpetrator nude. The perpetrator works to increase the cohesiveness of the group, often building in an element of fear, for these are keys to encourage cooperation and discourage disclosure (Lanning, 1992). There seem to be no significant characteristics of children involved in these rings.

Jenkins (1998) argues that physical sex rings in the United States are passé, owing to the openness and prevalence of pornography and sexual solicitation on the Internet. Admittedly, the introduction of the Internet as a tool to recruit and operate such rings increases the complications involved in detection.

CHILD PORNOGRAPHY, SEXUAL DEVIANCE, AND THE INTERNET

Today, pedophilia, pornography, and other types of sexual deviance related to children are made more accessible through the Internet. It is difficult to discuss one type of extrafamilial abuse of children without overlapping into another, as the ways in which perpetrators become involved with children are most often online.

Child Pornography

The production, possession, and distribution of child pornography are deeply interwoven in the activities of pedophiles, pederasts, and those involved in sex rings, sexual trafficking, and child prostitution. Both outlets and victims are often found through online activities. Pornography is a stimulant and a by-product, in many forms, of the sexual exploitation of children. Sometimes referred to as *kiddie porn*, child pornography is a multi-million-dollar business.

In his classic 1976 study, Robin Lloyd estimated that more than 260 child pornography magazines were being sold in the United States. Today, the number of pornographic Internet sites has far surpassed the number of magazines. With little effort, sometimes even by accident, children pull up a variety of pornographic images on the computer.

Pornography appears to be more available now than at any other time in history. Perhaps this is due to some misconception we have about it. Our society has come to believe that obscenity is in "the eyes of the beholder" and is also protected by the First Amendment. In reality, however, there are legal guidelines for what is considered to be pornographic and therefore illegal.

Some feel that pornography is either harmless or that it is an acceptable outlet for those who might otherwise act out sexually. Yet exposure to pornography has been found to desensitize individuals, so that some are more likely to play out their fantasies (Hughes, 1998). Research attests to the strong correlation between pornography and sexual abuse (Freeman-Longo and Blanchard, 1998; Curtis et. al., 2008; Flood 2009).

It is difficult to define *child pornography*. Usually, the definition includes sexually explicit material with children as the subject. According to the National Center for Missing and Exploited Children (NCMEC), child pornography is the "sexually explicit reproduction of a child's image, voice, or handwriting—including sexually explicit photographs, negatives, slides, magazines, videotapes, audiotapes, and handwritten notes." The NCMEC further classifies pornography as *commercial* (produced for wide distribution and sale) or *homemade* (intended for individual consumption).

Child erotica is "any material relating to children that serves a sexual purpose for a given individual." Types of erotica include souvenirs, letters, toys, games, and sexual aids. The difference between erotica and pornography is that in the production of the latter, children are victimized.

Pornography represents specific uses to the pedophilic consumer. First, it provides him or her with a means of sexual arousal. With pornographic pictures, films, tapes and websites, he or she stimulates his or her fantasies, often as a prelude to masturbation or sexual activity with children. Child molesters also use pornography to lower children's inhibitions (Cooper, 2002; Holmes and Holmes, 2009; Jenkins, 2001; Taylor and Quayle, 2003; van Dam, 2006; Curtis et. al., 2008; Wortley and Smallbone, 2012). Children who see peers engaging in sex and apparently enjoying it may be more likely to comply with the molester's demands. The exploitation of a child may include taking pictures or movies of the child, which the pedophile subsequently uses as a form of blackmail to compel the child to keep the sexual activities a secret.

Second, research shows that pornographic collections are important to pedophiles. Some perpetrators use the materials they have produced as a medium of exchange. By trading pornography with others, the pedophiles broaden their own collection and vary their stimuli. The Internet now makes such trades easier.

And finally, pornography is used for profit. Those who reap the most significant profit, however, do not appear to be pedophiles. Although those interested in children consume and sometimes produce the materials, commercial dealers, who reproduce and distribute, amass the bulk of the financial gains (Cooper 2002; Jenkins, 2001; Sher, 2008; Taylor and Quayle, 2003; Wortley and Smallbone, 2012).

Possessors of Child Pornography

As law enforcement techniques have increased in sophistication, there have been more arrests of people possessing child pornography. In fact, the profiles of Internet child pornographers (ICPs) are based almost entirely on data from those who were arrested (Wortley and Smallbone, 2012).

Detective Jim McLaughlin, a New Hampshire police detective and pioneer in apprehending online perpetrators, has made over 750 arrests of online perpetrators to date. He has also adopted the term *technophilia* to refer to those who use the computer to engage in sexual deviance involving children (McLaughlin, 1998).[1] After an extensive three-year study of sexual exploitation of children over the Internet, McLaughlin and his colleagues, funded by a grant from the Justice Department's Offices for Juvenile Justice and Delinquency Prevention, uncovered over 200 perpetrators of sexual solicitation and abuse via the Internet in 40 states and 12 foreign countries.

McLaughlin (1998) suggests that there is no real profile for offenders who engage in technophilia, but he suggests that many have similar characteristics. The typical offender is in his 30s to 40s and is often described as someone who isolates himself without many friends. He is probably not too involved with his extended family, and not one to accept social invitations. Instead he prefers to stay at home in front of his computer. He may care little about his surroundings, subsisting on take-out food while all of his energies are focused on the world that he has created online. He has some favorite chat rooms that he can access quickly through his computer icons. He usually has fictional aliases (usually posing as another child or teen) through which he chats with the children and youths who interest him sexually. His favorite activity involves the hunt for just the right child to "turn him on."

McLaughlin adds that this offender might or might not be married, might or might not have his or her own children, or might be involved in any type of profession. A list of offenders who have been investigated includes professions such as college or high school student, computer operator, teacher, laborer, nurse, engineer, self-employed, and so on(McLaughlin, 1998). In short, the individual who uses the Internet to lure children might be anyone fitting any of the offender typologies mentioned earlier. The relative anonymity of the computer world offers him or her a chance to groom a child before he or she ever has to take the risk of meeting that child. And this seduction can be done under the seemingly watchful eyes of parents.

McLaughlin (2000) and his colleagues have also identified several categories of perpetrators according to how they use the Internet and pornography. (At the same time, the authors caution that this categorization is an early attempt to understand.)

---

[1] McLaughlin, with the Keene, New Hampshire, police department, was part of the Regional Task Force on Internet Crimes Against Children. Along with the Portsmouth, New Hampshire, Police Department and the Education Center in Newton, Massachusetts, Keene received a grant from the Office of Juvenile Justice and Delinquency Prevention to study Internet Crimes Against Children through the formation of this task force.

Some offenders, identified as *collectors*, expect to generate their own collection of pornography and chat with children as well. Others, *travelers*, are most interested in meeting the child; this is their ultimate goal. *Manufacturers* produce their own pornography by photographing sometimes unsuspecting children and sharing what they produce with others online. *Chatters* are mainly interested in talking with children and in presenting themselves as an adult who can be trusted (McLaughlin, 2000).

The largest study of ICPs to date has been through the Crimes Against Children Research Center (CACRC) in New Hampshire (Wolak, Finkelhor, and Mitchell, 2011). Researchers in these studies report that there have been comparatively a small number of arrests of ICPs, suggesting that there are numerous individuals involved in such pornography who are never apprehended. Another interesting fact pointed out by the CACRC study is that while the incidence of child sexual abuse in the United State appears to decline (by 53 percent from 1992 to 2007), the arrest of ICPs has more than doubled from 1,713 arrests in 2003 to 3, 672 arrests in 2006 (Wortley and Smallbone, 2012).

The latest speculation about an ICP is that an ICP is most likely male. Most are in their later 20s and older, although younger adults (18–26 years) are becoming increasingly more represented. ICPs are usually white, non-Hispanic (89 percent), and most are employed full time (61 percent). About a third were either married or living with a partner, and about 21 percent living with children. These offenders live in all types of settings (urban, suburban, rural, etc.) and come from all walks of life—from professionals to blue-collar workers (Wolak et al., 2011).

What motivates pedophiles who use the Internet to talk with and sometimes meet children are various types of thinking errors, or *cognitive distortions*. Offenders have significant fantasy lives, and their fantasies about sexualized children may surpass the reality (McLaughlin, 2004). Some offenders are striving to lure the child into a sexual meeting at some point. Others are more interested in an idealized friendship, a large component of which is sexual talk and sharing in the belief that a "total relationship" includes sex. Still others see themselves as older mentors who want to guide the child, which includes experiencing sexual intimacy (McLaughlin, 2004).

A variety of other studies have failed to present an accurate picture of these offenders. Some have identified depression and some antisocial and exploitive tendencies but have ruled out mental illness (Wortley and Smallbone, 2012). Studies have indicated that these offenders are more likely to be classic pedophiles than sexual offenders but less likely to sexually abuse an actual child. However, theorists also postulate that the viewing of pornography over time can reduce inhibitions and strengthen preferences for children. This, in turn, may lead to the ICP making contact (Babchishin et. al., 2011; Wortley and Smallbone, 2012).

As more and more of these offenders are studied and apprehended, more about them and their motivations will be learned.

Children at Risk

It is clear that a significant threat to children today is in their own homes via the Internet. A 2000 survey of 1,501 households disclosed that 74 percent of children had access to the Internet (Finkelhor et al., 2000; Mitchell, Finkelhor, and Wolak, 2003). Over a decade later that percentage is even greater (Jones et. al., 2012; Wolak, Finkelhor, Mitchell, and Ybarra,

2008; Wortley and Smallbone, 2012). Of those children who regularly use the Internet, many are subject to sexual solicitation, unwanted exposure to sexual materials, and sexual harassment.

As mentioned earlier, pedophiles seek to engage children for several purposes. If their intention is to engage in sexual chat or to collect pornography, this can easily be done online. When the goal of the perpetrator is sexual abuse, he has several options. Malls, arcades, parks, and playgrounds all provide opportunities for offenders to meet and engage children. Some may be interested only in molesting the child, but others may be intended to produce pornography as well.

There are few common characteristics to identify the victims of child pornography. Most fall between the ages of 10 and 16, but younger and older models are also used. Blondes are often preferred. Here is one case:

> Debbie is an example of a girl involved in pornography. At age 9, she frequented a local shopping mall, mainly to escape from her alcoholic mother who often beat her. From the ages of 3 to 5, Debbie had been molested by an uncle. When he was killed in a bar, Debbie was freed from his exploitation. Adult sex wasn't new to Debbie, either. She had observed her mother's activities with boyfriends on numerous occasions.
>
> At the mall, Debbie hung around the arcade. She was bored and lonely and thus quite vulnerable to a nice-looking man who began to pay attention to her and treat her to candy bars and soda. Before long, he was taking her to his apartment and videotaping her in various activities. She met his other "young friends" and heard how they "made movies." By the time her benefactor offered her "a movie contract" to do pornographic films, Debbie was thoroughly enmeshed in his way of life. For her, the type of acting required of her meant little, but the attention and status she gained for doing it meant everything.

Male victims are often engaged by peers. Certain characteristics make some boys vulnerable to being lured into pornography: boys without close religious affiliation, with no strong father figure, in need of money, or upset by family unrest (such as death, divorce, or a recent move). Boys and girls who are runaways, come from broken or impoverished homes, or are estranged from their families make excellent targets for the pornographer (Flowers, 2001; Hughes, 1998; Curtis et. al.; 2008).

Although some children are still approached in public places and engaged in person, perpetrators are more likely to use the Internet, as this gives them a significant advantage. Online, a would-be perpetrator can engage a child initially yet maintain relative anonymity until he or she feels secure in giving personal data (e.g., phone or address) or arranging to meet. Knowing the child also feels safe in his or her own home gives the online abuser another advantage. Moreover, the perpetrator feels secure in the belief that he or she has plenty of time for the engagement. If the seduction goes awry with one child, another is always close at hand.

The engagement of children for pornography can follow several steps. The amount of contact the perpetrator has with the child as he or she undertakes this engagement depends on how the child has been recruited. The perpetrator, whether in person or online, first uses *enticement* by offering psychological or material rewards. Children who meet perpetrators online in chat rooms may be intrigued by the attention of an adult, or they may assume that the person with whom they are chatting is a peer. Many online perpetrators pose as peers to gain knowledge of the child. However accomplished, enticement involves understanding the child—his or her likes and dislikes—in order to begin to know what will interest him or her (Cooper, 2002; Hughes, 1998; McLaughlin, 2000, 2004). Fostering trust and a certain intimacy helps the perpetrator progress. Many children are now recruited via the computer and may never even meet the pornographer. In addition, producers of such materials may generate cyberpicture composites (one child's head, another's body) to further escape detection and prosecution.

With live models, *excitement* is the next step. Self-conscious children with fragile egos and awkward, growing bodies find excitement in the perpetrator's assurances that they have "movie-star quality." The perpetrator then encourages them to pose for pictures, flattering them and inviting them to display more and more of their bodies. When a perpetrator meets a child online, he or she may suggest ways that the child can photograph himself or herself or be photographed by peers. The child is then asked to electronically scan the picture and send it via e-mail to the pornographer. Sometimes, these pictures are altered to appear sexual when they were not taken for that reason (Hughes, 1998). Eventually, children are talked through "action shots" of sexual acts with other victims or with adults. Drugs may be used to heighten the excitement or lower the child's resistance.

The child who begins to feel guilty and wants to tell someone then becomes a victim of *entrapment*, making him or her feel unable to escape the relationship. "After all I have done for you," the perpetrator insists, and the child feels compelled to continue and to keep their activities secret. Perpetrators use a variety of methods to avoid detection. They may threaten to blackmail or harm the child or may play on the child's fondness for them. If a child is involved in a pornography circle, pressure from peers may encourage the child to keep the secret.

Exit, or disclosure, takes place in many ways. For some children, exit comes with their parents' realization that their activities on the computer need intervention. Some children and teens have met the perpetrator and even run off with him or her. For children recruited initially in person and involved in a sex ring, exit comes about in a number of ways. The most difficult part of disclosure for a child is overcoming the guilt of having voluntarily participated.

The long-term effects for children involved in pornography are not unlike those of children in sex rings. Certainly, the duration of the incident, the degree of contact with the perpetrator, and the depth of involvement of the child—including how much he or she has been made to shoulder the blame—make a difference in the degree of trauma. Even with brief contacts online, Finkelhor et al. (2000) found that some of the children in their study felt stress and fear about the contacts (see also Mitchell et al., 2003). Those more involved suffered to a greater degree.

For children who have become deeply involved in pornography, the most significant problems seem to involve the direction and values of their lives. They may have difficulty separating love and sex, gaining a true sense of their own worth, and seeing themselves on par with their peers. Because their experiences differ so completely from normal children, pornography victims may find themselves becoming involved in a deviant lifestyle. Sex is something they know; using sex for attention, for a feeling of importance, or to make money is part of their history. It is not surprising that pornographic stars often continue in the business or turn to prostitution. It is not unlikely for such individuals to later become involved in the production of child pornography (Flowers, 2001).

Sexting

The advent of cell phones has created a new way to produce and distribute pornography. So-called youth-produced sexual images have come to the attention of law enforcement agencies and are addressed under criminal statutes—a fact that has not always been obvious to those who create them.

When Jared took a picture on his cell phone of his girlfriend, Abby, they were both high on the pot that Jared had lifted from his older brother's stash. Both high school juniors at the time, they joked about Jared using it as a pin up in his school locker. But a month later Jared discovered Abby had gone out with his best friend and was extremely angry. Thinking to get even with her, he forwarded her nude picture to several of his friends one of whose mother had accidentally switched phones with him. Jared had no idea until an officer came to his home that he could be arrested for his act of vengeance.

Sexting refers to sending explicit sexual messages or images electronically via cell phones or posting them on the Internet. The concern in recent years centers around sexting as practiced by teens and how to distinguish these practices from child abuse (Lenhart, 2009; Walker et. al., 2011).

Wolak and Finkelhor (2011) explain that acts of sexting can be divided into two categories: experimental and aggravated. *Experimental* incidents involve pictures taken by young people themselves usually either with romantic intent, for attention seeking or to share with peers. They have no ill intent toward their subjects many of whom may have participated in the picture taking. *Aggravated* incidents, on the other hand, involve additional elements often with criminal intent. Adults may be involved, minors may be abused, there may be threats or coercion of the victims, and/or the pictures may have been taken against the subjects will or without their knowledge. In general, there is the intent to harm or profit from the images (Lenhart, 2009; Walker et. al., 2011).

How specific sexting incidents are evaluated may depend on a variety of factors: who intercepts them, the ages of those pictured, the history of those pictured (e.g., victims of sexual abuse or involvement with criminal justice agencies), whether the pictures were taken under coercion, the nature of the pictures, and how they are disseminated (Wolak and Finkelhor, 2011).

Some experts argue that the prosecution of sexting by teenagers blurs the lines between teen experimentation and those who commit sexual crimes. In a well-publicized case, an 18-year-old boy sent nude pictures of his 16-year-old girlfriend to numerous friends after an argument with the girl. He was subsequently arrested, and charged with a felony for which he will be required to register as a sex offender until he is 43 years old (Brimer and Rose, 2012). Victims of texting may be nonetheless harmed by this practice. Anxiety, shame, post-traumatic stress disorder, and even suicide can result (Lenhart, 2009; Walker et. al., 2011; Brimer and Rose, 2012).

CHILD PROSTITUTION

Child prostitution has long been a concern of child advocates. In the 1970s, after three years of study, Lloyd (1976) estimated there were 300,000 males under age 16 prostituting in the United States. The studies by Densen-Gerber and Hutchinson (1978) and

Densen-Gerber (1980) suggested that there were equally as many girls. Today, child prostitution continues to be a problem of significant importance in the United States, with an increased number of teens running away from dysfunctional homes and falling into prostitution. Because only one in two is known to police and agencies, the exact number is difficult to compute (Flowers, 2001, 2005, 2010).

Child prostitution is rooted in antiquity. More recently, the history of various cultures abounds with reports of child prostitution. For example, early Chinese immigrants included girls who were sold by their fathers and brought to the United States to serve as prostitutes (Mass, 1991). Why, then, has it only recently come to the attention of researchers, therapists, and theorists? Perhaps several factors have contributed to its incidence and to its study.

The so-called hippies and the counterculture of the 1960s was one that brought this type of exploitation into focus. In the Haight-Ashbury district of San Francisco, the urban working-class residences gave way, in the mid-1960s, to the hippies—middle-class young people dedicated to the overthrow of the political and social views of the previous generation. Approximately 7,000 young people were said to have inhabited this one district. The hippies espoused the power of innocence, the importance of "doing one's own thing," and a life of instant gratification, which encompassed sexual permissiveness.

This sexual laissez-faire attitude—compounded by the transient nature of their lifestyle and the often immediate need for food, shelter, and money to live—created a vulnerability for involvement in prostitution. Groups seeking to deal with the burgeoning problem were faced with epidemics of venereal diseases and drug abuse. Although the hippie problem died out quickly, their existence had a great impact on our culture.

The hippie population was commonly made up of teens who had fled their homes. The problem of runaways began to take on its own identity as the media told the story and social agencies explored new solutions. In the early 1970s, the mass murder in Houston of young runaways further highlighted the problem. The general public was alerted to the issues by countless articles and by Ambrosino's popular book *Runaways* (Ambrosino, 1973). The attention given the problem culminated in the Runaway Youth Act in 1974. The legislation offered funds and technical assistance to communities seeking to combat the problem (Flowers, 2005).

Lloyd's *For Money or Love: Boy Prostitution in America* (1976) was one of the first studies to illuminate the prostitution of male children as a by-product of the runaway problem. Lloyd's book made a formal connection between runaways and prostitution and intensified the focus on both. Several newer studies (see Flowers, 2001, 2005) have supported Lloyd's findings.

The child abuse movement has helped reveal the widespread problem of child prostitution. Many feel that child prostitution is the most overlooked form of child abuse today. As professionals explored the after-effects of maltreatment, prostitution was noted as a major consequence. Prostitution was also found to be intertwined with pornography, physical abuse, and other types of exploitation. In 1974, the Child Abuse Prevention and Treatment Act expanded the definition of *sexual abuse* to include "negligent treatment or maltreatment," which, by many, is interpreted to include child prostitution.

The children's rights movement is the last significant influence on our attitude toward child prostitution. Surfacing in the mid-1960s, children's rights have been the basis for a variety of court decisions. The Gault case in the late 1960s had a major impact on the recognition of the rights of children. When 15-year-old Gerald Gault was placed in a detention center after allegedly making an obscene phone call, neither he nor his parents were offered legal counsel. The result was Gault's incarceration in the Arizona State Industrial School, ostensibly until his majority. The American Civil Liberties Union eventually brought the case to the U.S. Supreme Court on May 15, 1967, and established the precedent that children—like adults—have constitutional rights to counsel, to face the accuser, and to avoid self-incrimination (Giovannoni and Becerra, 1979). The Gault decision alerted the public and the legal system to the importance of children's rights.

Throughout the 1970s, the movement for the rights of children blossomed. Today, the recognition of these rights includes protection from exploitation and abuse. In 1977, Congress concluded that the sexual exploitation of children is an extension of the concerns over child abuse as well as children's rights. The concerns stressed the harm done to children through their engagement in prostitution and the inefficiency of current laws dealing with the problem. Since that time, the National Center on Child Abuse and Neglect has awarded four grants to study child prostitution and pornography, through which more has been learned about child prostitution and exploitation.

Today, agencies such as NCMEC emphasize the seriousness of the problem and urge intervention.

Profile of Prostitutes

Background

Juveniles who enter prostitution are often from similar backgrounds. Most are from dysfunctional family systems. James (1980) discovered that 70 percent of the girls in prostitution reported the absence of one or more parent during childhood. Silbert and Pines (1981) stated that 75 percent, or three-fourths, of the girls in their study were raised by one parent. Juvenile prostitutes report poor relationships with parents and other family members (Finkelhor and Ormond, 2004; Flowers, 2005, 2010; NCMEC, 2002). Some girls had mothers who were themselves prostitutes. Many of these juveniles begin their careers as young as 12. Some have been as young as 9 (Flowers, 2001, 2005; Klain, 1999).

Sexual abuse in the family of origin has long been associated with later prostitution in adulthood. Juvenile prostitutes also report incestuous experiences in their younger years (Finkelhor and Ormond, 2004; Flowers, 2001, 2005, 2010; Klain, 1999; NCMEC, 2002; Silbert and Pines, 1981). The sexual abuse they suffered at home was often of long duration. Many thus became runaways (Flowers, 2001, 2005).

Acquaintance with sexuality in this exploitive manner teaches the young girl that sex can be used. She learns to separate her feelings from the sexual experience—a technique that accounts for her survival and now enables her to prostitute herself. Many girl prostitutes report being raped at least once in their lives. Immigrant children, exposed to sexual assault in their native countries, may also fall into prostitution when they reach this country.

The association between sex and violence further insulates the prostitute from emotional involvement. Most female child prostitutes were physically abused—many with extreme brutality—prior to their emancipation (Flowers, 2001, 2005, 2010; Klain, 1999; Silbert and Pines, 1981). Other girls are from neglectful homes. Some have spent their lives in institutions and see prostitution as a means of escape (Densen-Gerber, 1980; Finkelhor and Ormond, 2004; 2001, 2005; Klain, 1999).

Boys enter prostitution from similar backgrounds. Many are raised by one caregiver. The indifference or hostility in their family of origin is marked. It is not unusual for boy prostitutes to have had different caregivers during their younger years. A few may have spent time in institutional care (Flowers, 2001, 2010; Weisberg, 1985). Physical and emotional abuse are often significant elements in the boys' backgrounds. The emotional abuse tends to center on belittling the youth or derisive comments about his budding homosexuality.

An even larger percentage of young male prostitutes are victims of neglect. Some felt compelled to leave their homes, whereas others were forcibly evicted by unconcerned parents. These boys were often exposed to early sexual experiences, though they may not label it as abuse.

> When he was 9 years old, Teddy was molested by a man in the men's bathroom at a park. As Teddy started to come out of the bathroom, the man pushed him back in, locked the door, pulled a knife, and insisted that Teddy comply with his demands. At first, Teddy was frightened. Once the man felt Teddy would not resist, he began to be more gentle and even talkative.
>
> On several other evenings, Teddy found himself returning to the park—almost hoping to meet the man. Anything was more enjoyable for him than listening to the fights of his alcoholic mother and her equally drunk boyfriend. On the fourth meeting, Teddy's acquaintance gave him five dollars. That was the last time he saw the man, but this was Teddy's initiation into prostitution.
>
> Teddy does not see his experience as abusive. Rather, he sees it as a bright spot in his childhood.

Boys and girls seem to have somewhat different reasons for going into prostitution. Girls are reported to be motivated by the rage, depression, and a sense of helplessness they experience as a result of deprived childhoods. They feel worthless and can therefore be easily exploited by pimps, who praise their worth as sex objects (Flowers, 2001, 2005, 2010; Klain, 1999). Flight from dysfunctional homes often leads to being picked up by pimps who provide some security. Police estimate that a runaway seeking to exist on the streets of a city will be driven to prostitution within four days. Although some authors suggest that girls usually start prostituting themselves when they are on their own and need money to survive, other authors argue that although economic issues are important, the meeting of other needs is more influential in their entrance into prostitution (Flowers, 2005). NCMEC (2002) explains that most girls do have a poor self-concept and seek the money as compensation.

Boys, on the other hand, cite money as the primary factor in choosing to prostitute themselves. Weisberg (1985) indicates that 87 percent of her respondents engaged in prostitution for the money. Many youths described their earnings as "easy money" (Flowers, 2001). Boys who consider themselves homosexual reported that they were drawn to prostitution for the sexual contacts (27 percent), for adventure (19 percent), and for sociability (11 percent); only a few boys in Weisberg's study prostituted to obtain drugs (3 percent) or to seek attention (5 percent). Both boy and girl prostitutes may also be motivated by the need to buy drugs or may prostitute themselves as a form of barter (Flowers, 2001, 2005, 2010; Klain, 1999).

Lifestyle

Not all juvenile prostitutes pursue their trade full time. Flowers (2005) has identified two categories of young female prostitutes: true prostitutes and part-timers. The true prostitutes may be *outlaws*, who ply their trade without pimps; *rip-off artists*, who masquerade as prostitutes in order to steal from customers; *hypes*, who prostitute to support their drug habit; *ladies*, who are termed this because of the way they carry themselves and conduct their business; *old-timers*, who are seasoned prostitutes who lack the class of ladies; and *thoroughbreds*, who are young professional prostitutes (p. 110). Part-timers include amateurs or "hos" and may be considered by their full-time sisters having no style.

The setting of the hustling also varies. Street solicitation takes place on roadways (hitchhiking), in truck stops, arcade game rooms, tourist locales, bus and train terminals, city parks, bars, convenience stores, and military bases. Sheltered settings include sex clubs, adult book stores, homes, escort services, hotels, massage parlors, and pornographic theaters (Flowers, 2001; Weisberg, 1985).

The life of a boy prostitute, or "chicken," varies according to his age, his degree of experience, and the setting of his activities. While one boy, called a "hustler," waits on the street for customers, or "chickenhawks," another is "on call" at his apartment, waits for his client to come to him ("call-boys"). Other boy prostitutes pick up customers in movie houses or at train or bus stations. If the men do not choose to rent a hotel room, boys are adept at servicing their customers in a darkened theater or restroom. The street boy is often of lower socioeconomic origin. Middle-class boys often use hitchhiking as their introduction to clients.

Violence is a constant threat for young male prostitutes. Unprotected by pimps, they must be constantly watchful of the men they accommodate. It is not uncommon to be assaulted by a customer. On the other hand, boys have been known to rob their clients, often with the help of a juvenile colleague.

Boys may very well be taking or selling drugs. In fact, prostitution may be the way they support their habit. Drugs not only relax the defenses but also may be a medium of exchange instead of money.

The girl prostitute usually depends on a pimp for her connections and her protection. She may engage in one or more types of prostitution. Some girls are "on the street," meaning they solicit their own customers. The encounter is often brief, lasting only about 30 minutes from the initial contact until parting. The girl attracts her customers, and the two agree on a price as well as the services that will be provided. The prostitute directs the customer to a location—often, an inexpensive hotel catering to by-the-hour traffic. Young prostitutes learn to service customers in cars and other settings as well (Flowers, 2001, 2005, 2010).

Another girl may be involved in the "circuit" or in a bordello. The circuit is a string of cities in which a child prostitute works—usually, for a period of two to four weeks. A booking agent or sometimes the girl's pimp arranges where she will go, transportation, and the length of the stay. The agent is compensated for this service by a commission; in the case of the pimp, his girl's "take" is enough. The girl is met immediately when she arrives to ensure that she keeps the agreement. This type of arrangement is difficult to intercept because investigation requires a lengthy, costly, and cumbersome cross-state search (Klain, 1999, Flowers, 2001).

Bordellos are often used to house girls who work the circuit. Bordellos are especially favored by pimps because the girl can be easily watched and cared for by the owner of the house. The prostitute's earning power increases as she need not hunt for customers on the street.

Although somewhat safer than the street girl, the bordello girl still worries about violence. Customers may beat her or rob her. Possession of large sums of money makes girls vulnerable to violence and robbery. Pimps, too, use violence to keep their girls in line. This can be particularly difficult as she depends on her pimp for managing and keeping her money, clothes, protection, and making her feel important. Pimps are often loved by their girls (known as their "stable"), and pimps guide and teach them during their earlier years. The girls turn over their earnings; the pimp, in turn, protects them from the police, violent customers, and sometimes pregnancy (Flowers, 2001, 2005).

In addition to all these risks, prostituting youths face significant health risks. Klain (1999) has estimated that 83.7 percent of homeless youths have unprotected sexual encounters. A large number of them are prostitutes. There is therefore a significant threat of HIV/AIDS and venereal disease facing these prostitutes on a daily basis. Even if they want to use condoms, client resistance usually prevents them. Many are also involved in drugs and alcohol, making the risks related to substance abuse a significant threat in their young lives (Flowers, 2005, 2010).

Pimps or personal managers play a significant role in the lives of juvenile prostitutes. Pimps have usually come from dysfunctional families themselves and often learned early about prostitution and the possibility of making money by selling it. They have frequently learned from experienced pimps in bars, reform schools, and other gathering places. Sometimes young male prostitutes "graduate" to becoming managers. Their self-importance then becomes derived from exploiting and controlling others (NCMEC, 2002). Pimps are often involved in other deviant activities, such as drugs and crime. In addition, they may use violence to maintain control over their prostitutes (Flowers, 2001, 2005).

Pimps range from those who recruit largely from the runaway population, maintain their cooperation through violence, and have few emotional ties with their prostitutes to more stable, less violent ones who use psychological manipulation rather than violence and may align themselves with particular girls. At the far end of the spectrum, pimps may be more professional, good businessmen who manage their stable well (Flowers, 2001).

Both male and female prostitutes lead precarious and often short lives. Their earnings may be significant, but they rarely have the opportunity to fully enjoy them.

The Impact of the Victims of Trafficking and Violence Protection Act

As mentioned in Chapter 6, the passage of the Victims of Trafficking and Violence Protection Act of 2000 (TVPA, Public Law 106-386, amended and reauthorized in 2003 as P.L. 108-193, 2006 as P.L. 109-164 and 2008 as 11-457) has had an influence on how child prostitution and pornography are addressed. Under TVPA these acts become federal crimes. Once primarily the concern of international organization, the more recent emphasis on sexual trafficking of children has focused on the United States (Finklea et. al., 2012).

Increasingly states have incorporated the term *child sexual trafficking* into their child abuse legislation, and Child Protective Services (CPS) agencies have sought to educate workers about this phenomenon. Currently, although the victims of child sexual trafficking may come to the attention of CPS, this agency is not always sufficiently trained to handle these cases. At the same time, the punishment of the traffickers falls under the responsibility of the Departments of Justice and Homeland Security. According to some critics, the administration of TVPA requires additional scrutiny and organization (Finklea et. al., 2012).

MISSING CHILDREN

Every year, thousands of children turn up missing from their homes. A recent study conducted by the U.S. Department of Justice suggests that missing children fall into six categories: (1) nonfamilial abduction; (2) stereotypical kidnapping; (3) familial abduction; (4) runaways or throwaways (e.g., children told to leave by parents); (5) children who are missing involuntarily, lost, or injured; and (6) children who are missing with a benign explanation (Sedlak, Finkelhor, Hammer, and Schultz, 2002). The latter two categories refer to situations in which the parents do not know the child's whereabouts, are alarmed, and may report their concern to law enforcement.

Custody disputes during divorce proceedings may also result in children being taken from one parent by another. Some see parental kidnapping as a form of emotional maltreatment, and such a problem must be addressed by courts settling divorce and custody cases. The remaining categories, however, often place a child at risk for being raped, sexually molested, or involved in pornography, prostitution, or even murdered (Flowers, 2001). Thus, the issue of missing children may be influenced by efforts to protect them against physical or sexual abuse and exploitation.

For more information on missing children, see NCMEC's website www.missingkids.com. Only by recognizing the need to join forces, society can truly ensure the protection of its children.

SUMMARY

Recognition that a significant percentage of children are abused by family members does not negate the need to consider those children abused or misused outside the home. The first component necessary for a child to be abused outside the family is for the perpetrator to gain access to the child or have the opportunity. Children are abused by pedophiles—individuals who either prefer children sexually or for whom sexual contacts with adults have become too conflicted. Pedophiles could have contact with children in a variety of ways—as friends, teachers, coaches, ministers and priests, or through the Internet.

Pederasty is another type of exploitation of children. Pederasts prey on young boys whom they befriend and initiate into sexuality. Since pederasty is illegal in this country, pederasts often operate in underground groups such as NAMBLA, the René Guyon Society, and the Childhood Sensuality Circle. Organizations of pederasts are guided by a code of ethics and see themselves as benefiting, rather than harming, the child. There is some controversy over whether or not inclusion in pederasty has lasting traumatic effects for the young victim.

Children are sexually abused and exploited in a variety of situations. Recently, the media has been filled with reports of abuse by clergy. Clerical perpetrators may fall into any category psychologically but may be attracted to ecclesiastical life as a result of pre-existing pathology. Fortunately, the majority of clergy are not abusive. The impact on the victims of abuse within the church can be profound, often robbing them of their faith as well as other trauma.

In the last decade, there have been a number of high-profile reports of sexual abuse in day care settings. These cases have resulted in an increased awareness of the importance of screening staff and using other safety measures.

Sex rings are another threat to children. These rings consist of groups of children and one or more perpetrators who now often use the Internet for recruitment, arranging to meet children whom they plan to molest or use for prostitution and for the production of pornography.

Child pornography is a significant problem in the United States giving rise to considerable efforts to curb this type of exploitation of children. Pornography is used to engage children in sexual abuse in relationships and may also be the end product of the perpetrator's exploitation. Today, the Internet figures prominently in an offender's access to children and ability to seduce them. Both male and female children are used in pornography. The child is enticed and entrapped by the skillful perpetrator and may find that the only alternative is through continuing in the career, often as a producer or through prostitution.

Recently, there have been concerns about sexting—the practice of transmitting sexually explicit messages or images electronically. Some controversy exists about the type of consequences there should be for teens who sext and how these consequences may blur the lines between these experimental acts and the actions of adult sexual abusers and pornographers.

Child prostitution, although an old form of exploitation, has more recently been brought to light by several groups: (1) the hippies in the 1960s, (2) runaways and their helpers, (3) the child abuse movement, and (4) the children's rights movement. Both male and female children, often seeking refuge from disturbed or abusive homes, become involved in prostitution. Boys are less likely to be sponsored by pimps but are more subject to violence. Girls typically are "managed" by adult males who do so either as surrogate fathers or lovers or from a purely business perspective. Some pimps are abusive and use threats and blackmail to ensure cooperation. Children are indoctrinated into prostitution by skilled adults. Boys are promised money and freedom, whereas girls value the attention and a sense of belonging provided by pimps—as well as the promise of financial gains. Boys are often able to exit from prostitution and lead relatively normal lives, but girls are more likely to go into adult prostitution as a means of survival.

Our nation continues to be concerned over the plight of missing children. Children are abducted by parents, and many run away or are lured away by perpetrators. Until society fully understands the dangers to children who are separated or unsupervised by caregivers, it will be difficult to provide our children with the protection they need and deserve.

Chapter 9

Psychological Maltreatment of Children

"You're a stupid, lousy kid, and I wish you'd never been born!" shrieked Delvina at her wailing toddler. Motherhood was more than she had ever imagined, and Delvina, at age 17, felt ill prepared to deal with it. Perhaps sharing her frustration in their less than satisfactory relationship, 2-year-old Allen cried frequently or banged his head against any available surface. His behavior stimulated his grandmother's screams at his mother.

"What's your problem, girl? You too dumb to take care of a baby? Well, I just can't abide that wailing no more!" Invariably, these words preceded her exit, and Delvina once more turned her angry words on her plaintive child.

The pattern in baby Allen's family is one of emotional abuse—a pattern that long preceded his birth.

PSYCHOLOGICAL MALTREATMENT DEFINED

Emotional and psychological maltreatment remains the most difficult type of abuse or neglect to define or isolate. Some child development experts argue that almost all parents are guilty of emotional maltreatment of children at some time or other. The ambiguous messages we give to children in our culture have even been considered to be abusive. For example, consider these mixed messages: A mother teaches her children not to lie but then comments, "Do not tell Dad I bought this today!" A father belittles his child by saying, "I don't understand why you can't do better in school. In my day, I worked to buy my books and walked three miles to school. *I* realized the value of an education." The clear message to the child is "What's wrong with *you*?"

In fact, emotional/psychological maltreatment underlies all types of abuse or neglect. Survivors tell us that the results of the physical blows do not last as long as the messages that accompany them. By the same token, it is the psychological manipulation on the part of the perpetrator of sexual abuse that creates and/or intensifies the scars for his or her victims.

The attempt to define *psychological maltreatment* has had a long history. Binggeli, Hart, and Brassard (2001) explain that many legal statutes simply refer to *mental injury* without defining the term. Earlier terms were *mental cruelty* and *emotional maltreatment*.

Today, many theorists separate the definition into two parts: emotional/psychological abuse (including verbal or emotional assaults, threatened harm, or close confinement) and emotional/psychological neglect (including inadequate nurturance, inadequate affection, refusal to provide adequate care, or knowingly allowing maladaptive behavior such as delinquency or drug abuse) (Barlow and MacMillan, 2010; Garbarino and Eckenrode, 1997; Iwaniec, 2006; O'Hagan, 1998; Whitman, 2002; Wiehe, 1997). Such fine distinctions are often muddled in the face of reality, however. Some parents both emotionally abuse and emotionally neglect, and in some situations, it is difficult to discern one from the other.

The consensus today is that emotional or *psychological maltreatment* is not an isolated event but rather a *pattern* of psychically destructive behavior that may include any of the following:

1. *Rejecting*—The adult refuses to acknowledge the child's worth and the legitimacy of the child's needs.

2. *Isolating*—The adult isolates the child from normal social experiences, prevents the child from forming friendships, and makes the child believe that he or she is alone in the world.

3. *Terrorizing*—The adult verbally assaults the child, creates a climate of fear, bullies and frightens the child, and makes the child believe that the world is hostile and unsafe.

4. *Ignoring*—The adult blocks the child from having stimulation, stifling emotional growth and intellectual development.

5. *Corrupting*—The adult encourages the child to engage in destructive and antisocial behavior, reinforces the deviance, and makes the child unfit for normal social experience (Barlow and MacMillan, 2010; Binggeli et al., 2001; Garbarino and Eckenrode, 1997; Iwaniec, 2006; Whitman, 2002).

Wiehe (1997) adds two additional behaviors to this list: destroying personal possessions and torturing or destroying a pet. He also suggests that siblings, as well as parents, can be emotionally abusive.

Although all of these behaviors may be seen in conjunction with or as an integral part of physical abuse, neglect, or sexual abuse, emotional/psychological maltreatment is perhaps the only type of assault on children that can also stand alone. The hurtful words, the serious inattention, or the hostile attitude can be enough to leave severe scars.

Consider the case of Alicia:

Alicia never felt "good enough." She was convinced that her mother's departure in her (Alicia's) infancy was a direct result of her birth. The youngest of six girls, Alicia knew without a doubt that the fact that she was not a boy had sealed her fate. Her father virtually ignored her, leaving her care to her oldest sisters. When one sister left home, her nurturance passed to the next oldest, but these sisters seemed incapable of giving much either. Perhaps they too blamed her for her mother's leaving.

At age 16, Alicia became involved with a friend of her father's—a man her father's age. She knew he was married, but it didn't matter. When their affair ended, she drifted from the arms of one older man to another, never quite able to find the love and approval she lacked. By age 25, she had attempted suicide four times.

The move from terming this type of abuse emotional to defining it as psychological is supported by numerous contemporary theorists. O'Hagan (1998) suggests that the following terms currently used in the literature are more in the realm of the psychological: (1) *psychological torture* (frequently seen in ritualized abuse); (2) *psychological terror* (creating extreme fear in the child); (3) *mental injury* (acts that have an impact on the child's mental well-being); and (4) *psychological unavailability* (being absent in the care of the child). This author goes on to distinguish between the terms *emotional abuse* and *psychological abuse* in the following manner:

> Emotional abuse is the sustained, repetitive, inappropriate emotional response to the child's expression of emotion and its accompanying expressive behavior. (p. 28) . . . .
> *Psychological abuse is the sustained, repetitive, inappropriate* behavior which damages, or substantially reduces, the creative and developmental potential of crucially important mental faculties and mental processes of a child; these include intelligence, memory, recognition, perception, attention, language and moral development. (p. 34)
> (Emphasis is the author's)

Proposing a clear definition of *psychological maltreatment* is further complicated when one considers the different practices of the cultures that make up the melting pot of this country. Several cultures use shame as a powerful tool to ensure obedience and acceptable behavior from their children. Referred to as *tiu lien* in Chinese, shame and shaming are used traditionally to help reinforce familial expectations and proper behavior within and outside family. An individual who behaves improperly will "lose face" and also may cause the family, community, or society to withdraw confidence and support (Fontes, 2008; Lum, 2007).

Some families of African or Native American origin threaten their children with the cultural approximate of the "bogeyman" when they perceive the need arises. As previously mentioned, the behavior of ethnic minorities closely tied to their origins must be seen in that context (Fontes, 2008). In other words, psychologically abusive behavior is that which implies rejection or in some manner impedes the development of a child's positive self-concept.

Is there a difference between psychological maltreatment and *growth-inducing challenge*? Many authors contend that there is. Growth-inducing challenge, when it occurs in the context of a caring, supportive relationship, is designed to enhance the sense of self and build the character. Psychological abuse, on the other hand, attacks or fails to nourish the individual in fundamental ways. Thus, the culturally accepted practice intended to strengthen the child's character is probably not abusive in the eyes of parents and children and therefore not likely to leave scars (Binggeli et al., 2001; Brassard and Hardy, 1997; Garbarino, Guttmann, and Seeley, 1986; Hart et al., 2002; Iwaniec, 2006; O'Hagan, 1998).

Another problem arises, however, when parents, closely tied to ethnic origins, use techniques long employed by their culture with a child who has become acclimated to a different value system. Mass and Geaga-Rosenthal (2000) describe the care of an 11-year-old, third-generation Chinese American boy who was sent to a child guidance clinic as a result of his development of an involuntary facial tic. The diagnosis determined that the boy's tic had developed as a result of the intense pressure his more traditional Confucian family had put on him over grades. For this family, their son's Bs and Cs were tantamount to his failure—and to the family's "losing face" (pp. 123–124).

To further define psychological maltreatment in a way that helps us take into consideration cultural variations, we can say that it involves acts or omissions by parents that jeopardize the development of healthy self-esteem, the ability to gain and maintain intimacy and relationships, and the development of social competence (Barlow and MacMillan, 2010; DeRobertis, 2004; Garbarino and Eckenrode, 1997; Iwaniec, 2006; O'Hagan, 1998; Skogrand, De Frain, and De Frain, 2007; Wright, 2008).

Even after one has defined psychological abuse operationally, intervention can be hampered by the fact that protective services must have proof that the abuse has occurred. There must, therefore, be three observable components: (1) identifiable parental behavior; (2) demonstrable (here and now, as opposed to the future scars) harm to the child; and (3) a causal link between the parental behavior and the harm to the child (Bross, Krugman, Lenherr, Rosenberg, and Schmitt, 1988, p. 544). Many child-rearing practices, as previously mentioned, are so imbedded in our cultural values that we find it difficult to discern when they are abusive. Thus, it may not be easy to determine that the child who has a poor self-concept and does poorly in school is doing so *because* of the extreme pressure being put on him or her to succeed, rather than as a result of some other factors.

THE ROOTS OF PSYCHOLOGICAL MALTREATMENT

> Our children are victims of the increasingly prevalent view that parenting is a messy, frustrating job that gets in the way of one's own growth and life, rather than enriching it. . . . To ask a young woman who is raising two toddlers, "But what are you doing with your life?" is to tell this mother that what she is doing—the job of parenting—is not worthy of respect. When a culture removes status from the role of mother or father, the self esteem from assuming that role is lessened. It is as if society is punishing parents rather than respecting them for tackling a tremendous task. Only jobs in the "real world" seem to earn such respect. (Covitz, 1990, p. 7)

The prevailing attitude of much of society that parenting is an unrewarding task certainly sets the stage for psychological maltreatment. Even families in which the family unit is the most valued social structure find themselves in conflict as their children adopt the predominant lifestyle of this country and question (or totally reject) old-world values. But Covitz (1990) goes on to say that beyond the societal atmosphere, emotional/psychological maltreatment results from "the healthy narcissistic needs" (p. 6) of the parents not being met. Garbarino and Eckenrode (1997) contend that psychological maltreatment is rooted not only in dysfunctional family communication patterns but also in the societal pressures impacting on the family. Family disruption, an inharmonious marital relationship, divorce, and outside stressors such as poverty, unemployment, mobility, and isolation can provide an atmosphere for this type of maltreatment. Prejudice, too, takes its toll, as revealed in this case:

> *The Rao family, Brahmans (the highest caste in Indian culture), were well-educated professionals, newly arrived in the United States. All light complected, the Raos were extremely distressed when their third child was born. His dark complexion was met by his maternal grandmother with the comment "Where did he come from? Our family has never been dark! He looks like the village people!" (often from a lower caste). While the*

Raos at first tried to overlook their son's different coloring, they felt that he was rejected by relatives. The subtle pattern of ignoring this child, which they developed, and their practice of keeping him away from others as much as possible, was detected by teachers when he reached school age. The family was referred for counseling. Although initially, they denied any differences in their feelings for this child, they were eventually able to deal with their issues around his coloring.

How much do children themselves contribute to being psychologically maltreated? As in physical abuse, psychologically abused children are often perceived by their parents as more difficult, different, or representing something that stimulates the parent to anger. Thus, the child may trigger his or her own maltreatment, but he or she is not necessarily the cause. Rather, it is how this child is perceived by the abuser. The hyperactive child, for example, while stimulating abuse by one type of parent may find understanding and help from the other parent. Once again, it is often the parents' expectations of their children that determine how well they are able to deal with the children.

There has always been a tendency to link emotional disturbance to maltreatment by parents. Garbarino et al. (1986) contend that "emotionally disturbed children are not by definition psychologically maltreated. There are multiple possible origins for disturbed personality development" (p. 5).

CHARACTERISTICS OF THE PSYCHOLOGICALLY MALTREATED CHILD

Children who are emotionally maltreated by a parent or even siblings suffer feelings of being inadequate, isolated, unwanted, or unloved. Their self-esteem is low, and they consider themselves unworthy (Barlow and MacMillan, 2010; Binggeli et al., 2001; Brassard and Hardy, 1997; Burnett, 1993; DeRobertis 2004; Hart et al., 2002; Iwaniec, 2006; O'Hagan, 1998; Skogrand et al., 2007; Wright, 2008).

Children respond to such messages in one of two ways: They fight back, becoming hostile, aggressive, and exhibit behavior problems, or they turn their anger inward, becoming self-destructive, depressed, withdrawn, or suicidal. Some of these children also develop somatic complaints (e.g., headaches, asthma, colitis, nervous habits) or sleep disturbances. These two cases illustrate the two different responses:

Gil was a child who responded to his abuse by striking out. In his 12 years, he had been constantly belittled and rejected at home. Feeling he and his accomplishments were worthless, Gil began sabotaging the efforts of other children. At school, he destroyed other children's papers and broke into and vandalized lockers; he wrecked the contents of lunch boxes, returning them crushed, soggy, and filled with insects or in some other way spoiled.

Inga, on the other hand, reacted to her parents' rejection by turning inward. She frequently scratched herself with sharp objects, seemingly mesmerized by watching the marks she made bleed. Every week at school was punctuated by at least two visits to the nurse's office with myriad medical complaints. When she was pronounced well or given some type of treatment, Inga wanted to be allowed to sit and talk with the nurse. The nurse soon realized that this emotionally starved child needed psychological treatment more than physical.

The negativity expressed by emotionally/psychologically maltreated children is often pronounced. Their behavior seems designed to draw attention. Some develop eating disorders, attempt suicide, or drift into delinquency. By the time the child is an adolescent, the consequences of maltreatment have often become an integral part of his or her personality (Garbarino and Eckenrode, 1997; O'Hagan, 1998; Skogrand et al., 2007).

FAMILY DYNAMICS

The scene is often set for emotional abuse and neglect long before children are born. Covitz (1990) suggests several situations that make the family ripe for maltreatment of their children. Parents "marry the wrong mate" (p. 29), become disillusioned with their partner, and consciously or unconsciously look for substitutes on whom to vent their anger and disillusionment. Parents who have unwanted pregnancies or desire children for unrealistic reasons may find their frustrations are vented on these children. Parents whose own needs have not been met in childhood may be so involved in finding an outlet for their neediness that a child becomes a burden to them (Dutton, 2007; Iwaniec, 2006; O'Hagan, 1998; Whitman, 2002).

Consider this case:

> Edith, the child of an alcoholic mother and a father no one had seen in years, saw Rick as the "answer to her prayers." He was a steady worker and seemingly reliable. But two children later, Rick found Edith's extreme neediness too draining and asked for a divorce. Furious, Edith refused but paradoxically took the children and left. For several months, they were homeless, living in shelters. Shelter staff complained that Edith left her children often and expected whoever was there to care for them. "And those children do nothing right in their mother's eyes," a shelter worker complained. Feeling harassed by the complaints, Edith moved in with a man she met at the unemployment office. Once again, she felt she would be cared for, but he disliked children. At first, Edith bullied the children into silent compliance. Eventually she took them to a neighbor—saying she'd return soon—and disappeared with her new boyfriend.

This mother's search for emotional fulfillment meant psychological abuse for her children and eventually abandonment.

Morrow (1987) contends that psychological abuse can be the natural by-product of alcoholism, suggesting that when parents are alcoholics, children can be victims of a different types of abuse. Even when overt abuse is not present, these children nonetheless are emotionally deprived, alienated from their parents, and feel socially isolated. Children in alcoholic and drug-addicted families are not only subject to possible emotional abuse by their parents but also suffer a secondhand emotional abuse in the form of shame and humiliation, as illustrated by this case:

> I never knew what my father would do. Sometimes when he was drinking, he'd be as sweet as could be, and sometimes he was even funny. But he was also cruel and inappropriate. One time, he threw the cat across the room in front of my friend. Another time, he came into my party wearing a lampshade on his head and nothing else. I was so embarrassed. I never knew whether to trust him. In fact, I never knew whether to love him or hate him.

Today, with the high incidence of separation and divorce, children may become the innocent victims of psychological warfare between their feuding parents. Certainly, the dissolution of the parental union has an impact on children in any case. Children are torn by their loyalties to each parent, they fear for their futures, and they feel guilt over what they perceive they must have done to cause this unrest. Handling by concerned, caring parents can help children to weather this storm to some degree. However, parents who are caught up in their own anger and bitterness may inflict additional psychological abuse on their children. These parents may not only be unaware of the daily needs of their children, but they also may insist that the children take sides. They may also lose sight of the fact that the spouse whom they so despise and criticize is one half of the child's heritage. Therefore, to continually slander this partner is to do so to the child as well (O'Hagan, 1998).

O'Hagan (1998) also suggests that some parents with mental illness may be more likely to exhibit "inappropriate emotional responses to their children's emotional expressions" (p. 89). In addition, the very fact that these parents may be in and out of the home, due to hospitalizations, will have an impact on their children.

And finally, adolescent parents who are children themselves may find that the demands of parenthood are too great:

> *"The baby just needed so much!" said 15-year-old Tanya. Although usually attentive to her baby's needs, Tanya found that she was frustrated by having little time to herself. She began screaming at her son, assuming that as long as she was feeding and changing him, she was a good caretaker. "He's too young to know how I feel," she argued. She was surprised when, several months later, she noticed that the baby cringed when she came near him.*

It is fairly safe to say that parents who psychologically abuse do so either because they had inappropriate (emotionally abusive) models of parenting or because they are waging their own internal emotional battles. Unfortunately, their children become the innocent victims of the parents' confusion.

Difficulty in Detecting and Treating Psychological Abuse

Often, emotional abuse is expertly hidden amid the child-rearing practices of our culture. It is therefore very difficult to recognize what is actually abusive. Usually, the recognition comes from the results—a child who cries out, withdraws, or lets us know he or she needs help. Unfortunately, intervention by protective services often depends largely on the ability of agencies to document and perhaps support the existence of the abuse in court through tangible, observable, concrete evidence. Emotional abuse is not easy to prove or document and thus may go unnoticed or untreated. Increasingly, however, states and protective agencies are developing statutes or policies that address emotional abuse. These certainly represent progress. It may be that our children will not be protected from emotional abuse until we, as a society, learn to value them more. Then the rights children deserve, as well as their protection, will follow.

Ritual abuse is another type of maltreatment that has an emotional impact on children. Due to the relatively new recognition of this form of child abuse, it is often difficult to diagnose and treat.

RITUALISTIC ABUSE

It is difficult to determine the appropriate section under which to include discussion of ritualistic child abuse. Most often, it falls into the realm of sexual abuse, but there are also decidedly physical aspects. I have chosen to discuss the phenomenon under psychological abuse as seemingly the most traumatic element is the psychological impact of such trauma.

The question then arises: Is there such a thing as ritualistic child abuse? Some authors argue that there is not and that the reports of so-called survivors fall into the realm of false memories (Faller, 2003; Fraser, 1997; Jenkins, 1998; Noblitt and Noblitt, 2008; Snedeker and Nathan, 2001). Jenkins (1998) explains that, despite numerous reports to child protection agencies, media coverage, and publications, no firm proof exists that satanic cults practicing ritualistic abuse exist and is "an eerily postmodern dominance of created illusion over supposedly objective reality" (p. 177). On the other side of the argument are authors and reported survivors who contend that this type of abuse is very real (see Noblitt and Noblitt, 2008; Noblitt and Perskin, 2000).

Faller (2003) outlines several reasons the belief in satanic cults and ritualistic abuse has been questioned more recently. First, many felt that there was a dearth of physical documentation in the reports of survivors of such cults. The best-known cases reported as ritualistic abuse were the McMartin preschool in Manhattan Beach, California, and the Country Walk case in Miami, Florida. Despite the media attention, both cases involved a myriad of questionable facts. A second reason the existence of ritualistic abuse has been questioned is due to the failure of law enforcement to uncover an organization of satanists behind the reported practices. Finally, the rigorous campaign against those who report such abuse has proved a deterrent to such reports (Faller, 2003).

Those who report abuse in cults describe sexual abuse in the form of group sex, child rape, and insertion of various objects into the vagina and rectum; physical abuse in the form of burning, cutting, and other forms of torture; emotional abuse by being threatened, disoriented, witnessing killing, and sexual abuse of others; being subjected to mind control, confinement, and pornography; and being compelled to ingest bodily secretions (Faller, 2003; Hedges, 1997; Noblitt and Noblitt, 2008; Noblitt and Perskin, 2000).

The question remains as to how clinicians and other professionals should respond to reports of ritualistic abuse from children and adult survivors. Hedges (1997) suggests that whether or not the phenomenon exists is not as crucial to therapists as the ability to deal with the psychological implications of the remembered abuse. At the same time, law enforcement continues to uncover factual evidence about this type of abuse.

SUMMARY

Psychological maltreatment has long been the subject of debate. What *is* psychological abuse? Although this maltreatment underlies physical and sexual abuse and neglect, it may also exist alone. Some authors, in an effort to define *emotional maltreatment*, divide it into emotional abuse and emotional neglect. Most agree that it involves rejecting, isolating, terrorizing, ignoring, and corrupting in their definition. Wiehe (1997) adds destroying personal possessions and torturing pets to the list.

Because the United States is a compilation of many cultures, it is sometimes difficult to determine when cultural practices are emotionally abusive. One question to ask may be, "What effect do these practices have on the children involved?" Psychological maltreatment has its roots in a variety of societal and personal deficiencies. Children who are emotionally/psychologically abused demonstrate anger, behavior problems, depression, withdrawal, and somatic complaints. Negativity is pronounced.

Parents who emotionally maltreat are often disillusioned with their own lives, are emotionally needy, or perhaps are substance abusers. Often, these parents have had inadequate models of parenting from their own parents. Because psychological maltreatment is so difficult to document, children who are abused or neglected do not always get the services to which they are entitled.

Chapter 10

Intervention
Reporting, Investigation, and
Case Management

The dynamics of child maltreatment are complex, and the complexity is heightened when the social service system becomes involved. These helping professionals strive to refine the intervention process so as to cause the least harm and upset for the already traumatized child. These efforts will become more successful as the professionals continue to assess the intervention process. Case management is the final piece in the helping process.

CULTURALLY SENSITIVE INTERVENTION

Child abuse or neglect is not an easy subject to discuss with any parent, and when cultural differences exist between worker and client, the picture becomes even more complex. Effective intervention—that is, to intervene so as to cause the least damage and prove the most helpful—with culturally diverse populations necessitates several areas of expertise on the part of the worker and agency (Fontes, 2008; Leigh, 1998; Lustig and Koester, 2009; Lynch, 2011; Rothman, 2007).

First, workers must become acquainted with cultures other than their own. If the agency has numerous potential clients from a particular culture, it is vital that the agency educate workers about the values, customs, and attitudes of those clients. For example, one city's demographics indicated that there was an increasing Hispanic American population. Efforts were originally made by the social service agency in the area to hire Hispanic caseworkers. After a year of recruitment, there was only one Spanish-speaking caseworker within 50 miles. Concerned about the increasing demands of Hispanic American clientele, several agencies joined together to establish training in the values and customs of this particular culture (predominantly South American) and required workers to take part in this training. Also, Spanish-speaking paraprofessionals were recruited from the community to work with non-Spanish-speaking caseworkers as translators.

While learning more about broad ethnic groups is important, it is also important not to generalize completely. In other words, workers must know about Hispanic or Asian Pacific Islander values in general, but if their caseloads are peopled by Mexican or Filipino clients, workers must learn more specifically about these cultures. Another pit-fall in the pursuit of becoming culturally diverse in case management and treatment of victims and families is the assumption that because something happens within a cultural context, it is normal. One worker reported having a case of a pregnant African American 14-year-old. The girl had been raped by her aunt's white boyfriend. The worker wanted to file a sexual abuse complaint, but the girl adamantly refused:

> *"My Mama says that Black women has always been raped by white men, right back to slave time. She was raped by a white man, her Mama was, and her Mama. Way back. So why is it so different for me? That's just the way it is."*

It was difficult for the worker to communicate to this teen that just because something seemed to have happened, it need not be considered right (Young, 1997).

The language values and customs of particular groups may also be affected—in the case of new immigrants—by the situations from which they came. For example, many refugees from totalitarian countries are extremely suspicious and even fearful of any government or institutional representative (Fontes, 2008; Heras, 1992; Lustig and Koester, 2009; Lynch, 2011; Webb and Lum, 2001). A social worker who has the power to intervene may well be seen as just that—a government representative.

Several other cultural values of ethnic families may be difficult for workers not familiar with the culture to understand. The emphasis on family cohesion may mean that the family would rather stick together, ignoring or discounting the abuse, than be separated. Often, the family is dependent on the abuser and can see no other way than to tolerate whatever he is doing. The family also takes precedence over the marital dyad. The American culture sees the marital couple as the cornerstone of the family, whereas other cultures view alternative family subsystems as equally as important. Trying to strengthen the marital dyad may mean weakening the family structure.

Another dynamic for many Asian cultures is the need to save face. If family members feel ashamed of something that they have done or another family member has done, they may deny it at all costs in order to save face. To the uninitiated worker, this may look like denial and resistance. And finally, the indirect communication style employed in many cultures may be confusing. Clients who are urged to express their feelings or tell someone something directly may leave the agency, rather than behave in a manner so foreign to their value systems (Fontes, 2008; Heras, 1992; Lustig and Koester, 2009; Lynch, 2011; Webb and Lum, 2001).

The importance of having interventionists who understand the practices and history of such cultures cannot be stressed enough. Areas where there is a large Asian population (such as Los Angeles County, California) have established a specialized Asian unit in the Department of Children's Services to investigate and serve Asian clients who are referred because of suspected abuse and neglect. When it is not feasible or practical to provide bilingual, bicultural staff for direct service, it is important to have consultants who can be available to line staff to advise and educate on the cultural aspects of the case Webb and Lum, 2001).

In addition to participating in training groups or using consultants, the worker who is not bicultural must be aware of his or her own values and attitudes. No matter how aware a worker may be of cultural differences, if he or she has preconceived negative attitudes toward a particular population, the client will not receive optimum service. Agencies should be responsible for effective as well as cognitive training of staff before these workers become involved in the intervention process.

UNDERSTANDING THE INTERVENTION PROCESS

Before considering the process, it is important to consider intervention itself. The goal of intervention is to stop the abuse and neglect of the child or children in question. The children's current safety is paramount. But there are also several future dimensions to the effort. The children's future safety must be ensured. Ideally, parents can be helped to change—to adopt different coping skills and perhaps even alternative values about child rearing. Another goal—too often overlooked—is to give the children positive parenting models so they can grow into nonabusive adults.

Although these ideals are not always attainable, given the limited resources and the relatively young art of protective social work, it is toward these ends that the system strives. The way in which the system functions to help abused children and their families differs from state to state. Figure 10.1 charts the usual process protective cases follow. Variations depend on numerous legal and human factors.

The intervention process can be divided into several phases: reporting; investigation and assessment; and case management. Each phase requires the professionals as well as the families involved to make decisions that take steps to interrupt the abuse and protect the children in the future. These actions are accompanied by a variety of feelings and responses that will also be discussed.

Reporting

Changes in the 1970s brought legislation that mandated the identification and reporting of child maltreatment to designated social service agencies. States enacted their own laws and identified specific professionals who were mandated to report child abuse and neglect. The term *mandated reporters* refers to individuals who, in their professional relationship with the child and family, may encounter child maltreatment. Some states are more specific than others as to those who are mandated, but those who list these professionals usually include physicians, other medical professionals, counselors, social workers, and school personnel.

In addition to who shall report, most state laws spell out several other guidelines for mandated reporters. Most state laws indicate the following:

1. *To whom the report should be made.* Departments of social or human services, child welfare, or child protection are usually designated to be the recipients of these reports. Some states indicate that a report to a law enforcement agency is also appropriate.
2. *Under what conditions a mandated reporter must report.* State laws give one of three answers: suspicion of abuse and neglect, reasonable cause to believe, and reasonable cause to suspect.
3. *A time period during which the report must be investigated by social services.* These periods range from 2 hours to 30 days.

Figure 10.1   Overview of Child Protective Services Process

Source: Reprinted from *Child Neglect: A Guide for Prevention, Assessment, and Intervention*, by D. DePanfilis, Washington, DC: Children's Bureau, U.S. Department of Health and Human Services, 2006 (p. 44).

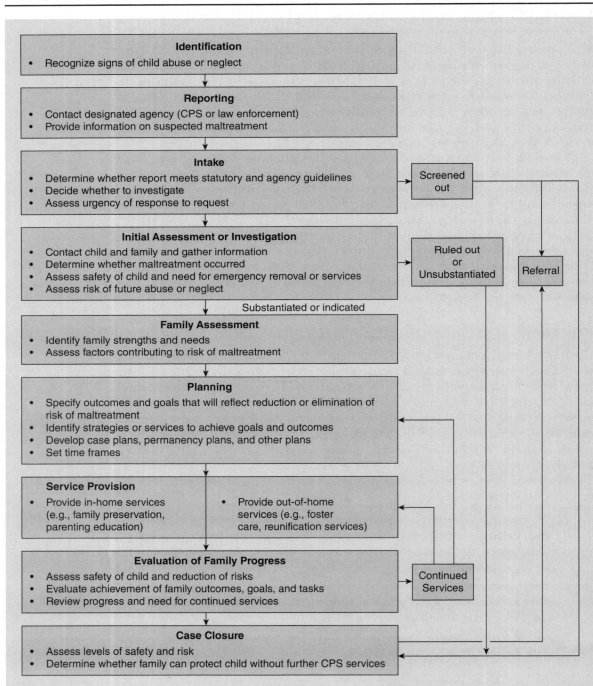

4. *The type of action taken if mandated reporters do not report.* Most state laws indicate that a mandated reporter who does not report is subject to a fine or imprisonment or will be charged with a misdemeanor.

5. *The type of immunity provided mandated reporters who make a report.* All states indicate some type of immunity from civil or criminal action (Weber, 1997).

While the law compels mandated reporters to disclose child abuse and neglect, other citizens are encouraged to do so. This often presents problems for the average person. Many people have no idea where to report. Although phone directories list protective agencies, people who have not had experience with social services may not know what these agencies are called. In fact, any law enforcement office, welfare office, or school can provide the name of the appropriate protective agency.

Another dilemma for people is whether to become involved. Abuse and neglect are not always easily recognizable and clearly defined. Even if they are, people wonder if they have the right to intervene in another's life. What would you have done in the following instance?

I was in an ice cream shop in mid-January. It was extremely cold, and it had recently snowed. Incongruous as it may seem, those of us waiting in line for ice cream were well bundled in coats, scarves, and mittens. As we waited, a mother and her toddler came into the store. The child was probably about 2 years old and wore only a diaper and a short-sleeved cotton shirt. She was barefoot. Her legs and arms looked chapped and red. Her face was dirty and her nose encrusted. The mother, dressed in slacks and a long-sleeved cotton blouse, paid little attention to the child, who coughed and snuffled her way to a nearby spot on the floor where she sat quietly.

In addition to not knowing where to report and not feeling the right to intervene in other's lives, most people prefer not to entangle themselves in the workings of a bureaucracy. Yet it is important that the average individual become better informed about reporting and take the risk in order to save a child from potential or continued harm.

Most agencies accept anonymous reports of child abuse and neglect, but they prefer not to for several reasons. Having the name of the reporter enables the agency to call back, if necessary, to clarify information. Some agency staff believe that giving one's name indicates more commitment to help the family. Agencies are quite familiar with vindictive calls from feuding neighbors, relatives, and ex-spouses, although fortunately, these calls are rare.

Well-meaning mandated reporters have asked if they can report anonymously, rather than chance having the family discover their identity. Although some states allow this, anonymity creates problems. First, many agencies require the staff to investigate reports from mandated reporters but allow them to use their own judgment on anonymous calls. Second, the mandated reporter could actually be fined or imprisoned for not reporting, and anonymity would provide no later proof of the reporter's identity. Thus, mandated reporters are always encouraged to give their names with the understanding that most agencies will not disclose their identities. Certainly, the reporter has the right to request anonymity.

Despite this hesitancy on the part of reporters to be known to the family, it can be beneficial for a family to know who has called child protective services (CPS), for several reasons. First, the reporter can make it known to the family that it was her or his intent to open the door for them to get help rather than a punitive gesture. Secondly, this step begins the process in the open, rather than continue the secret keeping that is an integral part of the family pathology. The reporter can work with the family to turn anger or defensiveness into energy for positive outcomes. Finally, not knowing who has made such a report can make families feel slightly paranoid. They often exert a great deal of energy trying to uncover the identity of the reporter, energy that could be better channeled in therapeutic efforts.

Should a family be told that their situation has been reported to CPS? This will depend on the circumstances. In general, CPS agencies often recommend that reporters do contact the family when they are making a report. However, if such a report will put the child at risk for greater danger or if the family is likely to flee, it might not be advisable to inform them that a report is being made until after CPS can respond and provide a safety net for all involved. The question is often asked by mandated reporters: Will an abuser come after me? Although there are cases when an abuser might seek to retaliate against a reporter, this is rare. More often families are frightened and defensive, and although a few will threaten, a reporter who seems concerned for their welfare and not his or her own is more likely to engage them in a positive manner.

Reporting suspected child abuse and neglect is not easy, but the step is vital to securing help for children and their families (see Figure 10.1).

Child Protection Teams

Over the last decade, more and more schools, medical facilities, and other agencies have recognized the usefulness of having child protection teams (CPTs). These teams, usually comprised of staff from different disciplines, are designed to meet when the need arises to discuss a particular situation in order to determine if a case requires reporting to the local child protection authorities.

Schools, especially, have found this approach helpful. The school-based CPT usually includes an administrator or his or her assistant, a guidance counselor, possibly the school nurse, and one or two other representative educators. If someone within the school suspects that a child is being maltreated, he or she brings those suspicions to a member of the CPT. The CPT then convenes as soon as possible to discuss the matter. If the team agrees with the reporter that the child protection agency should be notified, either the designated CPT member or the original reporter (depending on the protocol that the school has established) makes the report to child protection. If the original reporter and the team disagree, the reporter may still report the case, but he or she often does so after having fully considered the facts involved. No matter what the outcome, the CPT holds such discussions in strictest confidence (see Crosson-Tower, 2002).

CPTs have been used effectively not only in schools but also in medical and psychiatric facilities and other such agencies. More recently, churches have recognized the necessity for having prevention plans and protocol and are developing such teams (Crosson-Tower, 2006). The advantage of a CPT is that the reporter feels supported by other colleagues who also provide a sounding board. In addition, it is not just one person who has the responsibility for reporting. Reporters who have collegial support and an opportunity to share their concerns often feel more secure in the fact that they have made a report.

Investigation and Assessment

A report to a social service agency starts a complex chain of events. Substantiation is the determination by the initial or intake social worker that abuse or neglect is in fact present. The decision whether to substantiate is usually made after the social worker has made some basic inquiries.

Reports come in by phone or through written referrals. The reporter is questioned on the phone or sometimes interviewed to determine the validity of his or her concerns. If the report is anonymous and little information is available, the screening or intake worker's job may be extremely difficult. This preliminary investigation requires the worker to talk with the children and their parents and perhaps other family members as well. Children are often interviewed at school or in another neutral setting, providing an opportunity for the worker to see the child alone. This is important to prevent the child from feeling overwhelmed or inhibited by the presence of the parent(s) who may also be the abuser(s).

In the course of the investigation, the intake worker may conclude that the report was inappropriate. For example, in a housing rather than a protective situation, the case would be referred to a different agency. If the worker determines that there is too little information to conclude that abuse or neglect exists or if the family appears to be coping without evidence of maltreatment, the case is "unsubstantiated," and no further contact is made. Some agencies keep the report on file for a period of time to see if other reports are made. New legislation protecting individual privacy in some states requires that the report be destroyed after a specific interval.

As we consider intervention, it is vital to look more closely at the reactions that the family involved may be exhibiting.

Family Reactions

It is safe to assume that the family is in a state of crisis or disequilibrium when disclosure takes place. Certainly, fear is very much a part of the clients' experience—fear of what will happen next, fear of authority, fear of having their children removed or of family breakup, and fear of their own feelings of helplessness. Fontes (2008) suggests that immigrant families may also have fears around deportation. Yet clients respond to this fear in different ways, based on their personality as well as cultural background. Denial is a common defense, especially in abusive situations and regardless of clear-cut evidence attesting to the abuse (Faller, 2003; Stone, 2005).

Often, clients project their problems or the cause of their problems onto others. A sexually abusive father responds, "If my wife had stayed home and had been there for me, I wouldn't have turned to my daughter." A mother accurately identifies the myriad stresses in her life as the cause of her battering her child. A father assumes that a child knows how tired he is and acts out to "get to him" (Azar and Cote, 2005). Some clients see the system as the problem, rather than their behavior or the behavior of a family member. Incestuous families frequently displace their anger onto the helping system, rather than face the threat of losing the perpetrator and the dissolution of the family unit (Joyce, 1997).

Some children also feel loyalty toward the perpetrator and want him or her to stay home. Unable to accept their underlying anger and repulsion for him or her, the family members instead develop antagonism for the social service system that has forced them to open this painful wound. These negative feelings are further augmented if the social worker in any way speaks out against the perpetrator. The family then sees this worker as unfeeling, uncaring, and unconcerned with the pain the perpetrator feels at his own victimization by the system. Such an unfeeling individual, the family deems, cannot possibly be of any help to them. This reaction should be considered in the context of the family's desperate need to regain a balance (Faller, 2003; Fontes, 2008; Forkey, Hudson, Manz, and Silver, 2002; Lynch, 2011; Seagull, 1997).

The abusive and neglectful family may demonstrate its fear through withdrawal or hostility. Withdrawal may take the form of missed appointments, inhibited affect, or refusal to talk. All of these reactions reflect an effort at self-protection and control. For Asians, it may be to "save face." Other minorities might exhibit similar behavior that should be seen within a cultural context. Hostility, although based on the same needs, may manifest itself in threats, verbal abuse, or passive resistance:

> *Mrs. Basil greeted the worker with an angry "Oh, it's you again." Although she allowed the worker to enter, the door was slammed forcibly, and followed by a tirade: "I don't know why you damn nosy people can't leave us alone." Mrs. Basil responded to the worker's questions with angry one-word answers and hurled verbal admonishments at her three young children.*

Although this client felt she had to cooperate to some extent, she nevertheless needed to express her frustration and helplessness through her verbal attacks. Also consider this response:

> *Mrs. Desmond, on the other hand, expressed her hostility by compulsivity. She compulsively cleaned and demonstrated a rigidity with her household and communicated a message to the worker that Mrs. Desmond was finally able to verbalize: "I'll show you I can be a good mother." The worker recognized her extreme vulnerability, and rather than point out that her rigidity was actually producing an opposite effect, was able to identify with her underlying feelings of powerlessness.*

Some clients experience and demonstrate depression, often precipitated by their feelings of failure and hopelessness. An easing of this depression can be translated into an attachment or overdependence on the worker. The message becomes "I can't take care of things. I'm overwhelmed. Take care of me." For some clients, this initial clinging to the helper provides the basis for a trusting relationship, on which they can build their future independence. Others feel so incapable that they can only transfer their dependence from one worker to another over the years.

Developing a case management or service plan for some clients can be a challenge. One of the most important aspects of deciding what type of services will be necessary is to assess the client's strengths within the context of his or her cultural values.

Since trust is the fundamental basis for the helping relationship, the worker must initially assess the client's ability to trust. One way to determine this is to explore the quality of significant relationships he or she has had in the past. Have there been some people on whom the client could count? Or have all the past relationships been punctuated with betrayals? Certainly, the client who has had some close trusting relationships will have a better capacity to invest in treatment. There are also cultural implications in the client's ability to trust. African American, Hispanic American, and Asian clients, faced with a predominantly white system, may feel they cannot trust. The client whose life has been permeated with disappointments, whether involving intimates or related to prejudice, will necessitate a long, patient period of engagement that may be characterized by an approach and avoidance as he or she learns that it is possible to trust. But trust is not always easy to establish between protective social worker and client.

Although the worker is fundamentally interested in helping the client, protective services also functions as part of the legal system. A worker has the power to remove children, and most clients are very much aware of this. Further, the worker cannot sacrifice accountability to the legal system in the interest of establishing a relationship. If the client chooses not to cooperate, the worker must take a legal role and possibly render a further trusting relationship impossible.

The concern the client demonstrates for the children is also significant. Poor judgment can cause parents to inadvertently harm their children. Stress may have the same effect, but if the parent has a fundamental love for the child, this love can be strengthened. Some recognition of their children's needs provides a useful strength on which to build. In addition to caring, the parent who expresses pride in his or her children can be helped to accept disappointments and adjust unrealistic expectations. Pride frequently derives from a sense of self. Although most protective clients exhibit poor self-esteem, many have some sense, albeit small, of their own worth. Self-esteem often can be enhanced if the client has had some previous successes of which he or she is proud. Further, clients who demonstrate an absence of chronic self-destructive patterns have a better prognosis for treatment (Azar and Cote, 2005; Seagull, 1997).

Many workers find that clients demonstrate determination. The same manipulation of the system, so often seen in multiproblem families who enlist the support of numerous agencies, can be used, with direction, as a strength to marshal community resources such as advocacy, housing services, financial aid, and so on.

Most workers hope for a willingness to change as an important ingredient in treatment planning. Unfortunately, this is not always likely at the onset, and sometimes clients are never willing to change. Above all, case management and treatment require patience. The rewards are significant, however, for the concerned worker who sees a client finally able to cope with and care for the children.

Home Visiting

Traditionally, the home visit has been the realm of the protective social worker. The abusive and neglectful parents are mostly involuntary clients. In most cases, they resent social service intervention and therefore are unlikely to seek it out or to respond to a call or letter requesting they keep an office appointment. On the other hand, sophisticated or aggressive clients (especially in sexual abuse cases) decide the best way to fight the intrusive system is with a good offense. These clients often appear at the office with little or no notice. Some cultural groups (e.g., Native Americans) protest by withdrawal or silence and most likely will not come to the office. Therefore, the worker must go to them.

For most protective workers, the first client contact is in the parents' home, which offers several advantages. First, the clients perhaps feel greater comfort and protection in their own familiar setting. The family may actually gain strength from this setting. From the worker's perspective, the home is an ideal diagnostic arena. The family drama is played out daily in this setting, and aspects of this interaction will continue, regardless of the presence of an outsider:

It became clear from visiting the Jenks's home that the primary rule was to pacify Mr. Jenks. Running of the household revolved around his return from work at 5:30. Whatever energy the severely ill mother, Kitty, was able to muster was directed toward her husband's comfort. But the furniture and the holes in the wall attested to the father's rage when his needs were not met by his wife and four children. Only 9-year-old Herbie, reported to the agency as a victim of severe abuse, did not subscribe to the family's mission and had obviously suffered for it.

After visiting on several occasions and at different times of the day, the worker realized that the family dynamics changed significantly depending on the presence or anticipated presence of Mr. Jenks. Midday was marked by relative calm, while the closer to 5:30 the family was seen, the more intense were their interactions.

In some cultures, one does not take problems outside the home. Thus, being in the client's home may enable the investigator to learn more about what originated the report.

Family patterns emerge as one observes members in their home. The quality of relationships becomes more clearly discernible; the unpredictable behavior of children and their parents' candid response to them provide workers with valuable information. Client strengths can be identified. For example, noticing a flair for creativity in home decoration may give a worker the opportunity to encourage outside interests for an isolated mother. Severe neglect of the home may indicate depression or a feeling of being overwhelmed by life and responsibilities. On the other hand, clients' compulsive and rigid neatness may reflect control, anger, or extremely high expectations that manifest themselves in child management. Less experienced workers may find that their own values about housekeeping standards must be acknowledged and not allowed to affect their view of the client's. It is important for workers not to generalize on the appearance of the home. The impressions gleaned from the home visit should instead be mentally filed for future use in diagnostic assessment.

Visits in the home also provide clients with an element of control as well as comfort—a fact that is not without frustrations for many social workers. Clients, for example, may not answer the door or not be home for appointments. In some instances, an unannounced home visit is made, but a letter is usually sent to clients alerting them to the worker's intention to visit.

Consistency and a caring attitude are both effective in working with a resistant client. Sometimes a note saying that the worker is sorry to have missed Mrs. Jones but will be back at the same time next week will indicate to the client that the worker intends to be persistent. The frustration itself represents interaction, and the engagement of the client has indeed begun. The worker hopes that consistency and persistence will be rewarded by some degree of client cooperation. If, however, the child is perceived to be at too much risk, court intervention may be immediately necessary.

Through the frustration of missed appointments and unopened doors, it is vital to remember the attitudes and motivations that underlie the resistance of protective clients. Resistance is, in fact, based on fear. We all fear unwanted intrusion in our lives, especially if it is accompanied by the perceived admonishment that we are not assuming responsibility as we should. Although workers are trained not to tell clients they are not parenting effectively, the fact of social service intervention nevertheless conveys the message. Further, clients often see protective services as the agency that takes away children. Although hampered perhaps in child rearing by their own childhoods, their attitudes, inabilities, or incapacities, most parents do love their children. Suggesting that children cannot stay at home makes parents feel branded as failures.

For the most part, protective clients have histories of deprivation and betrayals. Much of their relationship with the protective worker will be colored by the client's fear of being betrayed and abandoned once again. Clients who learn to trust the worker may become greatly dependent on him or her. Thus, allowing a social worker to enter one's life can provoke anxiety.

Clients control and resist during interviews. They also control by missing interviews. The too-loud TV, ringing phone, or frequent demands of children provide distractions behind which some clients hide. Again, perseverance and the polite and patient suggestion that these issues are important and must be discussed may help. Clients often surround themselves with neighbors or relatives who either speak on their behalf or ensure that the conversation remains superficial. The worker may need to request to see the client alone. It is important to remember, however, that the kinship values of some cultures means that the presence of relatives and intimates is not as much resistance as inclusion. In these situations, recognition of these cultural variations may actually enhance the relationship between worker and client.

Clients use a variety of resistance techniques. A young social worker describes her experience with a neglectful mother whose child had been placed in foster care by the courts:

> Star was sullen and withdrawn during our interview. We talked about the action she would need to take to have her daughter returned. Suddenly she got up, walked through a nearby door, and shut it. I heard the lock click. I assumed she had gone to the bathroom until I saw that the bathroom door was open—and the room was empty. I waited and waited. All I could think of was, "No one ever told me what to do about this!" I must have sat there for 20 minutes and finally called to her. No answer. I knocked on another door and asked, "Are you okay?" No answer. I then realized that Star had no intention of coming out. I wrote her a note telling her when I would be back and left it on the table. Not knowing what else to do, I left.

The home visit provides opportunities to engage the client; befriending a much-loved pet, admiring a possession, or appreciating a cup of coffee helps clients witness the worker's concern. Hispanic American clients may actually be more cooperative if they see the worker as a warm, friendly individual who could be part of the family. Above all, however, it is important to remember that seeing clients at home is entering their sanctuary. The home is the most intimate area of one's life. Respecting this sanctity while still doing effective protective work is the art of home visiting.

ASSESSING RISK AND PROTECTIVE FACTORS

Assessment begins the moment the social worker assumes a case. Discussions with the reporter, reading old files and new reports, and contacts with collaterals (e.g., teachers, neighbors, therapists, or others involved with the family) are all important. However, the first interview with the client must provide information pivotal to the case. Initially, the social worker must answer four questions:

1. Is the child at risk from abuse or neglect and to what degree?
2. What is causing the problem?
3. What are the strengths or protective factors that could be built on with services to alleviate the problem?
4. Is the home a safe environment or must the child be placed? (Forkey et al., 2002; Hewitt, 2012; MacDonald, 2005; Righthand, Kerr, and Drach, 2003; Weber, 1997).

Risk to the child must be fully investigated. Can the child remain at home? It is vital to look at risk in the context of the type of abuse, the family history, and the family's attitude toward the child. Neglect, although disturbing, usually has been going on for years, if not for generations. Unless the family decides to flee to avoid intervention or unless the child's health is severely endangered, the situation is perhaps not overly volatile. Physical abuse, on the other hand, is much less predictable. The report itself can precipitate further abuse. Yet for some families, the intervention of authority, represented by protective services, is enough to give the child some protection.

Familial sexual abuse has probably gone on over a period of time, and unless pregnant, infected with venereal disease, or showing evidence of physical harm, the child may not be in immediate danger. However, several factors tend to cause protective service agencies to see sexual abuse as a high-risk situation. First, society in general believes sexual contact between adults and children so abhorrent that it must be stopped. Second, once disclosure has taken place, with its initial crisis, confusion, and disorganization, an incestuous family tends to mobilize itself to preserve its existence. If intervention does not begin immediately at disclosure, the family may persuade the child to recant, protect itself with legal help, or even flee. And finally, after disclosure, the chance of suicidal thoughts or actions on the part of the child or the perpetrator or both is high, and immediate intervention may be needed.

In addition to assessing the risks of further abuse to the child, current child welfare practice also assesses the protective factors in the case. These may be the strengths that the child or the family have or that are inherent in the environment. It is on these strengths that services must be based.

Although risk assessment currently is the primary tool used by most CPS agencies, there is a trend nationally to emphasize a strengths-based perspective, rather than a risk-assessment perspective. This shift will most likely inform practice in the future. For now, both risk factors and protective factors are assessed thoroughly (see Table 10.1).

The next few sections reflect the current practice of interviewing to further assess risk. Before this interviewing is undertaken, it is important that the worker determine which conditions present low risk and which present high risk for dependent children. Risk may be assessed according to several interdependent yet situation-specific factors: child specific, caregiver related, perpetrator specific, incident related, and environmental. Table 10.1 outlines these factors and provides a method of assessing the degree of risk to the child or children.

Table 10.1 **Assessing Risk for Child Maltreatment**

Risk Factors Related to Child	Low Risk	More Concerning Risk	High Risk
Age	Adolescent	Elementary school age child	Infancy 0–3 years
Circumstances surrounding birth	Few complications in pregnancy and birth	Some difficulty/complications in pregnancy and birth	Unwanted, problem pregnancy; difficult birth; low birthweight; exposure to drugs/ETOH
Evidence of trauma	Mild or little trauma earlier in childhood	Some trauma or question of past abuse	Serious trauma or abuse in past
Personality/temperament	Ability to self-calm few behavior or development problems	Tendency toward being withdrawn or mildly aggressive	Behavior problems; ADHD
		Mild behavior issues	Aggressive or severely withdrawn
		Mild learning disabilities	
Health and development	Mild or no health problems; relatively normal development	Some health problems; some developmental delay	Chronic or serious illness, physical disability, limited cognitively, poor development
Social adjustment	Relatively normal peer relationships	Some difficulty with peers	Difficulty with or isolation from peers due to child's preference or peer reaction to child
Childhood history	Relatively normal development; secure attachment with own parents; no apparent abuse as child	Some childhood difficulties; another sibling with problems; some difficulty with attachment; some parental conflict	Difficult childhood marked by abuse, neglect, domestic violence, or substance abuse
			Parental conflicts
Use of substances	Little or no drinking or use of drugs; if drinks, only socially	Drinking—can be excessive. Significant use of prescription drugs—marijuana or other drugs—in social situations	Alcoholism or heavy use of prescription or street drugs
Personality	Relatively easygoing, effective problem solving, able to self-calm, low anxiety	Marked anxiety in stressful situations. Tendency toward depression, insecurity, some difficulty trusting, some difficulty taking responsibility for actions	Low frustration tolerance; poor impulse control; feels controlled by outside events; depressed or anxious; feels insecure; has difficulty trusting

(continued)

Table 10.1 **Assessing Risk for Child Maltreatment (*continued*)**

Risk Factors Related to Child	Low Risk	More Concerning Risk	High Risk
Relationship issues	Fairly stable relationships; has intimate relationships and an adequate support system	Some difficulty making and keeping friends; tends to have multiple intimate relationships over time; feels lonely and sometimes isolated; involved in problematic divorce	Relationship characterized by change, stress, and conflict; multiple unsatisfying relationships
			Relationships may be based on drinking together or other such escape or violence, domestic violence, divorce disputes, and custody battles
Parenting potential	Was desirous of children; enjoys parenting; sees children as individuals, spends time with children	May not have wanted children but accepted them or wanted them but did not realize amount of work; has time for children when convenient; attends to children's basic needs but also needy; may compete with children for partner's attention	Did not want children; sees them as a burden; resents the time they take; prefers company of partner or friends; high stress level; conflicted parent–child interaction; negative attitudes about children's behavior
			Inadequate knowledge of child development or unrealistic expectations
Family structure	Functioning two-parent family or single parent with healthy support system or close relationship with extended family	Single parent with limited support system/family support; two parents experiencing some conflict	Single parent with few supports or two parents in conflict using children as pawns; domestic violence, single mother with frequent male relationships
Mental health	Relatively stable, able to handle stress and problem solve	Some indication of psychological problems but under control or treatment	Mental illness (borderline personality, bipolar, psychotic, etc.)
Explanation for behavior	Accidental	Minor injury; may have resulted from too vigorous discipline, but parent takes responsibility	Injury resulting from desire to harm child
			Feels the need of severe corporal punishment
Economic status	Relatively secure financially with little economic stress	Some economic stress; insecure employment; past unemployment	Severe economic stress; unemployment

Table 10.1 (*conitnued*)

Risk Factors Related to Child	Low Risk	More Concerning Risk	High Risk
Safety	Safe, stable neighborhood; feels safe in environment	Some neighborhood unrest	Violent/dangerous neighborhood; family feels unsafe
			Exposure to environmental toxins
			Victims of racial prejudice
Access to resources	Fair knowledge of community resources and willingness to use them	Some knowledge of community resources but hesitant to use them	Little or no knowledge of resources
			Rejection of community resources
			Poor or dangerous schools
Physical condition of home	Clean with no apparent safety or health hazards	Trash, garbage, animal excrement visible	Unsafe conditions due to building structure, trash, garbage, animal/human feces that are unattended to and present health hazard

Protective Factors

• Protective factors are in contrast to risk factors and serve to protect the child from possible abuse. Significant protective factors might be as follow:

Protective Factors Related to Child

• Child is in good health and result of a normal pregnancy and birth

Or

• Mother receives and accepts support around any current or past problems with child
• Child has above-average intelligence
• Child has easy temperament, is well bonded with caretakers, and feels secure
• Child has healthy self-esteem, is able to problem solve (age appropriate), and shows age-appropriate degree of autonomy
• Child has good peer relationships
• Child has experienced relatively healthy development free from trauma
• Child has hobbies or interests

Protective Factors Related to Parents/Family

• Positive parent–child relationship with secure attachment
• Appropriate structure/family rules with fair, nonphysical discipline
• Parents model healthy self-esteem and good problem-solving abilities
• Presence of concerned and caring extended family
• Higher parental educational level
• Family expects prosocial behavior

(continued)

Table 10.1	**Assessing Risk for Child Maltreatment (*continued*)**

Protective Factors Related to Environment

- Access to health and educational resources
- Consistent parental employment
- Adequate housing
- Mid to high socioeconomic status
- Family is affiliated with religious faith community
- Presence of other positive and influential adult models

Source: Adapted from www.childwelfare.gov. Accessed April 13, 2009.

Children

The child-specific factors to consider are age and physical or mental abilities. The younger the child, the more vulnerable he or she is to the abuse; for example, the same force may cause more injury to an infant than to an older child. Further on the continuum, the worker considers the mental and physical capacities of the child to protect himself or herself. Children who are mentally retarded, physically disabled, congenitally malformed, premature, chronically ill, or physically affected by the parents' use of drugs or alcohol during pregnancy are at higher risk for maltreatment (Hewitt, 2012; Righthand et al., 2003).

Caregivers

Initially, the worker notes the level of cooperation and capabilities shown by the caregivers, remembering to frame this within a cultural context. Parents who recognize there is a problem present a better prognosis and less risk to the children than those who demonstrate hostility or refuse to cooperate. The physical, mental, and emotional capabilities of the parent—as evidenced by their expectations of the child, ability to protect the child, and ability to control anger and other impulses—indicate the degree of risk to the victim. Parents who are unaware of children's needs or demonstrate poor judgment or concept of reality present a high risk to the dependent child.

Perpetrators

Here, the worker is concerned with the abuser's rationality of behavior and access to the child. The adult who intentionally abuses or who has a history of abusive or sadistic behavior places the child in greater danger than the accidental abuser. Further, the greater the perpetrator's access to the child, the more likely the abuse will be repeated.

Incidence and Environment

The incident itself is weighed in the light of future potential harm to the child. The worker determines the likelihood of permanent harm, the location of the injury, the previous history of abuse or neglect, and the physical conditions of the home. Environmental factors provide additional information. Parents who do not use support systems place the child at higher risk, for example, than those who can reach out for help. The degree of stress in the home also affects the likelihood of abuse. Death, divorce, incarceration of a parent, unemployment, career change, residence change, and birth of a child can all place a child at greater risk. Again, all these factors must be evaluated within a cultural context.

EXPLORING CAUSES AND SERVICES

The causes of child maltreatment are myriad. Assessment begins at the first meeting with the client and continues throughout treatment. Whether there are existing services to provide aid or otherwise help the situation is a factor in assessing risk to the child. A family for whom little can be done—because of the severity of their problems or their unwillingness to use services—provides greater risk for the child. Removal of the child may therefore be indicated.

One particularly difficult aspect of assessment is that it is usual for the family to initially deny the report of maltreatment. Subsequent interviews will be much more productive if the worker is able to identify with the client's underlying feelings and need to deny rather than with the denial itself. The worker must also be cognizant of the culture of the client and how that may affect his or her presentation (Fontes, 2008; Lynch, 2011; Webb and Lum, 2001). Recognizing feelings, rather than assigning blame, often elicits the client's recounting of his or her perception of the situation.

During the client's presentation of the facts, the worker gathers clues in order to "begin where the client is." Does the father feel overwhelmed by the problems of inadequate housing? Does the mother see her frustrations increased by an alcoholic husband? Does the parent try to cope with new cultural mores combined with the stresses of finding a place for himself or herself in a seemingly hostile culture? Worker–client engagement can be enhanced by the worker's ability to give direct support to the client.

For example, Mrs. Clemens, defensively recounting her problems, mentioned the difficulty of feeding her seven children. Being sure Mrs. Clemens would be eligible, given what was already known about the family, the worker suggested food stamps. "Oh, I've heard of them little coupons," the mother responded, "but I never knew where you got 'em." The worker arranged to take Mrs. Clemens to get food stamps, and the mother was then more amenable to discussing the problems of her children.

Some parents do not deny the report and instead feel they were justified in their actions. Mr. Alverey, for example, acknowledged that the belt marks on his son's legs were punishment for the boy's misbehavior. "My father punished me that way," he contended, "and I turned out okay." The worker was able to identify with this father's concern for his son but tried to help him use less forceful disciplinary methods. Met with Mr. Alverey's resistance to change, the worker had to firmly stress that the beatings must stop or court intervention would be necessary. If the practice that caused the abuse is accepted in another culture but not in the United States, the family must be helped to understand this.

On the first visit, an assessment of immediate risk and protective factors for the child is vital. If the worker begins to engage the parents by recognizing their feelings and needs, future intervention should go more smoothly.

HANDLING EMERGENCIES

At the onset or at any time during the intervention process, the protective case may reach the point of emergency. What constitutes an emergency is debatable, but agencies generally acknowledge three conditions: imminent danger of physical harm to the child, a dangerous home situation, or abandonment of the child. Immediate responses may include the police taking custody or hospital staff detaining children whom they deem to be in danger. In some states, protective services workers may also remove children from their homes in an emergency. Immediately following the emergency removal, a court order (authorizing custody) must be obtained. Most states recommend that if the emergency is during working hours, a court order be obtained prior to removing the child.

In some emergency situations, protective services workers rely on police to aid them in the removal of children. For example, if the home situation is volatile or there is danger to the worker as well as the child, police may be asked to help. A worker who fears violence or retaliation from the parent or who has reason to believe that the parents will flee may seek police support. Police officers can be invaluable in handling hostile or aggressive parents while the worker attempts to calm and pack for overwrought children.

Emergencies require particular skills of protective workers. Assessment must be made quickly while weighing carefully the risk of the child and the rights of the parents. Actions must be purposeful while still recognizing the feelings of those involved. In most cases, the worker has time to interview and assess, but emergencies do occur.

ASSESSMENT INTERVIEWING

Interviewing Adults

Validating the existence of abuse or neglect without antagonizing parents (and thereby closing the door to their help in the future) or precipitating an emergency is not easy. Not only does the worker have particular questions that should be answered to assess risk to the child, but he or she must also use good interviewing skills to elicit the responses and engage the client. The investigative worker must seem confident, skilled, relaxed, and assertive without losing the ability to communicate concern and compassion.

How an interview progresses depends on the worker's style and attitudes as well as on the client's responses. Table 10.2 lists interviewing techniques. Several other factors go into successful interviewing.

The worker must recognize the level of sophistication of the parents. Neglectful mothers, for example, may demonstrate verbal inaccessibility or a limited ability to communicate, especially in relation to their thoughts and feelings (Crittenden, 1999; Iwaniec, 2004; MacDonald, 2005; Polansky, Borgman, and DeSoiz, 1972; Polansky, Chalmers, Buttenweiser, and Williams, 1990). It is important, therefore, to use simple language to explain things carefully and to encourage client feedback to test for understanding. Although more sophisticated clients have a better command of language, they may still be unfamiliar with the process of the social service system or with social work jargon. Certainly, a worker must be careful to refrain from language that implies blame or connotes particular values.

Clients for whom English is a second language or who are relatively new to the culture may also need to have things explained slowly and carefully. Workers (in interviewing)

Table 10.2	Skills Used in Interviewing
1. Listening	
Attending	—The process by which the interviewer communicates interest and encouragement to the client. Attending involves Establishing eye contact;* Maintaining a posture indicating interest; Using gestures to communicate message; and Verbalizing statements that relate to the client's statements.
Paraphrasing	—The method of restating the client's message to test the interviewer's understanding of what has been said.
Clarifying	—The process of bringing the client's message into clearer focus by the interviewer's restating or asking for clarification.
Perception-checking	—The process of the interviewer verifying his or her perceptions by paraphrasing what was heard, requesting feedback on the validity of the perception, and then correcting the perception as necessary.
2. Leading	
Indirect leading	—Inviting the client to tell his or her story by saying, for example, "What would you like to discuss?" or "Tell me more about that."
Direct leading	—Focusing the topic by a suggestion to do so, for example, "Can you tell me about the last time you saw welts on Johnny?"
Focusing	—Bringing the client back to the topic that the interviewer needs to discuss, for example, "Could you think about what it is that annoys you about his behavior?" or "What are you feeling right now after we've been talking?"
Questioning	—Using open-ended questions (those that require more than a yes or no answer) to further explore the client's message.
3. Reflecting	
Reflecting feelings	—Paraphrasing the client's feelings in an effort to make clearer those that were vaguely expressed. The clients are thus given an opportunity to own their own feelings by hearing what they said.
Reflecting experience	—Relating to what the client is experiencing as he or she talks, the interviewer comments on body language, such as rapidity of speech, gestures, eye contact, or postures.
Reflecting content	—Repeating in fewer words the ideas expressed by the client. Through the use of additional vocabulary words—to help the client express himself or herself better, or through more concise phrasing—to get to the point, which has been lost in an abundance of words, the worker clarifies the client's ideas.

(continued)

Table 10.2   Skills Used in Interviewing (*continued*)

4. Summarizing	
	—Trying to aid the client by picking out various themes or overtones as the client speaks. The interviewer can aid the client by picking out the major ideas and feelings in a total interview, which helps both interviewer and client focus on the essence of the interview.
5. Confronting	
	—Pointing out to the client what is actually happening by giving feedback about his or her behavior. The risk in confronting is that the client may not be ready to hear what the interviewer has observed.
6. Interpreting	
	—Explaining the meaning of events to clients to enable them to see their problems in a new light. The interpretations may be given in terms of the particular philosophy or model of the interviewer. For example: "You are concerned that your daughter favors her father and seems to reject you. Many little girls at three are going through a stage when this is very natural." Sometimes the interviewer uses metaphors or stories to help interpret the client's behavior or feelings.
7. Informing	
	—Giving information, the most common of which is advice. Although it is often tempting to give advice, the interviewer must be aware of the client's readiness to receive it. For a variety of reasons, clients frequently ask for advice and then do not follow it. Advice may be based on the interviewer's values and not conform to the client's.
8. Guiding	
	—Informing clients about what to expect in certain instances, for example, when they go to court. Guidance provides clients with information that may direct their actions and responses.

*Where culturally appropriate.

Source: Adapted from Brammer, Lawrence M., and Ginger MacDonald. *The Helping Relationship: Process and Skills,* Seventh Edition. Published by Allyn and Bacon/Merrill Education, Boston, MA. Copyright © 2002 by Pearson Education. Reprinted by permission of the publisher.

must also be aware of cultural variations. For example, most people have been taught that eye contact is important, but some cultures (e.g., Asian) see it as disrespectful. Many cultures (e.g., Hispanic) will be resistant unless the worker has taken time to become acquainted through answering questions about himself or herself and chatting. The Hispanic parent will need to respect this person before he or she will disclose (Fontes, 2008; Hildebrand, Gray, and Phenice, 2007; Lum, 2000; Webb and Lum, 2001).

The purpose of the interview is to gather facts or information in order to assess the danger to the child. Direct questioning is likely to put the parent on the defensive. Asking a series of open-ended questions or reflections or giving the parent an opportunity to express his or her own feelings and attitudes toward the child is more effective (Steele, 2012). Another technique to uncover previously hidden facts or discrepancies is to ask the parent to recount in detail the incident that resulted in the child's injury—for example, "Could you show me what happened when Susie fell off the bed?"

Careful observation not only of the parent's description but also of his or her emotional response and manner in telling the story will help the worker to gather more information, as revealed in the following:

> Mrs. Hall tearfully explained how she had been in the other room when she heard 1-year-old Susie scream. Her husband had been there with the baby. When asked to describe the fall, Mr. Hall responded angrily, "What do you mean describe to you how she fell? If you fall off a bed, you just fall off a bed." As the worker discussed the situation further with this father and mother, she recognized the inconsistencies in their accounts. A fall from the height of the bed could not have caused Susie's type of injury. The mother often confused facts and seemed more concerned with her story than with Susie's welfare. She was defensive, although the worker had implied no blame.
>
> Finally, Mrs. Hall tearfully admitted that she had been with Susie and had been so angered by her constant crying that she had slapped her. The blow was so hard the child was thrown off the bed with enough force to fracture her arm. The father's inability to explain the accident, in addition to other discrepancies, had given the worker her first clue.

Although the facts of abusive incidents are important, particular areas should also be explored during the first few interviews in order to gather information for validation, including the following:

Parental History and Functioning

- How does the parent feel about the parental role? Are there cultural variations to this role?
- How did the parent's own parents discipline? Has the parent adopted the same methods that result in physical abuse or neglect?
- Was the parent sexually abused as a child?
- Did the parent experience early deprivation (which may hamper the parent's own ability to nurture) or abuse?
- Did the parent experience abandonment, death, or divorce as a child?
- Were the parent's parents alcoholic, drug dependent, or involved in criminal activity?
- Does the parent show evidence of extreme rigidity, excessive dependency needs, or borderline or state of psychosis?
- Has the family newly immigrated or is she or he part of a minority community with different values?

Parent's View of the Child

- What kind of expectations does the parent have of the child?
- Does the parent appear to understand the child's developmental needs?
- Does the parent see the child as difficult, unusual, hard to care for, or even "evil"?
- Does the parent describe the child in negative terms?
- Does the parent touch the child lovingly or talk to the child with affection? Or does the parent seem unable to comfort the child and perhaps stiffen when touched?
- Can the parent provide a history of the child's developmental milestones?

- Does the parent ignore the child or talk negatively about him or her in the child's presence?
- Is the parent frequently frustrated with the child? Is the child a scapegoat?
- Is the parent jealous or extremely overprotective of the child?
- Does the parent compare the child negatively to anyone else in the family?
- Does the parent describe the child as having any significant health or behavior problems?
- Is the parent overly seductive with the child?
- Does the parent engage in role reversal with the child? Is the child expected to assume adult responsibilities and take care of the parent?

Functioning of the Family

- Does one parent significantly dominate the other? (Is this culturally appropriate?)
- Are the parents openly antagonistic to each other?
- Are the conflicts between parents taken out on the children?
- Do there appear to be no family rules or extremely rigid rules?
- Is there marked role reversal between parents and children?
- Are the generational boundaries blurred?
- Do the parents appear to be covering up for each other?
- Is there undue stress on the family (e.g., significant losses, unemployment, alcoholism, residential moves, prejudice, or one parent absent)?
- During stress, do family members appear to abandon each other, or do they become neurotically overdependent on one another? (Keep in mind that some cultures are more family oriented than others.)
- Do family members engage in eye contact or physical contact?
- Do family members engage in activities together?

Environment

- Are there chronic environmental stresses or long-term problems that sap the parents' energies? (Are there, e.g., feuds with relatives or neighbors, poverty, discrimination, infestation by rodents, inadequate sanitation, significantly different cultural mores, or inadequate space and privacy?)
- Are there neighborhood factors that threaten the child's safety? (Is there, e.g., drug trafficking, unsafe housing, an unprotected body of water or wells, a condemned building, or a high crime rate?)
- Are there conditions around the home that endanger the child's safety? (For instance, are there easily accessible poisons, sharp objects, broken glass, exposed electrical wiring, rotten or moldy food, or small objects dangerous to a child under 2 years old?)

Family's Support System

- Does the family appear to be isolated either geographically or in terms of having someone close they could call on?
- In a time of crisis, does the family have friends or relatives they feel they can ask for help?
- Does the family depend more on formal social service systems than on informal systems?

An assessment of the family's support system—that is, who they have available to go to in time of crisis or to share good times—is particularly important. Research attests that a major cause of abuse is isolation. A family that is isolated is more vulnerable to intrafamily and environmental stresses. Later treatment may help family members make connections with others who can be of support emotionally, especially in times of crisis.

Although not all these questions can be answered in one interview, the astute protective worker gains a great deal of insight by careful observation as well as from verbal interchange on this interview (Steele, 2012).

Interviewing Children

Children—both victims and their siblings—provide valuable information in the investigation of protective cases. It is important to remember several important facts about children, however.

Expression

Children often speak in metaphors, whereas adults usually give a more literal interpretation of a situation. Children often relate their experiences in stories (especially in cases of sexual abuse). Children's drawings, especially, symbolize what they are attempting to express (see Willats, 2005). With this in mind, the investigative interviewer takes care to consider what the child has said at many levels.

Time

Children may have difficulty understanding time in the way adults do. A day, a week, or a year may mean little to a young child. On the other hand, the interviewer learns to use milestones such as "the time you got up" or "how long before Christmas."

Attention

Children are not used to being interviewed in the way we traditionally talk with adults. Indeed, their attention spans may not be sufficient to cover the entire story at one time. For this reason, a variety of techniques are used with children. They may be encouraged to draw, to act out the incident themselves, or to use dolls or talk to puppets.

Setting

Children perceive adults as authority figures, and this may color their responses. The wise interviewer engages the child in a nonthreatening manner, often sitting on child-sized chairs or even on the floor to come down to the child's level.

Memories

Children's memories differ from those of adults. Does fantasy distort children's memories? Although it is often assumed that children have poorer recall than adults, this seems to be related more to their insufficient experience and lesser ability with the language than to their ability to retain information. In fact, because children's heads are less cluttered with extraneous details, they may have a better recall of certain events (Steele, 2012).

It is often debated whether children are able to differentiate between fact and fantasy. This has been an especially controversial topic in the consideration of the testimony of children in sexual abuse cases and continues to be debated.

Developmental Level

If one considers the developmental level of a young child and the child's understanding of sex, as witnessed by their play (see Table 10.3), it is not likely that the details of oral and genital sex, for example, will be in the child's frame of reference. Therefore, the child has not imagined doing it and does not have these imaginings to confuse with reality.

Table 10.3 Stages of Sex Play

0–18 months	Child begins awareness of ability to experience pleasure from own body, including genital exploration.
2½ years	Child shows interest in different postures of boys and girls when urinating and interest in physical differences between the sexes. Genital exploration continues.
3 years	Verbally expresses interest in physical differences between sexes and in different postures in urinating. Girls attempt to urinate standing up. May feel increased need for genital masturbation.
4 years	Extremely conscious of the navel. Under social stress may grasp genitals and may need to urinate. May play the game of "show." Also, verbal play about elimination. Interest in other people's bathrooms; may demand privacy for self, but be extremely interested in bathroom activity of others.
5 years	Familiar with but not too much interested in physical differences between sexes. Less sex play and game of "show." More modest and less exposing of self. Less bathroom play and less interest in unfamiliar bathrooms.
6 years	Marked awareness of and interest in differences between sexes in body structure. Questioning. Mutual investigation by both sexes reveals practical answers to questions about sex differences. Mild sex play or exhibitionism in play or in school toilets. Game of "show." May play hospital and take temperature. Giggling, calling names, or remarks involving words dealing with elimination functions.
7 years	Less interest in sex. Some mutual exploration, experimentation, and sex play, but less than earlier. Sexually oriented dreams and fantasies begin, commonly resulting in "wet dreams." Strong feeling of modesty and privacy needs beginning to be expressed.
8 years	Interest in sex rather high, though sex exploration and play are less common than at six. Interest in peeping, smutty jokes, provocative giggling. Children whisper, write, or spell "elimination" or "sex" words.
9 years	May talk about sex information with friends of same sex. Interest in details of own organs and functions; seeks out pictures in books. Sex swearing and sex poems begin.
10 years	Considerable interest in "smutty" jokes. Feelings of modesty. Privacy continues. Onset of secondary sex characteristics may begin.

Note: Some cultures differ markedly from this chart. Cultural variations must be considered.
Source: From *Child Behavior: Specific Advice on Problems of Child Behavior* by Frances L. Ilg, MD and Louise Bates Ames, PhD, et al. Revised Edition. Copyright © 1981 by Louise Bates Ames, Frances L. Ilg, Sidney M. Baker, and Gesell Institute of Child Development. Reprinted by permission of HarperCollins Publishers, Inc.

Language

Children use different terminologies and language. During an interview, especially when validating sexual abuse, the interviewer needs to verify the child's terminology, especially about body parts. This can be done by having the child point to areas of his or her own body or by using anatomically correct dolls or pictures. Once the meaning is clear, it may be more comfortable for the child to use his or her own terminology (Faller, 2007; Friedrich, 2001; Steele, 2012).

In addition to all these factors, the interviewer of children must take into consideration the child's age, maturity, language and communication skills, and emotional readiness to be interviewed.

Setting up an interview with a child requires more care than for an interview with an adult. Children are usually seen alone or sometimes with a *functioning ally*—that is, a concerned adult who takes the child's side and protects him or her from further abuse. Workers often try to see the child at school or in another neutral setting, where parental intervention will not cause the child undue concern. In this case, to alleviate guilt, the child is often assured that the parent will be told of the interview. The parent is subsequently notified.

Sometimes, it is necessary to see a child in the home. The parents' cooperation will then need to be secured. Certainly, the child is entitled to as much confidentiality as an adult, and the parents are helped to understand this. The setting of the interview (if one has control over this) should be free of distractions but equipped with a few necessary resources—such as paper, crayons, dolls and other toys, and materials designed to enable the child to explain what has happened. Interviewers are usually cautious about having too many toys in the room, as they can serve to distract. Older children are often aided in their talking by playing board games.

The actual interview usually involves engaging the child, establishing the interviewer's credibility, fact finding, allaying the child's anxiety, and helping the child to anticipate the future.

Engaging begins with helping the child feel comfortable by letting the child explore the room, ask questions, or talk about school, friends, or activities. This spontaneous small talk makes the child feel comfortable and also assists the interviewer to discern the child's emotional style, maturity, and ability to communicate. The interviewer explains to the child why he or she is there.

This may lead naturally into establishing the credibility of the interviewer. Comments such as "I've talked to many other boys and girls who had this kind of problem" help the child see the worker as someone others have trusted. The child may also feel less alone in his or her problem. During these opening phases, the worker should be especially sensitive to any anxiety the child is feeling and reflect on this. By feeling that he or she has agreed to give this information, the child is helped to feel in control. The abused child is one who has felt out of control for a long time, so giving the child an element of control through the interview can be the beginning of the therapeutic process.

Fact finding with children is not as simple and straightforward as it may be when interviewing adults. Children have short attention spans. They may not want to discuss the abuse. As a result, they may change the subject frequently or want to end the interview. Such an interview takes mental agility and creativity. One 5-year-old boy, being interviewed by a worker and observed behind a one-way mirror by a team of professionals, refused to discuss the "games" his mother's boyfriend played with him. After undressing anatomically correct dolls and asking the child to identify the body parts, as well as numerous other techniques, the worker was at a loss. She assured the child she would return and went to talk with her colleagues. As soon as she left, the child scrambled under the table with the male doll and furtively sucked on its cloth penis. He then took out his own penis and attempted to insert it in the doll's mouth. With this obvious demonstration of what had been done to the boy, the worker returned and began gently questioning him about male penises, without disclosing what she had seen. Eventually, the boy began to talk about the boyfriend's sexual abuse of him.

Although open-ended questions are a good place to begin, the worker may need to be more direct without leading the child into specifics. For example, the interviewer might say, "I've talked with children who have had adults touch them in the private places of their bodies. Has that ever happened to you?" Or in the case of physical abuse, the interviewer might say, "Some kids say that they had accidents because they are afraid to say that someone had hit them." It may seem natural to the interviewer to ask the child direct questions that will confirm what the worker believes has happened. However, it is important that questions be kept nonleading. Although small children do not usually lie, especially about sexual abuse, they may easily be led to make erroneous statements by their desire to please adults.

For example, one interviewer believed that a child had been sexually abused by her father and communicated this belief to the child. With anatomically correct dolls, the worker placed the adult male doll on the girl doll and asked, "Is this what your father did to you?" The child—having roughhoused with her father in the past—was confused. She had not felt what she and her father had done was wrong. She sensed, however, that the worker did and wanted her to respond affirmatively. Her mother, too, had pressured her, so the child decided she had better agree that this had happened. Such obvious leading of a child to accuse the father, who turned out to be innocent, causes great pain for all involved.

Prejudicing juvenile witnesses jeopardizes court cases that are brought against guilty perpetrators. For this reason, interviewers are being taught to be especially careful. Some agencies videotape or record the interview to ensure that they have an accurate record of what—and how—the child was asked.

Instead of talking to the worker, the child may prefer to draw what happened without saying anything. The interviewer then encourages the child to explain the picture. Puppets are useful because a child can engage in a conversation with the worker's puppet or through his or her own puppet, without having to talk to the interviewer directly.

The worker must be particularly sensitive to the feelings of the child during the telling of the abuse. Children experience fear, anxiety, guilt, shame, and myriad other emotions. In addition, children do not always have the same view of the abuser that an adult may. An abusing parent may still be beloved because the child internalizes the guilt. On the other hand, expressions of extreme rage and hatred may be difficult for the worker to accept.

Other validating information to assess the further risk to the child may be necessary after the interview, but the child's own assessment of safety is often quite accurate. Questions about what precipitated the abuse may indicate what steps will be needed to protect the child in the future.

Sometimes, it is useful to ask the child to reconstruct the event. The effectiveness of this technique must be weighed against possible trauma to the child of remembering in such detail. If remembering appears to be beneficial rather than detrimental, the worker might ask the child to recall the setting, what he or she was wearing, where the abuser was, where others were, and how the abuse occurred (Faller, 2007; Seagull, 1997; Steele, 2012). If the child is from a culture with distinct taboos against talking about sex, the interview may be more difficult.

In the case of sexual abuse, the worker should consider certain validating factors: multiple incidents over a period of time, progression of sexual activity, elements of secrecy, elements of pressure or coercion, and explicit details of sexual behavior (Faller, 2007; Friedrich, 2001). Since most sexual abuse includes multiple incidents over time, the interviewer can discover from the child if this was the case. As discussed in previous chapters, sexual abuse usually involves a progression of sexual activity that becomes more intimate over time. In almost all situations, the perpetrator of sexual abuse pressures or coerces the victim and then compels secrecy. And finally, the child who recounts in explicit detail will not have sufficient knowledge for such a description unless he or she has been abused.

deYoung (1986) suggests a variation on this framework as a means of judging the truthfulness of the allegations of young children in sexual abuse that still has weight. These factors continue to be considered today. She cites clarity, celerity, certainty, and consistency as indicators of the validity of the reports. But children between the ages of 2 and 7 (the ages of children in her study) demonstrate problems in these areas. In terms of clarity, children of these ages may have difficulty in expressing themselves accurately. They must rely on their limited experience for elaboration. Thus, "ejaculation" becomes "urination," as the latter is the only function of the penis with which they are familiar. Their thinking is concrete and has insufficient subtlety to recognize objects in an altered form. The relationship between the erect and flaccid penis therefore confuses them. Children may also delay telling anyone about their abuse. Such delays actually give credence to the child's report, as delay is the rule rather than the exception. It must also be noted that delays are not a result of the child's doubt of what has happened but of the perpetrator's demand for secrecy.

The lack of certainty, often pointed to in the testimony of abused children, relates to their perception of reality. The abuser may have told the child that the sex interaction was normal, while other adults are now saying it is not. The child, therefore, is required to sort out or reinterpret the abuse and is often confused.

The last factor deYoung (1986) cites as considered in the testimony of sexually abused children is consistency. There is a great deal of pressure on the child to recant or amend the accusation. Further, the way in which the child tells the story to a given adult may differ according to the adult's style and manner of interviewing.

If these four validation points are compromised with young children, how then can the allegation be verified? deYoung (1986) suggests that the answer is found in specific details: The child who is asked to describe the acts of sexual abuse and can do so in detail—especially if these details exceed the child's level of understanding and maturity—is more likely to be believed. The context of the abuse should also be described. Asking the child to describe exactly where the abuse occurred and where others were at the time elicits further specific details. In addition, the more specific the child can be about how the perpetrator elicited secrecy, the better. Did the abuser threaten or bribe the child or suggest harm to others?

And finally, the way in which the child recounts the abuse—the child's affect—is important. Did the child experience pleasure, pain, confusion? The child will often describe mixed emotions—pain at the penetration but happiness and warmth at the amount of attention received from the perpetrator. The victim may not feel negative toward the abuser. And this fact can confuse the less experienced or even the informed interviewer.

In validation, much use can also be made of the past trauma factors suggested by Finkelhor and Browne (1985) and deYoung (1986): An abused child will demonstrate traumatic sexualization (using sexual behavior to manipulate others or demonstrating age-inappropriate sexual knowledge); indicate a feeling of betrayal (by those previously trusted); evidence disempowerment (by feeling that all his or her needs will be overridden and by exhibiting fear and anxiety about the sense of powerlessness); and indicate a feeling of being stigmatized (evidenced by shame, guilt, blame, and low self-esteem). If these factors are present, a child is more likely to be believed.

Although most researchers and practitioners report that young children, especially, rarely fabricate stories of sexual abuse on their own and should be believed, the court system, in prosecution of perpetrators, has required more attention to the validity of allegations. A particular concern is still expressed over the accusation of sexual abuse by adolescents. Are adolescents more likely to fabricate the sexually abusive experience?

Because adolescents are engaged in battles for control and separation, some may use allegations of sexual abuse as tools in this conflict. Although there is certainly this possibility, the skilled interviewer concentrates on adolescents' details and considers their clarity, celerity, certainty, and consistency that smaller children tend to distort. If it is found that the adolescent has used the accusation as a weapon, some investigation should be undertaken as to why this particular weapon was used. Was the adolescent traumatized at an earlier time by someone else?

Once the child or adolescent has told the interviewer about the abuse in depth, he or she may feel anxious, fearful, and guilty about having disclosed so much or about what the abuser might do. The child needs assurance of protection. Fears must be allayed—not that the situation will immediately improve but that the worker is willing to help. The child should be told that he or she is not to blame and that it was important that he or she was able to talk with the interviewer.

Children wonder and should be helped to anticipate what will happen in the future. The thorough interviewer finds out what the child expects or wants to happen. Despite some assumptions, the child may not want to return home. The worker makes clear to the child, however, that what does happen depends on many factors and not just the interview. Children should not be given false hopes that their desires will prevail, nor should they be left with the feeling that they are to blame for the outcome. In the balance between assisting children in feeling somewhat in control and recognizing that they are still children—and therefore subject to the decisions of parents, social services, and the courts—workers face a difficult problem. Some element of control can be found, however, in knowing what might happen. The child can be told that the worker will see the parents and may talk with the child again. If the worker is sure that the court will be part of the process, the child may be helped by seeing the courtroom and knowing who will stand where. The worker's encouragement of the child's questions may strengthen the bond and elevate the trust between worker and child.

Interviewing a child necessitates skill, calm, self-assurance, and both cultural and personal sensitivity. The worker who does not enjoy or appreciate children or who is not familiar with the particular child's culture is not a good candidate for this task. For this reason, the worker who interviews children should be carefully chosen.

Anticipated prosecution of abusers in sexual abuse situations has stimulated the search for more accurate methods of validation that will not put increased stress on the victim. Videotaping of the allegedly abused child is one area in which advances are being made to alleviate the stress on the child. Prior to videotaping, a child is asked to repeat the account to numerous people—social workers, police, therapists, the judge, and myriad others. Videotaping places the child and just one experienced interviewer in a room with anatomically correct dolls, drawing materials, puppets, and other tools through which the child can find expression. The interview can be watched behind a one-way mirror by police, district attorneys, psychiatric or medical consultants, or other professionals who are or will be involved in the case. The tape provides visual evidence to assess the child's credibility. There has been much controversy over whether or not such a tape can be used in court in lieu of the child's testimony. The justice system grants the right to everyone accused to face his or her accuser and has not yet settled on a provision for the unique situation of abused children.

Some states are, however, addressing this issue with specific legislation. To ensure the protection of all parties, states that allow videotaping stipulate requirements. Some mandate that no attorney may be present at the taping of the interview. The video equipment must be operated by competent, experienced operators and the voices on the tape must be fully identified. The child must not be asked leading questions, and the worker interviewing the child must be experienced and trained in interviewing. Requirements may stipulate that the interviewer must be available to testify or be cross-examined at the court proceedings. The child, too, may be called to testify if the court deems it necessary, although this would be done in the judge's quarters rather than the open court. And finally, the defendant should be allowed to see the child, but the child need not be required to face him or her (through the use of closed-circuit TV or a one-way mirror). So far, such a ruling seems to be effective and is, in fact, being employed or explored in other states.

Not only can videotapes prevent children from being needlessly and repeatedly interviewed, but they can demonstrate to the nonabusing parent or to the perpetrator the validity of the child's story. This is done with much preparation and care, however, by ensuring that the child knows the adults will see the tape and ensuring that the child will be protected from pressure or harm after the viewing.

Another much-debated issue is the ownership of the videotape. Since the tape is an important and confidential piece of evidence, it is often retained by the district attorney or the court, which regulates its viewing. The efficacy, ethics, and usefulness of videotaping are still under discussion, and only time will tell what the outcome will be.

Custody of the Children

Custody and possible placement of children during the investigative process are controversial and entail careful scrutiny of a number of factors. The infant requiring a consistency in caregivers for bonding and the toddler's needing comfort in expressing individuality and autonomy are just two such factors. The 3- to 5-year-old's pursuit of identity through continuity and feeling loved by the caregiver is also recognized. The school-age child seeks stability in order to form a healthy conscience and self-concept and begins to seek relationships outside the family. Adolescents need to know they can return to dependency, even as they pursue their painful journey from childhood to adulthood. Amid the recognition of these different needs, the debate centers on whether constancy with parents who are functioning at a barely minimal level is preferable to separation and placement in a setting where the children's needs will be met more adequately.

Theoretically, children are placed during investigatory periods only when it is deemed that the risk of their remaining home is inordinately high. Someone—whether worker, supervisor, or both—must decide that the danger to the child outweighs the need for constancy (Hewitt, 2012; Knight, Chew, and Gonzalez, 2005; Weber, 1997).

There are many factors that affect this decision. The family's cultural background may have a significant influence. The parents' ability to handle stress and their past histories of substance abuse or other episodes of child maltreatment also figure in the equation. Input from other agencies involved with the family is significant in the assessment. Finally, to avoid removal whenever possible, families should be helped to use available resources to minimize risk to the child. If the family is unable or unwilling to use these resources or unwilling to cooperate, this fact would be considered, as well.

However, social workers are often criticized for their perceived lack of creativity and perseverance in eliciting cooperation from parents. Although this criticism may be justified in some instances, the protective services case can be extremely frustrating and draining on an individual worker.

Currently, much attention has been paid to the traumatic effects of separation on the children. Many experts contend that children feel abandoned, rejected, helpless, worthless, and humiliated as a result of being removed from their homes. These feelings produce anger, which is sometimes directed toward the parent but more often turned inward. Children may feel inherently bad or tend to isolate themselves. This sense of isolation sometimes combines with an intense need to retaliate. Fantasies about retaliation give rise to the fear of punishment that the child perceives will result from this retaliation.

Attempts are now being made to find alternative methods to separation in order to protect the child. Abusers, especially in sexual abuse cases, are being separated from the family rather than the child. The problem with this intervention exists when the nonabusing parent does not cooperate in the enforcement of the separation. Certainly, the preference of protective services agencies is, whenever possible, to keep the family unit intact. In cultures with strong kinship ties, it is vital that social services explore the feasibility of placing children with relatives or friends of the family rather than with strangers. In fact, in most cases today, CPS will look at which family members might be able to foster the child. Being placed with people the child knows can minimize the separation trauma.

After making the difficult decision to remove a child, the social worker must prepare the child for removal, which ideally includes, over time, familiarization with the foster home (or institutional setting), meeting the family, preliminary visits, explanations about the placement, conveying the child's likes and dislikes to the foster parents, and finally placement. The reality is that most placements during the preliminary stages of the social services process (i.e., investigation and initial case management) are emergencies. These increase the trauma for the child and require sensitivity on the part of the worker and foster parents to manifestations of this trauma.

Early placement produces trauma for the child and adds to the helplessness of the parent. Removal has different effects on the future of the client–worker relationship.

For some parents, removal forces them to realize they must cooperate in order to regain custody of their children. Other parents, however, see the loss of their children as the ultimate failure and withdraw by total noncooperation or even flight. The effect of child removal on parents is often difficult to predict.

Removal of children is, in most cases, involuntary for the parents. In an attempt to protect the children, the court authorizes placement. There are instances, however, when placement is a voluntary, preplanned, and therapeutic event. Some states allow voluntary placement of children when the ego strength of the parent is sufficient to allow them to contract with protective services. In these cases, placement permits the parents to mobilize their own resources toward the reunification of the family unit. During the agreed-upon time, the parents receive treatment or in some other way prepare themselves so that the risk to their children is minimized. Because significant motivation on the part of the parents is necessary, this solution is often impractical.

Although involuntary placement is painful for both children and their parents, it is in some instances necessary to protect the victims during the preliminary stages of casework. Chapter 14 considers placement in the context of treatment, rather than as an emergency measure, and discusses the implications for foster parents.

OTHER PROFESSIONALS INVOLVED IN THE INTERVENTION PROCESS

Protective service social workers depend heavily on other professionals within the community for reporting, assessment, and treatment of abused and neglected children and their families. It is important to consider the contributions of all these professionals in order to appreciate what their concerted efforts might achieve.

The Medical Team

Recognition and reporting of child abuse owe much to the medical community. From radiologist John Caffey, who first brought to the attention of others what he felt could only be explained as nonaccidental injuries, to C. Henry Kempe, who labeled the phenomenon the *Battered Child Syndrome*, physicians, nurses, and medical social workers have been vital in shaping the services now provided for child maltreatment cases (see Kempe, 2007).

Physicians

Physicians, whether private family practitioners or pediatricians on the hospital staff, provide input into the social service process in three important ways: (1) as reporters when they discover cases of child maltreatment, (2) as diagnosticians to aid in validation of maltreatment, and (3) as consultants in planning treatment.

The physician is mandated in all states to report suspected child abuse and neglect (Reece, 2008). Many physicians are hesitant, however, to report their suspicions to social services for several reasons. First, they may be unsure that the injury or condition is undeniably attributed to abuse. Second, they may not have faith in the social service system because of lack of knowledge or because of past situations they deemed were not handled well by social service staff. Physicians may fear that reporting the maltreatment will put the child in more danger or that it will negatively affect the doctor–patient relationship. Many physicians fear that a report will involve them in court proceedings, which will take time from their other patients. Some private physicians are so involved with their patients that it is difficult for them to even consider that those individuals could be abusive.

Although there may be some truth behind these reasons of hesitancy, the problems can be circumvented. Renewed dialogue among social service agencies, physicians, and other medical personnel has improved communication. In addition, noted physicians like Ray Helfer and Suzanne Sgroi were particularly influential in enlisting the support of their colleagues. With an understanding of the system, the physician can assess it much more effectively. Clearer laws mandating reporting by physicians have compelled their increased involvement.

The physician's role in validation cannot be understated. Radiology plays an important role in the documentation of physical abuse (see Smith, 1997). Skeletal abnormalities, unexplained fractures, and multiple fractures are conditions that necessitate further study to rule out abuse. A skeletal survey aids the physician in gathering validating material. Radiologic findings that are seen frequently in abused children include spiral fractures (often from twisting); transverse fractures in the middle of long bones or fingers (from the extremities being "rapped"); unusual fractures, such as rib or clavicle breaks in infants; traumas to the head, such as skull fractures; and other unusual fractures (Dale, Green, and Fellows, 2005; Feldman, 1997; Reece, 2008; Smith, 1997). All of these can be detected through x-rays.

Physicians can diagnose symptoms of neglect. Comparison with normal growth curves may validate the suspicion of the failure-to-thrive syndrome. Long-unmet medical needs attest to the neglect of the child's health care. The physician may also confirm the social worker's concerns over the child's inappropriate affect.

A physical examination often validates sexual as well as physical abuse. Sgroi (n.d.) suggests that "every child has the right to receive a complete examination by a competent and knowledgeable examiner if sexual assault is suspected." The thoroughness and type of examination, however, depend on the nature of the sexual abuse. If the abuse has continued for a considerable period of time, there is less likelihood of force or violence and thus the chance of observing vaginal or rectal tears is minimized. Or if the abuse took place some time before, evidence of physical trauma may no longer be obvious.

For these reasons, a complete physical exam should be considered only if the abuse has just occurred and physical damage to the child is likely. Certainly, the physician should screen for venereal disease and possible pregnancy in all cases, whether by an actual physical exam or through asking the child or parents pertinent questions.

Some physicians contend that an examination allows them to assess the degree of physical harm. Since almost all children fear that physical harm has been done to them, an exam allows the professional to assure the unharmed child that no damage has been found. Whether or not to do a physical exam should be considered carefully to ensure that the child's best interests are served.

If an examination is done, the physician is directed to screen for evidence such as the following (Giardino and Giardino, 2003; Reece, 2008; Sgroi, n.d., 1982; Sgroi, Porter, and Blick, 1982):

1. Sperm in the vaginal, genital, or rectal region
2. Trauma to the genital or rectal area

3. Gonorrhea infection of the vagina, rectum, urethra, and throat

4. Foreign bodies in the vagina, urethra, or rectum

5. Syphilis

6. Symptoms of pregnancy

7. Signs of other type of maltreatment, abuse, or neglect

The medical examination should be done by a physician who is knowledgeable about the signs of sexual abuse, who is relaxed and calm, and who can offer reassurance to the child. An internal examination for a small girl can be especially anxiety provoking, unless accompanied by a great deal of sensitivity toward the child. The physician will want to develop a rapport with the child, answer any questions, and provide some explanation as the examination progresses (Reece, 2008; Sgroi et al., 1982). The examining physician should also be aware of and make notes on any comments the child makes during the exam that might later be helpful for the investigating agency.

Whether examining for physical abuse, sexual abuse, or neglect, the physician is mindful of the child's need for control. Although the victim is not often given the opportunity to consent to the exam, an explanation of what will take place may help the child feel more in control. In sexual abuse situations, especially, the child is often concerned about having been damaged. Assurances that the physical examination will help to determine this and will not be painful often elicits the child's cooperation.

The physician is also a valuable consultant in planning treatment for abused and neglected children. Broken bones or other medical problems that require frequent visits allow medical personnel the time to observe the child's affective behavior as well as tend to the physiological needs. Pregnancy or venereal disease will require continual involvement. Physicians can maintain contact with social services to aid in case management. The sensitive physician can be a vital part of the total therapeutic team.

Nurses or Nurse Practitioners

Nurses see abused and neglected children in many areas other than the office or the hospital emergency room. School nurses are in one of the best positions to recognize maltreatment. Public health and visiting nurses often enter an abusive or neglectful home long before social services becomes involved. Thus, nurses should be well versed in not only the symptoms of abuse and neglect but also the necessity and procedure for reporting.

Because the nurse is often the first medical contact with the family and child in the office or hospital setting, she or he is in a unique position to gather important information about the injury, the family history, the parent–child interaction, and the affect of both parents and children. For example, clues about the abusive or neglectful behavior can be gleaned by attention to such details (see Giardino and Giardino, 2003; Helfer 1997; Powell, 2007):

- How does the parent speak to the child?
- Does the parent comfort the child or in other ways react to his or her crying?
- Does the parent hold the child and, if so, how?
- Is there obvious role reversal between parent and child?
- Does the parent seem aware of the child's needs?
- Does the parent speak negatively about the child?
- Can the parent provide a history of the child's development?

The nurse can also set the tone for later interviews with the child and parent. The nurse can engage, comfort, and generally put the child at ease. The child can be helped to realize that he or she is not to blame for the abuse and is welcome to talk and ask questions. Calming the child will be extremely beneficial for the later examination. In fact, the nurse can explain to the child in a soothing manner exactly what the examination will entail.

The nurse can engage parents, as well. Since the parents probably feel vulnerable, unsure, and perhaps even guilty, the nurse is in a position to empathize with them and make them feel as comfortable as possible. It may be difficult not to make judgments on these parents, but careful observation of their behavior, especially with the child, can be an important part of the assessment done by the total medical team. Some nurses are asked to explain the legal responsibility of the office or the hospital to report abuse and neglect. Although false assurances as to the outcome are not possible, it is important to allay parents' fears about the process—for example, their fears that their children will be immediately whisked away from them (if, indeed, that does not seem warranted).

In talking with the parent, the nurse often secures certain important information (Giardino and Giardino, 2003; Helfer, 1997; McGovern, 2007), such as the parents' explanation of the injury or condition, the history of previous health problems or trauma, the preventive health measures such as immunizations and tests that have been done to date, the dietary history, and the parents' assessment of the child's general health and temperament. Although many of the questions asked and assurances given may fall within the realm of the physician's exam, the nurse is usually the first professional seen and is, therefore, in a pivotal role to set the stage for a productive and comfortable relationship between the patient and the medical team.

The office or hospital nurse also provides a valuable service in preventive medicine. Often, abuse or neglect can be predicted by prenatal, perinatal, or postnatal indicators. Parents who present extremely negative attitudes toward pregnancy or attempt to deny the pregnancy, parents who lack emotional support, mothers who wanted to terminate the pregnancy but did not, and parents who do not appear to want their child can be at high risk to abuse or neglect.

Studies have shown that some experiences at birth place children at higher risk for abuse. A difficult delivery, combined with a lack of support for the mother; a negative response to the baby, evidenced by not wanting the baby; and an inability to attend to the infant's needs, especially with a high-risk infant, are all factors that may indicate later maltreatment. Parental behavior that should be noted includes anxiety around the baby, negative reactions to the baby, withdrawal from the baby, complaints about nonexistent problems, and maternal depression. Another indicator is apparent isolation or lack of support for the parents.

According to the laws of most states, little can be done about child maltreatment until it actually happens. However, parents who appear to be at risk can be referred to support services and, perhaps, helped to prevent maltreatment.

Nurses have long been valued in child abuse prevention for their teaching role with parents. Modeling of appropriate infant and child care as well as education on nutrition and health issues for unsure parents are especially helpful. Education for professionals on how to recognize bruises that do not fit the explanation, untreated medical problems, and venereal disease is valuable in the validation and treatment of child abuse by social service workers, teachers, lawyers, and others.

Medical Social Workers

The duties of the social worker employed in the hospital or other medical setting differ from institution to institution. Theoretically, the social worker is the coordinator for information pertaining to a case of abuse or neglect and the liaison with the social service system. The worker should be well versed in the questions protective services will ask and the procedures that will be undertaken. The social worker may be in a position to provide support to the child or family during the investigation process. A vital part of the role may be pulling together existing evidence such as x-rays, various physicians' opinions, test results, records, and diagnoses for the protective services personnel. It may fall to the medical social worker to explain to the parents the process both at the hospital and in the protective services system.

If the child returns home, the medical social worker may be instrumental in treatment planning. Placement in a foster home may warrant an interview with foster parents to acquaint them with the child's needs and medical treatment. When protective services dismisses a case, because it is deemed neither abuse nor neglect or because there is insufficient evidence, the social worker on the hospital staff may want to ensure that the parents are referred to services that will aid them in practicing more effective child care (e.g., parent support groups, visiting nurses, or homemaker services).

The responsibility for coordination of an abuse or neglect case is not always clear. Medical professionals may prefer to deal with protective services directly. The medical social worker needs to be guided by the knowledge of hospital policy and the political atmosphere. Also, abusive or neglectful situations sometimes elicit counterproductive negative or emotional feelings from hospital staff. Ideally, the medical social worker should be in a position to help other medical professionals come to grips with their feelings. In some hospitals, this professional is adequately utilized. In others, however, the medical hierarchy takes precedence, and medical professionals themselves report or deal with the abuse without the intervention of social services.

The best possible solution for the abused or neglected child and the family, however, is for the medical team to function as a unit, providing valuable validation, case management, and treatment planning material to the protective services workers.

The Legal Team

Police

The police officer's involvement in cases of child abuse and neglect differs from state to state and from community to community. Traditionally, the public assumes that police officers are responsible for the protection of life and property and for the preservation of peace in the community they serve (Cross, Finkelhor, and Ormond, 2005; McGovern, 2007; Shepherd, 1997). But when child abuse is involved, there are vast differences in the duties of the police officer.

In some areas, the police have the primary responsibility for taking reports and investigating allegations of abuse and neglect, while in the majority of jurisdictions, the police play a supportive role to protective services agencies. How states address the maltreatment of children in their legal statutes also varies. In many states, sexual abuse by a family member or relative comes under the jurisdiction of social services, whereas abuse by a nonrelated perpetrator is solely a police matter. Prostitution and pornography usually are considered the realm of law enforcement, yet the victims of these crimes are often eligible for services from child protective workers. Thus, any attempt to generalize the exact role of the police officer is fruitless. But currently, a majority of the 50 states mandate the involvement of the police through reporting, assisting child protection agencies, and, in some cases, doing investigations (Cross et al., 2005; Giardino and Kolilis, 2002; McGovern, 2007; Shepherd, 1997).

The police officer is an important member of the intervention process for several reasons. First, the officer is easily identifiable (much more so than a protective social worker) and is frequently well known in the community. Children are taught, for the most part, to see the police as protectors. Second, the police are easy to locate and can be quickly dispatched to the scene of an emergency. And finally, no community is without some police service, but some smaller communities are quite far removed geographically from protective services offices.

Police officers, in general, perform three functions: take reports of abuse and neglect, investigate reports (either independently or in a supportive role to the department of social services), and respond to emergencies (e.g., domestic violence, severe abuse, abandonment) (American Prosecutors Research Institute, 2004; Giardino and Kolilis, 2002; Kiwala, 2000; McGovern, 2007). Most individual officers will, at some time, take reports and respond to emergencies, but some precincts have special child abuse units trained to investigate allegations of abuse.

A report comes to a police officer in one of several ways. In some cases, it is the patrol officer who notices something as he or she surveys a neighborhood. Or a direct report is made by the victim who is willing to describe the abuse and give information; the victim can often lead the officer to the scene or to the perpetrator. If a child reports, the parents must be notified as soon as possible. The department of social services may also be contacted if state law dictates. (In every state, the police are mandated reporters to the designated agency, and if that agency is social services, it must be notified.)

An indirect report is made by a parent or other caregiver after the victim has disclosed the abuse and often after some time has elapsed or when the parent has observed an injury and has become concerned. It is not uncommon for reports to be made in custody cases, when one parent perceives that the estranged spouse or ex-spouse has in some way harmed the child. Obviously, such cases are difficult to handle and not always clearly defined. Police also take reports when a child has died from abuse (Giardino and Kolitis, 2002).

The referral report comes from a community agency such as a school, hospital, or other social service agency. The proactive report is one in which the police officer discovers child abuse or neglect in the process of investigating another complaint, such as a domestic disturbance, a suicide attempt, or a runaway child.

Several problems exist in the police detection of child abuse. The first is that police are becoming increasingly hesitant to intervene in cases of domestic violence, partly because this situation is certainly the most volatile and dangerous to the police themselves. If a call appears to be spousal violence rather than child abuse, the police are sometimes less willing to intervene. A second issue concerns runaways. Only fairly recently has the connection between running away and abuse at home been clearly demonstrated. In the past, runaways were not taken so seriously. The assumption was that the child would probably return or that the likelihood of the child's running away again was fairly slim. As a result, the symptom—running away—was passed over with little exploration of the cause. The well-trained and competent police officer should evaluate the situation (to the extent possible) to determine if child abuse is indicated.

Once a report is received, the police officer must decide what action should be taken. The case can be closed, based on the assumption that no abuse or neglect actually existed or because of insufficient evidence. Recognition that the child is abused or neglected necessitates further action—through referral to the police department's child abuse unit for investigation, referral to the local department of social services, or both. If the situation requires removal of the child or if the child is abandoned by his or her caregiver, the officer may need to refer the case directly to juvenile or family court (Cross et al., 2005; Giardino and Kolilis, 2002; Shepherd, 1997).

Rarely are abusive and neglectful parents arrested. Exceptions include when the injury to the child is extremely severe or obviously sadistically inflicted, when a crime has been committed, when the parents present a danger to others, or when arrest is the only way to preserve peace. Current regulations in some states, however, require the arrest of sexual abusers. If prostitution or pornography is involved, arrest is also indicated.

Child abuse and neglect investigation is an area that is not usually expected of police by the public and one that, in many ways, seems to contradict the other roles performed by police. As a result, their involvement in abuse and neglect investigations raises problems for police agencies. First, police officers must have adequate training to recognize and deal with child abuse situations (Shepherd, 1997). In the past—prior to increased recognition of the need for police training—decisions to dismiss or refer child abuse cases for further investigation were based on the personal judgment of the officer involved, rather than any legal mandate. Second (and in relation to the first problem), more personnel are needed for units established specifically to deal with juvenile matters such as child abuse. These officers should receive more comprehensive training. Third, there is a need for social service agencies and police agencies to work more closely together in coordinating their roles in child abuse cases. Although this does exist in some communities, the cooperation could be much more widespread. Fourth, police agencies should keep abreast of new abuse legislation and its implications in their practice. And finally, police and other community agencies should participate in interdepartmental planning for the protection of children and the prevention of child abuse and neglect (American Prosecutors Research Institute, 2004; Cross et al., 2005; McGovern, 2007; Shepherd, 1997). Although many police departments provide safety training (including children's personal safety from abuse) in schools, there is often little coordination with social service prevention programs. More coordination would provide a better opportunity for the effective education of children.

The role of the police and their place on the CPT is a vital one. Many child abuse reports are made in the evening, when child protective workers may not be available to respond. Most communities now have hotlines, but police may be the first to respond. The response time of police officers averages about 26 minutes. In emergencies, responsive service is important to adequately protect children. Police authority cannot be minimized, and social workers often benefit from police protection from difficult clients. The incentive to cooperate with the police is therefore mutual.

The police have long been recognized as protectors; without their input, along with others on the CPT, a vital part of the process is overlooked.

Courts

The role of the courts will be covered extensively in Chapter 11.

The Educational Team

Teachers

The teacher is in a unique position to detect and report child abuse and neglect. Teachers are in closer contact with children for more hours in the day than any other adult—often more than the parents. Those dedicated to the teaching of the whole child perceive impediments to the child's learning including attention to the perceptual learning problems in children. Schools spend many hours addressing the needs of and teaching children who are disabled. Yet the residual effects of child abuse and neglect can be just as detrimental to learning as other types of disabilities (Crosson-Tower, 2002).

As stated earlier in this chapter, the teacher is also a mandated reporter in every state. Until recently, teachers were not sufficiently educated either to detect the signs of abuse and neglect or to realize their responsibility to report and the importance of their role in child abuse prevention. More recently, training for educators to help them recognize and respond to child maltreatment has enabled these professionals to recognize the importance of their role.

Despite increased training, many teachers still verbalize fears and problems about their role in the intervention process. One fear is that they will not really be able to recognize abuse and neglect in any given child. Further education of teachers appears to be the key: Teachers take courses or extensive training in child maltreatment intervention and learn to look for specific physical and behavioral clues in both children and their parents. This education emphasizes that all state statutes dictate that teachers who suspect abuse or neglect *must* report, and it also leads to the understanding that trained protective workers investigate and validate, rather than the teachers themselves.

Teachers also fear the responsibility involved in reporting an abusive or neglectful family. The responsibility may seem overwhelming, but compared to the guilt over a seriously injured child whose situation was not reported before additional abuse occurred, reporting can easily be seen in perspective.

Some teachers are concerned that reporting will destroy their relationship with the child's parents. Although this is a possibility, it need not happen. Intervention by protective services is often frightening for parents. Teachers can provide supportive relationships to help them through the process. Teachers may also have observed problems that inhibit the parents' child-caring abilities. Relating these problems to the social worker can help the parents. Consider the following case:

> *A concerned teacher filed a report regarding 7-year-old Anita Reynaldi, who appeared to be severely neglected. The teacher had had her brother Roberto in class several years before and had found Mrs. Reynaldi a concerned and cooperative mother. Why this mother now ignored requests to come in to talk about Anita or to remedy the situation in any way was a mystery. However, in talking with the social worker, the teacher outlined the mother's strengths and her previously cooperative attitude. The teacher was also able to reach out to the mother once the social worker had visited. Totally overwhelmed by*

recent developments in her life and by Anita, a hyperactive child whom she felt she could not handle, Mrs. Reynaldi responded to the teacher and, through her, gained support during the intervention and treatment.

Unfortunately, not all parents are as cooperative as Mrs. Reynaldi. Teachers describe parents who are angry and hostile when a report has been made. However, the safety of the child is of more importance than the teacher's relationship with the parents. If that safety requires intervention, the concerned teacher should act.

The school administration is not always supportive of teachers' reporting. (The reasons for this are discussed in the next section.) Teachers who feel they should file a report of child abuse or neglect have met with opposition from school principals or vice principals. The teacher is in a difficult position and must decide whether to abide by the superior's wishes or to report independently, thus jeopardize the relationship with the superior or even his or her own job. Some teachers do not know that reporting to an administrator does not constitute the teacher's legal responsibility of reporting. Nor does reporting anonymously cover the teacher as a mandated reporter.

Another major fear teachers have expressed is that nothing will be done by social services once the report is made. Teachers complain that they never hear from the social worker or that the family situation does not appear to change. More communication between teachers and social workers greatly enhances the trust each has for the other. If treated as an integral part of the CPT, the teacher is a valuable resource in keeping the social worker up to date on the child's progress.

Teachers learn of abuse or neglect situations in one of several ways. First is through their own observation of the child in class. Children who are abused or neglected manifest behavioral indicators that can be detected by the sensitive teacher. Although many behavioral problems can be associated with other disturbances, some point more specifically to maltreatment. Sometimes, children themselves disclose to those concerned educators with whom they have developed a trusting relationship. In these situations, the teacher must take the responsibility for seeing that the child is protected from further abuse. Immediate involvement with protective services ensures this protection. The child's peers may recognize abusive or neglectful situations and tell their teacher. In some instances, contacts with the parents have uncovered practices of inappropriately severe discipline or other forms of abusive behavior.

Once teachers receive a report, they should be aware of the procedure or protocol followed by their particular school system. Sometimes, reports are made to the school nurse, the counselor, or an administrator who then files a report with protective services. In other schools, teachers must notify the administration but are expected to make the actual contact with the social services agency themselves. In many states, the social service agency responds to the reporter and assures the reporter that the case is being investigated. Rules of confidentiality usually prohibit that specific information be given to the teachers. Because of the fears and hesitations mentioned earlier, more and more schools are using the CPT approach and developing more formal protocol.

Reporting is not the only area in which teachers are involved. During the course of treatment, the social worker monitors the child's progress. A mirror to this progress is the child's behavior in school. Teachers provide valuable input in helping determine the direction for treatment.

Recently, teachers have also become increasingly involved with the prevention of abuse. Since the child trusts these adults and since these adults often provide a constant influence in what is sometimes a chaotic life, teachers are in an ideal position to introduce abuse and neglect prevention materials into the curriculum.

The teachers' influence on and importance to children make them particularly important members of the intervention team.

Administrators

Administrators see themselves as responsible for the effective running of their educational community. Yet an educational community is not effective unless the rights of each child to an education are being protected. Although the attention to individual children is usually left to line workers—in this instance, teachers—it is the administrator's role to lend support to the staff. Therefore, the detection and reporting of child abuse are as much responsibilities of the administrator as they are of the teacher.

As mentioned, teachers sometimes complain that administrators are not supportive of their need to file reports of child maltreatment. Administrators appear cautious about reporting for several reasons. First, they may fear that reports of child abuse will reflect on their school. Will reporting antagonize parents? Will reporting abuse gain the principal or the school a reputation for making trouble and perhaps cause funds to be cut in the future? Yet concerned principals, vice principals, superintendents, and assistant superintendents realize that most parents value consideration of the whole child—including attention to learning barriers.

Some administrators are not fully aware of their reporting responsibilities or of their liability when they do not report. More and more, supervisory staff have begun to attend training for teachers, as well as training geared specifically toward administrators. Many administrators also find the CPT to be an effective tool. Still, administrators, like teachers, voice frustration that not enough is being done in child protection cases. Again, only effective communication with community agencies and recognition of the options available to protective services can fully dispel these frustrations.

Pupil Personnel Services

Pupil personnel services include those professionals involved in enhancing a child's education: the school nurse, guidance counselor, school adjustment counselor, psychologist, and other staff.

The school nurse is in the school system. It is often the nurse to whom teachers turn for support in the process of recognizing and reporting child abuse and neglect. Nurses are asked to examine bruises and talk with children and are often invited to give their opinions as to whether to report. Because of their medical training, school nurses can validate that a bruise does not fit the explanation or, in some other manner, give the teacher confidence in the ability to recognize abuse. Nurses are also frequently involved in prevention education, and some feel more comfortable discussing topics such as sexuality than some teachers. The nurse can help by teaching hygiene to children whose parents are not meeting this need.

In some schools, the nurse has the responsibility of reporting child abuse and neglect. This removes the teacher, who is in constant contact with the child and may see the parents, from the role of reporter (although the teacher is still legally mandated to see that a report is made). In some instances, this distance allows the teacher more flexibility in the ability to relate to the parent in a helpful way.

School counselors and psychologists are used in a variety of ways. Traditionally, the guidance counselor helped with scheduling and career choices, the adjustment counselor provided a link with the parents, and the psychologist administered testing. As funds became limited and the number of personnel decreased, the roles merged or overlapped in many schools. Today, it is difficult to generalize as to who sees the child for counseling or has contact with the parents. Counselors who see children in a guidance or counseling capacity frequently learn that a child has been maltreated. In fact, teachers often send children to counselors to validate their own suspicions. Children may reach out to counselors either to report the abuse or to seek help with issues that are symptoms of the abuse.

By functioning as a team along with teachers and administrators, nurses and counselors help to ensure that the child's right to learn without the impediment of abuse or neglect is more fully protected.

The Mental Health Team

The term *mental health professional* refers to a variety of professions: psychologists, psychiatrists, clinical social workers, expressive therapists, and possibly other therapists responsible for clinical intervention.

Mental health professionals may become involved in child abuse and neglect cases in several ways. Their juvenile patients may disclose that they are currently being or have been abused or neglected, or other patients (parents, spouses, relatives, or friends) may report that the child is being abused by someone with whom they are involved. Abusers may report their own acts of maltreatment, although this is the exception rather than the rule. And finally, protective service agencies may refer children for counseling or for psychological testing.

Mental health professionals, like physicians, police, and educators, are mandated reporters under the child abuse reporting laws. Since reporting can be somewhat controversial, some mental health facilities designate a particular staff member to be the liaison with protective services and in that capacity be responsible for reporting as well as accepting referrals.

Psychiatrists, psychologists, psychiatric social workers, and other counselors often voice concerns over the obstacles to reporting from a therapist's perspective. Some therapists prefer not to become involved. Others argue that the reporting laws jeopardize the therapeutic relationship between therapist and client.

From the point of view of the therapist, these concerns may be justified. Yet telling the therapist may be a client's plea for help. Further, failure of mental health professionals to report may place children in dangerous situations. Encouraging clients to self-report is one method of circumventing this problem. In addition, some states allow agreements between mental health professionals and protective services by which abusers who continue to seek therapy and receive treatment are exempt from services other than periodic case review by protective social workers.

Mental health professionals provide a valuable resource for protective service agencies. It is often helpful to the validation process or in the course of treatment planning to refer a child, an abuser, or a nonabusive parent for psychological testing. In addition, psychiatrists, psychologists, psychiatric social workers, and other counselors are often asked to use their skills in the treatment of victims, perpetrators, and families.

Clergy and Church Staff

Undoubtedly as a result of the child abuse scandals involving clergy and churches, religious communities have recognized the need to develop policies and reporting protocols, as well as forge cooperative relationships with agencies serving abused and neglected children. The Archdiocese of Boston, for example, has undertaken to train all the adults and children in their schools and parishes in child abuse prevention. As a result of the Cardinal's Commission on Child Protection, the archdiocese developed policies to guide church personnel in responding to abuse allegations.

Protestant churches have also been called to demonstrate their desire to protect children through developing protocol that outlines how reports should be made and how clergy and church staff should be screened (see Crosson-Tower, 2006).

The Community

Many states acknowledge in their reporting laws that any member of a community might be in a position to recognize and report child maltreatment. Some states mandate that any person who suspects that a child is being abused or neglected report it. In the last few years, church communities and youth organizations have taken responsibility for their part in child abuse intervention.

Toward a Total Team Approach

Certainly, the most effective method of combating child abuse and neglect within a particular community is to employ the skills of all of the medical, legal, educational, and mental health professionals in the formation of a communitywide CPT. In addition to including a variety of professionals, the team must include racial and cultural representatives of the clientele served.

Numerous communities have demonstrated the effectiveness of such an approach by improving communications among professionals, eliminating unnecessary and costly overlap of agency services, and coordinating more effective prevention programs. Only through a total team effort can children be adequately protected from future abuse and neglect.

SUMMARY

The trauma caused by child abuse and neglect can, unfortunately, be increased by the intervention system. For this reason, professionals continue to evaluate and change the intervention process so that it can be as helpful as possible to victims and their families.

The intervention process involves a series of complex steps: reporting, investigation and assessment, and case management. Treatment planning and treatment, evaluation and follow-up are discussed in Chapter 11. The intent of this process is to stop the current abuse and neglect. Hoped-for outcomes include protecting the child from future maltreatment, teaching the parents coping skills, and possibly even changing parental attitudes toward child rearing.

The first step in the process falls on the reporters. Many professionals—such as physicians, counselors, social workers, police, and teachers—are designated by law as mandated reporters. The mandated reporter is required to report the abuse or neglect to the appropriate agency, usually to the state or county department of social services, and can be penalized for failure to report.

Following the report, the social service agency decides whether maltreatment is present. This may necessitate talking with the alleged victim, with the parents, and with other knowledgeable people about the situation. If the case is substantiated or the conclusion made that maltreatment is a fact, further investigation ensues. The family's reaction to intervention must also be considered. Not only must workers look at the family's fears and the defense mechanisms they use, but they must evaluate the family's strengths, as well. A unique aspect of protective services is that much of the interviewing is done in the client's home. Home visiting involves a variety of issues not present in office interviews and requires a worker to develop additional sensitivity, along with a different set of diagnostic and interviewing skills.

Protective workers involved in the assessment process learn to ask specific questions designed to assess the potential risk of the home situation to the child and the capacity of the parents to cope with child rearing. The interviewing process is an integral part of assessment. Different skills are required for interviewing adults than for children.

Sometimes, the social worker has time to investigate and assess a particular case. In other instances, however, the child is in too much danger or the parents will not cooperate. Such cases are considered emergencies and require an immediate decision on whether to involve the court system, remove the child from the home, or both. Part of assessment will be to determine who should have custody of the children and the impact that this will have on them.

Validation, especially in the area of child sexual abuse, is not always easy. New techniques to improve the quality of intervention are constantly being explored.

A variety of professionals are involved in the intervention process, and each of their roles must be understood individually. The medical team—consisting of the physician, nurse or nurse practitioner, and medical social worker—is in the position to report, validate, and sometimes treat maltreatment cases. Police officers are often the first to discover child abuse or neglect through reports from children and adults or in the course of their investigation of other police matters.

The educational team—consisting of teachers, administrators, and pupil personnel services staff—is a vital link in the intervention process. As a result of their constant contact with children, these professionals are more frequently in a position to recognize abuse or neglect, provide valuable input during the intervention and treatment process, and participate in prevention programs to educate children about abuse and neglect.

Although mental health professionals may be in the position to recognize child maltreatment in their cases, some are reluctant to report. Mental health services play an important role, however, in validation and treatment of protective situations.

There is increased emphasis on the need for others in communities to report. Clergy and church personnel have been called on to develop reporting protocol.

As a society, our best hope of intervention in cases of child abuse or neglect is for community professionals to communicate and work as a team. The team approach has been implemented in many communities and appears effective.

Chapter 11

The Legal Response to Child Abuse and Neglect

I n dealing with protective cases, the hope is that intervention is sufficient to protect the child until treatment is established and implemented and that parents see the need for their cooperation with social services—an ideal that is frequently difficult to achieve. It may be necessary, therefore, to bring the structure and authority of the court system into the overall picture.

Referral to the court system is one type of intervention available. Court action is generally considered when the child is in imminent danger or the parents are unable or unwilling to cooperate with the social service agency in improving the care of their children. There are other instances, however, when involvement with the court system might also be considered:

- The parents are unable to provide the child with proper care because of the hospitalization, incarceration, or physical or mental incapacity of one or both parents.
- The parents abandon their children, and an emergency placement must be arranged.
- Treatment is necessary and can only be obtained by a court order, not through the informal resource channels of social services.
- The parents are denying the child medical attention, and the lack of this attention may be life threatening.
- The case involves death of a child or severe physical injury inflicted on the child by the parent.
- The case involves sexual abuse and state statutes indicate that sexual abuse is punishable by law (Dale, Green, and Fellows, 2005; Davidson, 1997; Faller, 2003; Katner and Plum, 2002; Myers, 2011).

Before deciding definitely on court action, the concerned caseworker weighs the positive and negative aspects. Could this case be handled in another manner than those already tried and that does not involve court proceedings?

There are some definite disadvantages to involvement in the court system. First, whether juvenile or criminal court, the proceedings have adversarial overtones (Bartollas and Miller, 2010; Duquette, 1997; Faller, 2003). Parents feel antagonistic and want to mobilize their resources against the social service agency. Lawyers arguing for their clients may seem, for some, reminiscent of popular TV shows, in which an attorney goes all out fighting to win for his client. Although juvenile court, especially, is quite unlike the TV version of courtroom scenes, the fact remains that court intervention can be an upsetting experience and one that may make the participants feel they must take sides. Second, the authority of the court and its decisions can be anxiety provoking for parents and children alike. Third, after all the preparation and emotional upheaval, the court may find insufficient grounds for further intervention, leaving the parents mistrustful of social services and the caseworker with few other options.

From the agency's perspective, the preparation of evidence, the writing of the court report, and the interviewing of witnesses account for a significant output of time for the social worker. Further, court delays and postponements require long hours of waiting and schedule changes. However, the caseworker and the agency may find that the positive aspects of court action—that is, the protection of the child and possible rehabilitation of the parents—outweigh all the negatives.

THE LEGAL RIGHTS OF PARENTS AND CHILDREN

In the court process, participants have particular rights (Masson and Oakley, 2001; Noel, 2013; Stein, 1998). Those of the parents include the right to notice, counsel, a hearing, be informed of their rights, and to confront and cross-examine.

The right to notice means notification that the parents are suspected of being abusive or neglectful and will need to appear in court. Parents are encouraged to engage an attorney, or one can be appointed for them by the court. Parents also have a right to demand the specifics of the allegations from the individual(s) who brought the case to court attention. In criminal court, parental rights increase. Here, parents have the right to a jury trial, the right to face their accuser, and the privilege against self-incrimination. Hopefully, non-English-speaking clients will have access to a translator or someone who can help them understand what is taking place. Rather than being a right per se, providing this service more often depends on the particular court or social agency involved.

Although children also have rights in court proceedings, these are not always as clear. They definitely have a right to counsel, and an attorney is usually assigned to them by the court. Technically, they have the right to notice of the hearing dates, but once an attorney or guardian has been appointed, notice usually goes to the surrogate. Children have the right to a hearing and cannot be removed from their home without a hearing. Some states, however, allow removal on parental consent or in an emergency, followed by a court order when necessary. Children, like their parents, are allowed the right to a hearing (Davidson, 1997; Harris and Teitelbaum, 2002; Myers, Diedrich, Lee, Fincher, and Stern, 2002; Noel, 2013).

Another right, interpreted in different ways by different states, is the child's right to a family life. Some states mandate that attempts be made to rehabilitate and reestablish the family unit. Some legal codes insist that a permanent, stable plan be made for the child whether he or she be to remain in the biological home or to be placed in substitute care. Children also have the right to a hearing in most states, although the case may be settled out of court before this occurs. Once in court, however, the child's lawyer, on behalf of the child, may cross-examine or confront witnesses (Duquette, 1997; Myers et al., 2002; Stein, 1998; Noel, 2013).

Intervention with Native American children is guided by the 1978 Indian Child Welfare Act (Jones, 2006; Simmons and Trope, 1999). This federal legislation supplants normal state procedures, as well as substantive law, when dealing with Native American children. Failure to meet the requirements of this act can have extensive repercussions, including the invalidation of court action years after it is supposedly final. The Indian Child Welfare Act is based on years of research, which uncovered the fact that Native American children had long been removed from their homes by social services because of the misapplication of middle-class norms to such families (Thorne, 1991). Through the Indian Child Welfare Act, the federal government has empowered some reservations to establish legislative bodies, such as courts, to handle abuse cases. Different tribes interpret their rights under this law differently. Some handle cases totally independently, whereas others work closely with non–Native American agencies (Earle and Cross, 2001; Faller, 2003; Simmons and Trope, 1999).

TYPES OF COURT INTERVENTION

Civil courts usually deal with child abuse and neglect. Most courts have within their civil court system a juvenile or family court that holds a session at least one day a week or whenever needed. Juvenile courts are usually responsible for juvenile matters—delinquency, statute offenses (such as running away or truancy, which, if committed by adults, would not come to the attention of the court), and the acceptance and disposition of protective petitions on behalf of children (Jones, 2006; Myers et al., 2002; Noel, 2013). Such a petition, often initiated by the protective services worker, attorney, or probation officer, brings to the attention of the court a child who is in need of protection from abuse and neglect.

How each juvenile court or session addresses the filing of a protection petition differs greatly and can only be generalized. In general, juvenile court is more informal than other court settings. Hearings are closed to the public and emphasize planning for the best interests of the children.

Some states prefer to address the protection of maltreated children through a guardianship procedure in probate court. In this instance, gaining legal guardianship of the child enables the protective worker, as the agency's representative, to regulate the quality of care available and the place of residence based on the child's best interests. In both of these proceedings, emphasis is on the child's needs, rather than censure of the parents.

In very few situations are physically abusive or neglectful parents involved in criminal procedures. Criminal court action would usually be taken in instances of severe or sadistic abuse or death, and some states' criminal court procedures are initiated when otherwise deemed necessary.

A recent trend, however, has been to prosecute sexual abuse cases. States cannot agree on whether all sexual abuse should come to the attention of criminal court or on what constitutes criminal sexual abuse. While sexual intercourse with a juvenile is a crime in all states, variations (e.g., age, identity of partner) may or may not be covered by the law.

The initiation of criminal proceedings may go directly through the police or district attorney, or the protective service agency may initiate the complaint after initial screening. In juvenile court matters, the individual who investigates the case usually has a great deal of input in the decision or the outcome of the case, but this is not always true in criminal cases. The primary purpose of criminal proceedings is to punish the perpetrator, and the court deems to know the best method. In this instance, the victim serves as a witness to facilitate conviction. In the past, only a minimum of attention (if any) was given to the needs of the victim. Fortunately, there is now a trend toward supporting the child through the court process (Davidson, 1997; Devon, 2010; Faller, 2003; Jones, 2006; Noel, 2013).

Today, it is also possible for a sexual abuse case to become a civil court action if adult survivors or adults, on behalf of victimized children, sue perpetrators, the institutions where they were abused, or the insurance company that provides coverage for that institution (Faller, 2003).

Given the differences in the types of court action that address abuse and neglect, one must consider the process in each, keeping in mind that each state differs in its interpretation of the legal statutes and the execution of the process.

Juvenile Court

The Process

The juvenile court process is initiated by filing a petition on behalf of the child and follows a sequence (see Figure 11.1), depending on the variables in the case. The *petition* is a formal document that alleges that on a specific date, at a certain time, and in a designated place events occurred that placed the child in question in danger from abuse or neglect. The filing of this petition gives the parents notice that court action is being taken. The signer of the petition—usually the child protective worker—is referred to as the *petitioner*. In many states, someone other than the protective worker may file a petition. If the case has gone directly to juvenile court and has not been initiated by a protective services agency, the agency must be notified and is usually then involved in the process.

The petition is reviewed in some states, often by the clerk of the court, to determine its clarity and seriousness. In some instances, a conference or a pretrial hearing is held (sometimes called a show-cause hearing), often in conjunction with the probation department, to determine the credibility of the petition. Although all those represented in the petition must be present at such a hearing, they need not then be represented by counsel. Although the hearing is geared toward fact finding, sometimes decisions are made. The petition may be withdrawn because of insufficient facts or evidence, or the child may be ordered to receive medical care or psychological evaluation. Also, the child may be placed temporarily in foster care. Occasionally, agreements or settlements preclude the need to carry the process further, but more often the case proceeds to an initial hearing (Duquette, 1997; Katner and Plum, 2002; Noel, 2013).

Sometimes, the protective services worker deems that between the filing of the petition and the adjudication, emergency removal of the child is warranted. A hearing must then be held to present the facts to support the removal and obtain an official removal order from the judge (Myers et al., 2002). The way in which emergency removals are handled differs greatly from state to state.

At the initial hearing, the petitioner must prove the facts in the petition are accurate. The petitioner does this by providing the court with written documentation or records and by calling witnesses to testify to the validity of the allegations. These witnesses provide an important multidimensional view of the case (Lyon, 2002). The parents can in turn bring forth their own evidence or refute the charges. This procedure is usually presided over by

Figure 11.1   Juvenile Court Process Flow Chart.
Source: Reprinted from Working with the *Courts in Child Protection*, by W. G. Jones, Washington, DC: Children's Bureau, U.S. Department of Health and Human Services, 2006.

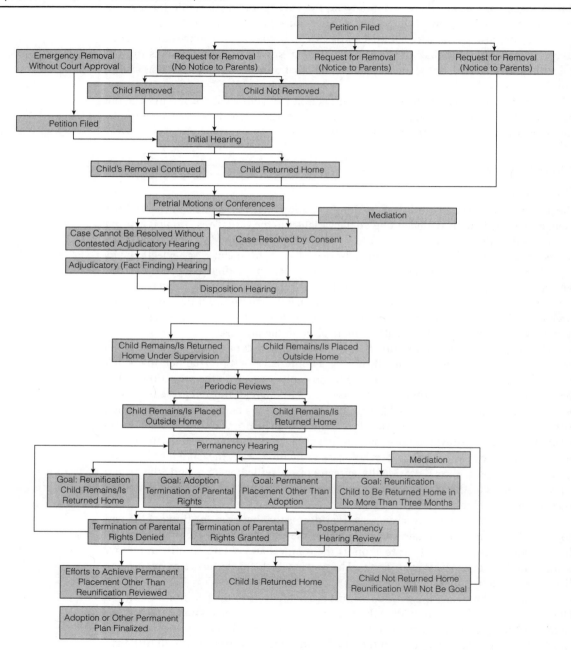

a judge. Some states also require that the child be present at this initial hearing to be identified by the court as the individual on whose behalf the petition has been filed. For small children, especially, this argument over their welfare, and seemingly against their parents, can be quite upsetting. Recognizing this, courts often allow the children to be taken from the courtroom once the identification has been made.

The layperson frequently pictures a formal and forbidding courtroom setting for this and other juvenile hearings. To minimize the trauma to children, juvenile court is much less formal than its sister courts and may look like a classroom or a meeting room. Of course, when the civil court holds a juvenile session or when space is limited in juvenile court, a standard courtroom may be used. Even so, the atmosphere tends to be more relaxed and informal, with an emphasis on social goals rather than punishment (Duquette, 1997; Faller, 2003).

At the initial hearing, attorneys who have been appointed for both parents and children (if the parents have not chosen to secure their own attorney) present their respective sides of the case. Until recently, the protective services agency was usually not represented by legal counsel. However, due to the increased complexity of cases and the liability issues involved, most agencies now have legal staff who will often represent the agency's interests in court.

The purpose of the initial hearing is fact finding. Based on these facts, several important decisions are made at this hearing (Ichikawa, 1997; Jones, 2006; Masson and Oakley, 2001; Noel, 2013; Peters, 1997; Stein, 1998). First, the validity of the case is determined. If the judge concludes that the petition is not supported by testimony, the case is dismissed. Then, an investigator is appointed by the court and given a prescribed period in which to complete a report of his or her findings. The investigator may be a social worker, an independent attorney, or an employee of the court who handles such investigations.

If the petition appears to be supported, the process continues as follows: The custody of the child is determined. Once abuse or neglect is found, the court takes jurisdiction over the child and then reserves several options: (1) Both legal and physical custody of the child can be given to the protective agency. The child would, in these circumstances, be placed in a foster home pending the next hearing. (2) The child can be placed with relatives. (3) The child can be allowed to return home during the investigation. If the child does return home, custody is often awarded to the protective agency to facilitate emergency removal should it be necessary.

Much discussion surrounds the placement of children during the investigatory period. Although an investigator cannot make a clear assessment of parenting skills if the children are not in the home, some child protection advocates still feel that a case that necessitated court action is usually serious enough to require removal. Because of this debate, it is difficult to predict where the children will reside during the investigation.

The investigation is that period between the initial hearing and the dispositional hearing in which the appointed investigator gathers additional facts to determine the severity and the causes of maltreatment. In addition, the investigator formulates recommendations for treatment or future actions to present to the court. The role of investigator is an important one. This individual should be fair and competent in searching out collaterals (e.g., teachers, neighbors, and others interested in the case) and exploring all the factors in the case. The court may have ordered medical or psychological evaluations of the parents or child or both, and the results are included in the investigator's report at the next hearing.

While the investigator seeks information to determine what will be in the best interests of the child, the parents' attorney seeks to help his or her clients form a plan whereby the child remains in or is returned to their care. Some attorneys encourage the parents to seek treatment during this interim period so they might argue more convincingly at the hearing. Indeed, for some parents, the reality of the court experience is enough to motivate them toward positive action.

Once the investigation is completed within the specified period, all the participants—usually excluding the child—again appear in court for the dispositional hearing. This proceeding is designed for decision making (Devon, 2010; Myers et al., 2002; Stein, 1998). It determines the custody of the child and the steps the parents must take to eventually resume the full care of their child if it is felt that this is possible. To make these determinations, several things happen at this hearing. First, the investigator's report is presented. (If the report is written, the judge and perhaps the attorneys have had some time to read it before the hearing.) The report includes the following:

- A description of the type of harm done to the child
- Background information on the family
- Information supplied by collaterals
- Recommendations of services for the family
- Possibly a timeframe in which these goals should be accomplished

Witnesses may be called to support the information in the report. Other types of evidence (e.g., records, letters, medical files) may be entered to support the report. And finally, the parents' attorney has the right to cross-examine witnesses and produce evidence to refute the allegations that the parents have abused or neglected their child.

Witnesses in this type of hearing can be few or many, depending on the complexity of the case. The layperson may testify from direct observation of the situation and may express opinions or make assessments. Witnesses are encouraged to recount as much direct observation as possible, however. For example, a teacher may be able to recount how he or she saw the bruises on Johnny or that Johnny confided that he had been beaten. These witnesses are asked to testify as to what they smelled, heard, saw, or touched. Neighbors, teachers, social workers, and others with firsthand knowledge may be called to testify. Only rarely is a character witness for the parents brought in to testify on their behalf.

The next most frequently used witness in protection hearings is one who gives expert testimony. This expert's credentials give him or her the sanction to give opinions in his or her area of expertise and answer hypothetical questions (Lyon, 2002). For example, a psychologist who has tested the child in question might be asked, "In your expert opinion and having done extensive testing with Johnny, would it be emotionally damaging for this child to continue to reside in this home?" Physicians, psychologists, some social workers, and others in specialized fields can appear as expert witnesses. Recently, some courts have allowed more controversial experts, such as graphologists (who are able to detect character traits from handwriting), to untangle the often complex factors in a case.

Sometimes, children are allowed to testify, but very young children may be in question as to their competency. In some states, especially in sexual abuse situations, evidence may include information told to a qualified third party by the child. This prevents the child from having to testify. Other states prefer to use videotaped interviews with the child. The testimonies and the evidence must prove that harm was done to the child. It is not enough to prove that the parents' behavior is abusive. Rather, the effect this behavior has had on the child must be established.

Several dispositions can be made as a result of this proceeding (Faller, 2003; Katner and Plum, 2002; Noel, 2013). These also vary considerably from state to state:

- The case can be dismissed if the judge deems that insufficient evidence has been presented to support the allegations of maltreatment.
- The judge may suspend judgment based on the parents' willingness to comply with the court's recommendations. In other words, the court may order the parents to undergo treatment or follow some other prescribed plan. They are given a time-frame—usually, six months to a year—in which they must meet certain conditions; at the end of this time another hearing is held. If the parents have failed to comply with the order, a judgment is made. If they have complied, the case may be dismissed or it may be continued to a later date to ensure the parents' compliance or consistency over time.
- The judge may order custody of the child to the protective agency. The child will then either (1) remain at home but be visited regularly by a social worker who assures the court of the safety of the child; (2) be placed in a foster home pending the parents' compliance with treatment; or (3) be placed with relatives in a kinship home.
- The judge may terminate parental rights based on the court's perception that the parents are unable to adequately care for their child. If this step is imminent before the hearing, the parents are notified of the court's intent. Most states now allow parents a period of up to 18 months to demonstrate that they can provide what is best for the child. Jones (2006) explains that other reasons for the termination of parental right might be that the child has been in foster care for 15 of the last 22 months, the child has been abandoned by the parents, or the parents have done serious bodily harm to the child or have committed, aided, or attempted the murder of a sibling. The termination of parental rights is not an arbitrary decision but rather is based on specific conduct or inaction. In addition, the child protection agency must show that it has made "reasonable efforts" at preserving the family (Davidson, 1997). In other words, the court observes that the child be further harmed if the parents regained custody or that remaining home is not in the child's best interests. In some states, this termination of parental rights frees the child immediately for adoption. In some other states, an additional petition outlining the best interests of the child and possibilities for future placement is necessary to set into motion the actual adoption procedure.

Throughout the court protection process, the parents have the right to appeal to a higher court, although procedures on such an appeal differ from state to state. If the appeal is heard, it is designed to review the case to ensure that the trial court correctly interpreted and followed existing law. The higher court may uphold the juvenile court decision, overturn its decision, or order the juvenile court to hear the case again if there was a violation of due process (Faller, 2003; Katner and Plum, 2002).

The juvenile court process is usually lengthy. Courts attempt to keep to a minimum the time between filing the petition and the first hearing, usually 24 to 72 hours. But because of multiple dispositional hearings and delays and cancellations, the process can drag on for years. During this time, the child may be moved from home to foster home in a seemingly endless cycle of separation and loss. This unfortunate situation can be somewhat ameliorated by competent social workers preparing and supporting the child during this period. It is with this in mind that most states have instituted the specific timeframe mentioned above.

The Participants

Before examining criminal court intervention, it may be helpful to look at the participants in the juvenile court process. While many have an idea (albeit colored by TV, other media, and fiction) of the role of judges, lawyers, and prosecutors in criminal court, few understand the differences and subtleties of a juvenile court hearing. The informality, the fact that children are involved, and the fact that juvenile court is not specifically concerned with adversary proceedings changes the style in which participants operate.

Judges   The role of the judge in juvenile court is not easy. Most judges are aware they serve as authority figures but understand that children should not be intimidated more than they already are. From the initial petition, it might be easy for judges to see parents as cruel and intentionally hurting their offspring. A closer look often promotes the understanding that the parents are frightened, deprived, overburdened individuals who may not have had the models to parent properly themselves. The judge must both protect the constitutional rights of the parents and consider the child's rights as well (Faller, 2003; Jones, 2006; Katner and Plum, 2002; Myers et al., 2002). Some courts use magistrates for this role.

Deprived of the support of a jury (in most cases), the judge or magistrate must base the final decision on the report of the investigator, on what has been heard in the courtroom, on the judge's own experience, and often on an assumption of what will be best for all concerned. The judge is also aware that the ruling may be subject to public outrage or overturned by a higher court.

Courts seek to determine guilt or innocence, but the juvenile court process emphasizes treatment. The judge must be able to assess how amenable the parents are to treatment and what resources are actually available in the community to help them. The judge must also face the shortage of placement and treatment resources for children (Harris and Teitelbaum, 2002).

Since people's motivations are never predictable, the juvenile court judge realizes there is no assurance that a child will be safe when returned home or happy in placement. Using only best judgment and the hope that it is correct, the judge renders the decision.

Children's Advocates   The attorney who represents the child has an important role in protecting the child's interests but often works with little or no information or feedback from the underage client. Representation of infants requires the attorney's judgment of what will be best for the child. With an older child, the counselor may adopt an approach that explores the child's feelings and hopes for the outcome. Then the attorney is faced with deciding whether the child will be more at risk at home or more traumatized by placement.

Understanding the impact on the child, not only of the abuse or neglect but of the implications for staying in the home, is essential. This attorney must be single-minded and constantly aware of the effects of the treatment suggested or the decisions made for the young client (Duquette, 1997; Faller, 2003; Katner and Plum, 2002). Attorneys for children do not assume the adversary role of attorneys in other proceedings but act here, as their alternate title implies, as guardians of the children's best interests. The lawyer is in close contact with the protective services agency to ensure what they propose for the child will indeed be the best plan (Duquette, 1997; Litzelfelner and Petr, 1997; Peters, 1997; Ventrell and Duquette, 2005).

Lawyers representing children sometimes function in an advisory role, acquainting their clients with what will transpire in court or even giving a tour of the courtrooms to minimize the intimidation when the child must be present. Some lawyers prefer to leave this preparation to social workers. Not every lawyer is interested in representing children. In fact, counsel for children are chosen differently, depending on the state and court. Some attorneys specialize in representing children and become proficient in balancing the needs of the children with their obligations to the court. Others are appointed—often as part of a training process when they first begin with a firm or an agency. The attorneys' feelings about child representation can greatly affect their manner of dealing with their clients.

Children are not always represented solely by lawyers. Some courts appoint a specially trained volunteer to protect the child's interests. One such volunteer program, known as CASA (court appointed special advocate), was created by Judge David Soukup, of the King County Superior Court in Seattle, Washington. In 1970, Soukup was concerned about the children in the cases coming through his court. His idea of using trained volunteers became established in January 1977. During the first year of this program (then known as the GAL, or guardian ad litem, program), there were 110 volunteers serving 498 children. The program is now nationwide, and by 1986, there were 201 CASA programs in 43 states.[1]

The concept of using special advocates arose from the fact that many lawyers did not feel comfortable being the sole representatives of children. There was little consistency in how this representation was carried out, and few lawyers were trained for child welfare responsibilities. Many felt ill prepared for the untraditional legal responsibilities of interviewing and sometimes counseling children (Faller, 2003; Katner and Plum, 2002; Litzelfelner and Petr, 1997; Myers et al., 2002).

The court-appointed special volunteer (who may be a layperson) plays a part in both juvenile and probate court proceedings. In probate court custody cases, CASA volunteers investigate the home situation and follow up to ensure the children's welfare until the case is decided by the court. In juvenile court cases, even though an investigator has already been appointed, the CASA volunteer continues to monitor the home once the investigation is over. The goal in this monitoring is to be sure the child is safe and that the parents are doing what they can for the child's well-being (Hood, 2006).

Although this program has been successful in many areas, some attorneys feel uncomfortable using lay volunteers. Volunteers, in turn, often complain that they are not being taken seriously by the courts. Those programs using volunteers hope that increased training and communication will ameliorate this problem.

Parents' Attorneys   While the children are being represented by an attorney, a CASA volunteer, or another court-appointed advocate, the parents also have representation. The parents' attorney is either hired by them or appointed by the court. This attorney may

---

[1]Based on an interview with Sue Scrogin, project director, the CASA Project, Worcester, Massachusetts.

need to overcome negative feelings about what has been done to the child in order to understand and defend the needs and rights of the clients. Considering that neglectful and abusive parents often have difficulty trusting others, forming relationships, and following through, the lawyer's role is often marked with frustration.

The main roles of the parents' attorney are to refute the allegations brought by the petition and to convince the court that the parents do have their children's interests in mind. This counselor attempts to evaluate the clients' problems and helps them and the court discover ways to minister to these problems. The lawyer advises the clients as to what might help minimize the court's concerns. For example, the lawyer might suggest that the court would look more favorably on the case if the clients secured housing not so structurally dangerous and rat infested as their current dwelling. Further, the counsel may help the clients get in touch with a housing agency through which better accommodations could be found. The parents' attorney may also advise them to cooperate with the protective services agency by following the prescribed treatment plan.

The attorney who fights vigorously for abusive or neglectful clients is not always popular. Yet this advocate serves to ensure that the court consider all sides of the problem. The presence of this counsel protects the parents' rights to due process (Duquette, 1997; Faller, 2003; Katner and Plum, 2002; Noel, 2013; Ventrell and Duquette, 2005). The attorney may also be operating as a spokesperson for those inarticulate parents who otherwise might not be given a fair hearing.

Agency Attorneys   Until recently, the protective services attorney did not always follow the case into the courtroom. More often, this individual functioned in an advisory role to the protective services worker on whom the burden of proof has fallen.

Today, agency attorneys are more likely to accompany social workers to court proceedings. This attorney is familiar with the court system and recognizes how to use it to the best advantage in securing an equitable plan for the child. The attorney is also familiar with the functioning of the protective services agency and can help to interpret this to the court. Knowing both areas, this attorney is better able to aid caseworkers in preparing reports and assisting them in the preparation of their testimony. When the attorney does go into the courtroom, it is to provide firsthand legal advice to agency representatives.

Social Workers   Social workers can serve several roles in a court hearing, although the roles they take differ greatly from state to state and agency to agency. The original reporter may have been a social worker who then came to court to testify, or a social worker may have been assigned to either the family or the children separately. This worker may then be asked to provide support to his or her clients and pertinent information during the hearing. It is often extremely difficult for workers who have been giving service to a family to seemingly choose sides in court.

Some agencies assign one or more social workers to advocate for either parents or children just before or following the initial hearing. These social workers are usually responsible for helping the clients to carry out the directives of the court (e.g., receive treatment, find adequate housing). Social workers may be in the employ of state, county, or private agencies, depending on who has responsibility for the case.

One of the most widely described problems for social workers going into court is that their views usually conflict with those of the attorneys. Attorneys are trained to listen for facts and to search out evidence, but social workers are often trained to make judgments on experience, psychological analyses, and even intuition. For this reason, some attorneys complain that social workers cannot articulate in a manner that is beneficial to their case (Copen, 2000; Stein, 1998).

Since both professions have their strengths, there is an increased trend toward dialogue between them. Social workers are learning to be more comfortable and articulate in court proceedings, while they strive to make attorneys more aware of how to interview children and how to determine what will be in the best interest of these children. To demonstrate this increasing counter awareness, every major child abuse conference in the last few years has featured numerous workshops from the legal perspective.

Witnesses   Anyone, but especially someone involved with child welfare services, may be called to appear in juvenile court as a witness. First-time experiences in court can be anxiety provoking, but the witnesses should remember they are there on behalf of the child (or the parent) and not on trial themselves.

Faller (2003) suggests pointers for those who must appear in court. A witness should prepare ahead. Notes about dates and events can help with recall, but these should not be read verbatim. Nor should the testimony be memorized. Appropriate dress is essential. Courts are still often conservative.

It is natural to be nervous. The stress of an unfamiliar courtroom, combined with the requirements that the witness answer under oath, often make the witness uncomfortable. Speaking more slowly and somewhat louder and more distinctly than usual will help get the testimony across. Most attorneys prefer to develop the case without having witnesses furnish extraneous details. Therefore, the attorney may ask questions that can easily be answered by yes or no. On the other hand, an attorney may direct the witness to furnish a good deal of information at once. For example, the witness may be told, "Tell us what you observed and what happened when you went to the Jones's home on March 15th." Answers should be factual and contain a minimum of hearsay or secondhand information. (In the event of an undue amount of hearsay, the opposing attorney may object.) A witness should confine himself or herself to that which is known, rather than guess or assume.

Cross-examination can be especially anxiety provoking. Although the witness must tell the truth, his or her words can often be twisted to appear to mean something else. This is especially true if a question is in two parts or is meant to be a trick question. Experienced witnesses learn that it is important not to be rushed. They consider the question calmly and then answer it as positively as possible. Two-part questions, for example, can be broken into their parts before being answered. If there is an objection, witnesses learn to stop talking until a ruling has been made.

With experience, court appearances become considerably easier and can actually make one feel involved and helpful in the cause of protecting children.

Alternatives

Settlements resulting from negotiations between attorneys sometimes preclude the need for a hearing. Unlike negotiations in other types of cases (e.g., criminal), these negotiations are often more complex. The fact that there are more participants, each perhaps with different viewpoints, and the fact that the children cannot speak for themselves add to this complexity (Ichikawa, 1997; Katner and Plum, 2002).

A settlement usually takes the form of what the parents will do in order to avoid a court appearance and have the child remain with them. The advantages of a settlement to the child must be fully weighed. For this reason, the agreement made is often written up in the form of a treatment plan.

There are advantages to settlements in juvenile court cases. First, a hearing may make the participants feel they are in an adversary relationship; people feel forced to take sides, even though the issue for everyone should be what is in the best interest of the child. Second, a recapitulation of the facts surrounding the abuse may increase the parents' feelings of guilt and elevate their defenses to compensate. Third, hearings and the preparation for them can be lengthy and require an inordinate amount of time for lawyers, social workers, and other court personnel (Katner and Plum, 2002; Myers et al., 2002).

The disadvantages to settlements, however, include the instances of parents who later regret that they had not presented their side. They may have felt pressured into negotiating. Without a hearing, pertinent information that could have a profound impact on the case may not be uncovered or parents may agree to the court recommendations just to avoid further court appearances, rather than with any sincerity or intention to follow through. It is vital, therefore, that the ramifications of the case be studied thoroughly prior to or during negotiations and that all parties feel comfortable with the settlement agreement.

Some states use voluntary placement of children to circumvent juvenile court hearings. An agreement is made between the parents and the protective agency that the children will be placed in a foster home while the parents undergo treatment or make other arrangements for their return. That was the case with Rochelle:

Rochelle Duclas, a 22-year-old mother of two, entered into such an agreement with the department of protective services. Rochelle maintained an apartment that she frequently shared with a boyfriend, Al, who was subject to extreme bouts of temper. The year before, Rochelle's two children, ages 2 and 3, had been removed by the juvenile court after it was discovered they had been severely abused by Al. It was the decision of the court that this mother could not or would not separate from her boyfriend long enough to ensure the safety of her children. The children therefore remained in foster care while the department petitioned to have them legally freed for adoption.

When Rochelle gave birth to a third child, she recognized the danger to the infant from Al, who had recently returned. She thought she could get her boyfriend to leave but needed more time. Rochelle approached the department and asked that she be allowed to place her child, temporarily, while securing a better apartment and a restraining order against Al. Feeling that this plan was preferable to the possible abuse of the baby, the department agreed.

One of the problems with voluntary agreements is that in many jurisdictions, they can be easily broken by the parents. The protective agency is then left with little alternative but to seek court action.

Not all states use the juvenile court in every instance. Sometimes, a guardianship petition is filed in probate court to avoid the lengthy juvenile court process. Guardianship is provided for a child when the parent is absent, incapable, or unfit to care for him or her. This course of action is usually undertaken when the parent seems unlikely to be able to resume care of the child. Guardianship is also used to protect the child when an agreement for voluntary placement is broken (Katner and Plum, 2002).

Advantages and Disadvantages of Juvenile Court

The consideration of advantages and disadvantages of the juvenile court system prompts a look at this system from a historical perspective. Prior to the late 1800s, children were rarely considered in courts as anything other than extensions of their parents. In 1899, due largely to the efforts of child advocates, the first juvenile court was established in Chicago.

Advocates of this seemingly new progressive system felt that children should be separated from adults in court proceedings for three reasons. First, when children committed infractions or crimes, they did so not because they were evil (a common perception about adults) but because they were in pain or conflict. These attention-seeking behaviors warranted help, not punishment. Second, children whose families abused or neglected them required careful evaluation and help that would protect their interests. Careful attention must be given to the rights of the children as well as the rights of the parents. And finally, those responsible for making these legal decisions about the welfare of children should have an interest in and expertise about children (Faller, 2003; Myers et al., 2002; Noel, 2013).

Over the years, juvenile courts have taken on more informality and less dependence on rigid legal protocols. There has been an attempt to keep in focus the needs of the children and their welfare. In abuse and neglect situations, petitions are brought on behalf of children, rather than against their parents. This shifts the emphasis from punishment of parents for their actions or lack of action toward treatment that will strengthen the home environment if at all possible.

Yet as the sexual abuse of children became one of the most pervasive issues of this era, some authors argue that juvenile court may actually benefit the perpetrator as much, if not more, than the child. For this reason, more and more states are passing legislation that mandates the report of sexual abuse cases to district attorneys. In this way, criminal courts will often also be involved.

Criminal Court

Increasingly, and especially in cases of sexual abuse, criminal courts deal with perpetrators. Occasionally, when a child dies as a result of abuse or neglect or is severely harmed, the parents are also prosecuted. The goals of criminal prosecution are, theoretically, rehabilitation, removal of the perpetrator from society, deterrence from future crimes, and retribution. The problem is that it is only the defendant, if found guilty, who is required to receive treatment. In family situations, such a remedy ignores the fact that abuse is usually a family system problem (Davidson, 1997; Katner and Plum, 2002).

Criminal prosecution may be used instead of or in conjunction with juvenile court. When this occurs, the juvenile court judge suspends decision pending the outcome of the criminal proceedings. Unfortunately, this often leaves the child and other members of the family in uncertainty for an extended period. If criminal and juvenile court cases proceed simultaneously, it is vital that attorneys responsible for the criminal and the juvenile cases work closely in matters that affect custody release of the alleged perpetrator, visitation, and the timing of the trials (Davidson, 1997). In many states, nonfamilial sexual abuse is not within the responsibilities of protective services agencies, and the issue is handled only as a criminal matter.

Criminal procedures differ significantly from those in juvenile court. As in other criminal cases, a perpetrator can be released on bail. Plea bargaining (an agreement made between all the parties to minimize the charges or avoid going to trial) is another option—and a controversial one, in many cases. While in both instances, the lawyer for the perpetrator is seeking to get the best deal for the client, others concerned hope for adequate protection for the child. Therapists and victim–witness advocates are often used to ensure that the child's best interests are protected (Faller, 2003; Jones, 2006; Katner and Plum, 2002).

Threat of prosecution is used as leverage, especially in sexual abuse cases. In these situations, the perpetrator pleads guilty with the understanding that the sentence will be suspended or reduced if he cooperates with a treatment program.

Prosecution in criminal court is not without drawbacks for the child and the family. The court process can be traumatic to the victim. Multiple appearances in the courtroom are often required and thus extend the procedure. The participants' lives seem consumed with preparing for and then enduring the court experience. The assault(s) must be relived again and again in the presence of a jury and a possibly crowded courtroom. Victims who testify often feel fatigue and may begin to doubt their own stories. Videotaping spares victims the numerous appearances. Yet for the duration of the trial and often long afterward, the family feels the pressure of scrutiny.

Much depends on the actions and attitudes of the important figures in the criminal court process. The district attorney emerges early as a professional whose style can have an effect on the participants. A district attorney may appear indifferent to witnesses and give them little direction or support. Another district attorney may be extremely authoritative and matter of fact and may indicate that he or she knows how to proceed and is not willing to deviate. Fortunately for most families and victims, many district attorneys take a more humanistic approach. As abuse cases have become more frequent, district attorneys have sought training to become more sensitive to the needs of children and families. Many district attorneys take time or have staff to prepare the participants in order to minimize the trauma of appearing in court (Faller, 2003).

Another source of help for families is the increasing number of victim–witness advocates. Operating out of the district or county attorney's office, victim–witness programs supply workers to offer support to the child and the family, to provide transportation, and to prepare the participants for their roles in court. The victim–witness advocate is a friend for the child and a counselor on whom the child can depend when others in the child's life may feel under too much pressure to offer support (Noel, 2013).

Despite the delays, the uncomfortable cross-examination, and the trauma of feeling put on the spot, the trial comes to an end. The possibilities for outcome are varied. The abuser may be fined for damages or be required to undergo treatment. If the family is to remain intact or if this is the eventual plan, family counseling may be ordered or recommended. In some instances, the perpetrator will be incarcerated and treatment may or may not be available (Katner and Plum, 2002). Perhaps one of the most difficult rulings for the plaintiff is to have the case dismissed. The child may be vulnerable not only to future assaults but also to the guilt of family disruption.

While there was once a good bit of leniency given by the courts to perpetrators of child sexual abuse, public pressure has resulted in the use of harsher punitive measures. This movement to punish offenders, especially multiple-time offenders, more severely has its positive and negative points. On the one hand, recognizing what may await them, offenders may put more pressure on children to recant. And families, aware that they may lose their breadwinner, may be more likely to protect the offender from prosecution and removal. On the other hand, the hope is that more stringent sentences will go a long way toward deterring future offenses (Davidson, 1997).

Whether the perpetrator is convicted or not, therapy for the child is usually advisable. Unlike adults, who may try to forget the unpleasantness of what has happened, children are frequently more affected by the process. Even when the perpetrator was not a family member, the child may fear retaliation or carry guilt because of testifying.

The criminal process is not always smooth and can be painful for those involved. The system, however, has come a long way in becoming sensitive to the needs of the parties in this all too frequent type of case.

The Impact of Court on Children

A child who has been abused or neglected and who is then faced with the experience of going to court has an additional adjustment. Once children were the pawns to be moved to and fro in the legal maze. With attention to children's rights, more focus has been put on the children and their reactions to the court experience.

How traumatized are children by the experience of going to court? Lipovsky (1994) compared three studies to determine the degree of system-induced trauma to children. She found that when children do testify in court, which is not as frequent as one might imagine, they are in fact not unduly traumatized. Older children have more difficulty with the experience than their younger counterparts, and children who are exposed to lengthy court battles may show more negative effects. Maternal support was found to be a key factor. Children who had mother as an advocate fared better (Lipovsky, 1994).

Time delays are one issue that can compound trauma for children. The backlog of court cases means that a child may be placed in legal and emotional limbo while his or her court case is pending. Delays and continuances can stretch the court process into months or even years. For the child whose future rests in the hands of the legal system, a few years can seem like an eternity.

To minimize the trauma to children, Lipovsky suggests several interventions that courts and social workers should keep in mind. Education is an effective tool to decrease children's anxiety about the court experience. Both children and their parents can be educated about court process complete with trips to familiarize themselves with a courtroom. Stress management procedures, such as teaching deep breathing, muscle relaxation and focusing, also helped children to cope. Children respond well to role plays, which let them practice using these techniques.

Improving parental attitudes about court was another method of providing support to children. Parents who were fearful of or extremely negative about the experience communicated this to their children. Improving maternal support (or support from the nonoffending parent) is vital in enhancing the child's ability to feel safe and protected.

And finally, Lipovsky stresses that helping professionals should keep in mind the individual characteristics of the child. Older children, whom studies show are more traumatized by court experiences, are often overlooked with the assumption that because they are older they can take care of themselves. Each child should be seen individually from the perspective of age, gender, reactions to stress, and general psychological makeup. Through these simple procedures, children can be helped to cope with their court experiences (Copen, 2000; Faller, 2003; Lipovsky, 1994; Masson and Oakley, 2001).

SEX OFFENDER REGISTRATION

One controversial aspect of criminal prosecution of sexual offenders has been how to protect the public from future victimization by known, convicted offenders. This concern became paramount when on July 29, 1994, 7-year-old Megan Kanka was raped and murdered by a twice-convicted sex offender who was living near her home in New Jersey. The offender, Jesse Timmendequas, was rooming with two other previously convicted offenders in a neighborhood that was totally unaware of their backgrounds. After the death of her daughter, Megan's mother was so incensed by this fact that she began to wage a campaign for community notification. The result of that campaign was that on May 17, 1996, President Bill Clinton signed federal legislation that became known as Megan's Law (Simon, 2003; Laney, 2008; Walsh, 1997).

Although interpreted differently from state to state, Megan's Law enables the public to learn whether a convicted sex offender is living in the neighborhood. In some states, police are mandated to alert the community when a high-risk offender settles in the area. In other instances, a public citizen can request a list of sexual offenders by calling a number, accessing the information on the Internet, or appearing at the local police station. When offenders move into a community, they are required to register with the local police.

The controversy around the constitutionality of Megan's Law has caused some states to suspend registration for varying amounts of time. Critics argue that registration gives the public a false sense of security. As one police officer explained, "Convicted felons are not the only offenders. When the public is on the lookout for only those who were previously caught, they miss protecting their children from the offender who has never come to the attention of the legal system." Further, sexual offenders who have received help and are trying to repair their lives feel that they are targeted when the general public knows who they are and may even object to their presence in the community. Many feel that it is like being tried twice.

A recent New Jersey study disputed the efficacy of offender registration, reporting that Megan's Law had no effect on reducing the number of victims or offenses (Zgoba, Witt, Dalessandra, and Veysey, 2008).

Although the intent of the sexual offender registry may have been to protect the community, the controversy still mounts. Only time will tell how it will be resolved.

THE MEDIA AND THE COURT

As child abuse and neglect cases appear more and more frequently in both juvenile and criminal court, the media have given greater coverage to the issue. Media interest stimulates the controversy over the public's right to know about these proceedings and the child's and family's rights to privacy. Media attention can also aggravate an already emotionally charged atmosphere. Critics of media coverage have expressed the opinion that perpetrators are condemned by public outrage and therefore have less than a fair hearing. The stigma is attached to the abusive and the nonabusive parent, as well.

In general, juvenile court hearings are open only to the participants and are closed to the media. Criminal hearings, however, may be opened to public scrutiny. Although it may be important to educate the public about what is being done in the area of court involvement in child abuse and neglect, the effect on children of not only the legal proceedings but of the attendant coverage cannot be minimized. Therefore, it should be with a great deal of sensitivity that the media be allowed to fully cover these cases.

SUMMARY

Court action in cases of child abuse and neglect takes place as a last resort when parents abandon their children, severely injure or kill them, place them in imminent danger, sexually abuse them, or fail to cooperate with the protective services agency. Going to court is not easy for the child or the family, and the positives and negatives must be considered carefully in the context of the entire case. Both parents and children have similar legal rights. These are the right to counsel, the right to be given notice, and the right to confrontation and cross-examination.

An abuse or neglect case may be handled in one of several courts. Civil court houses juvenile sessions or courts, in which a petition can be brought to request protection for dependent children. Criminal courts prosecute the perpetrators. In some states, probate or superior courts hear different types of maltreatment cases.

The juvenile court process differs from state to state. For the most part, it consists of three stages: the petition, the adjudication, and the disposition. Between each stage there can be variations, such as fact-finding conferences, an investigation, or out-of-court settlements. The parents and the child are each represented by counsel, and the hearings are tried on merits to determine what is in the best interest of the child. The juvenile court hearing is usually somewhat informal. Once the case has been investigated, the facts are presented and a plan of treatment for the parents may be required. The court also determines that the custody of the child be with the parents, relatives, or through the protective services agency.

The professionals involved in juvenile court are an important part of the process. The judge hears the case and makes the final decision based on the recommendations of the investigator, the protective agency, and the attorneys. The attorney for the child assumes the role of counselor for the client as well as represents the child's best interest. More recently, CASA provide support for the families and monitor the cases to ensure that court recommendations are followed.

The parents' attorney attempts to refute the allegations of abuse and neglect and represents the interests of the clients. Often, this role extends to helping the parents by making referrals for services that will enable them to provide a better environment for their children. The attorney for the protective service agency usually functions in an advisory capacity but may attend the hearings to provide support in more complex situations.

There are some alternatives to juvenile court hearings. Settlements resulting from negotiations between the attorneys of involved parties sometimes preclude a court hearing. Voluntary placement gives parents time to receive treatment or mobilize their resources in order to provide a better home for their children. Some protective agencies use probate court guardianship as an alternative to juvenile court.

When children have been killed, severely injured, or sexually abused, perpetrators are usually prosecuted in criminal courts. One of the most significant drawbacks about criminal court is the effect it can have on children and their families. Often, it is the participants' relationships with the district attorney, their own attorneys, and the victim–witness volunteers that minimize the trauma caused by this complex process.

Although court action can create a strain for the participants, it does provide a useful mechanism through which society can protect abused and neglected children.

Chapter 12

Treatment
Physical Abuse and Neglect

The identification and assessment of abusive and neglectful families have one goal: to protect the child. In years past, some people believed that the solution was to remove the child from the family if it was not providing appropriate care. Now, we realize that this alternative, in some instances, may actually be more damaging to the child. We have also learned that some families, with adequate supports, can begin to parent effectively. Treatment of families, therefore, becomes more essential in providing children with a safe and nurturing atmosphere. Unfortunately, if funds are cut from social services, it is often in the area of treatment. It is hoped that as more effective treatment methods are developed, funding sources will recognize how vital this area of the helping system is to children.

PREPARING TO PROVIDE TREATMENT

Professionals who are involved in treatment of abusive and neglectful families must be aware of several aspects of their work. First is in the area of *counter transference*—that is, the worker's reaction to the client (feelings, attitudes, thoughts, and behaviors), which is brought about by the helper's own past life experiences. This reaction may be based on the worker's own history of abuse, past relationships with parents or caretakers, previous life experiences, and relationships with intimates (Howe, 2005). If clients "push our buttons," we, as professionals, must become aware of it so that our actions do not negatively influence the service being provided.

A second area of importance is *confidentiality*. Every client has the right to privacy when he or she shares thoughts or feelings with a helping professional. In protective work, the parameters of confidentiality become more problematic. There are three areas in treatment that the client cannot expect the worker or therapist to maintain confidentiality: if the client has threatened or attempted suicide; if the client threatens to kill another; or if the client abuses or neglects a child. These situations should or must be reported.

What if a worker is treating a mother who admits in an interview that she has begun to beat her child *again* and asks the worker to keep this secret? After all, she is participating in services for the original report of abuse. For treatment to be effective, no secrets can be kept between worker and client. This would not be confidentiality but collusion. The skilled worker learns the difference.

PROVIDING TREATMENT

The recognition and reporting of abuse and neglect accomplish little for the victim and the family unless prompt, effective treatment follows. Treatment often takes the form of intensive case management, during which the services needed by the family are overseen by a social worker. Sometimes, families also participate in group or individual counseling. Unfortunately, prompt and effective treatment does not always become a reality for several reasons.

Client Resistance

Engaging families in treatment can be extremely difficult. Communicating to a family that its methods of child care are considered inadequate does not always convince them of the need for change. Families may resent the intervention and be concerned only with escaping from the scrutiny of the social service system:

> Mike Forrester was particularly resistant to treatment. He did not consider beating 5-year-old Timmy with a belt as abusive. His father had disciplined him in this manner. But social services insisted that he refrain from hitting Timmy. Mike therefore agreed with whatever was suggested, hoping "they'd get off his back." He agreed to see a counselor but never quite made the appointments, citing as excuses transportation and sick children whom he had to watch while his wife worked.
>
> It was not that Mike Forrester did not love his son. The 35-year-old father had been raised with particular values and with set methods of discipline. He could not believe that these would be any more harmful to Timmy than he felt they had been to him.

Some parents mistrust services and treatment methods or feel they will do no good. It should be remembered that seemingly negative patterns of interaction can keep families together. The sexually abusive family, for example, thrives on keeping the secret. Two isolated parents with extremely low self-esteem are threatened by exposure to the outside world. They have taught their children to be like them. Exposure to treatment means possible change and an upset of the delicate family balance. Treatment may force them to break their dependencies on one another. Family members feel this will intensify their isolation and leave them even more helpless.

Cultural differences may actually be perceived as resistance. If professionals do not take time to understand the culture and therefore fail to engage a minority client, the client is often labeled as resistant or difficult. For example, the African American client who believes that she should "leave things in the hands of the Lord" is often perceived as unmotivated to cooperate with treatment (Atkinson, Morten, and Sue, 2003; Fontes, 2008; Jackson and Brissett-Chapman, 1999).

Parents have expressed the fear that seeing a social worker or a counselor will label them. A young, neglectful mother was asked to take her son to a child guidance clinic to evaluate his multiple learning problems. Despite the fact that transportation was provided, alleviating her first concern, the mother refused to go. "My son ain't crazy!" she protested, "and I ain't takin' him to no shrink."

Individuals who have had difficult, deprived childhoods themselves have difficulty trusting. Establishing trust with a helping professional may be extremely hard for them. Some parents perceive that there is still a threat of removal of their children, and they are afraid to disclose too much.

Above all, treatment must be seen within a cultural context: How can the client be helped to parent more effectively within her or his own culture? How can a compromise be reached between the client's cultural values and the laws that govern this nation? When clients perceive that they are not being robbed of their cultural values, their resistance may be considerably less.

Client Response

Even after becoming engaged in treatment, families do not always follow through. Consistency may be a problem for many families who abuse and neglect children. They also have difficulty delaying gratification or looking toward final goals. For these families, participating consistently with the services provided to them can be frustrating and unrewarding. As one neglectful mother said, "If I'm such a lousy mother, either fix me NOW or forget it" (Williams and Crosson-Tower, 2013). Parents who have been able to recognize their need for change may not understand why it doesn't happen more quickly. They do not comprehend that change can involve pain, and at the first twinges of pain, they want to flee. Consider this case:

> Mrs. Hooper found it extremely difficult when 10-year-old Betty began to act like the child she was. Betty had been sexually abused by her father since she was 5, but she had cared for her sickly mother despite their poor relationship. Betty's father had been ordered out of the house by the court, and now the mother and daughter agreed to try to pick up the shattered fragments of their relationship.
>
> Since Betty had taken on all her mother's responsibilities and domestic roles, the change in this arrangement was difficult for both mother and child. Mrs. Hooper, who was able to see that her hypochondria was a bid for attention, recognized Betty's need to be a little girl. But the tasks and decisions that now fell to the mother seemed overwhelming to her. In reaction, she blamed the therapist for "causing her so much trouble" and refused to return to therapy.

In the treatment of neglectful parents, some authors (Cantwell, 1997; Dubowitz, 1999; Hecht, Chaffin, Bonner, Worley, and Lawon, 2002; Howe, 2005; MacDonald, 2005; Polansky, DeSaix, and Sharlin, 1972; Righthand, Kerr, and Drach, 2003; Stevenson, 2007) suggest that personality problems, such as extreme immaturity and difficulty with verbal communication, present major barriers to treatment. These authors characterize a majority of chronically neglectful mothers as "playing games" to resist treatment. One such game is "Look-how-hard-I'm-trying." The client with this outlook appears to do whatever is suggested by the worker but continually fails in her efforts to change, often because she sabotages her own efforts.

There may be several reasons why the treatment does not work for this mother. Changing may be too difficult for her. Or maybe she has been asked to change in a way that has not fully engaged her cooperation and has instead antagonized her. This mother may not even recognize the importance or necessity for change and her apparent efforts only because she has been told she must alter her lifestyle.

It is important to recognize that agreeing with the worker but not acting as promised may not be a game per se—as Polansky describes. For example, Asians value harmony; they would not contradict someone in authority. Therefore, rather than say no to the worker, some Asians might agree to change behavior but do nothing. This is another cultural nuance (Fontes, 2008; Lum, 2010).

Another game cited by Polansky and colleagues (1972) is the "Yes, but" maneuver. A client asks for advice, but to every suggestion she counters with the reason she cannot possibly carry it out. Another scenario includes the client who continues her old patterns of behavior, and when this is pointed out, she protests she did not understand what was expected of her. A difficult type of client enlists the worker's sympathy by apologizing profusely but claims the worker cannot expect much more from someone so incapable. The result of any of the preceding maneuvers is frustration on the part of the worker, who may want to transfer the case, close it, or invoke court action to remove the children.

Other clients respond to treatment with other defenses:

> *Mrs. Moss was being seen by a social worker and a private therapist. Because of busy schedules, these two professionals conferred only infrequently about Mrs. Moss's progress. Then the irate therapist called the social worker to complain that the worker was sabotaging Mrs. Moss's therapy. It took a good part of the conversation before the professionals recognized that their client had been playing them against each other by telling each suggestions that Mrs. Moss said the other had made. Until the worker and therapist finally talked, Mrs. Moss's therapy was in severe jeopardy.*

It is not uncommon for some clients to lure professionals into disagreements with each other. For this reason, open communication within the helping network is vital.

Clients who are resistant to treatment sometimes present their need as one involving a concrete service. For example, the client who requests housing assistance, welfare, or food stamps may agree to counseling to ensure that the concrete service is provided. Yet once the money or food stamps are in hand or the family moves into the new dwelling, the client no longer goes for counseling, despite telling the worker that he or she would. These clients have difficulty seeing help as anything except the tangible. To them, change is having some commodity they did not have before. These clients, like the ones who play games and have difficulty following through, present a particular problem to those offering treatment.

Eligibility Criteria

Limited funding forces agencies to have clear eligibility criteria. Families who do not fit into these guidelines may not receive adequate service. The Sung family, for example, was not eligible to receive group therapy at a clinic that served only low-income families because their income was above the guidelines. The only other similar program for abusive families was at an agency that served an area outside the Sungs' neighborhood. The solution to this problem, perhaps, is for agencies to exercise as much flexibility as possible.

Limited Community Resources

There are often limited resources within the community to treat families (especially those who have limited English-language skills). Until recently there were very few programs in smaller communities to treat incestuous families. With increased publicity and more training in treating sexual abuse, this problem is slowly being remedied. Services in still other areas may be in short supply. For example, respite day care openings for the abusive mother who needs time away from her child to enhance her coping capabilities are not always available. Groups for physically or sexually abusive parents are all too few. Some therapists prefer not to accept clients for whom a sliding fee scale is necessary or who are funded by public assistance. Programs to train parents in their role or offer them support, such as parent aide programs and Parents Anonymous, cannot always find sponsorship.

The reasons for these shortages are many. Today, as more state and federal funds are cut, social services are often the first to suffer. And with the state of the national economy, those who volunteered in the past as parent aides or other roles may need to use their time to support their own financial survival.

Treatment Methods

While the social service system has developed somewhat adequate methods of recognizing, validating, and initially intervening in child abuse or neglect situations, treatment methods continue to evolve. Despite the progress that has been made in the area of treatment, some types of clients are difficult to help. Some cultural minorities are newly represented in this country, and many workers know little about working with them. The multiproblem family, for example, living from crisis to crisis, takes a great deal of time and consistency on the part of the helpers (Jones, 1997; MacDonald, 2005). In turn, workers experience frustration and often burnout.

Such families must be monitored, but programs continue to explore the most effective methods of treatment for the sexual offender with little real consensus. Advocates agree that new methods must be continually explored, but shortages in funding may make this impossible.

Who Provides Treatment?

Who actually treats families depends largely on the availability of services, finances, and expertise. Today, very few protective agencies have the funds or mandate to undertake treatment themselves in addition to case management. If more expertise exists elsewhere and the service can be funded in some way, treatment may be referred to another agency.

For example, a particular protective agency had traditionally assigned ongoing workers to see neglectful families regularly to help them provide better care for their children. These cases were extremely time-consuming; clients often missed appointments. Crises were a way of life for these clients and necessitated immediate responses from the workers. Transportation had to be provided, workers had to accompany clients to medical appointments, and so on. A large caseload of such families made the social worker relegate other cases to lower-priority status. The worker was also unable to perform those necessary administrative tasks, such as dictating and writing reports, completing authorization forms, and attending consultation, supervision, or staff meetings.

The trend now is for agencies, often with the aid of grants and independent of child protective services (CPS), to treat and otherwise provide a full range of treatment services for multiproblem families. For example, one worker supplies the family with a "friendly visitor" who was available to talk, respond to crises, or provide transportation. Another professional within the agency provides counseling for clients on an individual, group, family group, or family basis. This task often falls to community-based mental health centers, which often serve low-income communities by providing a variety of psychological services (Forkey, Hudson, Manz, and Silver, 2002).

Sexually abusive clients and families are usually also referred by CPS to other treatment agencies. Treatment for sexual abusers may be undertaken in prison or may be done at private agency facilities. Groups—currently the treatment of choice for not only offenders but for mothers and daughters—are sponsored by a wide variety of agencies and programs.

If treatment is referred out of the protective agency, which is usually the case today, the CPS social worker then maintains only a case management role, which means monitoring the case, keeping communication open among all parties, documenting progress, connecting the clients with additional sources of help, and eventually determining when the case can be closed.

As the chapter continues to discuss treatment, references to *the agency* will be to whatever agency has undertaken to treat the clients in conjunction with CPS.

Duration of Treatment

Length of treatment is impossible to estimate. Some families find that the resources available through social services and the knowledge of how to tap such resources in the future is sufficient. For these families, the process may be short. At the other end of the continuum are clients whose lives will be constantly intertwined with social services, as were the lives of their parents and grandparents. Their cases may be open with CPS for an extended period, or once the immediate service is provided, the case may be closed only to be opened again sometime later. The duration of treatment may also depend on how long funding for such services is available.

Given the variety of families who abuse and neglect and the numerous methods of treatment, how does the worker know when termination of protective services is indicated? Some generalized guidelines can be offered to answer this question.

Parents who have become aware of their needs, have found nonabusive ways to cope, and can reach for help in the future are probably ready for termination. Obstacles to future help must be minimal—in other words, parents have or know how to obtain access to transportation, telephone, and other methods of communication. The parents should have developed a support system—that is, a network of people to whom they can turn to share moments of joy, sorrow, and crisis. In this system, there should be someone who can recognize crises and help the family seek outside aid. Before terminating a case, the worker will want to be sure that any immediate crisis—such as poor housing, unemployment, illness, chronic alcoholism, and severe financial problems—has been resolved to alleviate stress for the client (Cantwell, 1997; Dubowitz, 1999; Forkey et al., 2002; Jones, 1997; Kellner and Crosson-Tower, 2013; MacDonald, 2005).

Communication is a vital skill for maltreating parents to develop. The parents must be able to recognize their own feelings, communicate them articulately, and appreciate the feelings of others. This may be especially difficult in cultures where the norm is not to talk about feelings. It is important that parents have improved self-esteem, recognize the growth they have made, and be proud of it. And finally, the way in which these parents see their children is important. They must perceive that the children are individuals with unique needs. Their expectations of their offspring should be realistic and their disciplinary methods appropriate. But most of all, it is hoped they find parenting more rewarding than they had before (Forkey et al., 2002; Jones, 1997).

Finding the type of intervention that will be most effective with a given client or family; determining how much time, effort, and financial resources can be devoted to that treatment; and deciding when termination is warranted are the challenges of working with clients who abuse and neglect their children. Treatment is not easy. There is a fundamental belief that parenting is something anyone can do. Intervening in this basic right often meets with hostility and lack of cooperation. Agencies, though well intentioned, may have different philosophies or fail to communicate effectively.

Treatment efforts cannot make everything all right for the family. The protective service system can only hope to make a difference. To give a more accurate picture of the treatment efforts necessary, each type of maltreatment and the implications of each follow.

FAMILY-CENTERED SERVICES

In years past, children who were abused or neglected were removed from their homes on a regular basis. But as increased attention was paid to how separation affects children, the philosophy of protective service agencies changed. Treatment, it is now believed, should be family based whenever possible. But how does a social worker visiting once or twice a month really help families to change? With some families it does not. The current trend is toward family-centered services. These intensive short-term, family-based services can be divided into two categories: family support and family preservation.

Family support services refer to voluntary services that are provided for families who are not yet in crisis. These services are actually designed to prevent crisis and promote healthy functioning. An example of such a service would be a home-visiting program that might be available for families of new infants. *Family preservation services* are mandated for families when a crisis is imminent or has already occurred—for example, when a report has been filed about a family to child protection and, after investigating the situation, the worker feels that the family should remain intact but needs intensive family services. These services are based on a strengths perspective and attempt to help the parents regain or develop the ability to meet their children's needs effectively. Families whose children have been placed in other homes may also qualify for such services as a prerequisite for reunification (Altstein and McRoy, 2000; Berns, 2009; Kellner and Crosson-Tower, 2013).

The Child Welfare League of America stresses the importance of such *intensive family-centered services*, or *IFPS*, to children (Pecora, Whittaker, Barth, and Maluccio, 2009). One of the oldest IFPS programs in the country is the HOMEBUILDERS, which was established in Tacoma, Washington in 1974. Described by some as a "behavior-modification program" (Sauer, 1994), models like this provide families with intensive skill building. Therapists use such techniques as values clarification, parenting training, problem solving, and other cognitive-behavioral methods. The program staff listens to families' problems and model problem solving to find solutions. This may necessitate connecting with concrete services such as housing, food supplements, transportation, medical care, employment training, and day care. Throughout the process, parents are encouraged to take as much responsibility as possible in meeting their own needs. It is the intensive support of the worker that enables them to do this (Bath and Haapala, 1993; Kellner and Crosson-Tower, 2013; Pecora et al., 2009).

Families become available for these IFPS services if their children are at risk for out-of-home placement or are being returned to the home after placement. Families are referred for intensive family services by the child protection agency. Some community agencies also have obtained grants to allow them to create intensive family services similar to or built on the HOMEBUILDERS model. With funding constraints resulting in program cuts, however, these programs are often the first to go. Advocates of such programs point out the painful irony that it is often the very services that might prevent a new generation of dysfunctional parents that are cut when funds become scarce.

IFPS programs are not for every family. Some parents are unable to comply with treatment plans, with the result that abuse can recur. This often places children in limbo, alternating between going home and foster care without a permanent plan. The failure of adequate permanency planning robs children of the ability to bond effectively, which is the basis of all future relationships.

Shared Family Care

The search for solutions to protecting children while enabling families to care for them has been a long one. While family preservation, as just discussed, may work for some, other families find it difficult to function with the 10 to 30 hours a week for 6 to 10 weeks that community-based programs usually provide.

> *Ms. Barber was drug addicted when she came to the attention of protective services for physically abusing her 5-year-old son. From an alcoholic family herself, Ms. Barber had a great many conflicts about parenting. She loved her son, but she did not feel confident to care for him.*
>
> *Initially, Ms. Barber attended a detox program while her son was placed in foster care. When she was released, it was felt that this mother would be able to care for her son and he was subsequently released to her. Social workers provided weekly visits to support and encourage the mother. Ms. Barber responded well. For a day or so after the social worker's visit, she was able to practice the suggestions given to her and give her child adequate care. But as the week passed, she would often become lonely and depressed and was at risk for returning to her drug taking.*
>
> *Feeling she could benefit, the agency referred Ms. Barber to a shared family care pilot project. The residence housed drug-involved women and their children. Along with support and counseling, the staff provided modeling for child care.*

Shared family care is the provision of out-of-home care in which host caregivers and the parent(s) care for the children simultaneously. The eventual goal is independent living for the family. Possible types of shared family care are (1) drug treatment programs for mothers with their children, (2) drug treatment programs for adults, which also offer treatment to the children, (3) residential programs for pregnant and parenting teens, (4) residential programs for children, which also offer live-in treatment programs for the parents, and (5) foster family homes for both the parent(s) and the children.

The advantage of such programs, if and when they are available, is that instead of the few hours a week, the parents can have the advantage of the support, modeling, and guidance on a 24-hour basis. Battered women's shelters have long provided this type of care, with success varying from center to center. Homes for unwed teens, too, are often structured so that the clients can continue living there after the baby is born. This model is especially important for mothers seeking drug treatment to enable them to avoid separation from their children. The crucial element of such programs is how well they foster independence so that family and children can return to the community.

Certainly, family preservation programs are sufficient for some families. But others, like the Barbers, cannot succeed on the limited services provided in the community. For these parents, shared family care and the subsequent return to a community setting, with additional skills and support, may be the difference between effectively parenting and having their children placed.

TREATMENT OF PHYSICALLY ABUSIVE FAMILIES

The primary goal of treatment with the physically abusive family is for the battering to cease, which often happens as soon as the social service system intervenes. The future protection of the child, however, depends on the parent learning to cope differently in instances that had provoked beating in the past. Prevention includes parents recognizing what feelings or events led to the initial abuse, learning to read the warning signals that immediately precede the abusive behavior, and learning alternative coping skills to handle anger and frustration. They may also gain more pride in themselves as parents and in their child and learn to understand child development so they can adopt realistic expectations of their children.

To accomplish these goals, it is necessary to assess and remove, to the extent possible, environmental stresses—inadequate housing or unemployment, for example. Services for children and other family members can be explored. One mother was particularly frustrated by a young child who "never listened." After testing, it was discovered the child had a substantial hearing loss and, in fact, could often not tell she was being spoken to. Providing a hearing aid and helping the mother realize that her daughter's slow development was a result of the hearing loss alleviated much of the anxiety between parent and child.

Another family was caring for the father's mother who had slowly deteriorated both physically and emotionally. The young wife with two babies at home (ages 2 and 4) had never wanted the care of her husband's mother. Now she not only resented the responsibility but felt overwhelmed in her role as a mother. Her husband was frequently away from home on business and gave her no support. Once this young mother was helped to verbalize her feelings and alternative arrangements were made for the paternal grandmother, the pressure was diminished and the battering of the 2-year-old ceased. Therapy was centered on developing better skills for future periods of heightened stress.

Treatment efforts also need to be directed toward an assessment of relationships within the family and with the extended family. Does the marital relationship or do the relationships with grandparents or parents' siblings require attention to reduce the stress that results in abuse? Abusive parents are frequently involved in pathological relationships with their families of origin. These may take the form of symbiotic, overly dependent, hostile-dependent, or rejecting relationships that sap the parents' energies and make it difficult for them to parent (Friedrich, 2002; Luby, 2009). Because abusive parents are usually products of unsatisfying childhoods themselves, the conflicting feelings they have toward their families of origin are more understandable.

One of the most obvious aspects of abusive parents is their negative self-image. Helping professionals need to help the parent identify his or her own strengths. Many protective services' clients find it difficult to believe they do anything well. In fact, they often sabotage their own successes. Treatment may include helping parents engineer small successes so they can be convinced of their own potential for handling larger problems. Being able to praise and nurture one's self is actually a prerequisite for the healthy nurturance of others (Filcheck, McNeil, and Herschell, 2005; Luby, 2009; Runyon and Urquiza, 2012; Williams and Crosson-Tower, 2013).

What about the parents who do not think their treatment of their children is a problem? Parents who respond to their children as their own parents treated them often claim there is nothing deviant about their child-rearing practices. In other instances, some parents abuse their children as part of religious or cultural beliefs or values that differ from the larger society. Some ethnic subcultures use corporal punishment. The issue here becomes a legal one. The law is interpreted by agencies who define abusive behaviors. Anyone living under these laws is expected to abide by them. Therefore, treatment in such cases may involve letting families know which laws must be respected and making them aware of appropriate disciplinary techniques. Failure to comply or adapt may mean removal of the children. However, the skillful worker will understand the cultural values of a family and endeavor to help that family to maintain their cultural integrity while still abiding by the dictates of their adopted home (Fontes, 2008; Jackson and Brissett-Chapman, 1999).

Parents who do not perceive they are harming their children may never gain insight into the effect their behavior has on them. If the family is able to maintain at least adequate child-rearing practices, the child usually remains with his or her parents. This is preferable to the trauma of separation. These families may be maintained on the CPS caseload for what is technically called *supervision* (i.e., periodic visits by a CPS worker to monitor the situation). More recently, however, budget cuts have meant that funding must be cut from many of these long-term supervision cases, sometimes setting marginally healed families adrift.

Treatment of the Abused Child

The tasks for professionals providing treatment for the physically abused child are myriad and complex. It is impossible to undo what the child has missed in development and the ability to attain healthy attachment. However, the goal of treatment is to provide remedial help as well as emotional security and psychological healing.

When treatment was first being done with abused children, the assumption was that the medical issues were paramount. Certainly, the medical needs must be addressed, but tending only to them is like putting a small dressing on a huge wound. Medical treatment is but one of the many services needed. These include but may not be limited to medical care, developmental remedial services, educational remedial services, socialization services, and psychological services. In addition, the child must be provided with future safety and security in his or her own home or in another placement.

Remedial Services

Developmentally, abused children are often somewhat behind. Healthy development necessitates an absence of conflict in order to accomplish the tasks that are required. When a child is constantly concerned about being harmed, it is difficult to think about anything other than self-protection. Home visitation programs may help the child, but teaching the parent to provide stimulating and age-appropriate tasks designed to aid in development is also important.

Occupational therapy may be used to develop the child's motor skills. For example, one mother had tied her toddler to his crib because she could not handle his heightened activity. As a result, by age 3, the child had not learned to walk and was deficient in other motor skills. Treatment included the services of an early intervention specialist, who helped the mother not only to massage and stimulate the child's limbs but also taught her games that would get him to use his muscles. At the same time, this strengthened the relationship between mother and child.

Abused children often qualify for Head Start programs designed to compensate for social and cognitive deprivation in the early years. Head Start also provides parental support and encourages parental involvement. Older children, due to their underdeveloped skills, may fall under special education under the Individuals with Disabilities Education Act (IDEA), first passed in 1997 and reauthorized in 2004, which mandates that all children have the right to free and appropriate education. A multidisciplinary team involving school personnel and a variety of specialists meets to devise an individualized education plan (IEP) specific to the particular child's needs. As part of this service, testing to determine the areas in which the child needs remediation is also conducted.

Psychological Services

Until fairly recently, little attention was given to individual or group psychotherapy for abused children unless the child was displaying blatant pathology. Because children are characterized by ever-changing developmental stages, each with its own crisis, it is not always clear which behavior is age appropriate and which symptoms may become fixed and cause for concern. Certainly, prolonged regression—or the return to a previous stage and failure to continue normal development—should be addressed.

Treating abusive families has usually centered on work with the parents by protective services caseworkers who see their primary roles as ensuring that the child is protected within the home or monitored in placement outside the home. Large caseloads make in-depth treatment of the child impossible, and finally, parents, who themselves have been starved of affection, may have difficulty watching their caseworker give special attention to the child.

Numerous experts dealing with abused children, however, assert that children's psychological needs must be considered in conjunction with treatment of the parents. Physically abused children often demonstrate, to some degree, identifiable symptoms such as flat or depressed affect, hypervigilance, problems with trusting, an inability to play, hyperactivity, and destructive or self-destructive behavior. Their self-concept is usually extremely low, and they often indicate feelings of shame and doubt (Forkey et al., 2002; Williams and Crosson-Tower, 2013; Wilson and Ryan, 2006).

Two areas that are included in the treatment of abused children are the expression of affect and self-concept.

Expression of Affect   The child's expression of affect is addressed in therapy. Poor control, aggression, and sporadic impulse control are the most obvious dysfunctions. The assessment of these must be taken within a cultural context. Some cultures (e.g., African American) are more affective in the expression of feelings than they are verbal. The therapist must therefore discern the difference between spontaneity and poor impulse control.

Abused children have been surrounded by violence, which they mirror in their own lives by exhibiting aggressive behavior. Unfortunately, the expression of aggression creates for them an inescapable cycle of rejection. Unable to express their anger or aggression toward the parent from whom they learned it, the abused child finds substitutes in peers and unleashes these aggressive acts on them. Resentful of this behavior, peers resist, ignore, or retaliate against the abused child, causing the child to experience more anger, which he or she will usually attempt to diffuse again on peers (see Figure 12.1). The children are unable to express their anger toward their parents for fear of losing them. This may translate into a fear of expressing anger toward any adult; children act out this anger toward others whom they consider equals or less powerful than themselves in a clear identification with the aggressor.

Abused children lack role models to teach them how to delay gratification, suppress anger, and channel unacceptable drives, and they have little idea of how to handle their own impulses. The children may perceive some need to control impulses, but their ability is tentative at best. Often with little recognition of what is happening to them, the children's loss of control manifests itself in temper tantrums, destructive behavior, and other unpredictable displays of emotion. The therapist teaches the child how not to hurt himself

Figure 12.1   Abused Child's Expression of Aggression

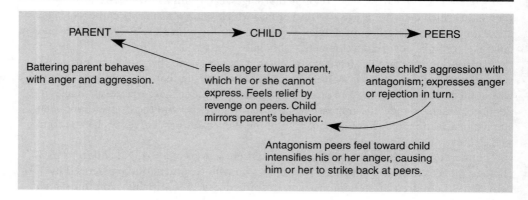

or herself or others. Eventually, the child can be helped to learn to recognize the breaking point of his or her control and how to sublimate this energy into functional channels for change (Cattanach, 2008).

Sexuality and aggression are closely allied and represent impulses that most children learn to control. Foster parents, as well as inexperienced therapists, are often surprised to encounter the amount of sexual acting out expressed by children who were physically abused. Although never actually sexually abusing, many immature parents never learned to channel their own sexual needs and may be seductive with their children. The affect of these parents, as well as their failure to protect the children from witnessing parental sexual exploits, causes confusion for the children.

Self-Concept   The children's negative self-concept is a result not only of what has been told them by the parent ("You're a stupid kid who can't do anything right") but of the conflicts about the parent's abusive behavior. Children depend on and love their parents as their primary source of nurturance. When the parent does not effectively nurture or is abusive, the child perceives that he or she has nowhere else to turn. It is too threatening to see one's only source of comfort as negative. Therefore, children turn the blame on themselves and assume that the abuse was deserved.

It is difficult to convince the child who has grown up feeling "no good" that he or she is worthwhile, but it is the therapist's task to provide a caring relationship to help the child manage little successes that eventually will improve the child's self-image. This low self-concept, combined with poor impulse control, creates in the child faulty development of the superego. What superego exists is often rigid, punitive, unyielding, and unreasonable in its demands, and since this superego has been developed at the hands of punitive, rigid parents, it could hardly be otherwise. When faced with a situation requiring the intervention of this internal conscience, the child often cannot tolerate the pressure. The result is usually a severe breach in the fragile code of ethics, a tantrum, or a total loss of control that only serves to reinforce the child's feeling that he or she is inherently bad. The self-concept, the fear of losing control, and the rigid superego severely limit the child's capacity for pleasure. Abused children are conspicuously lacking in their ability to have fun (Briere, 1992; Cattanach, 2008; Friedrich, 2002).

The therapist creates a relationship in which the child can observe and experience nonpunitive behavior as well as enjoy warm concern. The child's negative beliefs about himself or herself and others cause a need to test—often for extended periods of time. The child wonders, "Can this adult really love the *real* me?" The intensity of the child's need to test can be taxing for the therapist, but understanding that this is a necessary stage in the therapeutic process keeps the behavior in perspective.

Play is one of the most useful types of therapy with young children. Using dolls, puppets, games, drawings, and other media, children are helped to express their fears, anxieties, and conflicts by dramatizing their lives and seeking recognition or interpretation. The classic story of play therapy, *Dibbs in Search of Self*, by Virginia Axaline, gives a clear indication of the intricacies of the therapeutic process using this technique (see also Cattanach, 2008).

Older victims who cannot tolerate just talking often respond well to board games, leisure sports, and even athletics. Much has been accomplished with adolescents during rests from shooting baskets on the court or over a pool table. Therapists who deal specifically with teens have developed a number of methods to explore conflicts and build confidence while enhancing the capacity for play (Hecht et al., 2002).

In group therapy, children enhance their abilities to socialize, decrease their sense of isolation, and improve their relationships with peers. Knowing that others in the group have also been abused creates a bond among members that eases communication (Silovsky, 2005).

Therapy is not necessarily easy for abused children and can generate conflicts of its own. First, these children may never have been exposed to adults with values so different from their parents. Many school-age children have problems in understanding the difference in values expressed by their teachers and their parents. In therapy, the abused child hears that his or her parents' values (at least in the area of child rearing) are not what society expects. This is bound to create confusion. Second, a child is allowed to behave in therapy in ways that would never be tolerated at home. Instead of having to follow rigid adult rules, the child is asked to express himself or herself freely. Many children cannot believe there is no inherent danger in this freedom and wonder if they are being led into misbehavior for which they will later be punished.

Conflict in loyalties is often a problem for children in therapy, and the abused child from a home where loyalty is a rigid requirement may be especially conflicted. This may become especially problematic with Asian Pacific children because of the sense of family honor and devotion to and respect for parents that are so deeply embedded in the culture's value system. Not only do children feel attachments to their therapists, but they are also encouraged to talk about their parents in a negative manner. This may feel unsafe. The exercise of therapy itself involves experiencing pain as issues come to the surface. Used to pain at home, the abused child may be reluctant to experience it elsewhere (Friedrich, 2002).

Parents of abused children are not always entirely supportive of therapy, although they may have initially approved the idea. Acceptance that the child has problems that need treatment validates to the parents that they have failed in their roles. Further, the parents' resentment of their children's therapy can be based on their own backgrounds. Because of their own childhoods of deprivation and desperation to have their own needs met, some parents feel jealous of the attention their children are getting, as well as of the attachment that may be growing between children and therapist. In the abusive family, the children feed the parents emotionally. The narcissistic parent may feel threatened by the child's being nurtured in another adult–child relationship. And finally, therapy creates behavior changes in the child. The parents have an investment in their child's previous symptomatology. Change in the child necessitates change in them, as well, a change to which they feel resistant.

To alleviate or reduce the obstacles parents place in the way of their children's therapy, it is necessary for the therapist to meet with the parents periodically. It is also wise for the parents to have their own therapist(s) or caseworker, on whom they can depend.

Socialization Services

Abused children may have been unable to accomplish the developmental task of *attachment* (bonding with the caretaker in a manner that promotes trust and reciprocity), which will hamper their ability to have healthy relationships in the future. Some of the therapy for attachment disorder takes place in the home, as parents are helped to reconnect with their children, as well as in the child's individual psychotherapy. But the child's resulting inability to trust, failure to feel empathy for others, and difficulty with reciprocal relationships must be addressed specifically.

In addition to working to help the child articulate his or her needs and helping the parents to meet them, the child needs to connect with peers. School is not always the friendliest place for children with problems. Therefore, children may be placed in group treatment to encourage their ability to heal and develop socializations skills with children who have issues similar to their own. Exposure to other maltreated children may also help with the development of empathy.

Programs like Big Brother/Big Sister may also be beneficial for abused children. Having a Big Friend may not only provide them with an adult who can give them attention and guidance, but it may also give them one more opportunity to socialize and develop a relationship.

Treatment of the Parents

Goals of Treatment

Whether the parents in an abusive family are seen at home by a caseworker involved in family preservation or shared family care or are referred to therapy with another professional, the goals remain the same (see Table 12.1). The areas that therapy must address are threefold: the nurturing and reparenting of the parent, therapeutic work with psychic conflicts and pathology, and amelioration of the distorted parent–child relationship.

However, therapy with abusive parents has unique characteristics that set it apart from therapy with other types of clients. It is so important with abusive parents that they feel a part of goal setting. Rather than impose on them the need to reach the goals outlined in Table 12.1, the effective worker joins with the family to come up with mutual goals. A written contract is often helpful in assuring that everyone understands what is expected.

Table 12.1	**Treatment Goals for Physically Abusive Parents**

1. Cease battering behavior.
2. Recognize the feelings or events that lead to the initial abuse.
3. Recognize the warning signals that immediately precede the abusive behavior.
4. Learn alternative coping skills to handle anger and frustration.
5. Gain pride in themselves as parents.
6. Learn to appreciate their children.
7. Begin to understand child development in order to adopt more realistic expectations of their children.
8. Minimize or reduce environmental stresses.
9. Understand their symbiotic relationships and behave more independently.
10. Improve communication with extended families or cope with the recognition that this is not possible.
11. Engineer and appreciate their own successes.
12. Recognize and reduce their isolation.
13. Learn to make their needs known to each other.
14. Meet the medical needs of their children.

The abuse of a child is a family systems issue. The total system is dysfunctional and often exists in a delicate pathological balance. To treat one person—the abuser or the child—is to ignore that balance. If the family system is to operate in the future, all members must be treated and that treatment must be well coordinated. The common scenario in the abusing family is for one parent to abuse while the nonabusive parent supports that behavior by failure to intervene. This silent parent must be helped to see his or her own complicity in the abuse.

Treating abusive parents requires an abundance of patience, persistence, and outreach. Their own inability to trust creates a barrier to the formation of a therapeutic relationship. Often referred by the court, many clients do not perceive the need to change. Building a relationship will be a slow, tedious process. Once engaged, parents test the therapist by a variety of acting-out behaviors and avoidance techniques; the next visit, they may be so extremely dependent and needy that they sap the emotional strength of the most experienced therapist. Because of this, it is often advisable to employ more than one therapist in the treatment. For example, a caseworker goes to the home, but the client also sees a private therapist.

Caseworker and therapist must keep in constant communication. Due to the depth and longevity of the issues, treatment will not be short term. Even if the initial sessions span only a few months, the client needs permission to use the relationship as a lifeline. It is not unusual for the abusive parent who has learned to trust the therapist to reach out years later—by letter, phone call, or request—for an appointment. The therapist may be the first person in their lives for whom these parents can feel trust, and thus, this person is not easily dismissed.

For the therapist, abusive parents present other obstacles. It is difficult to acknowledge what has been done to a child and still provide the abuser with the nurturing and unconditional positive regard he or she needs. For this reason, some experienced therapists advise as little contact as possible between the parent's caseworker or therapist and the child. Further, the therapist or caseworker is tempted to take a blaming and angry or forgiving stance. The blaming is based on what the parents have done to their children, while the forgiving says "They had difficult childhoods themselves; they too are victims." Neither stance benefits the client. These parents must be understood but held accountable for past actions and future growth.

Within these goal areas, there will be specific issues that must be considered in treatment.

Nurturing and Reparenting

Nurturing and reparenting require consistent contact with the parents, during which they are treated as individuals of worth. The void of a deprived childhood can never be totally filled, but warmth and caring will help. In time, the client may begin to feel dependence on the therapist—often, the first person he or she perceives has provided positive reinforcement. To prevent prolonged dependence, the parents are taught how to ask to have their needs met.

Most of these clients have gone through life expecting to be nurtured and understood without ever asking. Their disappointment when others do not magically perceive their desires can be overwhelming for them. They may develop inappropriate methods of displaying their disappointment, such as battering their child for attempting suicide. Few recognize that they can ask for what they need.

Without proper intervention, couples in abusive families spend their entire lifetime hoping the partner will intuitively know what they need and being angry when the partner fails. Teaching couples to communicate helps each parent meet his or her own needs and may correct the dysfunctional marital bond. In addition, the parent can let go of the parentified child. Finding others on whom to depend, the parent can allow the child to be a child and relieve that child of the obligation of nurturing the parent.

Families who are newly immigrated may require an additional form of nurturing. It is often helpful to them to be guided into their new culture. The worker may actually be able to help them recognize that the parenting techniques they used in their culture of origin are not the only ones available. Since severe corporal punishment is illegal in the United States, for example, it is not an option. But there are other methods of ensuring the respect and obedience of children.

Acceptance by a therapist and improved communication toward having one's needs met help the parent adopt a more positive attitude toward self and others. Developing a client's more positive self-image is a long, arduous task for both client and therapist, however.

Addressing Psychic Conflicts and Pathology

The abusive parent comes to therapy with deep psychological conflicts and pathology. The client has developed life patterns that are extremely dysfunctional, and part of therapy will be to examine and hopefully change those patterns that have plagued the client.

The first of these, rooted deep in childhood, is *symbiosis*—the neurotic smothering bond with another individual, usually someone in the parent's family of origin. Harboring a poor self-image, the client feels a need to attach to another for strength, but ironically, this bond usually saps rather than supplying strength. The client frequently goes on to find such a symbiotic relationship with a spouse.

Part of breaking the symbiosis is in recognizing that it exists. Many abusive families have no idea how dependent they are on each other because the symbiotic bond has taken on hostile overtones. For example, a couple may describe their relationship as unsatisfying. They fluctuate between fighting violently for days at a time followed by periods of coldly ignoring one another. Yet they are always together and deeply dependent on this volatile relationship. These patterns can be identified in therapy, and steps can be taken to break this pattern. Often, it requires the partners contracting with each other to change their behavior.

Abusive parents demonstrate a marked degree of isolation from others. They have no one to whom they can turn in crisis or in joy. Group therapy especially helps break this isolation. Aiding them in better communication and in identifying a support system makes them better able to handle stress in the future. Since stress often translates into abusive behavior, breaking down this isolation also provides protection for the child (Briere, 1992; Filcheck et al., 2005).

Impulse control is as much an issue for the parents in an abusive family as it is for their children. Explosive tempers in some parents contrast with the internalization, somatization (manifesting conflicts in physical ills), and eventual breakdowns in others. Identifying appropriate ways to get their needs met may be helpful (Helfer, 1978). More recently, relaxation and hypnosis techniques have sometimes been used to help parents take charge of their outbursts.

Other dysfunctional patterns and self-destructive tendencies, such as obesity and passive–aggressive behavior, may need to be addressed.

Improving Parent–Child Relationships

The final area to stress is the improvement of the parent–child relationship. In wanting the child to be protected, the therapist often focuses on this area prematurely. In fact, until parents can nurture and understand themselves, they are unable to provide it for their children. When the parents feel better about themselves, they can work on the parent–child relationship. Some parents never become sufficiently stable to parent effectively, and their children are likely to be removed and their parental rights terminated. Through time, other parents are able to learn how to parent.

Abusive parents have been devoid of models of positive parenting, so an effective method of teaching is to provide them with models. Parents can watch the interaction between their child and others at day care centers, crisis nurseries, or other programs. Homemakers, visiting nurses, or social workers help the parent in the home. In some instances, the child's therapy includes allowing the parent to observe, frequently from behind a one-way mirror. Sometimes, foster mothers are asked to help the parent by teaching them to interact positively. Modeling positive interactions requires that the parents have some therapy themselves so they can view the other adult and their child without being inordinately threatened.

Parents are then encouraged to try out new ways of interacting with their children. Sometimes, playing with children while the therapist watches behind a one-way mirror is effective. After the play session, the therapist praises their use of specific interactions. The way the parents now interact with the child may be the result of their observance of models, attendance at a parent awareness class, or their new knowledge of child behavior. Since many abusive parents have little idea of child development or child management, a component of therapy may be to introduce them to classes on these issues.

As therapy for the parents progresses, they can be helped to understand the child's behavior and deal with it more effectively. A prerequisite for the parents' improved communication with the child is that the parents value the child. No longer can this child be a burden to the parent. The parent must see the child as a unique individual with needs, abilities, and potential. Without this recognition, developing a truly positive relationship between parent and child will be impossible.

Numerous therapeutic methods are used with abusive parents. Supportive casework in the home provides some support and treatment. If the parents have insurance or are eligible for particular agencies, they may individually or as a couple be referred for psychotherapy or marital therapy. Group psychotherapy is especially effective with abusive parents.

Family therapy is sometimes used with the total family unit to enhance better communication. This type of therapy is often most effective after the members have gained insight into their own individual issues. For cultures that value family unity (e.g., Asian), this approach may actually be a starting point.

Other Types of Family Treatment

Parent aides are especially helpful with parents. The aide or lay therapist provides nurturing of the parent and models positive interactions with the children. A homemaker is often brought in to help with housekeeping tasks and alleviate the pressures of maintaining the family.

Another effective therapeutic intervention is Parents Anonymous (PA). PA was founded in 1969 by an abusive mother, Jolly K., who felt that her needs were not being met by the social service system. Based on the Alcoholics Anonymous (AA) model, PA welcomes parents who maltreat their children and offers the support of others who have developed more healthy relationships with children and peers alike. A PA group is sponsored by an individual or an agency in the area but functions as an autonomous self-help organization. Parents come to PA voluntarily. At the weekly (or more frequent) meetings, members discuss individual histories and coping techniques and generally support one another. PA owes its success not only to the dedication of its members but also to the fact that the meetings help abusive parents break their isolation, share with others, and feel better about themselves.

Termination

There are two paramount questions in the treatment of abusive parents: When can the case safely be closed? and When are these individuals able to parent effectively?

What criteria should be used? First, parents should demonstrate decreased isolation and have developed an adequate support system. They should have people to whom they can reach out when they need help and not be afraid to do so. The parents should demonstrate better impulse control and know how to recognize and channel their anger before it becomes out of control. Through effective therapy, parents should have learned to feel better about themselves, be more realistic in their expectations of themselves, and find more pleasure in life. Stress should not be as much of a problem for these parents, now that they have learned to deal with it through a variety of new coping methods.

Above all, the successful rehabilitated abusive parent has a better relationship with his or her child. The parent sees the child as a worthwhile, enjoyable individual and can tolerate the child's age-appropriate or negative behaviors. Secure in asking for and receiving gratification from others, the parent need not look to the child to satisfy his or her needs. Rather, the parent can appreciate the child as a child and participate in a loving, nurturing relationship with him or her.

One of the biggest frustrations of protective services work is the knowledge that these goals must be accomplished before the client flees, the court dismisses the case, or the demands of bureaucracy necessitate closing the case.

Treatment of the Siblings

If only one child within the family is abused, the siblings are often forgotten in therapy. Yet they, too, have therapeutic needs. Siblings who know that a brother or sister is the object of abuse harbor fear of being next. Recognizing his or her powerlessness against an adult, this child tends to identify with the abuser either by silent collusion or by verbally or physically abusive behavior toward the victim. This sibling, too, learns violence as a manner of relating to others. He or she also lacks positive parenting models to use in the future.

Though not marked by the bruises and breaks of the abused child, siblings carry another type of scar—guilt. Survivors' guilt emerges variously. These individuals feel guilty that they survived while others did not. Similarly, siblings who watched their brother's or sister's abuse wonder how they escaped. At the same time, these children feel guilty they did not intervene on the victim's behalf, however impossible that might have been.

In situations where the victim is removed from the home, one or more siblings may become the abuser's next victim. When this happens, the sibling may demonstrate many of the feelings and behaviors of the originally abused child.

Whether in family therapy or through some type of individual therapy or program, the needs of the siblings should be addressed. They have experienced the same dysfunctional, abusive home setting as the victim and also have the potential to grow up to be unhappy, needy adults.

TREATMENT OF NEGLECTFUL FAMILIES

The treatment of neglectful families is perhaps one of the least frequently addressed issues in protective services literature. One reason is that neglect seems to permeate the lives and generational histories of the families involved and is difficult to combat, as is the depression that is so pervasive. Because of the depression, the antisocial behavior, and often the denial that there is a problem, neglectful families are difficult to engage in treatment.

Polansky and his colleagues (1972) have done extensive research with such clients and advise that

> one's leverage for entering the neglectful family and starting to work toward diagnosis and change is going to depend on the use of authority (with some associated fear) or the mother's transferring dependent strivings onto the worker—usually both. (p. 218)

There are, therefore, two forms of leverage that have the potential for engaging the neglectful family in treatment: (1) authority, based on the threat or intervention of the court, and (2) the satisfaction of a parent's need, which is usually tangible but sometimes merely a need for attention. When a referral originates from an agency dealing with a client who is seeking financial assistance or housing, a worker who meets these needs may more easily engage the client in additional therapeutic help.

Protective workers have discovered that one effective method of eliciting the trust of a neglectful parent is first to offer something tangible that the client wants, however small:

> *Mrs. Bates collected soda and beer cans from all over the country. Her interest in her hobby was almost childlike. The worker discovered that by bringing an occasional can that Mrs. Bates did not have, the mother was more open and willing to talk. The sessions frequently consisted of Mrs. Bates's bringing out all her collected cans and explaining how she had gotten them. In between these explanations, the worker was able to talk about Mrs. Bates's care of the children and other problems in her life.*

More than any other type of leverage, neglectful parents respond to their liking of the social worker or therapist. Since these clients have such difficulty trusting, an attachment to the worker must be highly valued. Through this fondness, the neglectful parent is more likely to model and try any advice given.

The social caseworker usually undertakes treatment of neglectful parents in the home. Neglectful parents often have difficulty attending therapeutic sessions with private therapists, although some will do so after they have established a trusting relationship with the caseworker or if they perceive that they can gain something by these visits. Since both the person and the environment must be considered in the treatment of neglect, the total picture is more visible in the home setting. The neglectful mother requires insight about how her uncontrolled impulses lead to the family's lacking necessities and endangering the children, and she also needs structure to help her function with some semblance of routine in the care of the children and the maintenance of the home. Casework services may help her in all these areas (Cantwell, 1997; MacDonald, 2005; Polansky, Chalmers, Buttenweiser, and Williams, 1981).

It is often necessary to call on other resources, as well. For example, a visiting nurse can provide the mother with help for the children's physical needs and hygiene and can teach infant care. One mother, newly eligible for food stamps and anxious to please the caseworker with her developing skills, had little idea of how to use them to feed her family nutritionally. A homemaker came for several visits to help her shop and cook creatively. Lay therapists, or parent aides, are especially effective with neglectful families. Because they have smaller caseloads, these lay professionals can visit the home regularly, provide guidance, support, and advocacy and, in general, give the parent a feeling that someone cares.

The social worker can provide numerous services to strengthen the family besides referral for other types of services. Table 12.2 outlines some of these supports. Two treatment models are applicable for neglectful parents: equilibrium maintenance and disequilibrium techniques.

Equilibrium Maintenance

Every family has a level at which it maintains itself most of the time. These conditions fluctuate, improve, or deteriorate. During a vacation, the family members may find that they enjoy each other's company and what they are doing together. On the other hand,

---

Table 12.2   What the Worker Can Do to Supplement the Neglectful Family

- Orchestrate the range of services the family needs to improve child care.
- Deal with the parents' emotional blocks to accepting services.
- Guide the family to needed services and facilitate the use of those services.
- Interview parents and help them improve interpersonal communication skills.
- Offer children individualized and supportive relationships.
- Reach out to family members with supportive counseling.
- Let family members know that someone is concerned about them.
- Provide parents with information and step-by-step guidelines for accomplishing tasks.
- Be a model for child-rearing techniques and for instilling family values.
- Help parents keep their fears and anxieties from growing out of proportion.
- Once mutual attachment is obtained, introduce expectations for the parents to meet.

Source: From C. Hally, N. F. Polansky, and N. A. Polansky, *Child Neglect: Mobilizing Services.* Washington, DC: U.S. Department of Health and Human Services, 1980.

when a death occurs, a parent is unemployed or ill, or one or more family members are experiencing a developmental crisis, the family functioning may be stressed.

Most families have the ability to call on resources to help regain and maintain equilibrium. An extended family member comes to help the parents rally and enable them to cope with whatever crisis exists. Or the family members recognize the need to reach out to community agencies. This mobilization requires that family members have sufficient ego strength and flexibility to respond (Hally, Polansky, and Polansky, 1980). These families are often good candidates for intensive family services (MacDonald, 2005).

Equilibrium maintenance is especially important with newly immigrated families that appear neglectful. Although the family's functioning was accepted in their original culture, it may not be in the United States. Or perhaps the family has been immobilized by the shock of being in a new and very different culture. With these families, the worker must build on their strengths to help them to once again gain a functional balance.

Neglectful families may not always have been neglectful, but in their current state they lack the resources to regain equilibrium. That was the situation with Cheryl:

> *Cheryl Levine gave adequate child care to her son, Harley, and daughter, Jenna, when they were infants. Her husband, Hank, was unemployed for a year and then Cheryl gave birth to twins. Her depression intensified, and her housekeeping and child care deteriorated. She began sleeping a good part of the day, expecting Hank to watch the children. But Hank, too, felt overwhelmed by the situation and began staying out more and more. Eventually, Harley's teacher, concerned about his listlessness and his stealing food from other children, alerted the protective agency.*
>
> *For the Levines, there was a standard to return to. After several months, casework services helped the family back on its feet. In foster care herself as a child, Cheryl was determined not to lose her children. Once trust was established, she readily complied with the agencies' suggestions.*

Sometimes, the care and concern shown by the social worker is enough to influence the parent's lifestyle:

> *Bertha Sills developed a relationship with her caseworker fairly quickly because of her desperate need to be cared for. Mrs. Sills began to observe the worker's clothes admiringly. She wondered how she, too, could look "that good." It wasn't long before Mrs. Sills began to take more pride in herself and in her care of her 3-year-old daughter. She began to resent the money that her boyfriend Ralph spent on drugs—money she realized could be used for her and her child.*
>
> *Using her relationship with the worker for strength and support, Mrs. Sills was able to sever her relationship with Ralph and make appreciable efforts toward better child care. When the protective agency felt it was safe to close the case, a referral was made to a volunteer agency to provide a weekly parent aide to enable Mrs. Sills to maintain her progress.*

Like Bertha Sills, some neglectful families can be helped to change by regular visits from a caseworker or an agency volunteer. This regular contact may be the first experience they have had with a caring individual and may also provide a model on which they can base their efforts at improved child care.

Disequilibrium Techniques

Other families demonstrate an equilibrium that is inadequate to ensure even minimally acceptable child care. In these cases, it is necessary to break old patterns in an attempt to raise the family's level of functioning. This means, in essence, throwing the family off balance to improve its situation and to involve them in more acceptable life patterns. This type of treatment is referred to as *disequilibrium* (Hally et al., 1980; Polansky et al., 1981).

To create this imbalance, protective agencies use a variety of mechanisms. First, the caseworker may need to inform the parents that their child care standards are inadequate. This is done in a firm but caring manner. Families must recognize that failure to improve child care may have legal consequences, as in this case:

The Long Bows, who recently moved to the northern United States from an Arizona reservation, were reported for neglect. They had been reported a month earlier but had not responded to the agency's help. The caseworker now explained to the Long Bows that it was not acceptable for the children to be dressed in lightweight, soiled clothing and holey sneakers during the coldest period of winter. Further, 1-year-old Janie must have supervision so that she did not play in the street outside the Long Bows' home. The piles of debris in the backyard were not only dangerous for the Long Bows' young children but were hiding places for rats. In addition, the two youngest children (ages 1 and 2½) could not be left alone in the care of 4-year-old Mona.

The Long Bows were at first resentful of having their lifestyle criticized. The worker sympathetically acknowledged their feelings but let them know that their continued lack of cooperation would necessitate court intervention.

The ultimate dislodging mechanism for some families is removal of the children. Removal sometimes impresses on the parents the seriousness of the neglect. This may cause them to put new energy into mobilizing their resources toward establishing an environment to which the children can safely return. For still other families, removal of the children is the ultimate blow, one against which they feel unable to fight:

Pat Parsons had been dealing drugs and prostituting for seven or eight years prior to the report to the protective service agency that she had two small children who were suffering from her deviant lifestyle. They were severely neglected. After reluctantly establishing a relationship with the social worker, Pat made several attempts to give up drugs and prostitution. She placed her children with a neighbor while she had men in her apartment and agreed to stop selling drugs. But her ties with her lifestyle were too strong. When 4-year-old Wendy was molested by one of Pat's clients, the agency removed both children.

Pat went into a deep depression, rousing herself only occasionally to visit her children in their foster home. Frequently, she appeared high on drugs, and the foster parents complained of the effect on the children. The caseworker confronted Pat. "They'd be better off without me," the mother admitted. She dropped out of sight, and eventually, the agency sought termination of parental rights through the court.

Unfortunately, all treatment efforts are not successful. In situations such as this, one can only hope to break the neglectful cycle so that the children can benefit.

One of the most overwhelming factors in the treatment of neglectful parents is dealing with their acute loneliness. Fearing intimacy, neglectful parents set up barriers between themselves and others, barriers that prevent their needs for others from being met. In a study of 156 low-income families, Polansky, Ammons, and Gaudin (1985) found that neglectful mothers were significantly lonelier and more isolated than other families in the same environment. Neighbors did not turn to these mothers when they needed assistance.

Although the social worker can help these neglectful families gain skills in developing and maintaining relationships, the task necessitates consistency and persistence. And the parents' sense of loneliness is so intense that it is often painful for the worker to empathize. Only through an adequate support system for themselves can the caseworkers resist being caught up in this permeation of loneliness and futility. For this reason, as well as the multitude of problems and the minimal progress demonstrated by some families, the neglectful family is among the most difficult to treat.

SUMMARY

The treatment of an abusive or neglectful family does not always progress smoothly, for several reasons:

1. Families are difficult to engage.
2. Families do not always follow through.
3. Families are not always eligible for treatment by appropriate agencies.
4. Resources to treat may be limited.
5. Treatment methods are not sufficiently refined to ensure success.

A relatively new concept in treatment is family preservation, which is the intensive community-based treatment of families.

The treatment of families may be undertaken by the protective service agency but is more often handled by referrals to other appropriate agencies, in which case the worker plays a case management role. The duration of these services is difficult to predict. Specific guidelines measure when families are ready for termination. For example, parents must do the following:

- Be more aware of their own needs and how to get them met
- Be able to reach out for help in the future
- Be able to communicate more effectively
- Have improved self-esteem
- Feel more positive toward their children

The primary goal with physically abusive parents is to stop the battering. In addition, it is hoped that these parents develop coping skills for the future. Treatment for the child necessitates attention to the medical problem resulting from the abuse, providing a safer environment, and attending to the psychological scars from the abuse.

Treatment of the parents necessitates patience and understanding. They must learn to trust the helper and learn to cope with the frustrations of their own lives in order to nurture their children. Such issues as symbiosis, isolation, poor self-concept, and impulse control must be addressed in treatment. The services for abusive parents may include group or individual therapy, marital therapy, the use of homemakers and parent aides, and participation in self-help groups such as PA. Ideally, cases are not closed until the battering has ceased and parents have developed coping mechanisms to deal with their frustrations.

Neglectful families can also be extremely difficult to treat because of their depression, antisocial behavior, and denial that a problem exists. The threat of authority—court involvement—is often used as leverage to engage them in treatment. Treatment is usually done in the home with an emphasis on building trust. The caseworker offers tangible as well as therapeutic services. Treatment usually involves equilibrium maintenance, which attempts, through services, to return the family to a level of adequate functioning, or disequilibrium techniques, which throw the family off balance and force them to reorganize more effectively. Because of the complexity of their problems, neglectful families are often the most difficult to treat.

Chapter 13

Treatment
Sexual Abuse

Even those experienced in working with physically abusive and neglectful parents are not fully prepared to deal with sexually abusive families. Although many of the problems are similar to and may be present in all types of maltreatment, sexual abuse and its treatment pose issues that other patterns of abuse do not.

ISSUES SURROUNDING TREATMENT

Deviant sexuality provokes reactions from society that, in turn, affect the worker engaged in treating sexually abusive families. People's desire to ignore the reality of sexual abuse often means they are uncooperative with the individual who investigates and treats it. Further, their rejection of the behavior of the client is often transferred to the worker. People wonder about the motivation of workers who specialize in sexual abuse. Is the worker obsessed with some kind of voyeurism or immoral interest? Along with the frustration of treating uncooperative clients, this suspicion from others puts a great deal of stress on workers.

Society's tendency to isolate both family and worker, combined with the family's secretiveness and will to bond in an effort to ward off intruders, makes treatment difficult. In this atmosphere, the worker, once allowed into the intimate family circle, may unintentionally collude with the clients and keep secrets from other professionals, thus exerting a negative rather than a positive influence on the family.

The helping system continues to struggle with how and who in the family to treat. Although familial abuse is a family problem, programs are not always available to treat all members of the family. The incarcerated offender, for example, may receive treatment, but his or her family may not. Individual therapy for the child victim may not be available.

Professionals advance new theories and treatment methods, but long-term testing and evaluation are either nonexistent or just beginning. Advances make professionals optimistic, but premature optimism about the incestuous family's rehabilitation is just as harmful as undue pessimism (Giardino, Lyn, and Giardino, 2010).

Most types of sexual abuse are performed by family members, though children are also abused by outsiders. Progress has been made in dealing with the incestuous family, but not many community services sufficiently address the needs of the children abused outside the home, nor is attention given to their parents. Although expected to support the victim, the parents themselves are dealing with their own conflicts about the abuse by someone outside the family. One possible reason for this lack of support is that familial abuse cases are handled by a social services agency, but extrafamilial abuse most often comes under the jurisdiction of the criminal justice system. Traditionally, the police and the courts exert control, rather than social services. Services for extrafamilial abuse cases improve, but the lack of resources remains a problem.

In cases of physical abuse or neglect, reports of maltreatment of both boys and girls are equivalent. But because boys are particularly liable to be sexually abused outside the home and more hesitant to report the abuse, they are often not treated.

ASSUMPTIONS ABOUT THE TREATMENT OF THE SEXUALLY ABUSIVE FAMILY

When treating a family in which there has been sexual abuse, it is important to make several assumptions. First, relational imbalances in the family were present before the incest occurred. In fact, incest could not develop within a family if there were not significant problems in communication and the manner in which members relate to each other. Thus, the problem of sexual abuse is not simply that but rather a symptom that results from a larger family problem.

In addition, sexual abuse is often a generational issue that has persisted through multiple generations as families within each generation have failed to communicate in an open, functional manner. One student in a sexual abuse class created a genogram (a diagram using symbols to show family members and relationship patterns) of his family going back for four generations. If any family member had been sexually abused or was sexually abusive, his or her symbol was drawn in red. When the student shared the chart with his fellow students in class, people were shocked at how colorful the chart had become. Thus, breaking the cycle of sexual abuse is not easy when it is based on a heritage of dysfunction.

Another consideration is that despite the dysfunction in the family, the imbalances may have felt comfortable to the family members on some level. For example, if a mother emotionally removes herself in a family harboring father–daughter incest, she may actually be relieved to have her daughter assume some of her tasks and roles. When treatment begins and she must reestablish her role as the disciplining parent, the housekeeper, or her husband's sexual partner, she may have difficulty. By the same token, the offender who has enjoyed the closeness with his daughter, not hampered by his wife's intervention, may now find the fact that he is allowed only supervised visits a very lonely prospect. The blurred generational boundaries may have worked for this family in some manner. Based on this fact, change may not be easy for them. All that they have known as a family unit is in upheaval and must be realigned for the benefit of all the members. In addition, the parents may have brought with them, from their own childhoods, expectations of how a family should function. Now those assumptions are being challenged.

Offenders, and sometimes their spouses, rationalize that the abuse is serving a purpose. For example, an offender may argue that he was educating his child about sexuality. At the same time, the nonabusing spouse sees that her husband and daughter are close and, sometimes even denying any suspicions she may have, is relieved that her child has a good rapport with her father. This may also leave the mother feeling freed of some of the responsibility of parenthood. Therefore, it will be necessary in treatment to discover what rationalization precipitates the behavior and find other ways to enable the parents to feel that this issue is being addressed (Gil, 1996).

Further, the assumption that either the family will stay together or they will separate should not be made. The ability of the family to remain a unit depends on many factors and may not be determined until well into treatment. The main goal for clinicians in treating the family will be to build therapeutic alliances with all members of the family system, emphasizing individual and family strengths, so that the family may make its own assessments about staying together.

Since sexuality is a subject surrounded by secrecy, conflict, and embarrassment in our culture, *it will be difficult for family members to talk about sexual issues*. The need to protect the "family secret" spills over into the therapeutic relationship. Thus, trust between the family and the therapist is essential before much real work can be done. This creates another problem in the treatment of incestuous families. While intervention usually involves case management by the child protection agency, *the policy of the agency is often to close the case once the initial steps are taken*. As one protective services worker put it:

> *Our agency requires the offender to leave while we assess whether the other parent can protect the child. If he or she can protect the child, we leave the child in the home. If not, foster care or placement with relatives might be the answer. We also try to connect all the family members with concrete services. For example, if the dad has an alcohol problem, we may make a referral for substance abuse treatment. It would be great if we could refer the whole family for treatment, but there are not too many agencies that are equipped to do that. And then, insurance becomes a problem. If the family doesn't have insurance, the options are even more limited.*
>
> *I hate to say it, but as long as the abuse has stopped, my agency has to close the case. That means that there are a lot of families out there who never get real treatment services.*

Fortunately, some innovations are being made in the treatment of incestuous families. It is hoped that these will increase.

TREATMENT MODELS

Of all the types of child maltreatment, sexual abuse is usually seen foremost as a criminal offense. Thus, an important part of intervention will be to determine how the offender can be held legally accountable for his offense and the impact that this will have on the whole family.

Unfortunately, too often, the intervention has been to prosecute the offender and perhaps secure treatment for the victim while forgetting that this is a total family system and should be dealt with accordingly. Many experts suggest a combination of family systems treatment combined with cognitive behavioral therapy to change the offender's behavior. Such combined therapies as marital treatment, family therapy, and even individual therapy are recommended by various experts in the field of sexual abuse.

Child Sexual Abuse Treatment Programs

One of the first programs to treat the sexually abusive family originated in the early 1970s. In 1971, Henry Giarretto was counseling victims and their families for the Juvenile Probation Department in Santa Clara, California. Recognizing that these families needed more services than the department or he could provide, Giarretto founded the Child Sexual Abuse Treatment Program (CSATP), which, by 1978, was serving more than 600 families. The three components of the program are the professional staff, lay volunteers, and self-help groups.

The professionals—social workers, probation officers, attorneys, and judges— orchestrate the treatment plan for the family and enlist support from the local protective agency and the court. The volunteers are student interns and others who provide transportation, one-to-one support to needy clients, and office duties. The self-help groups— Parents United, for abusive families, and Daughters and Sons United, for those molested as children—operate on the model of Alcoholics Anonymous and give support and group therapy to the members. Groups break the isolation experienced by families and help them to offer and gain from each other valuable insights (Giarretto, 1996).

Current family treatment programs offer different types of therapy and intervention, including individual therapy, marital or couples counseling, family therapy, and groups for victims, offenders, and nonabusive parents. Arts and expressive therapies might also be used to help children to express themselves when they are not comfortable with words.

Numerous programs have been adapted from the CSATP efforts. The threat of prosecution appears to be one of the most effective methods of engaging perpetrators in treatment. When perpetrators agree to participate in treatment, their sentences are often suspended.

TREATMENT METHODS

Issues Addressed in Family Treatment

An incestuous family is a system that is composed of subsystems and of individual members. For this reason, there are issues that involve the family system as a whole and each member individually.

As a whole, the sexually abusive family has some specific tasks. First, there must be a *realignment of generational boundaries* and roles (Gil, 1996; Gil and Johnson, 1993; Iwaniec, 2006; Sgroi, 1982). In the hierarchy of a family where the boundaries are clear, it is the adults who create a united front and have enough authority to enforce appropriate rules. But in incestuous families, the adults are split and the children may be parentified into assuming adult roles. Thus, it is necessary to establish a healthy hierarchy where both the marital/parental and the sibling subsystems are clear (Gil, 1996; Gil and Johnson, 1993; Righthand, Kerr, and Drach, 2003).

Second, treatment involves *teaching the family members how to communicate effectively* so that all might get their needs met. Part of this may also be *teaching the adults parenting skills*. It is difficult for children not to have structure. Helping the children to feel safe in the future will involve helping the adults to create not only boundaries but also healthy rules for the family to live by. Many families have rules that protect the family secret. For example, one family rule might be that no one talks about the fact that there are problems in the family. Yet it is this rule that protects and continues the dysfunction. Many parents bring with them *unresolved traumas* from their own childhoods, and these may need to be addressed. And each family member has issues individually that must also be addressed (Gil and Johnson, 1993; Howe, 2005; Iwaniec, 2006).

Phases of Treatment

Whatever the treatment method, James and Nasjleti (1983) describe the three phases that mark the incestuous family's progress from intervention through treatment: the disclosure–panic phase, the assessment–awareness phase, and the restructure phase. Despite the age of the research, the phrases still provide a helpful gauge.

Disclosure–Panic

The disclosure–panic phase is the most critical period for family and social worker alike. The family's initial defenses are anger and denial. They often project blame onto others, especially the protective worker who has intervened. Workers sometimes find it difficult to be supportive while they feel under attack. Families can so skillfully intellectualize that workers may doubt the accusation.

Despite the attempt to argue away the accusation of sexual abuse, the family is in acute crisis. The perpetrator and the victim are extremely vulnerable and may have suicidal thoughts. The family members tend to overreact, sometimes violently. Underlying these intense reactions is the fear of loss and separation. For Asian families, there may also be a sense of acute shame—that family honor has been lost. Loyalties vacillate. While some families blame the victim and assert that he or she is lying, others initially protect the perpetrator and accuse the social service system of unjust and unfounded allegations.

Throughout this phase, which lasts several weeks to several months, the worker uses crisis intervention techniques and empathetically supports each member. The child especially must be assured that he or she is believed by the worker and will be protected in the future. With the rest of the family, the worker firmly states that the abuse has occurred and that he or she is willing to help them face the consequences.

Each participant reacts characteristically in this initial phase. The father (usually the perpetrator) insists the allegations of abuse are false. He may express anger toward the victim and accuse the child of "wanting to send him to jail." When those around him believe the victim's story, the father may withdraw and threaten or attempt self-destruction.

The mother often denies the abuse and assumes her child is lying. There are too many painful thoughts to face if the allegation is true. Once she accepts the reality, she is hurt. ("How could he do this to me?" "Why am I not as desirable as my own daughter?") The anger she feels is directed toward the victim or the perpetrator, or she may vacillate. She is overwhelmed with shame, wondering what others will say. If she believes the child, she blames herself for not protecting her offspring. The mother also expresses concern about what will become of her. Will she lose her home and her economic support if her husband leaves?

The children who are victims blame themselves for the abuse. They are frightened by the fact that no one believes them. They may also feel they are to blame, not only for the abuse but also for the family disruption following disclosure. Above all, the victims protest they only wanted the abuse to stop; they never imagined the family disruption that would occur.

The siblings of the victim experience confusion—fear over what will become of the family and anger at the victim over the disruption.

Assessment–Awareness

The assessment–awareness phase occurs when the family members accept the reality of the abuse and assess what they actually have in the way of family relationships. They become dependent on the worker or therapist while exploring what lies ahead. This is a difficult period for the helper. Consistency and patience are mandatory. The clients may cling to the worker in a manner that seems stifling. As each member begins to examine his or her role in the abusive family structure, there is a great deal of pain.

During this phase, the therapist aids the family in realigning generational boundaries. Roles of parents and children must be redefined so that members recognize their appropriate roles in the future. The marital couple receives intensive therapeutic help in communicating. The worker assists in strengthening the mother–child bond in order to provide future protection for the child. This aspect of treatment takes time, because the child may feel as much if not more anger toward the nonabusive parent as toward the perpetrator. In turn, the mother feels guilt for not protecting her child, which may cripple her ability to relate to the child now, especially if she perceives the child's anger.

As the mother–child relationship becomes more functional, the father's future role with the children is considered. It is often helpful for the father to meet with the victim and acknowledge his responsibility for the abuse. Without this apology, many victims are never able to overcome the anger they feel.

If the father has left the home and if the family chooses not to continue in its present structure or to reunite, it is important for family members to receive therapy to help them with this separation. Loss has been a paramount fear since disclosure, so any separation will be particularly painful, no matter how necessary it appears. Issues such as potential visiting between the father and the children will be an integral part of the agreement to separate.

Throughout the assessment–awareness phase, family members experience conflicting feelings. Both mother and father may continue to consciously or unconsciously blame the victim or judge that the child somehow seduced the perpetrator. The therapist will recognize and understand this kind of emotional projection. For the father, the need for projection is obvious: If the victim is also to blame, he himself does not seem so bad. The mother's feelings of worth are at stake. If her daughter, for example, is totally blameless, then the mother wonders if she is unattractive, undesirable, or unwanted by her husband. The father and mother both play the blaming game of "If you had been … ." Husbands accuse their wives of not being responsive enough. Wives accuse husbands of being too demanding or under the influence of alcohol or drugs.

Bursts of insight that seem to preclude the need for further therapy are not uncommon during this phase. For example, the Moreno family began attending church regularly and felt they were now being guided by God. They wanted to terminate therapy, believing that the incest could never happen again. The therapist helped them recognize that their basic family patterns had not yet changed; although their faith might help them, the reasons for the original incest still existed.

Fear fluctuates with hope. The family fears a recurrence of the abuse, but as they begin to recognize the dysfunctional patterns and the need to make changes, they hope that their insights will sustain them in the future.

The victim is also in conflict during this phase. Anger mingles with the need for close nurturing relationships, especially with the mother. The child may be faced with paradoxical messages. As roles become realigned, the victim is encouraged to act like a child, rather than continue in a parental role. But if the child acts out in rebellion, the parents often chastise him or her. Victims begin to wonder where they fit, if they are somehow damaged or unlovable, or if they can ever trust again (Bratton, Ceballos, Landreth, and Costos, 2012; Cattanach, 2008; Fitzgerald and Cohen, 2012; Hunter, 1990; James and Nasjleti, 1983; Sgroi, 1982).

Restructure

Gradually, the sexually abusive family begins to adopt a more functional pattern of life. In the restructure phase, they are reunited and have more open and honest communication. They have probably been in treatment for several years and therefore have a better understanding of when to ask for help in the future. The therapist has helped them explore coping mechanisms to keep a healthy balance.

The father and mother both take responsibility for future positive parenting and admit their past mistakes. They have learned to maintain boundaries, to communicate effectively, and to give nonsexual stimulation and affection to their children. The victim feels more of a sense of power and confidence that he or she need no longer be the parent. The child recognizes that he or she has the power to resist and to ask for help if the molestation recurs. All members of the family—parents, victim, and siblings—feel greater self-worth and can empathize with the feelings of the others.

As the family members pass through the phases of treatment, each one attempts to handle different issues.

TREATMENT OF SPECIFIC FAMILY MEMBERS

The Child and Adolescent

Numerous issues surface for the sexually abused child. First, the abuse itself causes elements of conflict or trauma. The family disruption following disclosure also has an impact on the victim. And if exposure to the criminal justice system is involved, the child experiences additional feelings of confusion. By receiving individual treatment, in conjunction perhaps with family treatment, it is hoped that the child will be able to deal with his or her feelings more effectively and integrate the abuse as a life occurrence in order to continue with his or her life (Cattanach, 2008; Fitzgerald and Cohen, 2012; Gil, 1993, 1996; Howe, 2005; Iwaniec, 2006; Pollio, Deblinger, and Runyon, 2011; Righthand et al., 2003; Williams, 1993). Seeing the family along with the child should open communication, allowing family members to express their needs in the future and assuring the child that he or she is entitled to protection within the family unit. One must also keep in mind the cultural values of the family, adjusting treatment accordingly (Fontes, 2008).

The course of treatment for children depends on several variables:

- Whether and how much the family supports treatment
- Whether the child resides with the family or in a foster home
- Whether the abuse was perpetrated by a family member or nonfamily member
- Whether there is involvement with the criminal justice system
- Whether there are cultural variations in the family system (e.g., values or the need to use an interpreter)

Children coming to treatment are usually grappling with 10 important issues that need to be addressed (Fitzgerald and Cohen, 2012; Gil, 1993; Pollio et al., 2011; Hunter, 1990; Sgroi, 1982):

1. Feeling like "damaged goods"
2. Guilt
3. Fear
4. Depression
5. Low self-esteem, leading to poor social skills
6. Repressed anger and hostility
7. Difficulty trusting
8. Blurred generational boundaries and role confusion
9. Pseudomaturity, masking the failure to have completed certain developmental tasks
10. Control and mastery over self

The first five issues tend to affect all children who have been sexually abused, while the last five are more likely to be results of abuse within the family.

The fear of being damaged goods is twofold. Not only do children fear physical injury or damage from the abuse, but they also perceive society's message that they are changed by what has happened to them. Consider the case of Cleo:

When Cleo, at age 11, came to treatment, she had fears about her ability to have children. The uncle who abused her had continually asked her how many children she hoped to have as he rubbed and penetrated. She became convinced that by his perversity he had ensured, in some unknown way, that she would never be able to give birth. She felt different and cheated. To further compound her feelings of isolation, the adults in her life, learning of her uncle's arrest for her abuse, began to relate to her as though she was more sexually experienced. Feeling that she was perceived as mature yet could never (in her mind) have babies, Cleo became severely depressed and withdrew, causing her worried parents to seek help for her. Cleo's therapist helped her to realize that her fears were unfounded.

In Cleo's situation, the physical damage was not as great as she perceived, but abused children face vaginal and rectal tears, scarring of tissues, and venereal disease. The therapist supports the child through whatever remedial measures are necessary for these injuries and then helps the victim come to terms with the feelings associated with the damage or loss.

Adolescents often react to their perceived damage with promiscuity, feeling "So what, I'm damaged anyway!" Thus, they embark on other sexual encounters, often with a self-destructive purpose. This behavior stems from their feelings of being damaged and from an extremely low self-concept that tells them they are worth little. Their sexual behavior then only intensifies the conviction of those around them that they are sexually wise beyond their years.

Boys carry a special burden when they are sexually abused, especially those from cultures where male dominance is the norm. Boys feel as if they are weak and should have been in control. Although male victims may also fear physical damage, the prevailing fear centers around homosexuality. The boy abused by a man wonders if the encounter has somehow made him homosexual. Since many perpetrators of this type of abuse are family men who present a picture of normalcy, the boy becomes convinced that the fault must be within him.

The young male abused by a woman faces similar fears but for different reasons. In a society where sex between older females and younger males is viewed almost as a rite of passage, the boy wonders why he should be disturbed by such an encounter. Does his discomfort, therefore, attest to his homosexuality? Unfortunately, in both situations, society supports the boy's fears, further convincing him of the damage done (Finkelhor, 1984; Hunter, 1990; Stone, 2005).

Therapeutically, the child's fears of damage can be addressed through education, a physical examination, and by discussing the fears and misconceptions. The attitude of society is not so easily changed, but children can be helped to realize that this problem is not theirs.

Abused children feel guilt for a number of reasons. Much time in therapy is devoted to helping the child recognize that he or she did not elicit the sexual interaction. Children suffer guilt from the love they feel for the abusing parent, their delight in the attention they were given, or from the physiological pleasure they experienced. Often, the perpetrator has added to this feeling by telling them how seductive or desirable they are. Taught by society to be seductive, girls become convinced that the abuse was to be expected from their behavior. Taught to be assertive, boys agonize over their inability to protect themselves and label themselves "weak" or "sissies" (Gartner, 2001; Hunter, 1990; Stone, 2005).

Guilt also stems from the child's perception that he or she is responsible for the disclosure of the abuse and the subsequent disruption of the family. The Asian child may also see himself or herself as responsible for the loss of family honor. Whether the victim disclosed the abuse intentionally or accidentally, he or she feels guilt at betraying the relationship with the perpetrator. The abuser has probably predicted dire consequences ("You'll be sent away" or "I'll go to jail"), and the child becomes convinced that these things will come to pass. The guilt-ridden child had no way to anticipate the intensity of the atmosphere, once disclosure is a reality and the family is thrown into crisis.

These types of guilt can only be treated by helping the child understand that he or she cannot be responsible for the actions of an adult. The child should also be empowered for the future by giving the clear message of "You are not responsible for what has happened in the past, but you can be helped to take control in the future."

Fear appears in the thinking processes of child victims in several ways. Nightmares and flashbacks attest to children's fears about the consequences of the disclosure or the fear that the perpetrator will abuse again. Children fear separation from the family and even from the perpetrator. Again, identification of these fears helps children understand them and gain insight into the likelihood of these events occurring. Setting up a mechanism to protect the child as well as providing the victim with new trust relationships helps to alleviate much of the fear. Along with the fear, there will usually be some degree of depression in child victims. This depression, sometimes masked by somatic complaints, is stimulated by the child's inability to process and deal with the myriad conflicts he or she is experiencing. While the depression usually subsides as the child has an opportunity to reveal and explore these feelings, the most immediate concern is that the depression does not precipitate a suicide attempt or self-destructive behavior (Fitzgerald and Cohen, 2012; Gartner, 2001; Howe, 2005; Hunter, 1990; Iwaniec, 2006; Stone, 2005).

The dysfunctional incestuous family, the fear of damage, and the guilt over participation in and disclosure of abuse lead abused children to low self-esteem. Not feeling sufficiently confident, these children are also robbed of their ability to develop adequate social skills, which in turn reinforces their low self-concept. Boys who were abused outside the home feel they are unlike their male peers—that they don't "measure up." Effective treatment gives children an opportunity to express their negative feelings about themselves. Positive feedback, often in a group setting, allows them to explore their strengths and enhances their self-esteem. With greater self-esteem comes a desire to master age-appropriate tasks with more confidence (Gartner, 2001; Gil, 1996; Hunter, 1990; Iwaniec, 2006).

Anger, although it may be masked by somatic symptomatology or unexpressed fantasies, plagues most victims of sexual abuse, especially male victims and those from incestuous families. The anger is felt toward a number of people and expressed in various ways. The victims may feel anger toward the perpetrator for abusing them, toward themselves for their perceived acquiescence, and toward others (especially nonabusing family members) for failing to protect them. Boys, unused to being victimized in our society, experience rage that they have been put in such a position.

Many female victims repress the rage they feel. Girls may act out—especially sexually—but the behavior only serves to mask the anger. A girl may internalize her anger and become depressed or exhibit self-destructive behavior, such as suicide attempts, self-mutilation, or eating disorders (Gil, 1993). Although some boys repress their anger, they are more likely to act out their rage. Since this rage is related to their sense of powerlessness, they feel they can regain power by robbing someone else of control. It is for this reason that male victims are more likely to be aggressive toward younger children or to sexually abuse other people. Through therapy, these boys can be helped to redirect their anger so that they can take power over some activity that is not abusive and will not harm others. Knowing that they have choices in regaining their sense of control is also important (Hunter, 1990; Stone, 2005).

All victims can be helped to get in touch with their anger and to understand its source. Therapists can suggest ways for the child to gain control and experience mastery. As children learn to be assertive, they discover a new sense of control that will protect them in the future.

Children abused within incestuous families are faced with issues inherent in living in a dysfunctional or unprotective environment. Many of these issues relate to those dealt with in Chapters 6 and 7. Attachment issues often figure in the lives of these children. The original dysfunction in the family may mean that there was faulty bonding early on. The later abuse becomes one more assault that impedes their ability to relate to others. Or a tenuous attachment may have occurred only to be interrupted by the betrayal of the abuse (Howe, 2005; Rich, 2006). These children learn that they cannot trust adults. A seemingly nurturing relationship with the perpetrator led to betrayal and exploitation, and other adults did little to stop it.

Children become parents to their own parents, and this confusion in roles is imbedded in the family structure. As a result, while the victims appear to take on responsibility far beyond their years, they have actually failed to complete many developmental tasks that their peers have mastered. Such children often feel that they have little control over themselves and their own lives. They are neither children nor adults and find it difficult to discover where they fit (Kagan, 2004).

Much of the treatment in these areas rests with the therapist's ability to present the child with an opportunity for a new and genuine trusting relationship in an effort to remediate for the attachment issues that impede his or her ability to form these relationships. If this is accomplished, the child can be helped to recognize what his or her role is in the family and that it is acceptable to relinquish much of the responsibility previously forced on him or her. Treatment enables the child to explore the deficiencies in development and guides him or her along the road to appropriate maturity (Fitzgerald and Cohen, 2012; Gil, 1993; Howe, 2005). Group treatment is useful because children and adolescents join with peers who are at different levels of development.

More recently, children from 3 to 18 have benefitted from *trauma-focused cognitive behavioral therapy* (*TF-CBT*). TF-CBT is primarily used to address children's affective disorders such as fear, depression, mood instability, anger, and so on; behavioral problems such as avoidance, violent acting out, sexualized behaviors, and so on; and biologic (somatic symptoms) and cognitive (self-blame, shame, low self-esteem etc.) problems. The goals of TF-CBT are to manage stress and help victims to regulate their behaviors as well as helping them to achieve mastery over their trauma responses and make meaning of their abusive experience (Fitzgerald and Cohen, 2012).

No matter which type of treatment is used, therapists aid children in communicating with other family members and with peers. Education is also part of treatment. Knowledge of anatomy, normal sexuality, birth control, male–female relations, and parenting enhances their development. If the court system is involved, the victim will need to be carefully prepared for what is to come. Support during the court process is also a vital part of treatment.

Sexually abused children respond to different treatment techniques depending on their age, the degree of attachment issues, the type of abuse, the cooperativeness of the family, and the skills of the therapist. Individual therapy is useful in developing a trusting relationship on which the child can model other relationships. Such therapy often begins when the child is in crisis over disclosure. Consistency in the relationship is vital, as any breach of trust or confidentiality will convince the victim that the therapist is as untrustworthy as the other adults in his or her life. With younger children, play therapy enables them to express themselves in a manner that is less threatening (Cattanach, 2008). Older victims enjoy games or projects, over which they can talk while seeming to put their attention elsewhere.

Group therapy is especially effective with adolescent victims. Here, victims can ventilate anger in a safe environment and develop new socialization skills. Sex education is a topic that lends itself to group discussion (Gil, 1993; Rich, 2006). If both a male and female therapist work with the group, their relationship simulates a family situation and provides positive modeling for victims. As the therapists demonstrate their ability to communicate effectively and to protect the group members from harm, the victims learn that they have a right to expect from healthy parents.

Art therapy is useful in assessment and in treatment. Drawings portray the victims' reactions to the abuse, their self-image, confusions about role and gender, misconceptions about the abuse, and their emotional states. Various art forms release the children's energy and free them of the constraints of talking with an adult. Music, dance, movement, mime, drama, and poetry are all methods of release for some children. Often, a group or individual therapy session begins with a warm-up period. The particular type of therapy is introduced and the children or adolescents are encouraged to participate. If the session is videotaped, the discussion that follows provides both child and therapist with an integrated understanding of what has transpired (Bannister, 2004; Malchiodi and Perry, 2008).

Journal and story writing are techniques that have been widely used with adult survivors and are useful in work with children, especially with older victims. Keeping a diary or journal enables the child to vent in privacy and provides a means through which he or she and the therapist can begin to relate. Even stories written about hypothetical people allow the therapist to explore the child's fears and fantasies. Poetry has also been found to stimulate emotional release. Whether reading the poetry of others or creating their own, victims experience and identify emotions that enhance their treatment.

Children may be seen in therapy with other members of the incestuous family. Mother–daughter therapy, as a pair seen individually or in groups, helps to strengthen the bond, improves communication, and ensures protection for the child in the future. Later in treatment, it is also extremely beneficial for the perpetrator and child to meet and for the perpetrator to take full responsibility for his or her actions.

Whether a child is the victim of incest or an assault outside the home, therapy is extremely helpful to ensure his or her integration of the trauma and future healthy development.

The Mother or Nonabusing Parent

The goals of treatment with the nonabusing parent are primarily to strengthen his or her role in the future protection of the child. Because of the frequency of father–daughter incest, it is therefore the mother who is usually the nonabusive parent. It is certainly possible for a mother to be an abuser, but in those cases, the father is often absent. Because these cases are rare, there is not yet a clinical outline of treatment for nonabusing fathers.

The mother has needs of her own, and until these are met, she cannot be fully available for her child. The mother in an incest triad has often been a victim of abuse or of a dysfunctional family herself. This has left her with scars that hamper her ability to parent and protect (Bratton et al., 2012; Levenson and Morin, 2000; Strand, 2000).

The therapist will recognize the mother's acute feelings of inadequacy and strong dependency needs. Whether she appears passive and dependent or domineering and hostile, she will need unconditional acceptance and encouragement to take control of her life. This is an individual whose past history and marriage have been punctuated with messages that she is a failure. Overwhelmed by the intensity of this message, she has often lapsed into depression. Like the other members of her family, her impaired self-concept has caused her to isolate herself and has prevented her from developing adequate social skills.

For this reason, group therapy is especially effective with these mothers. They often need massive amounts of support, which can be better supplied by a group than by one therapist. In a group, the mother can also be encouraged to become more assertive, behavior that not only benefits her but also provides her with skills with which she can protect her child (Johnson, 1992; Karson, 2001; Levenson and Morin, 2000; Rosencrans, 1997; Strand, 2000).

Communication is a major problem for incestuous families. As one member of this family system, the mother is especially unable to express herself and make her needs known. She must learn, through therapy, to recognize her own feelings and to share them with others. Many of these women have spent their lives expecting others to perceive their needs and then fill them. Their disappointment when their needs remain undetected and unfulfilled does not prevent them from continuing to harbor unrealistic expectations of those around them. These mothers cannot admit that their marriages have disappointed them and that they have little communication with their children.

The mother's low self-esteem, lack of assertiveness, denial, and unrealistic expectations also prevent her from setting and enforcing limits in the family. In treatment, the mother is faced with the recognition that she failed to prevent the abusive behavior. When she comes to terms with this fact and begins to perceive herself as a responsible and autonomous person, the mother increases her ability to enforce role boundaries. If the family remains intact, she must be in a position to ensure that the incestuous father does not have the opportunity to abuse again. She must be sensitive to his behavior around the child and conscious of not leaving father and child alone. For this task, she must put aside her denial, see herself as capable and assertive, and be able to communicate her own needs and desires (Johnson, 1992; Rosencrans, 1997; Strand, 2000).

In working with these mothers, one must always keep their culture in mind. Although she must learn to protect her child, a mother who has also learned to be assertive and independent may become isolated in a male-dominated culture. Thus, a balance must be achieved between the needs of the child and cultural norms (Fontes, 2008).

The mother's anger and her inability to trust are two underlying elements that must be addressed. Her anger may be directed toward the perpetrator or toward the victim for their perceived betrayal. She may turn this anger inward or express it openly. Mothers from dysfunctional families of origin often carry anger as a remnant from childhood. Instead of expressing it overtly, the mother may have kept this anger hidden. Anger is not an emotion that hides well, however. It is often evidenced as passive behavior toward her family or is directed inward. In the safety of therapy, the mother can admit her feelings and express her rage. She can grieve over her unmet needs and ventilate her feelings about those who have failed to meet them.

Through her relationship with the therapist or with her therapy group, the mother also learns how to trust. This sense of trust is important for her to carry back to her own family. Through therapy, she learns that trust is based on communicating with others, being accountable, and holding others accountable for their actions.

The key word in treatment of the nonabusing mother is *support*. She may have so lacked nurturing herself that she needs to be given a great deal of support and guidance before she can give it to others.

Not all mothers opt to keep their families intact. For those who choose divorce rather than risk being betrayed again, therapy centers around supporting them through the process, enabling them to provide for and protect their children, and helping them to deal with their renewed feelings of failure, loneliness, and isolation. In addition, this mother must learn to recognize her self-abusive patterns so that the next man with whom she becomes involved does not have the same abusive tendencies as those of her husband.

Women whose husbands are incarcerated face different decisions, conflicts, and frustrations. Should she wait for his release and attempt to maintain communication across prison walls, or should she divorce him and risk being alone and perhaps feel that she has somehow betrayed him? The mother will need support in making this decision and in helping her children adjust to it. She will also need help in deciding how she will protect the child once the offender is released. Since jail/prison terms for sexual abuse are usually relatively short, this is a real concern.

Although individual therapy is effective, group therapy seems to provide more opportunities for support and growth. Sometimes, concrete services—such as financial assistance, child care, and transportation—are also essential. If the criminal justice system is involved, the mother as well as the victim may require anticipatory guidance and backing through this process.

The Perpetrator

The type of treatment for the perpetrator of sexual abuse depends on three interrelated factors: (1) the type of assault he or she committed; (2) where he or she resides when treatment is undertaken; and (3) the gender of the perpetrator.

At some point, the incestuous father usually has therapy sessions with the family. Although he may reside outside the home, he usually has contact with the family unit, especially when reunification is a projected goal. If the family chooses to exclude him, he may be seen alone or in group therapy to resolve his own issues (Flora, 2001; Flora, Duehl, Fisher, Halsey, and Keohane, 2007; Kirsch, Fanniff, and Becker, 2011). If the state in which he resides decrees automatic incarceration or if the assault on his child was violent or included other illegal aspects (e.g., production of pornography), the incestuous father may be imprisoned. Therefore, the type of treatment he receives, if any, depends on what he has done and what jurisdiction has custody.

The extrafamilial abuser is more likely to be incarcerated for several reasons. First, in many states, incest is reported to protective services, but extrafamilial abuse is brought to the attention of a law enforcement agency and likely leads to prosecution. Second, extrafamilial perpetrators are more often classic pedophiles, which means that they tend to abuse more frequently, begin their abusive patterns earlier in life, have more victims, and exhibit deeper pathology (Flora, 2001; Flora et al., 2007; Prendergast, 2004; Ward, Polaschek, and Beech, 2006). Only occasionally is he able to be involved with treatment outside the prison setting.

While male perpetrators come to the attention of the social service agencies and judicial system more frequently than female perpetrators, women also abuse children. However, women are less likely than men to be detected. For this reason, there are very few programs that specialize in female offenders. One program, Genesis II, in Saint Paul, Minnesota, does ongoing group therapy and educational intervention with women who have committed sexual abuse. The goals of the program (Mathews, 1998) are to help the women do the following:

- Take primary responsibility for their sexually abusive behavior.
- Increase their understanding of and empathy for the victim.
- Increase their awareness of their own emotional and psychological processes that led to the sexual abuse.
- Establish a way to meet their own sexual and interpersonal needs without victimizing others.

The women, some of whom reside in halfway houses and others at home, are referred to the program by child protection workers, probation officers, and private therapists. Women, too, become involved in relapse prevention (Eldridge and Saradijian, 2000).

Is there a "cure" for the perpetrator? Consensus is that child sexual abuse, like alcoholism, has no cure but can be controlled. For the incestuous father, whose needs are for nurturing and whose offense appears based on an imbalanced family system filled with stress, control means a combination of treating the family for its dysfunction and teaching the perpetrator other methods of coping with his response to stress. For the pedophile, whose patterns are based on compulsion and on an inability to cope effectively with life issues, control necessitates additional restraints. He must have no direct contact with children, and because many pedophiles will not monitor this themselves, other measures (e.g., registration or tracking by bracelet) must be taken.

When considering the treatment of sexual offenders, two issues arise. First are issues of risk—the public must be protected from their actions. The course of action based on this view is to incarcerate the offender. However, if an offender is to gain anything from intervention, he or she must receive treatment based on his or her own pathology. This necessitates assessing the strengths of the abuser and determining what must be remediated (Flora, 2001; Flora et al., 2007; Kirsch et al., 2011; Ward et al., 2006).

Prognoses for treatment depend on the type of perpetrator and his or her history (Flora, 2001; Flora et al., 2007; Ford, 2006; Ogilvie, 2004; Prendergast, 2004). At what age did he begin abusing? How long has the behavior lasted? What is the intensity or severity of the abusive behavior? How frequently do abusive episodes occur? If the perpetrator began his abusive career early in life and has continued to abuse regularly and with more intensity, his prognosis is much more guarded than the man who began in his adulthood and had abused one or two victims and only infrequently.

Te most effective approaches with offenders tend to be cognitive and behavioral or cognitive behavioral therapy techniques (Flora et al., 2007; McGrath, Cumming, Burchard, Zeoli, and Ellerby, 2010). These help the offender to examine his thoughts (cognition) and behavior in order to understand his cognitive distortions, ability to feel empathy and his deviant arousal patterns. The eventual goal will be to help the offender interrupt his behavior before offending again (relapse prevention).

Whatever the approach to therapy, there are specific goals to be met in working with both male and female perpetrators (Flora, 2001; Ford, 2006; Laws, Hudson, and Ward, 2000; Ogilvie, 2004; Prendergast, 2004; Ward et al., 2006):

1. Accept personal responsibility for the abuse.
2. Understand the sequence of feelings, events, stimuli, and circumstances that led to the sexual offense.
3. Learn to break the pattern at the first sign leading toward abuse.
4. Learn appropriate tools and mechanisms to break the pattern and control the behavior.
5. Develop a positive self-concept.
6. Have an opportunity to test new skills in a safe environment.
7. Have posttreatment support to prevent recidivism.

At the onset of treatment, abusers must be individually assessed. Personality testing can be particularly useful. In some programs, perpetrators write in-depth autobiographies, through which past experiences and thinking patterns can be analyzed. Exposing the man to groups of other offenders also provides assessment material. In behaviorally based programs, a physiological penile assessment may be administered. In this test, a small sensing device is attached to the penis to measure the individual's erection response to various stimuli. This test is used especially when some type of aversion therapy is anticipated.

Since the primary defenses of perpetrators are denial, rationalization, and projection of blame, an important step at the onset of treatment is to help the individual take responsibility for his abusive behavior. "My daughter was too seductive" or "My wife went to work and neglected me" is not an acceptable excuse for the abuse. One method of getting the offender to take responsibility is to place him in a group of offenders who are at different stages of treatment. Many of these men have already admitted their own responsibility and openly confront a man who does not.

The habitual offender probably never looked at the pattern that led to abuse. Clues may be discernible through his past history:

Ray was abused by an uncle (his mother's brother) at family reunions. The relationship between Ray's mother and her brother was not harmonious, and Ray had the courage to tell her because he felt she would be sympathetic. Instead, the mother laughed derisively, "You can't even keep out of his way? He's such a wimp, but even you can't keep him away!" Ray remembers feeling shocked and betrayed and vividly recalls his reaction of uncomfortable warmth, sweating palms, and a dry mouth. His mother taunted him about his disclosure for years.

From his adolescence, Ray remembers being rejected by a classmate whom he had asked for a date. She laughed at his awkward attempt. He remembers having the same physiological feelings and emotional hurt he had experienced with his mother. Unconsciously, he then wanted someone else to feel as weak and as helpless as he. He sought out a younger neighbor boy, whom he molested. This boy was the first of many.

In treatment, Ray began to recognize that when he felt helpless or laughed at, especially by a woman, he developed the same physiological symptoms and the desire to molest. Once the perpetrator pictures the chain of events leading to his abusive behavior, he learns methods to control his impulses. Ray learned to not set himself up for rejection, and he also developed an exhaustive program of physical activity to channel any aggressive impulses more constructively.

A variety of behavior techniques are used to help the perpetrator break his pattern. Olfactory aversion, involving an extremely unpleasant smell (such as ammonia), eventually blocks the man's arousal response to certain stimuli. For example, an abuser watching a slide presentation of a naked child is made to break a net-enmeshed capsule of spirits of ammonia and hold it under his nose. The smell inhibits his arousal and prevents an erection. Eventually, he learns to associate the smell with seeing the child, and this stimulus no longer arouses him. Shocks using visual or verbal cues are other means of aversion therapy (Flora, 2001; Prendergast, 2004). (E.g., the perpetrator is shown slides, and a shock is administered when he sees the type of child he offended against. Or he is asked to tell of his offense in detail and is given a shock when he describes how he has victimized the child.) (See Flora et al., 2007, for more detail about treatment techniques.)

A more controversial method of reducing sexual response is with Depo-Provera (medroxyprogesterone acetate), a drug that decreases the functioning of the testes and inhibits the sexual drive. Currently, the drug is best known for its use at the Johns Hopkins University Hospital in Baltimore, where it is being administered weekly to a selected group of perpetrators. The concerns about this medication are based on questions of how effective it is and of its long- and short-term effects. In addition, the abuser may need continued doses after treatment. There is some question as to how these doses can be made available as the use of this type of therapy is currently experimental and somewhat controversial (Flora, 2001; Prendergast; 2004).

Whether his behavior is controlled psychologically, behaviorally, or through the use of drugs, the offender must still be helped to improve his feelings about himself. Male offenders see themselves as inherently powerless in a society that expects men to be assertive and take command. Their choice of a significantly weaker victim—a child as opposed to a peer—is clearly indicative of these feelings. An exploration of social stereotypes, combined with an assessment of their own individual strengths, enables perpetrators to develop more positive goals for themselves. Positive reinforcement as they take steps to reach this goal allows them to feel better about themselves. This is by no means a short process. Years of abuse at home and messages from others that they were inadequate have made abusers deeply lacking in self-respect (Flora et al., 2007; Prendergast, 2004).

The sexual abuser has also failed to develop social skills. Despite the nature of his crime, he probably has little understanding of sexuality. Sex, to him, is often negative and dirty. He sees sex as a method of degrading or humiliating others. In treatment, the perpetrator learns about anatomy and sexuality and that sex, properly used, is not negative. He is helped to reassess his values about sex. If the abuser is in family treatment, he and his spouse may be encouraged to explore ways in which they can develop a satisfying sexual relationship.

Part of the incestuous father's early problems with healthy sexual relationships was not only his distorted understanding of sexuality but also his inability to empathize with others. This appears to be a problem for all sexual abusers. Throughout his life, the abuser has had little insight into the feelings of others, especially his victims. One method of treatment brings him face to face with survivors of sexual assault. He, too, is possibly a survivor, and helping him explore this in therapy gives him an opportunity to recognize his feelings in others. The offender who sees a child as multidimensional and recognizes the harm to that child may have a better chance to control his abusive impulses in the future.

Since a major contributor to the abuse is the perpetrator's feelings of helplessness and need to control, treatment aids perpetrators to take control over their own lives through assertiveness training and control over their substance abuse. Vocational or educational training, along with other psychosocial education, allows the men to perceive themselves as worthwhile (Flora, 2001; Flora et al., 2007; Prendergast, 2004; Sawyer, 1999).

Two major limitations of treatment programs for sexual abusers are that there is no built-in opportunity for the perpetrator to test his new skills in a safe environment and that there is no insurance of follow-up services after treatment has ended. For example, incarcerated abusers who have received treatment in conjunction with a prison term often find themselves unsupported by social services following their release. In recognition of this oversight, many programs are now seeking to provide posttreatment support services. Another possible solution is for the perpetrator to become affiliated with a self-help group, such as Parents United. Support services are vital to help the perpetrator center his energies on controlling his impulses. Sexual offending is usually not a one-time occurrence and commitment to treatment is a life-long necessity.

Because sexual offenders are at risk for recidivism, there is currently a great deal of emphasis on the *relapse prevention model* (Flora et al., 2007; Laws et al., 2000; Ward et al., 2006). Relapse prevention involves individualized treatment that assesses the offender's own sexual fantasies, motivation, and offending cycle. It designs treatment that includes techniques for monitoring his or her ability to interrupt the impulses to abuse that could lead to recidivism. Programs using this method strive to strengthen the offenders' own self-control and, while motivating them in a desire to prevent themselves from reoffending, provide them with specific behavioral techniques to achieve these goals. To date, many of these efforts have been quite successful.

How are the treatment needs of the perpetrator addressed in various types of programs? Basically, the abuser may be treated in three structural frameworks that can, in some instances, overlap: (1) treatment in conjunction with the family unit; (2) treatment in the community but independent of the family; and (3) treatment while incarcerated.

Treatment in the Family Unit

In family counseling, the needs of each member of the family must, at some time, be addressed. Individual counseling assesses how each one's needs can be integrated with those of other family members. Individual counseling with the incestuous father explores his willingness to take responsibility and his understanding of his own abusive patterns and helps him learn to control his desires.

Skill building becomes a vital part of family therapy, and often, the man is joined by his wife to explore ways to communicate better, share family roles more equitably, enjoy a better sexual relationship, and learn to manage the stresses of family life. Together, these parents may be trained in parenting skills to enable them to feel more in control. Trust between these couples is another major treatment issue, as revealed in this case:

Dick and Susan Hawthorne were seen in therapy shortly after it had been disclosed that Dick had been abusing 9-year-old Michelle for several years. The court agreed to allow Dick to receive treatment. At first, Dick and his wife and daughter were each seen separately by different therapists. Dick readily admitted that he had abused Michelle, but it took several months before he was ready to take full responsibility for his actions. In addition to individual counseling, Dick also participated in a group of six other men that was largely responsible for his recognition of how he had betrayed his daughter.

After several months, Dick changed his regular individual sessions to weekly sessions with Susan. He continued to go to the fathers' group, and Susan and Michelle joined a mother–daughter group. Dick and Susan were guided in the exploration of their relationship from everyday communication and division of labor to their sexual compatibility. These weekly marital sessions lasted for several months.

When it was suggested that Dick and Susan were ready to have family therapy, Dick objected. He realized that Michelle was well aware of what had happened, but he had convinced himself that 12-year-old Phillip and 4-year-old Tracey had not been involved. Couple therapy continued until Dick realized the necessity of bringing the family together. In family therapy, the roles and expectations of both the parents and children were explored. Phillip expressed his hurt at what he perceived was his father's rejection of him. He was jealous of Michelle, despite his suspicion that something was wrong. Tracey was given an opportunity to ventilate her confusion. At her age, she knew little of the reality of what had occurred but was very much aware of the tension in the household. Susan was helped to deal with her family's anger at her for abandoning them because of her frequent meetings and busy schedule. Dick was encouraged to accept his part in the abuse and to assure Michelle that he alone was to blame. The family continued in therapy for a year while Dick remained in the fathers' group.

Fathers who receive therapy with their families may or may not be living at home. For those who live apart, rejoining the family occasionally helps them evaluate their ability to return to the home on a more permanent basis. Needless to say, this would not be possible without assurance that the children were protected and were in no real danger from renewed abuse.

Treatment in the Community

Not every incestuous father can be reunited with his family. Some seek or are compelled to seek treatment independent of their families. Pedophiles may not have a family or choose to receive treatment for their problem without involving other family members.

Treatment may be individual or in groups or a combination of the two, and the same issues described in the last section are addressed. In some instances, treatment is a component of the man's probation or is based on the agreement that if he cooperates with treatment, he will not be prosecuted. In these instances, the court might also have stipulations that must be met:

Lex was 22 years old when he came to the attention of the court for molesting a 5-year-old girl. Although he had had numerous fantasies about children in the past, he had never had an opportunity to act on them. Now he was unemployed, lonely, and depressed. The abuse, in his eyes, resulted from a several-month relationship with his victim.

Because it was his first known offense, the court put him on probation with the condition that he seek therapy at a local mental health clinic. It was also stipulated that he find employment and move to an area where there were not as many small children. Part of Lex's therapy, therefore, included job-skill training, finding a job, and renting an apartment in an adult building. The prospect of being completely surrounded by adults frightened him, however, and his sessions were often devoted to helping him deal with this issue by becoming more assertive and gaining more self-esteem.

It is uncommon for a perpetrator to seek therapy on his own. Sometimes, therapists discover clients who have abusive tendencies on which they may have acted. Then the dilemma for a therapist is that he or she is mandated by law to report child abuse. Some therapists hesitate to report, despite the consequences due to their fear that reporting will destroy the delicate balance of patient–therapist relationship.

Treatment in Prison

There is a heated controversy about whether the perpetrator should be punished or treated. There are those who contend that child sexual abuse is a heinous crime and warrants only punishment, but experience shows that incarceration does little good. Sentences are often short, and the perpetrator's life in prison is far from therapeutic. In the prison hierarchy, the child molester is even below the rapist. The sexual abuser of children is likely to be raped or beaten by his fellow inmates and usually must be kept in protective custody, away from the general population. As a result, when he is released, he is not only still a child abuser but an angry, bitter, and humiliated child abuser, who is apt to further degrade his victims by using the violence he learned in prison.

Incarceration without treatment serves to keep the offender out of the community for a short time but does little toward rehabilitation. Increasingly, prisons are initiating treatment programs that differ depending on whether the sex offender is housed as part of the general population, in a separate wing, or in a separate building (Flora, 2001; Flora et al., 2007; Prendergast, 2004):

1. Integrated programs periodically remove the prisoners from the general population and from their routines in order to attend group or individual sessions. The program is usually part of a model dealing with a variety of mental health problems, including abuse.

2. Programs that advocate housing offenders in a separate wing provide a more cohesive approach with more time for interaction between staff and offenders. The offenders' daily routine includes group therapy. Although this arrangement protects them from the general prison population, being clustered together in such a way labels and stigmatizes these inmates.

3. It is less common for inmates to be housed in separate buildings, largely because of financial, security, and space considerations, as well as the priorities of the particular prison. If security is ensured and a high staff–inmate ratio is maintained, such a structure can be effective.

Although treatment within the prison is preferable to no treatment at all, it does have its drawbacks. Critics contend that the closed, protective atmosphere generates an artificial setting of security and prevents the inmates from practicing their new skills in real-life situations. Unable to practice what they have learned, will the abusers be able to stand the stresses of living outside the prison environment? In addition, participation is usually voluntary. Openly admitting sexual abuse subjects the inmate to abuse from other inmates, so perpetrators are often hesitant to join treatment programs.

To date, few prisons offer offender treatment, and those programs that do exist are often understaffed and underfunded. Since the few programs are still so recent, accurate statistics on recidivism—or chances of success—are not available.

Successful in-house treatment programs find that offenders respond best when exposed to a variety of groups. These groups address issues such as these:

- Sex education
- Relationship with women
- Personal victimization
- Sociodrama (role-playing interpersonal conflicts)
- Communication skills
- Dealing with anxiety and tension
- Patterns of sexual assault and making the community aware of sexual assault (in which professionals from the community are invited to meet with offenders)

In addition, the inmate may participate in individual counseling and be given the opportunity to attend self-help groups, such as Parents Anonymous and Parents United. Such an approach provides offenders with a particularly well-rounded treatment program.

Occasionally, prison inmates are allowed to enter the community for counseling, especially when they have almost finished their sentences and attempts are being made for family reunification. Again, security is a paramount concern. Since therapists are community based, there will be more of a chance for the abuser to maintain contact and support after his release. These therapists may be particularly influential in helping him in the transition between incarceration and freedom.

Treatment of Juvenile Offenders

Juveniles are a growing population of sexual offenders. Some youth who act out sexually are erroneously labeled offenders when, in fact, they are acting out the trauma of their own abuse. For these children and adolescents, family-centered treatment, in conjunction with individualized therapy, is often successful. But when a youth exhibits more severe pathology, a piece of which is sexually molesting other children, there is a greater need for intensive treatment (Flora, 2001; Rich, 2003, 2009).

Depending on the degree of pathology, the youth may remain at home while participating in individual and group therapy as well as family treatment. Young people with more serious pathology are often placed in residential treatment settings, where they can benefit from more specialized therapy. Parental involvement is also encouraged.

Is Treatment Effective?

There is much controversy about the way in which sexual abusers should be handled. Some feel the solution is to "Slap them in prison and throw away the key," but the reality is that this does not benefit anyone. Certainly, the offender does not learn patterns other than deviant ones. And further, the prison system is such that the offender *will* usually be released into the community again. The untreated offender often returns angry about the treatment he has had in prison. It is this person who will not only reoffend but will do so with more force and anger.

The alternative, it would seem, would be to offer effective treatment. But does treatment work?

Offenders who exhibit more complex pathology have poorer treatment outcomes and more likelihood of relapse. Studies have found offenders involved in treatment have shown a decrease in deviant arousal, more internalized locus of control, fewer cognitive distortions, and an improved ability to cope with potential relapse situations (Rice and Harris, 2003). A recent Canadian study that compared 3,121 treated offenders to 3,625 offenders found that treated offenders were less likely to reoffend (Hanson, Bourgon, Helmus, and Hodgson, 2009).

From this and other recent studies, it would seem that treatment for offenders is effective. It is important to recognize, however, that it is erroneous to assume that one treatment method is appropriate for all offenders. Each offender must be assessed individually, and treatment must be geared specifically to him or her.

Preservation of Incestuous Families

Should incestuous families be kept together? Can a child be protected from further abuse? These questions are difficult to answer and are the subject of debate among social workers, therapists, police officers, attorneys, and judges (Kagan, 2004; Pope, Williams, Sirles, and Lally, 2005). Sexual abuse is often woven into the fabric of a family system. Reworking that fabric can be an exceptionally difficult task. Can parental rights be respected while protection of the child is ensured? In addition, what are the reactions and needs of the siblings of the victim? How can these be addressed? (See Baker, Tanis, and Rice, 2001.)

When protective services intervenes in an incest situation, the preferred intervention is to remove the offender in order to stabilize the family and protect the child. This necessitates that the nonabusive parent not only believes the child but is willing to protect him or her. Mothers in incestuous families have reported that this seems like an overwhelming task:

"I felt like I had to watch him every minute," reported one nonabusive mother. "When my daughter first told me that her father was abusing her, protective services made him leave. We got into therapy, and I figured we could get things straightened out. But there was so much pressure. I couldn't trust him anymore. I couldn't leave him alone with my daughter. It was like there was always a big black cloud over our heads."

Mothers who commit themselves to monitoring their spouse's behavior may find the stress too much. The offender experiences the pressure. Karl worked at home and found that his daughter's presence worried him:

I was afraid to be around her [his stepdaughter] ... afraid I would do something again. I didn't want to but I was still afraid. My wife and I had to make sure we planned things so that I never had to put her to bed or bathe her.

Intensive family intervention may help the family to achieve a balance that protects the child. But such patterns are difficult to break, and many families feel the need of follow-up services to maintain themselves. It may also require a great deal of motivation on each member's part for the incestuous family to be preserved.

Parents of Children Abused Outside the Home

Parents of children who were abused by those outside their families are rarely provided treatment. One reason for this oversight is that these cases are usually reported to law enforcement, rather than to child protection agencies. The goal then becomes apprehension and prosecution of the perpetrator. When the child exhibits undeniably associated symptoms, he or she receives treatment. Rarely, if ever, do the parents. Instead, they are expected to support their child and cooperate in the efforts to punish the perpetrator. Yet these parents often have conflicting feelings that make their support of the child difficult.

An overriding feeling for parents is guilt. No matter how unrealistic are their concerns, they chastise themselves for not having protected their child from harm. They agonize over "Why did I let her walk home from school alone?" or "Why did I allow him to play on that ball team?" or "Why did I choose that babysitter?" or "Why didn't I watch her more closely on the Internet?"

The reaction to these feelings, in addition to self-blame, is to overprotect the child, which leads to family conflict and often augments the child's problems. In therapy, the parents are helped to recognize that although adequate supervision is important, children need increasing amounts of responsibility and independence for healthy growth.

Parents also tend to project blame on each other ("Why were you late picking Sally up?" or "Didn't you watch him?"). Mothers and fathers who argue over their degree of responsibility for the child create problems in their own relationships. They may also blame the child, especially if he or she was not where they expected him or her to be. For example, one boy usually walked home from school by a predominantly residential route. One day, however, he decided to walk another way, which passed a local variety store. It was on this route where he met the man who then molested him. His parents had never told him that he could not take the business route, but when they learned of his abuse, they were extremely angry with him for "disobeying." Some parents blame the child for not stopping the abuse. They ask why the child didn't run or fight, forgetting that under their tutelage the child had learned to be in awe of and obey adults.

Parents sometimes resent the family disruption after the abuse has been disclosed. Police question family members, there may be court appearances, and the tenor of the family is usually one of anxiety and unrest. In response to a lengthy period of investigation, one father commented, "Maybe our son should never have told us about being molested; he probably would have forgotten it after a while." Despite the disruption, the parents must recognize that the child needs to feel protected. Reporting, investigation, and prosecution of the abuser give the message to the child that the abuser is to blame and not the child.

The parents' inability to recognize and cope with the trauma of the child's abuse may be related to their own past. Parents who were abused themselves as children find that residual conflicts are stimulated as they attempt to help their child through the aftermath of the experience. With therapy, parents can resolve some of their own issues.

It is natural for parents to be angry with the perpetrator. When their daughters are abused, fathers, in particular, describe wanting to retaliate by killing or maiming the abuser. They should be helped to explore their anger, recognize it as a reaction to feeling powerless, and be helped to channel their desires to act in a more appropriate way. Parents may also feel that their child is somehow permanently damaged by the abuse and express anger toward the perpetrator for this damage. Part of the child's recovery will depend on the parents' ability to lay to rest the fears about being damaged and help the child face the future. Until the parents are able to see the child as the same individual he or she was before the abuse and to love the child just as much, it will be difficult for them to be truly helpful. For these reasons, the parents of children abused by outsiders need support and insight into coping with the abuse and helping their child recover.

SUMMARY

Workers treating sexually abused children and their families need particular skills. In treating sexual abuse, the worker discovers that society's attitudes toward the clients and the workers themselves affect the treatment process. Helpers approach the treatment of incestuous families with several assumptions: the relational imbalances predate the abuse, these imbalances were comfortable for the family on some level, one must find replacements for the dysfunctional behaviors, one cannot predict whether the family will remain together, and it will be difficult for them to face the sexual issues.

One of the first programs to treat sexual abuse was the CSATP in California. Since the late 1970s, this program has treated families and perpetrators and become the model for numerous programs across the country. In treatment, an incestuous family goes through specific phases: disclosure–panic, assessment–awareness, and restructure. During each of these phases, the family members experience certain conflicts that must be addressed in treatment.

Each perpetrator, victim, or family member in sexual abuse has particular treatment needs. The child or adolescent must overcome feelings about being damaged, guilt, fear, and depression, along with feelings of low self-esteem. Children abused within their family have difficulty trusting again, exhibit pseudomaturity and loss of control, and feel anger toward the perpetrator and the nonprotecting parent. The goals of treatment with the nonabusing mother are to help her protect her child in the future. In order to do this, she must resolve her conflicts over her own collusion in the abuse, improve her own self-concept, learn to trust others, learn to make her needs known, communicate more effectively, and become more assertive. Underlying the mother's inability to protect is often a good deal of anger. She must learn to find the source of this anger and release it so that it can be channeled appropriately.

Treatment of the perpetrators depends on the type of assault (incestuous or extrafamilial), on their residence during treatment, and on their gender. There are few available data on the treatment of female offenders, but treatment goals for perpetrators—male and female—include getting them to take responsibility for the abuse, helping them to understand their abusive patterns and how to break them, and encouraging them to develop better self-concepts. In addition to treatment, perpetrators must have opportunities to test their new skills and have support following treatment.

The treatment of sexual abusers may be done in a variety of settings. Perpetrators are treated in conjunction with the family to facilitate future healthy family interaction. Other members in the family are given individual treatment, with emphasis on their own personal functioning. If a perpetrator is incarcerated, he may or may not have treatment, but without treatment, there is little hope for rehabilitation.

Treatment is rarely available to parents of children abused outside the home. Expected to support their children, these parents are often hampered by conflicts of their own. They feel guilt at having failed to protect their children and often blame their spouses or the victim for the abuse. They feel intense anger toward the perpetrator and see the child as somehow damaged. All of these feelings must be addressed before the parents can be truly supportive of their child.

Chapter 14

Foster Care as a Therapeutic Tool

Even with treatment of the family, children may not be able to remain in the home. Out-of-home care can be foster care or some type of group or residential setting. Ideally, if substitute care becomes necessary, it should not merely be a holding environment but a part of the therapeutic process. Family foster care is usually the first choice after the child's own home, but several factors can inhibit effective foster placement.

PROBLEMS WITH FOSTER CARE

Often, the court orders that children be placed in foster care for their protection and the parents are forced to comply. Or immediately after the disclosure of the abuse, the social service agency may decide that the children are in danger if left at home. Even if the placement is a voluntary agreement between the parents and the agency, the parents may think they are pleasing the social worker and that placement will be short-term. Many parents fail to recognize the implications of such a separation. If the separation is forced, the parents may well have difficulty accepting it. They may even sabotage the placement. Certainly, they feel powerless and resentful. Giving up their children to other parents is a clear sign of their own failure (Berrick, 2008; Grant, 2004; Karson, 2001).

Separation is traumatic for the children and causes conflicts and resistance. Sensitivity on the part of the social workers, foster parents, and natural parents is needed to support the foster child through the separation process.

There are elements of instability in foster care. Often, the social worker does not know that the court has ruled that the children be returned to their own home. Also, foster parents are free to request the removal of children. Children are, therefore, unsure of where they belong. In addition, about 30 percent of children will be returned to their birth parents only to reenter care (Kaufman and Grasso, 2006; Wulczyn, 2004).

The transitory nature of foster care placements has long been seen as a problem in the child welfare system. For children who already have attachment issues, these moves can create even greater problems (Barth, Albert, Berrick, and McCourtney, 2010; Goodyer, 2011; Grant, 2004; Howe, 2005; Rosenwald and Riley, 2010). The emphasis on permanency planning has been an attempt to address this detriment to children's well-being. However, Kaufman and Grasso (2006) argue that a definition of *permanency* must address not only achieving but also maintaining a permanent residence for a child.

In foster care, children are faced with myriad adjustments. Children must first adjust to separation, to a different lifestyle, new surroundings, possibly a new school, and the new parents' own children, neighbors, and friends. Children from different cultural backgrounds often lose not only their home but also their culture when they are placed in a foster home of a different culture. Even if they get used to all these things, the children are still aware of the instability of their situation.

ALTERNATIVES TO FOSTER CARE

For these and other reasons, foster placement is considered a last resort in protective work. What, then, are the alternatives to foster care?

First, the social worker must be creative in examining means to protect the children in their own homes. The concept of *family preservation* may be one alternative to placement. Today, agencies advocate the use of informal support systems, such as extended family members, neighbors, the school, religious affiliations, and community groups. African American *kinsmen* and Hispanic *compadres* often provide resources for children of their cultures. Research has shown that placement of Native American children with Native American families increases their stability and self-concept. Increasing emphasis is now placed on *kinship care*, or involving the extended family of children as placement resources. These homes offer the child increased continuity and can be an integral part of the therapeutic plan (Boyd-Franklin, 2006; Farmer and Moyers, 2010; Hegar and Scannapieco, 1999; Rosenwald and Riley, 2010; Webb, 2011). Finding these resources and contracting with them to provide support for the family as placement opportunities are time-consuming, which may account for social services not fully using these systems.

Second, the exact reason for placement must be analyzed. Is the child really in imminent danger, or does placement represent an easy solution? Working with maltreating families can be terribly frustrating, whereas coordinating services, aided by competent foster parents, may be less so. If the request for placement originates from the birth parents, their motivations must be fully explored. Do they feel compelled to place their child, or are they asking for placement in response to stresses that seem overwhelming? Often, these issues can be addressed therapeutically without the removal of the children. And finally, the social service system must examine the family's potential for providing adequate child care. Would a variety of remedial and support services strengthen the family sufficiently so that placement could be avoided?

THERAPEUTIC POTENTIAL IN FOSTER CARE

In some situations, foster placement is inevitable. In these cases, steps should be taken to ensure that foster care provides the greatest therapeutic atmosphere possible. With children from different cultures, placements in foster homes of similar cultures may enhance the therapeutic effect. There are several inherent positive aspects for the child in placement.

Foster care provides an opportunity for diagnostic screening. In a somewhat controlled atmosphere that is relatively independent of parental influence, social workers can assess delayed development and explore the children's language abilities. Infants with failure to thrive syndrome or who exhibit other problems related to nurturance are fed carefully and monitored. Based on these assessments, the workers can derive appropriate treatment plans.

Despite the pressures inherent in foster care, the foster home provides the child with some distance from the fears and conflicts of his or her home environment. Children learn that they need not fear abuse, that their needs are met, and that they can begin to predict the behavior of the adults around them. Admittedly, not all children respond immediately, but foster care provides an atmosphere where the healing can begin to take place (Berrick, 2008; Rosenwald and Riley, 2010; Webb, 2011).

Foster parents provide new and more positive models for their charges. Well-screened and well-matched foster parents promote positive growth and development in the children. They present reasonable expectations and consistent discipline. Ideally, the marital relationship demonstrates to children that people can live together in trust and harmony.

Inherent in this assumption is that the agency effectively screened the foster parents initially and also took care to match this particular child with the household. Inadequate screening can result in foster parents responding to the pathology of the foster child and themselves replicating the dysfunctional behavior of the natural parents.

With foster care, the agency can remedy problems in the child's developmental delays, nutritional deficits, and unmet medical needs. The family gives the child adequate stimulation, which begins to compensate for development delays. They make medical appointments and administer medication. The foster home represents a controlled environment, where some degree of consistency in these remedial procedures can be ensured (Crosson-Tower, 2013; Mallon, 2005; Pecora, Whittaker, Maluccio, Barth, and Plotnick, 2001; Webb, 2011).

One type of foster home that is much in demand is the home that is willing to accept children who are HIV infected. Some states have now developed specialized programs for these children. Most programs require certain qualifications of these foster parents. Similar to families that provide foster care for a child with any type of serious medical condition, these families must be ready to accommodate numerous medical appointments. In addition, these foster parents must be educated as to the transmission of HIV and the fact that their foster child may eventually die. This is not something that every foster family can take on. For that reason, these families are often aggressively recruited and require special training and support (Taylor-Brown, 1991).

The responsibility rests on protective agencies to structure the placement of the child in order to ensure the greatest therapeutic success. Screening of foster parents is important. Attempts should be made in recruiting to find foster parents from all cultures represented by the children placed. Protective workers must know the backgrounds of foster parents, lest they be put in situations that, replicating their own unresolved experiences, they are unable to handle. The agency should know what type of child behavior is unacceptable to these parents. The foster parents may have their own conflicts that prevent them from parenting particular children. Kinship care homes (mentioned earlier) provide excellent resources for children. But these homes must also be screened to ensure that the placement serves the best interests of the children.

If foster parents are considered part of a team effort to help the child, they will be more amenable to honesty in the screening process and cooperation with the agency. (Unfortunately, some agencies have not yet learned to regard these individuals as team members, adding to the difficulty of the foster parents' job.)

The birth parents, too, should be seen as part of the team, though traditionally this has not been practiced. The birth parents are seen as clients and, although in some respect they remain so, their roles change slightly after placement of the children. The goal is to ensure what is best for the children, and in this regard, the birth parents are as vital a resource as foster parents. Being encouraged to be team members may reduce the competition between these two sets of parents. It is also beneficial for the children to witness a good working relationship between their guardians. Successful placement depends on the continuation of ties between the children and their birth parents.

THE ROLE AND IMPORTANCE OF THE BIOLOGICAL PARENTS

Despite the maltreatment the children suffered from their biological parents, the children are, nevertheless, closely tied to and involved with these individuals. The children's experience of living with their parents caused them to adopt certain personality traits and habits. Children identify with their parents, and cutting off this relationship is like severing a part of the child from himself or herself. Criticisms of the birth parents are felt by the child as criticisms of himself or herself.

Because of these ties, children who are totally separated from their parents develop unrealistic ideas about them. They may idealize and deny or, conversely, exaggerate their maltreatment. For healthy growth, children need to learn to see their parents as multidimensional. Continued supportive contact can help them do this.

Feeling abandoned, foster children often perceive that their own weakness, inherent badness, or behavior caused their parents to leave them. Continued contact assures the child that the parents still care. The child may sincerely miss the parents he or she lived with since birth (Crosson-Tower, 2013; Grant, 3004; Karson, 2001).

Instead of engendering feelings of powerlessness and defensiveness, social workers can help natural parents play an integral part in the child's adjustment to foster placement and emotional growth and eventually facilitate the child's return home. Continued contact with the parents can actually help the child relate better to the foster parents. If children are able to process their feelings of separation and loss and take comfort that their parents care enough to visit, their energies will be freer to bond with the foster parents.

Visiting with the parents allows the child to see them more realistically. When the birth parents are relieved of the burden of continuous child care, they may be able to treat the child better during visits and lay the foundation for a more positive relationship. With treatment, parents may be changing and visits will allow them brief periods when they can try out their new understanding and their skills in child management (Crosson-Tower, 2013; Webb, 2011).

The more the birth parents feel part of the team, the easier the return of the child will be. Increasingly, agencies are considering kinship placements to keep the children within the extended family, making a transition home perhaps even smoother. Some agencies suggest that parents—as well as the foster parents—sign a contract that outlines their responsibilities. Such a contract gives the parents a sense of control and purpose, so that they will not need to feel in a position of having to fight about what is being done or sabotage the child's placement. Even when the outcome is the final termination of parental rights, the parents can be helped to believe that they have chosen what is best for the child.

There are always cases in which parents are not willing to cooperate. These situations are especially difficult for children, social workers, and foster parents alike. If parents have been approached as part of the therapeutic team and are still unable to respond in a positive manner, other steps must be taken (e.g., permanent termination of parental rights and adoption).

THE ROLE OF FOSTER PARENTS

It is understandable that foster parents may have difficulty seeing birth parents as part of the team. The biological parents have in some way harmed the child, a fact that most concerned foster parents cannot forget. The birth parents may be difficult to deal with, because their pathology often makes them uncooperative, inconsistent, and unpredictable. Their need for control and feelings of failure may result in the birth parents criticizing the foster parents. When children perceive this tension, they are apt to play one set of parents against the other.

Many foster parents describe the detrimental effects parental visits have on the children. Conflicted in a variety of ways, children respond to parental visits by regression, acting-out behaviors, and general periods of unhappiness. In their desire to protect the children, foster parents find themselves blaming and growing increasingly angry at the biological parents.

The intensity of these emotional conflicts might block cooperation between foster and birth parents. But when they are supported by the concerned social worker, foster parents can be extremely therapeutic in their approach to birth parents. Consider the following case:

> Anne Todd had been the foster mother to Jimmy for several months before his mother, Fran, began visiting. Jimmy, age 3, came into foster care because his severe neglect had caused major medical complications. When Fran requested visiting, Anne felt conflicted. Her family had grown to love Jimmy and deplored the condition in which he had come to them. But Anne also realized that the intent was to eventually return Jimmy to his mother. Not only must this mother be given an opportunity to learn to care for him, especially in light of his medical needs, but Jimmy missed his mother and talked of her often. With the support of the social worker, Anne set up regular visits with the birth mother.
>
> During these visits, the foster mother modeled proper care for Jimmy and encouraged Fran to emulate her. Fran began to confide in her son's foster mother and derived support from the relationship. Anne encouraged Fran to accompany her to Jimmy's frequent medical appointments and eventually suggested that Fran take the responsibility for these appointments herself. Although frustrated by Fran's failure to show up on occasion and having to explain this to Jimmy, Anne realized that her continued patience could only benefit her foster child. In fact, Jimmy seemed to bask in the positive relationship between his foster mother and his birth mother. He delighted in the security of having two families.
>
> When an agency conference finally concluded that Fran would never be able to adequately care for Jimmy's medical needs, Anne felt a mixture of sadness and relief. Now the foster mother was able to help Fran accept the future, and Anne felt she had done all she could to facilitate the most therapeutic environment for both mother and child.

Like Anne, foster parents can serve as models for birth parents, demonstrating appropriate child care. They can ease the transition for the child from home to placement and home again by careful explanation and by allowing the child to express feelings. The foster parent who recognizes the child's need for contact with birth parents, facilitates visiting, and helps to interpret the parents' inconsistencies so that the child sees sides of the natural parents is of great benefit to the child. Criticism of the child's parents not only puts the child on the defensive but also robs him or her of the opportunity to see how adults can cooperate despite their faults (Crosson-Tower, 2013; Sinclair, Wilson, and Gibbs, 2004).

Some foster parents act as advocates for the children and for their parents. For example, because they are in closer contact with the child than is the social worker, they often recognize problems that go undetected by the social service agency. Intervening with the school or with medical facilities on the child's behalf is a common task. Since foster parents are often present during visiting between the birth parents and children, they are in a position to advocate for parents who are interacting more positively with their children.

Being a foster parent is not easy. Foster parents must learn to cope not only with natural parents but also with children who have a variety of behavioral and emotional problems. As one foster mother described it, "Working with foster kids means learning to anticipate their needs. Most of these kids haven't learned to tell you what they want. When they are hurt, they are more apt to withdraw or to act out than to tell you. You try to figure out what's wrong, but it's not always easy" (Nutt, 2006).

In reaction to their past experiences, foster children arrive with established behaviors, some of which require the foster parents' patience and creativity. Chronic masturbation, stealing, lying, eating disorders, and pyromania are just a few problems foster parents face. In addition to the behavior of the children, foster parents must deal with the social service agency and its bureaucratic requirements, red tape, and high staff turnover. Each new social worker who takes a child's case may have a different way of operating and thus cause confusion for the foster parents. With heavy caseloads, social workers are not always available when foster parents most need them. Foster parents learn to be resourceful, but the support of the agency and an occasional pat on the back are still helpful.

The competent foster parent is integral in the treatment for the child. To retain competent foster parents and prepare them to meet the myriad crises they must handle, agencies are supplying more extensive and effective training, providing more consistent support, and making better resources available to them. When placements are well planned and when foster parents are well screened, trained, and given adequate support, the foster care system can be a valuable resource for abused children.

OTHER PLACEMENT FOR ABUSED
OR NEGLECTED CHILDREN

Two other types of placement—residential and adoptive—are considered as last resorts. Residential treatment usually indicates that the child's behavior has deteriorated so greatly that he or she would be too disruptive for a foster home. Adoptive placement terminates parental rights because the court or the social services system has determined that the parents are unable to care for the children.

Residential Treatment

As the culmination of unsuccessful attempts at placement in foster care, the abused or neglected child goes into a residential treatment setting. As a result, children arrive there with very little trust and with the firm conviction that they are failures.

The advantages of residential treatment include providing the children with a less intensive emotional atmosphere than may occur in relationships with parental figures. Since their ability to trust has been severely hampered, the children are often unable to tolerate close emotional ties. In addition, children have a greater variety of models, one or more of whom they might feel comfortable and identify with. Behavior—especially acting out—that would not be tolerated in a foster home is more easily accepted in a residential setting.

At the same time, residential treatment provides the structure needed by some disturbed children. The daily environment is regulated to be therapeutic, and the training staff oversees the children's activities and monitors their progress. The setting, the staff members, and peer-group pressure are conducive to concentrated treatment (Crosson-Tower, 2013; Pecora et al., 2001).

The assumption in residential treatment, as in foster care, is that the child will return to his or her home or will be placed for adoption. In an institution, the emphasis is on the rehabilitation of the child, rather than helping him or her await the parents' rehabilitation. The residential center staff acts as a therapeutic family, rather than a substitute family. By the time children reach residential placement, their problems are complex and their treatment needs are more intensive. Although classwork is often part of the program, sometimes the child goes to the public school but is monitored closely. In addition, the staff offers a variety of therapies that include counseling, group counseling, and particular remedial services (e.g., special education tutoring, medical, and dental treatment).

When it seems likely that the child will go home, the staff emphasizes communication with the family and the family's caseworker. Although family involvement is encouraged, the child's parents are not always ready or able to cooperate. By the time a child reaches residential care, the parents may be less than optimistic about their child rejoining the family. In fact, because of their guilt, they may feel relief that the child is in an institution. The parents sometimes justify that residential treatment proves the child's removal from the home was his or her fault and not theirs. Some parents may want to be involved but don't know how, and many institutions are geographically distant, so transportation is difficult (Crosson-Tower, 2013).

To ease the child's return home, the parents must be involved. It would be unrealistic to thrust a child into the same dysfunctional environment and expect him or her to thrive. Through parental involvement in the residential setting, the child can be helped to recognize the problem in their home environment, and the parents can be treated in support groups and individually to help them adjust to and handle the child's issues.

When a child is expected to return home, visits that increase in length and frequency aid both family and child to make the transition. When the child was put in residential treatment, the family balance changed, and only with careful preparation will the family be able to accept the removed child and attain a new sense of balance.

Adoptive Placement

A child deserves a stable environment, and if the family will never be able to provide it, adoption may take place. The adoption process with an abused or neglected child should be undertaken slowly and with much preparation. The child must grow to trust the adoption worker, whose role is to prepare him or her for adoption. The child needs time to grieve over the loss of the natural parents and to understand some of the reasons the parents could not keep him or her. Only after this grieving has been completed can the child bond with the new parents.

One practice now used by some agencies is the *life book* (see Webb, 2011), a written account or scrapbook depicting the child's life to date. Adoption workers encourage the child to create this book, which the child takes with him or her to the adoptive home. The adoptive parents can then talk openly with the child about his or her past and help the child see the natural parents as multidimensional human beings. Witnessing the past merging with the present enables the child to adjust more easily to adoption.

Parents who adopt abused and neglected children must be carefully screened and educated about the residual effects of maltreatment. Unlike babies, older maltreated children come with a past that may deeply inhibit their ability to trust. Many agencies now train parents more intensively to ensure the success of the adoptive placement.

SUMMARY

An abused or neglected child may need to be placed in foster care. Despite symbolizing failure to the parents and causing instability for the child, foster placement does have advantages. The child is provided with an opportunity to learn to trust in a more functional environment with models who, ideally, embody the more positive aspects of parenting. The agency can use this time for a more accurate diagnosis and supply remedial services when needed.

Although the tendency is for the birth parents to feel powerless and, in compensation, criticize both the foster parents and the agency, those parents who are considered part of the therapeutic team are more likely to be engaged in the best interest of the child. The foster parents must deal with difficulties presented by the birth parents as well as those inherent in taking a foster child. Many natural parents are able to look to their children's substitute parents as models for positive parenting.

Abused and neglected children who cannot tolerate foster care are often placed in residential settings. The positive aspects of such a placement are that the child is spared the more intense emotional relationships of a home setting; the child has available a variety of models with whom to identify; and the child is provided with much-needed structure, but the institutional setting can better deal with behavior not ordinarily tolerated in a home. If the child is expected to return home, it is important to include the parents as much as possible in the therapy and planning for the child.

When the parents do not appear to be capable of caring for the child in the future, adoptive placement is an option. Children who are placed for adoption require counseling and adequate preparation in order to ensure that this, the last resort in the treatment process, is therapeutically successful.

Chapter 15

Adults Abused as Children

The last few chapters have explored intervention and treatment of child abuse and neglect as a way of alleviating the child's suffering. When society intervenes, it does so with the hope that the children will at least be able to understand the abuse and neglect and thus allow them to face adulthood with the freedom to make appropriate choices. Although social service intervention is not always successful, past victims of abuse who had not disclosed are now coming forward and elaborating on how their isolation from any kind of help intensified their suffering.

SOCIETY'S MISCONCEPTIONS

Society has accepted as truth several myths regarding adults who were abused as children. There are, however, other perspectives to consider.

Myth #1

The individual who was abused or neglected will abuse or neglect his or her own children.

This myth is actually the misinterpretation of a much-used statistic gleaned from studies by several researchers that showed that of those parents who physically and sexually abuse their children, a large percentage had themselves been abused as children. This does not mean, however, that individuals who have been abused will necessarily become abusers. Healing the hurt and changing the pattern of abuse are possible. Sometimes, insight, understanding, and thought are sufficient to turn the abused from repeating the mistakes of their childhood.

On the other hand, neglect statistically tends toward a multigenerational pattern. Parents who neglect fail not only to meet their children's needs but also to provide adequate parenting models. But once again, adults who recognize the dysfunctional patterns of their families of origin may be better able to work toward overcoming them in their nuclear families.

Myth #2

Abused and neglected children become deviant adults, involved in crime, drugs, or prostitution.

Of those involved in crime, drugs, and prostitution, many were abused or neglected, but not all past victims lean toward a deviant lifestyle in adulthood. For every inmate of a correctional facility who was abused as a child, there may be 50 or more who were abused but have not turned toward deviant behavior. Abuse can create anger and bitterness, but each victim directs or channels this anger differently.

Myth #3

The effects of abuse or neglect are irreparable and render the future adult incapable of leading a fulfilling and happy life.

Once again, the myth distorts the whole picture. The abuse or neglect is irreparable only in that it is history: It happened, and that fact cannot be undone. The child is left with scars, but these scars need not prevent the emerging adult from leading a fulfilling life.

Successful survivors of child abuse say they have learned not to live in the past. The past—with its memories of abuse—represents pain and a sense of helplessness and powerlessness. Control of the individual's life was seen as outside himself or herself. To survive and succeed, the victim must recognize the following facts:

- The abuse or neglect did happen and exists as part of one's childhood history.
- At that time, the victim had little control (by virtue of being a child) over what was happening.
- Although the victim cannot change the past, he or she can affect the future.
- By taking control of one's own life, one can have a fulfilling life in spite of the residual scars of childhood.

Many past victims have learned to regain control of their own lives and have overcome what were the burdens of childhood. Whether or not they have complete control of their lives, the reality is that adults abused as children *survived* the abuse. For this reason, many authors and therapists refer to these individuals as abuse *survivors*. Some survivors point out that survival is not a destination but rather that surviving the after-effects of childhood maltreatment is an ongoing process.

REASONS FOR ADULTS' DISCLOSURE

If the survivor's history of abuse or neglect is not made obvious through some form of deviant behavior, how is it recognized? Some past victims never disclose that they suffered maltreatment. Although some do attempt to tell a therapist or friend, they are often not heard. They may not know the words to use, or more likely, the therapist or friend is not able to be receptive, possibly because of his or her own conflicts. One survivor's story emphasizes this problem:

"I was in therapy for almost nine years. I had problems in my marriage, an array of affairs, and an overwhelming fear of failure. I had pushed what had happened to me—the fact that my father sexually and physically abused me—out of my mind. But I began having nightmares—remembering only bits. I kept trying to describe the dreams to my therapist. Finally, I was able to piece it together. I remembered exactly what my father

had done. It was as if my therapist couldn't believe it. But who could make up the horrible, bizarre details of what happened!

"Soon after I told him, my therapist suggested we end our sessions. I was devastated. I vowed then to never again share my horrible secret. That was 12 years ago—and I haven't told anyone again—until now."

Fortunately, therapists are now becoming better trained in the area of abuse, especially sexual abuse. Part of this training should aim to make them aware of why they are reluctant to hear about child maltreatment.

Survivors disclose their sexual or physical abuse in later life for various reasons discussed in the following sections.

Relationships

Relationships often determine the decision to talk about the experiences and feelings that had previously been a well-guarded secret. Some survivors want to be completely honest with their partners. There may be an element of need—the need to be accepted and loved by intimates in spite of any event or relationship in the past.

Low self-esteem may also push the survivor to disclose sexual abuse. These individuals, consciously or unconsciously, feel they have been tainted by the abuse and will, therefore, be rejected by their loved ones (Courtois, 2010; Dorias, 2009; Flynn, 2008; Isley, Isley, Freiburger, and McMackin, 2008; Levenkron and Levenkron, 2008; Many and Osopsky, 2012). Their ability to trust is often so limited that they are sure that husbands, wives, or lovers will never accept the evil that they feel surrounds them. The survivors often disbelieve accepting and sympathetic mates, but rejecting mates reinforce their damaged trust.

Sexual dysfunction in the present affects relationships. Past victims often avoid sexual intimacy and isolate themselves from relationships that lead to sex. Conversely, they sometimes behave promiscuously, which excludes closeness or deep feelings of attachment. When a relationship does have meaning, however, the survivor often finds it difficult to feel comfortable. Consider the case of Lisa:

> Lisa was a college senior who sought counseling because she was deeply involved with a fellow student but could not tolerate his sexual advances. The two had dated for six months with no sexual contact. When Ed initiated sex with affection and tenderness, Lisa began having anxiety attacks. Subsequent counseling revealed that Lisa had been sexually abused by a brother for several years. She had felt close to this brother, but when the sexual abuse began, she felt betrayed and used. Now she saw Ed's sexual advances in the same light.

Sex therapists seeing couples who complain of sexual dysfunction often discover that one or both partners were victims of sexual abuse. There is some evidence that physical abuse also creates a mistrust of sexual involvement.

Pressures of Adulthood

Developmental issues also precipitate disclosure in the late teens and early adulthood. The first deeply intimate relationship is one such issue. However, stress and fears related to career or financial success may cause the survivor to feel undeserving or unprepared and thus precipitate disclosure. Past victims frequently do not relate these present issues with the abuse and usually only discover the connection while in therapy. The birth and growth of the survivor's own children stimulate memories of the individual's own dysfunctional childhood:

> "When Robbie was born, I kept wondering—no, more than wondering, I was obsessed with what kind of a mother I'd be. My mother was an alcoholic, and my father beat my brother and me. To make up for the way my mother neglected me, I was probably overprotective. But the worst part was that whenever Bill touched Robbie, I'd get really tense. 'Don't hurt him,' I'd say, as if my husband would. It got so bad that I'd hardly let Bill touch our son.
>
> I knew I had to get some help. I told my friend about the abuse. I'd never told anyone. Ours was such a perfect family. My mother hid her drinking well, and no one would have ever suspected that Dad beat us. But I began to realize that I was seeing all fathers as hurting their kids."

As children grow, parents see themselves in their offspring and consequently fear for their children's safety. Often, this fear leads the adults to talk about their abuse:

> Jane began having severe headaches and muscle pains when April was 8 years old. Concerned about her mother, April often came directly home from school to be with her. Jane's mother insisted that Jane seek medical advice. No organic reason could be found, and the physician suggested that Jane seek therapy. Jane refused. Several months later, April's teacher expressed her concern about April's preoccupation and inattention in school. When Jane realized that April's fears were of her dying, she sought help.
>
> Intensive therapy disclosed that at age 8, Jane had been repeatedly sexually abused by a neighbor. She began to understand her fears about April's walking to school or going out in the neighborhood as an intense need to protect her daughter from what had happened to her.

Loss, Depression, or Trauma

Loss is often a problem for those who have survived dysfunctional families. Losses in adulthood may precipitate a need to face the original loss—the deprivation of a loving, protecting, or nonabusive family. Thus, disclosure can be associated with death of a loved one, death of the perpetrator or nonprotecting parent, children leaving home, loss of a job, and various other normal changes in life.

And finally, some past victims begin to explore their childhoods to overcome persistent, nonspecific, and often nondebilitating depression, usually caused by low self-esteem:

> "I just never thought much of myself," said Bruce. "I don't know why, but I just figured I wasn't worth much." Bruce had been raised by two alcoholic parents who were severely neglectful. He had learned early how to survive and, as a result, had made a success of his life. It was not until he considered the pain of his childhood, though, that he could even begin to appreciate his own successes.

It is rare that a flash of insight prompts disclosure of an abusive or neglectful family background. Often, the perception and understanding of past dysfunctional family life are clouded by present life stresses. The pieces of memory emerge slowly and must be fitted together in an understandable pattern so that the victim can face them. Some individuals struggle for a lifetime to gain this understanding. Others prefer not to risk reexperiencing the pain and so never discuss what happened to them. Some sexual abuse survivors are jolted into reexperiencing and remembering childhood abuse by trauma in adult life (Courtois, 2010; Many and Osopsky, 2012). For example, many adult rape victims are reminded of issues they have repressed as they attempt to put the current rape in perspective.

For most survivors, the symptoms of the residual effects of the abuse precede the recognition of their origin. Therefore, it is important to consider the residual effects in some depth.

RESIDUAL EFFECTS OF CHILD ABUSE AND NEGLECT

In the 1970s, Ray E. Helfer—pediatrician, therapist, and expert in the area of child abuse—coined the acronym *WAR*, for the *World of Abnormal Rearing* (Helfer, 1978), to refer to the experiences of children who were exposed to dysfunctional families. Victims of WAR, Helfer says, have not learned some basic lessons. As mentioned in Chapter 5, these unlearned skills include the following:

1. How to get their needs met appropriately
2. How to delay gratification
3. How to make decisions
4. How to take responsibility for their own actions
5. How to separate feelings from actions

Because symptoms may mask the real problem, therapists often do not recognize that their clients did not learn these tasks. The residual effects of neglect, abuse, and sexual abuse are quite similar (see Table 15.1). However, there is value in considering the way in which these emotional scars manifest themselves depending on the type of maltreating family.

EFFECTS FROM THE NEGLECTING FAMILY

Studies about the residual effects of child maltreatment abound, as do self-help books for survivors. Although a significant number of adult survivors experienced neglect as children, little information concentrates on neglect alone. Thus, we must either use older studies, like those done by Polansky and his colleagues (1972, 1981), or assume that those studies that discuss childhood maltreatment in general also include survivors of neglect.

Some critics have suggested that the categories of abuse and neglect should be combined when discussing the residual effects. But I have chosen to discuss them separately, despite the fact that they may overlap to varying degrees.

Trust

The personalities of all types of maltreatment survivors exhibit difficulty with trust. Trust is a basic aspect of socialization, and the development of our ability to trust begins in the first years of life. Society expects babies to be nurtured by a loving parent or parents

Table 15.1	Residual Effects of Familial Maltreatment		
Physical Abuse	**Neglect**	**Sexual Abuse**	
Difficulty trusting others	Difficulty trusting others	Difficulty trusting others	
Low self-esteem	Low self-esteem	Low self-esteem	
Anxiety and fears	Anger	Anxiety and fears	
Physical problems	Impaired object relations	Shame and guilt	
Anger	Impaired parenting abilities	Physical problems	
Internalization of aggression	Lowered intelligence	Anger	
Depression	Impaired development	Self-abusive tendencies	
Difficulty with touching	Verbal inaccessibility	Depression	
Inability to play	Inability to play	Difficulty with touching	
Difficulty with relationships	Difficulty with relationships	Inability to play	
Abuse of alcohol and drugs	Abuse of alcohol and drugs	Distorted view of body	
Perception of powerlessness	Perception of powerlessness	Difficulty with relationships	
		Abuse of alcohol and drugs	
		Perception of powerlessness	
		Sexual problems	

who allow them to develop free from harm. A child who does not receive these entitlements may not recognize it initially, but as an adult, the individual will begin to realize that his or her parents were emotionally unavailable (Gold, 2000; Poston and Lison, 2001; Rodriquez-Srednicki and Twaite, 2006).

In adulthood, the betrayal is reflected by these characteristics:

- An inability to trust others
- An inability to trust oneself
- An inability to trust the environment

Parents of neglected children provided little, or at least inconsistent, nurturing and support. Indifference characterizes the parents' relationship with their children, which becomes a pattern on which the children model their own behavior. Their expectations of support, attention, and stimulation become a distant memory (Briere, 1992; Lew, 2004). As adults, they no longer expect that their needs will be met, but these individuals desperately desire nurturance.

The result is that many past victims of neglect demonstrate dependency with little underlying trust. History has taught them that people are not trustworthy. Polansky et al. (1972) have described neglectful mothers, most of whom had been themselves neglected as children, as demonstrating an "absence of intense personal relationships beyond forlorn clinging, even to [their] children" (p. 54). So pervasive is this lack of hope and trust that it often infects the helpers who deal with neglectful families.

Required to provide for themselves at an early age, survivors of neglect might be expected to develop some degree of proficiency. Although past victims demonstrate an ability to survive despite incredible odds, they lack a true sense of trust in themselves. Not only have they lacked encouragement and stimulation to develop a healthy self-image, but they have also modeled themselves on parents who thought little of themselves. Comprehending that one was not loved can be so devastating that the survivor turns inward and assumes he or she must have deserved being treated with such indifference (Briere, 1992; Polansky et al., 1981). Lack of trust in oneself is manifested by an inability to make decisions, extremely low self-esteem, an inability to accept one's own accomplishments, and other types of self-defeating behavior.

Often, neglected children are exposed to deviant subcultures, the members of which see themselves as different from the greater society. The school and the community frequently accentuate these differences. In addition, many of these children have learning disabilities. The case of Chico illustrates how different some children feel:

> "I kept hearing from day one that nobody understood where we was comin' from," said Chico, the past victim of neglect in a largely rundown neighborhood. "The bunch of us in our block stuck together. We smoked grass and just did our thing. Our parents didn't care, and no one else did. But we got a reputation, see. They said we was tough, and we maybe tried to prove how tough we really was. I got so as I knew that if you wasn't from Broad Street, you wasn't worth trusting."

Chico's inability to trust permeated his life. He had difficulty in school and was frequently suspended, thus reinforcing his feelings that he could trust no one.

Anger

Anger often creates problems for the survivor. Feeling robbed of childhood, betrayed, and powerless, the adult reacts to the injustice with anger, which can become an intense rage. The past victim may turn the anger inward or act out the anger toward others.

Anger turned inward results in depression and self-abusive tendencies. Adele, severely neglected as a child, had difficulty parenting her own children. She demonstrated an emotional numbness and a stubbornly negative attitude that social workers confused with chronic depression.

For some neglected children, anger is expressed through aggressive or delinquent behavior. Polansky et al. (1972) refer to the process that leads to delinquency or acting out of anger as the *deprivation–aggression sequence*. Failure to meet a child's basic needs results in frustration. Frustration translates into aggression. Bender (1948) also attributes aggressive behavior to unmet needs: "Since the child is under the impression that adults can satisfy his needs, he considers any deprivation an act of aggression and reacts accordingly.... A failure in this regard is a deprivation and leads to frustration and reactive-aggressive response" (p. 360).

The life histories of famous killers such as Lee Harvey Oswald, James Earl Ray, Sirhan Sirhan, Jack Ruby, and Charles Manson are examples of maltreated children. Polansky et al. (1972) categorize this type of guilt-free expression of aggression as part of the deprivation–detachment sequence:

> The massive inhibition of feeling that derives from indifferent and unempathetic mothering amounts, we think, to a kind of splitting in the ego. Since the person is unable to be aware of his own hurts and suffering, he is certainly unable to empathize with those of others. Such a person can inflict suffering on other people then, with coldness and calculation of which more normal persons would be quite incapable. (p. 7)

Relational Imbalances

A failure to trust and low self-esteem, in addition to repressed or aggressively expressed anger, hamper the survivor's abilities to form satisfying relationships. Experience with an inconsistent, withholding family of origin limits the later adult's ability to give. The expectation of being unfulfilled and unnurtured is reinforced by merging with a similarly emotionally needy individual (Briere, 1992; Polansky et al., 1981). Consider this case:

> Joan was severely neglected as a child. Her mother had little time or energy for her five children. The care of them was left largely to Joan and her older brother, Rick. Joan left school at age 16 and worked in a fast-food restaurant. She was quiet and timid and found meeting customers difficult. She eventually got a job in the kitchen, where she did well. Harry was a fellow cook, and although they talked little, she realized that Harry's background was not unlike her own.
>
> When Joan was 18 and pregnant, she married Harry. In the years that followed, Joan returned from work to care for the young children, but she fought with Harry over his sexual pursuits of other women. Her dreams of being loved, protected, and cared for soon became illusions.

Past victims of neglect may never have learned how to negotiate, compromise, or problem solve—skills that are vital for the endurance of relationships. Instead, their fairytale thinking, combined with no models for appropriate relationships and a severely limited ability to trust, greatly reduces the chance of having healthy relationships. Often, by recognizing these problems, survivors increase their chances of having satisfying relationships.

Low Self-Esteem

The neglected child feels at fault for the indifference of his or her parents, but the caregivers may have directly contributed to the feelings of blame or worthlessness. These and other such statements echo through the memories of many past victims:

> "If it weren't for you, your father would not have left."

> "You kids drive me nuts; that's why I drink."

> "Can't you do anything right, you stupid kid?"

Sanford and Donovan (1992), in their assessment of the origin of women's self-esteem, comment as follows:

> As children, we could not distinguish unfair expectations (which had nothing to do with us) from realistic assessments of who we were. And because we were absolutely dependent on our parents for our survival, we looked up to them. Hence, when they said, we are "plain," "stupid," or "lazy," we did not question their credentials, much less the fairness of their expectations. Their judgment became reality to us. We were not likely to pick and choose among the labels they applied to us. We integrated them all, to some degree, even when they were overwhelmingly negative. (p. 55)

Although these authors refer to only women's self-esteem, the integration of negative descriptors certainly describes the experiences of men, as well.

As children exemplify these negatives in their behavior, parents respond with increased rejection. School personnel, neighbors, and other children react to the symptoms of the child's distress, rather than the causes. Attention-seeking behavior is met with criticism, suspension, or expulsion from school. The culmination of these experiences is the individual's view of himself or herself as fundamentally at fault, unworthy, and a bad person.

Impaired Social Skills

Neglected children, feeling negative about themselves and perhaps about others, often demonstrate impaired social skills. Limited stimulation has impeded development and possibly lowered their intellectual abilities. Increased responsibilities and the need to fight for existence hamper the adults' ability to play or enjoy the simple pleasures of life. Past victims often describe their recreational activities as ways of escaping unfulfilled lives, rather than as enjoyments to be savored. The impulsivity that characterizes the neglectful family often creates adults who have difficulty with responsibility and who opt for escape when they feel stressed (Polansky et al., 1981).

Polansky and colleagues (1981) describe *verbal inaccessibility*—or the inability to effectively communicate—as a problem in dealing with neglectful families. A poor command of language and the inability to conceptualize and verbalize feelings stem largely from a lack of experience in talking with people other than on a superficial level. This verbal inaccessibility is often a contributor to, as well as a by-product of, impaired intellectual development. Until they develop proficiency in communication, survivors of neglect continue to feel isolated and misunderstood.

Substance Abuse

The use of drugs and alcohol is decidedly a cultural issue, but its prevalence as a form of escape or a means to ease social interaction is common in individuals with impaired social skills. The influence of addictive substances in the neglected child's life may have been significant, and the use of these substances as an adult may be a result of modeling, peer pressure, identification, or a variety of other issues. Even those who are not practicing alcoholics exhibit the symptoms of alcoholic behavior, and there ceases to be a personality distinction between the active alcoholic and those who suffer the effects of parental alcoholism.

Physical Problems

Insufficient care promotes health problems in later years. Nutrition alone has been tied to impeded growth, lower intelligence, poor teeth, and a variety of other problems (Dubowitz, 1999; Polansky et al., 1981). Some children suffer throughout life from the effects of neglect:

> At age 2, after he swallowed a product designed to unclog kitchen drains, Simon's mouth and throat had to be reconstructed. It was unclear whether Simon's swallowing the substance was accidental or intentional because his mother had been both neglectful and abusive in the past. Even after treatment, Simon had difficulty swallowing, and throughout his adulthood, he complained of feeling that he was choking.

The body responds to emotional as well as physical care. Past victims of neglect often complain of physical problems that originated in their physiological and emotional history. Physical symptoms require attention, but often the complaints are ill-defined remnants of a lifetime of poor care as well as chronic stress (Dubowitz, 1999; Gold, 2000; Polansky et al., 1972). Although often very real, victims' somatized problems require that they pamper themselves and ask for attention from others, a right they may have been denied in childhood.

Although the physical and emotional problems of adults, for whom neglect was a by-product of alcoholism or abuse, have been documented, little attention has been directed to the scars of neglect itself. Studies (Dubowitz, 1999; Polansky et al., 1981) attest to the continuation of the neglectful cycle from generation to generation. But the experience of the individual who breaks the pattern is not as well documented. "The adult's remembrance of childhood deprivation is masked by the merciful process of repression, which is part of the adaptability of the human ego" (Polansky et al., 1981, p. 6).

EFFECTS FROM THE PHYSICALLY ABUSING FAMILY

Many of the problems of the survivors of neglectful families are duplicated in the adults who were physically abused as children. The difference is that neglect is an *omission*, whereas abuse more often represents a *commission*. The neglected child may be chronically uncared for or unattended to, whereas the abused child may only suffer intermittently. However, the nonabusive periods—filled with parental stimulation, attention, and contrition—confuse the developing child.

Trust

Difficulty with trust becomes a manifestation of the recognition that life—and those who represent that life—is unpredictable. Life's unpredictability is a given, but the past victim of abuse has learned that the unpredictable event is usually hurtful. In an instant, a loving mother or father would instead scream, hit, or threaten. Therefore, to trust was to become even more vulnerable. To be cautious and anticipate the abuse, the child would hide and try to avoid the situation that seemed to stimulate the abuse. Many adult survivors become particularly adept at anticipating and avoiding conflict, while others flee from intimacy in the fear that closeness is synonymous with vulnerability to pain.

Isolation, based largely on their inability to trust others, is a significant problem for both abusive parents and for past victims of physical abuse (Briere, 1992). As adults, survivors feel that by not risking trust, they will not be betrayed or hurt. In fact, they often lack trust in their own ability to find others who will not hurt them. The result is a cautious, ever-vigilant individual who isolates himself or herself and often builds up a protective barrier. That was the case with Nancy:

"Anyone would have said I was the model of mental health," laughed Nancy, with a tinge of irony. "I was president of everything—from women's groups to PTA to Toastmistress to the historical society. You name it, and I was in a leadership role. And was I busy! I had little time for much else. I was probably a good leader in that I got things done, but my biggest problem was that I couldn't delegate. Once I tried, but the woman didn't do the task the way I thought it should be done. That clinched it. I knew that no one would follow through as I could.

"I guess that's what happened to my marriage, too. I just had trouble with closeness. Ned told me that I never trusted him. I really didn't, I guess. I was sure he'd find someone more interesting and more desirable. When he did, I wasn't at all surprised. It took me awhile before I found out though. I was so busy I didn't realize what was happening. When I did learn of his affair, I looked around for someone to commiserate with, but there was no one there. I realized that my hyperactivity was my way of shielding myself from trusting anyone enough to let them get to know me well. I had acquaintances from my committees but no real friends."

Anger

For survivors of abuse, anger is a familiar emotion but one that has been so integral to their upbringing that they often have difficulty recognizing it. The anger they feel over being abused and unprotected is turned inward or projected outward.

Turning anger inward usually results in depression or self-abusive behavior. The display of anger through aggression results not only from frustration but also from the child victim's identification with the aggressor. The physically abused child learned from observation that anger is synonymous with physical aggression. The child perceived that the abuser had power by virtue of his or her violent behavior.

As the child grew into adulthood, he or she felt that the only way to have power was to take it. This individual did not learn that the feeling of anger need not be followed by physical action. Frustrated, overwhelmed, and needy, the past victim, now a parent, may lash out at his or her own children. By learning to identify this anger as his or her own and learning to channel it, this parent can, however, avoid the abuse of his or her children.

Relational Imbalances

Crippled by the inability to fully trust and therefore to achieve true intimacy, the survivors of abuse seek out the familiar—people who behave similarly to the abuser or the nonprotecting parent of the past. By so doing, these individuals unconsciously predispose themselves to abusive treatment, such as battering, emotional abuse, and alcoholism (Bogarty and Toler, 2002; Lew, 2004; Many and Osopsky, 2012; Rodriquez-Srednicki and Twaite, 2006; Sonkin, 1998). Or past victims join together in symbiotic relationships with others who experienced the same types of emotional problems.

Symbiosis may occur with a shift from an enmeshed family of origin into a marital relationship. Feeling dependent on parents but often resenting that dependence, the survivor often marries young in the hope that this new husband or wife will provide a conflict-free and nurturing relationship. Yet the expectation on the part of each partner is to be taken care of by the other. But spouses' dependency on one another is not rewarded, partially because the individuals cannot fully trust each other and because both have deeply unmet needs and unrealistic expectations. The result is anger and disillusionment. Anger further alienates the couple but increases their need to cling to each other, in hostile dependency and the hope that their needs may somehow be met. Frustrated, the couple often turn to their children for nurturance. These children then carry the burdens of their parents' unfinished business into their own adulthoods.

Noted family therapist Murray Bowen (1966) terms this fusion and inability to break with the family of origin as *undifferentiation*. Undifferentiated individuals have great difficulty developing relationships with anyone but those who harbor similar needs (Bowen, 1966; Titleman and Schoenewolf, 2003).

Fear of physical contact often creates problems in intimate relationships. Touch may have been only hurtful in childhood and beatings the only physical contact the child experienced.

Low Self-Esteem

Children who are physically abused, like those who are neglected, attribute the cause of their parents' behavior to themselves. Abused children assume that the punishment inflicted on them resulted from their misdeeds, regardless of the fact that the misdeeds were not specified. The feeling of being inherently wrong or at fault follows children into adulthood and colors their behavior.

This thinking also creates distinct splits in how these adults view other people or issues. They often view the world in black-and-white or good-and-bad terms. They see their parents as good; otherwise, they would have to admit and grieve over their loss of nurturing. It follows, then, that the victims are all bad and that others in their lives surely are better than they are. Therefore, survivors of abuse continue to see themselves as unable to live up to the actions or the expectations of those around them.

For some, protection is the only recourse. They may assume an aggressive or even hostile demeanor. Some past victims use humor to justify their existence and protect themselves against the depression of never being good enough. The underlying drive for these individuals, whether they manifest it in their behavior or protect themselves against feeling inferior, derives from their inability to believe that anyone could find them worthwhile since their parents did not (Briere, 1992; Cloitre, Koenen, and Cohen, 2006; Gold, 2000; Schwartz, 2000).

Coping Skills

Like neglected children, adults who were physically abused as children battle feelings of powerlessness, have somatic symptoms, escape through substance abuse, and are unable to play or enjoy themselves. Unlike past victims of neglect, who may never accumulate enough psychic energy, survivors of abuse often compensate through overachievement.

Some achievement-driven past victims precipitate stress with which they have not learned to deal. Life at home was often controlled and regimented. Parents made decisions, and children's input was discouraged or discounted. As a result, survivors never learned to solve problems in a logical manner. As adults, their making even the smallest decision often causes a major crisis. Partialization may truly be out of their grasp. Many past victims find themselves easily overwhelmed, which leads to acute anxiety, physical symptoms, loss of control over temper, substance abuse, or a total inability to function. Learning to consciously separate problems into their various components and proceeding to function in a step-by-step fashion are necessary for the survivor to begin to feel in control (Cloitre et al., 2006; Gold, 2000; Sonkin, 1998).

LONG-TERM EFFECTS OF DOMESTIC VIOLENCE

The attention given to the long-term effects of domestic violence is relatively recent. In fact, it is only within the last decade that protective services agencies have developed units devoted to intervention with families in which children witness the battering of one parent by another. For this reason, the life-long trauma to the individual has been discussed more in antidotal form than as the subject of research findings. Increasingly, however, consideration is being given to the adults who witnessed violence as children.

In a recent study of 1,099 male batterers who were ordered by the court to receive treatment, Murrell, Christoff, and Henning (2007) found that there was an increased likelihood for these men to inflict on their wives and children the same violence they witnessed or experienced in childhood. In addition, the violence was often intensified. In contrast, some survivors who witnessed domestic violence as children have the opposite response. As Margarita put it:

> "I still abhor violence! I flinch whenever anyone yells, expecting that the blows will come next. I have trouble trusting men, especially those who have loud voices or who are big. And I don't trust anyone to protect me ... either man or woman. Neither my mother or father did when I was little. I cannot believe that anyone can now!"

More research needs to be done on adults who witnessed violence as children. The current interest in domestic violence may well lead to this additional research.

EFFECTS FROM A SEXUALLY ABUSING FAMILY

Because of the attention brought by survivors and by the women's movement, sexually abusing families are widely researched. Adult past victims of incest demonstrate many of the same symptoms as those from other dysfunctional families, but the taboo associated with sexual abuse—and especially incest—stimulates additional problems that plague adult past victims. The necessity of keeping the secret often augments adults' feelings of anger and guilt. Being beaten does not carry the same degree of censure in our society as being sexually abused within one's own family. Society, therefore, intensifies the symptoms and feelings of the adult who was a victim of child sexual abuse.

In their classic work, Finkelhor and Browne (1985) cite four major categories of trauma resulting from child sexual abuse: betrayal, traumatic sexualization, stigmatization, and powerlessness. These categories can be most useful in understanding the effects of this type of maltreatment.

Betrayal

Trust is as fundamental an issue for the sexual abuse survivor as it is for past victims of other maltreatment. Betrayal of this trust is often devastating. As a child, the individual trusted the parents and often felt that this trust was respected and understood. Recognition that the victim was used for the abuser's pleasure is confusing and hurtful:

> Donna describes the sexual abuse by her father as not fitting the picture. "He was the most loving, giving individual I ever met. He had infinite patience with me, unlike my mother, who could be abrupt and demanding. I just assumed that when he started touching me and telling me it was okay, he was right. I had a feeling that it was strange, but in those days, I believed my father implicitly. When a friend and I read a book about an unhealthy relationship between a father and daughter, I was really hurt by the disgust my friend registered. I was so confused. Now I'm just angry. How could he do that when I trusted him so much?"

Not only did one parent abuse the child, but the other failed to protect her. The result for the adult past victim is a sense of mistrust (especially of members of the sex of the perpetrator), anger, grief, and often depression. The adult feels not only unable to trust but inadequate to judge who is trustworthy. This, in turn, makes past victims more vulnerable to further victimization (Finkelhor and Browne, 1985; Levenkron and Levenkron, 2008; Many and Osopsky, 2012; Russell, 1999; Sonkin, 1998). Many minorities, especially African Americans, also experience betrayal at the hands of the system designed to help them. When racially imbalanced attitudes and policies further victimize the victim, her or his sense of betrayal is intensified.

Traumatic Sexualization

Traumatic sexualization refers to the child's premature indoctrination into adult sexuality and the confusion this process involves. During the years when children should be learning gradually about sexuality, the perpetrator equates sex with affection and rewards the child for sexual behavior. The result for adult victims is not only the confusion between sex and affection but also a distorted perception of sexual norms. Often, these individuals compensate in promiscuity or prostitution.

Promiscuity seems a consequence of self-destructive tendencies that may originate in repetition compulsion; that is, individuals attempt to alleviate their anxiety and perhaps recapture the pleasure experienced with the abusing parent. The original relationship's pain and pleasure and betrayal and intimacy become paradoxically entwined in the performance of sexual acts for recognition and attention (Maltz, 2012).

The motivation for prostitution seems similar. Although only a small percentage of incest victims (Russell, 1999) actually become prostitutes, a high percentage of prostitutes studied reported incest in their childhood (Nadon, Koverola, and Schluderman, 1998).

As a child, the individual learned from the perpetrator that sexual favors could be traded for rewards. As an adult, more sophisticated barter ensured a relatively lucrative, albeit dangerous, lifestyle.

Some theorists (Levenkron and Levenkron, 2008; Maltz, 2012; Schwartz, 2000) contend that promiscuity and prostitution are a combination of anger, mind–body split, feelings of worthlessness, and the attitude of "My body has been used already, so why not?" Or some feel that the promiscuous individual seeks acceptance and affection that she or he confuses with sexuality (Lew, 2004; Rodriquez-Srednicki, 2006).

Some past victims experience an aversion to sex, demonstrating such problems as arousal dysfunction, desire dysfunction, and difficulty in achieving orgasm (Courtois, 2010; Maltz, 2012). Some victims avoid or feel phobic about intimate encounters. Often sexual contacts stimulate flashbacks, as in the case of Helen:

> "Whenever I let anyone touch me," explained Helen, "I think of my father. My partner's hands become my father's hands in my mind, and the guilt and pain I feel over the incest turns off any positive feelings I have about having sex now."

Russell (1999) found that women who have been abused are more likely to reject sexual advances and, as a consequence, suffer more sexual violence, especially rape in marriage.

Confusion over sexual identity often plagues survivors. Finkelhor (1984) found that "boys victimized by older men were *four times* more likely to be currently engaged in homosexual activity than were nonvictims" (p. 195). He also noted, however, that it is difficult to discern whether the abuse was a precipitating factor in homosexual activity or whether boys with a predisposition toward a homosexual lifestyle were more vulnerable to abusers (see also Cassese, 2001; Sonkin, 1998). One explanation for this could be related to stigma. A boy who has been involved with an older man may see himself as homosexual not only because he has had the sexual experience with a man but also because his male abuser apparently found him sexually stimulating. The boy attaches authority and power to the adult and assumes that if the abuser sees him as homosexual, he must be. Thus, the boy chooses a homosexual lifestyle to be consistent with his image of himself and his perception of how others see him (Dorias, 2009; Maltz, 2012). Cassese (2001) suggests that gay men must learn to separate the crime of pedophilia from consensual intimacy.

Some women who choose female partners do so because, on some level, they have concluded that men are not to be trusted. A woman who was abused by her mother may adopt the same pathological symptomatology and choose women as sexual partners (Ogilvie, 2004).

Stigmatization and Self-Esteem

The child who was sexually abused incorporates deep feelings of guilt, shame, and "badness" in his or her self-image. As an adult, the individual has harbored the secret for some time. This need to guard the secret at all costs, compounded by the isolation necessary to feel safe in keeping it, makes the adult feel negatively toward himself or herself (Dorias, 2009; Ogilvie, 2004; Russell, 1999). Victims experience a sense of being damaged and in this tainted stance see themselves as different from others.

Some past victims think their bodies are marred and detestable. They may also feel anger toward their bodies, feeling that the flesh somehow acquiesced to the abuse while the spirit or the essence of the person did not. Some individuals describe feeling angry at their bodies for experiencing physical pleasure during the abuse. The image of the body becomes distorted; it is seen as deformed, too fat, too thin, or ugly (Cloitre et al., 2006; Maltz, 2012; Rodriquez-Srednicki and Twaite, 2006).

Survivors may somatize their conflicts, presenting anorexia nervosa, bulimia, headaches, nausea, menstrual or vaginal problems, colitis, and so on. These symptoms are based on both the impaired picture of self and on internalized anger and guilt. Some past victims describe seeing their bodies as so plagued by problems that they can focus on these and therefore not have to consider the psychological memories of the abuse (Briere, 1992; Levenkron and Levenkron, 2008; Rodriquez-Srednicki and Twaite, 2006).

Increasing attention has been given to the concept of dissociation in survivors and its relationship to self-esteem. *Dissociation* has been defined as "a defensive disruption in the normally occurring connections among feeling, thoughts, behavior, and memories, consciously or unconsciously invoked in order to reduce psychological distress" (Briere, 1992, p. 36). People dissociate to escape from the reality that is too painful or traumatic to face. Dissociation is a type of anesthesia, which allows the personality to cope.

Briere (1992) suggests three forms of dissociation that are common to survivors. These are disengagement, detachment/numbing, and observation. *Disengagement* involves moments of "spacing-out," in which one is oblivious to external events. These moments may be conscious or unconscious and rarely last more than a few seconds to several minutes.

When a survivor has extreme difficulty with negative events, *detachment* or *numbing* may occur. The individual psychologically removes himself or herself (not always consciously) so that he or she is unaware of the negative feelings triggered by certain memories, thoughts, and events. In its more extreme form, this type of dissociation may create someone who is totally unaware of feelings. The detached person can look at situations in an intellectualized nonemotional manner (Briere, 1992; Cloitre et al., 2006; Schwartz, 2000).

Observation occurs when individuals watch themselves involved in certain distressing activities. For example, some survivors speak of the mind and body as almost separate entities. Researchers and clinicians see the origin of this mind–body split in the victim experiencing so much emotional or physical pain during the actual abuse that the mind temporarily separates from the body:

> *Tessa describes feeling this mind–body split whenever she and her lover have sex. "When my father used to sexually abuse me, I would leave my body almost. Sometimes, I'd take my mind into a wall or the couch. I thought that he could abuse my body but not my mind. But that defense became so much a part of sex that now I can't stop doing it when I am making love. My therapist and I are working on helping me to 'stay' during lovemaking."*

This phenomenon should not be confused with more serious psychosis, unless it continues for extended periods and the thought processes become grossly distorted. The splitting of the mind and body has been referred to by some as *self-hypnotic anesthesia* (Courtois, 2010; Rodriquez-Srednicki and Twaite, 2006; Schwartz, 2000).

Some past victims, often those subjected to bizarre, ritualistic, or serious abuse, experience more severe forms of dissociation: amnesia or Dissociative Identity Disorder

(DID), formerly referred to as multiple personality disorder (MPD). *Psychogenic amnesia* is a way of avoiding deep-seated psychological conflicts. The individual has totally blocked out and cannot remember personal events or behaviors—a state that goes beyond normal forgetfulness. Past victims with *DID* exhibit two or more separate personalities that may or may not be aware of each other's existence (Briere, 1992; Courtois, 2010; Duncan, 2008; Schwartz, 2000).

Self-mutilation is another residual symptom of an abused past. Past victims report using substances such as drugs and alcohol to either punish the body, dull the senses, or escape the memories of abuse. Some past victims also cut or burn themselves. Nora describes her hospitalization and self-abuse as a result of being sexually abused:

> *"I had been hospitalized for severe depression. I was 19 years old, and my father had gone to jail because he'd molested me. But the trial had taken two years, and by then, I was pretty upset. I remember my mother calling me, saying my father had been beaten up by the other inmates. She berated me for almost an hour on the phone—about how it was my fault and all. I went back to my room really shaken. I don't even remember doing it, but the next thing I knew, I was running down the hall on fire. I'd set the leg of my jeans on fire—I didn't even know it."*

The ultimate destruction is *suicide*. Suicide, the last escape, may be attempted once or more frequently. At the root of these attempts are deep depression, self-blame, and a feeling of being so different that one cannot hope to be with others (Bogarty and Toler, 2002; Courtois, 2010; Dorias, 2009; Rodriquez-Srednicki and Twaite, 2006).

While some survivors see the body as the offending part of the self, others see the damage as more intrinsic. Both men and women feel shame and guilt not only about the incest, which they often feel they engendered or contributed to, but also about all that was wrong with the family. "If I could have been better" is often heard from guilt-ridden past victims. A fundamental part of the parentification process, guilt aided the abuser and now it continues to plague the past victim.

Another element of feeling different is the question "Why me?":

> Gert was one of seven children. At the age of 7, she was raped by her father. He continued to sexually abuse her for several years. Although she believes that at least one brother knew of the incest, no one ever mentioned it. Gert has no idea why her three sisters were never abused. Today, she has told two of them. They advise her to "put it behind you and live a happy life." Their attitudes infuriate Gert, who grapples daily with the anger and guilt over being her father's chosen victim.

Survivors often fantasize about what made them so different from their siblings who were not abused. If they discern a difference, they translate it into something negative and thus feel even more guilty and despicable.

Survivors' guilt is often an issue for past victims of incest. Here, the individuals realize that they have survived either emotionally or physically but that others close to them who also experienced the abuse did not. Incest survivors describe being plagued with guilt when they see brothers and sisters react with greater pathology to the abuse. The guilt and shame compound the survivors' sense of hopelessness and the feeling that they have neither the right nor the power to take control of their own lives.

Powerlessness

Feeling out of control or powerless becomes a major problem for the past victim of sexual abuse. Fears permeate his or her life. Nightmares, phobias, and attacks of anxiety keep the individual ever mindful of the abuse and of the terror or pain associated with it. Decisions become difficult. Survivors describe *feeling vulnerable*. There is, in fact, a high risk of future victimization for those who feel powerless to avoid or protect themselves from it.

Male survivors suffer significantly from feelings of *incompetence*. Although females also feel powerless, society accepts this in a woman. Men, on the other hand, feel stigmatized for their inability to take control, and their guilt compounds the problem. For some, this is translated into withdrawal and even sexual impotence. Other males overcompensate and become overly aggressive and sometimes abusive (Dorias, 2009; Hunter, 1990; Lew, 2004; Sonkin, 1998). Mike repressed the sadistic sexual abuse by his father until it surfaced in a recurring dream that attested to his sense of powerlessness:

> "I see my father coming at me with a pipe. He is dressed in black and looks very sinister. He smiles as he brings the pipe crashing down on me—again and again. I want to run or protect myself, but I can't. I can't scream. I can't cry out. I feel hot and wet and then I see it—a river of my own blood running past me. Then I envision the street, and I see the blood running down the gutter and into the sewer. I want to cry, 'Come back,' because it feels like with that stream all the strength—the life, in fact—has gone out of me."

Barbara, too, remembers her mother's sexual abuse of her. These flashbacks left her feeling anxious and perspiring profusely. Every detail of the abuse flashed before her, and she felt powerless to control the incidents. The events were so vivid in her mind that she worried that she was becoming seriously ill.

Some theorists describe these involuntary disturbances in perception among female incest survivors. The phenomenon results from an inability to control flashbacks and compounds the past victim's feelings of vulnerability and lack of control. Some individuals report an array of hallucinations or perceptions for which there seems to be no external stimulus (Courtois, 2010; Schwartz, 2000; Yehuda, 2002).

Past victims also describe *visual hallucinations*, such as shadowy figures reminiscent of traumatic elements of the incest experience; movement in the peripheral vision, which disappeared when confronted directly; and elaborate recreations of incestual events. Some women report hearing intruder sounds (e.g., scrapes, footsteps, breathing) as well as childlike cries for help. Inner voices can be comforting and helpful or can direct the past victim toward maltreatment of themselves or others. Touch and smell also play a part in the hallucinatory experiences of some of the women.

The feeling of powerlessness also results in an overall sense of impaired efficacy. Survivors feel they are less capable and less effective in their work. Some past victims somatize this feeling and develop physical ailments to excuse their failures. Conversely, others become compulsive overachievers and excel with an intensity and drive. One woman described her experience:

> "I knew I was a good bookkeeper, but that's all I believed I could do. So I was determined to become the best bookkeeper the company ever had. I worked at it constantly. In retrospect, I'm sure I drove everyone nuts. Their paperwork had to be just so. But I made myself nuts, too—or figuratively at least. I ended up in the hospital with exhaustion, severe depression, and a pretty lousy outlook on the world."

Anger

Survivors may feel powerless because of their inability to protect themselves, to perceive reality accurately, or to demonstrate competence. But they may also feel powerless to control their anger. The anger stems from being used or victimized, being out of control or vulnerable, and being unprotected. Some individuals feel anger over being robbed of childhood. Anger can be turned inward; the past victim may feel anger at himself or herself for what he or she perceives as ineffectual behavior or contributing to the abuse. Survivors may feel anger at their own helplessness or powerlessness. "Why wasn't I able to say no?" they agonize. In these situations, it is necessary to help the person recognize the variety of reasons children are not able to say no.

Anger is often directed toward the nonprotecting parent as well as the perpetrator. But often it is difficult to recognize, admit, or express this anger, as illustrated by this case:

> "My father came to me when he realized he was terribly ill. I was already angry with him and had been for years. But his reaching out to me infuriated me even more. How could he, after what he'd done to me! But then I felt guilty; he was sick. How could I turn him away? After all, he was my father. So I took care of him."

In the end, this past victim turned her anger inward because she was unable to direct it toward the appropriate person. She became depressed and ill until she was eventually helped to understand the origin of these symptoms.

A common technique used with survivors is to have the individual write a letter expressing this rage to the perpetrator or to the unprotecting parent. For some, the pain and sadness resulting from the writing are sufficient to exorcise much of the anger. For others, confronting the person—advisedly, with the support of a trusted therapist or intimate—is the best way to direct the anger appropriately.

Anger is not always directed inward or appropriately. Anger may be diffused throughout the individual's life or directed toward loved ones, intimates, children, or other substitutes. Perhaps the past victim does not even recognize what he or she feels is anger. Sometimes, the anger is expressed through actions, and the differentiation between the feeling and action is impossible for the survivor to make. Parents who were victims find themselves struggling to control their annoyance over their children's behavior. The spouse of a past victim may find that his or her mate acts illogically in disagreements. The degree of anger expressed can be mild, moderate, or even dangerously pathological.

Many rapists experienced a childhood fraught with conflict. They learn to express their anger toward the figures from their childhoods by displacing it onto others through sexual aggression.

The inability to cope with anger intensifies the survivor's feelings of powerlessness and further undermines his or her self-esteem. Since some people find the expression of or even the admission of anger is difficult to accept, past victims who recognize their feelings as anger wonder if they are unique in the intensity of this anger. "Why am I so angry?" "Does anyone else feel this way?"

Because anger is so deeply felt but so difficult for past victims to label or express appropriately, its existence often impedes the forming of healthy relationships.

Relational Imbalances

Relational problems are based on numerous factors, several of which relate to the following traits of the survivor:

- Need to repeat the past or gravitate toward the family of origin
- Difficulty trusting
- Inability to label and express feelings appropriately and thereby have meaningful communication with intimates
- Strong need to have others meet their needs
- Low self-esteem

For past victims, childhood did not provide security. But people find security in the familiar and are often frightened by the unknown. Victims of past familial injustices are particularly threatened by the insecurity of the unknown, and although they may vehemently protest their intentions to have a different homelife from that of their family of origin, they often marry individuals much like their parents or themselves.

Dysfunctional relationships have their roots in the formation of an incestuous family. Adult men who were abused or witnessed the abuse of a sister often seek the all-loving mother, who will give them the unconditional love their mothers did not. Feeling understood only by partners with similar backgrounds or feeling they deserve nothing more, these men also perpetuate the cycle of the dysfunctional family. In a society that prescribes action in males, these men are more likely to practice some type of abuse—emotional, physical, or sexual—on their wives and children.

Another issue for past victims of sexual abuse is that they may have grown up believing that the abuse they suffered was synonymous with being loved. Many have never learned to separate sex and affection and, given their fear of trust to achieve true intimacy, form superficial sexual attachments. But along with the sexual relationship comes the remembrance of being used or violated. Without even knowing why, victims find their relationships empty, unsatisfying, and even abusive. Some continue these dysfunctional liaisons because they are convinced they deserve no better or are panic stricken at the idea of being alone. Others fear risking and prefer to live with the familiar.

Incest survivors may have trouble both with spousal relationships and with their children. The past victims' own helplessness, low self-esteem, and difficulty handling anger impede their abilities to provide organizational structure, consistency, and an appropriate balance between affection and discipline. As mothers, many past victims are overwhelmed by the responsibility of child rearing. As a result, they may withdraw emotionally or retreat through drugs or alcohol.

These mothers demonstrate difficulties in setting limits. Their children quickly learn that because of her guilt, the mother can be cajoled, prodded, or often disobeyed beyond what she claims are her limits. Unfortunately, children then often blame their mother for her weakness, much as she blamed her own mother.

Families of origin frequently impinge on the lives of survivors and their new families and create a resurgence of old issues that confuse current roles. The perpetrator may attempt to molest the former victim's children, or the victim's mother may require care and plead with her daughter for help. Consider the following:

> *"My mother actually had the nerve to complain to me about my father. She'd sit at my kitchen table for hours, saying what a horrible man he was. I don't know what she expected from me. All I could think of was 'Where were you when I needed protection from him?' "*

Siblings often blame the survivor for his or her problems. If the siblings knew of the abuse, their guilt may prevent them from recognizing the past victim's feelings in light of their own complicity. Siblings who did not know of the abuse often cannot or will not believe it:

> *"Two of my sisters knew that my father had raped me, and one brother must have known. But my other brothers didn't know, I'm sure. But it didn't help for them to know. All my brothers and sisters kept telling me that I had to forget what happened. My father was dead, and I had to put it in the past. I think they blamed me for upsetting my mother by telling her. They also blamed me for my anxiety attacks when I'd call them and beg to talk. It was as if they couldn't hear what my father had done to me. It was easier to assume I was nuts!"*

Multiple Victimization

Research shows that individuals, especially women, who were victims of incest have a higher incidence of repeat victimization. Russell (1999) reported that of the 940 women she studied, 82 percent of incest victims again suffered some type of serious sexual assault, compared to only 48 percent of women who were not incest victims (p. 158). In addition, 46 percent of the incest victims reported physical or sexual violence in marriage, compared to 19 percent who had not been incest victims. And 53 percent were subjected to sexual harassment from an authority figure (p. 158).

Undoubtedly, at least for the women in Russell's sample, repeated victimization is a reality. Because women have been conditioned to be victims, they are more likely than men to be victimized again (Briere, 1992; Messman-Moore, Long, and Siegfried, 2000). However, even some men again experience exploitation, which creates feelings reminiscent of the abuse (Dorias, 2009; Lew, 2004; Sonkin, 1998).

Chapter 6 described the damaged-goods syndrome. The perception of damage is twofold. Not only do abused children feel inherently tainted, but society sees them as different from other children. Because the child was previously violated, another perpetrator, aware of the past abuse, does not feel inhibited. Perpetrators often rationalize that the child, or later the adult, is more knowledgeable—and even seductive (Russell, 1999). Some husbands of past victims need to abuse or violate them as a form of exorcism. Perpetrators sometimes find excitement from the knowledge that the victim had been part of an illicit activity. And finally, society often sees victims as responsible for their fate, a rationalization used frequently by those prone to violent physical and sexual behavior (Messman-Moore et al., 2000; Russell, 1999).

In addition to others' views of them, the survivors' views of themselves are manifested in an internalized powerlessness. The individuals often see themselves as vulnerable and do not perceive they have the right to resist effectively. Reactivated fears paralyze the past victim:

> "The worst thing that my father's abuse did was rob me of my ability to scream—literally. After I escaped the abuse at home, I was raped twice. The first time, I was 19, and I called my mother, crying. She told me it was my own fault if I went out at night. The second time, I was married and my husband and I were swimming with two other couples at night. A bunch of motorcycle guys came up. They dragged me off and raped me. I couldn't even scream. Afterward, my husband and the others were upset with me. They said I must have wanted to be raped. That really hurt. They just couldn't understand that I couldn't cry out. I was paralyzed."

Being robbed of anger or the ability to react can follow a survivor throughout life.

The propensity of former victims to repeat the past or gravitate toward the familiar often predisposes them to revictimization. One victim of incest married three times in an attempt to break the pattern of returning to the familiar:

> I got married when I was 19. I married a guy I realize now who came from the same kind of family I did. He had a sister who was a heroin addict and a prostitute, and I think his father had molested her. He used to constantly put me down.... My father was always putting me down, and I'd had it. So I left my first husband. My second husband was like my father, too. He was suffering from post-Vietnam stress and did some crazy [abusive] things to me, just like my father. I was only married to him for 10 months, and then I left. My third husband was quiet and passive.... You know, I married my father twice and then I married my mother.... My mother always ignored me. I was always looking for her love, but I never felt like I got it.

Another aspect of the survivor's sense of self is the impaired ability to avoid danger. Most children project tentative antennae and take risks, and if the world proves too much, they can run home for comfort. But if the hurt is at home as well as outside, the individual's sense of reality of what is safe or unsafe becomes distorted. Thus, as adults, these past victims are not always able to discern what situations are potentially harmful.

Janoff-Bulman (2002) explains that the psychological impact of victimization includes the shattering of some basic beliefs about the world. Most of us assume that the world is comprehensible and meaningful and that we are personally invulnerable. Once these perceptions become distorted, it is difficult for individuals to test and avoid danger. Often, they become victims again.

Survivors of dysfunctional families, whether neglectful or physically or sexually abusive, pay for their vulnerability. In time, the residual effects of family pathology can be reduced through greater self-knowledge.

EFFECTS FROM EXTRAFAMILIAL ABUSE

Since physical abuse and neglect are, by definition, at the hands of a caregiver, the only type of abuse possible outside the home is sexual assault or molestation. Chapter 8 discussed the range of abuse, from molestation by an acquaintance or a stranger to involvement in pornography and prostitution rings or satanic cults. Children molested or exploited outside their homes demonstrate similar problems to those who were victims of incest. Feeling damaged appears to be a universal, residual effect of sexual exploitation. The inner sense of damage and society's perception of damage intensifies the blame of self. Depression, self-destructive behavior, and low self-esteem result from the blame and guilt the victim carries (Flynn, 2008; Gold, 2000; Isley et al., 2008; Naparstek, 2006; Ryder, 1992). Many past victims describe fears that plague them in flashbacks, in nightmares, or in anxiety over future victimization. In the words of one survivor,

> *"I'm still frightened when a strange man passes me on the street after dark. Even when I'm with someone, I cling to that companion. I feel so vulnerable. I'm afraid that if anyone approached me again, I'd just freeze and let it happen."*

The particular fears the victim has often relate to the type of assault or the amount of force used. Sandra's abuse and her later reactions characterize a victim who was initially cajoled by the perpetrator:

> *Sandra had seen the perpetrator at the playground on several occasions. He frequently talked to the children or took their pictures. One day, he engaged several children, including Sandra, in a game of hide-and-seek. Sandra "found" him in the utility shed, and they began talking. He offered her money to remove her clothes. When she refused, the perpetrator drew a knife, threatened her into compliance, and molested her.*
>
> *Following the episode, Sandra ran home in tears but was afraid to tell anyone. She was sure she had led the man on and would be blamed for what happened. She withdrew from her friends, threw herself into schoolwork, and returned home immediately after school. Sandra remembers recurring nightmares, some about being victimized again and others that centered around her image of herself as tainted and "evil." She placed herself, unconsciously, in situations where she was again and again taken advantage of by boys she dated.*
>
> *When Sandra was 19 and in college, she was raped by an acquaintance at a party. Her reaction to the rape was to become completely hysterical—confusing in her uncontrollable sobbing the events of this rape with her experience as a child. In therapy, she was eventually able to separate the two events and to understand her feelings of being exploited and her sense of guilt, blame, and shame.*

While women feel a continued sense of powerlessness, male victims often describe intense fears about being out of control both at the time of the assault and in later adulthood. In order to gain control, some male victims become perpetrators. Although both males and females experience sexual fears and problems, males are more likely to express confusion about their sexual identity. Women, on the other hand, report increased sexual inhibitions and decreased sexual desire. It is not unusual for past victims of extrafamilial abuse to also be vulnerable for further victimization.

An increasing number of survivors of abuse by clergy have been speaking out and attesting to similar residual effects. Added to these effects is often the destruction of the individual's faith, which sometimes provides solace for other abuse survivors (Flynn, 2008; Isley et al., 2008). Increasingly, therapists and nonabusive clergy find themselves working together to help these individuals heal spiritually (Bilich, Bonfiglio, and Carlson, 2000).

More and more survivors of abuse by cults have also spoken up in the last few years. These survivors describe similar symptoms as other abuse survivors, but they also exhibit fears and behaviors peculiar to this type of abuse. Ryder (1992) points out that issues like extreme fear of circles, fear of being the center of attention, overreaction to supernatural films, fear of abandonment, and phobias about blood, robed figures, candles, demons, and snakes may be present in those who experienced ritualistic cult abuse. Because this type of abuse can be so bizarre and so out of one's frame of reference, it is often difficult for past victims to remember and make sense of what they have experienced.

Current statistics project that one out of three girls and one out of five boys will be sexually abused prior to the age of 18. Of this number, 40 to 60 percent will be victims of incest. This means that approximately half the victims experience exploitation outside the family unit. Yet very little has been written about these individuals as adults, so knowledge in this area is limited.

A WORD ABOUT RESILIENCY

When we consider the survivors of child abuse and neglect, we usually focus on the residual symptoms because they are the most obvious manifestations of maltreatment. What we sometimes forget is the resiliency of the human spirit. Many individuals survive their abuse despite all odds and turn their experiences into an opportunity for learning. Increasingly, researchers are considering what makes children resilient and how such resilience can be fostered in others.

Resiliency refers to the ability to survive or bounce back from pressure or crisis—a kind of emotional buoyancy. Valentine and Feinauer (1993) have identified several characteristics in the resilient female survivors of child sexual abuse that they studied. These individuals appear to have the ability to find supportive relationships outside their families of origin. They have also developed a sense of positive self-regard. They have used spiritual grounding, sometimes in the form of religion, to bring them through the difficult times. In addition, they have recognized their own personal power, bringing their locus of control inward while attributing blame and responsibility rightly to their abusers. And finally, resilient people have adopted a philosophy of life that leaves them open to learning and growth. Perhaps it is this philosophy that helps them to use their abuse as a means to learning and growth.

In considering resilience, one must be careful not to blame the victim who is not able to bounce back from the experience. Rather, we must continue to study and understand what helps one person to heal and hampers another from doing so effectively.

A variety of different methods are used to help survivors get in touch with their own strengths and potential. We will now consider some of them.

TREATMENT OF ADULTS WHO WERE
ABUSED AS CHILDREN

Chapters 12 and 13 discussed the treatment of abused and neglected children and their families. In recent years, there has been an emphasis on therapeutic services for adults who did not disclose the abuse in childhood. Many of these past victims have carried the abuse hidden deep in their memories for years.

Repressed Memories

"For years, I had a vague feeling that something had happened to me as a child. In fact, I couldn't remember much of my childhood. Following my divorce, I sought out a therapist, mainly because I was feeling like such a failure. And then the dreams started coming. I would dream that there was a shadow in my bedroom. I was petrified to have that dream. It took several years before the memories returned … the memories of my father coming to my room at night and sexually abusing me. Throughout those years I remembered things in bits and pieces … in smells and images."

It is not uncommon for people who have been traumatized to repress the memories of this experience or relegate them to the darkest part of one's mind. When this happens, these feelings and the recall of these experiences may lie dormant for years. Remembering them may be triggered by certain events. The occurrence of a similar situation (e.g., a mother's child is abused at about the same age she had been abused), the death of the perpetrator, the birth of one's child, becoming free of an addiction, feeling safe, or experiencing a new trauma (e.g., being raped as an adult when one had repressed the memory of childhood sex abuse) are all examples of triggers that can bring up old memories (Cloitre et al., 2006; Courtois, 2010; Duncan, 2008; Fredrickson, 1992; Schwartz, 2000).

The term *repressed memory syndrome* was developed to describe those who have no memory of the abuse they suffered. Some survivors, unlike the one quoted above, not only have no memory but no sense that anything happened to them. Only after the memories are triggered do they begin to emerge (Sheiman, 1993).

Currently, there is much controversy over the concept of repressed memories. Some critics have blamed therapists for leading their clients into "remembering" experiences that never happened and then falsely accusing others of abusing them. The fact that memories return in vague images that may require some interpretation compounds the argument. It is the wise therapist who helps the client make connections and interpretations rather than making them for him or her. As one therapist put it,

"Bev described memories and dreams she was having which sounded much like those recounted by my sexually abused clients. I felt fairly sure that eventually she would remember that she was abused. But when she asked me 'Do you think I was sexually abused?', my response had to be, 'Bev, that is for you to tell me, not for me to tell you.' And eventually she did remember and told me about her experiences."

Research tells us that survivors do repress memories of abuse—memories that are too painful to keep in their conscious mind (Duncan, 2008; Fredrickson, 1992; Rodriquez-Srednicki and Twaite, 2006; Schwartz, 2000; Sheiman, 1993). When adults abused as children seek therapy, there are several methods that might help them.

Individual Therapy

Traditional therapies can be helpful to the past victim, provided the therapist is educated and skilled in working with survivors, especially those of sexual abuse. Since sexual abuse is a painful issue, not all therapists are comfortable dealing with it, however,

"I finally told my therapist of 10 years that I'd been sexually abused by my father. He nodded and started asking me about something unrelated. I couldn't believe it. Here I'd gotten up the courage to mention it, and he wasn't even hearing me."

Tower (1988) states that in order to work with sexual abuse victims, a therapist must possess the following qualities:

- Be comfortable, informed, and skilled in discussing sexual issues
- Be comfortable, informed, and clear about his or her own sexuality
- Have achieved an awareness and comfortable relationship with his or her own family of origin
- Have developed a sense of autonomy
- Be comfortable with his or her own vulnerability

There are variations to individual therapy. Through *psychotherapy*, victims come to terms with the trauma that occurred and their guilt surrounding their perceived complicity. The individual is encouraged to develop connections between past and present and to enhance present coping capabilities.

A variety of different techniques may be used in individual therapy. *Gestalt therapy* focuses on the present, with less emphasis on the past or the future. The goal is to help the individual recognize the current feelings and to take responsibility for behavior. Gestalt therapists have patients conduct dialogues between parts of themselves (e.g., body parts, wishes, and feelings) to help victims accept themselves as whole people.

Past victims of childhood abuse are often suffering from *posttraumatic stress disorder (PTSD)*. Those who suffer from PTSD may behave as though they are living in the past and have no control over the future. Sensations and emotions trigger old memories over which they feel they have little control. One emerging therapeutic approach used with PTSD is *eye movement desensitization and reprocessing (EMDR)*. EMDR focuses on encouraging the client to bring up old memories and at the same time reprocess them through bilateral stimulation of one of the senses via flashing lights, waving fingers, hand taps, or alternating tones. The theory is that "the stimulation of both right and left hemispheres somehow unblocks traumatic memories that have been frozen at a time when the client was unable to process the overwhelming emotions of the traumatic event" (Ogilvie, 2004, p. 176). Proponents of EMDR believe that it has had significant success.

Guided imagery as part of the therapeutic technique has also had success. Guided imagery is a type of directed daydreaming in which the client is talked through imagery designed for a specific purpose. The use of such imagery by those who have expertise in the field has been found to improve functioning and actually change body chemistry (Naparstek, 2006).

Expressive therapies have also been found to be effective with survivors, although some caution that they not be used exclusively. Art therapy, for example, helps the survivor to express the feelings associated with the trauma (Meijer-Degen, 2006) and then take the opportunity to process them. Because the unconscious is brought out in expressive ways (art, drama, music, etc.), there may be more psychic material available to process than if the client were to just talk about it.

Therapists may draw from a variety of approaches and combine them. Victims should seek the therapist who meets his or her own particular needs.

Group Therapy

Many therapists prefer to use group treatment because past victims feel very isolated from others and unique in their circumstances. Meeting other individuals with similar issues dispels these fears and reduces feelings of loneliness. By interacting with other group members, survivors practice building or rebuilding their social skills. Group members also have an opportunity to reduce the pain they feel through ventilating their feelings. In sharing, members gain different perspectives on their experiences, which enables them to begin to recognize their feelings and understand their trauma.

Survivor groups are most often either all male or all female, but occasionally, groups are mixed. Such programs are sponsored by feminist organizations, mental health clinics, family service agencies, and other organizations.

Groups provide a variety of positive experiences. One past victim describes a group:

> "Our group combined everything. At first, we just shared our stories. In the beginning, we were asked to keep diaries or journals on our reactions to the group, on what we did well, and on how we didn't cope so well between group meetings. After a time, we read these journals aloud. It was scary at first, but we got used to it. Reading them aloud really helped. Occasionally, we had homework, such as having to answer questions or assess certain ideas or attitudes we had. Sometimes, we would agree to work on some particular behavior for a week. We also did role playing where we had to face an empty chair. When I did it, the chair was supposed to hold my father, and I could say whatever I chose. It really helped me realize how angry I was."

Role-playing, keeping journals, and writing (but not sending) letters help sexual abuse survivors. Journal writing encourages the identification of positive and negative feelings about the abuse, the perpetrator, and the nonprotecting parent. In writing down these emotions, survivors are helped to understand more clearly who they are. By keeping a journal over a period of time, the writer can also trace his or her progress. And finally, by placing the journal on a shelf, the survivor symbolically puts aside the memories when the therapy is over or the victim temporarily feels the need to separate from the hurt.

Through role-playing, past victims practice telling others of the abuse and their feelings or prepare to confront significant individuals. Confronting the perpetrator, for example, may at first be altogether too threatening, but in these exercises, victims rehearse what they will say and also anticipate possible reactions from the perpetrator.

Writing a letter to someone with whom the past victim has unresolved issues helps to express his or her feelings. Such a letter aids the person to prepare to talk or to revise and deliver the letter. Jane describes the use of her letter:

> "I had never intended to send my mother the letter. Writing it had really helped me. I was able to express feelings I'd never admitted to. But I finally decided I would give it to her. I went over to her house, handed it to her, and left the room while she read it. I couldn't be there. When I got the courage to return, she just sat there with tears in her eyes. 'I'm sorry,' she cried. 'I'm sorry I wasn't there for you, but I was so afraid of him myself.' At first, it seemed like her usual denial of my father's abuse of me, but then, I realized how vulnerable we both were. That letter opened up real communication between us."

Some groups, more issue-oriented than those described above, deal with topics such as sex education, coping with anger, communication skills, assertiveness, and building new skills. Group therapy, used extensively with past victims of sexual abuse, has also been effective with survivors of other childhood abuses. Whatever the focus of the group, victims can be helped to build and rebuild social skills and learn that they are not alone.

Self-Help Groups

Self-help groups, often modeled on Alcoholics Anonymous, have a history of effectiveness with individuals who feel isolated by their problems.

Parents Anonymous

Although originally designed for parents who physically abused their children, Parents Anonymous (PA) now attracts parents who are former victims of all types of maltreatment. The members build support systems while they learn to cease their abusive or potentially abusive behavior.

Adults Molested as Children

This group evolved from the Child Sexual Abuse Treatment Program in California (see Chapter 13) under the direction of Henry Giaretto and was designed for past victims of incest who felt the need of support. Giaretto's groups brought together women initially to express their anger, shame, and guilt. Here they learned that others shared similar feelings about their abuse and their lives. After at least two eight-week sessions, the participants joined a Recontact Group, composed of unrelated nonoffending and offending parents. The former victims—through contact with these parents—began to complete unfinished emotional business. Eventually, past victims found themselves bonding with these other parents and, in this way, reestablished trust and open communication. Survivors were then asked to transfer the confrontation to and to open communication with their own parents. Even when their parents were not available, past victims appeared to gain a significant amount from the group experience and were able to use their experiences in other relationships (Giarretto, 1996). From this original group, a variety of such groups have emerged to help adults who were victimized as children.

Writers Groups

In these groups, members express their feelings and their experiences through various literary forms. One past victim recounted how she started a writers' group.

> "I was affiliated with a woman's center, and they knew I wrote quite a bit. They invited me to lead a literary group. When I suggested a group for incest survivors, I think they were a bit taken aback, but they agreed. Initially, five women came. We met once a week and would write on a particular topic—for example, 'Was there any one person that you can point to who helped you to survive?' or 'What survival skills have you developed?' Rather than become immersed in the details of the abuse, we tried to focus on the survival aspect. I guess we were almost congratulating ourselves for surviving. You can't exactly run out and tell everyone you survived, but with special people or through writing, it's nice to celebrate your victories."

A variety of self-help groups are emerging. For instance, gay and lesbian groups and those specifically for men are gaining prominence. For the adult who was abused or neglected as a child, the support of peers is comforting and leads to understanding and recovery.

Legal Actions

Recently, there has been a move for survivors to take legal action against their perpetrators, often in the form of suit for money for therapy. Advocates of these actions describe them as not only just retribution but therapeutic and validating, as well (Friess, 1993). Other survivors report that the act of suing one's father alienates them from the rest of the family, making the past victim feel as alone and isolated as he or she did in childhood (Penelope, 1992). Friess, in her autobiographical book *Cry the Darkness* (1993), describes her suit against her father and the emotional toll it took on her and her family.

Certainly, any survivor contemplating legal action against a perpetrator should have the support of those around her or him. In addition, it is helpful for a therapist to review with the survivor her or his feelings and the impact that this action will have on the survivor and those close to her or him.

THERAPISTS' RESPONSES TO WORKING WITH SURVIVORS

Therapy with survivors of trauma can take its toll on therapists. Courtois (2010) suggests some typical countertransference issues that are often inherent in work with survivors. The incredible pain, confusion, and anger of past victims can leave the therapist with similar feelings or feeling drained and discouraged. In their study of a random sample of 383 therapists treating 111 survivors and 272 sexual offenders, VanDeusen and Way (2006) learned that these clinicians found significant disruptions in their ability to trust and be intimate with others (p. 80).

How does one who chooses to work with survivors protect against such vicarious trauma? First, supervision is vital. In an agency, this is usually available, but those therapists working privately and recognizing the need for supervision will often become involved in peer supervision groups with other therapists in the area. Second, it is important to monitor one's own feelings while doing this type of work and to have an opportunity to discuss these feelings in confidence with peers. And finally, the importance of personal support beyond the work environment cannot be overestimated.

SUMMARY

As society becomes more conscious of the existence of child maltreatment, an increasing number of former victims are coming forward to tell their stories. They disclose for a number of reasons. They may be troubled by symptoms seemingly unrelated to the abuse, by relational or sexual dysfunction, with problems of loss, or by issues related to the normal progress of their lives.

All types of child maltreatment leave scars. Often, these scars are similar, but the symptoms specifically related to neglect, abuse, or sexual abuse are somewhat different in their degree or expression.

Individuals who were neglected as children have difficulty trusting. The inconsistency and lack of nurturance in their childhoods makes it difficult for them to expect support from others or even to depend on themselves. These survivors feel anger over their parents' lack of care—an anger that may lead to depression, delinquency, or aggressive behavior. They may have trouble relating to others in any but a superficial manner. Their low self-esteem, combined with poor social skills, can promote difficulty in communication as well as in everyday functioning. Physical problems result from early malnutrition and poor emotional health.

Physically abusive families leave scars that hamper the victims' ability to trust, express and identify anger, and form and maintain relationships. Low self-esteem in these victims interferes with their coping skills and inhibits their ability to parent. There is a need for research into the effects of domestic violence on the lives of the adults who experienced it as children.

Victims of past sexual abuse experience wounds from feeling betrayed, traumatic sexualization, powerlessness, and stigmatization. They have difficulty trusting and often feel powerless to control their own lives. This powerlessness often results in sexual problems, revictimization, problems with relationships, confused sexuality, and impaired self-esteem. Because of their need to repeat the past, survivors may reconstruct the patterns of their childhoods if they do not seek help. Some past victims repress memories that are too difficult to handle.

Treatment of adult former victims can be given individually or in groups. Individual therapies include traditional psychotherapy and possibly the use of Gestalt, EMDR, guided imagery, and expressive therapies. Groups, however, are also considered to be very effective. Therapy groups use techniques such as journal writing, unsent letters, and role-playing to enable past victims to understand and deal with their trauma. Self-help groups also contribute to the therapeutic efforts. With therapy, survivors can be helped to take control of their own lives and live more effectively despite the traumas of dysfunctional childhoods.

Working with survivors of childhood trauma can have its effect on therapists. To compensate for these effects, it is important that those working with this population seek supervision, monitor their own feelings, and have adequate support systems.

Chapter 16

Working in Child Protection

Working in child protection requires multiple skills and perspectives. The protective social worker must be creative, resourceful, persistent, and dedicated. He or she must also be flexible enough to not only tend to everyday responsibilities on behalf of children but also keep an eye on prevention and the needs of the next generations.

A DAY IN THE LIFE OF TODAY'S PROTECTIVE WORKER

Gina Kirby has worked in a child protection agency for several years. She is a vivacious, enthusiastic, and competent worker who takes her job seriously. Gina described her most recent day:

> *"I got to the office at 8:45, my coffee and donut in hand, with a plan for my day. My first task was to pick up a 5-year-old at his foster home and take him to a hospital 20 miles away for a psychological evaluation. Since this appointment had been difficult to arrange, I was anxious to keep it. I was scheduled to sit in on a conference at a nearby school later in the morning. The school had recently enrolled one of our adolescent clients, and the staff felt the girl had some special learning problems. The meeting was to include her teachers, the psychologist, her parent, her parent's therapist, and several other professionals involved in the case. I hoped to return to the office for lunch with several of my fellow workers—something we had been planning but never seemed to manage. In the afternoon, after getting up to date on paperwork, I would visit two foster homes I was supervising and drop in on a neglectful mother I had been monitoring. A full day to say the least.*
>
> *As I was leaving to pick up Timmy for his psychological examination, my phone rang. A call from the police alerted me to a crisis on which I had to take immediate action, including filing a petition with the court for the protection of a 7-month-old baby and appearing at the emergency hearing that afternoon. At my computer, I quickly printed out the form our office had developed to simplify the procedure, after having added the necessary information. As I finished on the phone, I wondered how I'd rearrange my day to include this emergency. No time to check e-mail today!*
>
> *'I'll file the court petition for you,' assured a sympathetic voice. Harry Sloane, my supervisor, gave me his usual cheerful smile. 'Get going,' he urged. 'Mrs. Gomez is*

expecting you.' He took the intake form and waved me out the door, calling, 'I'll also cover your school meeting and cancel your afternoon visits. But keep your cell phone with you'. I am notorious for leaving my cell in the car when I am on a visit! Harry and I, as supervisor and worker, have a good working relationship. I keep him up to date on my activities and, as a result, he frequently covers for me when I am faced with the inevitable emergency calls.

As I hurried out, I passed the homefinder's desk. 'I have a 7-month-old girl going to court this afternoon; could you line up a foster home in case I need it?' I asked.

'Sure,' she said, already checking her computer. In our office, foster homes are found and screened by one unit of workers. When we need a home for a child, we give one of these workers the information, and they give us a listing on a foster home that seems appropriate and is available.

Marcia Gomez, Timmy's veteran foster mother, had him ready when I arrived. I was thankful for her efficiency. The drive to and from the hospital and the evaluation were uneventful. At noon, I received the awaited for text telling me that a foster home had been identified for my emergency placement. By half-past twelve, I was headed toward the office to pick up the foster home information. While Timmy was being tested, my supervisor had texted me at the hospital to let me know that the hearing was at 1:00 P.M.

With those time constraints in mind, I swung through a drive-in and got a burger and coffee for the road. So much for my lunch plans. Back at the office, I learned that the emergency foster mother had not been reached as yet. The homefinder assured me she hoped to hear back from this foster mother by the time I was out of court, so I arranged to return to the office to pick up the information.

By 1:00, I was at the courthouse, waiting and hoping my lunch would finally digest. Knowing I could wait anywhere from 15 minutes to 2 hours for our case to be heard, I made some mental notes about the clients with whom I'd soon be working. A mother sat on the opposite bench; she had reportedly left her severely neglected 7-month-old baby alone overnight. The neighbors had called the police. The mother looked more like a child herself. As I introduced myself and talked with her, I noticed that she was disheveled and pale and appeared terribly frightened. She held her infant daughter on her lap and smoked one cigarette after another. Between cigarettes, she texted distractedly on her cell phone. I suspected that she was trying to escape her pain and fear. The baby sat listlessly on her mother's lap. She was small for her age, barely able to sit up, and her uncombed hair seemed lifeless and lacking the luster of that of a healthy baby. Her nose was encrusted and she coughed frequently.

After half an hour, our case was heard. In a small room, which looked not unlike a classroom except for the elevated bench, the judge listened to police officers and neighbors, who described how Melanie Merchant had continually neglected baby Kimberly until all concerned feared for her safety. Considering the facts and since Melanie was about to be evicted from her apartment, the judge ordered that Kimberly be placed in a foster home while our agency worked with her mother.

Ms. Merchant showed little affect when I talked to her after the hearing. She seemed in shock, not believing that her child was being taken away from her. I tried to empathize with her, but found it difficult to penetrate her protective shell. 'We'll need to work on a service plan together,' I explained. 'This is a plan for helping you to visit Kim.' I further explained that the service plan would give us both guidelines and goals toward which we could work such as finding housing for her and eventually getting her daughter back. (Mentally I added, 'If that's what you want,' remembering clients who had decided eventually that parenting was just too overwhelming for them.) We agreed that Ms. Merchant would return home, get clothes and diapers for Kimberly, and meet me at the office in an hour. At that time, we could do the service plan, or if she preferred, we could just talk and complete the plan in a few days. She agreed and wordlessly handed me her daughter.

It always depresses me somewhat to take a child from a parent, no matter how much it seems warranted. This was no exception. The mother, who I learned was only 17, surely had her own needs too, and I hoped I could help her.

I put Kim's dirty jacket on her, walked out, and strapped her in a car seat. She watched me closely but made no overt response. I talked to her soothingly, explaining in soft tones what was happening. I'm not sure babies understand these words, but it always makes me feel better to tell them what's going on.

Back at the office, another worker, after first insisting on washing Kim, played with her. I chuckled to myself; when I first started as a protective worker, the condition of some of the children was difficult for me to take. Now I realized I had almost grown used to it. However, I also knew that the next time I saw this baby in her foster home, she would look different—clean and, very likely, more animated.

My supervisor greeted me with a report on the school meeting and several other messages that had come in for me. I returned three of the calls, learning that one of my adolescent clients had run away. Tomorrow would be spent trying to track him down.

The homefinder gave me the name of the competent foster mother whom she had finally reached. I called to confirm that I would be bringing the child and told her the little I knew about Kim. The foster mother said she'd be glad to take her. She hoped I'd be able to bring her soon, however, as the dinner hour became hectic and she would like to talk with me about the baby and any visiting arrangements that had been made. I promised I'd try to get there as soon as possible.

While I waited for Kim's mother, I filled out authorizations on our computerized system to place her in the foster home and forms so that the foster mother would start getting paid. Fortunately, the computer was not down, as it frequently is, so all went smoothly. I also secured a passbook that set up a system whereby Kim could receive medical treatment with a copy of the results of each visit coming to our agency for the file. In the newly opened file, I recorded what had gone on in court.

By 4:30, it was obvious that Kim's mother was not coming. This meant my going to see her within the next few days, but in the meantime, the baby had no diapers or other clothing. Hurriedly—remembering my promise to the foster mother—I put in a request for a purchase order for clothing and diapers, and with the now sleepy baby in my arms, I once again headed for my car. Juggling Kim on my hip, I bought the necessary items. By the time we reached the foster home, dinner preparations were well under way, but the foster parents greeted their new child and me warmly. I explained that visiting had not yet been established and told them what little I knew about Kim's background and needs. The baby, now safely tucked in a crib, slept as if the day had been too much for her. The foster family invited me for dinner, but I assured them that my own family would be awaiting my return.

By 6:30, I was driving home, exhausted. I thought of the events of the day and made a note of tomorrow's plans:

- *Call Melanie Merchant and arrange to talk with her.*
- *Call Kim's foster mother to find out how the night went.*
- *Begin searching for my runaway.*
- *Record the contacts with Kim's foster family.*
- *Reschedule today's planned visits.*

The list seemed to go on and on; I found myself thankful for the cooperation of my supervisor and fellow workers at the office. I knew how valuable their teamwork was to me. But I was especially glad for the family who was awaiting me at home."

Although it is difficult to call a day *typical*, Gina's experiences are not uncommon. Amid the crises and confusion, the worker often finds strength in his or her fellow workers and his or her own support system.

What exactly does it take to become a social worker handling a schedule such as this? (In this context, *social worker* does not mean the manner in which the person was trained but that most protective agencies call their employees social workers. Thus, someone with training in any discipline from human services—psychology, sociology, education, or even unrelated fields—could be called a social worker by virtue of the position.)

SKILLS AND QUALIFICATIONS NEEDED FOR CHILD PROTECTION

A social worker, whether protective or one who has another job description, is considered to be a professional (Popple and Leighninger, 2011; Segal, Steiner, and Gerdes, 2009; Weber, 1997). A professional is one who possesses the following:

- A systematic body of knowledge
- Authority because of his or her expertise
- Sanction from the community
- A code of ethics
- A professional culture
- An obligation to professionalism or to perform competently

Knowledge

For protective services, knowledge includes understanding of the abusive or neglectful family and what can be done to help them, as well as a familiarity with interviewing techniques, case reporting, advocacy skills, and so on. Workers should also bring a sensitivity to cultural differences in clients. If there is a high population of a particular culture in the worker's agency, he or she should become knowledgeable in the values of that culture. In addition, the worker must come to the job with (or develop on the job) a sense of how to use the system—from government to community to the agency—to best help the client. Since not all workers bring with them this knowledge, they should have a commitment to acquiring it as soon as possible, whether through orientation training, on-the-job training, or additional schooling.

Authority and Sanction

Clients and the community assume that protective workers have authority not only because of their knowledge and expertise but because of the authority accorded to them by the community by virtue of the agency in which they work. For example, the community recognizes that protective workers can go to a home and ask to speak with the parents about the maltreatment of their children. If the parents refuse to cooperate, the worker can gain entry with an order from the court. Again, by virtue of the legal or court system, the worker has the authority to place children in foster homes. For professionals, the possession of these three attributes—knowledge, authority, and community sanctions—are intertwined (Popple and Leighninger, 2011; Segal et al., 2009).

Ethics

A code of ethics, a professional culture, and an obligation to professionalism or competency are also interrelated for the protective services worker. Most social workers subscribe to the National Association of Social Workers Code of Ethics, but protective services is based on additional assumptions about clients or interpretations of the code. Most protective agencies believe the intact family benefits the child and strive to take this into consideration when making decisions about the client's future. The goal that one tries to carry out in practice is to do as little harm as possible to the child.

One aspect of any social service code of ethics that is vital to protective work is that of confidentiality. *Confidentiality* is defined as an implicit or explicit agreement between a professional and a client that the information given by the client will be kept private between counselor and client, except under very specific situations.[1] Clients often share very personal aspects of their lives with protective workers. In turn, they expect to have this information kept between the worker and them.

Because of the ambiguity of the nature of the information passed on to workers, it is important to have a good understanding of the issue of confidentiality. What information must be placed in the file and used for validation of abusive or neglectful behavior? This is sometimes a difficult judgment. Absolute confidentiality has other limits in addition to reporting information in the record or using it for validation in court. Certainly, case conferences with supervisors or consultants must include pertinent information. Protective workers, like numerous other professionals, are mandated reporters. Any new incidences of abuse must be substantiated. Workers may also release information to other professionals, provided they are authorized to do so by the client. Another aspect of confidentiality is that the client must know what can be kept between the worker and himself or herself and what must be shared.

Social service professionals are trained to assume that the client has worth and that he or she has the right to self-determination. Usually, *self-determination* is the right to govern and control one's own life—including accepting (or not accepting) treatment and focusing its content. In protective services, however, the concept is slightly altered. By law, parents

---

[1]In counseling situations, confidentiality may be set aside if the client makes a specific threat to harm himself or herself, to seriously harm another, or is suspected of abusing a child.

who abuse or neglect children are expected to cooperate with the protective agency. If they choose not to, they may be subject to court action. However, within the relationship between worker and client, the parent is encouraged to take as much control over his or her situation as possible. In fact, rehabilitation usually entails helping the parents take control of their own lives.

Professionalism

Protective workers are part of a professional culture that shares an interest in children and families. Theoretically, this interest should reflect universal beliefs from agency to agency and provide a great deal of support for those within the profession. Some of those interested in child abuse and neglect have a network to affirm those beliefs through such forums as the National Conference on Child Abuse and Neglect. At such gatherings, the obligation professionals feel toward abused and neglected children and their families is concentrated. Organizations such as the National Center on Child Abuse and Neglect, the National Committee to Prevent Child Abuse, and the C. Henry Kempe National Center for the Prevention and Treatment of Child Abuse and Neglect all provide technical Society on the Abuse of Children provides a newsletter, *The Advisor*, outlining developments in the field. This organization also strengthens the sense of identity of protective workers.

Some workers prefer to do their daily jobs without attempts to share or benefit from the work or ideas of others of their profession. The reality of a *professional culture*, therefore, is that the workers' underlying concern for families and the actions they take differ from agency to agency. In addition, social workers and administrators may hold divergent views on the needs of the clients within the context of overall agency responsibilities. Thus, there is a culture of related professionals who, despite similarities, are often quite different in their views and operations.

Ethnic Competence

As our country becomes more and more diverse in its cultural composition, protective workers must also develop what has been identified as *ethnic competence*. To develop this competence, one must do the following:

- Know one's personal values concerning minority persons.
- Distinguish between personal and professional values, and anticipate ways they may conflict with or accommodate the needs of minority clients.
- Develop interviewing skills reflective of the worker's understanding of the role of language in ethnically distinct communities.
- Refine the ability to relate to minority professionals in ways that enhance their effectiveness with clients.
- Develop one's capability to use resources—agencies, persons, research—on behalf of minority communities.
- Pursue knowledge of the history, traditions, and values of a minority group.
- Research the impact on minority clients of social service policies (Webb and Lum, 2001).

Personal Traits

Protective services require certain personal qualities in the workers. As a prerequisite, workers must exhibit warmth, sensitivity, sincerity, and a caring and nurturing attitude. These qualities are essential because so many abusive and neglectful clients need understanding and nurturance. The worker must also be sensitive to the clients' emotions and comfortable in dealing with their pain and helplessness.

Yet the same childlike affect that contributes warmth and sensitivity also requires structure. The protective worker will at some time have to be authoritative, confronting, and assertive. Quick decisions are necessary, and these decisions are not always popular. Workers, therefore, must also become comfortable with hostility, especially from clients. Good problem-solving skills and flexibility are vital to success in handling the constant crises and stresses.

The protective worker must communicate effectively. He or she should be open to working on a team or cooperating with other agencies on cases. Perhaps two of the most valuable assets in protective work are a sense of humor and an optimistic but realistic outlook. Although workers cannot minimize the client's problems by unwarranted optimism, they must continue to believe in the client's ability to change. This belief stimulates workers to search for more creative ways of approaching and dealing with client issues.

Effectively Juggling Tasks and Responsibilities

The duties of a protective services worker are myriad; Table 16.1 lists only a few of the most important (see also Crosson-Tower, 2003). To accomplish these, an individual needs to

Table 16.1   Basic Duties of a Protective Worker

With Clients	With Collaterals	With Colleagues in the Office
Interviewing for validation	Interviewing reporters for facts	Recording cases
Interviewing to give them emotional support	Discussing children's progress with teachers	Making calls to collaterals
Preparing children for placement	Interviewing relatives to determine best alternative plan for client	Selecting and interviewing approved foster homes
Seeing children regularly in foster homes or in clients' homes	Visiting foster homes	Setting up appointments for clients with other services, such as medical examinations or psychological testing
Visiting client regularly	Visiting schools	Completing forms (often on computer)
Providing transportation to medical and other appointments	Reviewing results of testing	Attending staff meetings
Arranging and orchestrating supervised visits between parents and children	Setting up treatment	Conferring with supervisor
Advocating for clients to obtain specific services	Discussing treatment progress with therapists	Presenting at and attending consultations
Appearing in court		Attending in-service training

have knowledge in several areas: basic helping skills, engagement skills, observation skills, communication skills, empathy skills, and cultural sensitivity.

The degree to which workers project empathy is sometimes difficult to keep in balance. Although workers become angry with clients who assault or neglect defenseless children, their desire to understand sometimes leads them to rationalize that the clients could not help it because their actions were precipitated by their own chaotic childhood or by the pressures placed on them. But these parents are not helped by either punishing them for their actions or by overlooking them. Instead, the protective worker must be aware of clients' pressures, yet hold them accountable for their actions in a helping, nonpunitive manner.

Dealing with Frustrations and Pressures

Protective services work is sometimes frustrating and filled with pressure (see Figure 16.1). For people interested in joining the profession, knowing about these frustrations and pressures is as important as knowing what qualities are useful and what duties must be performed.

Figure 16.1   Pressures on Protective Workers

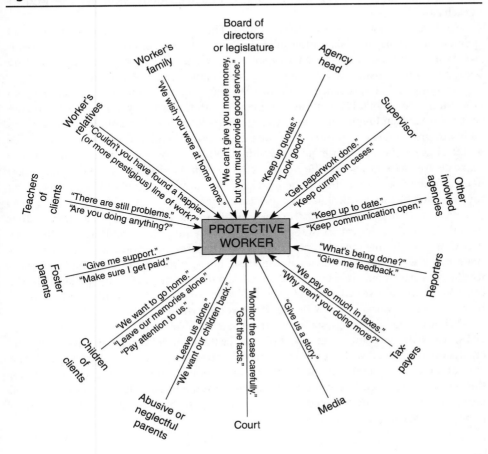

One basic problem for the worker is to resolve the impact of society's ambivalence toward the job it is asking him or her to do. On the one hand, society expects that children will be well cared for by their parents, but when parents fail, there is outrage. Many people feel that neglectful or abusive parents should be subject to some form of social control.

Thus, society supports the protective agencies that assume this task. In fact, the existence of such agencies assures society that something is being done. However, society gives protective agencies little real support. To many people, maltreatment of children is so abhorrent that they prefer not to become involved and hope instead that the agency deals with the family quickly and relatively quietly.

Therefore, the protective worker operates with a sense of isolation from the community—accepted on the one hand but mistrusted and ignored on the other. The dilemma is further intensified because the worker, acculturated by society, holds the same views as the general population and may be conflicted about his or her role. Thus, workers frequently feel stress over the conflict of values they feel and the role they must perform (Crosson-Tower, 2013; Weber, 1997).

Identification sometimes becomes a problem for protective workers. Some workers, especially those who experienced unsatisfactory relationships with their own parents, may overidentify with the maltreated child and create additional problems. An unbiased view—one that looks for strengths in both parents and children—is the goal for workers in each case.

Children are not always easy to work with. They lack inhibitions and are apt to react spontaneously. They may act hostile and aggressive, withdraw, or be decidedly uncooperative. Work with these small clients frequently requires shifting gears, changing plans, and being constantly sensitive to the need to explore feelings or offer explanations.

Working within a bureaucracy is also a challenge. A bureaucracy requires smooth and efficient operation that is not always compatible with the ideology of protective services. Rules, red tape, and regulations may seem to impede, rather than enhance, the worker's ability to provide service for his or her clients. Uniform regulations measure clients' eligibility, but people's needs are quite individual. While the bureaucratic system strives to make decisions for efficiency, the worker seeks to make choices that will be of maximum benefit to the client. In addition, the worker hopes these decisions will be reviewed and implemented by those with skill and expertise in the field.

But within the bureaucratic structure, decision makers and those in authority often hold their positions regardless of their skills (Zastrow, 2012). In a public agency, the rules may change each time there is a newly elected governor or other official. Because protective services work requires individuals capable of quick thinking, flexibility, and adaptability, the confines of bureaucracy can seem entirely too limiting for many workers. On the other hand, workers see clients who have very little structure in their lives, and it is often necessary for the worker to provide them with some structure.

While the bureaucratic system sometimes seems to bar effective administration of social services, this structure is, in fact, the only way these services can be provided. Bureaucracies are concerned with equity and with the equitable apportionment of limited time and resources. Agencies require rational decision making in areas of human emotions, but the policies and procedures of social agencies provide a much-needed structure. The ideal is to accept the necessity—indeed, the importance—of such a structure and learn to use it to better serve clients.

The typical individual who joins protective service sees himself or herself as tolerant, helpful, and understanding. A strong need to be liked can be difficult for those in protective services where one must often make unpopular decisions. The abundance of paperwork and frequent emergencies frustrate the organized worker who feels that it is impossible to ever finish a task. One worker's story is typical:

"I came in Monday morning, knowing that I had tons of paperwork (on the computer) from the week before. I had removed two children from their home, necessitating the completion of several forms. A foster mother had not been paid. I had to trace down an adolescent who had run away and placed herself in a friend's home. Not only did I have to check out that situation, but I also had to file the appropriate forms to okay it. Several other cases needed similar authorization. I also had to enter dictations on the computer on every case I had seen or acted on.

Braced by a strong cup of coffee, I sat down to tackle the work on my desk and bring my cases up to date. I had hardly gotten a good start when the phone rang. One of my clients was in crisis. Her husband had beaten their child, and the neighbors, hearing the child's cries, had threatened to call the police. 'Please come at once,' she begged. I felt frustrated at never seeming to get ahead of my cases, but as I put on my coat, I told myself that tomorrow was another day. Maybe tomorrow I'd be able to tackle the pile of paperwork again."

How do workers cope with the frustrations of protective work? One answer is that despite the fact that this type of work is terribly time-consuming, the worker must reserve time for himself or herself. Outside activities that provide pleasure and enable the individual to relax reduce the stresses of the job. Above all, it is important to maintain an adequate support system of people who care. A strong support system is one characteristic that distinguishes workers from their isolated clients.

These frustrations have the potential to cause burnout, which many experts contend is a higher risk for social workers, especially in protective services, than for many other professions (Shapiro, Dorman, Buckly, and Welker, 1999). *Burnout* can be seen as an attitude or state of mind characterized by an array of symptoms that include depression, emotional, physical and psychological fatigue, feelings of helplessness, and a lack of enthusiasm about work and even about life in general. The worker experiencing burnout is often short tempered, apathetic, cynical, and discouraged (Richards, 1999) and sometimes uses substances (drugs or alcohol) to excess (Schaufeli and Enzmann, 1998; Shapiro et al., 1999).

From a slightly different perspective, caregivers may lose their sense of commitment when they feel their work is not sufficiently valued. In protective services, workers face hostile clients who wish they had not become involved with the "helping system." Reporters and collateral agencies question whether workers are doing all they should to aid clients. And the general public, in an attempt to deny the problem of child maltreatment, often places little value on the role of the protective services worker.

A sense of commitment is born out of the workers' recognition of an explicit ideology, which then dictates the way in which their roles should be carried out. Approaches to problems are rarely clear cut. There is no one way to work with abusive and neglectful families, and each case requires ingenuity and initiating to decide what will work best. This planning requires an abundance of energy. Frustration results when well-conceived treatment plans must be revised again and again because clients appear unresponsive. With no clear how-tos, workers' energies are often sapped.

To avoid losing their energy and their interest in their work, protective workers require positive leaders and adequate support from both co-workers and administrators. But much of the satisfaction in their professional roles is self-generated. A sense of humanity and adequate self-esteem are vital for the worker to aid families who lack self-esteem and to survive in a system fraught with contradictions.

FACING THE CHALLENGES OF WORKING IN CHILD PROTECTION

The first challenge for a child protection worker is the mandate to *protect the children while striving to—if at all possible—preserve the family* while respecting the rights of all of those involved. Child protection services (CPS) workers will attest to the fact that they are often criticized by the public for not doing enough to protect children. As one worker explained:

> "We do the best we can. Most kids at least are given a chance to have a better life. Sure the system isn't perfect, but until someone designs a better one, it will have to do."

Working constantly with people in pain, many of whom have difficulty responding to help can also take its toll. Worker burnout is not uncommon resulting in a high turnover of staff. As one worker explained:

> Collegiality in a CPS office is crucial. You need the support of other workers whom you have gotten to know and worked along with. When you lose colleagues that you trust and are constantly having to work with new inexperienced people, it can be tough.

Training is key in protective services. The high turnover and constant demands may mean that *training is an area that does not get the attention needed.* Not only do workers need training on how to respond in their CPS roles to all types of clients but the geographic area in which they work may present other challenges. High minority populations require increased cultural awareness and training is often the only way to really achieve cultural competence.

CPS work also requires working with as *bureaucracy that often changes with the political climate.* A new administration cuts funds and new workers are not hired or old one laid off. This means higher caseload for those workers who remain. Good casework takes time. More cases means that people are being denied the face-to-face worker attention that they may need.

The *interface between bureaucratic systems* can also cause difficulties for clients and workers. One worker made this observation:

> "My office is right near a large army post. With the incredible stresses on military families, the frequent deployment and return of parents, and the general atmosphere in this time of war, we see parents who just can't handle parenting along with everything else. But the military has its own regulations and sometimes a slightly different take on the situation than we in child protective services do. Figuring out how to work together can sometimes become a challenge."

Technology has both helped and hindered the provision of services. Computerization enhances efficiency in completing forms and keeping track of clients and trends, but a disabled computer system has the potential to bring a busy office to a standstill.

Those who have worked in CPS often suggest to new social workers that they do the following:

- Know what knowledge you will need, and be sure that you are prepared.
- Request formal training when you begin working for an agency.
- Expect good supervision.
- Develop a personal support system both at work and in your personal life.
- Strive to find the best way to serve your clients in an impersonal bureaucracy.
- Request training in cultural competence.
- Learn when change is appropriate and work for it.

Even with its flaws, the social service system works well in intervening for abused and neglected children. As long as workers provide clients with caring and nurturing, see each one as an individual, promote consistency and cooperation within the structure, and strive to improve the system, there will be hope for doing the job even better.

AN EYE TOWARD PREVENTION

The prevention of child abuse and neglect is the responsibility of every member of society. Protection social workers often become involved in a variety of prevention efforts and work with other agencies and organizations within the community toward this end. Of the three types of prevention, *primary prevention* is the effort to educate the general population to prevent maltreatment; *secondary prevention* consists of efforts directed toward high-risk populations; and *tertiary prevention* is intervention to prevent abuse or neglect from continuing (Gonzalez and MacMillan, 2008).

Throughout the years, a variety of efforts have been aimed toward the prevention of child maltreatment. And seemingly, those efforts have paid off. The National Committee for Prevention of Child Abuse, founded in 1972 by Donna Stone, set as its goal the reduction of child abuse by at least 20 percent by 1990. In fact, between 1992 and 2000, there was a 40 percent decrease in the maltreatment of children (Portwood, 2006), and this trend has continued to a lesser degree. According to a recent survey, it is estimated that between 1992 and 2010, there have been significant declines in the rates of physical abuse (56 percent) and sexual abuse (62 percent), with a slight decline in neglect (10 percent) (Finkelhor, Jones, and Shattuck, 2011).

Does this information reflect the heightened awareness of both the public and professionals for the potential for child abuse and the need to intervene? A variety of organizations continue their efforts to work toward the goal of public awareness and education, specific prevention programs, advocacy, research, and evaluation. Although funding is always a problem, over the last few years, money has come from various sources, one of which is the Children's Trust Fund.

In the late 1970s, Dr. Ray Helfer founded the Children's Trust Fund to support states' prevention efforts. Currently, the Children's Trust Fund is employed in 40 states, raising monies for prevention through surcharges on marriage licenses, birth certificates, and divorce decrees or through specifically earmarked tax refunds. State advisory committees set up guidelines to govern the distribution of available monies.

More recently, states have been encouraged to develop Children's Trust Funds by the Child Abuse Prevention Federal Challenge Grant, which matches one-fourth of the money a state makes available for prevention funds (Plummer, 1999). Children's Trust Funds use these funds for a variety of prevention programs. For example, the Massachusetts Children's Trust Fund recently developed a booklet to help educators establish a child abuse reporting protocol in their schools. This agency has also been instrumental in the efforts of the Boston archdiocese to undertake a massive education and prevention program in its schools and parishes. In addition to state and federal resources, private industry, individual agencies, and communities are using more innovative methods to raise needed funds.

Prevention has been successful in four areas: in schools, with families, with professionals, and within the community.

PREVENTION EFFORTS IN SCHOOLS

Prevention efforts should begin in the schools, where the parents of tomorrow learn what will be expected of them. The hope is that if children are taught what abusive parents have never learned, they will have a better chance of becoming healthy adults and concerned parents. The school can aid in child abuse prevention by providing the following:

- Life skills training
- Preparation for parenthood
- Self-protection training
- Educational services for the community
- Help for at-risk families

Life Skills Training

To cope with our complex society, children need more—or at least different—skills from those of generations ago. This is especially true for newly immigrated children. Children today may not need to learn how to milk a cow or till a field; the skills they require are more subtle. The same learning that prepares them for the complexities of our society will help them become better parents, as well. Several basic and appropriate skills can be taught to children.

Coping with Stress

Schools can teach children to assign priorities in order to enable them to choose among myriad tasks. In developing problem-solving skills, children learn perspective. Some schools even teach relaxation techniques to help minimize physical and mental stress.

Coping with Crisis

Another life skill children need is the ability to cope with crisis. Some schools teach their students the appropriate people to approach when a crisis occurs. Officers from fire and police departments and representatives from other community organizations give talks to promote safety. More recently, children have also been educated on what to do during the crisis of being abused (e.g., say no, run away, and tell someone). By knowing the multitude of resources available to them, children are less likely to become isolated adults who do not know how to seek help.

Making Decisions

Helfer (1978) suggests that important skills that abusive parents failed to develop be taught to children to prevent their becoming abusive parents. Children need to learn to make decisions. To make choices is, in fact, fairly easy to impart, but the assumption must be that children have the right to choose. Increasingly, schools are creating more flexible curricula to encourage choices and develop this skill.

Learning Socialization

Children must also be encouraged to learn appropriate ways to get their needs met. When adults actively listen to children, they encourage children to express their needs. When children know that they have been heard, they are then more likely to be patient in waiting to have these needs met and to delay gratification. Teachers are learning to allow children to express their feelings more openly, and in this way, children find how to separate feelings from actions. In a society filled with violence, children must learn that violence need not follow feelings of anger. In whatever they do, children must learn to take responsibility for their own actions. In addition, children must learn to communicate with peers in ways that minimize conflict. Such training goes a long way to preventing future violence. Programs that utilize peer mediation have been helpful in teaching students to get along and build better relationships (see Portwood, 2006; Teolis, 2002).

Building Positive Self-image

School personnel know the importance of building a positive self-image for healthy adulthood. Books such as *Teen Esteem* (Palmer and Froehner, 2000), *Raising Boys Well* (Hartley-Brewer, 2006a), and *Raising Girls Well* (Hartley-Brewer, 2006b) address this issue and suggest exercises for teachers to use in helping children feel better about themselves. Building self-image is being more fully integrated into the curriculum, and teachers are helping children create and enjoy successes in order to feel better about themselves.

These are just a few of the life skills that children can be taught. In addition, vocational training, budgeting instruction, and time management practices are useful to prepare for adulthood. Teaching life skills should help children become healthy adults who feel capable of controlling their own lives and more comfortable in caring for and guiding their own children in the future.

Preparation for Parenthood

To prepare today's children to be tomorrow's healthy parents, they must be provided with knowledge about normal sexuality, child development, and parenting skills.

Healthy Sexuality

Since most members of sexually abusive families know little about healthy sexual relationships, teaching children more about their bodies and the sexual functions might actually protect them from being abused and abusing.

Normal sexuality should be part of the regular curriculum. As children mature, the amount of knowledge they require will increase; therefore, high schools need to help them integrate this knowledge. Teaching basic material should be addressed more fully than can be done in one high school health or biology course. Giving children age-appropriate material beginning in elementary school will increase their comfort with and broaden their understanding of their own sexuality.

When children learn about sexuality and that information becomes a normal, natural part of their education, they are better prepared to enter into healthy sexual relationships as adults. The ability to communicate sexual needs removes one of the many stresses in marriage. Poor communication between spouses greatly hampers each individual's ability to parent effectively.

Knowledge of Child Development

Adolescents who babysit should be acquainted with the developmental stages of children. If these teens become parents, having some knowledge on the subject will save them a great deal of worry and frustration. If adolescents are taught what to expect from children, child rearing might be viewed more realistically and less idealistically.

Learning Parenting Skills

Along with learning what to expect from children, students must learn parenting skills. Parenting skills involve the roles and responsibilities expected by society.

In one particularly useful exercise, students pair up as couples and care for an egg. The egg—representing their baby—must be kept warm and given proper care. The egg must not be left alone and must be protected from harm. At the end of the exercise, the participants discuss what they have learned about the joys and burdens of parenting. The exercise must not become a game, and the seriousness of the task must be emphasized. Some classes hold mock child abuse proceedings or court hearings when a "parent" has damaged the egg. Students may also be helped to grieve over their egg if it "dies." The students find the experience enlightening.

Discussions on a variety of parenting issues, both in mainstream U.S. culture and in others, are also helpful. Debates on discipline, the assignment of chores, the question of allowances and budgeting, and the facts about nutrition may even help children recognize how their own parents are feeling about and handling these issues. Children who learn what parenting entails may be less eager to become parents too early and may be more prepared to be effective when and if they do.

Self-Protection Training

Teachers

Schools have become increasingly involved in helping children protect themselves, especially in the area of sexual abuse. A prerequisite to classroom prevention programs, however, is the training of teachers to become involved with and committed to this aspect of child abuse prevention education. A number of programs strive to train teachers so that they will feel more comfortable bringing prevention into the classroom. School systems now offer this and other forms of in-service training to teachers and other school personnel and invite teachers to write proposals for grants to bring in experts to train the school staff.

Children

Once teachers become comfortable with the material, they can plan prevention programs for children. Such programs are becoming more prevalent. Basically, the numerous programs now available strive to (1) educate children about what sexual abuse is, (2) make children more aware of who potential abusers are, and (3) teach children what action to take when someone tries to abuse them (Kenny, Capri, Thakker-Kolar, Ryan, and Runyon, 2008; Plummer, 2004; Wurtele and Kenny, 2012). Program material addresses all ages of children, and total programs provide age-appropriate information from kindergarten through sixth grade (Plummer, 1999: Wurtele and Kenny, 2012).

Prevention efforts in classrooms emphasize that children have the right not to be hurt and that if they are being abused, they should tell a trusted adult. One reason teachers must be comfortable with this material is that with the programs' emphasis on seeking help, children are led to confide in adults—especially, teachers. Teachers must be receptive to children's attempts to tell them and must know where to go with the information.

How successful have these classroom efforts been? Beginning in 1984, attempts to look critically at the training began. A recent study of the efficacy of self-protection/child empowerment programs (Kenny et al., 2008) concluded that the children who participate in such programs demonstrate an increase in knowledge and skills. In addition, these children have reported that they feel safer after having taken part in such prevention efforts. For the most part, there were few, if any, negative side effects for the children involved. It was noted that people in some cultures—including Asian cultures, some Hispanic cultures, and African American and Native American cultures—may see assertiveness on the part of children to be disrespectful. In addition, some families might distrust the law enforcement or child protection agencies to which abuse would be reported. These concerns must be addressed.

One benefit of existing prevention programs, besides teaching children concepts that will protect them from possible sexual abuse, is that training stimulates disclosure. Children who have been abused tend to come forward to report once they have taken part in school training. Through these efforts, children communicate more openly both in the classroom and at home with their parents.

There are aspects of these programs that concern some schools. School districts that are hesitant to teach sex education are unlikely to institute sex abuse prevention training. Concerns include: Does sex abuse prevention training distort the picture of sexuality when deviance is taught before the normal role of sexual development? What happens to children who are later abused when programs suggest that saying no prevents abuse?

Hopefully, there will continue to be evaluation and revision of school-based prevention programs so that children can be adequately prepared to protect themselves.

Educational Services for the Community

Prescriptions for prevention include community awareness. Schools can further these efforts through workshops, opening their facilities to self-help groups, and through adult education.

Many school prevention programs expand the curriculum to include at least one workshop for the community. This can be done as part of a student and parent training program. A session for the community would acquaint the participants with the problems facing abusive parents, educate them as to resources available to combat child abuse or neglect, and engage them in a discussion of how to prevent child maltreatment in the future.

In addition to providing training for the community, schools offer support to other prevention programs by allowing the use of their facilities and resources. Self-help groups such as Parents Anonymous and Parents United appreciate the use of meeting rooms. Schools' films or books can also be made available for interested groups or individuals.

And finally, schools can provide adult education programs for parents. Along with the usual offerings designed to improve skills or introduce new interests, schools might include evening courses in child development, parenting skills, budgeting, stress reduction, and problem-solving skills to help parents expand their capabilities, feel more in control at home, and perhaps be less likely to abuse. At one innovative school, a course entitled "Understanding Child Abuse and Neglect for Parents" attracted a number of people, including several potential parents and one or two who admitted, well into the course, that they feared they were abusive. The instructor worked with these concerned individuals to improve their coping skills and to help them become more relaxed parents.

Schools Helping At-Risk Families

In every community, there are families who are potentially abusive or neglectful. Families need to minimize their stresses and strengthen their coping abilities. Schools can offer evening programs for parents who work or for those who need extra relief from child care responsibilities. Late afternoon recreation programs for adolescents might alleviate the stress that is commonly felt before the dinner hour.

Underutilized schools sometimes donate space to crisis nurseries. When parents feel the need of support or temporary relief from child care, they can stop in or leave their children for a while. As part of their course structure, high school students assist in these nurseries.

PREVENTION EFFORTS WITH FAMILIES

It is important to educate the parents of tomorrow so that they will not be abusive, but what of the families of today? There are many ways to help families cope with stress as a prevention for maltreatment. Some parenting enhancement programs are offered to those who are specifically designated as at high risk of abusive or neglectful behavior. Others are designed for parents who are interested or feel the need to take such courses.

The most effective models for parents are parent education programs that focus on improving their coping skills, educating them about child development, facilitating bonding and communication with their children, and increasing their ability to approach helping resources (Browne, Stratton, Hanks, and Hamilton, 2002; Chadwick, 2002; Daro, 2003; Dodge and Coleman, 2009; Fontes, 2008; Galano, 2007; Gonzalez and MacMillan, 2008; Gutterman, 2000; Huebner, 2002; Lutzker, Wolfe, and Bigelow, 2001; Wurtele and Kenny, 2012).

One of the earliest parent education and support programs is the Olds model, developed by Olds and colleagues. This prenatal/early intervention project, which began with home visitation by nurses during pregnancy, was initially evaluated in Elmira, New York, and found to have positive effects on parenting attitudes and behaviors during the first two years of a child's life. The model has now been evaluated extensively and become popular for reducing the number of nonaccidental injuries to children, in addition to promoting a home atmosphere that is more supportive of healthy development (Portwood, 2006; Wulczyn, Barth, Yaun, Harnden, and Landverk, 2006).

Another far-reaching parent education/early visitation program with the goal of preventing maltreatment is the Healthy Families America (HFA) program, an initiative that stimulated the development of numerous other programs based on it. HFA, launched in 1992 by Prevent Child Abuse America in partnership with the Ronald MacDonald House Charities, uses trained, professionally supervised paraprofessional home visitors to engage with the parents and help to address their parenting needs (Portwood, 2006; Wulczyn et al., 2006). This program was the precursor for Hawaii's Healthy Start model, which has been widely adopted (Daro, 2003; Galano, 2007; Portwood, 2006).

These programs and others like them work in similar ways. They begin by identifying and working with high-risk mothers early in their pregnancies by evaluating their needs, strengths, and support networks (Wurtele and Kenny, 2012). In fact, a great deal can be learned about the mother's support system whom she brings to prenatal visits and how she relates to these individuals. If she consistently comes alone, is this by choice or because she has no one to whom she can turn for support? How involved does the father seem in the pregnancy?

Once high-risk parents have been screened and identified, agencies offer in-home service to support and train families in order to prevent maltreatment of children. This approach seems especially useful with teenage parents. In this type of home service, a trained volunteer, professional, or team of professionals provides assistance to the mother or both parents on a regular basis. The home visitor may teach parenting skills, furnish transportation, assume an advocacy role, or perform other services. (These services are similar to those described in Chapter 12, but the difference here is that these parents have not yet abused or neglected their children.) Among the many benefits of in-home service is an increase in parental ability to recognize and respond to the child's emotional, physical, and developmental needs; a decrease in subsequent pregnancies; an increase in seeking out and using health care and job training resources; a decrease in the use of welfare; and an increase in the rates of employment and in the number of high school completions (Galano, 2007; Gutterman, 2000; Lutzker et al., 2001).

Evaluating Home Visitation Programs

Although the Olds model and the Healthy Families model have been widely evaluated, there are also numerous other models that differ somewhat in design. The design and delivery of such programs is particularly important and must be carefully assessed.

Wulczyn and colleagues (2006) report that these factors have been evaluated and a set of criteria deduced that optimize the effectiveness of intervention. Home visitation programs should (1) be long term (at least 6 months to 3 years), offering a significant number of contacts between helpers and the parents (weekly or biweekly); (2) connect with the parent either prenatally or in the immediate postpartum period; (3) have trained professionals (e.g., nurses) who have been the primary service deliverers, as opposed to exclusively paraprofessionals; (4) have a clear "theory of change" that is a clear expectation of what behavior or attitudes will be impacted by the service delivery; (5) have a developmental focus to the services, meaning that services must be tailored to the developmental needs of the children and their families; and finally (6) be comprehensive, offering a broad array of services to fully meet the parenting needs of the clients (pp. 141–142). Given these criteria, experts believe that parent education programs in the home can be particularly helpful in promoting child well-being.

Parent/Child Screening and Prevention

Some experts believe that parents and children must be screened carefully to determine if they are at risk. Helfer (1976) states that there are three times when there is a natural opportunity to screen and subsequently educate future and present parents: (1) at the high school level; (2) when they seek services for pregnancy and the impending birth of their children; (3) and when these children enter the school system.

Screening children for problems when they enter the school system is and should be routine in most, if not all, schools. The school needs to know the special needs of this child, his or her developmental level, possible barriers to future learning, and the general health of the child. Through interviewing the parent and talking with the child, there is an opportunity to assess the home environment. How does the child see himself or herself in the family system? Does he or she feel loved and protected or isolated? In discussion with the parents, many school personnel ask for a developmental history and not only listen for problems and delays but also observe how the parents describe the child. If the child is viewed as different, are there negative connotations? The parent–child interaction shows much about the relationship, and the teacher or counselor may detect the child's ability to trust and learn from another adult.

The question is, "What happens with this information?" The family's right to privacy cannot be ignored. How can this information aid the child in his or her school career? Information that helps remove barriers to the child's learning ability is valuable. The child may need remedial work, aid with self-esteem, or extra attention in his or her transition into the school setting. These needs may call for immediate referral or may simply be noted in the teacher's records.

Parent–child problems are slightly more difficult. Some parents just need support. Entrance into school, especially with the first child, is when parents' child-raising practices come under scrutiny. Parents may feel unsure of themselves and nervous about public exposure. Reassurance is helpful. Some parents perceive that there is a problem and ask for help. Other parents deny problems. If these parents are not receptive to offers of help, the school personnel will want to keep close track of this child and his or her progress, unless the child is in immediate danger.

Parent support groups address a variety of problems. Unfortunately, support groups are frequently considered to be for parents with problems, while average parents are expected to be more or less self-sufficient. Yet many parents describe moments when they question the effectiveness of their child management skills and would appreciate the support and advice of other parents.

Schools often become involved in parent support groups. One innovative school had a program, sponsored by the Parent–Teachers Association, that provided a series of groups focusing on children's specific developmental milestones. For example, the first of these was entitled "When Your Child Goes to School" and included sessions on the problems children encounter in the early grades, helping the child make the transition from home to school, parents' use of free time, sibling rivalry, and children and television. Each session took up a different topic, and parents came together to discuss their views. Another group dealt with "The Transition Year."

Many educators think that third grade marks the transition between socializing and more demanding learning skills, and this grade presents problems for some children. Taking courses such as "When Your Child Reaches Puberty" and "Your Values, the Schools', and Your Child's," along with the younger-age problems encountered, encouraged parents to reach out for help or gave them confidence in their own parenting abilities.

Information for immigrants is not easily imparted. In the late 1800s and early 1900s, immigrants were attracted to settlement houses like Hull House in Chicago (for more information, see Addams, 1910), where they were helped to assimilate our culture and child-rearing practices. Now, however, immigrants get little support, and practices that are well accepted in their culture may be considered abusive in ours—yet no one tells these parents this until society intervenes.

Many communities sponsor English as a second language (ESL) programs. Why not incorporate (especially for parents) information on the United States as a second culture? But do we have the right to dictate to those from other cultures how they should raise their children? When their practices violate federal or state laws, they are informed, but it seems fair to communicate this information early after their arrival, rather than subject these parents to notification by the protective service system.

As society becomes more aware of the incidence of child sexual abuse and increasingly committed to prevention, parents are being encouraged to train their children to protect themselves. Although parents have always sought to protect their children, they are now learning that the warnings of the 1950s and 1960s ("Don't get in a car with strangers" or "Don't take candy from strangers") were inadequate. Research proves that the danger from strangers is not as significant as abuse administered by parents or acquaintances.

Some parents do not feel the need or cannot talk to their children about sexual abuse. Some feel they supervise their children sufficiently, and therefore, preparation for the possibility of abuse is unnecessary. Others feel that they do not want to frighten their children needlessly. Yet these parents often alert their children to the possibility of kidnapping—a much more frightening concept for children.

Parents often do not feel they have the appropriate vocabulary to talk about sexual abuse. They may be unsure of their own values about sexuality and fear that a discussion of sexual abuse will uncover their ambiguity. For some parents, talking about molestation brings back painful memories of their own abuse or of other sexual conflicts. For whatever reasons, many parents are hesitant to educate their children on the subject.

Prevention educators want to train parents to talk with their children. Although women tend to be the primary attendees of such educational programs (and also the primary source of sexual education information for children), men should also be encouraged to participate, if for no other reason than to decrease the likelihood of becoming abusers themselves.

Some parents educate themselves in the interest of preventing their children from being abused, rather than fall back on incorrect information that they might have been given themselves as children. It is not always easy to broach the subject of sexual abuse with one's children. Some parents assume that when the child asks for information, they will alert them to the dangers of sexual abuse. But what if the child never asks? Other parents would prefer that children receive this education in other settings, such as schools, yet there are still those who protest against schools instituting such prevention programs. What, then, is the solution that will meet everyone's needs? It is clear that there is a need for a more coordinated and collaborative approach among home, schools, and community agencies to educate parents and involve them in prevention efforts.

In addition to educating their children, parents have an obligation to create a home atmosphere that discourages keeping harmful secrets, encourages open communication, and creates healthy sexuality. In addition, children can also be taught skills that make them less likely to be victims, like feeling good about themselves, and not being hampered by sexual stereotypes. In addition, when children know that they have parents who will listen and take their fears seriously, they will feel more secure.

The importance of parents educating their children about sexual abuse cannot be understated. Perhaps one of the most convincing testimonies to this concept comes from an inmate incarcerated for the sexual abuse of children:

> *"I look for the kid who looks vulnerable—you know—the one who doesn't have much confidence, who's probably been taught to obey adults no matter what. And I really know that I have it made if no one's explained anything about sex to the kid. Then I can tell him or her anything I want, and he or she will believe me. When parents don't talk to kids about sex or abuse and when the kid knows he or she can't ask questions, that's when I have no trouble getting a child to go along with me. Maybe parents should know that. If they want to protect their kids against someone like me, they should talk to them—tell them honestly what could happen."*

Culturally Sensitive Prevention

Fontes (2008) points out the necessity of being sensitive to cultural variations in prevention efforts. Yet recent studies have shown a lack of knowledge on the part of those who develop and implement prevention programs as to how to make them effectively culturally sensitive (Fontes, 2008; Kenny et al., 2008; Plummer, 2004; Lustig and Koester, 2009; Wurtele and Kenny, 2012). Since most programs are developed by the majority culture (white), Fontes contends that they do not address the needs of specific minority populations.

One way to address the needs of minority communities is to involve them in joint efforts to develop curricula. Not involving minority members but rather developing what are assumed to be culturally competent programs might be construed by minority communities as their being targeted as the problem (Fontes, 2008). Instead, encouraging the involvement of members of various cultural groups in prevention planning will make it clear that the need is universal (Diller, 2010).

EFFECTIVE PREVENTION

A significant part of prevention involves educating the public about how to prevent child abuse. Public awareness programs often include the distribution of pamphlets, public service announcements, sponsorship of speakers by civic groups and the availability of books at libraries.

How effective are such community education programs? The National Committee to Prevent Child Abuse has collected data to determine if the prevention efforts made in the last few years have had an impact on the general public (Daro and Gelles, 1992; Plummer, 2004). The results of numerous evaluative surveys demonstrate changes in several areas of public attitudes. First, there has been a decline in physical punishment during the last few years. Parents now seem to recognize the harmful effects of yelling and swearing at children on a long-term basis. African Americans, Hispanic Americans, and blue-collar workers are most likely to report spanking children, but the rate has declined. The surveys have also indicated that parents are more likely to stop and think before hitting. Most experts agree that the educational programs about child abuse have been effective in decreasing the maltreatment of children (Daro, 2003; Dodge and Coleman, 2009; Daro and Gelles, 1992; Plummer, 2004; Wurtele and Kenny, 2012).

To enhance future educational efforts, these authors divided families into three types: consumer families, dependent families, and resistant families. *Consumer families* are those who recognize their limitations in knowledge and voluntarily sign up for educational groups and parent groups. These families call hotlines and generally seek to keep from abusing their children. *Dependent families* need more help and need to know how to access education and services. They need outreach and follow-up. But it is the *resistant families*—those who are dysfunctional, abuse alcohol and drugs, have deficient parenting skills, and are resistant to efforts to change—that require the most attention. By categorizing families, prevention efforts can be tailored to the needs of specific populations (Wulczyn et al., 2006).

Demonstrating understanding of and support for agencies involved in the intervention and treatment of abuse is also vital. There is also an opportunity for all types of community groups to be involved in prevention programs. For example, the Campfire Girls undertook a popular prevention project in child sexual abuse, whereby children were trained to recognize and react to abusive situations. A community men's service group purchased prevention packages and sponsored training for teachers, parents, and interested citizens. A council of family service agencies hosted a series of parenting courses. The possibilities for involvement and the ideas for prevention activities are limitless.

On a national level, in 1988, Congress passed an amendment to the 1974 Child Abuse Prevention and Treatment Act that created an advisory board on child abuse and neglect. This board proposed a 31-recommendation report that suggested, among other points, areas in which prevention efforts might be made. According to Krugman (1997), the general nature of these recommendations caused the report to become lost in bureaucracy and prompted the advisory board to issue a second report that was much more specific. It focused on the need for the federal government to take a more active role in protecting children and to assess the current state policies to determine their efficacy.

In short, the United States was challenged to state its child protection policy and to be a driving force behind the protection of the nation's children. The report underscored the importance of efforts to strengthen families and neighborhoods, suggested new ways to coordinate federal efforts at intervention, and encouraged continued development of home visitation and neonatal services.

The signing of the Adoption and Safe Families Act of 1997, with its emphasis on improving permanency for children, caused many experts to be more optimistic about the future. It is too early to know the full impact of the national efforts to respond to the issue of child abuse and neglect. Many point out that we must do more to meet the needs of our children. Currently, on a federal level, there is some effort to keep track of how states are meeting their obligations toward maltreated children. The National Clearinghouse on Child Abuse and Neglect, under the Children's Bureau, tabulates summaries of reporting statutes and statistics for all states. Reporting laws tend to vary, but seeing the comparisons may stimulate more alignment.

The prevention of child abuse and neglect must be given increased priority in the future. Although efforts in intervention and treatment have had some success, they have only addressed a part of the problem. Effective prevention should mean that fewer children need ever be exposed to the hurt of being abused or neglected. Only a combined and coordinated effort can accomplish this goal.

Working Toward a Better Tomorrow

Prevention efforts are alerting people to the problem of child abuse and neglect and the need for intervention, but additional efforts must focus on three areas: changes in society, changes in the helping system, and additional research. Each area connects closely with the others, and all are vital in reducing the incidence of child abuse and neglect.

Nigel Parton (2006), in his book *Safeguarding Childhood*, traces societal changes in England, suggesting that the situation may be similar in the United States and Canada. During the late-nineteenth century, a great deal of emphasis was placed on the privacy of the family, which had a significant influence on policy and practice. Only when the family could not meet its responsibilities was intervention initiated.

Changes in society over the last few decades, as well as the economy, have placed additional stress on the family, making it more difficult for this structure to meet its needs unaided. Increased recognition that early intervention is crucial to child well-being, as well as a realization that uncoordinated and solely crisis-oriented service provision does not have a positive effect on children and families, has created a need to shift the emphasis of services to children.

At one time, the focus of children's services was the *protection* of the child, or the *child-saving approach*. The intervention was marked by investigation and assessment of risk and is backed by the legal powers that stand ready to remove the child if circumstances warrant it. Increasingly, the focus has changed, with the recognition that child maltreatment is enmeshed with family dysfunction, relationship issues, communication issues, and poverty and other sociological stressors. The approach has become one of helping the family to meet the demands of child raising through parental supports and education inherent in the family preservation model. With this approach, the emphasis also has changed from deficit assessment to the current strength-based perspective used by child protection agencies today. This approach looks at the parents' potential and the barriers that must be removed in order to promote successful parenting (Parton, 2006; Veith, Bottoms, and Perona, 2006).

Although the growing atmosphere of insecurity about morality, national safety and authority, the difficult economy, and the validity of social institutions and social experts, children—who are both vulnerable and sill developing—become the focus of our need to control the future (James and James, 2004; Parton, 2006). With this new insecurity about the stability of the future comes an emphasis on prevention as an effort to control what will evolve. Parton (2006) suggests that what "is being prevented is not so much the problem itself but the collapse of the various systems that have been in place to manage it" (p. 173). With the concepts of safety and risk as central, there is now increased attention on *surveillance*—surveillance of pedophiles (community notification), surveillance and accountability of professionals providing services (quality control through audit and computerization), surveillance of children (identification and increased safeguards), and even a concern about surveillance of any dealings with children.

Computerized systems bring together the pertinent data for recordkeeping as well as monitoring. Although in the past, it was professionals who were seen to hold the expertise for solving problems and serving children, technological systems are now seen to possess the pertinent keys. With this mindset, there is not only increased attention to confronting the current danger to children through intervention but also a fervent effort to anticipate the dangers of the future and prepare to meet them. The rub here, both in the scrutiny of existing services and policies and the efforts to prophesize the future needs of children, is that there is an expectation of a certainty that is impossible in child welfare (Parton, 2006).

Some might construe the current atmosphere as negative, but it has many positive aspects, as well. One positive aspect is the attention to personal rights and especially the rights of children. The rights of parents have always been paramount. Only when parents failed completely in their expected roles were these rights curtailed or revoked. With more allegiance to protecting the rights of children to have healthy and functional childhoods, there is potential for increased investment in methods to respond to the cries of their caretakers. For example, currently our legal system allows response to maltreatment only after the fact. Anticipating their own weaknesses, even parents who reach out for help may not be eligible for supportive services. Once the abuse occurs, however, the services are available.

Consider this case:

Wilma Fitz had had two children removed by the court and eventually placed for adoption. When she became pregnant again seven years later, she was determined to be a good parent to this child. But when the baby was several months old, Wilma found the baby's constant crying and need for attention aggravated her to the point where she was afraid she would again be abusive.

She approached a local agency and requested day care for several hours each day and support if she needed it. This protection agency informed her that there were no openings for day care available and referred her to another agency, which suggested she go into counseling. After several referrals that led nowhere, Wilma gave up. She attempted to cope in the same state of isolation that had characterized her previous parenting experience.

When the baby was 9 months old, the protective agency received a call from a local hospital, saying that the baby had been admitted with multiple breaks and bruises, the cause of which appeared to be abuse by the mother.

Granted, some communities might have found resources to help Wilma before she battered once again, but the ability to help before the fact depends more on worker or agency creativity than on any formal or national structure. Increased acceptance of the concept that it is up to a total community to safeguard and protect the rights of children, joining with parents who are unable to do so alone, will benefit both the Wilmas of the future and their children.

Surveys of community needs and concerns should more effectively anticipate children's needs as well as the needs of their parents. Some agencies survey providers and community members and ask what they perceive as the major gaps in services provided for children. Money is always an issue in the provision of services, and in the current economy, it is even more so. Needs assessments must document the reality of children's needs. Since much of public funding is provided through legislation, having a voice in the legislature is important. But children cannot vote for those services. Instead, the protection of their rights depends on interested advocates to further their causes. Needs assessments give advocates tools to make the point and substantiate it, based on the record of community concern (Chadwick, 2002).

How else can the community become acquainted with the needs and rights of children and their families and begin to advocate for more money to provide for these necessities? There is a need for creative programs that heighten public awareness. Removing the stigma attached to the intervention process with troubled families, promoting positive parenting, and making more people within the community aware of children's right and needs will also provide better alternatives to maltreatment.

Rethinking Child Protection

As more and more reports barrage CPS, agencies' ability to respond is often hampered by bureaucratic regulations, shrinking resources, and dwindling funds. In 1998, Waldfogel made suggestions about meeting the challenges faced by CPS works—suggestions that still have validity today and which cause CPS falling short in its ability to serve children in need of protective services. First, this author believes that there is *overinclusion*, meaning that some families who are referred to CPS never should be. For example, some experts express concern about the disproportionate number of minority children represented in the child welfare system (Fontes, 2008).

Second, Waldfogel (1998) points out that the *capacity* of CPS to provide services to families is exceeded by the number of referrals that it must address. And with an increased demand for services, workers face higher caseloads, which means that they cannot be as effective as they might otherwise in their provision of services. Third, and somewhat paradoxically perhaps, the same author cites *underinclusion*, in that there are families who could benefit from CPS services but are never referred. Even the most efficient reporting and screening procedures will miss some families who should have services.

Service orientation is also problematic. It is the mandate of CPS to perform two functions: to investigate cases of reported abuse and neglect and to intervene and keep families together whenever possible. Parent education programs that might appropriately use referrals for the second goal are not always available. Thus, because of these two sometimes competing goals, CPS is often criticized for being ineffective in whatever role it chooses to take. Finally, Waldfogel (1998) suggests that the *service delivery* that CPS provides falls short in that it can be uneven across communities, especially to minority clients.

The current emphasis on strengthening families paves the way for Waldfogel's (1998) three-part paradigm for child protection that features (1) more cross-agency service planning (where CPS could have access to the services of other agencies to meet their clients' needs), (2) better links with informal helpers (where CPS could make better use of such informal helpers as extended families, churches, and neighborhood resources), and (3) the ability to provide a differential response (where CPS and its partner agencies would customize their responses to a particular family's needs, with constant evaluation to monitor that family's progress). This paradigm would offer a community-based approach to child protection that is long overdue.

A community-based response is even more important in this time of economic upheaval. As agencies cut back and even close, informal helping systems may be the only hope for meeting the needs of families. Coordinating these resources is vital and must be addressed.

Creating a Unified Response

Despite the enactment of federal legislation for child abuse and neglect prevention and treatment, states have, for the most part, the freedom to interpret the act as they choose and form their own policies.

Initially, states adopted reporting laws in an attempt to demonstrate concern for children. Early laws reflected no cost figures but proved the legislators' desire to protect their weakest constituents. It soon became obvious that money had to be designated to augment protective agencies and expand treatment facilities. Some states appropriated more resources and financial backing to these services than others, and as a result, states differ significantly in the specificity of their reporting laws and in their commitment to helping the maltreated child.

For example, the penalty for not reporting abuse and neglect varies, from state to state, from a large fine or time in jail to a small fine or no penalty at all. In some states, incarceration of the convicted perpetrator is automatic; others mandate little for the treatment or punishment of sexual abusers. An abusive or neglectful parent may find numerous services available in one state but few in another. Depending on the court and the community interpretation of penalties, treatment plans for offenders and abusive parents also vary considerably.

To adequately address the problem of abuse and neglect, several steps should be taken. First, laws must be written more succinctly to be more specific and less subject to individual interpretation. National standards should enable agencies to have guidelines that standardize services. Communication among state agencies should ensure a more unified approach.

As efforts to encourage reporting from professionals on a national level increase, the type of follow-up offered must also improve. Consider this case:

> One particular school district received intensive training in the detection and reporting of child abuse. As a result, the number of reported cases of abuse within the school system doubled. But the community had an understaffed protective service agency that was overwhelmed by the number of these new reports. Much to the frustration of the teachers and other reporting professionals, the cases were not handled immediately. After a short period of time, mandated reporters began overlooking reportable cases because they realized little would be done if the report was made.

The solution to such an issue may be for the protective services agency to look for ways to bolster services. One method is to document the need versus the availability of personnel and request additional funding to hire more staff. Given the workings of government, this process can be extremely slow.

In the preceding example, the agency had not used all its appropriated contract funds, so the protective workers were primarily assigned intake responsibilities while private personnel were contracted to provide investigative services. Treatment was already a contracted service, but the worker who undertook treatment was from the same agency doing the investigation.

Whatever the plan, follow-up services must keep pace with the reporting to be truly effective.

Looking Within, Between, and Beyond Agencies

One of the biggest complaints among workers, especially new protective workers, is the lack of sufficient training. Although some agencies do give their workers initial and periodic training, many agencies think on-the-job training is best:

> When Sara Craft was hired by a large protective agency, she received only brief training on how to fill out appropriate forms. Directly out of college, with a major in English, Sara knew little about multiproblem families, nor was she familiar with the Hispanic culture, a strongly represented population in the area.
>
> After her two-day instruction on forms, she was assigned 10 cases, all of which had been uncovered for quite some time. Of these 10 cases, 4 were severely neglectful families who had proved a challenge to previous workers. On her fifth day of work, Sara was sent out alone to deal with these families, three of whom were Mexicans who spoke little or no English. Her inexperience and acute frustration soon became apparent.
>
> Although Sara's supervisor met with her before and after she visited the families, this neophyte worker lacked the knowledge of basic skills. When this same agency later instituted a two-week training period in which basic skills, knowledge of abusive and neglectful families, information about the Hispanic culture, and information about forms was imparted, the effectiveness of new workers was greatly increased. In addition, workers tended to demonstrate higher satisfaction with the job and stayed in their positions longer.

Periodic training is also necessary for social workers. Protective services is a rapidly developing field, requiring new ideas and skills. Workers must be informed of such advances. In addition, training makes many protective workers feel revitalized and helps them to aid clients in new ways.

Despite the importance of training, the cutting of state and federal funds means that agencies must determine their priorities. Ironically, training might be one area that is cut to prioritize service-related activities, which are quantifiable. Public attention, as well as formal evaluation, will focus on the efficiency with which agencies accomplish their mandate.

Colleges and universities may need to take a more active role in providing ongoing education to future and current professionals in child protection. Graduates of bachelor's programs that provide courses or certificates in child protection may appeal to agencies seeking employees. And once hired, child protection workers may be forced to seek academic courses to enhance their knowledge and skills. Colleges will then be called on to meet this demand.

Part of any social service training, whether agency based or academic, should focus on the needs of minorities. It is not enough to have one or two Spanish-speaking workers on a protective service staff; every member of the agency staff should be trained to recognize cultural problems and differences. In areas where there are Native American, Hispanic, and Asian populations, workers should have a knowledge of differing values in order to adapt their impressions and methods of dealing with individuals from these cultures. Some agencies now train or encourage workers to seek training in oppression issues. The more staff members are able to examine their own values, the more effective they will be with clients.

Other competencies may not currently be given sufficient attention in training protective workers. *Relationship competencies* have been identified as the most crucial. Consumers pointed to the need for workers to show respect for others, have effective communication skills, be comfortable with relationships, be nonjudgmental and nondefensive, and be calm in the face of crisis or client anger. Workers feel that they and their colleagues should demonstrate appropriate attitudes (e.g., nonjudgmental, nonaggressive, respect for clients' values), be able to communicate well, not prejudge, empower the client to participate, and recognize the impact that protective services can have on the lives of clients.

Nonetheless, it is often the interpersonal skills that are not adequately addressed in worker training. Agencies must become more aware that beyond training their staff to complete the necessary forms, relationship skills must be highlighted for both new and experienced staff. In addition, it is vital in this era when collaboration is crucial that workers can work in cooperation with other agencies without "turf battles."

Another important consideration is the *support* given to protective workers. Work with abusive and neglectful families is extremely demanding and can be quite draining. Workers need to know not only that they are supported in their decisions but also that they are encouraged to form strong support systems with fellow workers. Like private industry, which is now sponsoring recreational activities for its employees, social service agencies must recognize that playing as well as working together improves staff morale.

Many agencies, in addition to increased staff training and support, benefit from *consumer representation* on boards and committees. The low-income client or the formerly abusive parent could help restructure services to ensure maximum efficiency. From the days of Jane Addams and her contemporaries, large numbers of social workers have been recruited from middle-class and upper-middle-class backgrounds. These individuals have had little contact with the social system from a consumer perspective. Their values may be quite different from those of clients. Therefore, inviting those who have recently been or who currently are using social services to participate in planning and decision making could be extremely beneficial in making the workers more sensitive to the clients' needs and values.

Some agencies have citizen advocacy teams review cases periodically. These teams consist of professionals and consumers, and all members have input on how cases should be handled. The team recommendation is used by the protective agency for decision making.

The team approach has its problems, however. The instability that brought these clients to the attention of the system often makes interaction difficult. In addition, confidentiality must be strictly guarded. Consumers who participate in decision making must be aware of the importance of keeping what they learn about other clients confidential. Screening may be necessary to ensure that individuals are not reviewing their friends' cases.

To better serve clients, *communication between and within agencies* must improve, particularly in the area of duplication of services. In states' interpretation of mandatory reporting, laws designate one agency to receive and usually investigate abuse reports, thus eliminating competition. But there is still considerable overlap in treatment services, and paradoxically, one client can find several agencies willing to treat him or her yet another may find himself or herself ineligible for any agency service.

Many communities have excellent working relationships between agencies. In others, the competition between and duplication of services continue. This problem is especially prevalent between public and private agencies. Private agencies often have a superior attitude toward public agencies. Admittedly, many private agencies, able to maintain a higher percentage of trained personnel and lower caseloads, see themselves as providing higher-quality service than their public counterparts. Rarely do public and private agencies support each other. For example, staff from the public agency are as unlikely to recommend to a United Way or Community Chest that more money be allocated to a certain private agency as that agency is to testify at a public budget hearing in favor of the public agency's increased funding. Yet in a time when protective services are so much needed and funds are so limited, these agencies would find strength in mutual support.

Advocacy for children's needs is a next step in providing better protective services. Children and their families are sometimes trapped in the maze of bureaucracy or caught between agencies and their requirements. Children's advocates, either as employees of a separate advocacy agency or in the role of case managers, must see that children receive all the services to which they are entitled. With new programs being instituted and existing programs closing due to insufficient funding or resources, there is the need to explore the field thoroughly before making the decision as to what services can be provided.

The child advocate plays an important role in ensuring that the child and the family are adequately served. Sometimes, advocacy necessitates mediating between agencies and encouraging agencies to use flexibility in their interpretation of eligibility standards. Despite agency constraints, the client must come first, and advocacy often means finding the best way to provide service to a given client when agencies argue that it cannot be done.

More attention should be paid to the importance of community structures and working through community leaders. To be proactive in the field of social services, one must recognize the importance of intervention in the power structure. Knowing how and when to intervene can provide maximum help to clients.

BEYOND CHILD PROTECTION: THE NEED FOR SOCIETAL CHANGES

The helping system alone cannot solve the problems of child abuse and neglect. Society must also make some important changes.

Reversing the Trend Toward Socially Impoverished Families

If society truly cares for and wants to protect children, then it must make an investment in the families that nurture them. Unfortunately, our culture has come to value things over people. But money and goods alone, as witnessed by the insufficiency of welfare allotments, are not the only answer. We must also protect that which perpetuates and strengthens the family. Poverty, the erosion of neighborhoods, and geographic mobility are all destructive forces to the family. Poverty subjects children to a variety of stresses, including parents whose own problems sometimes rob them of the ability to be emotionally available for their children.

Whether or not the family can triumph over poverty, numerous other stresses that challenge family stability have been identified in the neighborhoods in which some maltreating families live. Garbarino and Sherman (1997) studied two neighborhoods—one that had a high rate of child maltreatment and one that had an extremely low rate. The high-risk neighborhood was inhabited by isolated families who described high levels of stress, in relief from which they expected no help from neighbors. There was little interaction, and this suspicion and mistrust transferred to the relationships between parents and children, as well. In the low-risk neighborhood, there was a spirit of cooperation and the feeling that this was a healthy place to raise children.

How does a community create and maintain a healthy neighborhood? Healthy neighborhoods are much like small towns, where small business supports community needs. Rezoning is one way such neighborhoods are being destroyed. Urban renewal entails demolishing old homes, often of lower-level socioeconomic groups, and building new apartments and condominiums that are well beyond the financial reach of former residents. Not until there is a commitment to refurbish existing neighborhoods in a manner that will still make them accessible to old neighbors will society maintain or regain the healthy neighborhood (Popple and Leighninger, 2011).

The low-income individual is not the only one whose support system suffers in today's society. Geographic mobility, which is frequently employment related, has caused families to separate from their relatives and friends. Those individuals with good interpersonal skills may readjust, whereas others remain isolated and feel unsupported in new communities. Still others, tired of frequent moves and making new friends who too will soon be left, isolate themselves through their job or other interests. As generation after generation experiences this trend, there will be an increasing breakdown of interpersonal relationships and an inhibited ability to trust and develop adequate support systems. Greater efforts on the part of communities to include citizens in planning and recreational projects may alleviate this problem somewhat. Businesses that move employees frequently must also take some responsibility for integrating workers and their families into new social environments.

Supporting Parenting

Until very recently, parenting was highly valued. Women were expected to care for and nurture their children, while men supported their efforts monetarily. Today, with more mothers in the workforce and more fathers wanting to be involved in parenting, modern technology often asks parents to choose between their children and their jobs. Long hours, the need for day care, and the inability to stay home with sick children put added stress on working parents.

What can businesses do to support parenting? Some companies support flex-time, in which employees put in the required amount of hours but begin work anytime between 7:30 and 10:00 A.M. This enables parents to tailor their days to their children's school hours. Still other businesses have job sharing—an arrangement whereby two employees share a full-time job. Thus, each works part time for prorated benefits. Increasingly, there is also more support for equal parenting. It is important that the father who wants to share responsibilities with the new family be granted paternity leave and flex-time, as well.

More recently, some industries have adopted the custom in the People's Republic of China of instituting onsite day care facilities for their employees. This way, even very young children can be visited by the parent throughout the workday. Parent centers are an innovation. Such centers offer literature, books, and classes and even lend large items of baby equipment, such as car seats. Even more important than these benefits is the attitude that employees can be effective parents, too. Perhaps another service that will come in time is employee-sponsored parent support or parent training groups. Here, employees could come during free hours to meet with and gain support from other working parents, to learn new skills to help them parent more effectively, and to handle parenting and employment with greater ease.

Today, when half the families in the nation have dealt with divorce (see Chapter 2), children have often become the victims of this emotional turmoil. Children's ability to cope with divorce is directly related to how their parents handle it. Increased emphasis must be placed on services to support divorcing parents and their children. In addition, as blended families become the norm, we must address the needs of all involved in this adjustment.

Realigning Societal Values

Our society holds several values that directly support the high incidence of child abuse and neglect. The assumption is made, for example, that anyone can parent and should be encouraged to have children. Typically, young couples are asked when they expect to begin their family. There is little question in most people's minds that it is only a matter of time before they will. The response that they do not intend to have children is met by parents, relatives, and even friends with surprise and disbelief and then with disappointment and often pressure to reconsider. Yet many of these couples have made this decision only after much thought. They may or may not change their minds, but for now, they have made their choice, a choice that should be respected by those around them.

Society should support parents in their roles, rather than perpetuate a romanticized idea of parenting. Parenting is hard work and should not be minimized by society's assumption that having children is not just a right but a duty. For no role in our lives do we receive less formal training than for that of being a parent.

One young woman who had become pregnant during adolescence related her feelings about giving up the baby for adoption:

"It's not that I don't think it was right for him," she relates. "His adoptive parents were great, and I'm sure he's really happy. It's the grief people gave me afterward. So many people said, 'How could you?' that I felt awful about it. In almost every conversation about adoption, someone will say, 'How could a parent ever give up a child?' I began to feel like some kind of monster for doing something I felt was best for my baby."

Pressure on individuals to become parents greatly contributes to their potential to be abusive or neglectful. When society recognizes the individual's right not to parent but offers support and education to those who choose to, it will be doing much to prevent child maltreatment.

Another contribution to child abuse is our culture's affinity for violence. Saturday morning cartoons feature violent encounters between animated characters. Children then graduate to TV shows, DVDs, and video games, in which people are killed savagely and with predictable regularity. The most popular movies feature power and vengeance. At sports events, fights between players are applauded more vehemently than the actual play of the game. Children learn patterns from their environment, so as adults, they may use violence not only for recreational escape but also to get their needs met.

Along with violence, our society also worships sex and, through advertising, communicates that sexuality can be used as a form of barter. Sex sells everything from jeans, hairspray, and cars to books on the best-seller list. When the sexually abusive father convinces his daughter that sex will buy her his attention and special favors, we should not be surprised that she accepts this. Some experts (Butler, 1996; Herman, 2000) argue that until we change sexual stereotypes, we will continue to predispose children to abuse.

Although there is much progress in providing a variety of models for children to emulate—assertive, self-sufficient, nonvictim women and men who can express fear, sadness, and other deep emotions—much more remains to be done. Unfortunately, the prevention of sex-role stereotyping goes beyond parents—although it must start with them. Clothes manufacturers still use pinks and pastels for girls and vibrant colors for boys. Rarely, if ever, does a commercial feature a boy playing with a doll.

WHAT DOES THE FUTURE HOLD?

It is difficult to know how the social welfare system will change over the next few years. There will continue to be concern over families who have traditionally been served by child protection. But increasingly, as the depressed economy influences not only unemployment but housing, as well, families who may not have needed social services in the past may be in need of help. Foreclosures affect the rates of both displacement and homelessness. Parents losing jobs and being unable to find other employment will clearly impact family stability. Such stressors may also impact parenting. And what will be the needs of military families, in which parents have been exposed to the traumas of war and must then return to their everyday lives with families who may have readjusted in their absence? State cutbacks in funds for the operation of a variety of child welfare and social service agencies will mean that fewer staff will be available to provide service to more consumers. Programs within agencies may be phased out in favor of performing essential tasks. How will these realities change the face of child welfare?

In every crisis, there is an opportunity for learning. What can we, in the child welfare field, learn from the constraints we currently face? How can we involve informal helping networks, such as churches and civic groups, and coordinate efforts to maintain boundaries, ethical standards, and competent social services for people in need? Certainly, the next decade of helping will call for creativity and perseverance. We may also need to rethink how families receive services. What does the future hold?

RESEARCH NEEDS

Research is an important component in the reduction of child abuse and neglect through prevention as well as planning for the future of intervention and treatment. The Children's Bureau (2008) suggested that there is a need for research into the investigation process for cases of child maltreatment. For example, what are the effects of the size of a worker's caseload on his or her ability to complete dispositions? What are the effects of differential response approaches to CPS? Do race, ethnicity, and socioeconomic status affect how cases are decided? Are children removed from the home in the face of different risk factors rather than confront those who remain in the home?

Proponents of prevention attest to the need to explore the efficacy of different types of prevention efforts. Evaluation of existing programs in prevention may well pave the way for the duplication of successful programs and the creation of others.

Since the greatest number of reported cases of child maltreatment are in the area of neglect, additional research into this area is clearly important. What factors lead to neglectful parenting, and how can neglectful parents be helped to meet the needs of their children?

Another area for research might be the nonabusive family. What skills do parents need to adequately fill their roles? What means do they use to cope effectively with the stresses of child rearing? Perhaps through isolating factors that contribute to a positive family atmosphere, we can offer more in the way of treatment to abusive families.

We also need more cross-cultural research. How do other societies define and deal with problems such as child abuse and neglect? What can these other cultures offer us in our attempt to combat child maltreatment?

And finally, people can learn a great deal from talking with survivors of abuse and neglect. When we encounter those who have experienced abuse and neglect but who go on to lead productive, uninhibited lives, we wonder what has made the difference for them. How can these survivors' experiences help us to help others?

Opportunities for research on child abuse and neglect abound, and it is this research that will enable us to better understand and intervene for our maltreated children.

SUMMARY

Protective workers are considered to be professionals who possess a systematic body of knowledge, authority, sanction by the community, a code of ethics, a professional culture, an obligation to competence, and ethnic competence.

The duties of such a professional require specific knowledge and skills, the most important of which are skills in basic helping, engagement, observation, and communication. Empathy is a primary personal trait required for the job.

Protective services work entails frustrations. Workers must first resolve any conflict about their role and how society views that role. Workers sometimes have difficulty overidentifying with clients—especially children. On the other hand, children are challenging clients; their spontaneity sometimes makes their behavior unpredictable and difficult to handle.

Bureaucracies present some difficulties to protective services workers. Following rules and regulations can be frustrating when the worker is concerned with the needs of clients and must be flexible in order to meet them. This same structure, however, provides a framework for equity and a model of consistency.

The stresses of protective work can result in burnout. For this reason, it is important that workers develop methods of reducing stress, especially through outside recreation and the maintenance of a healthy support system.

In spite of the frustrations of protective services, workers allude to the benefits brought about by the success stories. In addition to the client, who does make one feel needed, there is usually good support among co-workers. As one worker put it, "We work very hard at this job, so we play hard too." And it is good to know that through the efforts of the worker, children may be spared further abuse.

It is these benefits that make work with abused and neglected children an extremely rewarding profession. To face the future, workers must learn to anticipate the pitfalls of the work and develop their own cultural competence.

The target populations for prevention efforts are schools, families, professionals, and communities.

Schools are becoming increasingly aware of the need to integrate prevention materials into the curriculum. Children who are given training in basic life and parenting skills become healthy adults and better parents. Self-protection information enables children to be better prepared to resist abusive individuals or helps them recognize the importance of telling trusted adults when they are being abused or have been approached. Schools can lead community awareness programs on the problems of abuse and neglect and how to prevent them, donate space for support groups and prevention programs, and expand adult education to benefit parents. Schools can also sponsor or provide space for services to high-risk families.

Prevention efforts must also be directed toward families. Parenting education enables parents to perform their roles more effectively and can alleviate some of the stresses unsure parents feel. High-risk parents can be identified by medical, social services, or school personnel and can be offered additional resources. Parent support groups can promote more positive parenting if directed at specific behaviors. Such support, as well as culturally specific information, should be given to immigrant parents to help them understand appropriate and inappropriate child management practices. Parents who educate their children about potential sexual abuse make them less vulnerable to the advances of an abuser.

Allied professionals are becoming more aware of the need for prevention, but they need to concentrate on combating child pornography. Engaging teams of professionals and laypeople in prevention efforts should begin to make our communities safer places in which children can grow. But this commitment must be communitywide in order to make a significant impact.

Despite current prevention efforts, much more must be done to decrease the incidences of child abuse and neglect. Our efforts should be directed to changes in the helping system, changes in society, and additional research.

A fundamental change must take place in how we regard providing services to families. Instead of waiting until parents fail and intervention is necessary, we should anticipate needs through needs assessments and heed the cues of parents who reach out for help before abuse occurs. Perhaps taking these actions would help remove some of the stigma surrounding social services and their clients.

We must also promote a unified response to abuse reports from state to state and insist on prompt and adequate follow-up. To ensure better services within the protective agency, workers should be adequately trained and given ongoing support in their jobs. Some training in minority needs and issues would further improve worker effectiveness.

Consumers are important contributors to decision making and planning in protective services. The use of consumers requires more attention to confidentiality issues, but in the long run, it should promote more efficiency in service provisions.

Communication between agencies is necessary to maximize the services that can be provided. Agencies often duplicate each other's efforts counterproductively. Sometimes, advocacy is used to ensure that client interests are paramount.

Society, as well as the helping system, must make changes to reduce the rate of child abuse. Foremost, families must be supported in the nurturing of their children. Poverty, eroded neighborhoods, and geographic mobility endanger interpersonal relationships and pose a threat to healthy family life. Businesses must recognize and provide services to enhance the parents' ability to be both competent workers and effective parents. As a culture, our propensity for assuming anyone can and must parent, our fascination with violence, and our tendency to socialize children in sex-role stereotypes actively contribute to child maltreatment. All these things must end.

Perhaps one of our best hopes for the future lies in research, not only to further define and understand abuse but also to evaluate existing programs. Only through our commitment to change and our willingness to undertake research, will we create a better future and will we able to combat the growing problem of child abuse and neglect.

References for Chapter 1

Addams, J. (1910). *Twenty Years at Hull House.* New York: Signet.

Amrosino, R., Heffernan, J. J., Ambrosino, R., and Shuttelsworth, G. (2011). *Social Work and Social Welfare.* Stamford, CT: Cengage.

Bremner, R. (Ed.). (1970). *Children and Youth in America: A Documentary History.* Vol. 1. Cambridge, MA: Harvard University Press.

Caffey, J. (1946). "Multiple Fractures in the Long Bones of Infants Suffering from Chronic Subdural Hematoma." *American Journal of Roentgenology* 56:163–173.

Conte, J., and Shore, D. (1982). "Social Work and Sexual Abuse." *Journal of Social Work and Human Sexuality* I(1–2): 201–211.

Crosson-Tower, C. (2002). *From the Eye of the Storm: Experiences of a Child Welfare Worker.* Boston: Allyn & Bacon.

Crosson-Tower, C. (2006). *A Clergy Guide to Child Abuse and Neglect.* Cleveland: Pilgrim Press.

deMause, L. (1998). "The History of Child Abuse." *Journal of Psychohistory* 25(3): 1–20.

Eglinton, J. (1965). *Greek Love.* New York: Oliver Layton.

Freud, S. (1966). *The Complete Introductory Letters of Psychoanalysis.* New York: Norton.

Friedman, A. B. (1956). *The Viking Book of Folk Ballads of the English Speaking World.* New York: Viking.

Gardner, L. (1980). "The Endocrinology of Abuse Dwarfism: With a Note on Charles Dickens as Child Advocate." In *Traumatic Abuse and Neglect of Children at Home,* edited by G. J. Williams (pp. 375–380). Baltimore: Johns Hopkins University Press.

Herman, J. (1997). *Trauma and Recovery.* New York: Basic Books.

Hindman, H. D. (2002). *Child Labor: An American History.* Armonk, NY: M.E. Sharpe.

Hoffman, E. (1978). "Policy and Politics: The Child Abuse Prevention and Treatment Act." *Public Policy* 26:71–88

Inglis, R. (1978). *Sins of the Fathers.* New York: St. Martin's Press.

International Society for Prevention of Child Abuse and Neglect (ISPCAN). (n.d.). Retrieved from http://www.ispcan.org/?page=History on July 2, 2012.

Jackson, P. (1978). "Black Charity in Progressive Era Chicago." *Social Service Review* 52:400–417.

Jackson, S., and Brissett-Chapman, S. (1999). *Serving African American Children.* Washington, DC: Child welfare League of America.

Justice, B., and Justice, R. (1980). *The Broken Taboo: Sex in the Family.* New York: Human Sciences Press.

Kempe, H., Silverman, F., Steele, B., Droegemueller, W., and Silver, H. (1962). "The Battered-Child Syndrome." *Journal of the American Medical Association* 181:17–24.

Lazoritz, S. (1990). "Whatever Happened to Mary Ellen?" *Child Abuse and Neglect* 14:143–149.

Lennon, F. (1972). *The Life of Lewis Carroll.* New York: Dover.

Lenoir-Degoumois, V. (1983). "The Manifestations of Ill-Treatment of Children. Historical Background." *International Journal of Offender Therapy and Comparative Criminology* 27:55–60.

Malinowski, B. (1927). *Sex and Repression in Savage Society.* London: Routledge and Kegan Paul.

Mass, A. I., and Yap, J. (2000). "Child Welfare: Asian and Pacific Islander Families." In *Child Welfare: A Multicultural Perspective,* edited by N. Cohen (pp. 107–129). Boston: Allyn & Bacon.

Meiselman, K. (1992). *Incest.* San Francisco: Jossey-Bass, 1978.

Middleton, R. (1962). "Brother-Sister and Father-Daughter Marriage in Ancient Egypt." *American Sociological Review* 27:603–611.

Mintz, S. (2006). *Huck's Raft: A History of American Childhood.* Cambridge, MA: Harvard University Press.

Morgan, L. H. (1877). *Ancient Society.* Chicago: Kerr.

Myers, J. E. B. (2011). "A Short History of Child Protection in America." In *The APSAC Handbook on Child Maltreatment,* edited by J. E. B. Myers (pp. 3–15). Thousand Oaks, CA: Sage.

Nabokov, V. (1989). *Lolita.* New York: Knopf.

Olafson, E., Corwin, D. L., and Summit, R. (1993). "Modern History of Child Sexual Abuse: Cycles of Discovery and Suppression." *Child Abuse and Neglect* 17:7–24.

Parton, N. (1985). *The Politics of Child Abuse.* London: Macmillan.

Popple, P. R., and Leighninger, L. (2010). *Social Work, Social Welfare and American Society.* Boston: Allyn & Bacon.

Public Knowledge LLC. (2003). *Discipline and Development: A Meta-Analysis of Public Perceptions of Parents, Parenting, Child Development and Child Abuse.* Severna Park, MD: Author.

Richardson, C. (2003). "Physician/Hospital Liability for Negligently Reporting Child Abuse." *Journal of Legal Medicine* 23:131–150.

Righthand, S., Kerr, B. B., and Drach, K. M. (2003). *Child Maltreatment Risk Assessments.* New York: Haworth.

Rose, S. R., and Fatout, M. F. (2003). *Social Work Practice with Children and Adolescents.* Boston: Allyn & Bacon.

Rush, F. (1992). *The Best Kept Secret: Sexual Abuse of Children.* New York: Tab Books.

Sameroff, A. J., and Gutman, L. M. (2004). "Contributions of Risk Research to the Design of Successful Interventions." In *Intervention with Children and Adolescents*, edited by P. Allen-Meares and M. W. Frazer (pp. 9–26). Boston: Allyn & Bacon.

Sanders, L. (1982). *The Case of Lucy Bending.* New York: Berkeley.

Sgroi, S. (1988). *Handbook of Clinical Intervention in Child Sexual Abuse.* Lexington, MA: Lexington Books.

Shelman, E., and Lazoritz, S. (2003). *Out of the Darkness: The Story of Mary Ellen Wilson.* Lake Forest, CA: Dolphin Moon Press.

Smuts, A. (2005). *Science in the Service of Children, 1893–1935.* New Haven: Yale University Press.

Summit, R. (1983). "The Child Sexual Abuse Accommodation Syndrome." *Child Abuse and Neglect* 7:177–193.

ten Bensel, R. W., Rheinberg, M. M., and Radbill, S. X. (1997). "Children in a World of Violence: The Roots of Child Maltreatment." In *The Battered Child*, edited by M. E. Helfer, R. S. Kempe, and R. D. Krugman (pp. 3–28). Chicago: University of Chicago Press.

Tower, C. C. (1984). *Child Abuse and Neglect: An Educator's Guide to Recognition, Reporting and Classroom Management.* Washington, DC: National Education Association.

Turner, J. (2005). *Incest: Origin of the Taboo.* Boulder, CO: Paradigm.

Weber, M. W. (1997). "Assessment of Child Abuse: A Primary Function of Child Protective Services." In *The Battered Child*, edited by M. E. Helfer, R. S. Kempe, & R. D. Krugman (pp. 120–149). Chicago: University of Chicago Press.

Weinberg, S. K. (1955). *Incest Behavior.* Secaucus, NJ: Citadel Press.

References for Chapter 2

Bee, H., and Boyd, D. (2011). *The Developing Child.* Boston: Allyn & Bacon.

Berk, L. E. (2012). *Child Development.* Boston: Allyn & Bacon.

Berns, R. M. (2012). *Child, Family, Community: Socialization and Support.* Belmont, CA: Wadsworth.

Bevin, T. (2001). "Parenting in Cuban American Families." In *Culturally Diverse Parent-Child and Family Relationships: A Guide for Social Workers and Other Practitioners,* edited by N. B. Webb and D. Lum (pp. 181–201). New York: Columbia University Press.

Bird, S. R. (2009). *Light, Bright and Damned Near White: Biracial and Triracial Culture in America.* Santa Barbara, CA: Praeger.

Bonilla-Santiago, G. (2007). "Social Work Practice with Puerto Ricans." In *Social Work: A Profession of Many Faces,* edited by A. T. Morales, B. W. Sheafor, and M. E. Scott (pp. 552–577). Boston: Allyn & Bacon.

Chan, S., and Chen, D. (2011). "Families with Asian Roots." In *Developing Cross Cultural Competency,* edited by E. W. Lynch and M. J. Hanson (pp. 234–318). Baltimore: Paul H. Brookes.

Cheung, M., and Nguyen, S. (2001). "Parent-Child Relationships in Vietnamese American Families." In *Culturally Diverse Parent-Child and Family Relationships,* edited by N. B. Webb and D. Lum (pp. 261–282). New York: Columbia University Press.

Coalition for Asian American Children and Families. (2001). "Understanding the Issues of Abuse and Neglect and Asian American Families." Retrieved from http://www.cacf.org

Culhane-Pera, C. A., Xiong, P., and Vawter, D. (Eds.). (2003). *Healing by Heart: Clinical and Ethical Case Stories of Hmong Families and Western Providers.* Nashville: Vanderbilt.

Delgado, R. (2000). "Generalist Child Welfare and Hispanic Families." In *Child Welfare: A Multicultural Perspective,* edited by N. Cohen (pp. 130–156), Boston: Allyn & Bacon.

Edwards, E. D., and Edwards, M. E. (2007). "Social Work Practice with American Indians and Alaskan Natives." In *Social Work: A Profession of Many Faces,* edited by A. T. Morales, B. W. Sheafor, and M. E. Scott (pp. 489–513). Boston: Allyn & Bacon.

Fabes, R., and Martin, C. L. (2003). *Exploring Child Development.* Boston: Allyn & Bacon.

Fong, R. (2003). *Culturally Competent Practice with Immigrant and Refugee Children and Families.* New York: Guilford.

Garcia, E. C. (2001). "Parenting in Mexican American Families." In *Culturally Diverse Parent-Child and Family Relationships,* edited by N. B. Webb and D. Lum (pp. 157–169). New York: Columbia University Press.

Glover, G. (2001). "Parenting in Native American Families." In *Culturally Diverse Parent-Child and Family Relationships,* edited by N. B. Webb and D. Lum (pp. 205–231). New York: Columbia University Press.

Goldstein, J., Freud, A., and Solnit, J. (1998). *Beyond the Best Interests of the Child.* New York: Free Press.

Goode, T. D., Jones, W., and Jackson, V. (2011). "Families with African American Roots." In *Developing Cross Cultural Competency,* edited by E. W. Lynch and M. J. Hanson (pp. 140–189). Baltimore: Paul H. Brookes.

Hildebrand, V., Gray, M. M., and Phenice, L. A. (2007). *Knowing and Serving Diverse Families.* Upper Saddle River, NJ: Pearson.

Hill, R. B. (2003). *The Strengths of Black Families.* Lanham, MD: University Press of America.

Hughes, D. A. (2006). *Building the Bonds of Attachment.* Northvale, NJ: Jason Aronson.

Imber-Black, E., Roberts, J., and Whiting, R. A. (2003). *Rituals in Families and Family Therapy.* New York: W.W. Norton.

Jacob, N. (2011). "Families with South Asian Roots." In *Developing Cross Cultural Competency,* edited by E. W. Lynch and M. J. Hanson (pp. 437–462). Baltimore: Paul H. Brookes.

Joe, J. R., and Malach, R. S. (2011). "Families with American Indian Roots." In *Developing Cross Cultural Competency,* edited by E. W. Lynch and M. J. Hanson (pp. 110–139). Baltimore: Paul H. Brookes.

Leiberman, A. F. (1990). "Culturally Sensitive Intervention with Children and Families." *Child and Adolescent Social Work* 7(2):101–119.

Levy, T., and Orlans, M. (1998). *Attachment, Trauma and Healing: Understanding and Tracking Attachment Disorder in Children and Families.* Washington, DC: Child Welfare League of America.

Lum, D. (2003). *Social Work Practice and People of Color.* Monterey, CA: Brooks Cole.

Lum, D. (2007). "Social Work Practice with Asian Americans." In *Social Work: A Profession of Many Faces,* edited by A. T. Morales, B. W. Sheafor, and M. E. Scott (pp. 463–487). Boston: Allyn & Bacon.

Mass, A. I., and Geaga-Rosenthal, J. (2000). "Child Welfare: Asian and Pacific Islander Families." In *Child Welfare: A Multicultural Focus,* edited by N. Cohen (pp. 107–129), Boston: Allyn & Bacon.

McAdoo, H. B. (2006). *Black Families.* Thousand Oaks, CA: Sage.

Morales, A., and Salcido, R. (2007). "Social Work with Mexican Americans." In *Social Work: A Profession of Many Faces,* edited by A. Morales, B. W. Sheafor, and M. E. Scott (pp. 515–533). Boston: Allyn & Bacon.

National Characteristics: Vintage 2011. Retrieved from http://www.census.gov/prod/cen2010/briefs/c2010br-04.pdf on Sept 2, 2012.

Nelson, B. (1990). *Making an Issue of Child Abuse.* Chicago: University of Chicago Press.

Nguyen, T. D. (2007). *Domestic Violence in Asian American Communities.* Lanham, MD: Rowman and Littlefield.

Okamura, A., Hieras, P., and Wong-Kerberg, L. (1995). "Asian, Pacific Island and Filipino Americans and Sexual Abuse." In *Sexual Abuse in Nine North American Cultures,* edited by L. A. Fontes (pp. 269–277). Thousand Oaks, CA: Sage.

Prater, G. S. (2000). "Child Welfare and African-American Families." In *Child Welfare: A Multicultural Perspective,* edited by N. Cohen (pp. 84–106). Boston: Allyn & Bacon.

Rich, P. (2006). *Attachment and Sexual Offending.* Hoboken, NJ: John Wiley & Sons.

Scott, M. E., and Shears, J. K. (2007). "Social Work Practice with African Americans." In *Social Work: A Profession of Many Faces,* edited by A. Morales, B. W. Sheafor, and M. E. Scott (pp. 535–555). Boston: Allyn & Bacon.

Sharifzadeh, V. (2011). "Families with Middle Eastern Roots." In *Developing Cross Cultural Competency,* edited by E. W. Lynch and M. J. Hanson (pp. 392–436). Baltimore: Paul H. Brookes.

Shibusawa, T. (2001). "Parenting in Japanese American Families." In *Culturally Diverse Parent-Child and Family Relationships,* edited by N. B. Webb and D. Lum (pp. 283–303). New York: Columbia University Press.

Skolnick, A. S., and Skolnick, J. H. (2010). *Family in Transition.* Upper Saddle River, NJ: Prentice Hall.

Smith, R. L., and Montilla, R. E. (2006). *Counseling and Family Therapy with Latino Populations.* New York: Taylor and Francis.

Waites, C. (2008). *Social Work Practice with African American Families*. New York: Taylor and Francis.

Webb, N. B., and Lum, D. (Eds.). (2001). *Culturally Diverse Parent–Child and Family Relationships*. New York: Columbia University Press.

Willie, C. V., and Reddick, R. J. (2010). *A New Look at Black Families*. Lanham, MD: Rowan and Littlefield.

Wu, S. (2001). "Parenting in Chinese American Families." In *Culturally Diverse Parent-Child and Family Relationships*, edited by N. B. Webb and D. Lum (pp. 235–260). New York: Columbia University Press.

Zayas, L. H., Canino, I., and Suarez, Z. E. (2001). "Parenting in Mainland Puerto Rican Families." In *Culturally Diverse Parent-Child and Family Relationships*, edited by N. B. Webb and D. Lum (pp. 133–156). New York: Columbia University Press.

Zinn, M. B., Eitzen, D. S., and Wells, B. (2010). *Diversity in Families*. Upper Saddle River, NJ: Prentice Hall.

Zuniga, M. E. (2011). "Families with Latino Roots." In *Developing Cross Cultural Competency*, edited by E. W. Lynch and M. J. Hanson (pp. 190–233). Baltimore: Paul H. Brookes.

Allen-Meares, P., and Fraser, M. W. (2004). *Intervention with Children and Adolescents.* Boston: Allyn & Bacon.

Bancroft, L., and Silverman, J. G. (2002). *The Batterer as Parent.* Thousand Oaks, CA: Sage.

Batchelor, J. (2008). "Failure to Thrive Revisited." *Child Abuse Review* 17(3):147–159.

Bee, H., and Boyd, D. (2011). *The Developing Child.* Upper Saddle River, NJ: Prentice-Hall.

Berk, L. (2012). *Child Development.* Upper Saddle River, NJ: Prentice-Hall.

Brazelton, T. B. (1969). *Infants and Mothers: Differences in Development.* New York: Dell, Delacorte Press.

Child and Adolescent Development (CAD) and Diamond, L. M. (Eds.). (2006). *Rethinking Positive Adolescent Female Sexual Development.* Hoboken, NJ: John Wiley and Sons.

Cicchetti, D., and Toth, S. L. (2000). "Developmental Processes in Maltreated Children." *Nebraska Symposium on Motivation* 46:85–161.

Connor, P. D., Sampson, P. D., Bookstein, F. L., Barr, H. M., and Streissguth, A. P. (2001). "Direct and Indirect Effects of Prenatal Alcohol Damage on Executive Function." *Developmental Neuropsychology* 18:331–354.

Davies, D. (2010). *Child Development: A Practitioner's Guide.* New York: Guilford.

Dolgin, K. G. (2010). *The Adolescent: Development, Relationships and Culture.* Upper Saddle River, NJ: Prentice-Hall.

Erickson, M. F., and Egeland, B. (2011). "Child Neglect." In *The APSAC Handbook of Child Maltreatment,* edited by J. E. B. Myers (pp. 103–124). Thousand Oaks, CA: Sage.

Fabes, R., and Martin, C. L. (2002). *Exploring Child Development.* Boston: Allyn & Bacon.

Finkelhor, D., and Browne, A. (1985). "Traumatic Impact of Child Sexual Abuse: A Conceptualization." *American Journal of Orthopsychiatry* 55:530–541.

Flores, E., Cicchetti, D., and Rogosch, F. A. (2005). "Predictors of Resilience in Maltreated and Nonmaltreated Children." *Developmental Psychology* 41(2):338–351.

Gilgun, J. F. (2003). "Protective Factors, Resilience and Child Abuse and Neglect." Retrieved from www.epi.umn.edu/mch/Healthygenerations/hg4b.html

Goldstein, S., and Brooks, R. B. (2006). *Handbook of Resilience in Children.* New York: Springer-Verlag.

Iwaniec, D. (2006). *The Emotionally Abused and Neglected Child.* West Sussex, England: John Wiley and Sons.

Lamb, M. (Ed.). (2010). *The Role of the Father in Child Development.* New York: Wiley.

Masten, A. S. (2001). "Ordinary Magic: Resilience Processes in Development." *American Psychologist* 56:227–238.

Myers, J. E. B. (2011). *The APSAC Handbook on Child Maltreatment.* Thousand Oaks, CA: Sage.

Quyen, G. T., Bird, H. R., Davies, M., Haven, C., Jensen, P. S., and Goodman, S. (1998). "Adverse Life Events and Resilience." *Journal of the American Academy of Child and Adolescent Psychiatry* 37:1191–1200.

Ryan, G. (1998). "The Sexual Abuser." In *The Battered Child,* edited by M. E. Helfer, R. S. Kempe, and R. D. Krugman (pp. 329–346). Chicago: University of Chicago Press.

Shibusawa, T. (2001). "Parenting in Japanese American Families." In *Culturally Diverse Parent-Child and Family Relationships,* edited by N. B. Webb and D. Lum (pp. 329–346). New York: Columbia University Press.

Webb, N. B., and Lum, D. (2001). "Working with Culturally Diverse Children and Families." In *Culturally Diverse Parent–Child and Family Relationships*, edited by N. B. Webb and D. Lum (pp. 3–28). New York: Columbia University Press.

Winkler, K. (2003). *Cutting and Self-Mutilation: When Teens Injure Themselves*. Berkeley Heights, NJ: Enslow Publications.

Black, M. M., and Dubowitz, H. (1999). "Child Neglect: Research Recommendations and Decisions." In *Neglected Children*, edited by H. Dubowitz (pp. 261–277). Thousand Oaks, CA: Sage.

Cantwell, H. B. (1997). "The Neglect of Child Neglect." In *The Battered Child*, edited by M. E. Helfer, R. S. Kempe, and R. D. Krugman (pp. 347–373). Chicago: University of Chicago Press.

Chasnoff, I., and Lowder, L. A. (1999). "Prenatal Alcohol and Drug Use and Risk for Child Maltreatment." In *Neglected Children*, edited by H. Dubowitz (pp. 132–155). Thousand Oaks, CA: Sage.

Crittenden, P. (1999). "Child Neglect: Causes and Contributors." In *Neglected Children: Research Practice and Policy*, edited by H. Dubowitz (pp. 47–68). Thousand Oaks, CA: Sage.

DePanfilis, D. (2006). *Child Neglect: A Guide for Prevention, Assessment, and Intervention.* Washington, DC: U.S. Department of Health and Human Services.

DePanfilis, D., and Salus, M. (2003). *A Coordinated Response to Child Abuse and Neglect: The Foundation for Practice.* Washington, DC: U.S. Department of Health and Human Services.

Drake, B., and Pandy, S. (1996). "Understanding the Relationship Between Neighborhood Poverty and Specific Types of Child Maltreatment." *Child Abuse and Neglect* 20:1003–1018.

Dubowitz, H. (1999). *Neglected Children.* Thousand Oaks, CA: Sage.

Dubowitz, H. (2007). "Understanding and Addressing the 'neglect of neglect': Digging into the molehill." *Child Abuse and Neglect* 31(6): 603–606.

Dubowitz, H., and Black, M. (2002). "Neglect of Children's Health." In *The APSAC Handbook of Child Maltreatment*, edited by Myers et al. (pp. 269–292). Thousand Oaks, CA: Sage.

Dubowitz, H., Villas, M. T., Litrownik, A. J., Pitts, S. C., Hussey, J. M., Thompson, R., Black, M. M., and Bunyan, D. (2011). "Psychometric properties of a self-report measure of neglectful behavior by parents." *Child Abuse and Neglect* 35:414–424.

Erickson, M. F., and Egeland, B. (2011). "Child Neglect." In *The APSAC Handbook of Child Maltreatment*, edited by J. E. B. Myers (pp. 103–124). Thousand Oaks, CA: Sage.

Fontana, V. J. (1976). *Somewhere a Child Is Crying.* New York: New American Library.

Garbarino, J., and Collins, C. (1999). "Child Neglect: The Family with the Hole in the Middle." In *Neglected Children: Research, Practice and Policy*, edited by H. Dubowitz (pp. 1–23). Thousand Oaks, CA: Sage.

Gaudin, J. M. (1999). "Child Neglect: Short-term and Long-term Outcomes." In *Neglected Children: Research, Practice and Policy*, edited by H. Dubowitz (pp. 89–108). Thousand Oaks, CA: Sage.

Hally, C., Polansky, N. F., and Polansky, N. A. (1980). *Child Neglect: Mobilizing Services.* Washington, DC: U.S. Department of Health and Human Services.

Hampton, R. L. (2003). *Black Family Violence.* New York: Lexington Books.

Haworth, J. (2007). *Child Neglect: Identification and Assessment.* London: Palgrave Macmillan.

Joffe, M. (2002). "Child Neglect and Abandonment." In *Recognition of Child Abuse for the Mandated Reporter*, edited by A. P. Giardino and E. R. Giardino (pp. 39–54). St. Louis: G. W. Medical.

Kaplan, C., Schene, P., DePanfilis, D., and Gilmore, D. (2009). "Introduction: Shining Light on Chronic Neglect." *Protecting Children* 24(1):2–8.

Kelly, S. J. (2002). "Child Maltreatment in the Context of Substance Abuse." In *The APSAC Handbook on Child Maltreatment*, edited by J. E. B. Myers, L. Berliner, J. Briere, C. T. Hendrix, C. Jenny, and T. A. Reid (pp. 105–117). Thousand Oaks, CA: Sage.

Korbin, J., Coulton, C., Lindstom-Ufiti, H., and Spilsburt, J. (2000). "Neighborhood Views on the Definition and Etiology of Child Maltreatment." *Child Abuse and Neglect* 24:1509–1527.

Korbin, J., and Spilsbury, J. (1999). "Cultural Competence and Child Neglect." In *Neglected Children*, edited by H. Dubowitz (pp. 69–88). Thousand Oaks, CA: Sage.

Mass, A. I. (July 11, 1991). Personal communication.

McSherry, D. (2011). "Lest We Forget: Remembering the Consequences of Child Neglect—A Clarion Call to 'Feisty Advocates.' " *Child Care Practice* 17(2):103–113.

Oates, R. K., and Kempe, R. S. (1997). "Growth Failure in Infants." In *The Battered Child*, edited by M. E. Helfer, R. S. Kempe, and R. P. Krugman (pp. 374–391). Chicago: University of Chicago Press.

Pearl, P. S. (2002). "Educational Neglect." In *Recognition of Child Abuse for the Mandated Reporter*, edited by A. P. Giardino and E. R. Giardino (pp. 55–61). St. Louis: G. W. Medical Publishing.

Polansky, N. A., Borgman, N. D., and DeSaix, C. (1972). *Roots of Futility.* San Francisco: Jossey-Bass.

Polansky, N. A., Chalmers, M. A., Buttenwieser, E., and Williams, D. P. (1978). "Assessing Adequacy of Child Caring: An Urban Scale." *Child Welfare* 57:439–449.

Polansky, N. A., Chalmers, M. A., Buttenwieser, E., and Williams, D. P. (1983). *Damaged Parents: An Anatomy of Child Neglect.* Chicago: University of Chicago Press.

Polansky, N. A., DeSaix, C., and Sharlin, S. (1972). *Child Neglect: Understanding and Reaching the Parent.* New York: Child Welfare League of America.

Polansky, N. F., Hally, C., and Polansky, N. A. (1975). *Profile of Neglect: A Survey of the State of Knowledge of Child Neglect.* Washington, DC: Community Services Administration, Department of Health, Education and Welfare.

Ritchie, D., Silverman, J. G., and Bancroft, R. L. (2011). *The Batterer as Parent: Addressing the Impact of Domestic Violence on Family Dynamics.* Thousand Oaks, CA: Sage.

Sharpe, T. J. (2005). *Behind the Eight Ball: Sex for Crack Cocaine Exchange and Poor Black Women.* New York: Haworth.

Smith, M. G., and Fong, R. (2004). *The Children of Neglect.* New York: Brunner-Routledge.

Spohr, H., and Steinhausen, H. (2011). *Alcohol, Pregnancy and the Developing Child.* Cambridge: Cambridge University Press.

Stevenson, O. (2007). *Neglected Children and Their Families.* Oxford, UK: Blackwell.

Strathearn, L., Gary, P. H., O'Callaghan, M. J., and Wood, D. O. (2001). "Childhood Neglect and Cognitive Development in Extremely Low Birth Weight Infants: A prospective study." *Pediatrics* 108:142–151.

Straussner, S. L., and Fewell, C. H. (2006). *Impact of Substance Abuse on Children and Families.* New York: Haworth.

Taylor, J., and Daniel, B. (2005). *Child Neglect.* Philadelphia: Jessica Kingsley.

Trocmé, N. (1996). "Development and Preliminary Evaluation of the Ontario Child Neglect Index." *Child Maltreatment* 1(2):145–155.

Trocmé, N. (Oct. 14, 1997). Personal communication.

U.S. Census Bureau. (2012). "Statistical Abstract of the United States." Retrieved from http://www.census.gov/compendia/statab/2012/tables/12s0712.pdf on Sept 29, 2012.

U.S. Department of Health and Human Services, Administration for Children and Families, Administration on Children, Youth and Families, Children's Bureau. (2011). "Child Maltreatment 2010." Retrieved from http://www.acf.hhs.gov/programs/cb/pubs/cm10/cm10.pdf#page=61 on June 5, 2012.

Wolock, I., and Horowitz, B. (1979). "Child Maltreatment and Maternal Deprivation among AFDC Recipient Families." *Social Service Review* 53:175–184.

Wright, C. M. (2005). "What Is Weight Faltering (Failure to Thrive) and When Does it Become a Child Protection Issue?" In *Child Neglect*, edited by J. Taylor and B. Daniel (pp. 166–185). Philadelphia: Jessica Kingsley.

Zuravin, S. J. (1999). "Child Neglect: A Review of Definitions and Measurement Research." In *Neglected Children: Research, Practice and Policy*, edited by H. Dubowitz (pp. 24–46). Thousand Oaks, CA: Sage.

References for Chapter 5

Algood, C. L., Hong, J. S., Gourdine, R. M., and Williams, A. B. (2011). "Maltreatment of Children with Developmental Disabilities: An ecological systems analysis". *Children and Youth Services Review*, 33:1142–1148.

Allen-Meares, P., and Fraser, M. W. (2004). *Intervention with Children and Adolescents*. Boston: Allyn & Bacon.

Azar, S. T., and Gehl, K. S. (1999). "Physical Abuse and Neglect." In *Handbook of Prescriptive Treatments for Children and Adolescents*, edited by R. T. Ammerman (pp. 329–345). Boston: Allyn & Bacon.

Bancroft, L. (2005). *When Dad Hurts Mom*. New York: Penguin.

Barker, J., and Hodes, D. T. (2012). *Child in Mind: A Child Protection Handbook*. New York: Taylor and Francis.

Beckett, C. (2007). *Child Protection*. Thousand Oaks, CA: Sage.

Black, D. A., Heyman, R. E., and Smith-Slep, A. M. (2001). "Risk Factors for Child Physical Abuse." *Aggression and Violent Behavior* 6(2/3):121–188.

Brittain, C. R. (Ed.). (2005). *Understanding the Medical Diagnosis of Child Maltreatment*. Denver: American Humane Association.

Bugental, D., Blunt, L., Judith, E., Lin, E. K., McGrath, E. P., and Bimbela, A. (1999). "Children 'Tune out' in Response to Ambiguous Communication." *Child Development* 70(1):214–230.

Button, D. M., and Gealt, R. (2010). "High Risk Behaviors Among Victims of Sibling Violence." *Journal of Family Violence* 25(2):131–140.

Cadzow, S. P., Armstrong, K. L., and Fraser J. A. (1999). "Stressed Parents with Infants: Reassessing Physical Abuse Risk Factors." *Child Abuse and Neglect* 23(9):845–853.

Caffaro, J. V., and Conn-Caffaro, A. (2005). "Treating Sibling Abuse." *Aggression and Violent Behavior* 10:604–623.

Casselles, C. E., and Milner, J. S. (2000). "Evaluation of Child Transgressions, Disciplinary Choices, and Expected Compliance in a No-Cry and Crying Infant Condition in Physically Abusive and Comparison Mothers." *Child Abuse and Neglect* 24(4):477–491.

Children's Bureau. (2011). "Child Maltreatment 2010." Retrieved from http://archive.acf.hhs.gov/programs/cb/pubs/cm10/cm10.pdf on Sept 1, 2012.

Cobley, C., and Sanders, T. (2006). *Non-Accidental Head Injury*. London: Jessica Kingsley.

Cohen, J. A., Berliner, L., and Mannarino, A. (2000). "Treating Traumatized Children." *Trauma, Violence, and Abuse* 1:29–46.

Coohey, C., and Braun, N. (1997). "Toward an Integrated Framework for Understanding Child Physical Abuse." *Child Abuse and Neglect* 21(11):1081–1095.

Crosson-Tower, C. (2013). *Exploring Child Welfare: A Practice Perspective*. Boston: Pearson.

Daniels, J. A., and Bradley, M. C. (2011). *Preventing Lethal School Violence*. New York: Spring-Verlag.

Dopke, C. A., and Milner, J. S. (2000). "Impact of Child Compliance on Stress Appraisals, Attributions, and Disciplinary Choices in Mothers at High and Low Risk for Child Physical Abuse." *Child Abuse and Neglect* 24:493–504.

Farrington, D. P., and Welsh, B. C. (2008). *Saving Children from a Life of Crime*. New York: Oxford University Press.

Feldman, K. W. (1997). "Evaluation of Physical Abuse." In *The Battered Child*, edited by M. E. Helfer, R. S. Kempe, and R. D. Krugman (pp. 175–220). Chicago: University of Chicago Press.

Field, T. (1998). "Maternal Depression: Effects on Infants and Early Intervention." *Preventative Medicine* 27(2):200–203.

Flowers, R. B. (2008). *The Adolescent Criminal.* Jefferson, NC: McFarland.

Fontes, L. A. (2008). *Child Abuse and Culture.* New York: Guilford.

Ford, J. D., Racusin, R., Daviss, W. B., Ellis, C., Thomas, J., Rogers, K., Reiser, J., Schiffman, J., and Sengupta, A. (1999). "Trauma Exposed Among Children with Attention Deficit Hyperactivity Disorder and Oppositional Defiant Behavior." *Journal of Consulting and Clinical Psychology* 67:786–789.

Fraser, M. W. (2004). *Risk and Resilience in Childhood.* New York: National Association of Social Workers.

Friends National Resource Center (FNRC). (2008). *The Protective Factors Survey.* Manhattan: Kansas State University, Institute for Educational Research and Public Service.

Giardino, A. P., Lyn, M. A., and Giardino, E. R. (2010). *A Practical Guide to the Evaluation of Child Physical Abuse and Neglect.* New York: Springer-Verlag.

Graham-Berman, S. A., and Howell, K. H. (2011). "Child Maltreatment in the Context of Intimate Partner Violence." In *The APSAC Handbook on Child Maltreatment*, edited by J. E. B. Myers (pp. 167–180). Thousand Oaks, CA: Sage.

Hall, L. K. (2008). *Counseling Military Families.* New York: Routledge.

Hampton, R. L. (Ed.). (1998). *Black Family Violence.* New York: Lexington Books.

Helfer, R. (1979). Lecture given by Dr. R. E. Helfer in New Bedford, Massachusetts, March 1979.

Helfer, R. (1989). From an untitled lecture given in New Bedford, MA, March 1979, as cited in C. C. Tower, *Child Abuse and Neglect.* Washington, DC: National Education Association, pp. 59–60.

Helfer, R. E., and Krugman, R. D. (1997). "A Clinical and Developmental Approach to Prevention." In *The Battered Child*, edited by M. E. Helfer, R. S. Kempe, and R. D. Krugman (pp. 594–614). Chicago: University of Chicago Press.

Hobbs, C. J., Hanks, H. G., and Wynne, J. M. (1999). *Child Abuse and Neglect.* New York: Churchill Livingstone.

Howe, D. (2005). *Child Abuse and Neglect: Attachment, Development and Intervention.* New York: Palgrave MacMillan.

Howes, P. W., Cicchetti, D., Toth, S., and Rogosh, F. A. (2000). "Affective, Organizational and Relational Characteristics of Maltreating Families: A Systems Perspective." *Journal of Family Psychology* 14(1):95–110.

Iwaniec, D. (2006). *The Emotionally Abused and Neglected Child.* West Sussex, England: John Wiley and Sons.

Johnstone, H. A., and Marcinak, J. F. (1997). "Sibling Abuse: Another Component of Domestic Violence." *Journal of Pediatric Nursing* 12:51–54.

Kaplan, S., Pelcovitz, D., Salzinger, S., Mandel, F. S., and Weiner, M. (1998). "Adolescent Physical Abuse: Risk for Adolescent Psychiatric Disorders." *American Journal of Psychiatry* 155(7): 954–959.

Kiselica, M. S., and Morrill-Richards, M. (2007). "Sibling Maltreatment: the forgotten abuse." *Journal of Counseling and Development* 85:148–161.

Lasher, L. J., and Sheridan, M. S. (2004). *Munchausen by Proxy.* New York: Haworth.

Loiselle, J. (2002). "Physical Abuse." In *Recognition of Child Abuse for the Mandated Reporter*, edited by A. P. Giardino and E. R. Giardino (pp. 1–21). St. Louis: G. W. Medical.

Lustig, M. W., and Koester, J. (2009). *Intercultural Competence: Interpersonal Communication Across Cultures.* Upper Saddle River, NJ: Pearson.

Lynch, E. W., and Hanson, M. J. (Eds.). (2011). *Developing Cross-Cultural Competence.* Baltimore, MD: Paul H. Brookes.

Main, M., and Coolbear, J. (2002). "Munchausen by Proxy." In *Recognition of Child Abuse for the Mandated Reporter*, edited by A. P. Giardino and E. R. Giardino (pp. 93–107). St. Louis: G. W. Medical.

Miller, B. V., Fox, B. R., and Garcia-Beckwith, L. (1999). "Intervening in Severe Physical Child Abuse Cases." *Child Abuse and Neglect* 23(9):905–914.

Minns, R., and Brown, J. K. (Eds.). (2006). *Shaking and Other Non-Accidental Head Injuries in Children*. Hoboken, NJ: John Wiley and Sons.

Monteleone, J. A. (1998). *Child Abuse*. St. Louis, MO: G. W. Medical.

Mufson, S., and Kranz, R. (1994). "A Family History of Abuse Contributes to Child Abuse." In *Child Abuse: Opposing Viewpoints*, edited by K. de Koster and K. L. Swisher (pp. 107–113). San Diego, CA: Greenhaven Press.

Mullender, A., Kelly, L., Haque, G., and Imam, U. (2003). *Children's Perspectives on Domestic Violence*. Thousand Oaks, CA: Sage.

Olweus. (2011). "Bullying Prevention Program." Retrieved from http://www.violencepreventionworks.org/public/index.page on Sept 3, 2012.

Parnell, T. F. (2002). "Munchausen by Proxy." In *The APSAC Handbook on Child Maltreatment*, edited by J. E. B. Myers, L. Berliner, J. Briere, C. T. Hendrix, C. Jenny, and T. A. Reid (pp. 131–157). Thousand Oaks, CA: Sage.

Paulson, D. S., and Krippner, S. (2007). *Haunted by Combat*. Westport, CT: Praeger Security International.

Potzner, D. (2010). "A Theoretical Test of Bullying Behavior: Parenting, Personality and the Bully, Victim Relationship." *Journal of Family Violence* 25:259–273.

Reece, R. M. (2009). *Child Abuse: Medical Diagnosis and Treatment*. Elk Grove Village, IL: American Academy of Pediatrics.

Reece, R. M. (2011). "Medical Evaluation of Physical Abuse. In *The APSAC Handbook on Child Maltreatment*, edited by J. E. B. Myers (pp. 183–194). Thousand Oaks, CA: Sage.

Rentz, E. D., Marshall, S. W., Loomis, D., Casteel, C., Martin, S. L., and Gibbs, D. A. (2007). "Effect of Deployment on the Occurrence of Child Maltreatment in Military and Nonmilitary Families." *American Journal of Epidemiology* 165(10):1199–1206.

Ritchie, D., Silverman, J. G., and Bancroft, R. L. (2011). *The Batterer as Parent: Addressing the Impact of Domestic Violence on Family Dynamics*. Thousand Oaks, CA: Sage.

Rivers, I., Duncan, N., and Besag, V. E. (2009). *Bullying*. Lantahm, MD: Rowman and Littlefield.

Rodriguez, C. M., and Murphy, L. E. (1997). "Parenting Stress and Abuse Potential in Mothers of Children with Developmental Disabilities." *Child Maltreatment* 2(3):245–251.

Roesler, T. A., and Jenny, C. (2008). *Medical Child Abuse: beyond Munchhausen by Proxy*. Elk Grove Village, IL: American Academy of Pediatrics.

Runyon, M. K., and Urquiza, A. J. (2011). "Child Physical Abuse: Intervention for Parents Who Engage in Coercive Parenting Practices and Their Children," In *The APSAC Handbook on Child Maltreatment*, edited by J. E. B. Myers (pp. 195–2012). Thousand Oaks, CA: Sage.

Saunders, B. J., and Goddard, C. (2010). *Physical Punishment in Childhood: The Rights of the Child*. Hoboken, NJ: John Wiley and Sons.

Shapiro, M., and Nguyen, M. (2011). "Psychological Sequelae of Munchausen's Syndrome by Proxy". *Child Abuse and Neglect* 35, 87–88.

Swenson, C. C., and Kolko, D. J. (2002). *Assessing and Treating Physically Abused Children and Their Families*. Thousand Oaks, CA: Sage.

U.S. Department of Health and Human Services, Administration for Children and Families, Administration on Children, Youth and Families, Children's Bureau. (2011). "Child Maltreatment 2010." Retrieved from http://www.acf.hhs.gov/programs/cb/pubs/cm10/cm10.pdf#page=61 on June 5, 2012.

Vincent, A., and Kelly, P. (2010). "Retinal hemorrhages in inflicted traumatic brain injury: the ophthalmologist in court." *Clinical & Experimental Ophthalmology* 8(5):521–532.

Webb, N. B., and Lum, D. (Eds.). (2001). *Culturally Diverse Parent–Child and Family Relationships.* New York: Columbia University Press.

Weihe, V. R. (2002). *Sibling Abuse.* Springville, UT: Bonneville.

Weihe, V. R., and Herring, T. (1991). *Perilous Rivalry: When Siblings Become Abusive.* Lexington, MA: Lexington Books.

Wigg, J., Windom, C. S., and Tuell, J. (2003). *Understanding Child Maltreatment and Juvenile Delinquency.* Washington, DC: Child Welfare League of America.

Williams, J. J. (2002). "Violence Among Children." In *Recognition of Child Abuse for the Mandated Reporter*, edited by A. P. Giardino and E. R. Giardino (pp. 109–135). St. Louis, MO: G. W. Medical.

Zielinski, D. S., and Bradshaw, C. P. (2005). "Ecological Influences on the Sequelae of Child Maltreatment." *Child Maltreatment* 11(1):49–62.

American Psychiatric Association (APA). (2000). *Diagnostic and Statistical Manual of Mental Disorders* (Text. rev.). Washington, DC: Author.

Anechiarico, B. (1999). "A Closer Look at Sex Offender Character Pathology and Relapse Prevention—An Integration Approach." In *The Sex Offender*, edited by B. Schwartz (pp. 17-20–17-28). Arlington, NJ: Civic Research Institute.

Araji, S. K. (1997). *Sexually Aggressive Children.* Thousand Oaks, CA: Sage.

Baker, L. (2002). *Protecting Your Children from Sexual Predators.* New York: St. Martin's.

Bancroft, L. (2004). *When Dad Hurts Mom.* New York: Penguin.

Bancroft, L., and Miller, M. (2002). "Batterer as Incest Perpetrator." In *The Batterer as Parent*, edited by L. Bancroft and J. G. Sullivan (pp. 84–97). Thousand Oaks, CA: Sage.

Barbaree, H. B., and Marshall, W. J. (Eds.). (2008). *The Juvenile Sex Offender.* New York: Guilford.

Beech, A. R., Browne, K. D., and Craig, L. A. (2009). *Assessment and Treatment of Sex Offenders.* Hoboken, NJ: John Wiley and Sons.

Beech, A. R., Parrett, N., Ward, T., and Fisher, D. (2009). "Assessing Female Offenders' Motivations and Cognitions: An Exploratory Study." *Psychology, Crime and Law*, 15(2/3):201–216.

Berliner, L. (2011). "Child Sexual Abuse: Definitions, Prevalence and Consequences." In *The APSAC Handbook on Child Maltreatment*, edited by J. E. B. Myers (pp. 215–232). Thousand Oaks, CA: Sage.

Bolen, R. (2007). *Child Sexual Abuse: Its Scope and Our Failure.* New York: Plenum.

Bolen, R. M., and Scannapieco, M. (1999). "Prevalence of Child Sexual Abuse: A Corrective Metanalysis." *Social Service Review* 73(3):281–313.

Burgess, A., Groth, A. N., Holstrom, L., and Sgroi, S. (1978). *Sexual Assault of Children and Adolescents.* Lexington, MA: Lexington Books.

Carnes, P. (2001). *Out of the Shadows: Understanding Sexual Addiction.* Minneapolis: CompCare.

Chandy, J. M., Blum, R. W., and Resnick, M. D. (1997). "Sexually Abused Male Adolescents: How Vulnerable Are They?" *Journal of Child Sexual Abuse* 6(2):1–16.

Cooper, S. W., Giardino, A. P., Vieth, V. I., and Kellogg, N. (2006). *Medical, Legal and Social Science Aspects of Child Sexual Exploitation.* Philadelphia: Elsevier Health Sciences.

Corwin, D. (2002). "An Interview with Roland Summit." In *Critical Issues in Child Sexual Abuse*, edited by J. R. Conte. (pp. 1–26), Thousand Oaks, CA: Sage.

Courtois, C. (2010). *Healing the Incest Wound.* New York: W. W. Norton.

Coxe, R., and Holmes, W. (2001). "A Study of the Cycle of Abuse Among Child Molesters." *Journal of Child Sexual Abuse* 10(4):111–118.

Davin, P. A. (1999). "Secrets Revealed: A Study of Female Sex Offenders." In *Female Sexual Offenders*, edited by P. A. Davin, J. Hislop, and T. Dunbar (pp. 9–134). Brandon, VT: Safer Society Press.

Dorias, M. (2009). *Don't Tell: The Sexual Abuse of Boys.* Montreal, Canada: McGill–Queens University Press.

Dube, S. R., Anda, R. F., Whitfield, C. L., Brown, D. W., Felitti, V. J., Dong, M., and Giles, W. H. (2005). "Long-term Consequences of Childhood Sexual Abuse by Gender of Victim." *American Journal of Preventive Medicine* 28:430–438.

Durham, A. (2006). *Young Men Who Have Sexually Abused.* New York: John Wiley & Sons.

Erooga, M., and Masson, H. (2006). *Children and Young People Who Sexually Abuse Others.* New York: Taylor and Francis.

Faller, K. C. (2003). *Understanding and Assessing Child Sexual Maltreatment.* Thousand Oaks, CA: Sage.

Finkelhor, D. (1981). *Sexually Victimized Children.* New York: Free Press.

Finkelhor, D. (1984a). *Child Sexual Abuse.* New York: Free Press.

Finkelhor, D. (1984b). "How Widespread Is Child Sexual Abuse?" In *Perspectives on Child Maltreatment in the Mid-80s* (pp. 3–9). Washington, DC: National Center on Child Abuse and Neglect, Department of Health and Human Services.

Finkelhor, D. (1994). "Current Information on the Scope and Nature of Child Sexual Abuse." *Future of Children* 4(2):31–53.

Finkelhor, D. (2008). *Childhood Victimization: Violence, crime and abuse in the lives of young people.* New York: Oxford University Press.

Finkelhor, D., Mitchell, K., and Wolak, J. (2000). *Online Victimization: A Report on the Nation's Youth.* Arlington, VA: National Center for Missing and Exploited Children.

Finkelhor, D., and Ormrod, R. (2004). "Prostitution of Juveniles: Patterns from NIBRS." Retrieved from www.ojp.usdoj.gov/ojjd on Feb, 2, 2006.

Finklea, K. M., Fernandes-Alcantara, A. L., and Siskin, A. (2012). "Sex Trafficking of Children in the United States: Overview and Issues for Congress." In *Child Sex Trafficking in the United States*, edited by J. V. Higgins and C. M. Brady (pp. 1–59). New York: Nova Science.

Flora, R. (2001). *How to Work with Sex Offenders.* New York: Haworth.

Flora, R., Duehl, J. T., Fisher, W., Halsey, S., Keohane, M., Maberry, B. L., McCorkindale, J. A., Parson, L. C. (2008). *Sex-Offender Therapy.* New York: Haworth.

Flowers, R. B. (2001). *Runaway Kids and Teenage Prostitution.* Westport, CT: Praeger.

Ford, H. (2006). *Women Who Sexually Abuse Children.* New York: John Wiley and Sons.

Gardner, R. A. (1991). *Sex Abuse Hysteria: Salem Witch Trials Revisited.* Cresskill, NJ: Creative Therapeutics.

Gartner, R. B. (2005). *Beyond Betrayal.* New York: Wiley & Sons.

Gil, E., and Johnson, T. C. (1993). *Sexualized Children: Assessment and Treatment of Sexualized Children and Children Who Molest.* Rockville, MD: Launch Press.

Gilgun, J. F. (1990). "Factors Mediating the Effects of Childhood Maltreatment." In *The Sexually Abused Male*, edited by M. Hunter (Vol. 1, pp. 177–190). New York: Lexington Books.

Gilgun, J. F. (2009). *Child Sexual Abuse: From Harsh Realities to Hope.* North Charleston, SC: Createspace.

Gillespie, A. A. (2011). *Child Pornography: Law and Policy.* New York: Taylor and Francis.

Groth, A. N., Birnbaum, H. J., and Brecher, E. M. (2002). *Men Who Rape.* New York: Perseus.

Haugaard, J. J. (2000). "The Challenge of Defining Child Sexual Abuse." *American Psychologist* 55(9):1036–1039.

Healy, M. (1996). "Child Pornography: An International Perspective." Paper presented at the World Congress Against Commercial Sexual Exploitation of Children, August 1996, Stockholm, Sweden.

Herman, J. (1997). *Trauma and Recovery.* New York: Basic Books.

Herman, J., and Hirschman, L. (2000). *Father–Daughter Incest.* Cambridge, MA: Harvard University Press.

Higgins, M., and Swain, J. (2009). *Disability and Child Sexual Abuse.* London: Jessica Kingsley.

Iwaniec, D. (2006). *The Emotionally Abused and Neglected Child.* New York: John Wiley and Sons.

Jenkins, P. (2001). *Beyond Tolerance: Child Pornography and the Internet.* New York: Union Press.

Jones, D. (1997). "Assessment of Suspected Child Sexual Abuse." In *The Battered Child*, edited by M. E. Helfer, R. S. Kempe, and R. D. Krugmen (pp. 296–312). Chicago: Chicago University Press.

Jones, L. M., Mitchell, K. J., and Finkelhor, D. (2012). "Trends in Youth Internet Victimization: Findings from Three Youth Internet Safety Surveys 2000–2010." *Journal of Adolescent Health*, 50:179–186.

Karson, M. (2001). *Patterns of Child Abuse*. New York: Haworth.

Kasl, C. D. (1990). "Female Perpetrators of Sexual Abuse: A Feminist View." In *The Sexually Abused Male*, edited by M. Hunter (pp. 259–274). New York: Lexington Books.

Klain, E. (1999). *Prostitution of Children and Child Tourism*. Washington, DC: U.S. Department of Justice.

Kubik, E. K., and Hecker, J. E. (2005). "Cognitive Distortions About Sex and Sexual Offending. A Comparison of Sex Offending Girls, Delinquent Girls and Girls from the Community." *Journal of Child Sexual Abuse* 14(4):41–69.

Leberg, E. (1997). *Understanding Child Molesters*. Thousand Oaks, CA: Sage.

Lew, M. (2004). *Victims No Longer*. New York: HarperCollins.

Lyon, T. D., and Ahern, E. C. (2011). "Disclosure of Child Sexual Abuse: Implications for Interviewing". In *The APSAC Handbook on Child Maltreatment*, edited by J. E. B. Myers (pp. 238–252). Thousand Oaks, CA: Sage.

Mannarino, A. P., and Cohen, J. A. (1997). "Family Related Variables and Psychological Symptoms in Sexually Abused Girls." *Journal of Child Sexual Abuse* 5:105–120.

Marshall, W. L., and Barbaree, H. E. (1990). "An Integrated Theory of the Etiology of Sexual Offending." In *Handbook of Sexual Assault: Issues, Theories and Treatment of the Offender*, edited by W. L. Marshall, D. R. Laws, and H. E. Barbaree (pp. 257–275). New York: Plenum.

Mathews, R., Mathews, J., and Speltz, K. (1990). "Female Sex Offenders." In *The Sexually Abused Male*, edited by M. Hunter (Vol. 1, pp. 275–293). New York: Lexington Books.

McLaughlin, J. F. (1999). "Cyber Child Sex Offender Typology." *Knight Stick* 55:39–42.

Meiselman, K. (1992). *Incest: A Psychological Study of Causes and Effects with Treatment Recommendation*. San Francisco: Jossey-Bass.

Mollon, P. (2003). *Remembering Trauma*. New York: John Wiley and Sons.

Ney, T. (1995). *True and False Allegations of Child Sexual Abuse*. New York: Brunner/Mazel.

Ofshe, R., and Watters, E. (1998). *Making Monsters: False Memories, Psychotherapy, and Sexual Hysteria*. New York: Charles Scribner's Sons.

Ogilvie, B. (2004). *Mother–Daughter Incest*. New York: Haworth.

Olafman, S. (2008). *The Sexualization of Childhood*. Westport, CT: Greenwood.

Pecora, P., Whittaker, J. K., Maluccio, A. N., Barth, R. P., and Plotnick, R. D. (2000). *The Child Welfare Challenge*. New York: Aldine De-Gruyter.

Pomeroy, W. B., Kinsey, A. C., Gebhard, P. H., and Martin, C. M. (1998). *Sexual Behavior of the Human Female*. Indianapolis: Indiana University Press.

Preble, J. M., and Groth, A. N. (2002). *Male Victims of Same Sex Abuse*. Baltimore, MD: Sidran Press.

Prendergast, W. E. (1991). *Treating Sex Offenders in Correctional Institutions and Outpatient Clinics*. New York: Haworth.

Rich, P. (2003). *Understanding, Assessing and Rehabilitating Juvenile Sexual Offenders*. Hoboken, NJ: John Wiley & Sons.

Rich, P. (2006). *Attachment and Sexual Offending*. West Sussex, England: John Wiley and Sons.

Rich, P. (2009). *Juvenile Sexual Offenders*. Hoboken, NJ: John Wiley & Sons.

Ritchie, D., Silverman, J. G., and Bancroft, R. L. (2011). *The Batterer as Parent: Addressing the Impact of Domestic Violence on Family Dynamics*. Thousand Oaks, CA: Sage.

Rosencrans, B. (1997). *The Last Secret: Daughters Sexually Abused by Mothers.* Brandon, VT: Safer Society Press.

Rush, F. (1992). *The Best-Kept Secret.* New York: Tab Books.

Russell, D. (1984). *Sexual Exploitation.* Beverly Hills, CA: Sage.

Russell, D., and Bolen, R. E. (2000). *The Epidemic of Rape and Child Sexual Abuse in the United States.* Thousand Oaks, CA: Sage.

Ryan, G. (1997). "The Sexual Abuser." In *The Battered Child*, edited by M. E. Helfer, R. S. Kempe, and R. D. Krugman (pp. 329–346). Chicago: University of Chicago Press.

Salter, A. C. (2003). *Predators, Pedophiles, Rapists, and Other Sex Offenders.* New York: Basic Books.

Seto, M. C. (2008). *Pedophilia and Sexual Offending Against Children.* Washington, DC: American Psychological Association.

Sgroi, S. (1982). *Handbook of Clinical Intervention in Child Sexual Abuse.* Lexington, MA: Lexington Books.

Stevens, D. J. (2001). *Inside the Mind of Sexual Offenders.* San Jose, CA: Authors Choice Press.

Stone, R. D. (2005). *No Secrets No Lies: How Black Families Can Heal from Sexual Abuse.* New York: Broadway Books.

Taylor, M., and Quayle, E. (2003). *Child Pornography: An Internet Crime.* New York: Brunner-Routledge.

Tower, C. C. (1988). *Secret Scars: A Guide for Adult Survivors of Child Sexual Abuse.* New York: Viking/Penguin.

U. S. Department of Health and Human Services, Administration for Children and Families Archives. Retrieved from http://archive.acf.hhs.gov/programs/cb/laws_policies/cblaws/capta/ on April 11, 2013.

U. S. Department of Health and Human Services, Children's Bureau. (2011). "Child Maltreatment 2010: Reports from the States to the National Center on Child Abuse and Neglect." Retrieved from http://archive.acf.hhs.gov/programs/cb/pubs/cm10/cm10.pdf on Sept 3, 2012.

Urquiza, A., and Keating, L. M. (1990). "The Prevalence of Sexual Victimization in Males." In *The Sexually Abused Male*, edited by M. Hunter (Vol. 1, pp. 105–136). Lexington, MA: Lexington Books.

van Dam, C. (2006). *The Socially Skilled Child Molester.* New York: Haworth.

Ward, T., Polaschek, D. L. L., and Beech, A. R. (2006). *Theories of Sexual Offending.* West Sussex, England: John Wiley and Sons.

Weeks, K., and Widom, C. S. (1998). "Self Reports of Early Childhood Victimization among Incarcerated Adult Male Felons." *Journal of Interpersonal Violence* 13(3):346–361.

Wolf, S. C. (1985). "A multifactor model of deviant sexuality." *Victimology* 10:359–374.

Wortley, R., and Smallbone, S. (2012). *Internet Child Pornography.* Westport, CT: Greenwood.

Yates, P. M. (2003). "Treatment of Adult Sexual Offenders: A Therapeutic Cognitive-Behavioral Model of Intervention." In *Identifying and Treating Sex Offenders*, edited by R. Geffner, K. C. Francy, T. G. Arnold, and R. Falconer (pp. 195–212). New York: Haworth.

Alaggia, R. (2001). "Cultural and Religious Influences in Maternal Response to Intrafamilial Child Sexual Abuse: Charting New Territory for Research and Treatment." *Journal of Child Sexual Abuse* 10(2):41–60.

Baker, L. (2002). *Protecting Your Children from Sexual Predators*. New York: St. Martin's.

Bancroft, L., and Sullivan, J. (2002). *The Batterer as Parent*. Thousand Oaks, CA: Sage.

Berliner, L. (2011). "Child Sexual Abuse: Definitions, Prevalence, and Cnsequences." In the *APSAC Handbook on Child Maltreatment*, edited by J. E. B. Myers (pp. 215–232). Thousand Oaks, CA: Sage.

Bolen, R. (2007). *Child Sexual Abuse: Its Scope and Our Failure*. New York: Plenum.

Brady, K. (1979). *Father's Days*. New York: Dell.

Briere, J. N. (1992). *Child Abuse Trauma: Theory and Treatment of the Lasting Effects*. Newbury Park, CA: Sage.

Brown, J. (1990). "The Treatment of Male Victims with Mixed-Gender, Short-Term Group Psychotherapy." In *The Sexually Abused Male*, edited by M. Hunter (Vol. 2, pp. 137–169). New York: Lexington Books.

Brown, J., Cohen, P., Johnson, J. G., and Salzinger, S. (1998). "A Longitudinal Study of Risk Factors for Child Maltreatment: Findings of a 17-Year Prospective Study of Officially Recorded and Self-Reported Child Abuse and Neglect." *Child Abuse and Neglect* 22:1065–1078.

Browne, K., and Herbert, M. (1997). *Preventing Family Violence*. New York: John Wiley & Sons.

Butler, S. (1996). *Conspiracy of Silence*. San Francisco: Volcano Press.

Carrasco, N., and Garza-Louis, D. (1995). "Hispanic Sex Offenders—Cultural Characteristics and Implications for Treatment." In *The Sex Offender*, edited by B. Schwartz and H. Cellini (pp. 13-1–13-10). Kingston, NJ: Civic Research Inst.

Conte, J. (Ed.). (2002). *Critical Issues in Child Sexual Abuse*. Thousand Oaks, CA: Sage.

Courtois, C. A. (2010). *Healing the Incest Wound*. New York: W.W. Norton.

Deblinger, E., Hathaway, C. R., Lippman, J., and Steer, R. (1993). "Psychosocial Characteristics and Correlates of Symptom Distress in Nonoffending Mothers of Sexually Abused Children." *Journal of Interpersonal Violence* 8(2):155–168.

Dorias, M. (2009). *Don't Tell: The Sexual Abuse of Boys*. Montreal, Canada: McGill–Queens University Press.

Erooga, M., and Masson, H. (Eds.). (2003). *Children and Young People Who Sexually Abuse Others*. New York: Taylor and Francis.

Faller, K. C. (1990). "Sexual Abuse by Paternal Caretakers: A Comparison of Abusers Who Are Biological Fathers in Intact Families, Stepfathers, and Noncustodial Fathers." In *The Incest Perpetrator*, edited by A. L. Horton, B. L. Johnson, L. M. Roundy, and D. Williams (pp. 65–73). Newbury Park, CA: Sage.

Faller, K. C. (2002). *Understanding and Assessing Child Sexual Maltreatment*. Thousand Oaks, CA: Sage.

Finkelhor, D. (1979). *Sexually Victimized Children*. New York: Free Press.

Finkelhor, D. (1980). "Sex Among Siblings: A Survey of the Prevalence, Variety and Effects." *Archives of Sexual Behavior* 9:171–194.

Flora, R. (2001). *How to Work with Sex Offenders*. New York: Haworth.

Fontes, L. A. (2007). "*Sin Vergüenza*: Addressing Shame with Latino Victims of Child Sexual Abuse and Their Families." *Journal of Child Sexual Abuse* 16(1):61–83.

Fontes, L. A. (2008). *Child Abuse and Culture*. New York: Guilford.

Fontes, L. A., and Plummer, C. (2012). "Cultural Issues in Child Sexual Abuse Intervention and Prevention". In *Handbook of Child Sexual Abuse*, edited by P. Goodyear-Brown (pp. 487–508). Hoboken, NJ: John Wiley and Sons.

Forward, S., and Buck, C. (1988). *Betrayal of Innocence: Incest and Its Devastation*. New York: Penguin.

Froning, M. L., and Mayman, S. B. (1990). "Identification and Treatment of Child and Adolescent Male Victims of Sexual Abuse." In *The Sexually Abused Male*, edited by M. Hunter (Vol. 2, pp. 199–224). New York: Lexington Books.

Gartner, R. (2001). *Betrayed as Boys*. New York: Guilford.

Grauerholz, L. (2000). "An Ecological Approach to Understanding Sexual Revictimization: Linking Personal, Interpersonal and Sociocultural Factors and Processes." *Child Maltreatment* 5(1):5–17.

Groth, A. N. (1982). "The Incest Offender." In *Handbook of Clinical Intervention in Child Sexual Abuse*, edited by S. Sgroi (pp. 215–239). Lexington, MA: Lexington Books.

Hanson, R. F., Lipovsky, J. A., and Saunders, B. E. (1994). "Characteristics of Fathers in Incest Families." *Journal of Interpersonal Violence* 9(2):155–169.

Herman, J., and Hirschman, L. (2000). *Father–Daughter Incest*. Cambridge, MA: Harvard University Press.

Herzberger, R. J. (1999). "Brother–Sister Incest—Father–Daughter Incest: A Comparison of Characteristics and Consequences." *Child Abuse and Neglect* 23(9):915–928.

Jacobs, J. L. (1994). *Victimized Daughters*. New York: Routledge.

Jenkins, P. (1998). *Moral Panic*. New Haven: Yale University Press.

Johnson, J. T. (1992). *Mothers of Incest Survivors*. Bloomington, IN: Indiana University Press.

Joyce, P. A. (1997). "Mothers of Sexually Abused Children and the Concept of Collusion: A Literature Review." *Journal of Child Sexual Abuse* 6(2):75–92.

Karson, M. (2001). *Patterns of Child Abuse*. New York: Haworth.

Kinnear, K. (2007). *Childhood Sexual Abuse*. Santa Barbara, CA: ABC-CLIO.

Kinsey, A. C., Pomeray, W., Martin, C., and Gebhard, P. (1953). *Sexual Behavior in the Human Female*. Philadelphia: W. B. Saunders.

Krane, J. (2003). *What's Mother Got to Do with It?* Toronto: University of Toronto Press.

Laviola, M. (1992). "Effects of Older Brother–Younger Sister Incest: A Study of the Dynamics of 17 Cases." *Child Abuse and Neglect* 16(3):409–421.

Lew, M. (2004). *Victims No Longer*. San Francisco: HarperCollins.

Messman-Moore, T. L., and Long, P. J. (2000). "Child Sexual Abuse and Revictimization in the Form of Adult Sexual Abuse, Adult Physical Abuse and Adult Psychological Maltreatment." *Journal of Interpersonal Violence* 15(5):489–502.

Mitchell, J., and Morse, J. (1997). *From Victim to Survivor: Women Survivors of Female Perpetrators*. New York: Taylor and Francis.

Ogilvie, B. A. (2004). *Mother–Daughter Incest*. New York: Haworth.

Olafson, E. (2002). "When Paradigms Collide." In *Critical Issues in Child Sexual Abuse*, edited by J. Conte (pp. 71–106). New Haven, CT: Yale University Press.

Rich, P. (2006). *Attachment and Sexual Offending*. West Sussex, England: John Wiley and Sons.

Ricker, A. (2006). *The Ultimate Betrayal*. Tucson, AZ: See Sharp Press.

Ritchie, D., Silverman, J. G., and Bancroft, R. L. (2011). *The Batterer as Parent: Addressing the Impact of Domestic Violence on Family Dynamics*. Thousand Oaks, CA: Sage.

Rosencrans, B. (1997). *The Last Secret: Daughters Abused by Mothers*. Brandon, VT: Safer Society Press.

Russell, D. (1999). *Secret Trauma: Incest in the Lives of Girls and Women*. New York: Basic Books.

Schonberg, I. J. (1992). "The Distortion of the Role of Mother in Child Sexual Abuse." *Journal of Child Sexual Abuse* 1(3):47–61.

Schwartz, B. K., and Cellini, H. R. (1995). *The Sex Offender*. Kingston, NJ: Civic Research Institute.

Seto, M. C. (2008). *Pedophilia and Sexual Offending Against Children*. Washington, DC: American Psychological Association

Sgroi, S. M., and Dana, N. (1982). "Individual and Group Treatment of Mothers of Incest Victims." In *Handbook of Clinical Intervention in Child Sexual Abuse*, edited by S. Sgroi (pp. 191–214). Lexington, MA: Lexington Books.

Stern, M., and Meyer, L. (1980). "Family and Couple Interactional Patterns in Cases of Father-Daughter Incest." In *Sexual Abuse of Children: Selected Readings*, edited by B. Jones, L. Janstrom, and K. MacFarlane (pp. 83–86). Washington, DC: U.S. Department of Health and Human Services.

Stone, R. D. (2005). *No Secrets No Lies; How Black Families Can Heal from Sexual Abuse*. New York: Broadway Books.

Strand, V. (2000). *Treating Secondary Victims*. Thousand Oaks, CA: Sage.

Tower, C. C. (1988). *Secret Scars: A Guide for the Survivor of Child Sexual Abuse*. New York: Viking/Penguin.

van Dam, C. (2001). *Identifying Child Molesters*. New York: Haworth.

Whetsell-Mitchel, J. (1995). *Rape of the Innocent*. Washington, DC: Accelerated Development.

Wiehe, V. (1997). *Sibling Abuse: Hidden Physical, Emotional and Sexual Trauma*. Thousand Oaks, CA: Sage.

Wiehe, V. (2002). *Sibling Abuse*. Springfield, VT: Bonneville.

Ambrosino, L. (1973). *Runaways*. Boston: Beacon Press.

Babchishin, K. M., Hanson, R. K., and Hermann, C. A. (2011). "The Characteristics of Online Sexual Offenders: A Meta-Analysis". *Sexual Abuse: A Journal of Research and Treatment* 23(1):92–123.

Baker, L. (2002). *Protecting Our Children from Sexual Predators*. New York: St. Martin's.

Berry, J. (2000). *Lead Us Not into Temptation*. New York: Doubleday.

Bolen, R. (2007). *Child Sexual Abuse: Its Scope and Our Failure*. New York: Plenum.

Brimer, R., and Rose, R. T. (2012) "Sex Offenders and their Victims" workshop presented at the MASOC and MATSA 14th Annual Joint Conference on the Assessment, Treatment and Safe Management of Sexually Abusing Children, Adolescents, and Adults, on April 13, 2012 at Marlborough, Massachusetts.

Bruni, F., and Burkett, E. (2002). *A Gospel of Shame: Children, Sexual Abuse, and the Catholic Church*. New York: Perennial.

Cooper, A. (2002). *Sex and the Internet*. New York: Brunner-Routledge.

Cozzens, D. (2002). *Sacred Silence: Denial and the Crisis in the Church*. Collegeville, MD: Liturgical Press.

Curtis, R., Terry, K., Dank, M., Dombrowski, K., and Khan, B. (2008). *Commercial Sexual Exploitation of Children in New York City*. Washington, DC: U.S. Department of Justice and New York: John Jay College of Criminal Justice.

Densen-Gerber, J. (1980). "Child Prostitution and Child Pornography: Medical, Legal and Societal Aspects of the Commercial Exploitation of Children." In *Sexual Abuse of Children: Selected Readings*, edited by B. Jones, L. Jenstrome, and K. MacFarlane (pp. 77–82). Washington, DC: U.S. Department of Health and Human Services.

Densen-Gerber, J., and Hutchinson, S. (1978). "Medical, Legal and Societal Problems Involving Children—Child Prostitution, Child Pornography and Drug-Related Abuse: Recommended Legislation." In *The Maltreatment of Children*, edited by S. Smith (pp. 317–50). Baltimore: University Park.

Doyle, T. P., Sipe, A. W. R., and Wall, P. J. (2006). *Sex, Priests, and Secret Codes*. Los Angeles: Volt Press.

Ertz, D. J. (1995). "The American Indian Sexual Offender." In *The Sex Offender*, edited by B. Schwartz and H. Cellini (pp. 14-1–14-12). Kingston, NJ: Civic Research Inst.

Faller, K. C. (2003). *Understanding and Assessing Child Sexual Maltreatment*. Thousand Oaks, CA: Sage.

Finkelhor, D., and Ormond, R. (June, 2004). "Prostitution of Juveniles: Patterns from NIBRS." *Juvenile Justice Bulletin*. U.S. Department of Justice. Retrieved from http://www.ndacan.cornell.edu/cmrlpostings/msg02976.html on April 22, 2013.

Finkelhor, D., Mitchell, K., and Wolak, J. (2000). *Online Victimization: A Report on the Nation's Youth*. Arlington, VA: National Center for Missing and Exploited Children.

Finklea, K. M., Fernandes-Alcantara, A. L., and Siskin, A. (2012). "Sex Trafficking of Children in the United States: Overview and Issues for Congress". In *Child Sex Trafficking in the United States*, edited by J. V. Higgins and C. M. Brady (pp. 1–59). New York: Nova Science.

Flood, M. (2009). "The Harms of Pornography Exposure Among Children and Young People". *Child Abuse Review* 18:384–400.

Flora, R. (2001). *How to Work with Sex Offenders*. New York: Haworth.

Flowers, R. B. (2001). *Runaway Kids and Teenage Prostitution*. Westport, CT: Praeger.

Flowers, R. B. (2005). The *Prostitution of Women and Girls*. Jefferson, NC: MacFarland.

Flowers, R. B. (2010). *Street Kids: The Lives of Runaway and Throwaway Teens*. Jefferson, NC: McFarland.

Flynn, E. P. (2003). *Catholics at a Crossroads: Coverup, Crisis, and Cure*. New York: Paraview Press.

Fogler, J. M., Shipherd, J. C., Rowe, E., Jensen, J., and Clarke, S. (2008). "A Theoretical Foundation for Understanding Clergy-Perpetrated Sexual Abuse." *Journal of Child Sexual Abuse* 17(3–4):301–328.

Fontes, L. A., and Plummer, C. (2012). "Cultural Issues in Child Sexual Abuse Intervention and Prevention". In *Handbook of Child Sexual Abuse*, edited by P. Goodyear-Brown (pp. 487–508), Hoboken, NJ: John Wiley and Sons.

Freeman-Longo, R. E., and Blanchard, G. (1998). *Sexual Abuse in America: Epidemic of the 21st Century*. Brandon, VT: Safer Society Press.

Gartner, R. B. (2001). *Betrayed as Boys: Psychodynamic Treatment of Sexually Abused Men*. New York: Guilford.

Geiser, R. L. (1979). *Hidden Victims*. Boston: Beacon Press.

Gerdes, L. (2003). *Child Sexual Abuse in the Catholic Church*. Farmington Hills, MI.: Cengage Gale.

Giovannoni, J. M., and Becerra, R. (1979). *Defining Child Abuse*. New York: Free Press.

Groth, A. N. (1978). "Patterns of Sexual Assault Against Children and Adolescents." In *Sexual Assault of Children and Adolescents*, edited by A. Burgess, A. N. Groth, L. Holstrom, and S. Sgroi (pp. 3–24). Lexington, MA: Lexington Books.

Groth, A. N., and Birnbaum, H. Jean. (2001). *Men Who Rape*. New York: Perseus.

Holmes, S. T., and Holmes, R. M. (2009). *Sex Crimes: Patterns and Behavior*. Thousand Oaks, CA: Sage.

Hughes, D. R. (1998). *Kids Online*. Grand Rapids, MI: Fleming H. Revell.

James, J. (1980). *Entrance into Juvenile Prostitution*. Washington, DC: National Institute of Mental Health

Jenkins, P. (1996). *Pedophiles and Priests*. New York: Oxford University Press.

Jenkins, P. (2001). *Beyond Tolerance: Child Pornography on the Internet*. New York: New York University Press.

Jenkins, P. (2003). "The Celibacy Requirement for Priests Does Not Contribute to Child Abuse." In *Child Sexual Abuse in the Catholic Church*, edited by L. I. Gerdes (pp. 31–34). Farmington Hills, MI: Greenhaven Press.

Jenkins, P. (2004). *Moral Panic*. New Haven, CT: Yale University Press.

Jones, L. M., Mitchell, K. J., and Finkelhor, D. (2012). "Trends in Youth Internet Victimization: Findings from Three Youth Internet Safety Surveys 2000–2010". *Journal of Adolescent Health* 50:179–186.

Jost, K. (2003). "Child Sexual Abuse in the Catholic Church: An Overview." In *Child Sexual Abuse in the Catholic Church*, edited by L. I. Gerdes (pp. 13–21). Farmington Hills, MI: Greenhaven Press.

Kearney, R. T. (2001). *Caring for Sexually Abused Children: A Handbook for Families and Churches*. Downers Grove, IL: InterVarsity Press.

Kennedy E. (1972). *The Catholic Priest in the United States: Psychological Investigations*. Washington, DC: United States Catholic Conference.

Kennedy, E. (2001). *The Unhealed Wound: The Church and Human Sexuality*. New York: St. Martin's Press.

Kennedy, E. (2003). "The Celibacy Requirement for Priests Contributes to Child Sexual Abuse." In *Child Sexual Abuse in the Catholic Church*, edited by L. I. Gerdes (pp. 28–30). Farmington Hills, MI: Greenhaven Press.

Klain, E. (1999). *Prostitution of Children and Child Sex Tourism*. Washington, DC: U.S. Department of Justice.

Lanning, K. V. (1992). "A Law-Enforcement Perspective on Allegations of Ritual Abuse." In *Out of Darkness: Exploring Satanism and Ritual Abuse*, edited by D. K. Sakheim and S. E. Devine (pp. 109–146). New York: Lexington Books.

Laws, R., and Donahue, W. T. (Eds.). (2008). *Sexual Deviance*. New York: Guilford.

Lenhart, A. (2009). "Teens and Sexting." Pew Internet and American Life Project. Washington, DC: Pew Research Center.

Lin, H. (Ed.). (2002). *Truth, Pornography and the Internet*. Washington, DC: National Academy Press.

Lloyd, R. (1976). *For Money or Love: Boy Prostitution in America*. New York: Vanguard Press.

Mass, A. I. (July, 11 1991). Personal communication.

McGlone, G. J. F. (2003). "The Pedophile and the Pious: Towards a New Understanding of Sexually Offending and Non-offending Roman Catholic Priests." In *The Victimization of Children: Emerging Issues*, edited by J. L. Mullings, J. W. Marguart, and D. J. Hartley (pp. 115–131). New York: Haworth.

McLaughlin, J. F. (1998). "Technophilia: A Modern Day Paraphilia." *Knight Stick: Publication of the New Hampshire Police Association* 51:47–51.

McLaughlin, J. F. (2000). "Cyber Child Sexual Offender Typology." *Knight Stick: Publication of the New Hampshire Police Association* 55:39–42.

McLaughlin, J. F. (2004). "Characteristics of a Fictitional Child Victim: Turning a Sex Offender's Dream into His Worst Nightmare." *International Journal of Communication Law and Policy, Issue 9, Symposium on Cybercrime, Part I*. Retrieved from www.ijclp.net/issue on April 20, 2009.

Mitchell, K. J., Finkelhor, D., and Wolak, J. (2003). "Victimization of Youths on the Internet." In *The Victimization of Children: Emerging Issues*, edited by J. L. Mullings, J. W. Marguart, and D. J. Hartley (pp. 1–39). New York: Haworth.

National Center for Missing and Exploited Children. (2002). *Female Prostitution: Problem and Response*. Washington, DC: U.S. Department of Justice.

North American Man Boy Love Association (NAMBLA). (2012). Retrieved from http://www.nambla.org/welcome.html on July 11, 2012.

Pryor, D. W. (1999). *Unspeakable Acts: Why Men Sexually Abuse Children*. New York: New York University Press.

Rich, P. (2006). *Attachment and Sexual Offending*. West Sussex, England: John Wiley and Sons.

Rizzuto, A. (October 15, 2003) Personal communication.

Rossman, P. (1976). *Sexual Experience Between Men and Boys*. Wilton, CT: Association Press.

Rush, F. (1992). *The Best Kept Secret: Sexual Abuse of Children*. New York: Tab Books.

Schumacher, R., and Carlson, R. (1999). "Variables and Risk Factors Associated with Child Abuse in Daycare Settings." *Child Abuse and Neglect* 23:891–898.

Sedlak, A. J., Finkelhor, D., Hammer, H., and Schultz, D. J. (2002). *National Estimates of Missing Children: An Overview*. Washington, DC: U.S. Department of Justice.

Seto, M. C. (2008). *Pedophilia and Sexual Offending Against Children*. Washington, DC: American Psychological Association.

Shea, D. (2008). *Effects of Clergy Sexual Abuse on Adults Victimized as Children*. Germany: VDM Verlag.

Sher, J. (2008). *Caught in the Web*. New York: Perseus.

Silbert, M. H., and Pines, A. M. (1981). "Sexual Child Abuse as an Antecedent to Prostitution." *Child Abuse and Neglect* 5:407–411.

Sipe, A. R. (1999). *Bless Me Father for I Have Sinned*. Westport, CT: Praeger.

Taylor, M., and Quayle, E. (2003). *Child Pornography: An Internet Crime*. New York: Brunner-Routledge.

Terry, K., and Smith, M. L. for John Jay College of Criminal Justice. (2006). "The Nature and Scope of Sexual Abuse of Minors by Catholic Priests and Deacons in the United States." Supplementary Data Analysis. Washington, DC: United States Conference of Catholic Bishops.

Tracy, S. R. (2005). *Mending the Soul*. Grand Rapids, MI: Zondervan.

van Dam, C. (2001). *Identifying Child Molesters*. New York: Haworth.

van Dam, C. (2006). *The Socially Skilled Child Molester*. New York: Haworth.

Walker, S., Sanci, l. and Temple-Smith, M. (2011). "Sexting and Young People: Experts' Views". *Youth Studies Australia* 30(4):8–16.

Ward, T., Polaschek, D. L., and Beech, A. R. (2006). *Theories of Sexual Offending*. West Sussex, England: John Wiley and Sons.

Weisberg, K. (1985). *Children of the Night*. Lexington, MA: Lexington Books.

Wolak, J., and Finkelhor, D. (2011). *Sexting: A Typology*. Durham, NH: Crimes Against Children Research Center, University of New Hampshire.

Wolak, J., Finkelhor, D., and Mitchell, K. J. (2005). *Child Pornography Possessors: Arrested in Internet-Related Crimes*. Alexandria, VA: National Center for Missing and Exploited Children.

Wolak, J., Finkelhor, D., and Mitchell, K. J. (2011). "Child Pornography Possessors: Trends in Offender and Case Characteristics". *Sexual Abuse: A Journal of Research and Treatment* 23(1):22–42.

Wolak, J., Finkelhor, D., Mitchell, K. J., and Ybarra, M. L. (2008). "Online 'Predators' and Their Victims." *American Psychologist* 63(2):111–128.

Wortley, R., and Smallbone, S. (2012). *Internet Child Pornography: Causes, Investigation and Prevention*. Santa Barbara, CA: Praeger.

References for Chapter 9

Barlow, J., and McMillan, A. S. (2010). *Safeguarding Children from Emotional Maltreatment*. London: Jessica Kingsley.

Binggeli, N. J., Hart, S. N., and Brassard, M. R. (2001). *Psychological Maltreatment of Children*. Thousand Oaks, CA: Sage.

Brassard, M. R., and Hardy, D. B. (1997). "Psychological Maltreatment." In *The Battered Child*, edited by M. E. Helfer, R. S. Kempe, and R. D. Krugman (pp. 392–412). Chicago: University of Chicago Press.

Bross, D. C., Krugman, R. D., Lenherr, M. R., Rosenberg, D. A., and Schmitt, B. D. (Eds.). (1988). *The New Child Protection Team Handbook*. New York: Garland.

Burnett, B. B. (1993). "The Psychological Abuse of Latency Age Children: A Survey." *Child Abuse and Neglect* 17(4):441–454.

Covitz, J. (1990). *Emotional Child Abuse: The Family Curse*. Boston: Sigo Press.

DeRobertis, E. M. (2004). "The Impact of Long-Term Psychological Maltreatment by One's Maternal Figure: A Study of the Victim Perspective." *Journal of Emotional Abuse* 4(2):27–51.

Dutton, D. G. (2007). *Abusive Personality*. New York: Guilford.

Faller, K. C. (2003). *Understanding and Assessing Child Sexual Maltreatment*. Thousand Oaks, CA: Sage.

Fontes, L. A. (2008). *Child Abuse and Culture*. New York: Guilford.

Fraser, G. A. (1997). *Dilemma of Ritual Abuse*. Washington, DC: American Psychiatric Publishers.

Garbarino, J., and Eckenrode, J. (1997). *Understanding Abusive Families*. New York: John Wiley & Sons.

Garbarino, J., Guttmann, E., and Seeley, J. W. (1986). *The Psychologically Battered Child*. San Francisco: Jossey-Bass.

Hart, S. N., Brassard, M. R., Davidson, H., Rivelis, E., Diaz, V., and Binggeli, N. J. (2011). "Psychological Maltreatment." In *The APSAC Handbook on Child Maltreatment*, edited by J. E. B. Myers (pp. 125–144). Thousand Oaks, CA: Sage.

Hedges, L. E. (1997). *Remembering, Repeating, and Working Through Childhood Trauma*. Northvale, NJ: Jason Aronson.

Iwaniec, D. (2006). The *Emotionally Abused and Neglected Child*. West Sussex, England: John Wiley and Sons.

Jenkins, P. (1998). *Moral Panic*. New Haven: Yale University Press.

Lum, D. (2007). "Social Work Practice with Asian Americans." In *Social Work: A Profession of Many Faces*, edited by A. T. Morales, B. W. Sheafor, and M. E. Scott (pp. 463–487). Boston: Allyn & Bacon.

Mass, A. E., and Geaga-Rosenthal, J. (2000). "Child Welfare: Asian and Pacific Islander Families." In *Child Welfare: A Multicultural Perspective*, edited by N. Cohen (pp. 145–164). Boston: Allyn & Bacon.

Morrow, G. (1987). *The Compassionate School: A Practical Guide to Educating Abused and Traumatized Children*. Upper Saddle River, NJ: Prentice-Hall.

Noblitt, J. R., and Perskin, P. (2000). *Cult and Ritual Abuse*. Westport, CT: Greenwood.

Noblitt, R., and Noblitt, P. P. (Eds.). (2008). *Ritual Abuse in the Twenty-first Century*. Bandon, OR.: Robert D. Reed.

O'Hagan, K. (1998). *Emotional and Psychological Abuse of Children*. Toronto: University of Toronto Press.

Skogrand, L., De Frain, J., and De Frain, N. (2007). *Surviving and Transcending a Traumatic Childhood: The Dark Thread*. New York: Haworth.

Snedeker, M., and Nathan, D. R. (2001). *Satan's Silence: Ritual Abuse and the Making of a Modern Witch Hunt*. Lincoln, NE: iUniverse.

Whitman, B. (2002). "Psychological and Psychiatric Issues." In *Recognition of Child Abuse for the Mandated Reporter*, edited by A. P. Giardino and E. R. Giardino (pp. 137–173). St. Louis, MO: G. W. Medical.

Wiehe, V. R. (1997). *Sibling Abuse: Hidden Physical, Emotional and Sexual Trauma*. Lexington, MA: Lexington Books.

Wright, M. O. (2008). *Childhood Emotional Abuse*. New York: Taylor and Francis.

American Prosecutors Research Institute. (2004). *Investigation and Prosecution of Child Abuse*. Thousand Oaks, CA: Sage.

Azar, S. T., and Cote, L. R. (2005). "Cognitive Behavioral Interventions with Neglectful Parents." In *Handbook for Treatment of Abused and Neglected Children*, edited by F. Talley (pp. 65–181). New York: Haworth.

Crittenden, P. M. (1999). "Child Neglect: Causes and Contributors." In *Neglected Children*, edited by H. Dubowitz (pp. 47–68). Thousand Oaks, CA: Sage.

Cross, J. P., Finkelhor, D., and Ormond, R. (2005). "Police Involvement in Child Protection Investigations: Literature Review and Secondary Data Analysis." *Child Maltreatment* 10(3):224–244.

Crosson-Tower, C. (2002). *When Children Are Abused: An Educator's Guide*. Boston: Allyn & Bacon.

Crosson-Tower, C. (2006). *A Clergy Guide to Child Abuse and Neglect*. Cleveland: Pilgrim Press.

deYoung, M. (1986). "A Conceptual Model for Judging the Truthfulness of a Young Child's Allegation of Sexual Abuse." *American Journal of Orthopsychiatry* 56:550–559.

Dale, P., Green, R., and Fellows, R. (2005). *Child Protection Assessment Following Serious Injuries to Infants*. Hoboken, NJ: John Wiley & Sons.

Faller, K. C. (2003). *Understanding and Assessing Child Sexual Maltreatment*. Thousand Oaks, CA: Sage.

Faller, K. C. (2007). *Interviewing Children About Sexual Abuse*. New York: Oxford University Press.

Feldman, K. W. (1997). "Evaluation of Physical Abuse." In *The Battered Child*, edited by M. E. Helfer, R. S. Kempe, and R. D. Krugman (pp. 175–220). Chicago: University of Chicago Press.

Finkelhor, D., and Browne, A. (1985). "The Traumatic Impact of Child Sexual Abuse: A Conceptualization." *American Journal of Orthopsychiatry* 55:530–541.

Fontes, L. A. (2008). *Child Abuse and Culture*. New York: Guilford.

Forkey, H., Hudson, K., Manz, P. H., and Silver, J. (2002). "After the Call: Children and the Child Welfare System." In *Recognition of Child Abuse for the Mandated Reporter*, edited by A. P. Giardino and E. R. Giardino (pp. 351–378). St. Louis, MO: G. W. Medical.

Friedrich, W. N. (2001). *Psychological Assessment of Sexually Abused Children and Their Families*. Thousand Oaks, CA: Sage.

Giardino, A. P., and Kolilis, G. H. (2002). "The Role of Law Enforcement in the Investigation of Child Maltreatment." In the *Recognition of Child Abuse for the Mandated Reporter*, edited by A. P. Giardino and E. R. Giardino (pp. 279–308). St. Louis, MO: G. W. Medical.

Giardino, E. R., and Giardino, A. P. (2003). *Nursing Approach to the Evaluation of Child Maltreatment*. St. Louis, MO: G. W. Medical.

Helfer, M. E. (1997). "Communication in the Therapeutic Relationship: Concepts, Strategies and Skills." In *The Battered Child*, edited by M. E. Helfer, R. S. Kempe, and R. D. Krugman (pp. 107–119). Chicago: Chicago University Press

Heras, P. (1992). "Cultural Considerations in the Assessment and Treatment of Child Sexual Abuse." *Journal of Child Sexual Abuse* 1(3):119–124.

Hewitt, S. (2012). "Developmentally Sensitive Assessment Methods in Child Sexual Abuse Case". In *Handbook of Child Sexual Abuse: Identification, Assessment and Treatment*, edited by P. Goodyer-Brown (pp. 121–142), Hoboken, NJ: John Wiley & Sons.

Hildebrand, V., Gray, M. M., and Phenice, L. A. (2007). *Knowing and Serving Diverse Families.* Upper Saddle River, NJ: Pearson.

Iwaniec, D. (2004). *Children Who Fail to Thrive.* Indianapolis: J. Wiley & Sons.

Joyce, P. A. (1997). "Mothers of Sexually Abused Children and the Concept of Collusion." *Journal of Child Sexual Abuse* 6(2):75–92.

Kempe, A. (2007). *A Good Knight for Children.* Bangor, ME: Booklocker.com.

Kiwala, L. (2000). *Guidelines for Police Training on Violence Against Women and Child Abuse.* London: Commonwealth Secretariat.

Knight, M. O., Chew, J., and Gonzalez, E. (2005). "The Child Welfare System: A Map for the Bold Traveler." In *Handbook for the Treatment of Abused and Neglected Children*, edited by P. F. Talley (pp. 25–37). New York: Haworth.

Lamb, M., Hershkowitz, I., Orbach, Y., and Esplin, P. W. (2008). *Tell Me What Happened: Structured Investigative Interviews of Child Victims and Witnesses.* Hoboken, NJ: John. Wiley & Sons.

Lum, D. (2000). *Social Work Practice with People of Color.* Monterey, CA: Brooks/Cole.

Lustig, M. W., and Koester, J. (2009). *Intercultural Competence: Interpersonal Communication Across Cultures.* Upper Saddle River, NJ: Pearson.

Lynch, E. W. (2011). "Developing Cross-Cultural Competence". In *Developing Cross-Cultural Competence: A Guide for Working with Children and Their Families*, edited by E. W. Lynch and M. J. Hanson (pp. 41–77). Baltimore, MD: Paul H. Brookes.

MacDonald, G. (2005). "Intervening with Neglect." In *Child Neglect*, edited by J. Taylor and B. Daniel (pp. 279–290). London: Jessica Kingsley.

McGovern, J. (2007). *Protecting Powers.* Hoboken, NJ: John Wiley & Sons.

Polansky, N., Borgman, N. D., and DeSoiz, C. (1972). *Roots of Futility.* San Francisco: Jossey-Bass.

Polansky, N., Chalmers, M. A., Buttenweiser, E., and Williams, D. (1990). *Damaged Parents: An Anatomy of Child Neglect.* Chicago: University of Chicago Press.

Powell, C. (2007). *Safeguarding Children and Young People: A Guide for Nurses and Midwives.* Columbus, OH: McGraw-Hill.

Reece, R. M. (2008). *Child Abuse: Medical Management and Treatment.* Elk Grove Village, IL: American Academy of Pediatrics.

Righthand, S., Kerr, S., and Drach, K. (2003). *Child Maltreatment Risk Assessments: An Evaluation Guide.* New York: Haworth.

Rothman, J. C. (2007). *Cultural Competence in Process and Practice: Building Bridges.* Upper Saddle River, NJ: Pearson.

Seagull, E. W. (1997). "Family Assessment." In *The Battered Child*, edited by M. E. Helfer, R. S. Kempe, and R. D. Krugman (pp. 150–174). Chicago: Chicago University Press.

Sgroi, S. M. (n.d.). "Examination for Child Sexual Assault." Mimeographed.

Sgroi, S. M. (1982a). *Handbook of Clinical Intervention in Child Sexual Abuse.* Lexington, MA: Lexington Books.

Sgroi, S. M. (1982b). "Pediatric Gonorrhea and Child Sexual Abuse: The Venereal Disease Connection." *Sexually Transmitted Diseases* 9:154–156.

Sgroi, S. M., Porter, F. S., and Blick, L. C. (1982). "Validation of Child Sexual Abuse." In *Handbook of Clinical Intervention in Child Sexual Abuse*, edited by S. M. Sgroi (pp. 39–79). Lexington, MA: Lexington Books.

Shepherd, J. R. (1997). "The Role of Law Enforcement in the Investigation of Child Abuse and Neglect." In *The Battered Child*, edited by M. E. Helfer, R. S. Kempe, and R. D. Krugman (pp. 251–259). Chicago: Chicago University Press.

Smith, W. L. (1997). "Imaging in Child Abuse." In *The Battered Child*, edited by M. E. Helfer, R. S. Kempe, and R. D. Krugman (pp. 221–247). Chicago: Chicago University Press.

Steele, L. C. (2012). "The Forensic Interview: A Challenging Conversation". In *Handbook of Child Sexual abuse: Identification, Assessment and Treatment*, edited by P. Goodyer-Brown, (pp. 99–119). Hoboken, NJ: John Wiley & Sons.

Stone, R. D. (2005). *No Secrets No Lies: How Black Families Can Heal from Sexual Abuse.* New York: Broadway Books.

Webb, N. B., and Lum, D. (2001). *Culturally Diverse Parent–Child and Family Relationships.* New York: Columbia University Press.

Weber, M. W. (1997). "The Assessment of Child Abuse: A Primary Function of Child Protective Services." In *The Battered Child*, edited by M. E. Helfer, R. S. Kempe, and R. D. Krugman (pp. 120–149). Chicago: Chicago University Press.

Willats, J. (2005). *Making Sense of Children's Drawings.* New York: Taylor and Francis.

Young, C. (1997). "Psychodynamics of Coping and Survival of the African American Female in a Changing World." In *Counseling American Minorities*, edited by D. R. Atkinson, G. Morten, and D. W. Sue (pp. 75–87). Dubuque, IA: Wm. C. Brown.

References for Chapter 11

Bartollas, C., and Miller, S. J. (2010). *Juvenile Justice in America*. Upper Saddle River, NJ: Pearson.

Copen, L. M. (2000). *Preparing Children for Court: A Practioner's Guide*. Thousand Oaks, CA: Sage.

Dale, P., Green, R., and Fellows, R. (2005). *Child Protection Assessment Following Serious Injuries to Infants*. Hoboken, NJ: John Wiley & Sons.

Davidson, H. A. (1997). "The Courts and Child Maltreatment." In *The Battered Child*, edited by M. E. Helfer, R. S. Kempe, and R. D. Krugman (pp. 482–499). Chicago: University of Chicago Press.

Devon, R. T. (2010). *Working with the Courts in Child Protection*. Hauppauge, New York: Nova Science .

Duquette, D. N. (1997). "Lawyer's Roles in Child Protection." In *The Battered Child*, edited by M. E. Helfer, R. S. Kempe, and R. D. Krugman (pp. 460–481). Chicago: University of Chicago Press.

Earle, K. A., and Cross, A. (2001). *Child Abuse and Neglect Among Native American/Alaska Native Children: An Analysis of Existing Data*. Portland, ME: National Resource Center for Organizational Improvement, University of Southern Maine.

Faller, K. C. (2003). *Understanding and Assessing Child Sexual Maltreatment*. Thousand Oaks, CA: Sage.

Harris, L. J., and Teitelbaum, L. E. (2002). *Children, Parents, and the Law*. New York: Aspen.

Hood, K. J. M. (2006). *A.S.A. Court Appointed Special Adovocate: A Basic Guide*. Spokane, WA: Whispering Pines Press.

Ichikawa, D. P. (1997). "An Argument on Behalf of Children." *Child Maltreatment* 2(3):202–211.

Jones, W. G. (2006). *Working with the Courts in Child Protection*. Washington, DC: U.S. Department of Health and Human Services.

Katner, D., and Plum, H. J. (2002). "Legal Issues." In *Recognition of Child Abuse for the Mandated Reporter*, edited by A. P. Giardino and E. Giardino (pp. 309–350). St. Louis: G. W. Medical.

Laney, G. (2008). *Sex Offender Registration*. Haupauge, NY: Nova Science.

Lipovsky, J. A. (1994). "The Impact of Court on Children." *Journal of Interpersonal Violence* 9(2):238–257.

Litzelfelner, P., and Petr, C. (1997). "Case Advocacy in Child Welfare." *Social Work* 42(4):392–402.

Lyon, T. D. (2002). "Scientific Support for Expert Testimony on Child Sexual Abuse Accommodation." In *Critical Issues in Child Sexual Abuse*, edited by J. Conte (pp. 107–138). Thousand Oaks, CA: Sage.

Masson, J. M., and Oakley, M. W. (2001). *Out of Hearing: Representing Children in Court*. Indianapolis, IN: John Wiley.

Megan's Law. (1996). Pub. Law No. 104–105.

Myers, J. E. B. (2011). "Legal Issues in Child Abuse and Neglect Practice." In *The APSAC Handbook on Child Maltreatment*, edited by J. E. B. Myers (pp. 361–375). Thousand Oaks, CA: Sage.

Myers, J. E. B., Diedrich, S. E., Lee, D., Fincher, K., and Stern, R. (2002). "Prosecution of Child Sexual Abuse in the United States." In *Critical Issues in Child Sexual Abuse*, edited by J. Conte (pp. 27–69). Thousand Oaks, CA: Sage.

Noel, J. (2013). "Court Services on Behalf of Children." In *Exploring Child Welfare*, edited by C. Crosson-Tower (pp. 231–250). Boston: Allyn & Bacon.

Peters, J. K. (1997). "The Lawyer for Children at the Interdisciplinary Meeting." *Child Maltreatment* 2(3):226–244.

Simmons, D., and Trope, J. (1999). *Issues for Tribes and States Serving Indian Children*. Portland, ME: National Resource Center for Organizational Improvement, University of Southern Maine.

Simon, J. (2003). "Managing the Monstrous: Sex Offenders and the New Penology." In *Protecting Society from Sexually Dangerous Offenders*, edited by B. J. Winick and J. Q. LaFond (pp. 301–316). Washington, DC: American Psychological Association.

Stein, T. (1998). *Child Welfare and the Law*. New York: Longman.

Thorne, W. A. (July, 15 1991). Personal communication.

Ventrell, M. R., and Duquette, D. N. (2005). *Child Welfare Law and Practice*. Denver, CO: Bradford.

Walsh, E. (1997). "Megan's Law—Sex Offender Registration and Notification Statutes and Constitutional Challenges." In *The Sex Offender*, edited by B. K. Schwartz and H. R. Cellini (pp. 24-1–24-6). Kingston, NJ: Civic Research.

Zgoba, K., Witt, P., Dalessandra, M., and Veysey, B. (2008). "Megan's Law: Assessing the Practical and Monetary Efficacy." Retrieved from ncjrs.gov/pdffiles1/nij/grants/225370.pdf on April 20, 2009.

Altstein, H., and McRoy, R. (2000). *Does Family Preservation Serve a Child's Best Interests?* Washington, DC: Georgetown University Press.

Atkinson, D. R., Morten, G., and Sue, D. W. (2003). *Counseling American Minorities*. Dubuque, IA: Wm. C. Brown.

Bath, H. I., and Haapala, D. A. (1993). "Intensive Family Preservation Services with Abused and Neglected Children: An Examination of Group Differences." *Child Abuse and Neglect* 17(2):213–225.

Berns, R. M. (2009). *Child, Family, Community: Socialization and Support*. Belmont, CA: Wadsworth.

Binggeli, N. J., Hart, S. N., and Brassard, M. R. (2001). *Psychological Maltreatment of Children*. Thousand Oaks, CA: Sage.

Briere, J. (1992). *Child Abuse Trauma*. Newbury Park, CA: Sage.

Cantwell, H. (1997). "The Neglect of Child Neglect." In *The Battered Child*, edited by M. E. Helfer, R. S. Kempe, and R. D. Krugman (pp. 347–373). Chicago: University of Chicago Press.

Cattanach, A. (2008). *Play Therapy with Abused Children*. London: Jessica Kingsley.

Dubowitz, H. (Ed.). (1999). *Neglected Children*. Thousand Oaks, CA: Sage.

Filcheck, H. A., McNeil, C. B., and Herschell, A. D. (2005). "Parent Interventions with Physically Abused Children." In *Handbook for the Treatment of Abused and Neglected Children*, edited by P. F. Talley (pp. 285–314). New York: Haworth.

Fontes, L. A. (2008). *Child Abuse and Culture*. New York: Guilford.

Forkey, H., Hudson, H., Manz, P. H., and Silver, J. A. (2002). "After the Call: Children and the Child Welfare System." In *Recognition of Child Abuse for the Mandated Reporter*, edited by A. P. Giardino and E. Giardino (pp. 351–378). St. Louis: G. W. Medical.

Friedrich, W. N. (2002). "An Integrated Model of Psychotherapy for Abused Children." In *APSAC Handbook on Child Maltreatment*, edited by J. B. Myers, L. Berliner, J. Briere, and J. C. Hendrix (pp. 141–157). Thousand Oaks, CA: Sage.

Hally, C., Polansky, N. F., and Polansky, N. A. (1980). *Child Neglect: Mobilizing Services*. Washington, DC: U.S. Department of Health and Human Services.

Hecht, D. B., Chaffin, M., Bonner, B., Worley, K. B., and Lawon, L. (2002). "Treating Sexually Abused Adolescents." In *APSAC Handbook on Child Maltreatment*, edited by J. E. B. Myers, L. Berliner, J. Briere, C. T. Hendrix, C. Jenny, and T. A. Reid (pp. 159–174). Thousand Oaks, CA: Sage.

Helfer, R. E. (1978). *Childhood Comes First*. East Lansing, MI: Ray E. Helfer.

Howe, D. (2005). *Child Abuse and Neglect*. London: Palgrave.

Jackson, S., and Brissett-Chapman, S. (1999). *Serving African-American Children*. New York: Child Welfare League of America.

Jones, D. P. H. (1997). "Treatment of the Child and the Family Where Child Abuse and Neglect Has Occurred." In *The Battered Child*, edited by M. E. Helfer, R. S. Kempe, and R. D. Krugman (pp. 521–542). Chicago: University of Chicago Press.

Kellner, L., and Crosson-Tower, C. (2013). "Family Preservation or Child Placement? Serving the Best Interests of the Child". In *Exploring Child Welfare*, edited by C. Crosson-Tower (pp. 211–230). Upper Saddle River, NJ: Pearson Education.

Luby, J. L. (Ed.). (2009). *Handbook of Preschool Mental Health*. New York: Guilford.

Lum, D. (Ed.). (2010). *Culturally Competent Practice: A Framework for Understanding*. Stamford, CT: Cengage.

MacDonald, G. (2005). "Intervening with Neglect." In *Child Neglect*, edited by J. Taylor and B. Daniel (pp. 279–290). London: Jessica Kingsley.

Polansky, N. A., Ammons, P. W., and Gaudin, J. M. (1985). "Loneliness and Isolation in Child Neglect." *Social Casework* 66:33–47.

Polansky, N. A., Chalmers, M. A., Buttenweiser, E., and Williams, D. P. (1981). *Damaged Parents: An Anatomy of Child Neglect*. Chicago: University of Chicago Press.

Polansky, N. A., DeSaix, C., and Sharlin, S. (1972). *Child Neglect: Understanding and Reaching the Parent*. New York: Child Welfare League of America.

Righthand, S., Kerr, B., and Drach, K. (2003). *Child Maltreatment Risk Assessments*. New York: Haworth.

Runyon, M. K., and Urquiza, A. J. (2011). "Child Physical Abuse: Intervention for Parents Who Engage in Coercive Parenting Practices and Their Children". In *The APSAC Handbook on Child Maltreatment*, edited by J. E. B. Myers. (pp. 195–2012). Thousand Oaks, CA: Sage.

Sauer, M. (1994). "Create Family Preservation Programs." In *Child Abuse: Opposing Viewpoints*, edited by K. deKoster and K. L. Swisher. San Diego, CA: Greenhaven Press.

Silovsky, J. F. (2005). "Group Therapy with Children Who Have Experienced Maltreatment." In *Handbook for the Treatment of Abused and Neglected Children*, edited by R. F. Talley (pp. 231–266). New York: Haworth.

Stevenson, O. (2007). *Neglected Children and Their Families*. Hoboken, NJ: John Wiley & Sons.

Williams, L. T., and Crosson-Tower, C. (2013). "Counseling for Families and Children." In *Exploring Child Welfare*, edited by C. Crosson-Tower (pp. 145–172). Upper Saddle River, NJ: Pearson Education.

Wilson, K., and Ryan, V. (2006). *Play Therapy*. Philadelphia: Elsevier Health Services.

References for Chapter 13

Baker, J. N., Tanis, H. J., and Rice, J. B. (2001). "Including Siblings in Treatment of Child Sexual Abuse." *Journal of Child Sexual Abuse* 10(3):1–16.

Bannister, A. (2004). *Creative Therapies with Traumatized Children*. London: Jessica Kingsley.

Bratton, S. C., Ceballos, P. L., Landreth, G. L., and Costos, M. B. (2012). "Child-Parent Relationship Therapy with Nonoffending Parents of Sexually Abused Children." In *Handbook of Child Sexual Abuse*, edited by P. Goodyear-Brown (pp. 321–339). Hoboken, NJ: John Wiley & Sons.

Cattanach, A. (2008). *Play Therapy with Abused Children*. London: Jessica Kingsley.

Eldridge, H., and Sradijian, J. (2000). "Replacing the Function of Abusive Behaviors for the Offender: Remaking Relapse Prevention in Working with Women Who Sexually Abuse Children." In *Remaking Relapse Prevention with Sex Offenders*, edited by P. Laws et al. (pp. 402–426). Thousand Oaks, CA: Sage.

Finkelhor, D. (1984). *Child Sexual Abuse*. New York: Free Press.

Fitzgerald, M. M., and Cohen, J. (2012). "Trauma-Focused Cognitive Behavioral Therapy". In *Handbook of Child Sexual Abuse*, edited by P. Goodyear-Brown, (pp. 199–228). Hoboken, NJ: John Wiley & Sons.

Flora, R. (2001). *How to Work with Sex Offenders*. New York: Haworth.

Flora, R., Duehl, J. T., Fisher, W., Halsey, S., and Keohane, M. (2008). *Sex-Offender Therapy*. New York: Taylor and Francis.

Fontes, L. (2008). *Child Abuse and Culture*. New York: Guilford.

Ford, H. (2006). *Women Who Sexually Abuse Children*. Hoboken, NJ: John Wiley & Sons.

Gartner, R. B. (2001). *Betrayed as Boys*. New York: Guilford.

Giardino, A. P., Lyn, M. A., and Giardino, E. R. (2010). *A Practical Guide to the Evaluation of Child Abuse and Neglect*. New York: Springer-Verlag.

Giarretto, H. (1996). *Integrated Treatment of Child Sexual Abuse*. Palo Alto, CA: Science and Behavior Books, Kluwer Academic Press.

Gil, E. (1993). "Individual Therapy." In *Sexualized Children*, edited by E. Gil and T. C. Johnson (pp. 179–210). Rockville, MD: Launch Press.

Gil, E. (1996). *Systematic Treatment of Families Who Abuse*. San Francisco, CA: Jossey-Bass.

Gil, E., and Johnson, T. C. (1993). *Sexualized Children*. Rockville, MD: Launch Press.

Hanson, R. K., Bourgon, G., Helmus, L., and Hodgson, S. (2009). *A Meta-Analysis of the Effectiveness of Treatment for Sexual Offenders: Risk, Need and Responsibility*. Ottawa, Ontario: Public Safety Canada.

Howe, D. (2005). *Child Abuse and Neglect*. London: Palgrave.

Hunter, M. (1990). *The Sexually Abused Male*. New York: Lexington Books.

Iwaniec, D. (2006). *The Emotionally Abused and Neglected Child*. West Sussex, England: John Wiley & Sons.

James, B., and Nasjleti, M. (1983). *Treating Sexually Abused Children and Their Families*. Palo Alto, CA: Consulting Psychologists Press.

Johnson, J. T. (1992). *Mothers of Incest Survivors*. Bloomington, IN: Indiana University Press.

Kagan, R. (2004). *Rebuilding Attachments with Traumatized Children*. New York: Haworth.

Karson, M. (2001). *Patterns of Child Abuse*. New York: Haworth.

Kirsch, L. G., Fanniff, A. M., and Becker, J. (2011). "Treatment of Adolescent and Adult Sex Offenders". In *The APSAC Handbook on Child Maltreatment*, edited by J. E. B. Myers (pp. 289–305). Thousand Oaks, CA: Sage.

Laws, D. R., Hudson, S. M., and Ward, T. (2000). *Remaking Relapse Prevention with Sex Offenders*. Thousand Oaks, CA: Sage.

Levenson, J., and Morin, J. W. (2000). *Treating Nonoffending Parents of Child Sexual Abuse*. Thousand Oaks, CA: Sage.

Malchiodi, C. A., and Perry, B. D. (2008). *Creative Interventions with Traumatized Children*. New York: Guilford.

Mathews, J. K. (1998). "An 11-Year Perspective of Working with Female Offenders." In *Sourcebook of Treatment Programs for Sexual Offenders*, edited by W. M. Marshall, T. Ward, S. M. Hudson, and T. A. Reid (pp. 259–272). New York: Plenum.

McGrath, R. J., Cumming, G. F., Burchard, B. L., Zeoli, S., and Ellerby, L. (2010). *Current Practices and Emerging Trends in Sexual Abuser Management: The Safer Society 2009 North American Survey*. Brandon, VT: Safer Society Press.

Ogilvie, B. A. (2004). *Mother–Daughter Incest*. New York: Haworth.

Pollio, E., Deblinger, E., and Runyon, M. (2011). "Mental Health Treatment for the Effects of Child Sexual Abuse". In *The APSAC Handbook on Child Maltreatment*, edited by J. E. B. Myers (pp. 267–288). Thousand Oaks, CA: Sage.

Pope, S. M., Williams, J. S., Sirles, E. A., and Lally, E. M. (2005). *Family Preservation and Support Services: A Literature Review and Report on Outcome Measures*. Anchorage: Casey Family Programs, University of Alaska, School of Social Work.

Prendergast, W. E. (2004). *Treating Sex Offenders*. New York: Haworth Press.

Rice, M. E., and Harris, G. T. (2003). "What We Know and Don't Know About Treating Adult Sexual Offenders." In *Protecting Society from Sexually Dangerous Offenders*, edited by B. J. Winick and J. Q. Fond (pp. 101–111). Washington, DC: American Psychological Association.

Rich, P. (2006). *Attachment and Sexual Offending*. West Sussex, England: John Wiley & Sons.

Rich, P. (2009). *Juvenile Sexual Offenders*. Hoboken, NJ: John Wiley & Sons.

Righthand, S., Kerr, B., and Drach, K. (2003). *Child Maltreatment Risk Assessments*. New York: Haworth.

Rosencrans, B. (1997). *The Last Secret*. Brandon, VT: Safer Society Press.

Sawyer, S. P. (1999). "Measuring Treatment Efficacy Through Long-Term Follow-Up." In *The Sex Offender*, edited by B. Schwartz (pp. 24-1–24-13). Kingston, NJ: Civic Research Institute.

Sgroi, S. M. (Ed.). (1982). *Handbook of Clinical Intervention in Child Sexual Abuse*. Lexington, MA: Lexington Books.

Stone, R. (2005). *No Secrets No Lies: How Black Families Can Heal from Sexual Abuse*. New York: Broadway Books.

Strand, V. C. (2000). *Treating Secondary Victims*. Thousand Oaks, CA: Sage.

Ward, T., Polaschek, D. L. L., and Beech, A. R. (2006). *Theories of Sexual Offending*. West Sussex, England: John Wiley & Sons.

Williams, M. B. (1993). "Assessing the Traumatic Impact of Child Sexual Abuse: What Makes It More Severe?" *Journal of Child Sexual Abuse* 2(2):41–59.

References for Chapter 14

Barth, R. P., Albert, V., Berrick, J. D., and McCourtney, M. (2010). *From Child Abuse to Foster Care: Child Welfare Services Pathways and Placements*. Piscataway, NJ: Transaction

Berrick, J. D. (2008). *Take Me Home: Protecting America's Vulnerable Children and Families*. New York: Oxford University Press.

Boyd-Franklin, N. (2006). *Black Families in Therapy: Understanding the African American Experience*. New York: Guilford.

Crosson-Tower, C. (2013). *Exploring Child Welfare*. Boston: Allyn & Bacon.

Farmer, E., and Moyers, S. (2010). *Kinship Care: Fostering Effective Family and Friends Placements* London: Jessica Kinsley.

Goodyer, A. (2011). *Child-Centered Foster Care: A Rights Model for Practice*. London: Jessica Kingsley.

Grant, L. T. (2004). *Breaking Up Families*. Jamaica, NY: Yacos.

Hegar, R. L., and Scannapieco, M. (1999). *Kinship Foster Care*. New York: Oxford University Press.

Howe, D. (2005). *Child Abuse and Neglect: Attachment, Development and Intervention*. Houndsmills, Basingstoke, Hampshire, England: Palgrave MacMillan.

Karson, M. (2001). *Patterns of Child Abuse*. New York: Haworth.

Kaufman, J., and Grasso, D. (2006). "The Early Intervention Foster Care Program." *Child Maltreatment* 11(1):90–91.

Mallon, G. P. (2005). *Toolbox: Facilitating Permanency for Youth*. Washington, DC: Child Welfare League of America.

Nutt, L. (2006). *The Lives of Foster Carers*. Philadelphia: Taylor and Francis.

Pecora, P. J., Whittaker, J. K., Maluccio, A. N., Barth, R. P., and Plotnick, R. D. (2001). *The Child Welfare Challenge: Policy, Practice, and Research*. New York: Aldine DeGruyter.

Rosenwald, M., and Riley, B. N. (2010). *Advocating for Children in Foster and Kinship Care: A Guide to Getting the Best Out of Our System and Practitioners*. New York: Columbia University Press.

Sinclair, I., Wilson, K., and Gibbs, I. (2004). *Foster Placements*. London: Jessica Kingsley.

Taylor-Brown, S. (1991). "The Impact of AIDS on Foster Care: A Family-Centered Approach to Services in the United States." *Child Welfare* 70(2):193–209.

Webb, N. B., (2011). *Social Work Practice with Children*. New York: Guilford.

Wulczyn, F. (2004). "Family Reunification." *The Future of Children* 14(1):95–113.

Bender, L. (1948). "Psychopathic Behavior Disorders in Children." In *Handbook of Correctional Psychology*, edited by R. Lindner and R. Seliger (pp. 360–377). New York: Philosophical Library.

Bilich, M., Bonfiglio, S., and Carlson, S. (2000). *Shared Grace: Therapists and Clergy Working Together*. New York: Haworth.

Bogarty, D. J., and Toler, S. (2002). *Daddy Can't Hurt Me Anymore*. Fredrick, MD: America House.

Bowen, M. (1966). "The Use of Family Theory in Clinical Practice." *Comprehensive Psychiatry* 7:345–374.

Briere, J. N. (1992). *Child Abuse Trauma*. Newbury Park, CA: Sage.

Cassese, J. (Ed.). (2001). *Gay Men and Childhood Sexual Trauma: Integrating the Shattered Self*. New York: Haworth.

Cloitre, M., Koenen, K. C., and Cohen, R. (2006). *Treating Survivors of Childhood Abuse*. New York: Guilford.

Courtois, C. A. (2010). *Healing the Incest Wound: Adult Survivors in Therapy*. New York: Norton.

Dorias, M. (2009). *Don't Tell: The Sexual Abuse of Boys*. Montreal: McGill-Queens University Press.

Dubowitz, H. (1999). *Neglected Children*. Thousand Oaks, CA: Sage.

Duncan, K. (2008). *Healing from the Trauma of Childhood Sexual Abuse*. Westport, CT: Greenwood.

Finkelhor, D. (1984). *Child Sexual Abuse*. New York: Free Press.

Finkelhor, D., and Browne, A. (1985). "The Traumatic Impact of Child Sexual Abuse: A Conceptualization." *American Journal of Orthopsychiatry* 55:530–541.

Flynn, K. A. (2008). "In Their Own Voices: Women Who Were Sexually Abused by Members of the Clergy." *Journal of Child Sexual Abuse* 17(3–4):216–237.

Fredrickson, R. (1992). *Repressed Memories*. New York: Simon & Schuster.

Friess, D. (1993). *Cry the Darkness*. Deerfield Beach, CA: Health Communications.

Giarretto, H. (1992). *Integrated Treatment of Child Sexual Abuse*. Palo Alto, CA: Science and Behavior Books.

Gold, S. N. (2000). *Not Trauma Alone*. Philadelphia, PA: Taylor & Francis.

Helfer, R. E. (1978). *Childhood Comes First: A Crash Course in Childhood for Adults*. East Lansing, MI: Ray E. Helfer.

Hunter, M. (1990). *The Sexually Abused Male*. Newbury Park, CA: Sage.

Isley, P. J., Isley, P., Freiburger, J., and McMackin, R. (2008). "In Their Own Voices: A Qualitative Study of Men Abused as Children by Catholic Clergy." *Journal of Child Sexual Abuse* 17(3–4):201–215.

Janoff-Bulman, R. (2002). *Shattered Assumptions: Toward a New Psychology of Trauma*. New York: Free Press.

Levenkron, A., and Levenkron, S. (2008). *Stolen Tomorrow*. New York: Norton.

Lew, M. (2004). *Victims No Longer*. San Francisco: HarperCollins.

Maltz, W. (2012). *The Sexual Healing Journey: A Guide for Survivors of Sexual Abuse*. New York: HarperCollins.

Many, M. M., and Osopsky, J. D. (2012). "Working with Survivors of Child Sexual Abuse." In *Handbook of Child Sexual Abuse*, edited by P. Goodyer-Brown (pp. 509–529). Hoboken, NJ: John Wiley & Sons.

Meijer-Degen, F. (2006). *Art Therapy: Coping with Loss and Trauma Through Art*. Delft, Netherlands: Eburon.

Mendel, M. P. (2008). *The Male Survivor*. Thousand Oaks, CA: Sage.

Messman-Moore, T., Long, P., and Siegfried, N. (2000). "The Revictimization of Child Sexual Abuse Survivors: An Examination of the Adjustment of College Women with Child Sexual Abuse, Adult Sexual Assault and Adult Physical Abuse." *Child Maltreatment* 5(1):18–27.

Murrell, A., Christoff, K., and Henning, K. (2007). "Characteristics of Domestic Violence Offenders: Associations with Childhood Exposure to Violence." *Journal of Family Violence* 22(7):523–532.

Nadon, S. M., Koverola, C., and Schluderman, E. H. (1998). "Antecedents to Prostitution: Childhood Victimization." *Journal of Interpersonal Violence* 13(2):206–222.

Naparstek, B. (2006). *Invisible Heroes: Survivors of Trauma and How They Heal*. New York: Bantam.

Ogilvie, B. A. (2004). *Mother–Daughter Incest*. New York: Haworth.

Parker, S. (1990). "Healing Abuse in Gay Men: The Group Component." In *The Sexually Abused Male*, edited by M. Hunter (Vol. 2, pp. 177–198). New York: Lexington Books.

Penelope. (1992). "Suing My Perpetrator: A Survivor's Story." *Journal of Child Sexual Abuse* 1(2):119–124.

Polansky, N., Borgman, R. D., and DeSaix, C. (1972). *Roots of Futility*. San Francisco: Jossey-Bass.

Polansky, N., Chalmers, M. A., Buttenwieser, E., and Williams, D. (1981). *Damaged Parents: An Anatomy of Child Neglect*. Chicago: University of Chicago Press.

Poston, C., and Lison, K. (2001). *Reclaiming Our Lives: Hope for Adult Survivors of Incest*. Lincoln, NE: iUniverse.

Rodriquez-Srednicki, O., and Twaite, J. A. (2006). *Understanding, Assessing and Treating Survivors of Childhood Abuse*. Lanham, MD: Jason Aronson.

Russell, D. (1999). *Secret Trauma*. New York: Basic Books.

Ryder, D. (1992). *Breaking the Circle of Satanic Ritual Abuse*. Minneapolis, MN: CompCare.

Sanford, L., and Donovan, M. E. (1992). *Women and Self-Esteem*. Garden City, NY: Doubleday Anchor Press.

Schwartz, H. L. (2000). *Dialogues with Forgotten Voices*. New York: Basic Books.

Sheiman, J. A. (1993). "I've Always Wondered If Something Happened to Me: Assessment of Child Sexual Abuse Survivors with Amnesia." *Journal of Child Sexual Abuse* 2(2):13–21.

Sonkin, D. J. (1998). *Wounded Boys, Heroic Men*. Avon, MA: Adams Media.

Titleman, P., and Schoenewolf, G. (2003). *Emotional Cutoff: Bowen Systems Theory Perspective*. New York: Haworth.

Tower, C. C. (1988). *Secret Scars*. New York: Viking Penguin.

Valentine, L., and Feinauer, L. (1993). "Resilience Factors Associated with Female Survivors of Child Sexual Abuse." *American Journal of Family Therapy* 21:216–224.

VanDeusen, K. M., and Way, I. (2006). "Vicarious Trauma: An Exploratory Study of the Impact of Providing Sexual Abuse Treatment on Clinicians' Trust and Intimacy." *Journal of Child Sexual Abuse* 15(1):69–85.

Yehuda, R. (2002). *Treating Trauma Survivors with PTSP*. Arlington, VA: American Psychiatric Publishers.

References for Chapter 16

Addams, J. (1910). *Twenty Years at Hull-House.* New York: Signet.

Browne, K. D., Stratton, P., Hanks, H., and Hamilton, C. (Eds.). (2002). *Early Prediction and Prevention of Child Abuse.* New York: John Wiley.

Butler, S. (1996). *Conspiracy of Silence.* San Francisco: Volcano Press.

Chadwick, D. (2002). "Community Organization of Services to Deal with and End Child Abuse." In *The APSAC Handbook on Child Maltreatment*, edited by J. E. B. Myers, L. Berliner, J. Brierre, C. T. Hendrix, C. Jenny, and T. A. Reid (pp. 509–523). Thousand Oaks, CA: Sage.

Children's Bureau. (2008). "Child Maltreatment 2007." Retrieved from www.acf.hhs.gov/programs/cm07/stats_research/index.htm

Daro, D. (2003). "Child Abuse Prevention: Accomplishments and Challenges." *APSAC Advisor* 15(2):3–4.

Daro, D., and Gelles, R. J. (1992). "Public Attitudes and Behaviors with Respect to Child Abuse Prevention." *Journal of Interpersonal Violence* 7(4):517–531.

Dodge, K. A., and Coleman, D. L. (Eds.). (2009). *Preventing Child Maltreatment.* New York: Guilford.

Crosson-Tower, C. (2003). *From the Eye of the Storm: Experiences of a Child Welfare Worker.* Boston: Allyn & Bacon.

Crosson-Tower, C. (2013). *Exploring Child Welfare.* Upper Saddle River, NJ: Pearson Education.

Diller, J. V. (2010). *Cultural Diversity: A Primer for the Human Services.* Stamford, CT: Cengage.

Finkelhor, D., Jones, L. and Shattuck, A. (2011). "Updated Trends in Child maltreatment, 2010." Crimes Against Children Research Center. Retrieved from http://www.unh.edu/ccrc/pdf/CV203_Updated%20trends%202010%20FINAL_12-19-11.pdf on October 31, 2012.

Fontes, L. A. (2008). *Child Abuse and Culture.* New York: Guilford.

Garbarino, J., and Sherman, D. (1997). "High-Risk Families and High-Risk Neighborhoods." *Child Development* 51:188–198.

Gonzales, A., and MacMillan, H. L. (2008). "Preventing Child Maltreatment: An Evidenced-Based Update." *Journal of Postgraduate Medicine* 54(4):280–286.

Gutterman, N. B. (2000). *Stopping Child Maltreatment Before It Starts.* Thousand Oaks, CA: Sage.

Hartley-Brewer, E. (2006a). *Raising Boys Well.* Cambridge, MA: DaCapo.

Hartley-Brewer, E. (2006b). *Raising Girls Well.* Cambridge, MA: DaCapo.

Helfer, R. E. (1976). "Basic Issues Concerning Prediction." In *Child Abuse and Neglect: The Family and the Community*, edited by R. E. Helfer and C. H. Kempe (pp. 363–375). Cambridge, MA: Ballinger.

Helfer, R. E. (1978). *Childhood Comes First.* East Lansing, MI: Author.

Herman, J. (2000). *Father–Daughter Incest.* Cambridge, MA: Harvard University Press.

Huebner, C. E. (2002). "Evaluation of Clinic-Based Parent Education Program to Reduce Risk of Infant and Toddler Maltreatment." *Public Health Nursing* 19(5):377–389.

James, A., and James, A. L. (2004). *Constructing Childhood: Theory, Policy and Social Practice.* Basingstoke, England: Palgrave.

Kenny, M. C., Capri, V., Thakker-Kolar, R. R., Ryan, E. E., and Runyon, M. K. (2008). "Child Sexual Abuse: From Prevention to Self-Protection." *Child Abuse Review* 17(1):36–54.

Krugman, R. D. (1997). "Child Protection Policy." In *The Battered Child*, edited by M. E. Helfer, R. S. Kempe, and R. Krugman (pp. 627–641). Chicago: University of Chicago Press.

Lustig, M. W., and Koester, J. (2009). *Intercultural Competence: Interpersonal Communication Across Cultures.* Boston: Allyn & Bacon.

Lutzker, J. R., Wolfe, D. A., and Bigelow, K. M. (2001). *Reducing Child Maltreatment.* New York: Guilford.

Palmer, P., and Froehner, M. A. (2000). *Teen Esteem: A Self-Direction Manual for Young Adults.* Atascadero, CA: Impact.

Parton, N. (2006). *Safeguarding Childhood.* New York: Palgrave.

Plummer, C. (1999). "The History of Child Sexual Abuse Prevention: A Practitioner's Perspective." *Journal of Child Sexual Abuse* 7(4):77–95.

Plummer, C. A. (2004). "Prevention Is Appropriate, Prevention Is Successful." In *Current Controversies on Family Violence*, edited by R. Gelles and D. Loeseke (pp. 288–305). Newbury Park, CA: Sage.

Popple, P. R., and Leighninger, I. (2011). *Social Work, Social Welfare, and American Society,* 7th edition. Boston: Pearson Education.

Portwood, S. G. (2006). "What We Know—and Don't Know—About Preventing Child Maltreatment". In *Ending Child Abuse*, edited by V. I. Veith, B. L. Bottoms, and A. R. Perona (pp. 55–80). New York: Haworth.

Schaufeli, W., and Enzmann, D. (1998). *The Burnout Companion to Study/Practice.* Philadelphia: Taylor & Francis.

Segal, E. A., Steiner, S., and Gerdes, K. E. (2009). *An Introduction to the Profession of Social Work.* Stamford, CT: Cengage.

Shapiro, J. P., Dorman, R. L., Buckly, W. M., and Welker, C. J. (1999). "Predictors of Job Satisfaction and Burnout in Child Abuse Professionals: Coping, Cognition and Victimization History." *Journal of Child Sexual Abuse* 7(4):23–42.

Teolis, B. (2002). *Ready-to-Use Conflict-Resolution Activities for Elementary Students.* Philadelphia, PA: John Wiley.

Veith, V. I., Bottoms, B. L., and Perona, A. R. (2006). *Ending Child Abuse.* New York: Haworth.

Waldfogel, J. (1998). "Rethinking the Paradigm of Child Protection." *The Future of Children* 8(1):104–119.

Webb, N. B., and Lum, D. (2001). *Culturally Diverse Parent–Child and Family Relationships.* New York: Columbia University Press.

Weber, M. W. (1997). "The Assessment of Child Abuse: A Primary Function of Child Protective Services." In *The Battered Child*, edited by M. E. Helfer, R. S. Kempe, and R. D. Krugman (pp. 120–149). Chicago: University of Chicago Press.

Wulczyn, F., Barth, R. P., Yaun, Y. T., Harnden, B. J., and Landverk, J. (2006). *Beyond Common Sense: Child Welfare, Child Well-Being and the Evidence of Policy Reform.* New Brunswick, NJ: Aldine Transaction.

Wurtele, S. K., and Kenny, M. C. (2012). "Preventing Childhood Sexual Abuse: An Ecological Approach." In *Handbook of Child Sexual Abuse*, edited by P. Goodyer-Brown (pp. 120–149). Hoboken, NJ: John Wiley & Sons.

Zastrow, C. (2012). *The Practice of Social Work.* Stamford, CT: Cengage.

Index